THE PROTECTION OF NON-TRADITIONAL TRADEMARKS

The Protection of Non-Traditional Trademarks

Critical Perspectives

Edited by
IRENE CALBOLI
Professor, Texas A&M University School of Law
MARTIN SENFTLEBEN
Professor, Vrije Universiteit Amsterdam

OXFORD
UNIVERSITY PRESS

OXFORD
UNIVERSITY PRESS

Great Clarendon Street, Oxford, OX2 6DP,
United Kingdom

Oxford University Press is a department of the University of Oxford.
It furthers the University's objective of excellence in research, scholarship,
and education by publishing worldwide. Oxford is a registered trade mark of
Oxford University Press in the UK and in certain other countries

First Edition published in 2018

Published in the United States of America by Oxford University Press
198 Madison Avenue, New York, NY 10016, United States of America

British Library Cataloguing in Publication Data
Data available

Library of Congress Control Number: 2018952546

ISBN 978–0–19–882657–6

Acknowledgments

This collective Book is the result of joint and intensive efforts of many people. While the undersigned conceived the theme and the structure of the Book, the publication was possible only thanks to our contributors. We thus want to express our deepest gratitude to these distinguished scholars and practitioners for their excellent chapters. The readers will appreciate the depth of their analysis and benefit from the wealth of information that is offered in every chapter of the Book. The completion of this project is an example of the possibility of international cooperation of authors across different jurisdictions and legal traditions.

The publication of this Book has been made possible also thanks to the intense work of many editors and reviewers. In this respect, we would like to thank our research assistants, Lee Chedister and Rebecca Ward Helterbrand, who collaborated with us throughout the entire editing process of the manuscript, for their excellent work in reviewing all the chapters of the Book. Additional thanks are due to Taylor Allan for her editorial assistance in the final stage of preparation of the manuscript. We would also like to thank Oxford University Press (OUP), in particular Alex Flach and Imogen Hill, for their support during the development of this project from the Book proposal to final publication. In addition, we want to express our gratitude to the members of the OUP editorial team who assisted us, with patience and professionalism, during the final stages of production. Above all, we are again grateful to our contributors for their insightful writings. These writings certainly present the most complete collection of scholarly contributions to this important area of trademark law to date. Together with the contributors, we discussed the conceptual contours of the different chapters during an academic workshop in January 2017 which was held at, and partially sponsored by, the Singapore Management University School of Law, where one of the editors was a Visiting Professor until May 2018. Two years after this project was started, several meetings, many emails, and phone calls later, this Book has finally become a reality thanks to our contributors and many other colleagues involved.

It is our hope that the Book will serve as a compass in the ongoing debate on the protection of non-traditional marks and a useful source of reference for policymakers, trademark examiners and attorneys, judges, and academics alike for what we believe is a growing and increasingly important area of trademark law, and intellectual property law in general. In this respect, we are particularly grateful to Dean Goh Yihan for his support, and to Singapore Management University School of Law for providing us with the necessary funding to publish this Book in open access. Last but not least, we are grateful for having had the opportunity to collaborate and co-edit this Book. Our different experiences and geographical locations have allowed us to create a collection of essays that we hope reflects a variety of diverse perspectives. This Book is dedicated to our contributors and to all trademark scholars who, like us, believe that the challenges arising from the protection of non-traditional trademarks constitute one of the most relevant issues of modern trademark law, and will become an even more relevant topic of analysis and debate in the years to come.

Irene Calboli and Martin Senftleben
September 2018

Table of Contents

List of Figures ix
List of Tables xi
Table of Cases xiii
Table of Legislation xxv
List of Contributors xxix

Introduction 1
Irene Calboli and Martin Senftleben

PART I ASSESSING THE LEGAL FRAMEWORK AND UNRESOLVED CHALLENGES

1. Making a Large Universe Visually Perceptible: The Development of Non-Traditional Trademarks in WIPO Treaties 13
Denis Croze
2. Non-Traditional Trademarks: An Empirical Study 37
Mitchell Adams and Amanda Scardamaglia
3. Paying the Price for Admission: Non-Traditional Marks across Registration and Enforcement 59
Dev S. Gangjee
4. Yellow Dictionaries, Red Banking Services, Some Candies, and a Sitting Bunny: Protection of Color and Shape Marks from a German and European Perspective 89
Annette Kur
5. Non-Traditional Trademarks and the Dilemma of Aesthetic Functionality 107
Justin Hughes
6. Should Trademark Law Protect Non-Traditional Trademarks? A Look at How Marketing Practices Try to Capture Essences 125
Deven Desai
7. Absolute Bans on the Registration of Product Shape Marks: A Breach of International Law? 147
Ng-Loy Wee Loon
8. What Should Constitute Infringement of a Non-Traditional Mark? The Role of "Trademark Use" 165
Michael Handler
9. Protecting Non-Traditional Trademarks in China: New Opportunities and Challenges 185
Haochen Sun

PART II ASSESSING THE IMPACT ON COMPETITION AND CULTURE

10. The Protection of (Three-Dimensional) Shape Trademarks and Its Implications for the Protection of Competition 203
Gustavo Ghidini

11. Non-Traditional Trademarks: The Error Costs of Making an Exception the Rule 217
Glynn S. Lunney, Jr.

12. Assessing the Impact of Registering Non-Traditional Marks: A European Union Competition Law Analysis 235
Lavinia Brancusi

13. The Economics and Management of Non-Traditional Trademarks: Why, How Much, What, and Who 257
Carolina Castaldi

14. Non-Traditional Trademarks in the Pharmaceutical Sector: Non-Traditional Barriers to Access to Medicine? 271
Arul George Scaria and Kavya Susan Mammen

15. Hands Off "My" Colors, Patterns, and Shapes! How Non-Traditional Trademarks Promote Standardization and May Negatively Impact Creativity and Innovation 287
Irene Calboli

16. A Clash of Culture and Commerce: Non-Traditional Marks and the Impediment of Cyclic Cultural Innovation 309
Martin Senftleben

17. Non-Traditional Trademarks and Inherently Valuable Expression 337
Lisa P. Ramsey

18. Non-Traditional Trademark Protection as (Non-Traditional) Means of Cultural Control 363
Katya Assaf-Zakharov

Index 383

List of Figures

2.1	Trends in the number of non-traditional trademark registration applications filed 1996–2016	45
2.2	Trends in EUIPO applications 1996–2016	52
2.3	Trends in UKIPO applications 1996–2016	52
2.4	Trends in IPOS applications 1996–2016	54
2.5	Trends in JPO applications 1996–2016	55
2.6	Trends in IP Australia applications 1996–2016	56
3.1	Louboutin trademark	64
3.2	Image representing Louboutin trademark application in France	69
3.3	Louboutin reconceived image for trademark application	70
3.4	Apple's color representation of its retail store layout and design for its U.S. registration application	71
3.5	Photographic representation of the head of a lilac-colored mop registered by Mery & Celim as a figurative mark	74
3.6	Figurative mark denied registrability	75
3.7	Representation of a knife handle design submitted by Yoshida Metals	77
3.8	Representation of color mark for inhaler	79
3.9	Lindt image without word mark	84
3.10	Lindt image with word mark	85
3.11	Crocs application showing logo on three views	87
8.1	Philips' Australian registered trade mark 309250 & Remington's RR DT55 shaver	173
8.2	Australian registered trade mark 783465	179
8.3	Diesel SpA's Australian registered trademarks 986713 & 986709	180
11.1	Distribution of: (i) potential trade dress claims; and (ii) potential arbitrary and fanciful word mark claims	229
13.1	Yearly numbers of new filings and registrations of non-visual marks at the USPTO, 1947–2017	265
13.2	Percentage of trademark filings that are successfully registered, by year of filing, starting from 1995	265

List of Tables

2.1 Application and Registration by Mark Type and Filing Basis 1996–2016 46

2.2 Applications by International Class, 1996–2016 49

13.1 Types of non-visual marks and classification in trade/service marks based upon the primary class (goods vs. services) 266

13.2 Top 20 firms in terms of total number of filings for non-visual marks at the USPTO 268

Table of Cases

EUROPEAN UNION

Commission

Decision 82/897/EEC, [1982] O.J. L 379/19 (Case IV/ C-30.128 — Toltecs-Dorcet) 242
Decision 90/186/ EEC, [1990] O.J. L 100/32 (Case No. IV/32.736 — Moosehead/Whitbread). 240
Decision 92/553/EEC, [1992] O.J. L 356/10 (Case No. IV/ M.190 — Nestlé/Perrier) 253
Decision 96/435/EC, [1996] O.J. L 183/1 (Case No. IV/ M.623 — Kimberly-Clark/Scott) 240
Decision 98/531/EC, [1998] O.J. L 246/1 (Case Nos. IV/34.073, IV/34.395 and IV/ 35.436 — Van den Bergh Foods Ltd.). 252
Decision 98/602/EC, [1997] O.J. L 288/8 (Case No. IV/ M.938 — Guinness/Grand Metropolitan). 253

Court of Justice of the European Union (CJEU)

Joined Cases 56/64 and 58/64, Consten & Grundig v. Commission, 1966 E.C.R. 429 238
Case 24/67, Parke, Davis & Co. v. Probel, Reese, 1968 E.C.R. 00081 238
Case 40/70, Sirena v. Eda, 1979 E.C.R. 03169, 1971 C.M.L.R. 260 238
Case 192/73, Van Zuylen v. Hag, 1974 E.C.R. 731. 239
Case 16/74, Centrafarm v. Winthorp, 1974 E.C.R. 001183 239
Case 51/75, EMI v. CBS, 1976 E.C.R. 811. 238
Case 27/76, United Brands Co. & United Brands Continentaal BV v. Comm'n of the European Cmtys., 1978 E.C.R. 207 253
Case 85/76, Hoffmann-LaRoche & Co. AG v. Commission, 1979 E.C.R. 461 252
Case 102/77, Hoffman La Roche v. Centrafarm, 1978 E.C.R. 11139 239
Case 31/80, NV L'Oréal & S.A. L'Oréal v. PVBA "De Nieuwe AMCK," 1980 E.C.R. 03775. 252
Case 322/81, NV Nederlandsche Banden Industrie Michelin v. Comm'n of the European Cmtys., 1983 E.C.R. 03461 252
Case 35/83, BAT Cigaretten- Fabriken GmbH v. Comm'n of the European Cmtys., 1985 E.C.R. 00363, ...242
Case C-10/89, S.A. CNL-Sucal v. HAG, 1990 E.C.R. I-3711. 239
Case C-241/91, RTE (Magill), 1995 E.C.R. I-743 239
Case C-9/93, IHT v. Ideal Standard, 1994 E.C.R. I-2789. 238
Case C-337/95, Parfum Christian Dior v. Evora, 1997 E.C.R. I-6013. 215
Case C-63/97, BMW v. Deenik, 1999 E.C.R. I-905, ECLI:EU:C:1999:82. 97
Case C-342/97, Lloyd Schuhfabrik Meyer & Co. GmbH v. Klijsen Handel BV, [1999] E.C.R. I-3819 82
Case C-375/97, General Motors Corp. v. Yplon S.A., 1999 E.C.R. 122 . . . . 199, 329
Case C-228/99, Silos e Mangimi Martini v. Ministero delle Finanze, 2001 E.C.R. I-8401 208
Case C-299/99, Koninklike Philips Electronics NV v. Remington Consumer Products Ltd., 2002 E.C.R. I-5475, ECLI:EU:C:2002:377. . . . . 4, 39, 90, 206, 247, 310, 326
Case C-2/00, Hölterhoff v. Freiesleben, 2002 E.C.R. I-4187. 168
Case C-273/00, Ralf Sieckmann v. Deutsches Patent- und Marknamt, 2002 E.C.R. I-11737, ECLI:EU:C:2002:748 . . . . 61, 66, 90, 131–32, 134, 165, 273
Case C-292/00, Davidoff & Cie S.A. v. Gofkid Ltd, 2003 I-389, ECLI:EU:C:2003:9. . . . . . .213, 329
Joined Cases C-53/01 to C-55/01, Linde AG and Others, 2003 E.C.R. I-3161, ECLI:EU:C:2003:206 . . . . 3, 90, 206, 207, 320
Case C-104/01, Libertel Groep BV v. Benelux-Merkenbureau, 2003 E.C.R. I-3793, ECLI:EU:C:2003:244 . . . . 3, 62, 91, 132, 166, 311, 320, 325
Case C-206/01, Arsenal Football Club v. Deenik, ECLI:EU:C:2002:651 103

Case C-218/01, Henkel KGaA v. Deutsches Patent-und Markenamt, 2004 E.C.R. I-1725, ECLI:EU:C:2004:88 . . . . . 3, 132, 166, 320, 325, 327
Case C-218/01, P, Henkel v. Office for the Harmonisation in the International Market (OHIM), 2007 E.C.R. I-8109, ECLI:EU:C:2004:258 90
Case C-283/01, Shield mark v. Kist, 2003 E.C.R. I-14313, ECLI:EU:C:2003:197 (Opinion of Advocate General Ruiz-Járabo Colomer) 311
Case C-283/01, Shield Mark BV v. Kist, 2003 E.C.R. I-14313, ECLI:EU:C:2003:641 . . . . . 90, 165, 272, 311
Case C-408/01, Adidas-Salomon AG v. Fitnessworld Trading Ltd, 2003 E.C.R. I-12537 . . . . . 5, 210, 330, 331
Case C-418/01, IMS Health, 2004 E.C.R. I-5039 239
Joined Cases C-456/01 and 457/01 P, Henkel v. OHIM, 2004 E.C.R. I-5089 . . . . . 90, 215
Case C-49/02, Heidelberger Bauchemie, 2004 E.C.R. I-6129, ECLI:EU:C:2004:384 91
Case C-100/02, Gerolsteiner Brunnen v. Putsch GmbH, 2004 E.C.R. I-694, ECLI:EU:C:2004:11 . . . . . 104, 106
Case C-136/02, P, Mag Instruments v. OHIM, 2004 E.C.R. I-9165, ECLI:EU:C:2004 90
Case C-245/02, Anheuser-Busch v. Budvar, 2004 E.C.R. I-10989, ECLI:EU:C:2004:717 104
Case C-371/02, Björnekulla Fruktindustrier AB v. Procordia Food, AB, [2004] EURLex ECLI:EU:C:2004:275 295
Case C-228/03, Gillette v. LA-Laboratories, 2005 E.C.R. I-2337, ECLI:EU:C:2005:177 104
Case C-321/03, Dyson Ltd v. Registrar of Trade Marks, 2007 E.C.R. I-687, ECLI:EU:C:2007:51 76
Case C-361/04 P, Ruiz-Picasso and Others v. OHIM, 2006 I-643, ECLI:EU:C:2006:25 . . . . . 321, 324, 328–9
Case C-24/05, P Storck v. OHIM, 2004 E.C.R. I-5677 215
Case C-25/05, P Storck v. OHIM, 2004 E.C.R. I-5719 215
Case C-48/05, Adam Opel A.G. v. Autec A.G., 2007 E.C.R. I-1017 . . . . . 5, 98, 168, 330, 331
Case C-235/05, L'Oréal v. OHIM, 2006 E.C.R. I-00057, EU:C:2006:271 100
Case C-17/06, Céline SAR v. Céline SA, 2007 E.C.R. I-7041, ECLI:EU:C:2007:497 . . . . . 104, 330
Case C-171/06 P, T.I.M.E. ART v. OHIM, 2007 E.C.R. I-41 100
Case C-371/06, Benetton v. G-Star, 2007 E.C.R. I-7709, EU:C:2007:542 . . . . . 90, 111
Case C-533/06, O2 v. Hutchison, 2008 E.C.R. I-4231, ECLI:EU:C:2008:339 98
Case C-102/07 adidas AG and adidas Benelux BV v. Marca Mode CV and Others 2008 E.C.R. I-2439 ('Adidas II') 5, 204, 213, 330, 331
Case C-202/07, France Telecom v. Commission, 2009 E.C.R. I-2369 . . . . . 213, 214
Case C-252/07, Intel Corp. v. CPM U.K. Ltd 329
Case C-385/07 P, Der Grüne Punkt-Duales System v. Commission, 2009 E.C.R. I-6155 243
Case C-487/07, L'Oréal v. Bellure, 2009 E.C.R. I-5185, ECLI:EU:C:2009:378 . . . . . 98, 169, 132–33, 323, 330
Case C-498/07 P, Aceites del sur v. Koipe, 2009 E.C.R. I-7371 100
Case C-529/07, Lindt & Sprüngli v. Hauswirth, 2009 E.C.R. I-4893, EU:C:2009:361 (Golden Bunny I) 96
Case C-62/08, UDV North America Inc. v. Brandtraders NV, 2009 I-01279, ECLI:EU:C:2009:111 330
Joined Cases C-236/08 to 238/08, Google France SARL v. Louis Vuitton Malletier S.A. and Others, 2010 E.C.R. I-2417, ECLI:EU:C:2010:159 . . . . . 98, 330
Case C-48/09, Lego Juris v. OHIM, 2010 E.C.R. I-8403, ECLI:EU:C:2010:516 . . . . 4, 78, 90, 148, 206, 207, 208, 247, 249
Case C-323/09, Interflora v. Marks & Spencer, 2011 E.C.R. I-8625 . . . . . 133, 210
Case C-324/09, L'Oréal S.A. v. eBay International AG, 2011 E.C.R. I-6011, ECLI:EU:C:2011:474 330
Case C-457/10 P, Astra Zeneca v. Commission, ECLI:EU:C:2012:770 . . . . . 243, 252
Case C-98/11, Chocoladefabriken Lindt & Sprüngli v. OHIM, ECLI:EU:C:2012:307 209

Case C-98/11 P, Chocoladefabriken Lindt & Sprüngli v. OHIM, EU:C:2012:307 (Golden Bunny II) 96, 101
Case C-661/11, Martin Y Paz Diffusion, ECLI:EU:C:2013:577 210
Case C-42/12 P, Hrbek v. OHIM, 2008 E.C.R. I-4231, ECLI:EU:C:2012:765 100
Case C-65/12, Leidseplein Beheer BV v. Red Bull, ECLI:EU:C:2014:49. 210
Case C-252/12, Specsavers International Healthcare v. Asda Stores Ltd., ECLI:EU:C:2013:497 96
Joined Cases C-337/12 P to C-340/12 P, Pi Design & Ors v. Yoshida Metal, ECLI:EU:C:2014:129 . . . . .77, 78
Case C-383/12 P, Environmental Manufacturing LLP v. OHIM, ECLI:EU:C:2013:741 329
Case C-205/13, Hauck GmbH v. Stokke A/S, ECLI:EU:C:2014:2233. . . . . 4, 90, 136, 137, 148, 209, 247, 249, 309, 326–27
Joined Cases C-217/13 and C-218/13, Oberbank AG & Others v. Deutscher Sparkassen-und Giroverband eV, ECLI:EU:C:2014:2012. . . . .93, 352
Case C-421/13, Apple Inc. v. Deutsches Patent-und Markenamt, ECLI:EU:C:2014:2070 72
Case C-445/13, Voss of Norway v. OHIM, ECLI:EU:C:2015:303 209
Case C-182/14 P, MEGA Brands International v. OHIM, ECLI:EU:C:2015:187. 100
Case C-215/14, Nestlé v. Cadbury, ECLI:EU:C:2015:604 . . . . .103, 209
Case C-30/15 P, Simba Toys GmbH & Co. KC v. EUIPO, ECLI:EU:C:2016:849. . . . .78, 90, 247, 249
Case C-75/15, Viiniveria Oy v. Sosiaali, ECLI:EU:C:2016:35 207
Case C-515/15 P, Roland SE v. EUIPO, ECLI:EU:C:2016:298 298
Case C-163/16, Christian Louboutin and Christian Louboutin SAS v. Van Haren Schoenen BV, ECLI:EU:C:2017:495 (AG Szpunar, 1st opinion) 64, 65, 247, 298, 375
Case C-163/16, Christian Louboutin and Christian Louboutin SAS v. Van Haren Schoenen BV, ECLI:EU:C:2018:64 (AG Szpunar, 2nd opinion). 64
Case C-163/16, Christian Louboutin and Christian Louboutin SAS v. Van Haren Schoenen BV, ECLI:EU:C:2018:423 (Judgment). 60, 65, 67, 297, 298
Case C-417/16 P, August Storck KG v. EUIPO, ECLI:EU:C:2017:340. . . . .68, 73
Case C-488/16 P, Bundesverband Souvenir — Geschenke — Ehrenpreise v. EUIPO, ECLI:EU:C:2018:673 309
Joined Cases C-84/17 P, C-85/17 P and C-95/17 P, Société des produits Nestlé v. Mondelez UK Holdings & Services, ECLI:EU:C:2018:266 (Opinion of Advocate General Wathelet). 72
Joined Cases C-84/17 P, C-85/17 P and C-95/17 P, Société des produits Nestlé v. Mondelez UK Holdings & Services, ECLI:EU:C:2018:596 72

Court of First Instance/General Court

Case T-30/89, Hilti AG v. Commission., 1991 E.C.R. II-1439 252
Case T-51/89, Tetra Pak v. Commission, 1990 E.C.R. II-00309 243
Case T-83/91, Tetra Pak International S.A. v. Commission., 1994 E.C.R. II-755. 252
Case T-504/93, Tiercé Ladbroke S.A. v. Commission, 1997 E.C.R. II-00923 252
Case T-219/99, British Airways v. Commission, 2003 E.C.R. II-5917. 252
Case T-88/00, Mag Instrument v. OHIM, 2002 E.C.R. II-467 215
Case T-234/01, Stihl v. OHIM, 2003 E.C.R. II-2867) 203
Case T-129/04, Develey v. OHIM, 2006 E.C.R. II-611 215
Case T-201/04, Microsoft, 2007 E.C.R. II-3601. 239
Case T-321/05, AstraZeneca v. Commission, 2010 E.C.R. II-2805 252
Case T-435/05, Danjaq LLC v. OHIM, 2009 E.C.R. II-2097 314–15
Case T-137/08 BCS SpA v. OHIM, 2009 E.C.R. II-4047. 132
Case T-492/08, Wessang v. OHIM, 2010 E.C.R. II-82 100
Case T-508/08, Bang & Olufsen v. OHIM, 2011 E.C.R. II-6975 . . . . . 207, 208, 209
Joined Cases T-409/10 and T-410/10, Bottega Veneta International v. OHIM, ECLI:EU:T:2013:148 304
Case T-434/10, Hrbek v. OHMI, ECLI:EU:T:2011:663 99

Joined Cases T-395/14 and 396/14, Best Lock v. OHIM, contested decision: R 1695/2013-4, ECLI:EU:T:2015:380 209
Case T-411/14, Coca Cola v. OHIM, ECLI:EU:T:2016:94 209
Case T-579/14, Birkenstock Sales Gmbh v. EUIPO, ECLI:EU:T:2016:650 73
Case T-629/14, Jaguar Land Rover Ltd v. OHIM, ECLI:EU:T:2015:868 295
Case T-631/14 Roland SE v. OHIM, contested decision: R 1591/2013-1, ECLI:EU:T:2015:521 . . . . 132, 298
Joined Cases T-101/15 and T-102/15, Red Bull GmbH v. EUIPO, Opium Mark, ECLI:EU:T:2017:852 80
Case T-167/15, Bundesverband Souvenir — Geschenke — Ehrenpreise v. EUIPO, contested decision: R 28/2014-5, ECLI:EU:T:2016:391 310
Case T-580/15, Flamagas v. EUIPO, ECLI:EU:T:2017:433 209
Case T-20/16, M/S Indeutsch International v. EUIPO, ECLI:EU:T:2017:410 73
Case T-36/16, Enercon GmbH v. EUIPO, Gamesa Eólica, SL, ECLI:EU:T:2017:295 68
Case T-601/17, Rubik's Brand v. EUIPO, contested decision R 452/2017-1 209
Case T-691/17, hoechstmass Balzer v. EUIPO, contested decision R2331/2016-4, ECLI:EU:T:2018:394 . . . . 207, 215

EUIPO/OHIM

Case R-655/2001-1, Dyson v. OHIM, OHIM 1st BoA, (2002) 76
Case R 9/2008-3, Crocs Inc. v. Holey Soles Holdings Ltd., OHIM 3rd BoA (2010) 86
Case R-2272/2010-2, Christian Louboutin v. OHIM, 2nd BoA, 16 June 2011 (unreported) 70
Case R 2450/2011 G, Chocoladefabriken Lindt & Sprüngli AG, EUIPO Grand BoA (2017) 83, 88
Case R-412/2012-2, Meso Scale Diagnostics, 2nd BoA (2012) 75
Case 1176C, Confiserie Rohan v. Chocoladefabriken Lindt & Sprungli, OHIM Cancellation Division (2014) 84
Case R 339/2014-3, Hessy s.r.o. v. Crocs Inc., OHIM, 3rd BoA, 14 September 2015 88
Case File No. ICD 9830, Crocs Inc. v. Dobré boty s.r.o., 18 September 2015 86
Case File No. ICD 9889, Crocs Inc. v. Jin Shi International, 6 November 2015 86
Case R-2583/2014-5, Pirelli Tyre Spa v The Yokohama Rubber Co Ltd, 5th BoA (2016) 75
Case R 3021/2014-5, Lidl Stiftung & Co. KG v. Crocs Inc., OHIM, 5th BoA (2016) 86
Case File No. ICD 9961, Crocs Inc. v. FLAMEshoes, 1 September 2016 86
Case File No. ICD 10529, Crocs Inc. v. Nuvens de Fantasia, Lda. 2 June 2017 86
Case R 200/2017-2, Giro Travel Company v. Andreas Stihl, 2nd BoA, 23 January 2018 80

EFTA

Case E-5/16, Municipality of Oslo, EFTA Court 6 April 2017 (Vigeland case) 310, 311–12, 319, 334–36

WTO

United States — Section 211 Omnibus Appropriation Act of 1998, WTO Doc. WT/DS176/R (6 August 2001) (Panel Report) 15
United States — Section 211 Omnibus Appropriation Act of 1998, WTO Doc. WT/DS176/AB/R (2 January 2002) (Appellate Body Report) 161–62, 161–63

NATIONAL CASES

Australia

Anheuser-Busch Inc. v. Budìjovický Budvar, Národní Podnik, (2002) 56 I.P.R. 182 (Federal Court) 171

BP Plc v. Woolworths Limited, (2004) 62 I.P.R. 545 (Federal Court). 62
Christodoulou v. Disney Enterprises Inc., (2005) 156 F.C.R. 344 (Federal Court). 171
Coca-Cola Co. v. All-Fect Distributors Ltd., (1999) 96 F.C.R. 107 (Federal Court) 170, 179, 181
Coca-Cola Co. v. PepsiCo Inc. (No. 2), (2014) 109 I.P.R. 429 (Federal Court) 181, 182
E & J Gallo Winery v. Lion Nathan Australia Pty. Ltd., (2010) 241 C.L.R. 144 (High Court) 170
Global Brand Marketing Inc. v. YD Pty. Ltd., (2008) 76 I.P.R. 161 (Federal Court). 179–80, 181, 182
Guccio Gucci SpA v. Guess?, Inc., (2015) ATMO 71 301
Kenman Kandy Australia Pty. Ltd. v. Registrar of Trade Marks, (2002) 122 F.C.R. 494, [2002] 56 I.P.R. 30 (Federal Court). 41, 43, 174, 176, 177, 178, 180
Koninklijke Philips Electronics NV v. Remington Products Australia Pty. Ltd., (1999) 91 F.C.R. 167, (1999) 44 I.P.R. 551 (Federal Ct.), aff'd (2000) 100 F.C.R. 90 (Federal Court). 42, 172, 173–74, 175, 176, 178
Mayne Industries Pty. Ltd. v. Advanced Engineering Group Pty. Ltd., (2008) 166 F.C.R. 312 (Federal Court) 173, 175, 177
Nature's Blend Pty. Ltd. v. Nestlé Australia Ltd., (2010) 87 I.P.R. 464 (Federal Court) 170
Pepsico Australia Pty. Ltd. v. The Kettle Chip Co. Pty. Ltd., (1996) 33 I.P.R. 161 (Federal Court). 170
Philips v. Remington, 100 F.C.R. 90, 1 (2002) (Federal Court) 41
Philmac Pty. Ltd. v. Registrar of Trade Marks, (2002) 126 F.C.R. 525 (Federal Court). 42, 62, 175, 177
Polo/Lauren Co. LP v. Ziliani Holdings Pty Ltd., (2008) 173 F.C.R. 266 (Federal Court) 174
Scandinavian Tobacco Group Eersel BV v. Trojan Trading Co. Pty. Ltd., (2016) 243 F.C.R. 152 (Federal Court) 183
Sebel Furniture Ltd. v. Acoustic & Felts Pty. Ltd., (2009) 80 I.P.R. 244 (Federal Court). 174, 175, 177
Shell Co. of Australia Ltd. v. Esso Standard Oil (Australia) Ltd., (1963) 109 C.L.R. 407 170

Belgium

Christian Louboutin v. Dr. Adams Footwear, Tribunal of First Instance [Tribunal de Première Instance] [Civ.], Brussels, 2013 298
Anne Frank Foundation v. Benelux Office for Intellectual Property, Court of Appeals of Brussels [Hof van Beroep], Cases 2013/7132 and 2013/7133, 3 October 2013 310
Christian Louboutin v. Van Dalen Footnote BV, District Court of Brussels, Case AR 2013-6154, 20 March 2014 298
Christian Louboutin v. Dr. Adams Footwear, Court of Appeals of Brussels [Hof van Beroep], IEFbe 1119, decision 2014/AR/734 (Nov. 2014) 298
Anne Frank Foundation, OHIM App. Bd., Case R 2401/2014-4, 31 August 2015 310

China

Ferrero SpA v. Trademark Appeal Board of the State Administration for Industry & Commerce of the People's Republic of China], 9 C.T.M.R. 105 (Beijing First Interm. People's Ct. Nov. 12, 2007) 190
Hermès International S.A. v. Trademark Appeal Board of the State Administration for Industry & Commerce of the People's Republic of China (Thir Party: Nanjing Youqishi Co.), 2012 Zhixingchu No. 1387 (Beijing First Interm. People's Ct. Aug. 30, 2012) 197
Hermès International S.A. v. Trademark Appeal Board of the State Administration for Industry & Commerce of the People's Republic of China (Third party: Dafeng Garment Factory), 2013 Gaoxingzhong No. 615 (Beijing First Intermediate Ct. Apr. 28, 2013) 191, 193, 194, 195, 198, 199, 200
Hermès International S.A. v. Trademark Appeal Board of the State Administration for Industry & Commerce of the People's Republic of China (Third Party: HermesEpitek Corp.) (Hermès v. France Ai Ma Shi), 2013 Gaoxingzhong No. 1992 (Beijing High People's Ct. Apr. 11, 2014) 194, 195, 196, 197, 199, 200

Finland

Abloy Oy v. Hardware Group Finland Oy, Supreme Court of Finland, KKO:2017:42 (2017) 88

France

Court of Cassation [Cour de Cassation], Commercial Chamber, Christian Louboutin v. Zara France, Decision No. 11/20724, 30 May 2012 . . . . .69, 298
Court of Cassation [Cour de Cassation], Decision 367605, 19 March 2015 301

Germany

Federal Constitutional Court [Bundesverfassungsgericht - BVerfG], May 31, 2016, 1 BvR 1585/13, Sampling. 332
Federal Court of Justice [Bundesgerichtshof - BGH], Jun. 19, 1956, IZ R 104/54, 1960 GRUR 244, 245-46, Simili-Schmuck 366
BGH, Jul. 14, 1962, I ZR 44/59, 1962 GRUR 144, Buntstreifensatin. 367
BGH, Dec. 18, 1968, IZ R 130/66, 1969 GRUR 292, 294, Buntstreifensatin II 366, 370
BGH Mar. 25, 1999, 1999 GRUR 730. 92
BGH, Jun. 17, 1999, I ZR 213/96, 1999 GRUR 1106, Rollstuhlnachbau. 370
BGH, Nov. 28, 2002, I ZR 204/00, 2003 GRUR 712. 216
BGH, Dec. 5, 2002, I ZB 19/00, 2003 GRUR 332, Winnetou 327
BGH, Dec. 5, 2002, I ZR 911/00 Abschlusstück (Parker case) 215
BGH, Jan. 23, 2003, I ZR 171/00, Winnetous Rückkehr 327
BGH, Oct. 30, 2003, I ZR 236/97, 2003 GRUR 360, Pflegebett 367
BGH, Feb. 3, 2005, I ZR 159/02, 2005 GRUR 583, Lila Postkarte. 321–22, 331
BGH, Feb. 3, 2005, 2005 GRUR 414. 95
BGH, Sep. 15, 2005, I ZR 151/02, 2006 GRUR 79, Jeans I 367
BGH Oct. 26, 2006, 2006 GRUR 235. 96
BGH Jan. 25, 2007, 2007 GRUR 780 95
BGH, May 24, 2007, I ZR 104/04, 2007 GRUR 984, Gartenliege 367
BGH Oct. 25, 2007, 2008, GRUR 505 . . . . .95, 99
BGH, Apr. 24, 2008, I ZB 21/06, Marlene-Dietrich-Bildnis. 310, 327–28, 333
BGH, Apr. 30, 2008, IZ R 73/05, 2008 GRUR 349, 353, Klemmbausteine III. 366
BGH, Apr. 30, 2008, 2008 GRUR 793. 95
BGH, Apr. 2, 2009, I ZR 199/06, 2009 GRUR 1073, Ausbeinmesser. 367, 370
BGH, May 28, 2009, I ZR 124/06, 2010 GRUR 80, LIKEaBIKE 367
BGH Nov.19, 2009, 2010 GRUR 637 92
BGH, Mar. 31, 2010, I ZB 62/09, Marlene-Dietrich-Bildnis II. 328, 333
BGH, Apr. 22, 2010, 2010 GRUR 1103. 95
BGH, Jul. 15, 2010, 2011 GRUR 148 97
BGH, Nov. 24, 2011, I ZR 175/09, Medusa. 5, 331
BGH Mar. 27, 2013, 12557, Beck Rechtsprechungs-Sammlung (BeckRS) 97
BGH, Sept. 18, 2014, I ZR 228/12, 2015 GRUR 581, Langenscheidt v. Rosetta Stone 88, 92, 93
BGH Mar. 21, 2015, I ZR 23/14, Bounty Chocolate Bar 88, 99
BGH Jul. 9, 2015, 2015 GRUR 1012, NIVEA-Blue. 92
BGH Sept. 23, 2015, 2015 GRUR 1201 94
BGH Oct. 21, 2015, 2016 GRUR 197. 95
BGH Jul. 21, 2016, 2016 GRUR 1167. 93
Federal Patent Court [Bundespatentgericht - BPatG], Nov. 25, 1997. . . . . .310, 319, 323–24
BpatG, 24 W (pat) 188/96, 1998 GRUR 1022, Mona Lisa. 310
BpatG, Nov. 9, 2005, Porträtfoto Marlene Dietrich 327–28
BpatG, Mar. 8, 2013, 2013 GRUR 844, DSGV v. Santander, ...92, 93, 94
BpatG, Aug. 5, 2013, 2013 GRUR-RS 14164 92
BpatG, Jul. 8, 2015, 2015 GRUR 796 93
Higher Regional Court Frankfurt [Oberlandesgericht Frankfurt am Main - OLG], GRUR-RR 255, 2012, Lindt v. Riegelein Confiserie 85, 97

Higher Regional Court, Hamburg [Oberlandesgerichte Hamburg], 2003 Az I ZR 75/234, BeckRS 03 367
Higher Regional Court Munich [Oberlandesgericht Műnchen] Jun. 23, 2000, Case 29 U 5077/99 216
Higher Regional Court, Zweibrücken [Oberlandesgerichte Zweibrücken], 2000 Az. I ZR 98/06— BeckRS 367
District Court Elberfeld [Landgericht Elberfeld], Odol case (1924) 214

Italy

Court of First Instance, Milan [Tribunale di Milano], Decision 6095 (2013), Gucci v. Guess? Inc., ... 300–01
Court of First Instance, Venice [Tribunale di Venezia], 15 February 2012, Crocs, Inc. v. Supermarket Della Calzatura sas & Progetti srl 86
Italian Competition Authority [Autorità Garante della Concorrenza e del Mercato – AGCM], Decision A224, 17 December 1999, PepsiCo Foods & Beverages International v. IBG S./Coca- Cola Italy 239
AGCM, Decision C2641, 9 May 1997, Henkel v. Loctite 239

Netherlands

Supreme Court [Hoge Raad - HR], Case LJN AV3384, 8 September 2006, Benetton Grp. SpA v. G- Star International BV 315
HR, Eerste Kamer, Case 9098 (R97/163HR), 1999 Nederlandse Jurisprudentie 697, 16 April 1999, Bigott-Batco v. Doucal 315

New Zealand

Coca-Cola Co. v. Frucor Soft Drinks Ltd., (2013) 104 I.P.R. 432 (High Court) 177, 181, 182
Fredco Trading Ltd. v. Miller, [2006] N.Z.C.A. 151 (Court of Appeal) 175
Mainland Products Ltd. v. Bonlac Foods (NZ) Ltd., [1998] 3 N.Z.L.R. 341 171
Tasman Insulation New Zealand Ltd. v. Knauf Insulation Ltd., [2016] 3 N.Z.L.R. 145 (Court of Appeal) 170

Singapore

City Chain Stores (S) Pte Ltd. v. Louis Vuitton Malletier, [2010] 1 S.L.R. 382 (High Court) 168
Nation Fittings (M) Sdn Bhd v. Oystertec Plc, [2006] 1 S.L.R. 712 (High Court) 172
Société des Produits Nestlé v. Petra Foods Ltd., [2017] 1 S.L.R. 35 (High Court) 148, 149

South Africa

Triomed (Pty) Ltd. v. Beecham Group Plc, [2003] F.S.R. 27 148
Verimark (Pty) Ltd. v. Bayerische Motoren Werke AktienGesellschaft, 2007 (6) S.A. 263 168

Spain

T.S. [Tribunal Supremo], Mery y Celim v. Betis Textil S.A. (Lilac mop), Feb. 25, 2016, Appeal No. 2403/2013 74

Sweden

Stockholm District Court, Patent and Market Court [Patent och marknadsdomstolen], Crocs Europe v. Öob, (2017) 86

United Kingdom

Champagne Heidsieck et Cie Monopole Société Anonyme v. Buxton [1930] 1 Ch. 330 (Ch.) 171, 183
Coca-Cola Trade Marks, In re [1986] R.P.C. 421, (H.L.) 63, 204, 205
Dyson Ltd v. Registrar of Trade Marks [2003] E.W.H.C. 1062 (Ch.) 76
Edward Young & Co. Ltd. v. Grierson, Oldham & Co. Ltd. (1924) 41 R.P.C. 548 (C.A) 170

Glaxo Wellcome v. Sandoz [2016] E.W.H.C. 1537 (Ch.) 78, 79
Glaxo Wellcome UK Ltd v. Sandoz Ltd [2017] E.W.C.A. Civ. 335, [2017] F.S.R. 33 (C.A.) 65, 79, 165
Hodgkinson & Corby v. Ward [1997] F.S.A. 178 214
Hodgkinson Corby Ltd. v. Wards Mobility Servs. Ltd. [1995] F.S.R. 169 (Ch. D) 147
Hoffmann-La Roche & Co. A.G. v. D.D.S.A. Pharm. Ltd. [1972] R.P.C. 1, 20 (C.A.) 280
Irving's Yeast-Vite Ltd. v. Horsenail (1934) 51 R.P.C. 110 (H.L.) 170
James' Trade-Mark, Re [1886] W.N. 152 (C.A.) 205
J.B. Williams Co. v. H. Bronnley & Co. Ltd. (1909) 26 R.P.C. 765, 770 (C.A.) 147
J.W. Spear & Son Ltd, Mattel Inc and Mattel UK Ltd v. Zynga Inc. [2012] E.W.H.C. 3345 (Ch.); affirmed on appeal: [2013] E.W.C.A. Civ. 1175 76
Koninklijke Philips Electronics NV v. Remington Consumer Products Ltd. [2006] F.S.R. 30 (C.A.) 172
London Taxi Corp Ltd. v. Frazer-Nash Research Ltd. [2016] F.S.R. 20 148
London Taxi Corp. Ltd. v. Frazer-Nash Research Ltd. [2017] E.W.C.A. Civ. 1729 295
Philips Electronics v. Remington Consumer Products [1998] R.P.C. 283 (Ch.) 73, 205
Philips Electronics v. Remington Consumer Products [1999] R.P.C. 809 (H.L.) 203, 205
Philips Electronics NV v. Remington Consumer Products Ltd. [2003] R.P.C. 2 148
Procter and Gamble's Trademark Applications, Re [1999] R.P.C. 673 205
Smith, Kline and French Laboratories Ltd v. Sterling-Winthrop Group Ltd. (1976) R.P.C. 511 (H.L.) 203
Société des Produits Nestlé S.A. v. Cadbury UK Ltd. [2012] E.W.H.C. 2637 (Ch.) 78
Société des Produits Nestlé S.A. v. Cadbury UK Ltd [2013] E.W.C.A. Civ. 1174 (C.A.) 78, 131
Société des produits Nestlé S.A. v. Cadbury UK Ltd. [2014] E.W.H.C. 16 (Ch.) 103
Société des Produits Nestlé S.A. v. Cadbury UK Ltd. [2014] R.P.C. 7 (C.A.) 165
Société des Produits Nestlé S.A. v. Cadbury UK Ltd. [2017] E.W.C.A. 358 (C.A.) 41
Société des Produits Nestlé S.A. v. Unilever Plc [2002] E.W.H.C. 2709 (Ch.) 255
Starbucks (HK) Ltd and others v. British Sky Broadcasting Group plc and others [2012] E.W.H.C. 3074 (Ch.), ...91
Whirlpool Corporation and Others v. Kenwood Ltd. [2008] E.W.I.T.C. 1930 (Ch.) 205

United States

Abercrombie & Fitch Co. v. Hunting World, Inc., 537 F.2d 4 (2d Cir. 1976) 290, 295
Abercrombie & Fitch Stores, Inc. v. Am. Eagle Outfitters, Inc., 280 F.3d 619 (6th Cir. 2002) 140, 374
A.C. Gilbert Co. v. Shemitz, 45 F.2d 98 (2d Cir. 1930) 226
Adams v. Heisel, 31 F. 279 (C.C.N.D. Ohio 1887) 220
Adidas-Salomon AG v. Target Corp., 228 F. Supp. 2d 1192, 1193 (D. Or. 2002) 374, 375
American Safety Table Co. v. Schreiber, 269 F.2d 255 (2d Cir. 1959) 226, 367
Antioch Co. v. W. Tramming Corp., 347 F.3d 150 (6th Cir. 2003) 113
Apple, Inc. v. Samsung Electronics Co., Ltd., 920 F. Supp. 2d 1079 (N.D. Cal. 2013) 122, 143
Apple, Inc. v. Samsung Electronics Co., Ltd., 786 F.3d 983 (2015) 143
Aromatique, Inc. v. Gold Seal, Inc., 28 F.3d 863 (8th Cir. 1994) 367
Au-tomotive Gold, Inc. v. Volkswagen of America, Inc., 457 F.3d 1062 (9th Cir. 2006) 114, 123, 359
Board of Supervisors for Louisiana State University Agricultural & Mechanical College v. Smack Apparel Co., F.3d 465 (5th Cir. 2008) 113
Bern Unlimited, Inc. v. Burton Corp., 95 F.Supp.3d 184 (D. Mass. 2015) 346
Blonder-Tongue Laboratories., Inc. v. University of Illinois Foundation, 402 U.S. 313 (1971) 232
Borden, Inc. v. F.T.C., 495 F.2d 785 (7th Cir. 1974) 246
Borden, Inc. v. F.T.C., 674 F.2d 498 (6th Cir. 1982), vacated, 461 U.S. 940 (1983) 246
Bose Corp. v. Linear Design Labs., Inc., 467 F.2d 304 (2d Cir. 1972) 221
British Seagull Ltd. v. Brunswick Corp., 28 U.S.P.Q.2d 1197, 1993 WL 409141 (T.T.A.B. 1993) 115, 116

Brown Shoe Co. v. United States, 370 U.S. 294 (1962) 251
Brunetti, In re, 877 F.3d 1330, 1349–50 (Fed. Cir. 2017) 344, 350
Brunswick Corp. v. British Seagull Ltd. & Outboard Marine Corp., 35 F.3d 1527 (Fed. Cir. 1994) 43, 112, 115, 116, 118
Brunswick Corp. v. Spinit Reel Co., 832 F.2d 513, 518 (10th Cir. 1987) 110, 111
Burgess Battery Co. v. Marzall, 92 U.S.P.Q. (BNA) 90 (D.D.C. 1951) 224
Buzz Bee Toys, Inc. v. Swimways Corp., 20 F.Supp.3d 483 (D.N.J. 2014) 346
C5 Med. Werks, LLC v. CeramTec GmbH, 249 F.Supp.3d. 1210, 1218 (D. Colo. 2017), appeal docketed No 17-1173 (10th Cir. May 19, 2017) 351
Calvin Klein Cosmetics Corp. v. Lenox Labs., Inc., 815 F.2d 500 (8th Cir. 1987) 371
Central Hudson Gas & Electric Corp. v. Public Service Commission of New York, 447 U.S. 557 (1980) 343, 344
Christian Louboutin S.A. v. Yves Saint Laurent America Holding, Inc., 696 F.3d 206, (2d Cir. 2012) 83, 108, 111, 113, 232, 249, 297, 375
Christian Louboutin S.A. v. Yves Saint Laurent America Holding, Inc., 778 F.Supp.2d 445 (S.D.N.Y. 2011) 83, 141, 297, 379
Clarke, In re 17 U.S.P.Q.2d 1238 (T.T.A.B. 1990) 274
Clicks Billiards, Inc. v. Sixshooters, Inc., 251 F.3d 1252 (9th Cir. 2001) 374
Coats v. Merrick Thread Co., 149 U.S. 562 (1893) 220
Cohen v. California, 403 U.S. 15 (1971) 357
Compco Corp. v. Day-Brite Lighting, Inc., 376 U.S. 234 (1964) 226
Crescent Tool Co. v. Kilborn & Bishop Co., 247 F. 299 (2d Cir. 1917) 220, 226, 232
Dastar Corp. v. Twentieth Century Fox Film Corp., 539 U.S. 23 (2003) 309, 316
Day-Brite Lighting, Inc. v. Sandee Manufacturing. Co., 286 F.2d 596 (7th Cir. 1960) 220
Deere & Co. v. Farmhand, Inc., 560 F. Supp. 85 (S.D. Iowa 1982), aff'd, 721 F.2d 253 (8th Cir. 1983) 42, 112, 116–17, 118
Dippin' Dots, Inc. v. Frosty Bites Distribution, LLC, 369 F.3d 1197 (11th Cir. 2004) 249, 351
Dorr-Oliver, Inc. v. Fluid-Quip, Inc., 94 F.3d 376 (7th Cir. 1996) 367
Duraco Prods., Inc. v. Joy Plastic Enters., Ltd., 40 F.3d 1431 (3d Cir. 1994) 367
Elizabeth Arden, Inc. v. Frances Denney, Inc., 99 F.2d 272 (3d Cir. 1938) 220
Eppendorf-Netheler-Hinz GMBH v. Ritter GMBH, 289 F.3d 351, 358 (5th Cir. 2002) 108
Ernest Thompson Fine Furniture Maker, Inc. v. Youart, 16 U.S.P.Q.2d (BNA) 1386 (N.M. Ct. App. 1990) 367
Ex parte American Enka Corp., 81 U.S.P.Q. (BNA) 476 (Comm'r Pat. 1949) 224
Ex parte Babson Bros. Co., 103 U.S.P.Q. (BNA) 115 (Chief Exam'r 1954) 223
Ex parte Boye Needle Co., 100 U.S.P.Q. (BNA) 124 (Chief Exam'r 1953) 224
Ex parte Haig & Haig Ltd., 118 U.S.P.Q. (BNA) 229 (Comm'r Pat. 1958) 224
Ex parte Minnesota Mining & Mfg. Co., 92 U.S.P.Q. (BNA) 74 (Chief Exam'r 1952) 224
Facenda v. N.F.L. Films, Inc., 542 F.3d 1007 (3d Cir. 2008) 343
Feathercombs, Inc. v. Solo Prods. Corp., 306 F.2d 251 (2d Cir.), cert. denied, 371 U.S. 910 (1962) 220
Feist Publications, Inc. v. Rural Telephone Serv. Co, 499 U.S. 340 (1991) 292
Ferrari S.P.A. v. McBurnie, 11 U.S.P.Q.2d 1843 (S.D. Cal. 1989) 376
Ferrari S.P.A. v. Roberts, 944 F.2d 1235 (6th Cir. 1991) 376, 377, 378
Funeral Consumers Alliance, Inc. v. Service Corp. International, 695 F.3d 330 (5th Cir. 2012) 232
General Motors Corp. v. Keystone Automotive Industry, Inc., 453 F.3d 351 (6th Cir. 2006) 377
General Time Instruments Corp. v. United States Time Corp., 165 F.2d 853 (2d Cir.) 226
Globe-Wemicke Co. v. Fred Macey Co., 119 F. 696 (6th Cir. 1902) 221
Gray v. Meijer, Inc., 295 F.3d 641 (6th Cir. 2002) 367
Gucci America, Inc. v. Dart, Inc., 715 F. Supp. 566, 12 U.S.P.Q.2d 1912 (S.D.N.Y. 1989) 377
Gucci America, Inc. v. Guess?, Inc., 868 F.Supp.2d 207 (S.D.N.Y. 2012) 300–1
Gum, Inc. v. Gumakers of America, Inc., 136 F.2d 957 (3d Cir. 1943) 220, 228
Haig & Haig Ltd. v. Maradel Products., Inc., 249 F. Supp. 575 (S.D.N.Y. 1966) 231

Hermès International v. Lederer de Paris Fifth Avenue, Inc., 219 F.3d 104 (2d Cir. 2000) 374, 375, 376, 377
INS v. Cardoza-Fonseca, 480 U.S. 421 (1987) 222, 223
International News Service v. Associated Press, 248 U.S. 215 (1918) 214, 367
Inwood Laboratories, Inc. v. Ives Laboratories, Inc., 456 U.S. 844 (1982) 109, 111, 226, 231, 278–79
J.C. Penney Co. v. H.D. Lee Mercantile Co., 120 F.2d 949 (8th Cir. 1941) 221, 226
John H. Rice & Co. v. Redlich Manufacturing Co., 202 F. 155 (3d Cir. 1913) 221
Keds Corp. v. Renee International Trading Corp., 888 F.2d 215 (1st Cir. 1989) 376
Keene Corp. v. Paraflex Industry, Inc., 653 F.2d 822 (3d Cir. 1981) 110, 111, 117, 118, 225
Keene Corp. v. United States, 508 U.S. 200 (1993) 223
Kellogg Co. v. National Biscuit Co., 305 U.S. 111 (1938) 109–19, 218, 220, 232
Key West Hand Print Fabrics, Inc. v. Serbin, Inc., 244 F. Supp. 287 (S.D. Fla. 1965) 220
L.D. Kichler Co. v. Dacoil, Inc., 192 F.3d 1349 (Fed. Cir. 1999) 117, 118
Levi Strauss & Co. v. Abercrombie & Fitch Trading Co., 633 F.3d 1158 (9th Cir. 2011) 378
Levi Strauss & Co. v. Blue Bell, Inc., 632 F.2d 822 (9th Cir. 1980) 376
Lois Sportswear, U.S.A., Inc. v. Levi Strauss & Co., 799 F.2d 867 (2d Cir. 1986) 376, 377
Louis Vuitton Malletier v. Dooney & Bourke, Inc., 340 F. Supp. 2d 415, 431 (S.D.N.Y. 2004) 377
Louis Vuitton Malletier v. Dooney & Bourke, Inc., 454 F.3d 108 (2d Cir. 2006) 374
Lucien Lelong, Inc. v. Lenal, Inc., 181 F.2d 3 (5th Cir. 1950) 220
M-5 Steel Manufacturing., Inc. v. O'Hagin's Inc., 61 U.S.P.Q.2d 1086, WL 1167788 (T.T.A.B. 2001) 117–18
Maker's Mark Distillery, Inc. v. Diageo North American Inc., 679 F.3d 410 (6th Cir. 2012) 113, 122–23
Market Co. v. Hoffman, 101 U.S. 112 (1879) 223
Marvel Co. v. Pearl, 133 F. 160 (2d Cir. 1904) 221
Mastercrafters Clock & Radio Co. v. Vacheron & Constantin-Le Coultre Watches, Inc., 221 F.2d 464 (2d Cir. 1955) 375, 376, 377, 379
Matal v. Tam, 137 S. Ct. 1744 (2017) 344, 350, 352
McCoy v. Mass. Inst. of Tech., 950 F.2d 13 (1st Cir. 1991) 113
McDermott International, Inc. v. Wilander, 498 U.S. 337 (1991) 222
McLean v. Fleming, 96 U.S. 245 (1877) 222
Meccano, Ltd. v. Wanamaker, 250 F. 450 (2d Cir. 1918), aff'd, 253 U.S. 136 (1920) 220
Mishawaka Rubber & Woolen Mfg. Co. v. S.S. Kresge Co., 316 U.S. 203 (1942) 129
Modem Aids, Inc. v. R.H. Macy & Co., 264 F.2d 93 (2d Cir. 1959) 220, 221
Morissette v. United States, 342 U.S. 246 (1952) 222
Morton-Norwich Prods., Inc., Re, 671 F.2d 1332 (C.C.P.A. 1982) 248
Moskal v. United States, 498 U.S. 103 (1990) 223
NAACP v. Button, 371 U.S. 415 (1963) 345
Nabisco, Inc. v. PF Brands, Inc., 191 F.3d 208 (2d Cir. 1999) 230
Nachman Corp. v. Pension Benefit Guaranty Corp., 446 U.S. 359 (1980) 222
Nichol v. Pullman Standard, Inc., 889 F.2d 115 (7th Cir.1989) 113
Nor-Am Chemical v. O.M. Scott & Sons Co., 4 U.S.P.Q.2d 1316 (E.D. Pa. 1987) 112
Norwich Pharmacal Co. v. Sterling Drug, Inc., 271 F.2d 569 (2d Cir. 1959) 226, 278, 284
Pagliero v. Wallace China Co., Ltd., 198 F.2d 339 (9th Cir. 1952) 110, 111, 124, 226
Paramount Industry, Inc. v. Solar Prods. Corp., 186 F.2d 999 (2d Cir. 1951) 220
Pfizer, Inc. v. Gov't of India, 434 U.S. 308, 314 (1978) 233
Philadelphia Novelty Manufacturing Co. v. Rouss, 40 F. 585 (C.C.S.D.N.Y. 1889) 220
Platt v. Union Pacific R.R., 99 U.S. 48 (1878) 223
Polo Fashions, Inc. v. Craftex, Inc., 816 F.2d 145 (4th Cir. 1987) 376
Publications International, Ltd. v. Landoll, Inc., 164 F.3d 337, 342 (7th Cir. 1998) 339
Qualitex Co. v. Jacobson Prods. Co., Inc., 514 U.S. 159 (1995) 37, 39, 42, 61, 62, 108, 111, 112, 113, 114, 115, 117, 122, 123, 125, 129, 130, 136, 225, 231, 248, 272, 292, 346, 347, 357, 358

Ratzlaf v. United States, 510 U.S. 135 (1994) 223
In re Construction Research & Technology GmbH, 122 U.S.P.Q.2d 1583 (TTAB 2017) 77
In re Fantasia Distribution, Inc., 120 U.S.P.Q.2d 1137 (TTAB, 2016) 60
In re Florists' Transworld Delivery, Inc., 106 U.S.P.Q.2d 1784 119
In re Hollaender Mfg. Co., 511 F.2d 1186, 1189 (C.C.P.A. 1975) 109
In re Honeywell, Inc., 497 F.2d 1344 (C.C.P.A. 1974) 224
In re Kotzin, 276 F.2d 411 (C.C.P.A. 1960) 224
In re Mogen David Wine Corp., 328 F.2d 925 (C.C.P.A. 1964) 224
In re Morton-Norwich Products, Inc., 671 F.2d 1332 (C.C.P.A. 1982) 109, 224, 231
In re Nantucket, Inc., 677 F.2d 95 (C.C.P.A. 1982) 223
In re N.V. Organon, 79 U.S.P.Q.2d 1639, 2006 WL 1723556 (T.T.A.B. 2006) 120, 279
In re Owens-Corning Fiberglass Corp., 774 F.2d 1116 (Fed. Cir. 1985) 42, 224
In re Pollak Steel Co., 131 U.S.P.Q. 482, 1961 WL 7862 (T.T.A.B. 1961), aff'd 314 F.2d 566 (C.C.P.A. 1963) 119
In Re Primo Water Corp., 87 U.S.P.Q.2d 1376 (TTAB 2008) 77
In re Slokevage, 441 F.3d 957 (Fed. Cir. 2006) 292
Reebok International Ltd. v. Sung Hwa International Corp., 6 U.S.P.Q.2d 1233 (S.D.N.Y. 1987) 376
Reed v. Town of Gilbert, 135 S. Ct. 2218 (2015) 343
Reiter v. Sonotone Corp., 442 U.S. 330 (1979) 223
Remco Industry, Inc. v. Toyomenka, Inc., 286 F. Supp. 948 (S.D.N.Y. 1968) 220
Remington-Rand, Inc. v. Mastercraft Corp., 67 F.2d 218 (6th Cir. 1933) 220
Rock & Roll Hall of Fame & Museum, Inc. v. Gentile Productions, 134 F.3d 749 (6th Cir. 1998) 292
Roho, Inc. v. Marquis, 902 F.2d 356 (5th Cir. 1990) 367
Rolex Watch U.S.A., Inc. v. "Bud" Forrester, 2 U.S.P.Q.2d 1292 (SD Fla 1986) 376
Rolex Watch U.S.A., Inc. v. Canner, 645 F. Supp. 484 (S.D. Fla. 1986) 375, 376, 377, 378
Rolls-Royce Motors Ltd. v. A & A Fiberglass, Inc., 428 F. Supp. 689 (N.D. Ga. 1976) 376
Ross-Whitney Corp. v. Smith Kline & French Labs., 207 F.2d 190 (9th Cir. 1953) 276–77
Russello v. United States, 464 U.S. 16 (1983) 223
Sassafras Entertainments, Inc. v. Roshco, Inc., 915 F. Supp. 1 (N.D. III. 1996) 367
Savant Homes, Inc. v. Collins, 809 F.3d 1133 (10th Cir. 2016) 346
Saxony Products., Inc. v. Guerlain, Inc., 513 F.2d 716 (9th Cir. 1975) 371
Sears, Roebuck & Co. v. Stiffel Co., 376 U.S. 225 (1964) 226
Shire US Inc. v. Barr Labs. Inc., 329 F.3d 348 (3d Cir. 2003) 284
Sinko v. Snow-Craggs Corp., 105 F.2d 450 (7th Cir. 1939) 220
SK&F, Co. v. Premo Pharmacological Labs., Inc., 625 F.2d 1055, 1057–58 (3d Cir. 1980) 277
Smith v. Chanel, Inc., 402 F.2d 562 (9th Cir. 1968) 367, 371, 378, 379
Smith v. Krause, 160 F. 270 (C.C.S.D.N.Y. 1908) 226
Societe Anonyme de la Distillerie de la Liqueur Benedictine de L'Abbaye de Fecamp v. Puziello, 250 F. 928 (E.D.N.Y. 1918) 220
Societe Comptoir de L'Industrie Cotonniere Etablissements Boussac v. Alexander's Department Stores, Inc., 299 F.2d 33 (2d Cir. 1962) 371
Sorrell v. IMS Health Inc., 564 U.S. 552 (2011) 344, 350
Spence v. Washington, 418 U.S. 405 (1974) 352
Stone v. INS, 514 U.S.386 (1995) 222
Sunburst Products, Inc. v. Cyrk International, 98 F.3d 1358 (Fed. Cir. 1996) 375
Sylvania Electric Products v. Dura Electric Lamp Co., 247 F.2d 730, 732 (3d Cir. 1957) 109
Tabor v. Ulloa, 323 F.2d 823 (9th Cir. 1963) 223
Texas v. Johnson, 491 U.S. 397 (1989) 349, 352
Thomas & Betts v. Panduit Corp., 65 F.3d 654 (7th Cir. 1995) 367
Tinker v. Des Moines Independent Community School District, 393 U.S. 503 (1969) 349
T-Mobile US, Inc. v. Aio Wireless LLC, 991 F.Supp.2d 888 (S.D. Tex. 2014) 355

TrafFix Devices Inc. v. Marketing Displays Inc., 532 U.S. 23 (2001) 108, 112, 113, 114, 248, 295, 346, 347
Truck Equipment Service Co. v. Fruehauf Corp., 536 F.2d 1210 (8th Cir.), cert. denied, 429 U.S. 86 (1976) 121, 225, 227
Turner & Seymour Manufacturing Co. v. A & J Manufacturing Co., 20 F.2d 298 (2d Cir. 1927) 228
Turner Broadcasting Systems v. F.C.C., 512 U.S. 622 (1994) 344
Two Pesos, Inc. v. Taco Cabana, Inc., 505 U.S. 763 (1992) 225–26, 292
Ty, Inc. v. Perryman, 306 F.3d 509 (7th Cir. 2002) 227
United States v. Bell, 524 F.2d 202 (2d Cir. 1975) 113
United States v. E.I. du Pont de Nemours & Co., 351 U.S. 377 (1956) 253
United States v. Gantos, 817 F.2d 41 (8th Cir. 1987) 377
United States v. Gonzalez, 630 F. Supp. 894 (S.D. Fla. 1986) 377
United States v. Hon, 904 F.2d 803 (2d Cir. 1990) 377
United States v. O'Brien, 391 U.S. 367 (1968) 344
United States v. Stevens, 559 U.S. 460 (2010) 343
United States v. Torkington, 812 F.2d 1347 (11th Cir. 1987) 377
Virginia State Board of Pharmacy v. Virginia Citizens Consumer Council, Inc., 425 U.S. 748 (1976)) 350
Versa Products Co. v. Bifold Co., 50 F.3d 189 (3d Cir. 1995) 367
Villeroy & Boch Keramische Werke K.G. v. THC Sys., Inc., 999 F.2d 619 (2d Cir. 1993) 111, 118
Vision Sports, Inc. v. Melville Corp., 888 F.2d 609, 613 (9th Cir. 1989) 374
Vogue Ring Creations, Inc. v. Hardman, 410 F. Supp. 609 (D.R.I. 1976) 220
Wal-Mart Stores, Inc. v. Samara Brothers, Inc., 529 U.S. 205 (2000), 120 S. Ct. 1339, (2000) 110, 178, 215, 226, 228, 292, 374
Wal-Mart Stores v. Samara Bros., 529 U.S. 205 (2000) 113, 114
Wallace International Silversmiths, Inc. v. Godinger Silver Art Co., Inc., 916 F.2d 76 (2d Cir. 1990), cert. denied, 499 U.S. 976 (1991) 110, 111
Ward v. Rock Against Racism, 491 U.S. 781 (1989) 344
Warner Lambert Co., v. McCrory's Corp., 718 F. Supp. 389 (D.N.J. 1989) 120
West Point Manufacturing Co. v. Detroit Stamping Co., 222 F.2d 581 (6th Cir. 1955) 220, 221
William R. Warner & Co. v. Eli Lilly & Co., 265 U.S. 526 (1924) 218, 220, 221, 226, 232, 277–78
Wright v. Morris, 111 F.3d 414 (6th Cir. 1997) 113
W.T. Rogers Co., Inc. v. Keene, 778 F.2d 334 (1985) 115, 118
Zangerle & Peterson Co. v. Venice Furniture Novelty Manufacturing Co., 133 F.2d 266 (7th Cir. 1943) 220
Zazú Designs v. L'Oreal, S.A., 979 F.2d 499 (7th Cir. 1992) 290
Zenith Radio Corp. v. Hazeltine Research, Inc., 395 U.S. 100 (1969) 232

Table of Legislation

INTERNATIONAL INSTRUMENTS

Agreement on Trade-Related Aspects of Intellectual Property Rights (1994) (TRIPS) 8, 63, 186
- Art 2(1) 161, 163
- Art 15 . . . . 161, 162–64, 215, 289, 291, 294
- Art 15(1) 1, 2, 4, 13, 14, 25, 38, 61, 131, 148–49, 163, 164, 273, 290, 294
- Art 15(2) 163
- Art 15(3) 291
- Art 16 162
- Art 16(3) 7, 213, 289
- Art 18 289
- Art 21 243
- Art 31 243
- Art 40(2) 243

American Convention on Human Rights (1969)
- Art 13 341

Australia–United States Free Trade Agreement (2004)
- Art 17(2) 273

Convention for the Protection of Human Rights and Fundamental Freedoms *see* European Convention on Human Rights

European Convention on Human Rights (1950) 292
- Art 10(1) 341, 342
- Art 10(2) 342
- Art 10(3) 342

International Covenant on Civil and Political Rights (1966)
- Art 19(2) 341

Madrid Agreement Concerning the International Registration of Marks (1891) 16

Protocol (1989) 16, 55

Marrakesh Agreement Establishing the World Trade Organization (1994)
- Annex 1C *see* Agreement on Trade-Related Aspects of Intellectual Property Rights

Paris Convention for the Protection of Industrial Property (1883) 14–15, 16
- Arts 1 to 12 161
- Art 10*bis* 149
- Art 6 155–61
- Art 6 *quinquies* A(1) 15, 149–51, 161, 162
- Art 6 *quinquies* B 149, 150, 151
- Art 6 *quinquies* C 149
- Art 6(1) 152–62
- Art 6(4) 153, 155
- Final Protocol
  - para 4(1) 153–61
  - para 4(2) 155

Singapore Treaty on the Law of Trademarks (1994) 273, 294
- Art 2 20
- Art 2(1) 17
- Art 3 . . . . 17, 18
- Art 5(1) 34
- Art 8 20
- Regulations (2006)
  - r 3 . . . . 2, 17–20, 23, 32–33

Trademark Law Treaty (1994) 14, 15–17, 294
- Art 2(a) and (b) 16
- Arts 3 to 13 15
- Art 3 15
- Art 3(1) 16
- Art 3(a) 16
- Art 3(x) and (xi) 16
- Art 4 15
- r 3(2) 17
- r 3(3) 16–17

TRIPS *see* Agreement on Trade-Related Aspects of Intellectual Property Rights

United States–Singapore Free Trade Agreement (2003)
- Art 16(2) 273

Vienna Convention on the Law of Treaties (1969)
- Art 32 150

EUROPEAN UNION

Treaties

Treaty on the Functioning of the European Union (2007) (TFEU)
- Art 101 (ex Art 81, prev. Art 85) 237, 238, 240, 242
- Art 101(1) 241
- Art 101(2) 237
- Art 102 (ex Art 82, prev. Art 86) 237, 239

Regulations

Commission Regulation (EEC) No 556/89 of 30 November 1988 on the application of Article 85(3) of the Treaty to certain categories of know-how licensing agreements [1989] O.J. L 61/1 241
Council Regulation (EC) No. 40/94 of 20 December 1993 on the Community trade mark [1994] O.J. L 11/1. . . . . 101, 238
Art 7(e). 205
Art 7(1) 204
Council Regulation (EC) No. 6/2002 of 12 December 2001 on Community Designs [2002] O.J. L 3/1. 370
Art 4(2) 204
Art 25(1) 88, 292
Council Regulation (EC) No. 139/ 2004 of 20 January 2004 on the Control of Concentrations Between Undertakings [2004] O.J. L 24/1
Arts 2 and 3 239
Council Regulation (EC) No. 207/2009 of 26 February 2009 on the Community trademark [2009] O.J. L 78/1. 206
Recital 8 212
Art 7(1) 148
Art 37(2) 82
Commission Regulation (EU) No 330/2010 of 20 April 2010 on the application of Article 101(3) of the Treaty on the Functioning of the European Union to categories of vertical agreements and concerted practices [2010] O.J. L 102/1. 241
Recital 3 242
Art 2(3) 242
Commission Regulation (EU) No 316/2014 of 21 March 2014 on the application of Article 101(3) of the Treaty on the Functioning of the European Union to categories of technology transfer agreements [2014] O.J. L 93/17 237
Regulation (EU) 2015/2424 of the European Parliament and of the Council of 16 December 2015 amending Council Regulation (EC) No 207/2009 on the Community trade mark and Commission Regulation (EC) No 2868/95 implementing Council Regulation (EC) No 40/94 on the Community trade mark, and repealing Commission Regulation (EC) No 2869/95 on the fees payable to the Office for Harmonization in the Internal Market (Trade Marks and Designs) [2015] O.J. L 341/21 . . . . 148, 206
Art 9(2) 213
Commission Implementing Regulation (EU) 2017/1431 of 18 May 2017 laying down detailed rules for implementing certain provisions of Council Regulation (EC) No 207/2009 on the European Union trade mark [2017] O.J. L 205/39
Art 3(2) 65
Regulation (EU) 2017/1001 of the European Parliament and of the Council of 14 June 2017 on the European Union Trade Mark [2017] O.J. L 154/1 . . . . 146, 238
Art 4. 65, 131, 347
Art 4(b) 134
Art 7(1) 78, 213, 347
Art 7(3) 104
Art 7(e). 137
Art 9(2) 355
Art 14(1) 82, 101
Art 18. 102
Art 31. 65
Art 58(1) 102

Directives

First Council Directive 89/104/EEC of 21 December 1988 to approximate the laws of the Member States relating to trade marks [1989] O.J. L 40/1. . . . . 89, 238
Art 2. 61
Art 3(e). 205
Art 3(1) 39
Art 5(1) 98
Art 5(2) 94
Directive 98/71/EC of the European Parliament and of the Council of 13 October 1998 on the legal protection of designs [1998] O.J. L 289/28. . . . . 207, 292
Arts 4 and 5 292
Art 7(1) 208

Art 10 . . . 292
Art 10(1) . . . 208
Art 11 . . . 292
Directive 2008/95/EC of the European Parliament and of the Council of 22 October 2008 to approximate the laws of the Member States relating to trade marks [2008] O.J. L 299/25 . . . 39, 89, 206
Recital 11 . . . 212
Art 2 . . . 38, 61
Art 3(1) . . . 65, 90, 148, 204
Art 3(3) . . . 328
Art 5(1) . . . 98
Art 5(2) . . . 94
Art 5(5) . . . 94
Art 6(1) . . . 100
Directive 2015/2436/EU of the European Parliament and of the Council of 16 December 2015 to approximate the laws of the Member States relating to trade marks [2015] O.J. L 336/1 . . . 58, 89, 206, 238
Recital 13 . . . 66
Recital 16 . . . 212
Art 3 . . . 2, 39, 61, 65, 131, 289, 347
Art 3(2) . . . 67
Art 4 . . . 42, 90, 295
Art 4(1) . . . 39, 57, 72, 78, 148, 290, 347
Art 4(4) . . . 104, 328, 347
Art 9 . . . 102
Art 10(2) . . . 94, 95, 98, 213, 355
Art 10(6) . . . 94
Art 14(1) . . . 82, 101, 351
Art 16 . . . 289
Art 19 . . . 102

NATIONAL INSTRUMENTS

Australia

Trade Marks Act 1955 (Cth) . . . 172, 301
s 6 . . . 40
s 120(1) to (3) . . . 168
Trade Marks Act 1994 (Cth) . . . 41
s 39 . . . 41
Trade Marks Act 1995 (Cth) . . . 40–41, 172, 174, 348
s 6 . . . 40
s 41 . . . 41
s 120 . . . 355
s 120(3) . . . 170
s 122(1) . . . 351

Belgium *see* **Benelux**

Benelux

Uniform Law on Trademarks 1971
Art 1(2) . . . 205

Canada

Trademarks Act 1985 . . . 135

China

Recognition and Protection of Well-known Trademarks Provisions
Art 2 . . . 199
Trademark Law (Shangbiao Fa) 1982
Art 7 . . . 186
Trademark Law (Shangbiao Fa) 2001
Art 8 . . . 186–87
Trademark Law (Shangbiao Fa) 2010
Art 28 . . . 191
Trademark Law (Shangbiao Fa) 2013
Art 7 . . . 192
Art 8 . . . 187
Art 9 . . . 187
Art 11 . . . 187
Art 12 . . . 188
Art 13 . . . 198
Art 13(1) . . . 199
Art 13(2) . . . 193
Art 13(3) . . . 193, 196–97
Art 14 . . . 193
Art 14(1) . . . 193
Art 19 . . . 192
Art 45 . . . 192
Art 57(2) . . . 196
Art 68 . . . 192

Germany

Trademark Act (old) (Warenzeichengesetz - WZG) 1936
s 25 . . . 89, 205
Trademark Law (Markengesetz) 1994 . . . 205

India

Trade Marks Act 1999
s 2(m) . . . 273
s 2(zb) . . . 273

Italy

Civil Code
Art 15(1) . . . 208

Japan

Act on the Partial Revision of the Patent Act and Other Acts 2014 135
Trademark Act (Shohyo-ho) 1959
Art 2. . . . . .40, 297
Art 3(1) 40

Luxembourg *see* **Benelux**

Malaysia

Trade Marks Act 1976
s 38(1) 168

Netherlands *see* **Benelux**

New Zealand

Trademarks Act 1953
s 8(1) 170
Trademarks Act 2002
s 5 347
s 5(1) 134
s 18 347
s 89(1) 170
s 89(2) 170, 168

Singapore

Trade Marks Act 1998, c. 332
s 2 40
s 7(3) 40, 147–48

United Kingdom

Patents, Designs, and Trade Marks Act 1883 (46 & 47 Vict. c. 57)
s 64 156
Trade Marks Act 1905 170
Trade Marks Act 1938
s 4(3) 170
Trade Marks Act 1994 . . . . .39, 205
s 1(1) 38

United States

Constitution 1783
Art 1(8) 211, 291
Amendment 1 343
Lanham (Trademark) Act 1946 (15 U.S.C. Ch. 22: § 1051 et seq.) 217, 219, 371
§ 2(f) 221–22
§ 14 289
§ 21(a) 295
§ 43(a) 221, 223, 225, 234
§ 45 (15 U.S.C. § 1127) 61, 130, 274, 346, 352
§ 114 289
§ 115(a) 290
15 U.S.C. § 1051(a) 346
15 U.S.C. § 1052(e) 346, 356
15 U.S.C. § 1053 346
15 U.S.C. § 1056 .82
15 U.S.C. § 1058 289
15 U.S.C. § 1125 355
15 U.S.C. § 1125(c) 351
Omnibus Appropriate Act 1998
§ 211 161
Restatement (First) of Torts 1938
§ 742 109
Restatement (Third) of Unfair Competition 1995
§ 17 . . . . 111, 112
Trademark Dilution Revision Act 2006
15 U.S.C.A. § 1125(c) 378
United States Code of Laws
17 U.S.C. § 106 .292
35 U.S.C. § 112 .291
35 U.S.C. § 171 .292

List of Contributors

Mitchell Adams is a Research Associate at the Centre for Transformative Innovation at Swinburne University and the Swinburne Law School. His interest is in empirical studies in intellectual property law and in particularly the registered trademarks system in Australia. Mitchell is a registered trademarks attorney and an Australian solicitor with experience in intellectual property and entertainment law. He has worked in the Intellectual Property and Commercialisation group at CSIRO and before that, at a prominent entertainment law practice in Melbourne. He graduated from Monash University with LLB (Hons) and BSc degrees, and was awarded first class honours in law in the area of intellectual property law.

Katya Assaf-Zakharov is an Assistant Professor at the Law School of the Hebrew University and a member of the DAAD Center for German Studies. Her main fields of research are Intellectual Property, Law & Society, Law & Culture, Law & Psychology, Law & Philosophy, as well as Comparative Law. She gained her PhD from the Ludwig-Maximilian University of Munich and later worked as a Visiting Professor at the University of Illinois.

Lavinia Brancusi held her law degrees at Warsaw University, Faculty of Law (master, dr. iur.) with an awarded doctoral dissertation in design law. She is a lecturer at New Technologies Law Centre, Institute of Law Studies, Polish Academy of Sciences in Warsaw and an Of Counsel at AOMB Polska. Her research interests cover cumulative protection in intellectual property, with a specific focus on product protection, functionality in trademark and design law as well as the interface between trademarks (brands) and competition rules.

Irene Calboli is Professor of Law at Texas A&M University School of Law, and Transatlantic Technology Law Forum Fellow at Stanford Law School. She has been a visiting professor and scholar in academic institutions worldwide. Most recently, she was Visiting Professor, Lee Kong Chian Fellow, and the Founding Deputy Director of the Applied Research Centre for Intellectual Assets and the Law in Asia, a Centre that she headed from 2015 until 2017, at Singapore Management University School of Law. An elected member of the American Law Institute and associate member of the Singapore Academy of Law, she currently serves, inter alia, as member of the Council of the International Law Association (Singapore Branch), Chair of the Art Law Section of the Association of American Law Schools, and member of the Legislation and Regulation Committee of the International Trademark Association.

Carolina Castaldi is Associate Professor in "Innovation in Service-based Economies" at Eindhoven University of Technology, the Netherlands. She obtained her PhD from Sant' Anna School of Advanced Studies, Pisa, Italy and is a former Robert Solow Fellow. Her research deals with the economics and management of innovation. She has extensive expertise in intellectual property rights, both patents and trademarks.

Denis Croze is Director of the Regional Office in ASEAN of the World Intellectual Property Organization, located in Singapore, since June 2012. Prior to this, Mr. Croze held various positions at WIPO in the Office of the Director General, the Copyright and Enforcement Sector and the Economic Development Sector. As Head of the International Law Development Section, he was the Secretary of the Standing Committee on the Law of Trademarks, Industrial Designs and Geographical Indications (SCT). His previous experiences were with the French Patent and Trademark Office (INPI), the International Chamber of Commerce, and the Office of Legal Affairs of the United Nations in New York.

Deven Desai is Associate Professor and Area Coordinator of Law and Ethics at Georgia Institute of Technology, Scheller College and an affiliated fellow of the Internet Society Project at Yale Law School. He was also the first Academic Research Counsel at Google, Inc., and a Visiting Fellow at Princeton University's Center for Information Technology Policy. He has written extensively on the relationship between branding and marketing practices and trademark law. His work has appeared in the Georgetown Law Journal, Minnesota Law Review, and Notre Dame Law Review. He has handled intellectual property matters with Quinn, Emanuel, Urquhart, & Sullivan, LLP, and was part of the policy team for the 2002 Cory Booker for Mayor campaign.

Dev Saif Gangjee is an Associate Professor at the Oxford Law Faculty and Director of the Oxford IP Research Centre. Dev's research focuses on intellectual property, with a special emphasis on branding and trademarks, geographical indications, and copyright law. He is a Research Affiliate with IP Osgoode, Canada. Dev also serves as an Editorial Board member of the Modern Law Review and the Indian Law Review.

Gustavo Ghidini is Professor of Intellectual Property Law at the Luiss Guido Carli University, Rome and Milan University. He is a Past President of the International Association for the Teaching and Research in Intellectual Property (ATRIP) and was a Senior Fernand Braudel Fellow, European University Institute, Firenze (2011). He is the editor (with Peter Drahos and Hanns Ullrich) of *KRITIKA-Essays on Intellectual Property*. His latest book in English is *Rethinking Intellectual Property-Balancing Conflicts of Interest in the Constitutional Paradigm* (2018).

Michael Handler is a Professor in the Faculty of Law, University of New South Wales, Australia, and a member of the Intellectual Property Committee of the Law Council of Australia. He has published numerous books, journal articles, and book chapters on trademark law, and is the co-author, with Robert Burrell, of the Oxford University Press treatise *Australian Trade Mark Law* (2d ed. 2016).

Justin Hughes is the Hon. William Matthew Byrne Professor of Law at Loyola Law School, Loyola Marymount University, Los Angeles, where he teaches international trade and intellectual property. From 2002 until 2013, he taught at Cardozo Law School in New York. From 2009 until 2013, Professor Hughes also served as Senior Advisor to the Undersecretary of Commerce for Intellectual Property. In that capacity, he was the US chief negotiator for the Beijing Treaty on Audiovisual Performances (2012) and the Marrakesh Treaty for the Blind (2013). Professor Hughes was educated at Oberlin and Harvard.

Annette Kur is Affiliated Research Fellow at the Max-Planck-Institute for Innovation and Competition, Munich and an Honorary Professor at Ludwig-Maximilians-University, Munich.

Ng-Loy Wee Loon is Professor of Law at National University of Singapore. She is also a member of Singapore's Copyright Tribunal and a member of the Singapore Domain Name Dispute Resolution Policy Panel. In 2013, she was conferred the "Singapore Law Merit Award" by the Singapore Academy of Law in recognition of her contributions made to the development and advancement of Singapore law. In 2016, she was appointed "Senior Counsel *(honoris causa)*" by the Singapore Court of Appeal for her contributions to the legal profession, in particular her assistance to the Court in her role as *amicus curiae*.

J. Glynn Lunney holds a joint appointment at the School of Law and the College of Engineering at Texas A&M University. He holds an engineering degree from Texas A&M, a law degree from Stanford, and a PhD in economics from Tulane. Professor Lunney teaches and writes primarily in the field of intellectual property, with a focus on the economic analysis of legal issues. He is an internationally recognized scholar, has published a casebook, *Trademarks and Unfair Competition* (West 2d ed. 2015), and has a forthcoming book on copyright and music, *Copyright's Excess: Music and Money in the U.S. Recording Industry*.

Kavya Susan Mammen is currently working as an Associate at an intellectual property law firm in New Delhi. Kavya is a graduate of the National Academy of Legal Studies and Research (NALSAR) University of Law, Hyderabad (BA LLB (Hons)) and she also holds an LLM from the Munich Intellectual Property Law Centre (MIPLC), Munich, Germany. Previously she has worked as a Research Fellow at the Centre for Innovation, Intellectual Property and Competition (CIIPC) at National Law University Delhi and in the Data Privacy and Contracts teams of IT companies in Bangalore.

Lisa P. Ramsey is a Professor of Law at the University of San Diego School of Law, where she is a founding member of the Center for Intellectual Property Law and Markets. She teaches and writes in the areas of trademark law, intellectual property, and international intellectual property. She has given presentations on trademark law throughout the United States and around the world, including in Australia, Canada, China, Denmark, New Zealand, Singapore, and the United Kingdom. Before joining the USD law faculty, Professor Ramsey was an intellectual property litigator for several years at a law firm in San Diego, California.

Amanda Scardamaglia is the Department Chair of the Swinburne Law School. Amanda's area of research is intellectual property law with a special focus on empirical and historical studies in trade mark law, branding, advertising, and the consumer. She completed her LLB (Hons), BA, and PhD at the University of Melbourne and is admitted to practice as an Australian Legal Practitioner in the Supreme Court of Victoria. Amanda was a State Library of Victoria Creative Fellow in 2015–2016 and was awarded a residential fellowship at the Centre for Intellectual Property Policy & Management at Bournemouth University in 2017. She is the author of the book *Colonial Australian Trade Mark Law: Narratives in Lawmaking, People, Power and Place* (Australian Scholarly Publishing 2015) and editor of the peer-reviewed journal *Legal History*. Her second book, *Charles Troedel: From Stone to Print*, will be published by Melbourne Books in 2019.

Arul George Scaria is an Assistant Professor of Law and Co-Director of the Centre for Innovation, Intellectual Property and Competition (CIIPC) at the National Law University, Delhi. He did his doctoral studies at the International Max Planck Research School for Competition and Innovation (IMPRS-CI), which is a doctoral program jointly offered by the Max Planck Institute for Competition and Innovation and the Ludwig Maximilians Universität, Munich. His post-doctoral research at the Catholic University of Louvain (UCL), Belgium, was in the area of open access to large-scale research data. His publications include *Ambush Marketing: Game Within a Game* (Oxford University Press 2008) and *Piracy in the Film Industry: Copyright and Cultural Consonance* (Cambridge University Press 2014).

Martin Senftleben is Professor of Intellectual Property at the Centre for Law and Internet, Vrije Universiteit Amsterdam, Guest Professor at the Intellectual Property Research Institute, University of Xiamen, and Of Counsel at Bird & Bird, The Hague. His activities focus on the reconciliation of private intellectual property rights with competing public interests of a social, cultural, or economic nature. He holds a PhD from the University of Amsterdam. From 2004 to 2007, he was a legal officer in the trademarks department of the World Intellectual Property Organization (WIPO) in Geneva. Mr. Senftleben is a member of the Copyright Advisory Committee of the Dutch State. He provided advice to WIPO in several trademark and copyright projects. His numerous publications include *Copyright, Limitations and the Three-Step Test* (Kluwer Law International 2004) and *European Trade Mark Law—A Commentary* (with Annette Kur, Oxford University Press 2017).

Hoachen Sun is Associate Professor of Law and Director of the Law and Technology Center at the University of Hong Kong. His research and teaching focus is on the theoretical and policy foundation of intellectual property, Chinese intellectual property law, and international and comparative intellectual property law. His book tentatively entitled *Ethical Copyright: New Directions in Protecting the Public Interest* will be published by Cambridge University Press in 2019. He is the co-editor of *The Luxury Economy and Intellectual Property* (Oxford University Press 2015) and *The Cambridge Handbook of Copyright Limitations and Exceptions in Comparative Perspective* (Cambridge University Press, forthcoming 2019).

Introduction

Irene Calboli and Martin Senftleben

I. Expansion of the Trademark Domain

During the past decades, the domain of trademark law and the scope of trademark protection have been expanded significantly.[1] The flexible application of prerequisites for registration has paved the way for the recognition of a wide variety of signs as subject matter eligible for trademark protection. This includes single colors, shapes, sounds, smells, video clips, holograms, and even gestures.[2] With the elastic conceptual contours drawn in the trademark section of the 1994 Agreement on Trade-Related Aspects of Intellectual Property Rights (TRIPS),[3] this remarkable growth of the trademark universe—the inclusion of so-called "non-conventional" or "non-traditional" types of marks—has become a worldwide phenomenon. While not establishing an obligation to accept non-traditional types of marks at the national level, the 2006 Singapore Treaty on the Law of Trademarks reflects the willingness of policymakers across all continents to facilitate the registration of traditional and

[1] *Cf.* Irene Calboli, *Chocolate, Fashion, Toys and Cabs: The Misunderstood Distinctiveness of Non-Traditional Trademarks*, 49 Int'l Rev. Intell. Prop. & Competition L. 1 (2018); Martin R.F. Senftleben, *Trade Mark Protection—A Black Hole in the Intellectual Property Galaxy?*, 42 Int'l Rev. Intell. Prop. & Competition L. 383 (2011).

[2] With regard to the debate on non-traditional types of marks at the beginning of the new millenium, see Ivo Lewalter und Paul T. Schrader, *Die Fühlmarke*, Gewerblicher Rechtsschutz und Urheberrecht 476 (2005); Felix Hauck, *Aktuelle Entwicklungen bei der Eintragung von Farbmarken*, Gewerblicher Rechtsschutz und Urheberrecht 363 (2005); Annette Kur, *Alles oder Nichts im Formmarkenschutz?*, Gewerblicher Rechtsschutz und Urheberrecht—International Teil 755 (2004); Adrien Bouvel, *Qu'importe le flacon ... Le droit des marques malmené par les emballages*, Propriétés Intellectuelles 863 (2004); Ruth Arnet, *Markenschutz für Formen*, sic! 829 (2004); Jochen Pagenberg, *Trade Dress and the Three-Dimensional Marks—The Neglected Children of Trademark Law?*, 35 Int'l Rev. Intell. Prop. & Competition L. 831 (2004); Markus Bölling, *Der EuGH und die abstrakte Farbmarke—Von der bewussten Entwertung einer Markenform*, Markenrecht 384 (2004); Senta Bingener, *Das Wesen der Positionsmarke oder Wo die Positionsmarke hingehört*, Markenrecht 377 (2004); Alison Firth, Ellen Gredley, & Spyros M. Maniatis, *Shapes as Trade Marks: Public Policy, Functional Considerations and Consumer Perception*, Eur. Intell. Prop. Rev. 86 (2001).

[3] TRIPS: Agreement on Trade-Related Aspects of Intellectual Property Rights art. 15(1), Apr. 15, 1994, Marrakesh Agreement Establishing the World Trade Organization, Annex 1C, 1869 U.N.T.S. 299, 33 I.L.M. 1197 (1994) [hereinafter TRIPS].

non-traditional marks alike.[4] Recent bilateral and plurilateral international trade agreements continue on the same path.

The extension of the domain of trademark protection to non-traditional marks can be placed in the context of modern branding and marketing strategies. Today's marketers seek to create a brand experience for all senses that has the potential to become a product in its own right and a core asset of the trademark owner's business.[5] For this purpose, traditional word and figurative marks are supplemented with non-traditional brand insignia that are often more abstract and conceptual. Modern advertising campaigns may have success in educating consumers to make a connection between a specific color, design feature, or smell, and a particular origin of goods and services. Interestingly, trademark law and practice follow and support this trend in branding and marketing even though it blurs the concept of "trademark" by going far beyond traditional word and figurative signs.

This far-reaching support for modern branding and marketing strategies is not an international obligation. International law offers national legislators the opportunity to draw hard boundary lines and set limits to the expansion of the realm of trademark protection. For instance, WTO Members are free to make it a condition that trademarks be "visually perceptible".[6] Nonetheless, countries hesitate to avail themselves of this option to categorically exclude sound and smell from the circle of registrable signs. Additional room for an outright exclusion of certain categories of signs could follow from the invocation of traditional notions of trademark law, such as the distinction between the mark and the product. In theory, a trademark is a sign attached to the product. It should not constitute the product itself. Otherwise, indefinitely renewable trademark protection may impede the continuous evolution of new products in the marketplace. For the protection of products and product features, the intellectual property system offers innovation-based systems with a limited term of protection, such as patent, industrial design, and copyright law. Applying a strict mark/product dichotomy, trademark protection could be confined to signs that are attached to goods. In consequence, signs that form part of the goods themselves, such as product shape and other design features, would fall outside the domain of trademark law from the outset. In practice, however, lawmakers and judges have abandoned the traditional distinction between mark and product in many countries.[7] Apparently, it is deemed preferable to keep the doors to trademark

[4] See Rule 3, Regulations Under the Singapore Treaty on the Law of Trademarks (as in force on Nov. 1, 2011), http://www.wipo.int/treaties/en/ip/singapore/, which deals with a wide variety of non-traditional types of marks.

[5] J.E. Schroeder, *Brand Culture: Trade Marks, Marketing and Consumption*, *in* TRADE MARKS AND BRANDS—AN INTERDISCIPLINARY CRITIQUE 161 (Lionel Bently et al. eds., 2008); D. Scott, A. Oliver, & M. Ley-Pineda, *Trade Marks as Property: a Philosophical Perspective*, *in* TRADE MARKS AND BRANDS—AN INTERDISCIPLINARY CRITIQUE 285, 296 (Lionel Bently et al. eds., 2008); Ralph S. Brown, *Advertising and the Public Interest: Legal Protection of Trade Symbols*, 108 YALE L.J. 1619, 1622–34 (1999); Mark A. Lemley, *The Modern Lanham Act and the Death of Common Sense*, 108 YALE L.J. 1687, 1706–07 (1999).

[6] TRIPS art. 15(1).

[7] Article 3 of the EU Trade Mark Directive 2015/2436, for instance, provides the following illustrative list of signs that are eligible for trademark protection in EU Member States: 'personal names, or designs, letters, numerals, colours, the shape of goods or of the packaging of goods, or sounds.'

protection open, leave the filtering of inappropriate signs to trademark offices and tribunals, and the regulation of the scope of protection to decisions on infringement.

In the absence of clear-cut exclusions from trademark protection, open-ended legal instruments form the center of gravity in the regulation of non-traditional marks. On both sides of the Atlantic, courts are struggling with the application of the concept of technical and aesthetic functionality as a tool to police the borders of trademark protection and prevent encroachments upon freedom of competition and freedom of expression. To this day, however, neither U.S. judges nor their EU colleagues have found the sorcerer's stone for applying the functionality doctrine in a consistent manner.[8]

The kingpin of the trademark protection system—the basic requirement of distinctiveness—does not necessarily offer more satisfactory solutions. With regard to non-traditional types of marks, courts may make an attempt to pose additional obstacles by holding that consumers are not in the habit of making assumptions about the commercial origin of goods and services on the basis of product shape or color.[9] To establish distinctive character, brand owners will thus have to prove the acquisition of distinctive character through use in trade. Inherent distinctive character seems unlikely in the absence of exceptional circumstances. It remains to be seen, however, whether this configuration of the test of distinctive character is a robust normative correction or a mere empirical assumption. If it is based on the empirical observation that consumers are not used to non-traditional marks, then the assumption becomes weaker and weaker with every non-traditional identifier of commercial source which brand owners imprint in the minds of consumers.[10] With advertising campaigns educating consumers to understand shape, color, sound, and smell as indications of commercial origin, the argument of consumers having difficulty with the source-identifying function of these signs loses its power of persuasion.

Instead of functioning as a robust bulwark against the continuous expansion of the domain of trademark protection, the pinnacles and towers of the test of distinctive character are thus in danger of being demolished on the basis of empirical findings. Its remnants may be surmounted rather easily. In the context of trademark registration, distinctiveness has come to mean little more than "recognizable" by the human senses when it is applied to individual features of the signs for which

[8] *Cf.* Graeme B. Dinwoodie, *The Death of Ontology: A Teleological Approach to Trademark Law*, 84 Iowa L. Rev. 611, 685–91 (1999); Annette Kur, *Too Pretty to Protect? Trade Mark Law and the Enigma of Aesthetic Functionality* (Max Planck Institute for Intellectual Property & Competition Law Research Paper No. 11-16, 2011).

[9] *See, e.g.*, Case C-218/01, Henkel v. DPMA, 2004 E.C.R. I-1725, ¶ 52; Joined Cases C-53/01 to 55/01, *In re* Linde & Others, 2003 E.C.R. I-3161, ¶ 48; Case C-104/01, Libertel Groep v. Benelux-Merkenbureau, 2003 E.C.R. I-3793, ¶ 65.

[10] *Cf.* Lotte Anemaet, *The Public Domain is Under Pressure: Why We Should Not Rely on Empirical Data When Assessing Trademark Distinctiveness*, 47 Int'l Rev. Intell. Prop. & Competition L. 303 (2016); Martin R.F. Senftleben, *Public Domain Preservation in EU Trademark Law—A Model for Other Regions?*, 103 Trademark Rep. 775, 801–03 (2013); Lisa P. Ramsey, *Descriptive Trademarks and the First Amendment*, 70 Tenn. L. Rev. 1095, 1150 (2003); Robert C. Denicola, *Trademarks as Speech: Constitutional Implications of the Emerging Rationales for the Protection of Trade Symbols*, 1982 Wis. L. Rev. 158, 170 (1982).

trademark protection is sought. In line with the TRIPS Agreement,[11] signs only need to be "capable of distinguishing" commercial source under most legal definitions today. Even in countries, such as the U.S., that require secondary meaning to register certain categories of non-traditional marks, the bar to prove distinctiveness is low. This development seems to be a corollary of the international preference for a registration-based grant of protection. Following this approach, it is sufficient that a sign appears capable of fulfilling the basic trademark function of identifying commercial source to grant exclusive rights and afford the trademark proprietor the opportunity to develop genuine use activities in the coming years. Instead of focusing on whether the sign has already proven to function as a badge of origin, it is sufficient that the sign has the capacity of distinguishing products per se. Trademark applicants may thus argue that a sign is distinctive because it constitutes a specific, recognizable product feature. If trademark offices accept this focus on product features and refrain from establishing a high threshold for demonstrating a specific source-identifying effect, trademark protection will become widely available for non-traditional marks.

II. Problems Inside and Outside Trademark Law

In other words, the current system is in danger of becoming circular in the sense that any recognizable sign, including products and product features, is eligible for trademark protection. This could include the shape of Kit-Kat and Toblerone chocolates, the Lego manikin, the Rubic's cube, the red sole of Louboutin shoes, the shape of Bottega Veneta bags, and the shape of the London cabs—which are all recognizable design features (if not the products as such), but have never been intended to serve as identifiers of commercial source, but rather constitute designs or creative works which, as such, deserve protection under industrial design or copyright legislation.

In many jurisdictions, this risk of circularity following from an elastic concept of distinctiveness is coupled with a weak system of counterbalances—both in terms of absolute grounds for refusal and trademark defenses. For example, historically, shape marks could not be registered, at all, in several countries, including the United Kingdom and Germany. These categorical exclusions are long gone and have been replaced, in several countries, with more flexible registration criteria that prevent trademark registration to a much lesser extent. These include the aforementioned exclusions of signs are that "functional" from a technical or aesthetic perspective. In fairness, courts have increasingly resorted to these provisions to deny protection of non-traditional trademarks.[12] But these cases appear as the tip of the iceberg when

[11] TRIPS art. 15(1).

[12] Developments in the EU can serve as an example in this regard. See the decisions Case C-299/99, Philips v. Remington, 2002 E.C.R. I-5475, ¶ 82 and Case C-48/09 P, Lego v. OHIM, 2010 E.C.R. I-8403, ¶¶ 45, 53–58, about technical functionality which lead to a far-reaching exclusion of technical subject matter even if alternative technical solutions exist. In addition, the potential of the doctrine of aesthetic functionality has been enhanced significantly in Case C-205/13, Hauck v. Stokke, 2014 E.T.M.R. 60, ¶¶ 19–20, where the Court developed a list of flexible factors for the identification of signs that are to be excluded from trademark protection for this reason.

considering the numerous cases that are settled. Moreover, no sound defenses have been crafted to date to limit the use, and potential abuse, of exclusive rights relating to non-traditional marks. For example, it remains difficult to invoke the defense for using a mark in a descriptive or decorative manner in these contexts.[13]

Not surprisingly, the inclusion of non-traditional marks in the canon of protected signs raises severe problems within the system of trademark protection. The erosion of the traditional mark/product dichotomy, the risk of exhausting the spectrum of attractive signs and granting anti-competitive control over important signs in a given category, the tendency of over-protecting non-traditional marks in the absence of well-developed defenses, and the deterrent effect of excessive trademark infringement claims and related litigation costs are examples of legal-doctrinal and practical challenges. Courts across the world seem to share these concerns. Several courts have invalidated prominent non-traditional marks in recent years.[14]

Nonetheless, it seems safe to assume that these cases are just a small fraction of the claims that are brought (at times arbitrarily) by trademark owners. Most of the claims lead to settlements in secret, and often involve licensing or coexistence agreements, or simply acceptance by third parties of the prohibition to use signs coming close to a registered non-traditional mark. As only defendants with "deep pockets" can afford expensive and lengthy litigation, the potential chilling effect of protecting non-traditional marks should not be underestimated. Even though prominent marks have been cancelled, many are still registered.

The repercussions of the decision to protect non-traditional marks, however, go far beyond the trademark system itself. As the various chapters in this Book describe in detail, the recognition of new types of marks substantially broadens the areas of overlap between trademark, industrial design, and copyright protection. Three-dimensional objects may serve as shape marks. A short melody may constitute a sound mark. A computer animation may qualify as a motion mark. Even single colors—the raw material of paintings—are registrable. With this broader range of signs qualifying as trademarks, right holders obtain unprecedented opportunities to acquire an amalgam of trademark, industrial design, and copyright protection. New areas of overlap emerge with regard to applied art and other forms of cultural expression, in particular sculpture and plastic art, musical compositions, and audio-visual creations.

Given the different configuration of copyright and industrial designs law on the one hand, and trademark law on the other, it is not surprising that the cumulation

[13] For instance, see Case C-408/01, Adidas v. Fitnessworld, 2003 E.C.R. I-12537, ¶¶ 39–41, where the Court established an ambiguous test by holding that "the fact that a sign is viewed as an embellishment by the relevant section of the public is not, in itself, an obstacle to the protection conferred by Article 5(2) of the Directive where the degree of similarity is none the less such that the relevant section of the public establishes a link between the sign and the mark." For decisions illustrating the weakness of the descriptive use defence in this context, see Case C-102/07, Adidas v. Marca, 2008 E.C.R. 2439, ¶¶ 47–49; Case C-48/05, Adam Opel v. Autec, 2007 E.C.R. I-1017, ¶ 44; Case I ZR 175/09, "Medusa," German Federal Supreme Court, ¶¶ 19–20 (Nov. 24, 2011).

[14] The list of decisions in this respect is lengthy. We thus refer, here, to the cases cited and discussed in the various chapters published in this Book and the cases cited therein.

of rights leads to tensions and inconsistencies within the system of intellectual property protection: indefinitely renewable trademark rights may thwart the objectives underlying copyright and industrial designs law, in particular the aim to ensure the free availability of designs and literary and artistic works after the expiry of the limited term of copyright and industrial design protection.[15] Trademark rights that remain after the end of copyright and industrial design protection have the potential to seriously impede the cycle of innovation in product design and literary and artistic creations which the rule of a limited term of protection supports. Additional interferences with cyclic cultural innovation may follow from the fact that infringement criteria and limitations of protection are not harmonized across trademark, industrial design, and copyright law. A right holder enjoying cumulative protection may have success in bringing a trademark claim even though the allegedly infringing use would not amount to infringement in the light of copyright or industrial designs infringement standards.[16]

The proliferation of non-traditional trademark registrations, applications, and the recent wave of litigation in this area is thus symptomatic of a larger disease of intellectual property maximization on the basis of an accumulation of rights. Not surprisingly, some of the most heralded law suits in this area involve companies trying to prolong their exclusive rights on valuable products through trademark protection, as trademark law offers a relatively low barrier to protection at comparably low costs, and the prospect of potentially high rewards once protection is granted. Trademark rights, however, are supposed to relate to signs that are needed to distinguish products in the marketplace. They should not be available for every recognizable product feature just because an additional layer of trademark protection can benefit the manufacturers.

From the bird's eye perspective of fundamental rights, these problems can be placed in the context of freedom of competition and freedom of expression. The extension of trademark protection to non-traditional types of marks can have serious effects on market competition as these marks often protect products, or parts of products, per se. In addition, the protection of non-traditional marks can prevent socially and culturally valuable uses. The potential harm that the protection of these signs can entail for market competition as well as freedom of expression is even more dramatic when one considers that the protection granted to trademarks

[15] *Cf.* Martin R.F. Senftleben, Vigeland *and the Status of Cultural Concerns in Trade Mark Law—The EFTA Court Develops More Effective Tools for the Preservation of the Public Domain*, 48 Int'l Rev. Intell. Prop. & Competition L. 683 (2017); Irene Calboli, *Overlapping Rights: The Negative Effects of Trademarking Creative Works*, *in* the evolution and equilibrium of copyright in the digital age 52 (Susy Frankel & Daniel J. Gervais eds., 2014); Annette Kur, *Funktionswandel von Schutzrechten: Ursachen und Konsequenzen der inhaltlichen Annäherung und Überlagerung von Schutzrechtstypen*, *in* geistiges eigentum im dienst der innovation 23 (Gerhard Schricker et al. eds., 2001); D.W. Feer Verkade, *The Cumulative Effect of Copyright Law and Trademark Law: Which Takes Precedence?*, *in* intellectual property and information law—essays in honour of herman cohen jehoram 69 (Jan J.C. Kabel & Gerard J.H.M. Mom eds., 1998).

[16] For a discussion of this risk, see Martin R.F. Senftleben, *Overprotection and Protection Overlaps in Intellectual Property Law—the Need for Horizontal Fair Use Defences*, *in* the structure of intellectual property law: can one size fit all? 136–81 (Annette Kur & Vytautas Mizaras eds., 2011).

may last in perpetuity. In the case of non-traditional marks that acquire the status of well-known[17] or famous marks (U.S.), or the status of marks with a reputation (EU), trademark law enhances the corrosive effect of protection by extending the scope of protection to dissimilar goods and services and use in non-competitive situations. Trademark offices should thus (continue to) apply appropriate safeguards against registration, and trademark courts should (continue to) develop sufficient safeguards against over-enforcement of rights in non-traditional marks. This is crucial to ensure undistorted market competition and support freedom of expression, and ultimately prevent abuses of the trademark system.

III. Taking Stock

Against this background, the purpose underlying this Book, and the collection of essays published in it, clearly comes to light: as non-traditional marks have found their way into trademark registers worldwide, the time has come to take stock. Which law and practice has evolved with regard to these marks during the last decades? How do trademark offices and courts address the wide variety of issues—ranging from legal-doctrinal to competition-based and cultural concerns—that are raised by the inclusion of non-traditional marks in the trademark system? Which positions have evolved in the debate on the continuous expansion of the domain of trademark protection? Which repercussions does this expansion have on other branches of intellectual property protection and the intellectual property system as a whole?

Offering a fresh, critical, and interdisciplinary analysis of the questions raised by the acceptance of non-traditional marks, the contributions to this Book provide an insightful academic—and at the same time practical—review of the topic. Across different jurisdictions, trademark offices and courts have rendered decisions on non-traditional marks against the background of their individual national and regional doctrines and traditions. This pool of decisions serves as a starting point for a discussion and comparison of different approaches to non-traditional marks. Providing a comprehensive overview of the status quo in different regions and countries, the chapters in the Book offer a cutting-edge discussion of legal problems and solutions in the field of non-traditional marks. As Editors, we are confident that, given the richness and diversity of the contributions, the Book can offer a careful and comprehensive analysis of the legal-doctrinal, competition-related, and cultural issues arising from the protection of non-traditional types of marks.

The Book is divided in two Parts. The first Part assesses the status quo reached in the legal treatment of non-traditional trademarks, including the history leading to the current international and national protection, and the unresolved legal challenges that still affect the protection of these marks, especially the boundaries of trademark protection. Denis Croze's chapter opens this Part with a historical reconstruction of the international negotiations and protection of

[17] TRIPS art. 16(3).

non-traditional trademarks, with particular attention to the work of the WIPO Standing Committee on the Law of Trademarks and the WIPO treaties. This historical reconstruction is followed by a detailed empirical study by Michell Adams and Amanda Scardamaglia, which offers a twenty-year retrospective on non-traditional trademarks, using the European Union, the United Kingdom, Singapore, Japan, and Australia as case studies.

Several doctrinal chapters follow this empirical study. First, Dev Gangjee analyzes the current legislation and the changes that have been applied to the registration of non-traditional trademarks, primarily in the EU. In particular, he addresses the question whether the current legislative system can successfully manage the tensions that the registration of these marks generates. He suggests that an equivalent of prosecution history estoppel may be needed in trademark law to resolve several of these tensions. A comprehensive review authored by Annette Kur follows. It addresses the leading case law in Europe from the adoption of the First European Trademark Directive to date. Kur devotes specific attention to the reform of EU trademark law and new safeguards against overbroad protection of non-traditional marks that have arisen in this context, in particular the new limitation of protection which exempts fair use of non-distinctive signs and indications. This European analysis is followed by an exhaustive review of the leading and current cases and applicable law in the U.S. by Justin Hughes. This chapter addresses and criticizes, in particular, the birth and developments of the judicial doctrine of aesthetic functionality in the U.S. The following chapter also addresses the U.S., but from a different angle. Notably, Deven Desai turns to branding and the analysis of marketing practices to explain the rise of the expansion of trademark protection and the recent wave of registration of non-traditional trademarks. Ultimately, Desai argues against the protection of non-traditional marks.

The following chapter, authored by Ng-Loy Wee Loon, devotes attention to the dilemma surrounding the international community's attitude toward the protection of non-traditional trademarks and the acceptance of the functionality doctrine as a ground for refusal and important counterbalance, particularly in respect of shape marks. Ng-Loy highlights that the *travaux préparatoires* of the Paris Convention indicate that Paris Union members could not agree on a definition of a "trademark," particularly whether product shape marks could constitute trademarks. However, this resistance was later overcome with the definition that was inserted into the text of the TRIPS Agreement. Nonetheless, she sees room for the categorical exclusion of shape marks on the basis of functionality considerations—without violating international law. The following chapter by Michael Handler focuses on the infringement analysis in cases arising from the protection of non-traditional trademarks. The chapter focuses on the requirement that, in order to find trademark infringement, a sign should be "used as a trademark" and the possibility to use this requirement as a suitable safeguard against overbroad protection that would stifle free speech and free competition. Exploring the potential of the trademark use requirement, Handler's analysis sheds light on an important balancing tool at the infringement stage that may supplement—and potentially even substitute—functionality considerations at the registration stage.

Part I is concluded by the chapter authored by Haochen Sun, which addresses a series of cases litigated by Hermès in China with emphasis on the decision by the Chinese courts to reject Hermès' request to register the shape of its Kelly bag as a three-dimensional trademark in China.

Building upon this analysis, the second Part of the Book focuses on assessing the impact of the protection of non-traditional trademarks on market competition, culture, and freedom of expression. The first chapter of this Part is authored by Gustavo Ghidini, who provides a doctrinal review of the problems which the protection of non-traditional trademarks can cause with regard to market access to similar signs by competitors. In the following chapter, Glynn Lunney uses an analysis based on law and economics to argue against the protection of non-traditional marks, again based on the concern that they may lead to perpetual monopolies on product features that were not supposed to be protected as trademarks when trademark laws were originally adopted in a variety of jurisdictions. Lavinia Brancusi brings the analysis of market access and the challenges created by non-traditional trademarks within the realm of competition law in her chapter. In particular, she examines several leading cases from the EU in this context. This economic analysis is continued in the contribution authored by Carolina Castaldi, an innovation economist, who offers the first systematic empirical analysis of the extent of filings of non-traditional trademarks using data from the USPTO. Arul Scaria and Kaya Mannen conclude the series of chapters dedicated to the challenges that non-traditional trademarks bring to market competition with a contribution focusing on a specific angle of this phenomenon: the impact of this protection on the marketing of generic pharmaceuticals. Notably, the chapter shows that protection for non-traditional marks in the pharmaceutical sector could pose significant barriers to access to medicine, particularly by increasing transaction costs and creating new barriers to generic entry.

Moving beyond the analysis of challenges that non-traditional trademarks may have on market competition, Irene Calboli's chapter focuses on the impact that the protection of these marks may have on product creativity and innovation. She argues that, by recognizing and protecting as marks elements that are product design and aesthetic product features, the protection of non-traditional marks supports a system that promotes standardization and repetition of the same features. The following chapter, authored by Martin Senftleben, warns that non-traditional trademarks may have a corrosive effect on cultural follow-on innovation. As a solution, Senftleben argues for a broader application of public interest-related grounds for refusal which lead to a categorical exclusion of non-traditional signs from trademark protection. This focus on the public interest is continued in the chapter that follows, which is authored by Lisa Ramsey. In particular, Ramsey argues that the right to freedom of expression may be harmed by granting trademark rights in certain non-traditional marks. She explains that non-traditional trademarks may intrinsically convey information, ideas, or other messages unrelated to the trademark. Therefore, trademark laws regulating this inherently valuable expression should have a sufficient justification, and governments should repeal or revise laws protecting non-traditional marks when they do not directly further trademark law's goals and harm expressive values more than necessary. Katya Assaf-Zakharov, in her conclusive chapter, argues that protecting non-traditional trademarks may become a form of cultural control, which supports cultural dominance by a certain privileged few—the trademark owners and those who can afford their products—at the expense of the rest of society which is deprived of freedom to use imitations of these signs and, in turn, their cultural meaning.

PART I

ASSESSING THE LEGAL FRAMEWORK AND UNRESOLVED CHALLENGES

1

Making a Large Universe Visually Perceptible

The Development of Non-Traditional Trademarks in WIPO Treaties

*Denis Croze**

I. Introduction

As it is the case for most intellectual property (IP) rights, trademarks have been experiencing an extension in scope of protection in new domains which, in the case of brands, include areas at the border of marketing and advertising. Innovative marketing and communication strategies, new branding methods, massive use of the Internet and social networks by consumers, globalization of trade and global distinctiveness of signs, fierce competition among exporting companies, enhanced risks of trademark misappropriation prior to protection abroad; all these new trends have contributed to the expansion of the types of signs which are today capable of constituting a mark. Moreover, with an estimated 36.5 million active trademark registrations at 130 offices worldwide, 5.98 million trademark applications filed in 2015 (15.3% increase from the previous year), and 4.44 million trademark registrations recorded worldwide in 2015 (26.6% increase from 2014), available signs become scarcer and the extension of trademarks beyond traditional signs, such as words or figurative devices, becomes justified.[1]

In spite of their limited number of registrations at the international level, non-traditional trademarks (NTTMs) have paradoxically been the subject of extensive research and publications since their indirect recognition in Article 15.1 of the Agreement on Trade-Related Aspects of Intellectual Property Rights (TRIPS Agreement).[2] This derives from the fact that these types of trademarks do not have

* This contribution derives from the presentation which was made at the Roundtable on the protection of non-traditional marks: Critical perspectives, held in Singapore on January 26 and 27, 2017. It is mainly based upon and reproducing extracts of WIPO documents of the Standing Committee on the Law of Trademarks, Industrial Designs and Geographical Indications (SCT).

[1] World Intellectual Property Indicators 2016, Economic and Statistics Series, WIPO publication No. 941, http://www.wipo.int/edocs/pubdocs/en/wipo_pub_941_2016-chapter3.pdf (2016).

[2] TRIPS: Agreement on Trade-Related Aspects of Intellectual Property Rights, Apr. 15, 1994, Marrakesh Agreement Establishing the World Trade Organization art. 15.1, Annex 1C, 1869 U.N.T.S. 299, 33 I.L.M. 1197 (1994) [hereinafter TRIPS Agreement].

Making a Large Universe Visually Perceptible: The Development of Non-Traditional Marks in WIPO Treaties. Denis Croze. Published 2018 by Oxford University Press.

an internationally accepted definition today, and that their registration and protection have not been harmonized at the multilateral level.

Called "new types of marks," "unusual marks," or "non-conventional marks" until the World Intellectual Property Organization (WIPO) Standing Committee on the Law of Trademarks, Industrial Designs and Geographical Indications (SCT) decided at its seventeenth session to use the term "non-traditional marks," it is only recently that NTTMs have been the subject of discussions at WIPO.[3]

Although WIPO treaties have not specifically regulated NTTMs, their development has been extensively discussed at WIPO meetings and diplomatic conferences. Therefore, it is more the discussions and documents produced by the WIPO Secretariat at the request of the SCT, rather than WIPO treaties, that provide a thorough analysis of the challenges, practices, methods of representation, and description of NTTMs, as well as possible areas of convergence among WIPO Member States.

Following a chronological approach, Section II of this chapter will look first at the provisions on trademarks and NTTMs in WIPO treaties such as the Paris Convention for the Protection of Industrial Property (Paris Convention),[4] the Trademark Law Treaty (TLT),[5] and the Singapore Treaty on the Law of Trademarks (STLT).[6] Section III will then add an analysis of the discussions and working documents of the SCT on NTTMs, which leads to further discussions in Section IV over the Working Group on the review of Rule 3(4) to (6) of the STLT Regulations and the adoption of amendments therein. The chapter will briefly conclude with a summary of the convergences and compromises made to settle on the agreed principles found in the STLT.

II. The WIPO Treaties and Relevant Provisions on Non-Traditional Trademarks

A. The Paris Convention for the Protection of Industrial Property

The Paris Convention is silent on the definition of what constitutes a trademark.[7] The Paris Convention is also silent on the subject matter of NTTMs, since these

[3] *See* WIPO, Report of the Standing Committee on the Law of Trademarks, Industrial Designs and Geographical Indications, WIPO Doc. SCT/17/8 Prov., ¶ 15 (2007); WIPO, Report of the Standing Committee on the Law of Trademarks, Industrial Designs and Geographical Indications, WIPO Doc. SCT/18/2, ¶ 3 (2007).

[4] Paris Convention for the Protection of Industrial Property, Mar. 20, 1883, *as revised* July 14, 1967, 21 U.S.T. 1583, 828 U.N.T.S. 305 [hereinafter Paris Convention].

[5] Trademark Law Treaty, Oct. 27, 1994, S. Treaty Doc. No. 105-35, 2037 U.N.T.S. 35 [hereinafter TLT].

[6] Singapore Treaty on the Law of Trademarks, Mar. 27, 2006, S. Treaty Doc. No. 110-2 [hereinafter STLT].

[7] TRIPS Agreement, *supra* note 2, art. 15.1 (defining for the first time the protectable subject matter of a trademark).

types of marks were not common at the time of the adoption of the Paris Convention and its later revisions.[8]

Article 6 *quinquies* A(1) is the only provision of the Paris Convention that may have an impact on NTTMs and their registration.[9] The question of the protection of foreign trademarks "as is" in the countries of the Paris Union has continued to create a multitude of comments and just as many different positions regarding its interpretation.[10] Since this specific aspect is dealt with in another chapter of this book, it will not be addressed in this chapter.[11]

B. The Trademark Law Treaty

In general, trademark owners have a reasonable expectation that the rights they obtain in one jurisdiction will also be obtained in other jurisdictions based on the same, or very similar, administrative requirements. Even though there were limitations to this principle, it seemed possible and desirable that the principle itself is not constrained by purely administrative requirements. The TLT, finalized and adopted in October of 1994, facilitated the harmonization of these requirements.

In particular, the aim of the TLT is to standardize and streamline national and regional trademark registration procedures. This goal is to be achieved through the simplification and harmonization of certain features of those procedures. The great majority of the provisions of the TLT concern the procedures before a trademark office relating to applications for registration, changes after registration, and renewal.[12] The rules concerning each phase are constructed so as to clearly define the limited requirements for an application or a specific request. As to applications for registration, the TLT provides an exhaustive list of indications that a Contracting Party may require.[13]

In this context, it was particularly important to look at registration formalities concerning NTTMs at the time of adoption of the TLT. Notably, discussions at the SCT showed that relative unfamiliarity with these signs led some IP offices to introduce formality requirements that were more complex than necessary. It was also relevant to find ways of simplifying the registration processes, since reproduction is particularly important for those applications claiming priority under the Paris Convention.[14] In these cases, the reproduction of the mark in the country of origin

[8] Paris Convention, *supra* note 4, adopted Mar. 20, 1883; *as revised at* Brussels (Dec. 14, 1900); *at* Washington (June 2, 1911); *at* The Hague (Nov. 6, 1925); *at* London (June 2, 1934); *at* Lisbon (Oct. 31, 1958); *and at* Stockholm (July 14, 1967); *and as amended on* Sept. 28, 1979.

[9] Paris Convention, *supra* note 4, art. 6 *quinquies* A(1) (stating that "Every trademark duly registered in the country of origin shall be accepted for filing and protected as is in the other countries of the Union, subject to the reservations indicated in this Article").

[10] *See* Professor G.H.C. Bodenhausen, Guide to the Application of the Paris Convention for the Protection of Industrial Property, WIPO publication No. 611, 107–13 (1969); WTO Appellate Body, *United States—Section 211 Omnibus Appropriations Act of 1998*, WT/DS176/AB/R ("US-Havana Club"), ¶¶ 129–48 (2002).

[11] See chapter 7 in this volume (focusing specifically on Article 6 *quinquies* of the Paris Convention).

[12] *See* TLT, *supra* note 5, arts. 3–13.

[13] *See* TLT, *supra* note 5, art. 3.

[14] *See* Paris Convention, *supra* note 4, art. 4.

and in the country of new application should coincide for the mark to be registered in the latter. Therefore, it was important that at least some basic elements of the technique of representing trademarks in trademark applications should be common to all IP offices, in order to facilitate the further registration of these marks beyond the country of origin. This was very important not only in the framework of priority claims under the Paris Convention, but also in the context of the Madrid System concerning the international registration of trademarks.[15]

Ultimately, the scope of the TLT is defined in Article 2, and is explicitly limited to visible signs and explicitly excludes non-visible signs. This exclusion refers specifically to holograms, sound, and olfactory marks. In particular, Article 2 is titled "marks to which this treaty applies" and provides:

> (a) This treaty shall apply to trademarks consisting of visible signs, provided that only those Contracting Parties which accept for registration three-dimensional trademarks shall be obliged to apply this Treaty to such trademarks.
> (b) This treaty shall not apply to hologram trademarks and to trademarks not consisting of visible signs, in particular, sound trademarks and olfactory trademarks.[16]

Hence, the most important provision of the TLT regarding the registration of NTTMs is Article 3, which enumerates the requirements or elements which shall be contained in or accompanying a trademark application ("Indications or Elements Contained in or Accompanying an Application; Fee"). Article 3 only refers to color and three-dimensional trademarks and requires that a statement from the applicant be joined to the application:

> (a) Any Contracting Party may require that an application contain some or all of the following indications or elements:
> ...
> (x) where the applicant wishes to claim color as a distinctive feature of the mark, a statement to that effect as well as the name or names of the color or colors claimed and an indication, in respect of each color, of the principal parts of the mark which are in that color;
> (xi) where the mark is a three-dimensional mark, a statement to that effect; [17]

The details regarding the reproduction of a three-dimensional mark are further clarified in Rule 3(3) of the Regulations under the TLT ("Details Concerning the Application"):

> [Reproduction of a Three-Dimensional Mark]
> (a) Where, pursuant to Article 3(1)(a)–(xi), the application contains a statement to the effect that the mark is a three-dimensional mark, the reproduction of the mark shall consist of a two-dimensional graphic or photographic reproduction.
> (b) The reproduction furnished under subparagraph (a) may, at the option of the applicant, consist of one single view of the mark or of several different views of the mark.

[15] Protocol Relating to Madrid Agreement Concerning International Registration of Marks, June 27, 1989, S. Treaty Doc. No. 106-41, Hein's No. KAV 6242; Madrid Agreement Concerning the International Registration of Marks, Apr. 14, 1891, 23 U.S.T. 1353, 828 U.N.T.S. 389.

[16] TLT, *supra* note 5, art. 2(a)–(b).

[17] TLT, *supra* note 5, art. 3(a), 3(x)–(xi).

(c) Where the Office considers that the reproduction of the mark furnished by the applicant under subparagraph (a) does not sufficiently show the particulars of the three-dimensional mark, it may invite the applicant to furnish, within a reasonable time limit fixed in the invitation, up to six different views of the mark and/or a description by words of that mark.
(d) Where the Office considers that the different views and/or the description of the mark referred to in subparagraph (c) still do not sufficiently show the particulars of the three-dimensional mark, it may invite the applicant to furnish, within a reasonable time limit fixed in the invitation, a specimen of the mark.
(e) Paragraph (2)(a)(i) and (b) shall apply mutatis mutandis.[18]

The increasing protection of non-visible signs and three-dimensional marks in many jurisdictions around the world, together with the introduction of electronic filing systems by national IP offices, the lack of TLT Assembly (like in other WIPO treaties) due to a lack of consensus over the voting rights of intergovernmental organizations, the adoption of a set of provisions on trademark license recordal, and the need for provisions on relief measures when time limits are missed, led to the need to update the TLT and make several technical and substantive changes to the treaty in response to these developments.

C. The Singapore Treaty on the Law of Trademarks

Building on the TLT, the aim of the STLT was to create a modern international framework for the harmonization of administrative trademark registration procedures by having a wider scope of application (notably including the provisions on trademark licenses), and by also addressing more recent developments in the field of communication technologies.[19]

The STLT was finalized and adopted in August of 2006. Unlike the TLT, the STLT applies to all types of marks that can be registered under the law of a Contracting Party, including non-visible signs. In particular, Article 2(1) states, regarding the "nature of trademarks," that "[a]ny Contracting Party shall apply this Treaty to marks consisting of signs that can be registered as marks under its law."[20] In this respect, the STLT is the first international instrument dealing with trademark law that recognizes NTTMs, even though the STLT does not expressly mention these marks in its provisions.

With regard to the indications or elements to be contained in or accompanying an application, Article 3 of the STLT contains similar, although not identical, provisions to the TLT:

a) Any Contracting Party may require that an application contain some or all of the following indications or elements:

[18] Regulations under the Trademark Law Treaty, Oct. 27, 1994, T. Doc. 105-35, 2037 U.N.T.S. 35.

[19] Joint Recommendation Concerning Trademark Licenses, adopted by the Assembly of the Paris Union for the Protection of Industrial Property and the General Assembly of WIPO, Sept. 25–Oct. 3, 2000, http://www.wipo.int/edocs/pubdocs/en/marks/835/pub835.pdf.

[20] STLT, *supra* note 6, art. 2(1).

. . .

(x) Where applicable, a statement, as prescribed in the Regulations, indicating the type of mark as well as any specific requirements applicable to that type of mark

. . .

(xii) Where applicable, a statement, as prescribed in the Regulations, indicating that the applicant wishes to claim color as a distinctive feature of the mark.[21]

Because of the wide differences between approaches at the national level concerning the registration of NTTMs among WIPO Member States, as well as because new types of NTTMs may appear in the future and require an amendment to the treaty itself, it was decided that it would be more flexible if the more specific provisions would be dealt with in the Regulations.

Rule 3(2), 3(3)(b), 3(5), and 3(6) of the Regulations to the STLT provide the details concerning the national application process for these NTTMs:

3(2) [Mark Claiming Color] Where the application contains a statement to the effect that the applicant wishes to claim color as a distinctive feature of the mark, the Office may require that the application indicate the name or code of the color or colors claimed and an indication, in respect of each color, of the principal parts of the mark which are in that color.

(3) [Number of Reproductions]

(b) Where the application contains a statement to the effect that the applicant wishes to claim color as a distinctive feature of the mark, a Contracting Party may not require more than five reproductions of the mark in black and white and five reproductions of the mark in color.

. . .

(5) [Hologram Mark, Motion Mark, Color Mark, Position Mark] Where the application contains a statement to the effect that the mark is a hologram mark, a motion mark, a color mark or a position mark, a Contracting Party may require one or more reproductions of the mark and details concerning the mark, as prescribed in the law of that Contracting Party.

(6) [Mark Consisting of a Non-Visible Sign] Where the application contains a statement to the effect that the mark consists of a non-visible sign, a Contracting Party may require one or more representations of the mark, an indication of the type of mark and details concerning the mark, as prescribed by the law of that Contracting Party.[22]

While Article 3 of the STLT provides an exhaustive list of indications and elements, it also contemplates that any Contracting Party may require some or all of those indications and elements. Therefore, it is possible for the Office of any Contracting

[21] STLT, *supra* note 6, art. 3.

[22] Regulations under the Singapore Treaty on the Law of Trademarks, Mar. 27, 2006, S. Treaty Doc. No. 110-2, http://www.wipo.int/wipolex/en/treaties/text.jsp?file_id=290032 [hereinafter STLT Regulations].

Party to require the applicant to provide a statement concerning the type of mark, which may be a color mark, a three-dimensional mark, or any sign that can be registered according to the law of the Contracting Party.

The Regulations to the STLT contain two additional provisions regarding the representation of NTTMs in trademark applications. Rule 3(5) deals with the representation of several visible non-traditional signs such as holograms, motion, color, and position marks, and provides that indications as to the number and the form of the required reproductions are left to national law.[23] Equally, Rule 3(6) provides that in the case of a non-visible sign, Contracting Parties are free to determine the form and other details concerning the representation of the mark.[24] It should be noted that the choice of the term "representation" for non-visible signs was intended to cover both the graphic or photographic reproduction of a mark and any other means of representation; for example, descriptions or electronic data files. In particular, where a Contracting Party allows the transmittal of communications by electronic means, other techniques to satisfy the reproduction requirements may be used.

It is agreed that the provisions of the TLT had a harmonizing effect on the form and means of representation of three-dimensional marks and color as a feature of the mark among the Contracting Parties of that treaty. The STLT contained identical provisions as the TLT for those two types of marks. The STLT does not, however, harmonize the representation of hologram, motion, color per se, or position marks, nor any of the non-visible signs. In each of these cases, the IP Office of any Contracting Party may retain the possibility of requiring a statement related to the application concerning the type of mark applied for. However, the specific requirements concerning the reproduction or representation of the mark itself were left to the discretion of each respective national law.

While the STLT Diplomatic Conference reached agreement on the items in Rule 3(1) to (4) concerning marks that are reproduced/described in standard characters, several other issues remained unresolved and left to the discretion of individual members and their national laws.[25] This referred in particular to the following: marks claiming colors;[26] the number of reproductions;[27] certain issues relating to the reproduction of three-dimensional marks;[28] questions concerning the reproduction of hologram, motion, color, and position marks;[29] as well as the representation of marks consisting of non-visible signs.[30] In this context, it appears useful to recall that the term "representation"—the description of a trademark in the application—includes a mark's "reproduction" and any graphic or photographic reproduction of a mark as well as other means of representation of it, for example, descriptions or electronic data files.[31]

[23] *Id.* at Rule 3(5).
[24] *Id.* at Rule 3(6).
[25] *Id.* at Rule 3(1).
[26] *Id.* at Rule 3(2).
[27] *Id.* at Rule 3(3).
[28] *Id.* at Rule 3(4).
[29] *Id.* at Rule 3(5).
[30] *Id.* at Rule 3(6).
[31] WIPO, Notes on the Basic Proposal for a Revised Trademark Law Treaty and Regulations Thereunder, WIPO Doc. TLT/R/DC/5, Note 3.09 (2005).

As it was already stated in document SCT/17/2 by the WIPO SCT[32] regarding the existing international standards of the representation in a trademark application, it appears quite clearly that one of the most important hurdles that NTTMs had (and still have) to face is their capacity to be represented graphically, and whether this mandatory requirement may be either replaced or supplemented by other elements as part of the trademark application process.[33]

In this respect, it should also be noted that, notwithstanding the fact that the STLT identifies a certain number of new types of signs that can be registered, WIPO Member States wanted to make it clear that the STLT did not create an actual obligation for any Member State to mandatorily accept the registration of such signs in their national laws. This point was clarified in the Resolution supplementary to the STLT and its Regulations, which were also adopted by the Diplomatic Conference leading to the adoption of the STLT:

> Acknowledging the fact that the Treaty provides for effective and efficient trademark formality procedures for Contracting Parties, the Diplomatic Conference understood that Article 2 and 8 respectively, did not impose any obligations on Contracting Parties to:
>
> Register new types of marks, as referred to in Rule 3, paragraph (4), (5) and (6) of the Regulations
>
> ...
>
> Each Contracting Party shall have the option to decide whether and when to provide for the registration of new types of marks, as referred to above.[34]

This principle was systematically recalled in WIPO's discussions on NTTMs, and was clearly setting the limits of the multilateral effort to harmonize trademark law with regards to NTTMs. Member States, however, wanted to get a better understanding of the issue, in particular with regards to the specific national practices relating to the registration of new types of marks, and referred the work to the SCT. In the remainder of the chapter, I refer to this work in more detail.

III. Work of the Standing Committee on the Laws of Trademarks, Industrial Design and Geographical Indications

A. Sixteenth Session (November 13 to 17, 2006)

After the adoption of the STLT, and in spite of the discussions during the Diplomatic Conference that led to its adoption in Singapore, many questions remained open. These questions are summarized in the SCT document on New Types of Marks, which was published as part of the Sixteenth Session of the SCT. Notably, the

[32] *See* WIPO, Methods and Representation and Description of New Types of Marks, WIPO Doc. SCT/17/2, ¶ 58 (2007).

[33] *Id.*

[34] Resolution by the Diplomatic Conference Supplementary to the Singapore Treaty on the Law of Trademarks, Mar. 27, 2006, ¶ 3, S. Treaty Doc. No. 110-2, http://www.wipo.int/wipolex/en/details.jsp?id=12670.

document states that "[t]he use and registration of new types of marks raises a number of important issues that may require further study," and these issues include:

- the constant emergence of new types of marks as a consequence of steadily evolving means of communication and marketing techniques;
- a balance between the possible protection of new types of trademarks and the need to keep certain signs available for use by all traders;
- appropriate ways of applying established trademark principles, such as the requirement of distinctiveness, the exclusion of descriptive signs, the acquisition of distinctiveness through use, in respect of new types of marks;
- a need to develop complementary approaches and principles in trademark law in order to deal with the emergence of new types of signs and to ensure coherence with other fields of intellectual property protection;
- appropriate ways of representing new types of marks for the purpose of their registration.[35]

Some of these issues had been highlighted in an issue-paper on new types of marks, which the SCT requested WIPO to prepare before the STLT Diplomatic Conference as part of the Fifteenth Session of the SCT (November 28 to December 2, 2005).[36] The issue-paper describes various types of trademarks and discusses particular issues related to NTTMs.[37] It also contains in its Annex some examples of new types of marks, which WIPO received from some SCT Members on an ad hoc basis in order to illustrate the various ways of representing particular types of NTTMs.[38] This issue-paper was largely based on information provided by the WIPO Questionnaire on Trademark Law and Practice, and ad hoc contributions of individual SCT Members.[39] It was also the first in a series of working documents produced on NTTMs by the WIPO Secretariat from 2005 to 2009, concluded with the adoption of a document on "Representation of Non-Traditional Marks: Areas of Convergence."[40]

As mentioned by the Chair of the SCT at the opening of the Sixteenth Session (November 13 to 17, 2006):

> [T]he issue of new types of marks was likely to remain a topic of interest for trademark offices, as they seemed to be under pressure from two directions. Firstly[,] from manufacturers, who wish to publicize their products and identify their brands and secondly from consumers, who would like to prevent free-riding or deceptional confusion. Although new types of marks were not the dominant signs applied for registration, they seemed to be important for those brand owners who used them nationally and wished to use them across markets. Therefore,

[35] WIPO, New Types of Marks, WIPO Doc. SCT/16/2, ¶ 72 (2006).

[36] WIPO, Compilation of Proposals for Future Work of Standing Committee on the Law of Trademarks, Industrial Designs and Geographical Indications, WIPO Doc. SCT/15/2, p. 2 (2005).

[37] *Id.* [38] *Id.* at Annex I-XVI.

[39] WIPO, Summary of Replies to the Questionnaire on Trademark Law and Practice, WIPO Doc. WIPO/Strad/INF/1 (2010).

[40] WIPO, Representation of Non-Traditional Marks–Areas of Convergence, WIPO Doc. WIPO/Strad/INF3 (2009).

it appeared that the Committee could work on developing common approaches for dealing with these new types of marks.[41]

The first SCT Document on new types of marks on NTTMs recalls that the types of signs considered capable of constituting a mark have expanded beyond words and figurative devices, and that visually perceptible signs were being used in trade together with signs (which may not in themselves be visually perceptible, but have a potential for distinguishing goods and services).[42] Other signs may be visible and yet differ from the traditional notion of signs constituting trademarks by one or more features. Therefore, in an attempt to categorize various signs that may constitute a mark, the SCT Report grouped signs according to whether they are visually perceptible (three-dimensional marks, color marks, holograms, slogans, titles of films and books, motion and multimedia signs, position marks, gesture marks), or whether they may be perceived by senses other than the sense of sight (sound marks, olfactory marks, taste marks, texture or feel marks).[43]

Interestingly, the SCT Report also deals with cross-cutting issues, such as the evolution of NTTMs in the market place, the need to keep certain signs available, the application of trademark principles, the overlap with industrial design and copyright protection, and approaches to graphical representation.

While noting that the recognition of NTTMs increases the number of signs eligible for trademark protection, which commercial operators may use to distinguish their goods or services, the Report recalls that since a broader range of signs may become subject to individual exclusive trademark rights, it is important to keep signs available by applying the same standards used in regard to traditional trademarks.[44]

The Report states that this might be a lesser problem in connection with complex signs, such as product packaging combining a three-dimensional shape with several colors and figurative elements; a hologram constituted by pictures combining individual colors and drawings; or a video clip or a musical piece requiring specific instrumentation. However, the claim to trademark protection for more basic signs, such as simple containers using unmodified basic geometrical forms, a single color or a smell, brings forth the need to keep certain signs available for all business operators in a specific sector. In addition, the question may be asked to what extent consumers are capable of distinguishing within a potentially wide diversity of signs of a specific type. In theory, for instance, the diversity of color shades can hardly ever be exhausted. In practice, however, consumers may not be able to distinguish fine nuances of colors.[45]

With regard to registration procedures, the Report stresses that new types of marks give rise to the practical question of graphic or other type of representation, which is a requirement under many national trademark laws. A number of criteria, such as the clearness, preciseness, accessibility, intelligibility, durability, and objectivity of a graphic representation, may be considered in order to ensure that the trademark

[41] WIPO, Report of the Standing Committee on the Law of Trademarks, Industrial Designs and Geographical Indications, 16th Session, WIPO Doc. SCT/16/9, ¶ 19 (2007).

[42] WIPO, New Types of Marks, WIPO Doc. SCT/16/2, ¶ 72 (2006).

[43] *Id.*

[44] *Id.*

[45] *Id.*

register adequately reflects protected signs. In respect of the practical means of representation, new types of marks frequently offer different possibilities ranging, for instance, from a written description to digital reproductions. We have seen that Rule 3(4) to (6) of the Regulations under the STLT contemplates reproductions of visible signs and representations of non-visible signs as part of the application procedure.[46] However, indications as to the nature of the reproduction or representation are only given in the case of three-dimensional marks (i.e., the reproduction of the mark shall consist of a two-dimensional graphic or photographic reproduction). Therefore, the Report advocates for further clarification, and where appropriate, the development of a common approach to the representation of new types of marks in administrative trademark office procedures.[47]

Ultimately, the discussions during the Sixteenth Session of the SCT illustrated the variety of approaches among WIPO Member States. A number of countries, particularly developing countries, that excluded the registration of non-visible signs were interested in having an in-depth analysis in order to understand the implications for their legislation, as well as the impact of any change on the practices of their national IP Offices, because the examination of these marks could require additional expertise from the examiners or specific and sophisticated technologies. On the other side, other countries stated that they have developed specific examination practices to deal with them in an ad hoc manner and were welcoming the development of guidelines or best practices, since their main problem was knowing whether certain signs protected at the national level could be protected also in other jurisdictions.

Several additional issues were raised during the discussions: the possible overlapping protection on the same object for three-dimensional marks and color marks also protected under copyright law; the difficulties in publishing non-visible signs; the various problems of representation of or reference to colors (in color identification systems and shades of color); the length of a sound mark; the size of the reproductions (which may cause a problem with designations under the Madrid system); and reproduction of a 3D mark with perspective view, or views, from the top, the base and each of the sides, to mention a few.

At the end of its Sixteenth Session, the SCT decided to limit the scope of its work to the representation and description of NTTMs and to the application of trademark principles to them and asked the Secretariat to develop two papers for discussion at the next session:

[1.] A paper setting out existing methods of representation and description of new types of marks in SCT Members, identifying where there are areas of convergence and any issues raised including the possibility of additional costs, particularly in developing countries;

[2.] A paper exploring in greater detail the relation of established trademark principles to new types of marks. All principles including, inter alia, functionality,

[46] STLT Regulations, *supra* note 22, Rule 3(4)–(6).

[47] WIPO, New Types of Marks, WIPO Doc. SCT/16/2, ¶ 72 (2006).

specialty and distinctiveness would be considered, as well as issues of public interest, including safeguarding the public domain.[48]

B. Seventeenth Session (May 7 to 11, 2007)

At its Seventeenth Session, the SCT went a step forward in trying to identify existing methods of representation and description of NTTMs, and considered a document prepared by WIPO, "Methods of Representation and Description of New Types of Marks."[49] The document presents an overview of existing methods of representation and description of new type of marks (Section II), as well as possible areas of convergence (Section III).[50] Section III of the WIPO document also addressed considerations on publication and the possibility of additional costs of NTTMs.[51] However, due to lack of time, only certain portions of the document were discussed, namely those relating to three-dimensional marks, color marks, and sound marks. Also at this session, the SCT recalled that nothing in the document or the subsequent discussion implied an obligation on any Member State to protect any type of mark.

From the overview contained in the document on "Methods of Representation and Description of New Types of Marks," we note that certain categories of NTTMs are more frequently applied for registration than others.[52] Some common thinking seems to emerge around the means of representing marks, such as three-dimensional marks, holograms, color and combination of color marks, motion, position, and sound marks. The representation of the more exceptional marks still requires a case-by-case assessment. In general, it was agreed that the application for registration of a mark must include a representation that demonstrates the nature of the mark and shows each feature clearly enough to permit a proper examination. It was also agreed that a statement as to the type of mark sought to be registered is usually required, as well as, in most cases, a detailed description of the mark. In particular, the representation of the mark very often takes the form of a graphic representation, although in certain countries, national laws or regulations may authorize other modes of representation for particular kinds of marks.

One of the more salient points in the discussion was that the form of graphic representation used should allow the average consumer to understand the nature of the mark. This was also stated in the WIPO document:

> One key factor in determining the suitability of any representation of the sign is that it is clear enough for the public to understand the nature of the mark, and that it can be recorded on the registry and published in an appropriately intelligible form so that anyone interested can access the information.[53]

[48] WIPO, Report of the Standing Committee on the Law of Trademarks, Industrial Designs and Geographical Indications, 16th Session, WIPO Doc. SCT/16/9, ¶ 73 (2007).

[49] WIPO, Methods of Representation and Description of New Types of Marks, WIPO Doc. SCT/17/2 (2007).

[50] *Id.* §§ II, III.

[51] *Id.* § III.

[52] *Id.* ¶ 75.

[53] *Id.* ¶ 64.

This is why highly technical descriptions or unusual technical modes of representation would generally not be acceptable under the law of many Member States.[54]

In this respect, the document on "Methods of Representation and Description of New Types of Marks" looked at the existing international standards in relation to "graphical" representation as a possible area of convergence. I also stress that the term "graphical"—which is normally associated with the idea of a picture or writing capturing the main features of the mark—may pose certain problems for non-visible signs.[55] These problems arise from the fact that a majority of countries require that a trademark consists of a sign capable of being represented graphically, and have graphical representation as an element of the definition of a trademark under national law.

Yet it should be recalled that Article 15(1) of the TRIPS Agreement does not provide for graphic representation. Instead, the provision only authorizes that signs may be visually perceptible as a condition for registration.[56] The WIPO document highlighted that existing methods of representation for NTTMs in several countries take the form of a pictorial representation, a written description, or a combination of both, and stated that the challenge created by the national requirements of 'graphical representation' could be overcome by a more generalized use of new and cost effective information technologies for trademark registration procedures which may offer new possibilities for the representation of NTTMs.[57]

The document also provided some special considerations regarding the publication of NTTMs, since the type and extent of the information to be published was partially different from country to country. In particular, some IP Offices made available information regarding applications and registrations via the Internet, in addition to making that information available on paper through a gazette or other similar publication by the Office. According to the WIPO document, the information provided could range from publishing all of the images submitted with the application of a three-dimensional or hologram mark, to publishing only one view of the mark, even if several views were submitted. In relation to motion, multimedia signs, and gesture marks represented by still pictures, it was mentioned that the number of images would be limited to as many as can fit in an A4 sheet when published. Similarly, it was stated that, where the application of a specific mark requires a statement of the type of mark and/or a description, the statement and/or description may be published as part of the representation. This may be the case, for example, with three-dimensional marks, holograms, sound, color, position, motion, multimedia marks, etc. It remained less clear how such information will be treated if it is voluntarily submitted by the applicant.

In contrast, the publication of non-visible signs seemed to be non-problematic where descriptions of those signs are acceptable as sufficient graphic representation, or where other graphic elements such as musical notation may be provided. In countries that accept the deposit of material supports (CD or DVD) for music or motion

[54] *Id.* ¶ 7. [55] *Id.* ¶ 14. [56] TRIPS Agreement, *supra* note 2, art. 15(1).

[57] WIPO, Methods of Representation and Description of New Types of Marks, WIPO Doc. SCT/17/2 (2007).

signs, it was suggested that a notice could be published stating that the sound may be available to the public upon request. Similarly, it was suggested that in countries that already publish information related to the marks in their gazette on the Internet, or make the signs otherwise available through that medium, it would be foreseeable to provide a sound or a movie icon where the sound, melody, or video clip may be assessed by the public.

An additional issue raised during the Sixteenth Session of the SCT in connection with the representation and description of NTTMs was the possibility of additional costs that those types of trademarks could cause, particularly in developing countries.

However, there was not much debate with regards to the possibility of reproducing graphically three-dimensional marks, color marks, holograms, slogans, titles of films and books, motion or multimedia signs, position marks and gesture marks. With the exception of motion or multimedia signs, these marks can be reproduced and published in a manner that would not appear to be different from traditional marks. Concerning motion marks, some methods of reproduction, such as adding a description to the graphic representation of a number of images showing the "motion" effect of the sign, or the submission of a short film or video clip, can be envisaged. It has been noted, for example, that there is no additional cost for the Office when three-dimensional marks are technically treated as figurative marks. However, there could be an additional cost for publication of the paper trademark gazette in color, if it was previously printed in black and white only. One possible way to overcome this problem, it was noted, could be to issue regular trademark office publications in CD-ROM format, which is quite inexpensive. This could solve the problem of elevated printing costs for color illustrations.

Concerning non-visible signs, the WIPO document additionally identified sound marks, olfactory marks, taste marks, and texture and feel marks. In this respect, it was noted that since all these signs can be reproduced in one way or another in a graphic manner, the same consideration concerning additional cost for examination and publication would apply. Still, this remains a point of contention among the countries that do not protect these signs. The WIPO document concluded that, to the extent possible, trademark registration authorities should apply the same or similar requirements for the graphic representation of NTTMs as they do for all types of marks. Moreover, if specific requirements are needed for the representation of certain types of marks, these requirements need to follow the principle of accessibility. In general, it may be preferable to avoid the use of sophisticated methods of representation, as these would not be understandable to the average consumer. This trend is illustrated, for example, by the abolishment of sonograms as means of reproduction for sound marks.

The other document submitted by the WIPO Secretariat to the SCT at this session referred to the "Relation of Established Trademark Principles to New Type of Marks."[58] This document was interesting in that it explored the relation of established

[58] WIPO, Relation of Established Trademark Principles to New Types of Marks, WIPO Doc. SCT/17/3 (2007).

trademark principles to new types of marks and considers functionality, distinctiveness, and specialty in general, as well as particular aspects relating to certain marks.[59] The document additionally discussed the issue of public interest and the safeguard of the public domain. The principle generally stated in the submissions by SCT Members is that they apply the same criteria to the examination of traditional marks as they do to the assessment of NTTMs. It appears, however, that while established trademark principles and normal examination techniques seem suitable for the assessment of registrability of new types of signs, additional trademark law analysis and policy discussion to set the boundaries between different IP rights was needed regarding NTTMs. Unfortunately, due to lack of time, no discussion took place on this document at the Seventeenth Session of the SCT, and discussion was postponed to the following session of the SCT.[60]

At the end of the Seventeenth Session, the SCT requested the WIPO Secretariat to prepare a working document for consideration at the Eighteenth Session, taking into account the deliberations of the Seventeenth Session and presenting key learnings for Member States in relation to the representation of those types of marks that the SCT would have considered at its Seventeenth Session.[61]

C. Eighteenth Session (November 12 to 16, 2007)

Progressively, discussions of the SCT on NTTMs concentrated on finding "adequate" means of representation of these marks to avoid procedural requirements that would be too complex or onerous for applicants and IP Offices.[62] It has been noted that the representation of these types of signs should satisfy not only the Office, but also the general public (including potential competitors) who need to understand what is claimed as a mark.[63]

At its Eighteenth Session, the SCT requested the WIPO Secretariat to prepare a new document for the Nineteenth Session regarding the methods of representation and description of NTTMs. This document would identify possible areas of convergence, based on documents SCT/17/2 and SCT/18/2 and the discussions at the Eighteenth Session. In particular, the document would focus on those areas where there has been less widespread experience, and that have not been addressed comprehensively in the STLT.

D. Nineteenth Session (July 21 to 25, 2008)

At its Nineteenth Session, the SCT agreed on the areas of convergence relating to the representation of NTTMs.[64] In doing so, the SCT noted that the areas of

[59] *Id.* [60] WIPO, Summary by the Chair, 17th Session, WIPO Doc. SCT/17/7 (2007).

[61] WIPO, Report of the Standing Committee on the Law of Trademarks, Industrial Designs and Geographical Indications, 17th Session, WIPO Doc. SCT/17/8 (2007).

[62] WIPO, Non-Traditional Marks—Key Learnings, WIPO Doc. SCT/18/2 (2007).

[63] *Id.*

[64] WIPO, Representation and Description of Non-Traditional Marks: Possible Areas of Convergence, WIPO Doc. SCT/19/2 (2008).

convergence did not impose any obligation on Members of the SCT to provide for registration of NTTMs. Each Member remained free to decide whether to provide for the registration of such marks. The SCT understood that the areas of convergence constituted a body of reference that could be used by IP Offices, as well as by trademark owners and practitioners, who were moving into new marketing and advertising techniques for which they required flexibility as to the available subject matter that may be used to identify their goods and services.[65]

E. Twentieth Session (December 1 to 5, 2008)

At its Twentieth Session, the SCT continued to discuss the representation of NTTMs and confirmed the areas of convergence agreed to at the Nineteenth Session and presented in document SCT/20/2.[66] The SCT further agreed to introduce, in the title of the Annex to document SCT/20/2[67] a footnote to the term "Non-Traditional Marks" with the following text:

> The resolution by the Diplomatic Conference supplementary to the Singapore Treaty on the Law of Trademarks and the Regulations thereunder refers to three-dimensional marks, hologram marks, motion marks color marks position marks and marks consisting of non-visible signs as "New types of marks". It also agreed to add a new Note 1.02 with the following text: "In some jurisdictions, the scope of protection will be restricted to those characteristics disclosed in the original representation."[68]

At the closing of its session, the SCT agreed that the Secretariat would publish the document, with the amendments as agreed upon by the SCT at this session, in the WIPO/STrad/INF series of documents, and bring this document to the attention of the relevant WIPO Assemblies.[69]

The document divides NTTMs into two categories: those with areas of convergence among the Member States (three-dimensional marks, color marks, hologram marks, motion and multimedia marks, position marks, gesture marks, sound marks) and those without areas of convergence that could be agreed upon (olfactory marks, taste marks, texture or feel marks). For each NTTM, where relevant, Notes accompanied the text of the area of convergence among the Member States concerning the application for the representation of the NTTM. These Notes are reproduced hereafter since they constitute the results of four years of discussion in the SCT and the corpus of a set of agreed principles among the Member States.

[65] *Id.*

[66] WIPO, Representation of Non-Traditional Marks: Areas of Convergence, WIPO Doc. SCT/20/2 (2008).

[67] *Id.* at Annex.

[68] WIPO, Representation of Non-Traditional Trademarks Areas of Convergence, WIPO Doc. WIPO/Strad/INF/3 (May 5, 2009).

[69] *Id.*

1. *Application for the representation of three-dimensional marks (area of convergence no. 1)*

Regarding three-dimensional marks, the accompanying Note stated:

> With regard to an application for the registration of a three-dimensional mark, a sufficiently clear representation showing one single view of the mark is sufficient for the granting of a filing date. Nevertheless, Offices may require more views or a description of the three-dimensional mark for the purposes of examination.[70]

The Note also specified that if additional views and other elements, such as a description of the three-dimensional mark, are required, the applicant should be given reasonable time limits to supply the missing requirements, in accordance with STLT Rule 5(1). The Rule specifies that at least one month from the date of the invitation by the Office where the applicant's address is in the territory of the Contracting Party concerned, and at least two months where the applicant's address is outside the territory.[71]

The Note further mentioned that in some jurisdictions, the scope of protection will be restricted to those characteristics disclosed in the original representation, and that opinions as to how many views of a three-dimensional mark should be published by the Office when multiple views are submitted remained divergent.

2. *Application for the representation of color marks (area of convergence no. 2)*

The Note related to the representation of color marks stated that:

> With regard to an application for the registration of a color per se mark or a combination of colors without delineated contours, Offices may require that a representation of such marks consist of a sample of the color(s) on paper or in an electronic format. Offices may require a designation of the color(s) by using their common names. Furthermore, Offices should allow the indication of recognized color codes to be chosen by applicants. Offices may also require a written description on how the color is applied to the goods or used in relation to the services.[72]

The Note additionally indicated that, in the case of color combinations, certain Offices may require the applicant to indicate the ratio or distribution of the colors used. It also states that Offices may require a designation of the color(s) by using their common names, and that they should allow the indication of recognized color codes to be chosen by applicants. It further specifies that internationally recognized color codes are deemed to be precise and stable and their use in trademark applications contributes to clarify the nature and the scope of color marks.

70 WIPO, Representation of Non-Traditional Marks Areas of Convergence—Annex, WIPO Doc. SCT/20/2, Annex p. 1 (Oct. 15, 2008).

71 STLT Regulations, *supra* note 22, Rule 5(1).

72 WIPO, Representation of Non-Traditional Marks Areas of Convergence—Annex, WIPO Doc. SCT/20/2, Annex p. 2 (Oct. 15, 2008).

3. *Application for the representation of hologram marks (area of convergence No. 3)*

Regarding the condition to registered holograms as marks, the Note stated that:

> With regard to an application for the registration of a hologram mark, the representation of such a mark may consist of one single view of the sign which captures the holographic effect in its entirety or, where necessary, multiple views of the hologram from different angles. Offices may require an applicant to include a description of the hologram mark where a single drawing or a series of drawings does not accurately represent the hologram.[73]

The Note also stressed that opinions remain divergent among the Member States with regards to the number of views of a hologram mark which should be published by the Office, when multiple views of the hologram are submitted.

4. *Application for the representation of motion or multimedia marks (area of convergence no. 4)*

The Note elaborated on the requirements for an application for motion and/or multimedia marks:

> With regard to an application for the registration of a motion or multimedia mark, the representation of such trademarks may consist of a series of still images, which put together, will depict movement. Offices may require that the application include a written description explaining the movement. Alternatively, Offices may require a recording of the sign in analog or digital format. Where electronic filing is available, an electronic file may be submitted with the application.[74]

The Note highlighted that experience with the registration of motion or multimedia marks suggests that the character of such marks is best captured if the mark is represented in motion.

5. *Application for the representation of position marks (area of convergence no. 5)*

The Note specified the conditions for registration of position marks as follows:

> With regard to an application for the registration of a position mark, the representation of such a mark may consist of a single view of the mark. It may be required that matter for which protection is not claimed, be represented in broken or dotted lines. A written description explaining the position of the mark in relation to the product may also be required if the graphic representation supplied is not sufficient.[75]

In addition, the Note pointed out that under certain national systems, position marks are treated as a subset of other types of marks, such as figurative or three-dimensional marks.

[73] *Id.* at Annex p. 2. [74] *Id.* at Annex p. 3. [75] *Id.*

6. *Application for the representation of gesture trademarks (area of convergence no. 6)*

Regarding the representation of gesture marks, the Note stated that:

> With regard to an application for the registration of a gesture mark, the representation of such a mark may consist of a single picture when the mark is treated as a figurative mark or several frames depicting the gesture if the mark is considered a motion mark. A written description explaining the gesture may also be submitted. For the rest, the considerations under possible area of convergence No. 4 would apply.[76]

The Note also specified that the area of convergence concerning gesture trademarks is based on the understanding that the term gesture mark is used by industry, but not necessarily in legal statutes.

7. *Application for the representation of sound marks (area of convergence no. 7)*

Regarding the representation of sound marks in trademark applications, it was clarified that:

> Offices may require that the representation of such marks consist of a musical notation on a stave, or a description of the sound constituting the mark, or of an analog or digital recording of that sound, or of any combination thereof. Where electronic filing is available, an electronic file may be submitted with the application. However, for some jurisdictions, only a musical notation on a stave may be considered as adequately representing the mark.[77]

Moreover, the Note indicated that electronic files such as MP3 or.WAV (wave form audio format) may be filed with certain Offices, but that national legislation may still include the possibility to submit analog recordings.

8. *Application for the representation of olfactory marks (area of convergence no. 8), taste marks (area of convergence no. 9), and texture and feel marks (area of convergence no. 10)*

For these three types of marks, the SCT could not identify an area of convergence regarding their representation. Some jurisdictions have accepted that such marks may be represented through a description, whereas for other jurisdictions a description cannot adequately represent the character of such marks.

9. *Publication of non-traditional marks*

On the publication of NTTMs, the SCT noted that with the introduction of new technologies and an increased use of NTTMs, limitation of the size of representations were becoming less relevant, and Offices indicated that the clarity of the representation was more important.

[76] *Id.* at Annex p. 4. [77] *Id.*

IV. Assembly of the Singapore Treaty on the Law of Trademarks and Working Group

At its first ordinary session (September 22 to October 1, 2009), the Assembly of the STLT considered document STLT/A/1/3 on "Future Work," where reference was made to the areas of convergence concerning the representation of NTTMs agreed upon by the SCT in 2008 and described in the previous section.[78] In particular, the Assembly approved the initiation of a review of Rule 3(4) to (6) of the Regulations under the STLT with a view to align that Rule, where considered possible and appropriate, with the areas of convergence concerning the representation of NTTMs agreed upon by the SCT. The Assembly also agreed to the convening of one session of a Working Group to undertake preparatory work for the review of Rule 3(4) to (6).[79]

The working document on the "Review of Rule 3(4) to (6) of the Regulations under the STLT" was submitted to the Working Group at its first session (June 28–29, 2010). The working document contained suggestions for the possible alignment of Rule 3 with the areas of convergence concerning the representation of NTTMs agreed by the SCT, in the form of draft amendments to Rule 3 with accompanying text.[80] The suggested changes from the current text of Rule 3 were recapitulated in the Annex to the document. In particular, the changes were indicated by underlining for new text and strikethrough of the deleted parts of the old text.

Once again, it was recalled in the document that there was no obligation under the STLT to provide for the registration of any of the signs contemplated in Rule 3(4) to (6).[81] It was additionally clarified that the effect of the amendments, if adopted, would be that Contracting Parties accepting the registration of those types of marks would also be bound to accept that the representation of such marks could be deposited as contemplated in the Rule.

The Working Group further revised the proposals of the WIPO Secretariat, and referred the amended rule for adoption by the STLT Assembly at its following session. Seven categories of NTTMs were now specifically addressed in Rule 3: three dimensional-marks,[82] hologram marks,[83] motion marks,[84] color marks,[85] position marks,[86] sound marks,[87] and marks consisting of a non-visible sign other than a sound mark.[88]

At its second session (September 20 to 29, 2010), the Assembly of the STLT adopted the amendments to Rule 3(4) to (6) of the Regulations under the STLT as

[78] WIPO, Representation of Non-Traditional Marks–Areas of Convergence, WIPO Doc. STrad/INF/3 (May 5, 2009).

[79] WIPO, Report of the STLT Assembly, First (Ordinary) Session, WIPO Doc. STLT/A/1/4 (Oct. 1, 2009).

[80] WIPO, Working Group on the Review of Rule 3(4)–(6) of the Regulations under the Singapore Treaty on the Law of Trademarks, WIPO Doc. STLT/WG/1/2 (Feb. 22, 2010).

[81] *Id.* [82] STLT Regulations, *supra* note 22, Rule 3(4). [83] *Id.* at Rule 3(5).

[84] *Id.* at Rule 3(6). [85] *Id.* at Rule 3(7). [86] *Id.* at Rule 3(8).

[87] *Id.* at Rule 3(9). [88] *Id.* at Rule 3(10).

proposed by the Working Group. The Assembly set November 1, 2011, as the date for the entry into force for the new Rule and Regulation.[89]

Since the amendments to Rule 3 had to be accompanied by the corresponding amendments to the Model International Form No. 1 (in particular, footnotes 13 and 14, relating to points 8.6 and 8.9) appropriate changes to the Model International Form No. 1 were also proposed.[90] Accordingly, a Working Group on the Review of Model International Form No. 1 was created. The Working Group held a session on January 31, 2012, to work on amendments to Model International Form No. 1, and recommended to the STLT Assembly for the adoption of the text for a revised Model International Form No. 1.[91] At its Fourth Session (October 1 to 9, 2012), the Assembly of the STLT adopted the proposed amendments.[92]

V. Conclusion

The discussions conducted in the SCT on NTTMs for several years, and the amendments to Rule 3(4) to (6) of the Regulations under the STLT that were adopted by the Assembly of the STLT showed the wide differences of practices among IP Offices regarding the possibility to register NTTMs and the formalities for such registration. However, this discussion also demonstrated that a compromise between the views of many different delegations was possible in order to identify areas of convergence and agree on a set of common principles. In doing so, Member States kept a few paradigms in mind.

First, Member States agreed that a balance must be struck between achieving legal certainty and maintaining options and flexibility for IP Offices. Member States pointed out that using "shall" instead of "may" in the language of the provisions might restrict the acceptable means that an IP Office could use for the representation of NTTMs. In turn, this could result in excluding possible types of representation (i.e., a representation of a sound mark in a sound file provided by electronic means, or a representation of a hologram mark in an electronic file in a movie clip or an animation). For developing countries that were not yet ready to introduce these more sophisticated means of representation, maintaining flexibility and indicating any requirement as optional was very important.

Second, the work done by the SCT and the Assembly of the STLT must allow for an expansion of the number of adherents to the STLT. Again, in order to be inclusive in this expansion, this implies not accepting the introduction of textual elements into the provisions that may result in posing obstacles to this expansion. In this respect, it was clearly stated in the works of the SCT and the Assembly of the STLT

[89] WIPO, Report of the STLT Assembly, Second Session, WIPO Doc. STLT/A/2/2 (Sept. 29, 2010).

[90] WIPO, Report of the Working Group on the Review of Model International Form No. 1 of the Singapore Treaty on the Law of Trademarks, WIPO Doc. STLT/WG/MIF1/1/4 (Jan. 31, 2012).

[91] *Id.*

[92] WIPO, Report of the STLT Assembly, Fourth (Second Extraordinary) Session, WIPO Doc. STLT/A/4/2 (Oct. 9, 2012).

that requiring some types of representation of NTTMs as the general rule could deter several WIPO Member States from joining the STLT. Simply put, it was noted that several Member States were either not ready to apply the rules as drafted, or these Member States believed that specifically drafted rules could limit their choice of acceptable means of representation, to the disadvantage of their applicants.

Third, in spite of the number of divergent views on the interpretation of key elements, such as what constitutes a "sufficiently clear representation" of the mark as required by Article 5(1)(a)(iv) of the STLT, it was important to identify areas of convergence for trademark applicants and owners in order to facilitate and secure the protection of their right in other countries.

Ultimately, discussions at WIPO among Member States demonstrated that important differences on approaches, practices, and sometimes legislation exist in the field of trademarks. In particular, in spite of the adoption of the TLT and STLT, important areas of trademark law remain ambiguous and unclear, especially in relation to some types of marks, such as NNTMs. Yet, due to the number of issues that remain to be clarified in this area, there is still space for further harmonization as part of the future work of WIPO and the SCT. Past discussions indicate very positively that it is still possible for WIPO Member States to agree on areas of convergence, and this can include further harmonization of the legal treatment and requirements for registration of NTTMs.

Annex: WIPO Documents on Non-Traditional Marks

SCT Documents

SCT/16 (November 13 to 17, 2006)
SCT/16/2: New Types of Marks
SCT16/9 Report of the Sixteenth Session (paragraphs 18 to 73)
Available at: http://www.wipo.int/meetings/en/details.jsp?meeting_id=10983
SCT/17 (May 7 to 11, 2007)
SCT/17/2: Methods of Representation and Description of New Types of Marks
SCT/17/3: Relation of Established Trademark Principles to New Types of Marks
SCT/17/8: Report of the Seventeenth Session (paragraphs 14 to 98)
Available at: http://www.wipo.int/meetings/en/details.jsp?meeting_id=12643
SCT/18 (November 12 to 16, 2007)
SCT/18/2: Non-Traditional Marks—Key Learnings
SCT/18/10: Report of the Eighteenth Session (paragraphs 11 to 156)
Available at: http://www.wipo.int/meetings/en/details.jsp?meeting_id=13322
SCT/19 (July 21 to 25, 2008)
SCT/19/2: Representation and Description of Non-traditional Marks: Possible Areas of Convergence
SCT/19/9: Report of the Nineteenth Session (paragraphs 15 to 184)
Available at: http://www.wipo.int/meetings/en/details.jsp?meeting_id=15323
SCT/20 (December 1 to 5, 2008)
SCT/20/2: Representation of Non-Traditional Marks: Areas of Convergence

SCT/20/5: Report of the Twentieth Session (paragraphs 241 to 252)
Available at: http://www.wipo.int/meetings/en/details.jsp?meeting_id=15325

WIPO/STrad/INF/Series Document

WIPO/Strad/INF/3: Representation of Non-traditional Marks: Areas of Convergence (May 5, 2009)
Available at: http://www.wipo.int/sct/en/wipo-strad/

Singapore Treaty on the Law of Trademarks Assembly Documents

STLT/WG/1 (June 28 and 29, 2010)
STLT/WG/1/2: Review of Rule 3(4) to (6) of the Regulations under the Singapore Treaty on the Law of Trademarks
STLT/WG/1/4: Report of the Working Group on the Review of Rule 3(4) to (6) of the Regulations under the Singapore Treaty on the Law of Trademarks
Available at: http://www.wipo.int/meetings/en/details.jsp?meeting_id=20186
STLT/WG/MIF/1/1 (January 31, 2012)
STLT/WG/MIF/1/1/2: Review of Model International Form No. 1 of the Singapore Treaty on the Law of Trademarks
STLT/WG/MIF/1/1/4: Report of the Working Group on the Review of Rule 3(4) to (6) of the Regulations under the Singapore Treaty on the Law of Trademarks
Available at: http://www.wipo.int/meetings/en/details.jsp?meeting_id=25562

2

Non-Traditional Trademarks

An Empirical Study

Mitchell Adams and Amanda Scardamaglia

I. Introduction

This chapter provides a twenty-year retrospective on non-traditional trademarks, using the European Union (EU), the United Kingdom (UK), Singapore, Japan, and Australia as case studies. It presents findings from an empirical study on the application and registration of non-traditional marks in these jurisdictions from 1996 to present day. The aim is to assess, among other things, whether the appetite for non-traditional marks differs across jurisdictions and what impact, if any, differing regulatory regimes have on filing and registration activity. The study further aims to canvass the micro-trends emerging from these data in order to test, at a high level, prevailing assumptions about non-traditional marks. The policy implications of these findings will also be touched upon and contextualized against growing concerns about trademark depletion, which have to date focused on the diminishing number of available words[1] and colors[2] as trademarks, but may well extend to non-traditional marks more generally.[3] This chapter also sets out plans for future research arising from the data presented here.

II. Jurisdictional Differences and Legal Controversies

Today, "almost anything at all that is capable of carrying meaning" can function as a trademark.[4] Even so, the limits placed upon registration vary across jurisdictions. When it comes to non-traditional marks, the EU, the UK, Singapore, Japan, and

[1] *See* Barton Beebe & Jeanne Fromer, *Are We Running out of Trademarks? An Empirical Study of Trademark Depletion*, 131(4) Harv. L. Rev. 945 (2018).

[2] Jani L. McCutcheon, *How Many Colours in the Rainbow? The Registration of Colour per se under Australian Trade Mark Law*, 26(1) Eur. Intell Prop. Rev. 27 (2006).

[3] *See* Beebe & Fromer, *supra* note 1.

[4] Qualitex Co. v. Jacobson Products Co., 514 U.S. 159, 162 (1995).

Australia make for an interesting comparative study thanks to their geo-political differences and their differing registration requirements for non-traditional marks.

The key point of difference between the case studies presented in this chapter relate to the treatment of functional marks—namely functional shape marks. The registration of non-traditional marks in these jurisdictions also poses the usual series of legal dilemmas, which are frequently relied upon to frame normative arguments for (but mostly against) the registration of non-traditional marks. These jurisdictional differences and policy dilemmas will be discussed in the first part, before the empirical impact of these issues are unpacked in the remainder of the chapter, with a view to test some of the assumptions underlying the scholarly discussion on non-traditional marks.

A. Comparative approaches to functionality and non-traditional marks

In most jurisdictions, or at least those that are signatories to the Agreement on Trade-Related Aspects of Intellectual Property Rights (TRIPS), non-traditional marks are registrable so long as they are distinctive and visually perceptible. Such signs include but are not limited to "... in particular words including personal names, letters, numerals, figurative elements, and combinations of colours as well as any combination of such signs ...."[5] As this illustrative list is not closed, the trademark concept underlying the TRIPS Agreement is broad enough to capture two dimensional and three-dimensional shapes, sounds and scents, as well as movement marks and holograms.

As our study will show (the findings of which will be discussed later in the chapter), the most popular category of registered non-traditional marks is the three-dimensional (3D) shape mark. The law relating to shapes is largely similar in those countries who are signatories to TRIPS—providing some facility for the protection and registration of shapes as trademarks—whether that be elements of trade dress, get-up or product design and configuration. There are however some differences with respect to the assessment of distinctiveness and the treatment of functional shapes, be that utilitarian functionality or aesthetic or ornamental functionality, which will be outlined here.

In the UK for example, and consistent with Article 2 of the former EU Trade Mark Directive 2008/95 (EU Directive 2008),[6] a trademark is defined under section 1(1) of the Trade Marks Act 1994 as consisting of

> any sign capable of being represented graphically particularly words, including personal names, designs, letters, numerals, the shape of goods or of their packaging, provided such signs are capable of distinguishing the goods of one undertaking from those of other undertakings.[7]

[5] Agreement on Trade-Related Aspects of Intellectual Property Rights art. 15.1, Apr. 15, 1994, Marrakesh Agreement Establishing the World Trade Organization, Annex 1C, 1869 U.N.T.S. 299, 33 I.L.M. 1997 (1994).

[6] Council Directive 2008/95 art. 2., 2008 O.J. L299/2 (EC).

[7] Trade Marks Act, 1994, c. 26 (Eng.).

Thus, the shape of goods or elements of their packaging are all registrable subject matter in the EU and the UK.[8]

In the UK, the turning point was the introduction of the Trade Marks Act 1994, which dramatically widened what constituted a registrable trademark. In particular, the 1994 Act made way for the possibility of registering several types of signs not previously registrable, including 3D marks. Pursuant to this definition and the principles set out in *Koninklike Philips Electronics NV v. Remington Consumer Products Ltd.*,[9] a sign (including shapes) cannot be precluded from registration because it is prima facie incapable of acting as a badge of origin. Instead, any determination as to registration hinges upon the assessment of distinctiveness, whether that be *ab initio* or through the use which is made of the sign in trade.

Significantly, the EU Directive, and consequently UK trademark law, does impose some restrictions for signs consisting of shapes that result from the nature of the goods themselves, are necessary to obtain a technical result, or give substantial value to the goods.[10] Similar to the American functionality doctrine,[11] this prohibition is justified on the basis of " ... the public interest, in ensuring that natural, functional, or ornamental shapes may be freely used by all."[12] More specifically, "[t]he functionality doctrine prevents trademark law, which seeks to promote competition by protecting a firm's reputation, from ... inhibiting legitimate competition by allowing a producer to control a useful product feature."[13] In doing so, the doctrine draws a clear line between the province of trademark law and patent law, to guard against the granting of a monopoly over functional features, potentially in perpetuity, without regard to whether such features qualify as patents.[14]

The EU prohibition on functional marks has been expanded to some extent by a recent amendment laid down in Article 4(1)(e) of the EU Directive which broadened the existing restriction on the registration of " ... signs consisting exclusively of the shape of the goods to other types of signs ..." by adding the words " ... or another characteristic." This amendment places some types of non-traditional marks, which

[8] At EU level, this has been confirmed in art. 3 of the current EU Directive 2015/2436 which also refers explicitly to shape marks.

[9] Case C-299/99, Koninklike Philips Electronics NV v. Remington Consumer Products Ltd., 2 C.M.L.R. 52, 39–40 (2002).

[10] This limitation was already introduced into the original text of art. 3(1)(e) of the First Council Directive 89/104/EEC of December 21, 1988 to approximate the laws of the Member States relating to trade marks, [1989] O.J. L040/1 (EC). The provisions stated that "(1)The following shall not be registered or, if registered, shall be liable to be declared invalid: ... (e) signs which consist exclusively of (i) the shape which results from the nature of the goods themselves; (ii) the shape of a good which is necessary to obtain a technical result; (iii) the shape which gives substantial value to the goods"; the provision was confirmed, with the same language and numbering, in the text of the European Parliament and Council Directive 2008/95, [2008] O.J. L299/25 (EC), which replaced Directive 89/104. Lastly, in 2015, art. 4(1)(e) of Directive (EU) 2015/2436 of the European Parliament and of the Council of December 16, 2015 to approximate the laws of the Member States relating to trade marks, [2015] O.J. L336/1 (EU) [hereinafter 2015 EU Trademark Directive], expanded the provision and added the language "or another characteristic" in addition to the "shape of the good."

[11] *Qualitex*, *supra* note 4, 164–65.

[12] Arnaud Folliard-Mongurial, *Distinctive Character Acquired Through Use: The Law and The Case Law*, in TRADE MARK USE 409 (Jeremy Phillips & Ilanah Simon eds., 2005).

[13] *Qualitex*, *supra* note 4, 164–65. [14] *Id.*

could be considered as giving substantial value to the goods (including colors), under threat of being rejected without the possibility of overcoming this objection on the basis of acquired distinctiveness. It is unclear how the Court of Justice of the European Union (CJEU) will interpret the meaning of the term "another characteristic" but it may have an impact on trademarking patterns in the future.

A similar restriction on the registration of functional marks exists under Singaporean trademark law, under section 7(3)(b) of the current Trade Marks Act, which prohibits the registration of shapes necessary to obtain a technical result.[15] In Singapore, section 2 of the Trade Marks Act 1998 broadly defines a sign to include "any letter, word, name, signature, numeral, device, brand, heading, label, ticket, shape, colour, aspect of packaging or any combination thereof...."[16] In an attempt for greater harmonization, the Trade Marks (Amended) Act 2004 (Singapore) removed the requirement that a mark has to be "visually perceptible" in order to qualify for registration, meaning that marks such as sound and smell marks, which were previously denied registration, can now be registered.[17]

Section 7(3)(b) of the Trade Marks Act 1998 (Singapore) prohibits the registration of shapes that are necessary to obtain a technical result.[18] As in the EU, the purpose of this provision is to prevent a trademark monopoly on technical solutions or functional characteristics. A mark must also be refused under section 7(3)(a) if the shape results from the nature of the goods.[19]

Japanese trademark legislation was amended in 1996 to include shapes of goods and packaging as registrable subject matter.[20] There are some restrictions to registration. Under this Act, trademarks which consist solely of a mark indicating in a common manner, the shape (including the shape of packages) are to be refused.[21] It was only in more recent times, with changes to the Trademark Act, that Japan allowed for the registration of all types of non-traditional marks.[22] Japan therefore, is an interesting element to this case study as a new entrant to the non-traditional mark market. Prior to these abovementioned changes, a trademark was defined as "... any character, figure, sign, or three-dimensional shape, or any combination thereof, or any combination thereof with colors."[23] While this definition allowed for the registration of shapes, colors and sound marks were not registrable. Moreover, it was difficult to register motion marks, hologram marks, and position marks. This peculiarity is reflected in the data presented in the remaining parts of this chapter.

The final jurisdiction presented in this case study is Australia. In Australia, shapes including 3D marks are registrable pursuant to the expansive definition of a sign contained in the prevailing Trade Marks Act 1995, which includes "... any letter, word, name, signature, numeral, device, brand, heading, label, ticket, aspect of packaging, shape, colour, sound or scent."[24] The Trade Marks Act 1995, which replaced the 1955 Act, not only made explicit provision for the registration of colors,

15 Trade Marks Act 1998, c. 332, § 7(3)(b) (Sing.). 16 *See id.* § 2.
17 Trade Marks Act 1998, c. 332, (Sing.) (amended 2004). 18 *See id.* § 7(3)(b).
19 *See id.* § 7(3)(a). 20 Shōhyō-hō [Trademark Act], 127 of 1959, 2(1) (Japan).
21 *Id.* art. 3(1)(iii). 22 *Id.* art. 2. 23 *Id.* art. 2(1).
24 *See* Trade Marks Act 1995 (Cth) § 6 (Austl.).

sounds, and scents for the first time in Australia, but also expanded registrable subject matter to expressly include aspects of packaging and shapes.[25]

In Australia, there is no functionality doctrine to preclude the registration of functional shapes. Nor is there any explicit legislative provision or ground for refusal relating to functional shape marks, although such a limitation was included in the Trade Marks Act 1994, an Act which never came into operation.[26] This represents a significant point of departure between Australian trademark law and the other jurisdictions considered in this study.

In the absence of an express statutory prohibition, there does appear to be a judicial reluctance to permit the registration of shapes where doing so would mean that "... the proprietor of the mark will be in a better position than a patentee or the proprietor of a registered design, each of whom has a protection limited to the span of a relatively short time."[27] Even so, the judicial statements made on the issue are purely obiter,[28] and as the issue of functionality is subsumed into discussions of distinctiveness under Australian trademark legislation, it is still possible that functional shapes could be registrable if they in fact become distinctive of one trader's goods through use.[29] This peculiarity stems from the operation of section 41 and the standard of distinctiveness under Australian trademark law. This may explain why the three-dimensional shape of Nestlé's break-away Kit-Kat chocolate wafer bar is registered as a trademark in Australia[30] but was refused registration in the EU.[31]

B. Other policy concerns

In addition to the concerns around functionality, non-traditional marks raise a number of other policy concerns, which may, in theory, limit the ability to apply and register such marks. The requirement of graphical representation is one such issue. This is particularly an issue for sound and scent marks. It was always thought that the requirement of graphical representation would limit the kinds of non-traditional marks that were registrable. Trademark offices have sought to deal with this by providing specific guidelines for the representations of various types of marks.[32] In Australia for example, there is no specific stipulation around sound

[25] *Id.*

[26] *See* Trade Marks Act 1994 (Cth) § 39 (Austl.) (now repealed). The Trade Marks Act 1994 (Australia) was hastily enacted by Parliament to meet a deadline imposed under international law, but it was never commenced and was eventually replaced by the Trade Marks Act 1995 (Cth) (Austl.).

[27] Philips v. Remington, 100 F.C.R. 90, 1 (2002) (Austl.).

[28] *See also* obiter statements in Kenman Kandy Australia Pty Ltd. v. Registrar of Trade Marks, 122 F.C.R. 494 (2002) (Austl.) (where Burchett J. observed that "[t]he concerns expressed in both Philips v. Remington (Aust.) and Philips v. Remington (U.K.) about the prospect of trade marks creating monopolies related only to the registration of trade marks that would restrict access to functional features or innovations, and for this reason were well founded."). *Philips, supra* note 27; Philips v. Remington, R.P.C. 809 (1999) (UK).

[29] *See* Trade Marks Act 1995 (Cth) § 41 (Austl.).

[30] *See* Australian Trade Mark Application 849096 as registered with respect to class 30 to Société des Produits Nestlé SA, https://search.ipaustralia.gov.au/trademarks/search/view/849096.

[31] *See* recent Judgment in Joined Cases C-84/17 P Société des produits Nestlé SA v. Mondelez UK Holdings & Services Ltd, formerly Cadbury Holdings Ltd, and EUIPO, C-85/17 P Mondelez UK Holdings & Services Ltd, formerly Cadbury Holdings Ltd v. EUIPO, and C-95/17 P EUIPO v. Mondelez UK Holdings & Services Ltd, formerly Cadbury Holdings Ltd. *Also see* Société des Produits Nestlé v. Cadbury UK Ltd, [2017] EWCA Civ 358; [2017] E.T.M.R. 31.

[32] *See generally Trade Marks Office Manual of Practice and Procedure*, Pt. 21 (Austl.).

marks, but it is recommended that such marks be represented by musical notation.[33] For scent, taste, and texture marks, a precise and accurate description is sufficient. The position is much the same in the EU, although the abovementioned amendment to the EU Directive in 2015 has relaxed the requirements around graphical representation to the extent that authorities and the public are able "... to determine the clear and precise subject matter of the protection afforded to its proprietor."[34]

Another policy issue that has attracted the attention of scholars and the judiciary concerns color marks as non-traditional marks. Opponents have argued that the registration of single colors would result in "color depletion" which would in time, limit traders' choices when it came to packaging and advertising.[35] This concern was observed in the key Australian authority on color marks—*Philmac Pty Ltd v. The Registrar of Trade Marks* (*Philmac*), where Mansfield J. noted that while "[i]n a scientific context, the range of colors available to traders for application to goods is in fact infinite ... in the context of trade mark law that is not the case."[36] Similarly, in the United States (U.S.), the District Court for the Southern District of Iowa ruled that the color green was aesthetically functional for tractors and, therefore, no protection should be granted to such a color trademark unless the acquisition of secondary meaning is proven.[37]

Aside from color depletion concerns, there has also been judicial skepticism as to whether a single color could even be inherently distinctive. Such skepticism was expressed by the Registrar in *Philmac*[38] and confirmed by others including Lehane J at first instance in *Koninklijke Philips Electronics NV v. Remington Products Australia Pty Ltd.*, who remarked that "[i]t is not easy to imagine circumstances in which a

[33] *Id.* Pt. 10.3.3.3. [34] 2015 EU Trademark Directive, *supra* note 10, art. 4.

[35] The color depletion argument was rejected by the U.S. Supreme Court in *Qualitex, supra* note 4, at 162 (1995) and the U.S. Court of Appeal for the Federal Circuit in re Owens-Corning Fiberglass Corp., 774 F.2d 1116 (Fed. Cir. 1985). In Australia, scholars have also argued substantively against the color depletion theory. *See* McCutcheon, *supra* note 2, at 27.

[36] Philmac Pty Ltd. v. The Registrar of Trade Marks, F.C.A. 1551, 58–60 (2002) (Austl.). Mansfield J. went on to say:

> In the present application, the consequence of a grant of registration would be to prevent any other trader in goods of the same description from using not only that shade of terracotta specifically described and visually represented in the application in respect of the goods to which the application relates, but all other shades of colour that might be described as deceptively similar to that colour ... That is ... the limited palate of colours available to a trader at the very least renders it more likely that other persons trading in goods of the relevant kind and being actuated only by proper motives—in the exercise, that is to say, of the common right of the public to make honest use of the colours forming part of the common heritage, for the sake of the signification which they ordinarily possess - will think of a colour and want to use it in connection with similar goods in a manner which would infringe a registered trade mark granted in respect of it. Stating the proposition in that way equates it with what has become known in international jurisprudence as the "colour depletion argument.

Id. at 60.

[37] Deere & Co. v. Farmhand, Inc., 560 F. Supp. 85, 217 USPQ 252 (S.D. Iowa 1982). More recently, *see* Deere & Co. v. FIMCO Inc., No. 15-CV-105 (W.D. Ky. Mar. 8, 2017).

[38] *See Philmac, supra* note 36.

sign which is simply a color ... will be capable of registration, or of use, as a trade mark.'[39] In jurisdictions where the functionality doctrine operates, concerns about color depletion and color scarcity can be dealt with in that way. We have seen this in the U.S., where the Federal Circuit barred the use of black as a trademark on outboard boat motors because black has special functional attributes in decreasing the apparent size of the motor.[40]

III. Methodology

The last decade has seen the emergence of a wide range of easy access intellectual property application information services. Services have ranged from making bulk application data publicly available for the purposes of statistical research,[41] to offering search tools covering application data from multiple intellectual property offices in one online database.[42] Among the datasets and databases available is trademark application data.[43] With the introduction of non-traditional marks, national intellectual property offices have started tagging their trademark application data to indicate the nature of the sign for ease of searching.[44] This has enabled the collation of non-traditional trademark application data. For this study, data on non-traditional trademark applications were sourced from the trademark offices of the EU, the UK, Singapore, Japan, and Australia.[45] It is important to emphasize that the data contained in this study have been compiled from national offices into a single snapshot to make it easier for statistical analysis.[46] The data collected are unique as

[39] Koninklijke Philips Electronics NV v. Remington Products Australia Pty Ltd., (1999) 44 I.P.R. 551 per Lehane J at [46]. Similarly, *see* Kenman Kandy Australia Pty Ltd. v. Registrar of Trade Marks, [2002] 56 I.P.R. 30, 110 (Austl.).

[40] Brunswick Corp. v. British Seagull Ltd. and Outboard Marine Corp., 35 F.3d 1527 (Fed. Cir. 1994).

[41] For example, the United States Patent and Trade Mark Office (USPTO) teams with Google to Provide Bulk Patent and Trademark Data to the Public (June 2, 2010), https://www.uspto.gov/about-us/news-updates/uspto-teams-google-provide-bulk-patent-and-trademark-data-public; Similarly IP Australia also provides open data to the public. *See*, IP AUSTRALIA, IP GOVERNMENT OPEN DATA, https://www.ipaustralia.gov.au/about-us/economics-ip/ip-government-open-data.

[42] *See* EUROPEAN UNION INTELLECTUAL PROPERTY OFFICE, TMVIEW, https://www.tmdn.org/tmview/ and WIPO, Global Brand Database, http://www.wipo.int/branddb/.

[43] *Id.*

[44] Applications are typically tagged as either a specific category of non-traditional trademark (i.e., 3-D shape, color, scent, or sound). Some applications were allocated a category of non-traditional mark at offices such as the European Union Intellectual Property Office (EUIPO) and UK IP Office (UKIPO), which have categorized the marks as "other." Each trademark application was examined based on its graphical representation and supplementary description or endorsement text to categorize the type of sign. For the sake of consistency with national registers, some categories were left unaltered. As the largest category of non-traditional mark, all 3D shape marks were renamed to "3D Shape marks" for ease of reference in the study.

[45] These jurisdictions were selected by the authors based on geographical spread and access to non-traditional trademark applications.

[46] Either sourced from aggregated trademark database sources such as TMview, national online trademark registers, or contained in released national bulk datasets.

they contain detailed information about aspects of individual non-traditional trademark applications.

The dataset contains 22,321 observations with filing dates from January 1, 1996 to December 31, 2016.

The EU trademark data were collected from the EU Intellectual Property Office (EUIPO) online database.[47] Bibliographic data for non-traditional trademarks held by the UK Intellectual Property Office (UKIPO) database with a filing date earlier than December 31, 2016 were collected from their 2016 data release.[48] The Singaporean and Japanese non-traditional trademark application data were collected from the national intellectual property office online databases.[49] The Australian data were drawn from IP Australia's Intellectual Property Government Open Database (IPGOD).[50] IPGOD includes over 100 years of data on all intellectual property rights administered by IP Australia.[51]

As such, this study is substantially more detailed and expansive than any existing study into the registration of non-traditional marks, which provides information to discern more longitudinal trends, including possible extensions to registration after the expiration of the initial ten-year term of protection. Therefore, this dataset is uniquely placed to examine twenty years of applications for shape, color, sound, scent, motion, position, hologram, gesture, and texture trademarks. The trademark activities for these non-traditional signs were examined individually before looking at any applications containing combinations of non-traditional signs. Particular attention was given to the longitudinal filing rates, the proportion of marks currently registered, the number of classes claimed over this period and the types of classes claimed for the different types of marks. Registrations were also examined to reveal the rate of renewals for all categories of non-traditional marks.

IV. Overview of Application Data

Figure 2.1 shows the general trends in the number of non-traditional trademark registration applications filed at the EUIPO, the UKIPO, the Intellectual Property Office of Singapore (IPOS), the Japanese Patent Office (JPO), and IP Australia, per year from 1996 to 2016.

[47] Via TMview. The TMview database contains information from the European Intellectual Property Office (EUIPO) on trademark applications and registered marks. EUIPO, TMview, https://www.tmdn.org/tmview/.

[48] Last updated on Nov. 2, 2016.

[49] Intellectual Property Office of Singapore, IP^{2}SG, https://www.ip2.sg/RPS/WP/CM/SearchSimpleP.aspx?SearchCategory=TM; Japan Patent Office, Japan Platform for Patent Information (J-PlatPat), https://www3.j-platpat.inpit.go.jp/cgi-bin/ET/TM_AREA_E.cgi?1499986729480.

[50] IP AUSTRALIA, INTELLECTUAL PROPERTY GOVERNMENT OPEN DATA 2016, https://data.gov.au/organization/ip-australia. The data presented are current as at Feb. 12, 2016.

[51] Bradley Man, *Overview of the Intellectual Property Government Open Data* (Economic Research Paper No. 02, IP Australia, 2014), 6 https://www.ipaustralia.gov.au/sites/g/files/net856/f/reports_publications/ip_government_open_data_paper_-_final.pdf.

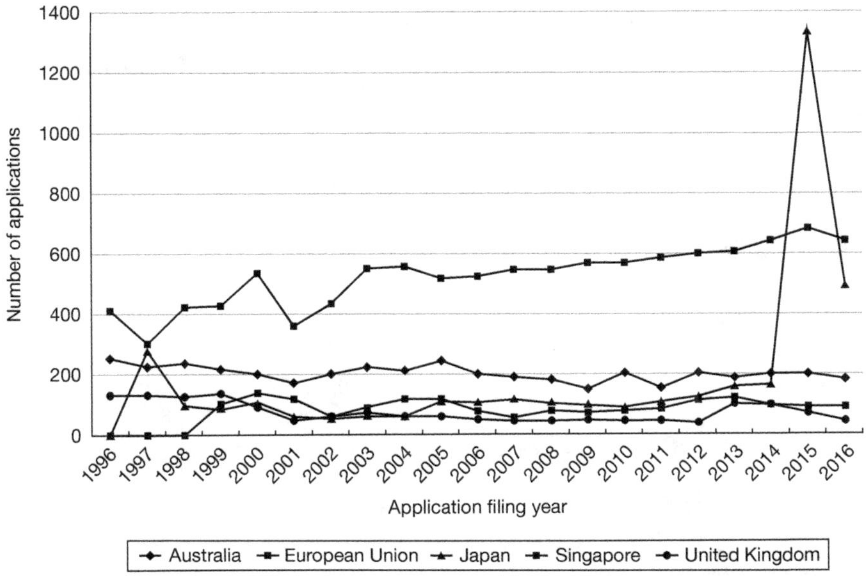

Figure 2.1 Trends in the number of non-traditional trademark registration applications filed 1996–2016

Over this twenty-year period, there has been a total 22,321 applications made in relation to the registration of non-traditional marks—that is, marks that have been classified as shape, color, sound, scent, hologram, movement, position, or gesture marks (or combinations of these kinds of marks).[52] As expected, the largest number of applications for Australia and the UK appear in 1996. For Australia, this was the first year during which the 1995 Act came into effect. The dramatic spike in total applications in 2015 corresponds with Japan legislating to accept non-traditional trademarks.

Previous to 2015, applications received by the JPO were predominantly 3D shape marks, indicating a general acceptance that shapes could function as a trademark. As Figure 2.1 shows, the trend in annual trademark applications remains steady for the UK, Singapore, Japan, and Australia. Conversely, the number of applications received by the EUIPO has slowly increased over the period. The peak in applications in 2000 and drop in 2001 interestingly corresponds with the Internet bubble.[53]

Table 2.1 reports the leading categories of non-traditional marks applied for at the five intellectual property offices. Over this twenty-year period, the overwhelming majority of applications has been for 3D shapes. The overall proportion of non-traditional marks currently registered for all applications filed from 1996 to 2016,

[52] There were some applications for non-traditional marks made in the years immediately preceding the change in legislation. For example, in Australia in 1995, seventeen applications for non-traditional marks were made, and a further nine applications were made between 1991 and 1994.

[53] ROGER LOWENSTEIN, ORIGINS OF THE CRASH: THE GREAT BUBBLE AND ITS UNDOING 101–26 (2004).

Table 2.1 Application and Registration by Mark Type and Filing Basis 1996–2016

Filing Country	Mark Type	Number of Applications	% of Total NTM Applications	Proportion Registered
AU	3D Shape	2,761	65.30	0.32
	Color	928	21.95	0.22
	Color-Shape	306	7.24	0.32
	Sound	106	2.51	0.52
	Position	58	1.37	0.45
	Movement	41	0.97	0.90
	Scent	19	0.45	0.05
	Hologram	8	0.19	0.50
	Gesture	1	0.02	0.00
	Subtotal	4,228	100.00	0.31
EU	3D Shape	9,042	81.89	0.56
	Color	1,210	10.96	0.41
	Position	381	3.45	0.32
	Sound	260	2.35	0.78
	Movement	123	1.11	0.56
	Hologram	10	0.09	0.30
	Scent	9	0.08	0.00
	Texture	4	0.04	0.00
	Font	2	0.02	0.00
	Subtotal	11,041	100.00	0.54
JP	3D Shape	2,428	64.13	0.88
	Sound	458	12.10	0.18
	Color	448	11.83	0.00
	Position	321	8.48	0.05
	Motion	116	3.06	0.43
	Hologram	15	0.40	0.53
	Subtotal	3,786	100.00	0.61
SG	3D Shape	1,100	64.63	0.39
	Colors	309	18.16	0.12
	Aspect of Packaging	193	11.34	0.34
	Sound	49	2.88	0.69
	3D Shape/Aspect of Packaging	30	1.76	0.33
	Movement	13	0.76	0.69
	Hologram	8	0.47	0.50
	Subtotal	1,702	100.00	0.34

Table 2.1 Continued

Filing Country	Mark Type	Number of Applications	% of Total NTM Applications	Proportion Registered
UK	3D Shape	1,337	85.49	0.65
	Color	149	9.53	0.70
	Sound	30	1.92	0.57
	Hologram	25	1.60	0.60
	Movement	18	1.15	0.39
	Position	3	0.19	0.33
	Texture	2	0.13	0.00
	Subtotal	1,564	100.00	0.65
	Total Applications	22,321	100.00	0.50

was 0.50. However, this was not reflected in individual categories of non-traditional marks. In general, movement marks receive positive treatment in each jurisdiction. The other categories do not fare as well. This may be due to increased scrutiny during examination.

Table 2.2 sets out the number of claimed classes of goods and services for which the application sought to register the non-traditional marks from each jurisdiction between 1996 and 2016. The forty-five classes of goods and services are taken from the international classification of goods and services or the Nice Classification.[54]

V. Focus on National (and Regional) Applications

The following sections will deal with non-traditional trademark applications filed in each jurisdiction.

A. European Union

The EUIPO received the highest number of applications for non-traditional marks, totalling 11,041 applications. Of these, 803 were Madrid Protocol applications. The majority of these marks fall into the shape category (9,042) followed by color trademarks (1,210). The EUIPO received 381 position mark applications, 260 sound applications, 123 movement applications, 10 holograms, nine scents, and four texture mark applications. Two applications contained type fonts. Of the total number of applications for non-traditional marks, 62.2% were initially accepted for

[54] Nice Agreement Concerning the International Classification of Goods and Services for the Purposes of the Registration of Marks (as amended on Sept. 28, 1979); Nice Classification (2017) (revised). For details see http://www.wipo.int/classifications/nice/en/index.html.

registration and currently 53.6% are registered as trademarks, while 3,743 (33.9%) were never registered after lapsing during examination. There are 429 applications (3.9%) currently pending. Around 63% of the applications registered from 1997 were renewed.

The EUIPO enjoyed the highest average number of filings over the period, with an average of 525.8 applications received per year. Figure 2.2 shows the peaks and increased growth in applications over the period along with a similar trend in the number of classes claimed per year. Interestingly the dip in 2001 correlates to the dot-com bust. The average annual growth rate over the period was 3.55%, the highest across the case study jurisdictions. More importantly, the number of classes claimed is increasing faster than the number of applications, with an average of 2.13 classes claimed per application over this period.

The most popular class claimed was 33 (alcoholic beverages, except beers), followed by 30 (including coffee, tea, cocoa, and confectionary), 3 (including soaps, perfumery, cosmetics), 9 (including computers), and 32 (including beers, mineral and aerated waters and other non-alcoholic beverages; fruit beverages and fruit juices). The most popular classes of services for which non-traditional mark applications were made included: 35 (including advertising), 42 (including scientific and technological services and research and design related thereto), 41 (including education), 39 (including transport), and 37 (including building and construction).

B. United Kingdom

The data from the last twenty years show that in total 1,564 applications were made to the UKIPO in relation to the registration of non-traditional marks.[55] Over the twenty-year period there were a total of 321 Madrid Protocol applications. Again, the majority of these marks fall into the shape category (1,337) followed by color trademarks (149). There were only thirty sound applications, twenty-five hologram applications, eighteen movement applications, three position applications, and two texture applications recorded. Of the total number of applications for non-traditional marks, 85.3% were initially accepted for registration and currently 65.2% are registered as trademarks, while 142 (9.1%) were never registered after being refused or withdrawn. Thirty-three (2.1%) are currently pending. Around 67% of the applications registered from 1996 were renewed.

The UKIPO received on average 74.5 applications per year, the lowest average compared to the other jurisdictions. Figure 2.3 shows interest peaked between 1996 to 1998 and slumped between 2001 to 2012. Interest picked up again between 2013 and 2015. The average annual growth rate over the period was 0.32%. The number of classes claimed did not necessarily match the number of filings. Interestingly the number of classes claimed during 2001 to 2012 peaked in 2005 and again in 2010.

[55] There were some applications for non-traditional marks made in the years immediately preceding 1996. For example, the data examined for this chapter showed in 1994, 100 applications for non-traditional applications were made, and a further 251 applications were made in 1995.

Table 2.2 Applications by International Class, 1996–2016

	International Class	AU		EU		JP		SG		UK	
		Number of Apps.	% of Total	Number of Apps.	% of Total	Number of Apps.	% of Total	Number of Apps.	% of Total	Number of Apps.	% of Total
1	Chemicals	74	1.14	291	1.24	47	0.72	19	0.90	16	0.57
2	Paints	29	0.45	118	0.50	19	0.29	16	0.76	3	0.11
3	Cosmetics and Cleaning Preparations	435	6.69	1,398	5.95	324	4.94	195	9.22	217	7.70
4	Lubricants and Fuels	62	0.95	270	1.15	49	0.75	20	0.95	35	1.24
5	Pharmaceuticals	295	4.54	780	3.32	331	5.05	110	5.20	119	4.22
6	Metal Goods	196	3.02	512	2.18	95	1.45	30	1.42	42	1.49
7	Machinery	195	3.00	564	2.40	155	2.36	44	2.08	95	3.37
8	Hand Tools	63	0.97	257	1.09	38	0.58	12	0.57	13	0.46
9	Electrical and Scientific Apparatus	413	6.35	1362	5.80	465	7.09	125	5.91	149	5.29
10	Medical Apparatus	146	2.25	361	1.54	109	1.66	17	0.80	36	1.28
11	Environmental Control Apparatus	168	2.58	526	2.24	101	1.54	31	1.47	52	1.84
12	Vehicles	129	1.98	433	1.84	95	1.45	20	0.95	55	1.95
13	Firearms	0	0.00	21	0.09	1	0.02	2	0.09	0	0.00
14	Jewellery	114	1.75	367	1.56	159	2.42	65	3.07	59	2.09
15	Musical Instruments	36	0.55	85	0.36	16	0.24	8	0.38	8	0.28
16	Paper Goods	242	3.72	1,039	4.43	279	4.25	91	4.30	112	3.97
17	Rubber Goods	78	1.20	230	0.98	27	0.41	12	0.57	18	0.64

(continued)

Table 2.2 Continued

	International Class	AU		EU		JP		SG		UK	
		Number of Apps.	% of Total	Number of Apps.	% of Total	Number of Apps.	% of Total	Number of Apps.	% of Total	Number of Apps.	% of Total
18	Leather Goods	110	1.69	425	1.81	130	1.98	48	2.27	40	1.42
19	Non-Metallic Building Materials	78	1.20	234	1.00	65	0.99	15	0.71	23	0.82
20	Furniture	170	2.62	632	2.69	146	2.23	35	1.65	39	1.38
21	Housewares and Glass	243	3.74	889	3.79	178	2.71	54	2.55	108	3.83
22	Cordage and Fibres	8	0.12	55	0.23	15	0.23	3	0.14	1	0.04
23	Yarns and Threads	1	0.02	9	0.04	3	0.05	2	0.09	1	0.04
24	Fabrics	50	0.77	152	0.65	47	0.72	12	0.57	19	0.67
25	Clothing	280	4.31	789	3.36	208	3.17	62	2.93	102	3.62
26	Fancy Goods	24	0.37	69	0.29	47	0.72	8	0.38	10	0.35
27	Floor Coverings	4	0.06	53	0.23	9	0.14	4	0.19	5	0.18
28	Toys and Sporting Goods	213	3.28	733	3.12	337	5.14	62	2.93	92	3.26
29	Meats and Processed Foods	162	2.49	1,135	4.83	250	3.81	75	3.55	102	3.62
30	Staple Foodstuffs	427	6.57	1,652	7.04	451	6.88	166	7.85	177	6.28
31	Natural Agricultural Products	94	1.45	238	1.01	70	1.07	19	0.90	10	0.35
32	Beers and other Non-Alcoholic Beverages	325	5.00	1,278	5.44	190	2.90	103	4.87	164	5.82
33	Alcoholic Beverages (except beers)	480	7.38	1,660	7.07	337	5.14	179	8.46	259	9.19

34	Smokers' Articles	56	0.86	187	0.80	29	0.44	55	2.60	30	1.06
35	Advertising and Business	313	4.82	1,208	5.15	392	5.98	92	4.35	131	4.65
36	Insurance and Financial	106	1.63	320	1.36	211	3.22	30	1.42	84	2.98
37	Building Construction and Repair	109	1.68	418	1.78	196	2.99	32	1.51	58	2.06
38	Telecommunications	64	0.98	342	1.46	79	1.20	28	1.32	39	1.38
39	Transport and Storage	86	1.32	451	1.92	120	1.83	17	0.80	52	1.84
40	Treatment of Materials	18	0.28	138	0.59	53	0.81	8	0.38	6	0.21
41	Education and Entertainment	152	2.34	572	2.44	256	3.90	79	3.74	83	2.94
42	Computer and Scientific	150	2.31	648	2.76	178	2.71	47	2.22	70	2.48
43	Hotels and Restaurants	50	0.77	338	1.44	112	1.71	43	2.03	49	1.74
44	Medical, Beauty, and Agricultural	36	0.55	134	0.57	64	0.98	15	0.71	13	0.46
45	Personal and Legal	16	0.25	106	0.45	74	1.13	5	0.24	23	0.82
	Total	6,500	100.00	23,479	100.00	6,557	100.00	2,115	100.00	2,819	100.00

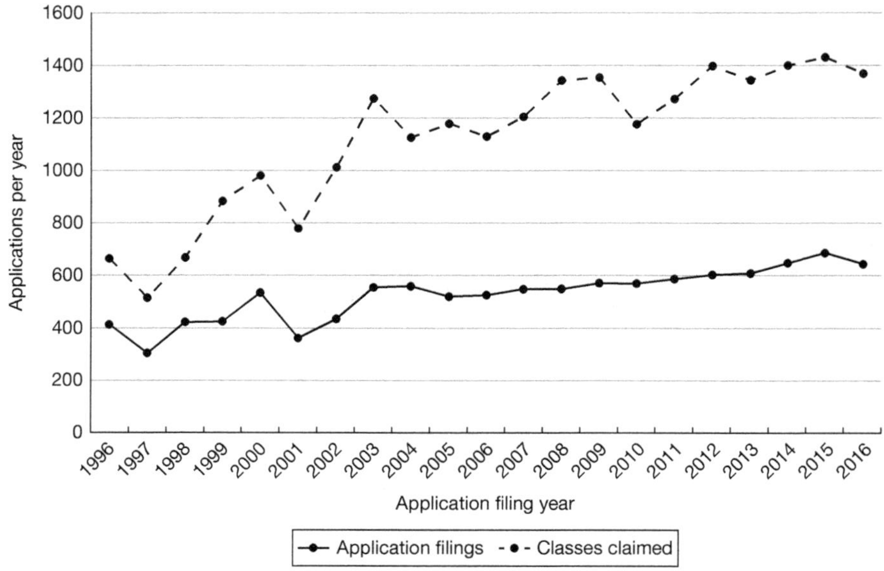

Figure 2.2 Trends in EUIPO applications 1996–2016

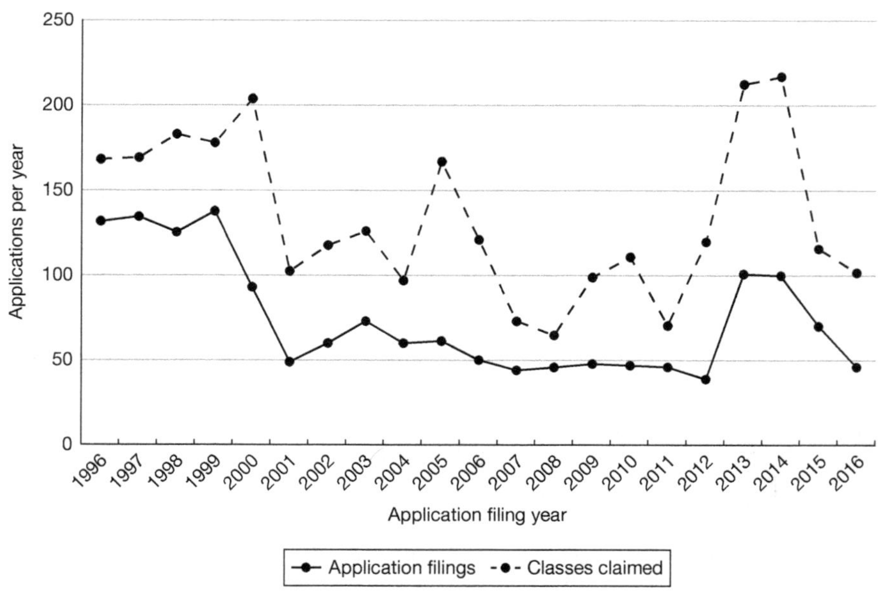

Figure 2.3 Trends in UKIPO applications 1996–2016

Overall, the average number of classes claimed was 1.80 per application. This was higher than the rate seen in Australia and discussed below.

Applications for non-traditional marks in the UK followed the general trend with the most popular claimed class of goods being international class thirty-three (alcoholic beverages, except beers) taking nearly 10% of total number of classes claimed in that the period. This was followed by classes 3 (including soaps, perfumery, cosmetics), 30 (including coffee, tea, cocoa, and confectionary), 32 (including beers, mineral and aerated waters, and other non-alcoholic beverages; fruit beverages and fruit juices), and 9 (including computers). The most popular classes of services for which non-traditional mark applications were made included: 35 (including advertising), 36 (insurance and financial services), 41 (including entertainment and education services), and 42 (including scientific and technological services and research and design related thereto).

C. Singapore

The data show Singapore was slow off the mark in terms of its non-traditional trademark applications. Between 1996 and 2016, 1,702 applications were made to the IPOS in relation to the registration of non-traditional marks with an average of 81.0 applications made per year. Three-dimensional shape marks dominate with 1,100 applications followed by color trademarks with 309 applications. Aspects of packaging is specifically tagged by the IPOS and indicated that 193 applications were made along with thirty applications for a combination of color and aspect of packaging. The remainder was made up of forty-nine sound applications, thirteen movement applications, and eight hologram applications recorded. Of the total number of applications for non-traditional marks, currently, 34.3% are registered as trademarks, the lowest seen in all five jurisdictions examined. One hundred and twenty-six applications (7.4%) are currently pending.

Figure 2.4 shows the peaks and troughs of total applications over the twenty-year period along with the number of Nice Classification classes claimed per year. As seen in the EU, the interest in non-traditional marks in Singapore peaked in 2000 and slumped in 2002, corresponding to the dot-com boom and bust. Overall the average annual growth rate over the period was 2.86%. The number of classes claimed closely follow the number of applications with an average of 1.24 classes claimed per application.

The most popular claimed classes of goods for which non-traditional mark applications were made included: class 3 (including soaps, perfumery, cosmetics), 33 (alcoholic beverages, except beers), 30 (including coffee, tea, cocoa, and confectionary), 9 (including computers), and 5 (including pharmaceuticals). The most popular classes of services for which non-traditional mark applications were made included: 35 (including advertising), 41 (including entertainment and educational services), 42 (including scientific and technological services and research and design related thereto), and 43 (hotel and restaurant services).

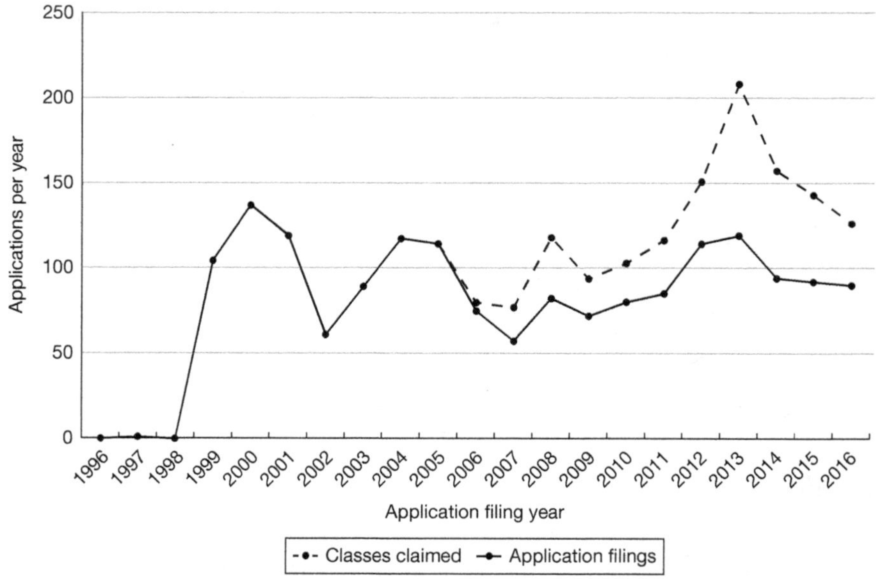

Figure 2.4 Trends in IPOS applications 1996–2016

D. Japan

Over the last twenty years, Japan displayed a healthy filing rate, despite the early legislative limitations. From 1996 to 2014, the JPO received 1,965 shape mark applications. Figure 2.5 below illustrates the continued interest with an average of 109.2 applications received per year from 1996 to 2014. Over the entire period, 3,786 applications in total have been made to the JPO in relation to the registration of non-traditional marks, with 342 being Madrid Protocol applications. Again, the majority of these marks falls into the shape category (2,428) followed by sound (458) and color (448) marks. The JPO received 321 position mark applications, 116 motion applications, and fifteen hologram applications. The spike in 2015 shown in Figure 2.5 was primarily driven by the interest in color and sound marks. Of the total number of applications for non-traditional marks, all marks appear to have been accepted for registration and currently 60.7% are registered as trademarks, while two international applications for shape marks were never registered after being withdrawn. Only one application was cancelled from the register (being a 3D shape mark). There are currently 1423 applications (37.6%) pending. Most of the shape applications registered before 2005 were renewed by the applicants. Figure 2.5 also shows the number of Nice Classification classes claimed per year. The number of classes claimed in Japan closely follow the other jurisdictions with an average of 1.73 classes claimed per application.

Unlike the other jurisdictions, the most popular claimed classes of goods were class 9 (including computers) making up 6% of total classes claimed, followed by 30 (including coffee, tea, cocoa, and confectionary), class 33 (alcoholic beverages, except

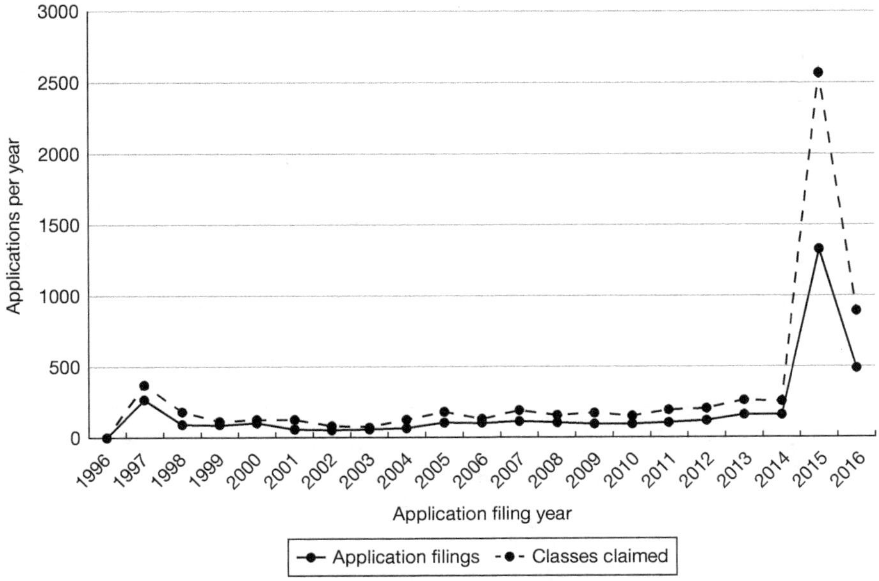

Figure 2.5 Trends in JPO applications 1996–2016

beers), 28 (toys and sporting equipment), and 5 (including pharmaceuticals). The most popular classes of services for which non-traditional mark applications were made included: 35 (including advertising) making up 6% of total classes claimed, 41 (including education), 36 (including insurance and financial services), 37 (including building and construction), and 42 (including scientific and technological).

E. Australia

The data from the last twenty years show that in total, 4,228 applications were made to IP Australia for the registration of non-traditional marks.[56] Over the twenty-year period, a total of 870 Madrid Protocol applications were made.[57] By far, the majority of these marks fall into the shape category (2,761) followed by color trademarks (928). There were only 106 sound applications, fifty-eight position applications, forty-one movement applications, nineteen scent applications, eight hologram applications, and one gesture application recorded. There were 306 applications recorded as combination shape and color marks.[58] Of the total number of applications

[56] There were some applications for non-traditional marks made in the years immediately preceding the change in legislation. For example, IPGOD data show that in 1995, seventeen applications for non-traditional applications were made, and a further nine applications were made between 1991 and 1994.

[57] Protocol Relating to the Madrid Agreement Concerning the International Registration of Marks, 15 U.S.C. § 1141a(b) (2004).

[58] These applications were categorized as a combination due to the IP Australia form allowing applications to indicate their non-traditional trademark via checkbox. *See* IP AUSTRALIA, APPLICATION TO REGISTER A TRADE MARK, https://www.ipaustralia.gov.au/sites/g/files/net856/f/tm00001_0415.pdf.

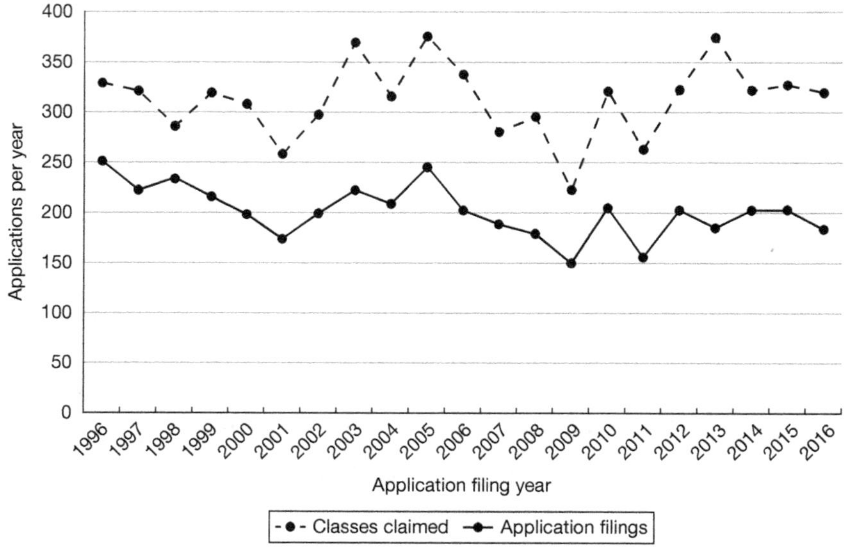

Figure 2.6 Trends in IP Australia applications 1996–2016

for non-traditional marks, 36.5% were initially accepted for registration. Currently, 30.6% of those applications are registered as trademarks, while 2,439 (57.7%) were never registered after lapsing during examination or were withdrawn. There were 281 applications (6.7%) refused or removed from the register; 214 applications (5.1%) are currently pending. Around 69% of the applications registered in the initial ten-year period (from the introduction of the Act) were renewed.

Figure 2.6 below shows the trend of total applications over the twenty-year period along with the number of Nice Classification classes claimed per year. As expected, the highest number of applications were received in 1996, the first year during which the 1995 Act came into effect. There are various dips including in 2001 and 2009 (which most likely correlates to the global financial crisis). The average annual growth rate over the period was -0.4%. As trademark applications can request more than one Nice Classification class, there are typically more filings in trademark classes than the number of trademarks filed. The number of classes claimed in Australia closely follow the number of applications with an average of 1.54 classes claimed per application.

The most popular claimed classes of goods for which non-traditional mark applications were made included: class 33 (alcoholic beverages, except beers), 3 (including soaps, perfumery, cosmetics), 30 (including coffee, tea, cocoa, and confectionary), 9 (including computers), and 32 (including beers, mineral and aerated waters, and other non-alcoholic beverages; fruit beverages and fruit juices). The most popular classes of services for which non-traditional mark applications were made included: 35 (including advertising), 41 (including education), 42 (including scientific and technological services and research and design related thereto), 37 (including building and construction), and 36 (including insurance and finance services).

VI. Conclusion

This chapter has presented the findings from the first comprehensive, longitudinal study of non-traditional marks across the EU, the UK, Singapore, Japan, and Australia. It has traced the filing activity in these jurisdictions over the last twenty years, including the number of applications and registrations across the various categories of non-traditional marks, as well as the classes of goods and services for which they have been applied and registered.

The data show that non-traditional trademarking activity was greatest in the EU, while Australia experienced negative growth over the period considered. Japan has enthusiastically embraced non-traditional marks, since the legal requirements for registration were relaxed to allow for the registration of all types of non-traditional marks, beyond shape marks. Singapore had the lowest filing rate.

Shape marks were by far the most popular category of non-traditional marks, followed by color marks, but combination shape and color marks also make up a significant proportion of the dataset. The last few years have also given rise to a growing number of movement marks, gesture marks, and holograms. The data also showed significant growth in position marks, especially in Japan. Almost as many position marks were registered in Japan as in the EU, where position marks were the third most popular category of registered non-traditional marks. The data would indicate that we are not running out of non-traditional marks. Rather, firms are shifting their attention to different forms of non-traditional marks, beyond the first wave of non-traditional marks of shapes and colors.

Furthermore, this data appears to dispel some of the concerns around non-traditional trademarks. As already noted, most applications relate to shapes. As such, many of the concerns around scent and sound marks and the requirement of graphical representation, have not arisen because those types of applications are so few in comparison to the other categories of non-traditional marks.

Moreover, concerns about color depletion also seem to be overstated. Many of the color marks registered were actually combination marks, and in Japan, more sound marks were registered than color marks. This might indicate that the functionality doctrine (and the doctrine of distinctiveness in Australia) may have had a cooling effect on the demand for these kinds of marks.

This data also presents several opportunities for future research. The first point of research concerns Article 4(1)(e) of the EU Directive and the broadening of the traditional functionality doctrine relating to the registration of "... signs consisting exclusively of the shape of the goods ..." to other types of signs by adding the words "... or another characteristic." There is speculation about whether this amendment will limit the types of non-traditional marks capable of registration. The dataset collated for this study provides the perfect base point to make this assessment, to test the impact of this change to the Directive.

This study also provides a perfect base from which to examine whether the amendment to the EU Directive in 2015, which has relaxed the requirements around graphical representation, may in fact change registration practices in the EU. Again, this dataset provides a base point for future research to test the impact of this change. Finally, this data provides fertile ground for further research into the experience of Madrid System applications in national offices—and whether they are treated differently in different jurisdictions.

3

Paying the Price for Admission

Non-Traditional Marks across Registration and Enforcement

*Dev S. Gangjee**

I. Introduction

This is an argument for joined-up thinking in relation to non-traditional signs in trademark law. Over the past three decades, trademark registration has moved from up-front exclusions for certain categories of signs (no shapes, no colors) toward cautious and incremental acceptance. However the policy concerns generated by the grant of legal monopolies in such signs remain equally relevant today. The grant of an abstract color mark to one trader closes off a part of the color spectrum to others. Can we therefore allow such signs into the system while successfully managing the tensions generated by their admission?

Responding to this challenge, this chapter explores two potential responses. First, when permitting such marks to be registered, should we correlate the mark as characterized at the time of registration—agreeably modest in its scope and ambitions—with the mark as deployed in an enforcement context, where it tends to be read more generously? By way of an illustration, does it make sense to insist upon a precise shade of color being used for very specific goods at the time of registration, if the scope of protection granted in the context of infringement rapidly expands across a broader spectrum of shades and contexts of use? Second, when it comes to regulating non-traditional marks, should we move beyond historic upstream solutions—in the form of exclusions from registrability—and proactively consider additional scope limitation mechanisms when applying infringement tests and defenses?

Drawing on a range of EU and U.S. decisions across various categories of non-traditional marks, the chapter argues that both questions should be answered affirmatively. Section II reviews the manner in which non-traditional marks came to be accommodated within trademark registration systems. Section III focuses closely on

* The author wishes to thank the editors and fellow contributors to this volume for feedback during the roundtable at the Singapore Management University on January 26–27, 2017. Lisa Ramsey and Michael Handler provided valuable insights during the roundtable, while the chapter benefitted from subsequent comments by Ansgar Ohly, David Musker, Richard Arnold, Barton Beebe, Luis Porangaba, Justin Hughes, and Graeme Dinwoodie.

Paying the Price for Admission: Non-Traditional Marks Across Registration and Enforcement. Dev S. Gangjee.

the characterization of the mark at the time of registration. Trademark registration calls for a non-traditional mark to be depicted or represented (always), described (often), and classified according to type (where possible). Characterization clearly matters, as the ongoing *Louboutin* (C-163/16) red-soled shoes litigation before the Court of Justice demonstrates. Once characterized, the mark is then channeled into the relevant stream of substantive examination analysis. Since characterization has consequences, applicants have learned to adapt in order to overcome obstacles to registration. However where such techniques have been used to subvert substantive criteria, registries and courts have responded by overriding the applicant's own preferred characterization with an objective assessment of the mark's content. Section IV outlines the importance of consciously connecting the scope of the mark as characterized for the purposes of registration with its scope for the purposes of infringement. Section V concludes.

II. Opening Up to Non-Traditional Marks

When it comes to registration, the "types of signs that are nowadays considered as being capable of constituting a trademark have expanded beyond words or figurative devices."[1] The universe of registrable signs is divided into those which can be perceived visually and those which are experienced through the other senses.[2] Visual signs have developed beyond the core of words and figurative marks or logos (such as the Nike "swoosh" or the Starbucks "mermaid"), extending to (i) three-dimensional marks, including product shape and external packaging; (ii) color marks, which refer to single colors without contours, or combinations of such colors; (iii) holograms, which optically store and retrieve an image in three dimensions; (iv) motion marks, where the moving image may be depicted via a short video clip or sequence of still images (including so-called gesture marks and fluid marks); (v) multimedia signs which include sound in addition to visuals; and (vi) position marks, where a sign appears at a specific location on a product.[3] Visual signs continue to evolve and pattern marks are a sub-category presently attracting attention.[4] They consist of a set of elements which are repeated regularly and have been applied for in the textile and

[1] World Intellectual Property Organization (WIPO), New Types of Marks, Sep. 1, 2006, Standing Committee on the Law of Trademarks, Industrial Designs and Geographical Indications (SCT), SCT/16/2, at ¶ 3.

[2] *Id.*; Qian Zhan, *The International Registration of Non-traditional Trademarks: Compliance with the TRIPS Agreement and the Paris Convention*, 16 World Trade Rev. 111, 112 (2017); *See also* the European Union Intellectual Property Office (EUIPO) classification of mark categories on eSearch plus, its search tool for accessing trademark records in its databases, https://euipo.europa.eu/ohimportal/en/esearch; and the classification of mark categories on TMView, a global trademark search tool that provides data about marks from the participating intellectual property offices, https://www.tmdn.org/tmview/welcome#.

[3] Variants of word marks potentially include slogans, titles of films or books, and more recently hashtags, although each of these is contested. Since they do not raise representation challenges in the same way as (say) a scent, they are not considered at any length.

[4] *See* In re Fantasia Distribution, Inc., 120 U.S.P.Q.2d 1137 (TTAB, 2016) (concluding that a diamond pattern on electronic hookahs is decorative and non-distinctive).

apparel sectors.[5] Signs that are perceived by the remaining senses predictably cover (vi) sound marks, both musical and non-musical; (vii) olfactory or scent marks; (viii) gustatory or taste marks; and (ix) tactile marks.

The accommodation of this range of subject matter relies upon the adoption of an open-ended definition of a trademark. Article 15(1) of the Agreement on Trade-Related Aspects of Intellectual Property Rights (TRIPS Agreement) acknowledges that any "sign, or any combination of signs, capable of distinguishing the goods or services of one undertaking from those of other undertakings, shall be capable of constituting a trademark."[6] United States (U.S.) statutory language takes a similar form: a trademark is a designation which includes, "any word, name, symbol, or device, or any combination thereof [which] serves to identify and distinguish [the mark owner's goods] from those manufactured or sold by others and to indicate the source of the goods, even if that source is unknown."[7] As the U.S. Supreme Court observed, since "human beings might use as a 'symbol' or 'device' almost anything at all that is capable of carrying meaning, [the statutory definition] read literally, is not restrictive."[8] The Court of Justice of the European Union (CJEU) echoed this in *Sieckmann*.[9] While the illustrative list of marks (words, personal names, letters, the shape of goods, etc.) in Article 2 of the EU Trademark Directive 1989 (TMD 1989) were all capable of being visually perceived, marks perceived by the other senses could also in principle be recognized.[10] An open-ended definition thus emphasizes that a trademark is what a trademark does. The candidate sign should have the potential to be distinctive, by indicating a product's commercial origin and thereby distinguishing that product from others on the marketplace. Moreover, trademark law recognizes that producers can educate the relevant public into perceiving practically any sign that is being used as a trademark, through the doctrine of acquired distinctiveness or secondary meaning.[11]

However this openness is a relatively recent development. For much of its history, the law of registered trademarks approached non-traditional signs with circumspection. This is evident in bureaucratic and judicial responses to claims for abstract color marks, without defined contours or boundaries—the color red per se, as opposed to a red square or circle. One part of the explanation for this has to do with technologies

[5] European Union Intellectual Property Office (EUIPO), Guidelines for Examination of European Union Trademarks, Part B, § 4, Ch. 3—Non-Distinctive Trademarks, 29–32 (Oct. 2017) [hereinafter EUIPO Guidelines].

[6] Agreement on Trade-Related Aspects of Intellectual Property Rights, Apr. 15, 1994, Marrakesh Agreement Establishing the World Trade Organization, Annex 1C, 1869 U.N.T.S. 299, 33 I.L.M. 1197 (1994) [hereinafter TRIPS Agreement].

[7] 15 U.S.C. § 1127 (Lanham Act § 45).

[8] Qualitex Co. v. Jacobson Prods. Co, 514 U.S. 159, 162 (1995).

[9] Case C-273/00, Sieckmann v. Deutsches Patent- und Markenamt, 2002 E.C.R. I-11737, ¶¶ 43–45 (CJEU).

[10] First Council Directive 89/104/EEC of Dec. 21, 1988 to Approximate the Laws of the Member States relating to Trademarks, [1989] O.J. L40/1 [hereinafter TMD 1989]. An open-ended definition continues to be found in its successors: art. 2 of the Trademark Directive 2008/95/EEC of Oct. 22, 2008, [2008] O.J. L299/25 [hereinafter TMD 2008]; and art. 3 of the Trademark Directive (EU) 2015/2436, [2015] O.J. L336/1 [hereinafter TMD 2015].

[11] TRIPS Agreement, *supra* note 6, art. 15(1).

of registration. In the context of late nineteenth-century British trademark law, "the decision to exclude colour from the scope of what could be registered as a mark was the result not of principled argument but arose from the practical difficulties in the way trademarks were registered."[12] Applicants were required to submit a wood-block or electrotype of the mark to be published in the trademark journal, and the chromo-lithography technology of the time could not rise to the challenge of reliably printing the precise shade that was being claimed as a mark. Representation challenges continue to impede olfactory and gustatory marks today.[13] However as practical representational challenges dropped away for most categories, the focus has increasingly shifted to policy arguments and public interest concerns.

This transition can be illustrated by the category of color marks, which present two problems.[14] The first is referred to as "exhaustion" or "depletion," where a party successfully claiming one color from the limited pool of available colors has the right to exclude others from using it. However other traders may have legitimate reasons for wishing to use that color. It may be the natural color of the product, have an ornamental or aesthetic function, be associated with a pre-existing and culturally contingent meaning (red for danger, luck, or seduction), or have a utilitarian function (hide dirt, reflect light, or radiate heat better). Exclusive rights would foreclose such uses, leading to undesirable marketplace distortions and unreasonable commercial speech restrictions. The second and related concern can be summarized as "shade confusion." Color depletion is compounded by the doctrinal mechanics of infringement analysis. The ability of the consuming public to differentiate between shades of colors is limited, since it is assumed that consumers are rarely in a position to directly compare the plaintiff and defendant's products side by side; they will have to rely on the imperfect recollection of their memories, where one shade of red may look indistinguishable from or very similar to another. In practice, the scope of the legal monopoly will therefore extend beyond the precise shade that is registered to cover a range of proximate shades, which inevitably favors the trademark owner or at least encourages speculative litigation. Cumulatively, depletion and shade confusion could lead to an increasingly propertized color spectrum, where trader A may effectively claim a large part of the blue spectrum for certain products, trader B may do the same for green and so on.

Historically, the response to such policy concerns has been up-front exclusion filters. Notably, certain categories of non-traditional marks were *de jure* excluded from the universe of registrable signs. Shape marks were problematic in light of the principle that trademark law should protect the mark as opposed to the product

[12] BRAD SHERMAN & LIONEL BENTLY, THE MAKING OF MODERN INTELLECTUAL PROPERTY LAW: THE BRITISH EXPERIENCE, 1760–911, 190 (1999).

[13] WIPO, Methods of Representation and Description of New Types of Marks, Mar. 29, 2007, SCT/17/2, ¶¶ 34–40.

[14] Surveyed in: *Qualitex, supra* note 8, 162; Philmac Pty Ltd v. the Registrar of Trademarks, (2002) 56 I.P.R. 452 (Federal Court of Australia); BP Plc v. Woolworths Limited, (2004) 62 I.P.R. 545 (Federal Court of Australia); Case C-104/01, Libertel Groep BV v. Benelux-Merkenbureau, [2003] E.C.R. I-03793 (CJEU), ¶¶ 47–55; *See also* Ann Bartow, *True Colors of Trademark Law: Greenlighting a Red Tide of Anti-Competition Blues*, 97 KY. L.J. 263 (2008–2009).

itself. If the law were otherwise, the mechanisms of acquired distinctiveness and indefinitely renewable terms of protection would permit enduring claims to product shapes or containers, raising the spectre of a "total and perpetual [legal] monopoly" in them.[15] Therefore in several jurisdictions including the United Kingdom (UK) and Germany, product shapes were categorically unregistrable.[16] The resulting patchwork of international protection was a longstanding concern and attempts were made to introduce a harmonized, open-ended trademark definition in the context of revisions to the Paris Convention.[17] It was with the establishment of the EU's harmonized trademark regime and the TRIPS Agreement that the major breakthroughs were achieved.[18] Today many jurisdictions have done away with categorical exclusions of subject matter.[19] However as a result of the former categorical exclusion mentality with its binary in/out filter (all shapes or abstract colors are *de jure* prohibited), techniques for addressing the underlying policy concerns *after* a non-traditional mark has been registered remain neglected.

To be clear, this chapter is not arguing that up-front exclusion filters are unimportant. They are—and ought to be—the primary filtration mechanism for excluding problematic non-traditional marks. The very act of successfully registering a mark enables the rights holder to threaten or initiate proceedings. Yes despite significant hurdles, in the form of demanding subsistence requirements, non-traditional marks are finding their way on to trademark registers. This chapter provides a framework for continuing to balance interests even after such marks have been registered.

III. Characterization at the Time of Registration

Characterizing a mark (1) according to its general category or type, while (2) describing its individual parameters and boundaries via representation and description, is a crucial first step. Many of the available statutory or doctrinal policy levers that regulate the availability and scope of trademark protection are influenced by this initial characterization. As we will see, there is considerable scope for tactical

15 In re Coca-Cola Trade Marks, [1986] R.P.C. 421, 457 (H.L.) (Considerable evidence to suggest the shape of the fluted Coke bottle was distinctive was overridden on policy grounds).

16 See Robert Burrell, Huw Beverley-Smith & Allison Coleman, *Three-dimensional Trade Marks: Should the Directive be Reshaped, in* PERSPECTIVES ON INTELLECTUAL PROPERTY VOL 7: TRADE MARKS RETROSPECTIVE 139, 143–46 (Norma Dawson & Alison Firth eds., 2000); Annette Kur, *Harmonization of the Trademark Laws in Europe—An Overview,* 1 INT'L REV. INTELL. PROP. & COMPETITION L. 2, 16–17 (1997).

17 Friedrich-Karl Beier & Arnold Reimer, *Preparatory Study for the Establishment of a Uniform International Trademark Definition,* 45 TRADEMARK REP. 1266, 1268–69 (1955).

18 See respectively: Kur, *supra* note 16; Lutz G. Schmidt, *Definition of a Trademark by the European Trademarks Regime—A Theoretical Exercise?,* 24 INT'L REV. INTELL. PROP. & COMPETITION L. 738, 739 (1999) (on EU law); Marshall A. Leaffer, *The New World of International Trademark Law,* 2 MARQ. INTELL. PROP. L. REV 1 (1998); NUNO PIRES DE CARVALHO, THE TRIPS REGIME OF TRADEMARKS AND DESIGNS 297 (2nd ed., 2011) (on TRIPS).

19 WIPO, Summary of Replies to the Questionnaire on Trademark Law and Practice, Jan. 25, 2010, SCT/11/6 (illustrating the national responses to questions concerning the registrability of product shapes, colors, etc.).

Figure 3.1 Louboutin trademark

behavior by applicants at this stage. The question arises as to whether a registry or court can be constrained by the applicant's preferred characterization. Alternatively, how far can tribunals go in overriding the applicant's own preferences? At the time of writing, this is a live issue in the EU, in the context of the reputed designer Christian Louboutin's registration of red soled high-heeled shoes as a trademark. Louboutin describes the mark as consisting "of the colour red (Pantone 18.1663TP) applied to the sole of a shoe as shown (the outline of the shoe is therefore not part of the trademark but serves to show the positioning of the trademark)" for high-heeled shoes (except orthopaedic footwear) in class 25.[20] The mark is reproduced in Figure 3.1.

More pertinently, Louboutin argued that the mark was neither a pure color, nor a three-dimensional or shape mark but a position mark, with a specific shade of red being the sign positioned on the under-soles. However, the District Court of the Hague and subsequently the Advocate General of the CJEU disagreed.[21] Both re-characterized the application as one fitting within the concept of a shape mark in Article 3(1)(e) of the TMD 2008, which contains the functionality exclusions from registrability but applies, on the face of it, only to shapes.[22] The Advocate General had concluded that the registration should be invalidated, on the basis

[20] For example, EU Trademark, Registration No. 008845539 (Louboutin red heels).

[21] Case C-163/16, Christian Louboutin SAS v. Van Haren Schoenen BV, (June 22, 2017) ECLI:EU:C:2017:495 (AG Szpunar). Given the importance of the issues relating to the lack of transitional provisions between the older and newer EU legislation, the dispute was reassigned to the CJEU's Grand Chamber. Oral arguments were re-opened, leading to a second Opinion, which confirmed and elaborated upon the conclusions of the first opinion: (Feb. 6, 2018) ECLI:EU:C:2018:64.

[22] *See* TMD 2015, art 4(1)(e) (in the latest legislative recast, this provision now extends beyond shapes to also cover "another characteristic" of the goods, which includes color); functionality prohibitions—such as a rule excluding signs which are necessary to produce a technical result—filter out features essential to a product's use or purpose, or characteristics affecting the cost or quality of the product, which should remain open for all competitors. For an overview of functionality, see Chapters 5, 7, & 10 in this volume.

of adding substantial (aesthetic) value to the goods, but the CJEU eventually disagreed, finding that the mark was not a "shape."[23] For non-traditional marks, characterization clearly matters.

A. The purpose of the description and categorization requirements

A mark needs to be identified via a representation at the time of registration. This is a mandatory legal requirement which takes the form of graphical representation (recently changed to adequate or enabling representation) in the EU[24] and the drawing requirement in the U.S.[25] For a simple word mark, the representation would be the word itself in standard characters, without stylization, whereas for a three-dimensional mark consisting of a product shape, representation could take the form of isometric line drawings or photographs. The mandatory representation requirement can be supplemented by a description of the mark, which adds contextual information.[26] The description plays a subordinate role and must correspond with the representation:

> The representation of the trademark shall define the subject matter of the registration. Where the representation is accompanied by a description . . . such description shall accord with the representation and shall not extend its scope.[27]

Descriptions are usually optional, but for certain types of non-traditional marks they are encouraged or even mandatory.[28] Especially for non-traditional marks, the representation and description must be read together to define the scope of the mark being claimed. Where a description is provided, it matters.[29] Descriptions

[23] The Advocate General's first opinion, *supra* note 21, argued that the sign as registered would either fit within a broader interpretation of the functionality exclusions in art. 3(1)(e) of the TMD 2008, which extended to a sign combining color and shape ([AG49]–[AG66]) or that the sign should be appropriately characterized as one consisting of the shape of the goods and seeking protection for a color in relation to that shape, rather than consisting of a colour per se ([AG28]–[AG41]). Classification of the type of mark was a factual question for the referring court, which was not bound by the registrant's choice of category ([AG31]). By contrast, the CJEU Grand Chamber held that the prohibition only applied to shapes and Louboutin's mark was not a shape; (June 12, 2018) ECLI:EU:C:2018:423.

[24] *See* TMD 2015 art. 3. *See also* Regulation (EE) 2017/1001 of the European Parliament and of the Council of 14 June 2017 on the European Union Trade Mark [2017] O.J. L154/1 arts. 4, 31(1)(d), and 31(3) [hereinafter EUTMR 2017].

[25] 37 C.F.R. § 2.52 (stating that the drawing shows the mark for which registration is sought); 37 C.F.R. § 2.21(a)(3) (stating that a clear drawing is a precondition for obtaining a filing date); *see* generally, USPTO, Trademark Manual of Examining Procedure (Oct. 2017) § 807.01 [hereinafter TMEP].

[26] *See,* e.g., U.K. Trademark Application Form TM3 (Rev. 01/2017). Representation is mandatory in Section 5. Description is optional in Section 7 and flagged up as useful for indicating non-traditional marks.

[27] *See* Commission Implementing Regulation (EU) 2018/626 of 5 March 2018 laying down detailed rules for implementing certain provisions of Regulation (EU) 2017/1001 of the European Parliament and of the Council on the European Union trade mark, and repealing Implementing Regulation (EU) 2017/1431, [2018] O.J. L104/37, art. 3(2).

[28] 37 C.F.R. § 2.52(e) (stating in the U.S., sound, scent, and non-visual marks do not require a drawing, but a detailed description of the mark is mandatory).

[29] Glaxo Wellcome UK Ltd v. Sandoz Ltd, [2017] E.W.C.A. Civ. 335, ¶¶ 34–43 (Kitchin LJ).

additionally allow the applicant to state whether the mark is an exotic or *sui generis* non-traditional mark, that is one which does not fit into any of the increasingly recognized categories available at the time of filing.[30]

Finally, trademark registration systems usually make provisions for the applicant to identify the mark's type or category (e.g., word, 3D, sound, or color) at the time of registration.[31] In the EU, if the applicant does not volitionally categorize the mark, the registry may assign a category based on the representation or else indicate that there is a formal deficiency with the application.[32] The UK position is illustrative of a national registrar's approach:

> We allocate a mark type [word, figurative, 3D, sound, etc.] to every application. This is an administrative action which aids the search for similar marks. If the mark type is unclear from the answer on the form, we will resolve this before we record the information on the application form.[33]

Read in conjunction, the representation, description, and categorization of type identify the precise subject matter that is being claimed as a mark and define its scope.

In the EU, the representation requirement has proved to be significant in the context of non-traditional marks. In *Sieckmann*, where the CJEU concluded that a scent could not be graphically represented, the Court emphasized the centrality of this requirement for the effective functioning of the registered trademark system.[34] Representation identified the protected subject matter with precision and thereby allowed the mark to be placed on a public register from where it would be accessible. Those accessing this information included not just the trademark bureaucracy, for the purposes of conducting effective examinations of applications, but also the general public including competitors, who have a commercial interest in being adequately notified of claims to exclusive rights. Representations therefore had to be comprehensible and clear. These teachings are now summarized in Recital 13 of the 2015 revision of the EU Trademark Directive (TMD 2015), which jettisons the "graphical" requirement and embraces other technological means for representing a mark.

> In order to fulfil the objectives of the registration system for trademarks, namely to ensure legal certainty and sound administration, it is also essential to require that the sign is capable of being represented in a manner which is clear, precise, self-contained, easily accessible, intelligible, durable and objective. A sign should therefore be permitted to be represented

[30] *See* WIPO Guide to the International Registration of Marks, B.II.16, ¶ 07.53 (2018) (discussing Rule 9(4)(a)(xi)).

[31] Specific types of marks are recorded by registries in the form of WIPO's Internationally Agreed Numbers for the Identification of Data (INID) codes. The codes are a convenient shorthand method for recording bibliographic data in relation to trademarks as well as other IP rights. The codes are contained in WIPO Standard ST.60, Recommendation Concerning Bibliographic Data Relating to Marks. For example, (554) indicates three-dimensional marks, (555) indicates holograms, and (557) indicates olfactory marks.

[32] EUIPO Guidelines, Part B, Section 2—Formalities, ¶ 9.

[33] U.K. IPO, Trademarks Manual, ¶ 2.2 (2017).

[34] *Sieckmann*, *supra* note 9, ¶¶ 48–54 (CJEU). For its significance, see Robert Burrell and Michael Handler, *Making Sense of Trade Mark Law*, Intell. Prop. Q. 388 (2003).

in any appropriate form using generally available technology, and thus not necessarily by graphic means, as long as the representation offers satisfactory guarantees to that effect.

The desire for specificity is also reiterated in Article 3(2) of the TMD 2015.

[A mark should be represented] in a manner which enables the competent authorities and the public to determine the clear and precise subject matter of the protection afforded to its proprietor.

The categorization of the mark according to its type serves similar purposes. According to the EU Intellectual Property Office (EUIPO):

The categorisation of marks serves a number of functions. Firstly, it establishes the legal requirements for each type of mark; secondly, it can help the Office and other economic operators to understand what the applicant is seeking to register; and finally, it facilitates searches in the Office database.[35]

The provision of accurate and sufficient information, via the representation, description, and categorization of type requirements, has foundational significance for the operation of the registration system.

B. The channeling implications of classification

Once a mark is classified, there are formal as well as substantive implications. Non-traditional marks will have to satisfy representation criteria specific to that category. Taking color per se marks in the EU as an example, this calls for "a representation of the colour or colours without contours in one single JPEG file or on one single A4 sheet. Where there is more than one colour, the reproduction must show the systematic arrangement of the colour combination. It is mandatory to file a reference to a generally recognised colour code, such as Pantone, Hex, RAL, RGB or CMYK."[36]

Besides specific procedural requirements, the applicable substantive tests will also vary. As *Louboutin* (above) showcases, until recently, only shape marks were subjected to functionality analysis in the EU. From the applicant's perspective it was important to clarify that the mark being claimed was a color, or figurative mark, or position mark and *not* a shape. More generally, a variation of the inherent distinctiveness test—assessing whether a mark possesses the ability to indicate commercial source *ab initio,* without acquired distinctiveness—applies to many categories of non-traditional marks such as color, shape, and sound.[37] Consequently, applicants sometimes argue that they have applied for a figurative mark depicting an image and not a shape or color, in order to escape the more demanding distinctiveness requirements for such non-traditional marks. In one such recent case concerning blue and white external packaging for confectionaries, the CJEU addressed the "figurative element" claim while reiterating its standard approach to shape marks was applicable:

[35] EUIPO Guidelines, Part B, Section 2—Formalities, ¶ 9. [36] *Id.* ¶ 9.6.
[37] See Chapter 15 in this volume.

The criteria for assessing the distinctiveness of three-dimensional marks consisting of the shape of the product itself are no different from those applicable to other categories of trade marks . . .

However, when those criteria are applied, the perception of the relevant public is not necessarily identical in relation to a three-dimensional mark consisting of the appearance of the product itself as it is in relation to a word or figurative mark which consists of a sign independent of the appearance of the products which it designates.

Average consumers are not in the habit of making assumptions about the origin of products on the basis of their shape or the shape of their packaging in the absence of any graphic or word element, and it could therefore prove more difficult to establish distinctiveness in relation to such a three-dimensional mark than in relation to a word or figurative mark . . .

In those circumstances, only a mark which departs significantly from the standard or customs of the sector and thereby fulfils its essential function of indicating origin is [distinctive] . . .

That case-law, which was developed in relation to three-dimensional trade marks consisting of the appearance of the product itself, also applies in respect of figurative marks consisting of the two-dimensional representation of the product . . .[38]

Thus attempts to evade the modified distinctiveness enquiry for non-traditional marks by "disguising" a shape mark as a figurative mark—or in this case, shape plus figurative element—have not enjoyed much success before EU tribunals. Similar reasoning is evident in a long-running dispute relating to a color mark consisting of progressively lighter shades of green in a vertical tapering column for wind energy convertors in class 7. It was successfully established that the mark represented the decorations visible on the actual vertical column of a wind turbine. Such a decoration would be perceived in aesthetic terms, rather than having origin-indicating significance. The CJEU confirmed that having initially characterized the mark as a color, the applicant could not subsequently re-characterize it as a figurative mark, in order to avoid the stricter distinctiveness scrutiny applicable to color marks.[39]

C. The applicant's freedom to define

While representation and characterization are clearly important for channeling the mark into the relevant stream of examination scrutiny, applicants retain considerable room to maneuver. Repeat players learn through experimentation that certain approaches to satisfying these subsistence requirements can be more successful than others.

Let us retrace our steps back to Louboutin's red-soled shoes. One of the initial national trademark applications in France (November 2000) was for a composite, that

[38] Case C-417/16 P, August Storck KG v. EUIPO, (May 4, 2017) ECLI:EU:C:2017:340, ¶¶ 33–36 (internal citations omitted) (the unsuccessful appellants had argued that the inclusion of a figurative element meant that the case law on assessing distinctiveness for shapes should not apply, since it was no longer a pure shape. However, the figurative element here was held to be commonplace and decorative. It did not alter the nature of what was effectively a packaging i.e., three-dimensional mark).

[39] Case T-36/16, Enercon GmbH v. EUIPO, Gamesa Eólica, SL, (May 3, 2017) ECLI:EU:T:2017:295 (illustrating that the stricter distinctiveness scrutiny for colors is very similar to shapes: average consumers are not usually in the habit of reading origin indicating significance into such signs).

Figure 3.2 Image representing Louboutin trademark application in France

is word and figurative, two-dimensional mark that was far less defined and qualified. It was held to be invalid on the basis of being inadequately graphically represented as well as insufficiently distinctive.[40] The French registration (No. 3067674) was for the sole of a shoe in the color red for "shoes" in class 25. The application was represented by an image of a red outsole which included a word element (Figure 3.2) and the description "*semelle de chaussure de couleur rouge.*"

The French Supreme Court confirmed the Paris Court of Appeal's reasoning for invalidating the mark. The image by itself did not conclusively represent a shoe sole, but was intelligible only together with the written description. Furthermore, a simple reference to the color red did not allow accurate identification of this color, since the depicted outsole contained several shades of red. Acquired distinctiveness could not help since evidence of its well-known status related to the concept of the red under-sole and not to a specific mark as such. Concepts could not acquire distinctiveness. The mark was subsequently reconceived as a stylized red sole (Figure 3.3) and described as claiming the color "red,"[41] but the U.S. trademark registry required further clarifications and there was concern that the (relatively abstract) mark as depicted was not the mark actually being used, which left it vulnerable to a counterclaim for revocation during infringement proceedings.[42]

The application continued to evolve and one only has to turn back a few pages to see how the final version has been "refashioned"[43] into a position mark relating to a precise shade of red specifically situated on the underside of high heel shoes in particular. It now appears sufficiently robust to withstand graphical representation

[40] Société Christian Louboutin et Monsieur Christian Louboutin v. Société Zara France, Cour de cassation [Court of Cassation], Chambre Commerciale, May 30, 2012, No. 11/20724.

[41] French Registration No. 063414903 (2006); U.S. Registration No. 3,376,197 (2008).

[42] *See* Anne H. Hocking and Anne Desmousseaux, *Why Louboutin Matters: What Red Soles Teach Us about the Strategy of Trade Dress Protection,* 105(6) TMR 1337 (2015) (for the evolution of Louboutin's strategy).

[43] Admittedly, a pedestrian pun.

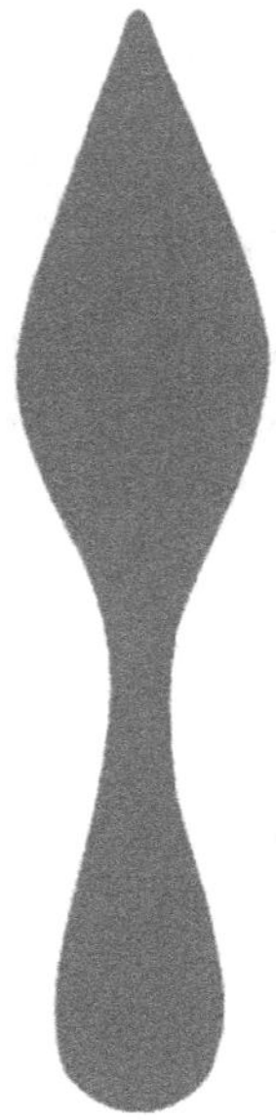

Figure 3.3 Louboutin reconceived image for trademark application

and distinctiveness challenges.[44] It has been suggested that the experience of filing in the U.S., which requires specimens of use showing the actual manner of use, set Louboutin on the path toward a narrow representation and description—a red sole contrasting with the upper of a woman's shoe, depicted to reflect the position of the color in relation to the shoe, as it would be actually perceived by the relevant public—as well as a narrow class of goods in the EU as well.[45]

Iterative adaptation is also evident in Apple's applications to register the interior layout or design of its retail stores as a service mark in class 35, for retail store services for computers and consumer electronics. The successful U.S. service mark applications were depicted in both black and white, claiming all colors[46] and in color.[47] Both are described in the following terms:

> The mark consists of the design and layout of a retail store. The store features a clear glass storefront surrounded by a panelled facade consisting of large, rectangular horizontal panels over the top of the glass front, and two narrower panels stacked on either side of the storefront.

[44] Case R-2272/2010-2, Christian Louboutin v. OHIM, 2nd BoA, Jun. 16, 2011 (unreported). However, the reasoning confirming its distinctiveness as a EUTM is questionable. Evidence of acquired distinctiveness "lite" (how consumers and the press actually reacted) was used to suggest inherent distinctiveness (how a notional consumer would hypothetically react when seeing the mark for the first time). Given the "substantial (aesthetic) value" findings of the Advocate General, *supra* note 21, it is more likely that consumers view the red soles as a stylistic feature which lends itself to acquired distinctiveness over time, as opposed to functioning as a trademark *ab initio*.

[45] Hocking & Desmousseaux, *supra* note 42, at 1340–41.

[46] U.S. Registration No. 4,277,914 (retail store services featuring computer, etc.).

[47] U.S. Registration No. 4,277,913 (the store features a clear storefront, surrounded by a panelled, steel gray façade).

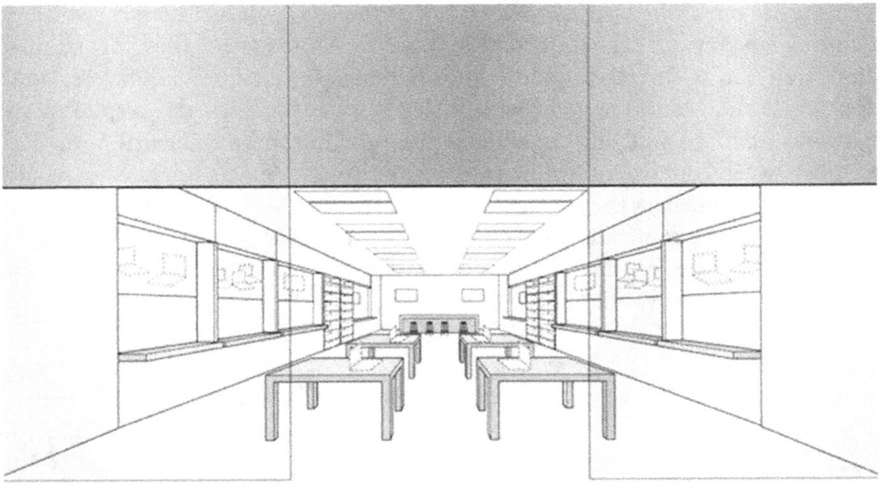

Figure 3.4 Apple's color representation of its retail store layout and design for its U.S. registration application

Within the store, rectangular recessed lighting units traverse the length of the store's ceiling. There are cantilevered shelves below recessed display spaces along the side walls, and rectangular tables arranged in a line in the middle of the store parallel to the walls and extending from the storefront to the back of the store. There is multi-tiered shelving along the side walls.

And the representation of the color version is depicted in Figure 3.4.

Apple drew on its experiences during the U.S. registration process when navigating several subsequent national applications across Europe.[48] First, Apple's initial U.S. application in 2010 was (i) for a broader, more abstract description of the mark ("distinctive design and layout of a retail store") and (ii) based on inherent distinctiveness. The latter was challenged by the U.S. Patent and Trademark Office (USPTO) on the basis that the retail store design was likely to be perceived as "decoration or ornamentation." Apple successfully changed tack and went down the secondary meaning or acquired distinctiveness route. It narrowed down the mark being claimed by adding detail to the written description. Apple also submitted directly relevant evidence—such as consumer surveys, direct consumer testimony, and unsolicited media coverage of its design in use—relating to its (more detailed) store design, in order to demonstrate that it signaled commercial source unaided, without reliance on its other logos or word marks.[49] Since Apple's U.S. experiences had suggested that acquired distinctiveness may need to be argued, it was aware of the implications of this for an EU trademark (EUTM) application. Acquired distinctiveness

[48] *As described in*: Simon Tracey & Teresa Lee, *Can Retail Store Designs be Protected as Trade Dress or 3D Marks?*, 44 World Trademark Rev. 87 (2013); Ben McEniery, *Trade Marks for the Design and Layout of Retail Premises*, 24 Austral. Intell. Prop. J. 1 (2014); Alexander von Mühlendahl, *European Trade Mark Law: Registrable Signs, Service Marks*, 9 J. Intell. Prop. L. & Prac. 160 (2014).

[49] *See* Tracey & Lee, *supra* note 48.

needs to be established across the entirety of the EU's internal market, which is a considerable evidentiary burden.[50] It therefore subsequently filed for national protection across several European jurisdictions, via an international registration under the Madrid system, with mixed results. Interestingly, despite many target jurisdictions applying the same harmonized European standards, some EU members accepted inherent distinctiveness arguments—Apple's store design would function as a trademark the very first time it was seen by the relevant public—while others rejected the application and called for evidence of acquired distinctiveness.[51] Since acquired distinctiveness is easier to satisfy on a country-by-country basis, favoring national applications as more pragmatically achievable seems to have been a wise choice.

Second, Apple applied for *retail services* in class 35. This allowed it to sidestep a major obstacle. Functionality objections in general and those across the EU in particular are engaged when a mark is applied for in relation to *goods*.[52] The irrelevance of functionality objections was confirmed by the CJEU in 2014, on a reference from Germany as to whether the application satisfied the definition of a trademark.[53] Third, during the U.S. trademark prosecution episode, Apple encountered the objection that its stores vary in appearance in significant ways (glass-fronted or silver-panel fronted; varying widths in shopping malls, etc.), which threatened acquired distinctiveness. Was there a stable sign being used as the anchor for acquiring distinctiveness? Apple effectively countered this by contending that a significant proportion of its stores were substantially similar to the design it was seeking to protect as a trade dress. Variations existed only at the level of non-substantive details.

The unease generated by the potential for "real world" variations led to the third strategy. The German trademark registry and Bundespatentgericht were concerned by the possibility of variations, but this concern was ultimately dismissed by the CJEU.[54] The German registry had interpreted EU requirements for graphical representation to require "indications of the absolute dimensions in metres or of

[50] Acquired distinctiveness must be established throughout the territory in which the trademark did not, *ab initio*, have distinctive character. Non-traditional marks are presumed to be lacking in inherent distinctiveness—consumers look at a shape or color and don't immediately perceive it as a trademark—so they require acquired distinctiveness and this needs to be established across the EU as a whole. The evidentiary burden this imposes on applicants has been extensively debated in the Kit Kat (shape of a chocolate bar) litigation: Joined Cases C-84/17 P, C-85/17 P and C-95/17 P, Société des produits Nestlé v. Mondelez UK Holdings & Services (Apr. 19, 2018) ECLI:EU:C:2018:266 (AG Wathelet); (July 25, 2018) ECLI:EU:C:2018:596 (CJEU).

[51] Nicholas Hohn-Hein, *Registering Store Design as a Trademark in the United States and Germany: A Comparative Analysis*, 105(6) Trademark Reporter 1295, 1297 (2015) at footnote 18 ("Extension of protection was granted by: Benelux, Israel, Spain, Italy, Poland. It was denied by: China, Germany, Great Britain, Sweden, Singapore, Australia, Japan, Korea, Russia, Turkey"); *see also* von Mühlendahl, *supra* note 48.

[52] TMD 2015 art. 4(1)(e); *cf* TMEP § 1202.02(a)(vii) (extending functionality to cover service marks as well in the U.S.).

[53] Case C-421/13, Apple Inc. v. Deutsches Patent-und Markenamt, [2014] E.T.M.R. 48, ¶ 24. The fact that goods were also sold in these stores did not detract from the fact that other services intended to induce those sales of goods—such as in-store product demonstrations, which did "not form an integral part of the offer for sale of those goods"—also took place at those stores (at ¶¶ 25–26).

[54] Hohn-Hein, *supra* note 51, at 1326.

relative dimensions with indications as to proportions," presumably with an eye to enhancing precision. In rejecting such a demanding standard, the CJEU instead reasoned that a two-dimensional representation of a layout design—in keeping with other forms of two-dimensional representations as figurative marks—clearly satisfied graphical representation. Stated simply, the line-drawing image submitted was stable and therefore adequate representation. The question of whether the mark-as-used was faithful to the representation-as-submitted was seemingly displaced to distinctiveness analysis.[55] Here, evidence of acquired distinctiveness can be used to establish that the actual layout and design of stores substantially corresponds to the graphical representation. It usually does not matter if there are "minor amendments to the sign that do not alter its distinctive character" during actual use and it "is possible to prove acquired distinctiveness of a sign that has been used together with other trade marks" such as the Apple logo.[56] From the applicant's perspective, distinctiveness is relatively more favorable doctrinal terrain as it permits some degree of variation. The Louboutin and Apple experiences suggests that sophisticated repeat players can successfully adapt by learning across jurisdictions.

D. Limits to this freedom—an objective assessment

In general, applicants should be free to adapt and to arrive at a characterization of the mark which is mutually acceptable to both registry and applicant. However an application may be crafted to superficially satisfy the characterization requirements of representation, description, and classification of mark type while simultaneously attempting to bypass substantive examination criteria based upon policy concerns. In such circumstances, registries and courts retain the discretion to override the applicant's characterization of the mark and substitute it with their own reading.

1. The type of mark

One tactical move which has obvious advantages is to claim that a mark belongs to a more conventional category. As we saw above, it has been argued that representations of products or their features—often in the form of line drawings—should be treated as two-dimensional figurative or "logo" marks, which are part of the conventional core of trademark law.[57] It is now well settled in the EU that the registrability principles "developed in relation to three-dimensional trademarks consisting of the appearance of the product itself, also applies in respect of figurative marks consisting of the two-dimensional representation of the product."[58] This conflation of the

[55] *Apple, supra* note 53, ¶¶ 18–23.

[56] EUIPO Guidelines, Part B, Section 4, Ch. 14—Acquired Distinctiveness, at ¶ 8.5.

[57] This argument continues to be attempted in the context of pattern marks: Case T-579/14, Birkenstock Sales Gmbh v. EUIPO, (Nov. 9, 2016) ECLI:EU:T:2016:650; appeal pending as C-26/17 P (the representation submitted was not a conventional figurative mark but consisted instead of a repeating pattern that would be applied to the surface of the goods. As a form of surface pattern, it was banal and indissociable from the appearance of the goods, thereby lacking distinctiveness).

[58] *August Storck KG, supra* note 38. The question of 2D (as represented) or 3D (in effect) arose much earlier. *See e.g.*, Philips v. Remington, [1998] R.P.C. 283, 288 (Ch.) (Jacob J) ("It would be quite

Figure 3.5 Photographic representation of the head of a lilac-colored mop registered by Mery & Celim as a figurative mark

image of a shape and the shape itself seems to be a considered response to the underlying policy concerns associated with three-dimensional marks, as a recent Spanish Supreme Court decision illustrates.[59] A two-dimensional photographic representation of the head of a lilac-colored mop had been registered by Mery & Celim as a figurative mark (Figure 3.5) in class 21, which includes household cleaning implements.

Presented as such, the application avoided the more demanding distinctiveness scrutiny reserved for shape marks. Infringement proceedings were subsequently commenced against a competitor, Betis Textil, making a similar-looking product but which carried the competitor's own packaging and name. The flattened two-dimensional image was effectively being re-inflated and used to proceed against the competitor's three-dimensional product. The Spanish Supreme Court was alive to this tactical dimension, and affirmed the lower courts' decisions. While the validity of the mark was upheld, its scope was narrowed to avoid a finding of infringement. The image of the mop as registered had to be compared against the defendant's actual mop with packaging, including its own word marks, with the overall differences carrying the day.

artificial to regard a straight picture of a thing, and the thing itself, as significantly different under a law of trade marks which permits shapes to be registered").

[59] T.S, [Tribunal Supremo], Mery y Celim v. Betis Textil SA (Lilac mop), Feb. 25, 2016, Appeal No. 2403/2013 (Spain).

Figure 3.6 Figurative mark denied registrability

Therefore construing the application based on the manner in which the sign is related to the underlying products, in order to identify what is *really* being applied for, makes sense from a policy perspective. EUIPO examiners and Boards of Appeal have relied on the goods or services being applied for, to read context into superficially innocuous figurative marks. So a device mark consisting of four identically sized circles was reinterpreted as the pattern actually formed at the base of the goods in the context of "multi-well plates that can be used in chemical or biological analysis using electrochemiluminescence for scientific, laboratory or medical research use" in class 9.[60] It would be perceived as a simple pattern conveying technical information—representing reagents or electrodes—and therefore non-distinctive. And an "upside down hockey bat" figurative mark (Figure 3.6) was construed—in light of the tyres applied for in class 12—as a true-to-life tyre groove design which was sufficiently functional to deny registrability.[61]

Yet this investigative freedom has outer limits. It stands in contrast to the general principle that the informational integrity of the register requires that the mark must be assessed in light of the application as submitted and not according to how it has been actually used by the applicant.[62] While functionality analysis seems to provide a license to look for context, distinctiveness analysis may not to the same extent.

[60] Case R-412/2012-2, Meso Scale Diagnostics, EUIPO, 2nd BoA (2012).

[61] Case R-2583/2014-5, Pirelli Tyre Spa v. The Yokohama Rubber Co Ltd, EUIPO, 5th BoA (2016).

[62] Case T-20/16, M/S Indeutsch International v. EUIPO, (June 21, 2017) ECLI:EU:T:2017:410, ¶¶ 33–37 (reading the applicant's actual use practices into the application was not permitted when assessing distinctiveness).

Another strategic possibility relating to the type of mark is for an applicant to resort to the open-ended "other" category at the EUIPO, potentially bypassing any classification according to the type of mark. In the past, this has given cause for concern where an attempt is made to register an abstract concept which may have a technical or otherwise desirable purpose. Such "many for the price of one" attempts have been refused for a range of reasons, as exemplified by Dyson's attempt to register a mark which consisted "of a transparent bin or collection chamber forming part of the external surface of a vacuum cleaner as shown in the representation."[63] Along with this description, Dyson also submitted representations in the form of photographic images of two vacuum cleaner models with external bins, but the mark as claimed extended beyond these two exemplars. An externally mounted transparent collection bin has functional utility; customers can visually verify when the bin needs emptying while it is easy to detach. However since it was very emphatically characterized as *not* being a shape, the (then applicable) EU functionality objections did not apply.

Some tribunals were concerned that the relatively loose association between a technical concept and a specific producer—nurtured during the finite term of patent protection—was insufficient for the purposes of acquired distinctiveness.[64] If the *de facto* production monopoly dropped away after the patent expired, would consumers still rely on this product feature as a trade source indicator once other producers could also legitimately incorporate it? In parallel proceedings involving an EUTM application, the EUIPO—in its previous incarnation as Office for the Harmonization in the Internal Market (OHIM)—concluded that graphical representation was not satisfied since the combined description and representations did not give the reader a clear and unambiguous idea of what the mark was when used in connection with vacuum cleaners.[65] A multitude of shapes and sizes could fit within the description. The range of variations also concerned the CJEU, which held that the application did not satisfy the definitional requirement that a mark must be a sign.[66] The application related to non-specific subject matter which performed technical functions. Admitting such a functional concept as a registrable mark would give Dyson an unfair competitive advantage, by converting finite patent protection into indefinite trademark exclusivity. Situating the mark within the open-ended "other" category should not allow it to escape these policy prohibitions.

While the USPTO is relatively more generous than the EUIPO when it comes to the drawing and written description requirements, it too stops short of registering mutable marks amounting to concepts. This is reflected in the rejection of so called "phantom marks." These are marks with a "phantom" element; a word,

[63] U.K. Trademark Reg. No. UK00002195417. Another example is provided by the attempt to register the concept of a Scrabble tile. It was robustly rejected: JW Spear & Son Ltd, Mattel Inc and Mattel UK Ltd v. Zynga Inc., [2012] E.W.H.C. 3345 (Ch.) (Arnold J); affirmed on appeal: [2013] E.W.C.A. Civ. 1175.

[64] Notetry Ltd's Application, O/295/02, U.K. Trade Mark Registry, Jul. 23, 2002; Dyson Ltd v. Registrar of Trade Marks, [2003] E.W.H.C. 1062 (Ch.).

[65] Case R-655/2001-1, Dyson v. OHIM, OHIM 1st BoA, (2002).

[66] Case C-321/03, Dyson Ltd v. Registrar of Trade Marks, [2007] E.T.M.R. 34.

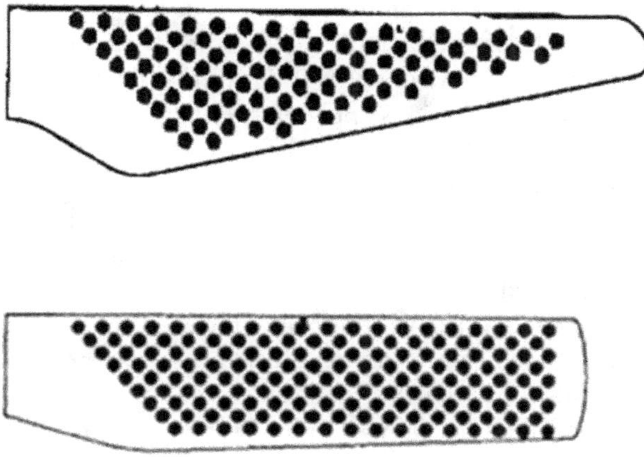

Figure 3.7 Representation of a knife handle design submitted by Yoshida Metals

alpha-numeric designation, or other component that is subject to change and represented by dotted lines or "XXXX" in the case of variable words.[67] The mark as registered does not accurately reflect the mark as used and diminishes the effectiveness of the register as an informational resource, with third parties being unsure as to the nature and scope of the mark. Some interesting tactical gambits are thus revealed when exploring residual or exotic categories of non-traditional marks.

2. *Representations and restrictive framing*

To what extent is a trademark examiner bound by the representation of the mark submitted by the applicant? Can the applicant rely on a restrictively framed representation to avoid substantive subject matter exclusions such as functionality? Or is the examiner permitted to range beyond the representation while construing the mark being applied for? By this stage, the reader will be forgiven for wondering whether trademark law has patent law pretensions, in terms of the approach to construing the intangible subject matter being claimed. This extent to which the representation-as-submitted is binding represents a broadening out of the "two-dimensional figurative mark or three-dimensional shape" issue considered above. The CJEU had an opportunity to directly address this in a dispute where the applicant Yoshida Metals had submitted the representation in Figure 3.7 for goods in classes 8 and 21, including knives and kitchen utensils.[68]

It did not help that the applicant had prevaricated as to the nature of the representation. It had initially classified it purely as a figurative mark sans description. Upon encountering objections from the examiner, the applicant clarified—if that is the

[67] In Re Primo Water Corp., 87 U.S.P.Q.2d 1376 (TTAB 2008); In re Construction Research & Technology GmbH, 122 U.S.P.Q.2d 1583 (TTAB 2017).

[68] Joined Cases C-337/12 P to C-340/12 P, Pi Design & Ors v. Yoshida Metal, OHIM, [2014] E.T.M.R. 32.

word—that it was the "'shape of a product', namely the handle of a knife . . . or that it represented the 'design of knife handles,' before finally settling on 'an arbitrary geometrical figure' or a 'pattern of dots.' "[69] This ultimate description was intended to avoid the functionality objections applying specifically to shapes. If the representation did in fact represent real-world knife handles, then its essential features, including a series of concave "dots" to improve the user's grip, were necessary to achieve a technical result. Drawing upon the wide-ranging functionality assessment remit established in *Lego*,[70] the CJEU confirmed that while the graphical representation requirement had a scope definition objective—"in order to determine the precise subject of the protection afforded by the registered mark to its proprietor"—that could not be abused to "restrict the competent authority's examination under" the functionality objections.[71] The EUIPO was entitled to look beyond the representation and consider the application in the round, as well as "the actual use made of the trade mark following its registration" provided that use shed light on the situation at the time of filing the application.[72]

The CJEU has subsequently confirmed that an examiner is permitted to range beyond the representation when assessing functionality objections.[73] The applicant seeking to protect the famous Rubik's Cube toy puzzle as a three-dimensional mark argued that the surface-level, black and white isometric drawing of the cube with grid lines—looking merely like a "cage"—did not reveal the underlying rotational capacity of segments, which would otherwise engage the technical functionality objection. In other words, the examination should stop at the surface or skin of the representation. The CJEU eventually held otherwise endorsing the view that during functionality analysis, examiners are permitted to look beyond the representation and make an overall assessment of the subject matter being claimed. And the functionality exclusions have been broadened out beyond shapes to cover "another characteristic" of the product, such as color or sound, which suggests that looking beyond the representation-as-submitted is permissible for the full range of non-traditional marks in these circumstances.[74]

3. *Representation versus description?*

The third situation which requires examiners and courts to objectively determine the content of the mark being applied for is when the representation and written description do not align and one is drafted more broadly than the other. In a case concerning a color mark (Figure 3.8) for the combination of purple for respiratory inhalers in class 10, the question arose as to how "a trade mark application or registration be construed where there is no strict congruence between the visual representation and the description."[75]

[69] *Id.* ¶¶ 14–15.
[70] Case C-48/09, Lego Juris v. OHIM, Mega Brands, [2010] E.T.M.R. 63.
[71] *Pi Design, supra* note 68, ¶¶ 57–58. [72] *Id.* ¶¶ 60–61.
[73] Case C-30/15 P, Simba Toys v. EUIPO, (Nov. 10, 2016) ECLI:EU:C:2016:849.
[74] TMD 2015 art. 4(1)(e); *see also*: EUTMR 2017 art. 7(1)(e).
[75] Glaxo Wellcome v. Sandoz, [2016] E.W.H.C. 1537 (Ch.), ¶ 39.

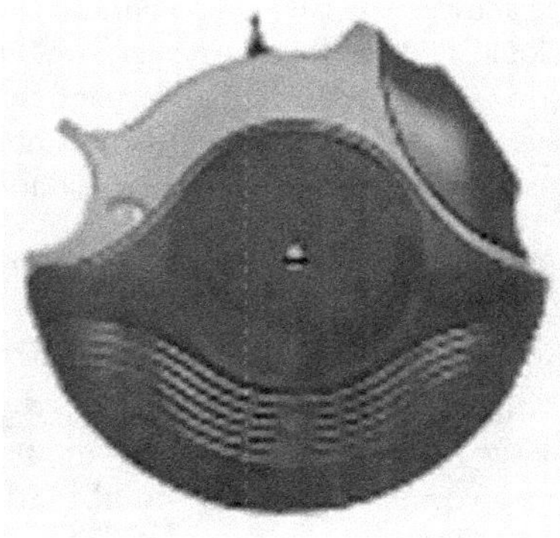

Figure 3.8 Representation of color mark for inhaler

The mark was described as consisting of "the color dark purple (Pantone code 2587C) applied to a significant proportion of an inhaler, and the color light purple (Pantone code 2567C) applied to the remainder of the inhaler." Defining the scope of the mark became relevant because it was at risk of failing the graphical representation requirement, to the extent that it permitted unlimited permutations and combinations of the two shades of purple. As a photograph of one particular model of Glaxo's inhaler, the graphical representation, with "spikes and all," was specific. Yet there was binding precedent which established that the language of the description, which referred to "significant proportions" of the inhaler, was too ambiguous.[76] In order to save the mark, could "the freedom of variation allowed by the description [be] qualified and narrowed to a single sign by the visual representation?"[77] The Court concluded that in these circumstances, an objective assessment by the assessing authority was called for, as opposed to viewing this from the perspective of the relevant consumers. Glaxo had argued that since the representation was mandatory and the description only optional, the representation should be prioritized. The High Court rejected this argument, concluding:

> [There] is no automatic precedence as between the visual representation and the description. If an application or registration is designated with INID code 558 [which signifies a colour mark *per se*], that provides an inflexible starting point: the mark must be construed as consisting exclusively of one or several colours. Thereafter the court must do its best to reconcile the visual representation and the description if there is no strict congruence between them.[78]

The Court of Appeal confirmed that the mark presented those consulting the register with a puzzle:

[76] Société des Produits Nestlé SA v. Cadbury UK Ltd., [2012] E.W.H.C. 2637 (Ch.) (affirmed in relevant part: [2013] E.W.C.A. Civ. 1174).

[77] *Glaxo Wellcome UK Ltd, supra* note 29, ¶¶ 34–43 (Kitchin LJ).

[78] *Id.* ¶ 43. This approach was confirmed on appeal: *Glaxo Wellcome UK Ltd, supra* note 29, ¶ 45.

It is not a two-dimensional figurative mark having the appearance of the pictorial representation; nor is it a three-dimensional mark having a particular shape and coloured in a particular way. Further, anyone inspecting the register would understand that, as a colour per se mark, registered in respect of inhalers, it is at least implied that it is not limited to the colours as applied to the particular shape of inhaler depicted in the registration.[79]

The final conclusion was that the mark being claimed was the one in the description, with the photograph being just one possible interpretation of it. The description allowed too many permutations of purple and was insufficiently precise to satisfy the graphical representation requirement.[80]

Meanwhile the same issue was being contemporaneously litigated before the EU's General Court, in the context of a color combination registration by Red Bull, the well-known energy drinks manufacturer.[81] A broad written description relating to the "juxtaposition" of specific shades of blue and silver was accompanied by one particular graphical representation. Rejecting the argument that the graphical representation effectively narrowed down the written description or took precedence over it, the General Court (i) confirmed the EUIPO's approach to reading the description in combination with the representation; and (ii) observed that the applicant's own extensive evidence of acquired distinctiveness showed that it used the two colors "very differently in comparison to the vertical juxtaposition of the two colors shown in the graphic representation included in [the] applications."[82] So in reality, an impermissibly broad color combination was indeed the object of trademark protection.

IV. Reconciling Scope: Registration and Infringement

Section III outlined the representation, description, and mark-type requirements that help to characterize a non-traditional mark for the purposes of examination by the registry. It also illustrated the potential for iterative learning and adaptation by applicants, in order to overcome obstacles to registration. However, where characterization techniques have been used to subvert substantive and procedural legal requirements, registrars and courts in the EU have been prepared to read between the lines and objectively construe the marks at issue. The final section of this chapter underlines the significance of correlating the scope of the mark as characterized for the purposes of registration and its scope for the purposes of infringement. It is time to consider whether trademark law needs functional equivalents to prosecution history or "file wrapper" estoppel in patent law. Prosecution history estoppel is

[79] *Glaxo Wellcome UK Ltd, supra* note 29, ¶ 75.

[80] *Id.* ¶¶ 79–80 (also referring to the application as a real "head scratcher").

[81] Joined Cases T-101 to 102/15, Red Bull GmbH v. EUIPO, Opium Mark, (Nov. 30, 2017) ECLI:EU:T:2017:852.

[82] *Id.* ¶ 79. For similar reasoning, *see also* Case R 200/2017-2, Giro Travel Company v. Andreas Stihl, 2nd BoA, Jan. 23, 2018 (the mere juxtaposition of gray (on top) and orange below as a color mark for chainsaws allowed for too many variations to satisfy graphical representation; the description—which should be read with the representation—did not sufficiently narrow down the mark).

a doctrine of claim construction directed at preventing a patentee from regaining a breadth of scope for the patent at the time of infringement, which they had given up during the prosecution (i.e., application) process. "Under the rule of prosecution history estoppel, patent applicants who amend their claims during the course of patent prosecution assume a significant risk: the risk that a court will later construe the changes as concessions that should be read to limit patent scope."[83] Stated simply, conditions and qualifications relating to the grant of rights continue to affect the subsequent exercise of those rights.

Making this correlation is increasingly important not just for trademark law but across all IP regimes. Identifying the scope of rights as *the* fundamental question underlying IP regimes, Lemley and McKenna observe:

> When infringement is at issue, IP owners tout the breadth of their rights, while accused infringers seek to cabin them within narrow bounds. When it comes to validity, however, the parties reverse their positions: IP owners emphasize the narrowness of their rights in order to avoid having those rights held invalid, and accused infringers argue the reverse .... Because of the separation between validity, infringement, and defences, a party may often successfully argue that an IP right means one thing in one context and something very different in another. And decision makers won't necessarily detect the problem because they are thinking of only the precise legal issue before them.[84]

In the U.S. context, the mismatch in approach between trademark registrability and infringement is aptly depicted by Tushnet: "Applicants and the [US]PTO spend much time and effort crafting the equivalent of an exquisitely detailed origami crane: a precisely delineated valid mark. Rather than considering the details, courts then ask the equivalent of 'is this paper folded?' by according presumptive validity to what the mark, at first glance, appears to be."[85] The wide ranging scope of the infringement enquiry undermines the potential for delimiting the protected subject matter at the time of registration.[86] This is primarily because the infringement enquiry depends on the relevant consumer's perception of the signs in question and consumers are deemed to view signs as a whole, without an awareness of any limits or qualifications entered upon the register.

A. Discarding disclaimers?

In the EU, this scope disconnect is most clearly reflected in the decision to no longer permit disclaimers at the time of registration.[87] Previously the EUIPO could require the applicant to disclaim any exclusivity over non-distinctive elements of the mark:

[83] Douglas Lichtman, *Rethinking Prosecution History Estoppel*, 71 U. Chicago L. Rev. 151 (2004).

[84] Mark A. Lemley & Mark P. McKenna, *Scope*, 57 Wm. & Mary L. Rev. 2197, 2200–201 (2016)

[85] Rebecca Tushnet, *Registering Disagreement: Registration in Modern American Trade Mark Law*, 130 Harv. L. Rev. 867, 872 (2017). *See also* Robert Burrell, *Trademark Bureaucracies*, *in* Trademark Law and Theory: A Handbook of Contemporary Research 95, 108 (2008).

[86] Robert G. Bone, *Notice Failures and Defences in Trademark Law*, 96 B.U. L. Rev. 1245 (2016).

[87] EUIPO Guidelines, *supra* note 5, Part B, Section 3, Ch 1, Absolute Grounds: General Principles, at ¶ 8. However the disclaimer seems to have resurfaced as a defense; the use of non-distinctive elements

Where the trade mark contains an element which is not distinctive, and where the inclusion of that element in the trade mark could give rise to doubts as to the scope of protection of the trade mark, the Office may request, as a condition for registration of said trade mark, that the applicant state that he disclaims any exclusive right to such element.[88]

However, disclaimers were infrequently requested in practice.[89] Despite their explicit scope-defining purpose, they were also inconsistently applied when it came to their relevance for infringement proceedings:

When determining conflicts, the overall impression of the conflicting marks is decisive, and it is difficult to see how a disclaimer (of which the public to which the marks are addressed is entirely unaware) can change the outcome. This is the more doubtful because of the de facto absence of disclaimers in registered CTMs and the absence of such disclaimers in most marks protected in Europe.[90]

These limitations to the scope-defining potential of disclaimers at the time of registration have parallels in U.S. trademark law as well.[91] The demands of infringement analysis apparently cancel out the effects of disclaimers.

An approach which assumes that the public interprets each mark as a whole is entirely reasonable. It sounds empirically plausible and has become entrenched as a central feature of both distinctiveness as well as infringement analysis. However it is worth recalling that the perspective of the average consumer—the vantage point in infringement analysis—is a hybrid construct, part-empirical and part-normative.[92] For instance, no matter how careless consumers might be in real life, EU trademark law assumes that the "average consumer of the category of products concerned is deemed to be reasonably well-informed and reasonably observant and circumspect."[93] The insight that infringement analysis allows us to view marks through normative filters is liberating. If marks are restricted at the time of registration, that scope reduction should follow them through to enforcement and the infringement tests do have the normative capacity to accommodate this reconciliation. It may be premature to give up on the logic underlying disclaimers.

of marks does not fall within the scope of infringement under TMD 2015 art. 14(1)(b), and EUTMR 2017 art. 14(1)(b).

[88] Community Trade Mark Regulation (EC) No. 207/2009 art. 37(2) of Feb. 26, 2009, on the Community trademark [hereinafter CTMR 2009].

[89] Max Planck Institute, *Study on the Overall Functioning of the European Trade Mark System*, 74–76 (2011).

[90] *Id.* at 75.

[91] *See* 15 U.S.C. § 1056 (allowing the USPTO to require that an unregistrable component of a registered mark, such as a purely descriptive element, is disclaimed at the time of registration). However, the scope-defining disclaimer does not remove the element from the mark when evaluating similarity between marks for the purposes of likelihood of confusion analysis. See the authorities cited in: TMEP, §1213.10.

[92] Graeme B. Dinwoodie & Dev S. Gangjee, *The Image of the Consumer in European Trade Mark Law*, *in* THE IMAGE(S) OF THE CONSUMER IN EU LAW 339 (Dorota Leczykiewicz & Stephen Weatherill eds., 2016); *cf.* Kimberlee Weatherall, *The Consumer as the Empirical Measure of Trade Mark Law*, 80 MODERN L. REV. 57 (2017).

[93] Case C-342/97, Lloyd Schuhfabrik Meyer & Co. GmbH v. Klijsen Handel BV, [1999] E.C.R. I-03819, ¶ 26.

B. Connections and disconnects in EU trademark law

For those familiar with the intricacies of non-traditional marks, the recent U.S. approach to Louboutin's position/color mark claim has intuitive appeal. Louboutin asserted its rights in a specific shade of red against Yves Saint Laurent (YSL), who were producing a bright red outsole as part of a monochromatic design in which the entire shoe was red. Louboutin was effectively asserting its rights to a specific shade of red, in the abstract, for high-heeled shoes. The trial Court invalidated Louboutin's mark based on aesthetic functionality.[94] However the appellate Court sidestepped an all-or-nothing approach in two moves. First, it confirmed the validity of Louboutin's registered mark but narrowed its scope to a position mark involving a color contrast, holding that "the lacquered red outsole, as applied to a shoe with an 'upper' of a different colour, has 'come to identify and distinguish' the Louboutin brand … and is therefore a distinctive symbol that qualifies for trademark protection."[95] Very significantly, the scope of the mark was limited based on the evidence of acquired distinctiveness, since it had been used as a red outsole *contrasting* with the remainder of the shoe. This is a point to which we return below. With the mark remaining valid but diminished, the infringement claim was dismissed at the second stage. Consequently, "the red sole on YSL's monochrome shoes [was] neither a use of, nor confusingly similar to, the Red Sole Mark."[96] The Court consciously drew parallels between the scope of the mark as registered and its reach during infringement analysis.

Across the EU, we are beginning to see disputes where some courts and tribunals have engaged in a similar mode of analysis, while in others decision makers seem to be considering issues in isolation, with detrimental consequences. Shape or three-dimensional trademarks provide us with examples of "joined-up" as well as "independent silos" modes of analysis. Litigation relating to the three-dimensional marks associated with the Lindt golden rabbit for chocolate products in class 30 illustrates the former approach. Lindt had applied in several registries for two variants of a three-dimensional mark relating to the shape and packaging of its chocolate bunny—one without any word mark on the golden packaging in Figure 3.9, and one with words such as "LINDT GOLDHASE" in Figure 3.10.[97]

Obtaining an EUTM for the version without any word element as in Figure 3.9 has proved challenging, with Lindt being unable to satisfy the EUIPO that it has surmounted the high threshold of acquired distinctiveness across the EU.[98] By contrast, the mark depicted in Figure 3.10 could be registered on the basis of inherent

[94] Christian Louboutin v. Yves Saint Laurent Amer. Holding, Inc., 778 F.Supp.2d 445, 449 (S.D.N.Y. 2011) (stating that "[b]ecause in the fashion industry colour serves ornamental and aesthetic functions vital to robust competition, the Court finds that Louboutin is unlikely to be able to prove that its red outsole brand is entitled to trademark protection, even if it has gained enough public recognition in the market to have acquired secondary meaning.").

[95] Louboutin v. Yves Saint Laurent Amer. Holding, Inc., 696 F.3d 206, 227 (2d Cir. 2012).

[96] *Id.* at 228.

[97] Variations of the shape and word mark include just the word "LINDT"; *see* Lindt, EUTM Registration No. 008577298.

[98] An overview of previous decisions rejecting the three-dimensional bunny mark (sans word) is found in Case R 2450/2011 G, Chocoladefabriken Lindt & Sprüngli AG, EUIPO Grand BoA (2017). However, Lindt has obtained several national registrations for this mark (noted at ¶ 9).

Figure 3.9 Lindt image without word mark

distinctiveness, primarily due to the word element which was distinctive. This word element enabled it to successfully withstand a cancellation application, where the EUIPO Cancellation Division reasoned as follows:

> The Cancellation Division considers that there is a recognisable generic shape and look to a chocolate Easter bunny and that no manufacturer is entitled to monopolise that image. There must be some additional distinguishing features that enable the sign to function as a badge of commercial origin . . .
>
> In the present case, the manufacturer's name ("Lindt Goldhaser)" appears clearly readable and prominently displayed on the Easter chocolate bunny representation. It is this feature which enables consumers to distinguish the CTM proprietor's sign (and the source of the products sold under that sign) from those of other traders . . .
>
> Therefore, notwithstanding the generic shape, colours and stylisation of the contested CTM, the sign is distinctive by dint of the words "Lindt Goldhaser" that appear clearly displayed on the Easter chocolate bunny.
>
> [While the registration is therefore valid] this ought not to sanction or permit the CTM proprietor to *overextend the scope of protection* it enjoys for its mark by *seeking to attack and oppose the registration of competing Easter chocolate bunnies which do not carry words which are similar to "Lindt Goldhaser."*[99]

[99] Case 1176C, Confiserie Rohan v. Chocoladefabriken Lindt & Sprungli, OHIM Cancellation Division, at ¶¶ 31–36 (2014) (emphasis added).

Figure 3.10 Lindt image with word mark

This is an explicit steer: the word element—crucial for obtaining a successful registration—should subsequently narrow the scope of exclusivity in the mark in the context of enforcement. A similar line of reasoning is found in German case law, where Lindt brought infringement proceedings against a competitor producing chocolate bunnies wrapped in gold but with a brown ribbon and its own trademark visible on the packaging.[100] The Frankfurt Court concluded that the word element of the mark was highly distinctive whereas the distinctiveness of the trade dress elements was low, given the fact that there were many similarly shaped bunnies on the market. Since there was no similarity as regards the highly distinctive elements (i.e., the words), but only similarity as regards the weakly distinctive trade dress elements (shape and color), the Court decided that the overall impression of the marks was dissimilar. As the first stage of the infringement analysis (are the signs sufficiently similar?) collapsed, infringement was not made out.

If *Lindt* represents a successful attempt at connecting the scope of the mark determined at the time of registration to the scope at the time of enforcement,

[100] Oberlandesgericht Frankfurt am Main [Higher Regional Court Frankfurt], Lindt v. Riegelein Confiserie, [2012] GRUR-RR 255 (Germany). An appeal to the BGH was denied in 2013, since it did not raise any fundamental issues of law.

litigation relating to Crocs—the reinvented clogs—represents more of a work in progress. Our story begins with the registered community design (RCD) for Crocs being invalidated in 2010 on the basis that it lacks both novelty and individual character.[101] Crocs' own advertising and sales in North America, prior to the RCD application in the EU, were found to be novelty destroying. Crocs then turned to trademark law and filed both national and EUTM applications for three-dimensional marks in two variants. One consisted of six views of the shoe *without any accompanying word or logo marks*[102] while the other was almost identical except for (i) *the addition of the Crocs crocodile logo in the representation* and (ii) *a written description* which expressly included the following text: "The mark consists of the shape of an article of footwear incorporating a logo featuring a stylised crocodile."[103] Sufficiently determined squinting should enable the reader to discern the logo in three views in Figure 3.11.

The "two variants" filing strategy is by now a more familiar tactic. Under EU trademark law, the "pure" three-dimensional mark is vulnerable to a functionality challenge, on the basis of adding substantial aesthetic value to the goods. This was the conclusion of at least one Italian Court, where the Italian mark for Crocs was invalidated.[104] Given that Crocs had applied for registered design protection as well, this is confirmation that aesthetic appeal motivated the design of the shoe shape.[105] By comparison, the variant which includes the crocodile logo has fared better. The EUIPO rejected a cancellation action on the basis that the logo was a non-functional yet essential feature of the shape mark, whereas *all* the essential features of such marks are required to fit within a given functionality exclusion. Here the crocodile logo was considered to be "a decorative or imaginative element that plays an important role in the depiction of a shape" and the crucial ingredient which insulated the rest of the three-dimensional mark from a functionality challenge.[106]

Despite having lost its finite RCD protection, Crocs could nevertheless potentially enjoy indefinite trademark protection for the shape of its shoes. Crocs relies on its national Swedish trademark for the "pure" shape as the basis for trademark infringement claims[107] as well as for invalidating RCDs relating to similar shoes filed by third parties.[108] It does so on the basis of provisions of EU design law which recognize prior rights in trademarks as the basis for objecting to confusingly similar

[101] Case R 9/2008-3, Crocs Inc. v. Holey Soles Holdings Ltd., OHIM 3rd BoA (2010).

[102] *For example*, mark referring to equipment for footwear, Swedish TM No. 400514.

[103] *For example*, mark without text, EUTM No. 006543516.

[104] Court of First Instance—Venice, Feb. 15, 2012, Crocs, Inc. v. Supermarket Della Calzatura sas & Progetti srl, (Italy). However claims by Crocs were successful under unfair competition law.

[105] For some, at least; as style icons these shoes are divisive.

[106] Case R 3021/2014-5, Lidl Stiftung & Co. KG v. Crocs Inc., OHIM, 5th BoA, ¶ 36 (2016).

[107] *See, e.g.*, Stockholm District Court, Patent och marknadsdomstolen [Patent and Market Court], Crocs Europe v. Öob, (2017).

[108] *See, e.g.*, the following EUIPO RCD Invalidity decisions: Case File No. ICD 9830, Crocs Inc. v. Dobré boty s.r.o., Sep. 18, 2015; Case File No. ICD 9889, Crocs Inc. v. Jin Shi International, Nov. 6, 2015; Case File No. ICD 9961, Crocs Inc. v. FLAMEshoes, Sep. 1, 2016; Case File No. ICD 10529, Crocs Inc. v. Nuvens de Fantasia, Lda. June 2, 2017.

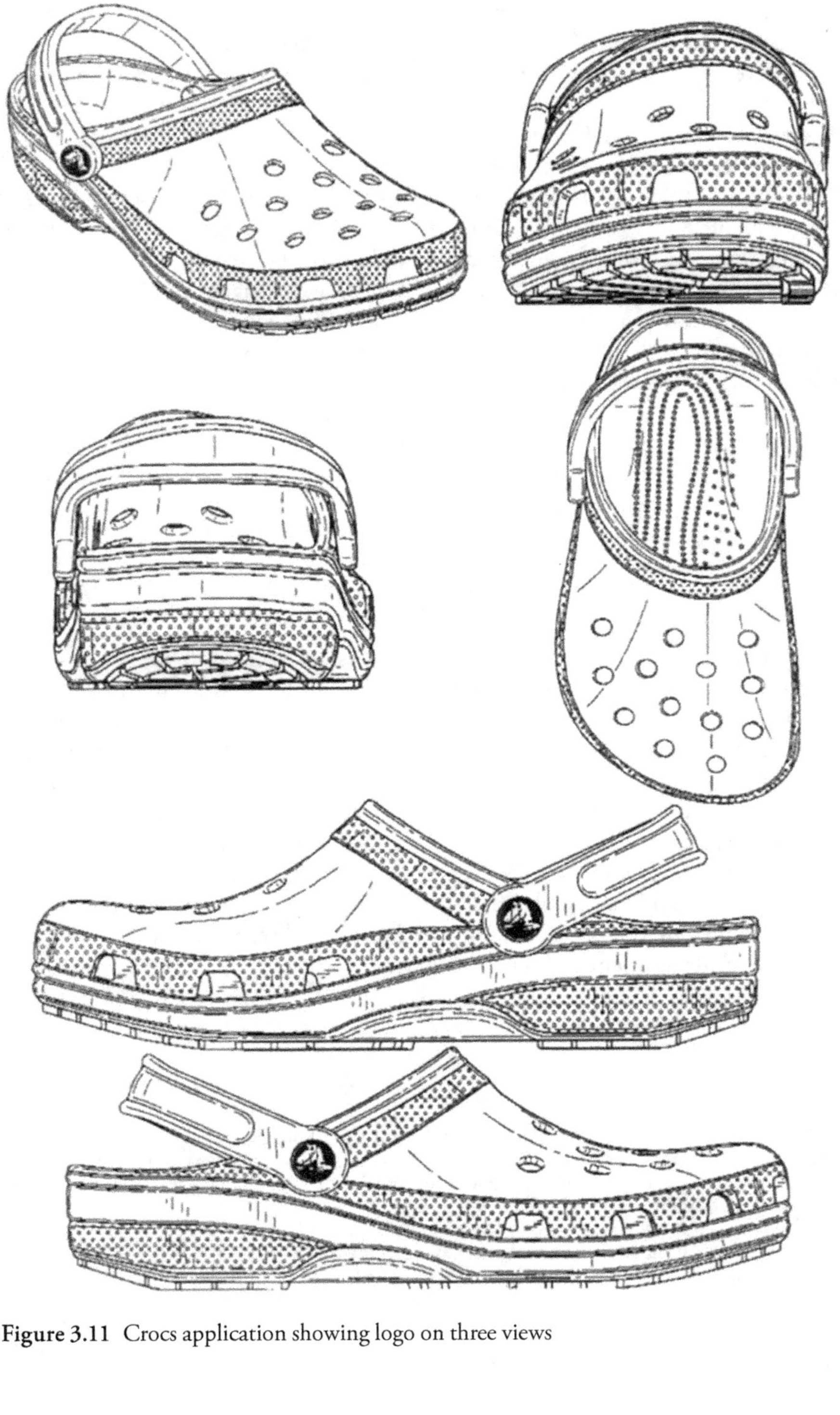

Figure 3.11 Crocs application showing logo on three views

designs.[109] This is notwithstanding the vulnerability of the "pure" shape Swedish mark to an aesthetic functionality/substantial value challenge.

However if Crocs' "pure" shape Swedish mark were to be invalidated on functionality grounds, to what extent could it rely on its "shape and logo" EUTM? Drawing inspiration from *Lindt*, could a competitor argue that since—by Crocs' own admission—the crocodile logo is an essential feature of its "shape and logo" mark, the use of the competitor's own distinctive logo would counteract a finding of infringement? Some guidance is provided in an RCD invalidation decision where a competitor successfully argued that the differences between its clogs and those of Crocs—including the use of its own COQUI word marks and "smiling frog" logo on its shoes—suggested that the competitor's design would not infringe Crocs' rights under its EUTM.[110] Along with differences in design features, the differences in logos and word marks were considered significant enough to avoid infringement. It would be incongruous if Crocs were allowed to emphasize the presence of its logo in order to escape a functionality challenge during registration and then de-emphasize it when comparing shape-for-shape (as the main or dominant elements) during infringement analysis.

V. Conclusion

This chapter has argued that it is increasingly necessary to correlate the mark as characterized at the time of registration with the mark as deployed in an enforcement context. Making this correlation is especially relevant for non-traditional marks, bearing in mind the gradual erosion of categorical exclusions. Otherwise the conventional approach encourages us to focus on a binary issue—in light of the underlying policy concerns, should a non-traditional mark be registered or not? Less thought has been given to the balancing of interests *after* such a mark has been registered. Connecting scope across registration and enforcement is one such method for redressing this imbalance. It should be considered alongside upstream exclusionary filters (such as adequate representation, distinctiveness, and functionality) as well as other limits to the scope of infringement and general defenses.[111]

[109] Council Regulation (EC) No. 6/2002 of 12 December 2001 on Community Designs art. 25(1)(e) (establishing that a Community design may be declared invalid if a distinctive sign is used in a subsequent design, and Community law or the law of the Member State governing that sign confers on the right holder of the sign the right to prohibit such use).

[110] Case R 339/2014-3, Hessy s.r.o. v. Crocs Inc., OHIM, 3rd BoA, Sep. 14, 2015, ¶ 35.

[111] *See generally* Chapter 8 in this volume. Courts in the EU have begun to explore the following issues: (1) Is the defendant using the colour or shape as a trademark, as a precondition for infringement? (*see* Langenscheidt Yellow, Case No. I ZR 228/12 (BGH), 46 Int'l Rev. Intell. Prop. & Competition L. 372 (2015); Bounty Chocolate Bar, I ZR 23/14 (Mar. 21 2015) (BGH)); (2) Is the use of the defendant's own word marks on an otherwise similar shape enough to counteract any confusion (*see* Abloy Oy v. Hardware Group Finland Oy, Supreme Court of Finland, KKO:2017:42 (2017))?

4

Yellow Dictionaries, Red Banking Services, Some Candies, and a Sitting Bunny

Protection of Color and Shape Marks from a German and European Perspective

Annette Kur

I. Introduction

When the first European Trade Mark Directive (TMD)[1] was implemented in the first half of the 1990s, it opened the door to registration of signs which, in some European jurisdictions such as Germany, were previously precluded from full trademark protection. This was of particular practical relevance for colors per se and for the shape of products.[2] In the early years after implementation of the TMD many entrepreneurs tried to make use and test the limits of the novel options. While exact data are lacking, there is reason to assume that such attempts were successful in a substantial number of cases, with patent offices—including the Office for Harmonisation in the Internal Market (OHIM; now the European Union Intellectual Property Office (EUIPO)) in Alicante—being uncertain how to deal with the applications.

The jurisprudence of the Court of Justice of the European Union (CJEU) has changed the picture, however:[3] while the CJEU emphasizes the openness of

[1] Council Directive 89/104/EEC to approximate the laws of the Member States relating to trade marks, 1989 O.J. L40/1 (EC) [hereinafter TMD 1989]; a codified version was published in 2008 (Directive 2008/95/EC, 2008 O.J. L299/25) [hereinafter TMD 2008]. In 2015, a Recast of the Directive was enacted (Council Directive 2015/2436 of the European Parliament and of the Council of 16 December 2015 to approximate the laws of the Member States relating to trade marks, 2015 O.J. L336/1 [hereinafter TMD 2015]. The changes have to be implemented by January 2019 (with the exception to changes concerning administrative procedures which only have to be implemented by January 2023).

[2] Previous to implementation of the TMD 2015, such signs could only be protected in Germany as "get ups" (Ausstattungen) if they were known to the general public as the distinctive sign of a particular enterprise (WARENZEICHENGESETZ [WZG] [(OLD) TRADEMARK ACT], § 25 (1996)). Registration was not possible. The legal situation was similar in Austria, Italy, and Greece.

[3] For a more detailed discussion of the developments see ANNETTE KUR & MARTIN SENFTLEBEN, EUROPEAN TRADEMARK LAW 148 (2017).

Yellow Dictionaries, Red Banking Services, Some Candies and a Sitting Bunny: Protection of Colour and Shape Marks from a German and European Perspective. Annette Kur. © Annette Kur 2018. Published 2018 by Oxford University Press.

the register to all types of unconventional signs,[4] it also signals that marks not conforming to the traditional scheme of words, graphics, and combinations thereof are unlikely to be perceived as indications of commercial origin.[5] The chance for registration of product shapes was further narrowed when the CJEU developed its markedly restrictive attitude toward shapes that are banned from protection due to their functional character (shapes exclusively resulting from the nature of goods,[6] being necessary to obtain a technical result,[7] or giving substantial value to the goods).[8] And even where that hurdle is cleared—or where the functionality ban at least until recently did not apply, as in regards to colors per se[9]—the option of establishing distinctiveness through use in the course of trade presents enormous challenges, if registration at the European Union (EU) level is envisaged.[10] Only very few colors or product designs have ever been successful in showing that, in spite of being inherently indistinctive, they have become distinctive in the entire territory of the EU.

While the cumulative effect of those developments severely reduces the number of unconventional signs in the form of colors per se and (pure) product designs that are validly registered at EU level, this does not mean that conflicts between such signs and identical or similar configurations used in the course of trade have become a non-issue. Several reasons account for that. First, there is an unknown number of signs that were registered during "generous" phases of office and court practice in spite of falling short of the standards enunciated in CJEU jurisprudence. Enforcement of such signs is risky, of course, as the alleged infringer could hit back by initiating nullity proceedings.[11] Nevertheless, such signs may have a certain

[4] *See e.g.*, Case C-283/01, Shield mark v. Kist, 2003 E.C.R. I-14313, ECLI:EU:C:2003:641, ¶ 35 (concerning sound marks). In principle, that also includes olfactory marks; however, they were (and still are) excluded from registration due to the fact that they cannot be represented in the register in a manner which allows an exact appraisal of the subject-matter, as set forth in Case C-273/00, Sieckmann v. Deutsches Patent- und Markenamt, 2002 E.C.R. I-11737, ECLI:EU:C:2002:748, ¶ 44, 55, 73. While the requirement of "graphical" representation was deleted by the European Union (EU) trademark reform, the substantive criteria enunciated in the decision are still valid and continue to bar access to trademark registration of smells and tastes.

[5] Joined Cases C-53/01-55/02, Linde, Winward and Rado, 2009 E.C.R. I-09889, ECLI:EU:C:2003:206, ¶ 48; Case C-218/01 P, Henkel v. Office for the Harmonisation in the International Market (OHIM), 2007 E.C.R. I-08109, ECLI:EU:C:2004:88, ¶ 52; Joined Cases C-456 & 457/01 P, Henkel v. OHIM (washing tablets), 2004 E.C.R. I-05089, ¶ 38; Case C-136/02, P, Mag Instruments v. OHIM, 2004 E.C.R. I-09165, ECLI:EU:C:2004:592, ¶¶ 30, 31.

[6] Case C-205/13, Hauck v. Stokke, 2014 EUR-Lex-62013CJ0205, ECLI:EU:C:2014:2233.

[7] Case C-299/99, Philips v. Remington, 2002 E.C.R. I-05475, ECLI:EU:C:2002:377; Case C-48/09, Lego Juris v. OHIM, 2010 E.C.R. I-08403, ECLI:EU:C:2010:516; Case C-30/15, Simba Toys v. European Union Intellectual Property Office (EUIPO), 2016 EUR-Lex-62014TJ0687, ECLI:EU:C:2016:849.

[8] Case C-371/06, Benetton v. G-Star, 2007 E.C.R. I-07709, EU:C:2007:542; Hauck, *supra* note 6.

[9] Before the EU trademark law reform of 2015, the "functionality ban" only applied to shapes; *see* TMD 2008 art. 3(1)(e). It has now been extended to all kinds of product characteristics; *see* TMD 2015 art. 4.

[10] For more details *see* KUR & SENFTLEBEN, *supra* note 3, at 193.

[11] The risk increases in proportion to the discrepancy between the standards previously applied and those enunciated by the Court of Justice of the European Union (CJEU). For instance, the German Federal Court of Justice [Bundesgerichtshof, hereinafter BGH] used to endorse a pointedly narrow application of the functionality ban. Inter alia this resulted in the registration of the seamed packages of Ritter Sport chocolate, and of the rectangular shape of dextrose tablets with slightly slanted edges. Both registrations were challenged by competitors in the course of infringement suits. Based on the stricter

leveraging power, especially vis-à-vis economically weak parties shunning any risk of litigation. Second, while establishing acquired distinctiveness for colors or product shapes is hardly feasible at the EU level, the option is more realistic in the national context. And indeed, once protection has been obtained by use on the (national) market, such signs can become very powerful, eventually posing a serious threat to competitors.[12] Third, for product design, an obvious way to master the legal hurdles is to add a distinctive feature, often in the form of a word mark or figurative element. It seems to be common practice in the EU that with such additions, even if they are small, product configurations can be registered as shape marks, irrespective of the indistinctive or functional character of the shape as such.[13] Only in infringement (or opposition) proceedings will it then be decided whether and to what extent the shape itself attracts some degree of protection in spite of being non-registrable as such.

This chapter addresses typical issues arising in conflicts over the use of colors or product configurations that are protected as trademarks. To illustrate the topic, a number of exemplary German court cases are presented in Section II. A comparison is then made of the principles applied in the national decisions with the practice established on the EU level by the General Court of the European Union (GCEU) and the CJEU, in Section III. Finally, the question is addressed whether the inclusion of "indistinctive" signs into the catalogue of limitations by the recent law reform can have positive effects in regards to harmonization of practice and a fair balance of interests. This is addressed in Section IV. The chapter ends with some brief conclusions in Section V.

II. Exemplary Cases from Germany

A. Color marks

Once it had been accepted in German practice that colors could be registered without being spatially limited,[14] a number of colors and color combinations

standards announced by the CJEU in Hauck, *supra* note 6, both marks were declared invalid and incapable of ever attracting trademark protection. At the time of writing, appeals were pending before the BGH. Those appeals were successful, so that the registrations remain intact.

[12] This is true in particular for protection of colors per se; see below, cases related under Section II A.

[13] In the words of Justice Arnold such additions may be called a "figurative fig leaf"; *see* Starbucks (HK) Ltd and others v. British Sky Broadcasting Group plc and others [2012] E.W.H.C. 3074 (Ch.), 2 Nov. 2012, ¶ 117 (regarding the figurative mark "NOW").

[14] This was initially contentious. In its first decision after the implementation of the TMD 1989 the German Federal Patent Court [Bundespatentgericht, BPatG] held that colors and color combinations can only be registered in a spatially limited form; BPatG Nov. 27, 1999, Gewerblicher Rechtsschutz und Urheberrecht (GRUR) 428, 2000. The decision was vacated by the decision in BGH Dec. 10, 1998, Neue Juristische Wochenschrift [NJW] 1186, 1998. The registrability of colors per se was ultimately clarified by the CJEU, *see* Case C-104/01, Libertel v. Benelux-Merkenbureau, 2003 E.C.R. I-03793, ECLI:EU:C:2003:244 (color orange); for color combinations *see* Case C-49/02, Heidelberger Bauchemie, 2004 E.C.R. I-06129, ECLI:EU:C:2004:384.

were accepted for registration,[15] in most cases based on acquired distinctiveness.[16] Enforcement of those marks has led to extensive infringement litigation, at times triggering decisions by the German Federal Court of Justice (Bundesgerichtshof, BGH).[17] Among the more recent cases are the lawsuit between a large publisher of dictionaries, Langenscheidt, and Rosetta Stone regarding the color yellow, and the dispute over the color red pending between the German association of savings banks (Deutscher Sparkassen- und Giroverband, DSGV) and Banco Santander.[18] In both cases, the respective color marks had been accepted for registration by the German Patent and Trademark Office (Deutsches Patent- und Markenamt, DPMA), but the alleged infringers challenged the registrations. Due to the bifurcation system applying under German law, infringement and invalidity claims must be assessed in separate proceedings, with infringement being dealt with by the ordinary courts[19] and invalidity being appraised by the DPMA.[20] However, the BGH has the ultimate say on points of law emerging in both types of proceedings.[21]

In both cases, *Langenscheidt v. Rosetta Stone* and *DSGV v. Santander*, the BGH denied the requests filed by the respective defendants for cancellation of the color marks yellow and red. Though both marks were not considered inherently distinctive, they had acquired distinctiveness through use. Inter alia this finding requires that the color is perceived by the public not as mere decoration, but as a sign distinguishing commercial origin. In *Langenscheidt*, the German Federal Patent Court (Bundespatentgericht, BPatG) had held that the requirement was fulfilled inter alia because the public had grown used to the fact that in the sector concerned, publishers distinguish the commercial origin of their products by using specific colors.[22] The issue was left open by the BGH; however, in view of the long duration

[15] The first one of these was the color violet for Nestlé (milk chocolate). For an early account of the rather critical reception of color marks in early German practice *see* Detlef von Schulz, *Die Farbmarke—ein Sündenfall?*, GRUR 714, 1997.

[16] Though not always, depending on the unusualness of the color and the breadth of protection claimed. Registration without showing acquired distinctiveness was accepted inter alia in BGH Mar. 1, 2001, GRUR 2001, 1154 (purple for cat food); BGH Sept. 19 2001, GRUR 2002, 538 (green for processor casings).

[17] Apart from those mentioned in the footnotes above and in the following text, these are, e.g., BGH Jul. 9, 2015, GRUR 2015, 1012 (NIVEA-Blue); BGH Nov.19, 2009, GRUR 2010, 637 (yellow for supply of electricity and products connected therewith); BGH Mar. 25, 1999, GRUR 1999, 730 (grey/magenta for telecommunication services).

[18] For an earlier infringement case *see* BGH Oct. 7, 2004, GRUR 2005, 427 (alleged infringement of Nestlé's violet color mark). Similar to what is reported in the text above about *Langenscheidt v. Rosetta Stone*, the finding of infringement appears rather questionable. It concerned the violet background of packages for pastry, with none of the verbal or graphical elements reminding even remotely of Nestlé's products, and not even the color being in the same tone.

[19] Such lawsuits are filed at the District Courts (Landgericht, LG) whose decisions are subject to an appeal to the appeal courts (Oberlandesgericht, OLG) and can lead to an appeal on points of law to the BGH.

[20] Appeals against decisions by the patent office are directed to the BPatG. With permission of the BPatG, an appeal on points of law can be filed with the BGH.

[21] See the brief account of the judicial hierarchy in civil and administrative cases in the two previous footnotes.

[22] BPatG Aug. 5, 2013, GRUR-Rechtsprechungssammlung (GRUR-RS) 14164, 2013.

and wide extent of the use made of the color yellow on the trademark holder's dictionaries, the BGH saw no reason to reverse the decision by the BPatG.[23]

In *DSGV*, the BPatG was of the opinion that acquired distinctiveness had not been established at the relevant date, and that the mark must therefore be invalidated. To make the decision immune against potential objections by the BGH, the deciding judges sought support from the CJEU by referring the question whether it was correct to assume that the color red for banking services only meets the required level of distinctiveness if at least 70% of the relevant public associate it with the party claiming the right.[24] When the CJEU—foreseeably—declared that the law does not permit defining such minimum thresholds,[25] the BPatG nevertheless ruled that the evidence procured in support of acquired distinctiveness had not been sufficient.[26] To that the BGH agreed insofar as lack of establishing distinctiveness at the time of application was concerned. However, the BGH contended that on points of law it must be accepted that distinctiveness had been acquired at the time when the BPatG issued its decision in the nullity proceedings.[27]

With validity of both color marks being confirmed, the question remains whether the use made by the defendants of the respective colors was actually infringing. As pointed out above, the infringement proceedings were conducted separately from the nullity proceedings. This means that, depending on the circumstances, the infringement claim can be decided even before a final decision on validity is made.[28] Thus, in *Langenscheidt v. Rosetta Stone*, the BGH issued its judgment in the infringement proceedings shortly before deciding on the invalidation claim.[29] The judgment is remarkable—to use a neutral expression—for the sweepingly broad scope accorded to the color mark. Although the color yellow is only registered for "bilingual dictionaries in printed form" the BGH held that it extends to Rosetta Stone's use of a similar color for software products containing language teaching programs. On that basis Rosetta Stone was prohibited from using yellow as the basis color on the packages of its products as well as in analogue or digital advertising or on its website. It did not matter that for an ordinary consumer an actual likelihood of confusion between the brands is rather unlikely, as Langenscheidt's dictionaries are marked, in addition to using the color yellow, by the letter "L" in large print and light blue color, while Rosetta Stone uses yellow only as a background for its word mark and further pictorial and graphical elements (thereunder the small, stylized image of a blue stone plate) that are unmistakably different from those of Langenscheidt.

[23] BGH Oct. 23, 2014, GRUR 581, 2015. [24] BPatG Mar. 8, 2013, GRUR 844, 2013.

[25] Joined Cases C-217 & C-218/13, Oberbank, 2014 EUR-Lex-62013CJ0217, ECLI:EU:C:2014:2012 ("Oberbank" is the name of another banking company who had joined with Santander and others in the nullity claim).

[26] BPatG Jul. 8, 2015, GRUR 796, 2015. [27] BGH Jul. 21, 2016, GRUR 1167, 2016.

[28] On request of the parties, infringement courts can also suspend the proceedings until the validity issue has been decided. However, this is rarely done; most courts prefer to move on with the decision. This is one of the grounds for criticism of the bifurcation system, which also applies in patent law. For an empirical study on the practical effects in patent litigation see Katrin Cremers, Fabian Gaessler, Dietmar Harhoff, Christian Helmers, & Yassine Lefouili, *Invalid but Infringed? An Analysis of the Bifurcated Patent Litigation System*, ZEW Discussion Paper No. 14-072 (2014).

[29] BGH Sept. 18, 2014, GRUR 581, 2015.

In *DSGV v. Santander* it is clear that DGSV must tolerate use of Santander's logo (white script and stylized flame on a red background), as the application was made at a time when the distinctiveness of DSGV's color mark had not been sufficiently established. Still pending in various lawsuits conducted before several German courts is the question to what extent the color red can be used as an element in advertising and other public relations designated to maintain a homogeneous image (corporate identity) within the EU market. A non-final decision by the BGH in one of those lawsuits was issued before the validity of the color mark was finally established.[30] The case concerned inter alia the prominent display of Santander's logo in perimeter advertising at sports events sponsored by the firm. The BGH held that no trademark infringement in the form of likelihood of confusion could be ascertained insofar as use of the logo including the color red only served to boost the renown and profile of the company, without being used for concrete goods and services. However, it was added that protection might be granted in case that DGSV's color mark qualifies as a "mark having reputation" in the meaning of Section 14(2) no. 3 of the German Trademark Act, and therefore qualifies for extended protection against conduct that makes unfair use of, or is detrimental to, the reputation or distinctive character of the mark.[31] Although the provision, just as the protection granted against likelihood of confusion, applies only to use which serves to distinguish goods and services, Article 5(5) of the TMD 2008/95/EC stipulates that Member States are free to grant such protection *mutatis mutandis* also when a mark is used for other than distinguishing purposes.[32] With those instructions the case was handed back to the Court of Appeal. The outcome of this and parallel cases remains uncertain at the time of writing.

Apart from in particular issues concerning extended protection for marks having a reputation, a key issue in these and similar cases is the question under which circumstances it can be assumed that a color is "used as a mark"; that is, to identify and distinguish goods and services. The same issue is frequently of relevance in proceedings involving product shapes, as is reported below.

B. Shape marks

1. *Use as a mark*

The specific relevance of the "use as a mark" criterion in shape mark infringement cases was first elaborated by the BGH in a dispute concerning a special (allegedly Russian) type of chocolate-covered éclair. The shape of the product had been registered for bakery products, jellies, marmalade, and jam. A competitor sold very similar-looking éclairs, imported from Ukraine, in packages showing images of the product together with the competitor's trademark. Being sued by the trademark

[30] BGH Sept. 23, 2015, GRUR 1201, 2015.

[31] The provision implements TMD 1989 and TMD 2008 art. 5(2). Basically the same provision is enshrined in TMD 2015 art. 10(2)(c).

[32] Now set out in TMD 2015 art. 10(6).

proprietor, the competitor filed an invalidation request which was pending on appeal when the BGH rendered its judgment in the infringement suit.[33] The BGH first emphasized that under the bifurcation system, courts dealing with infringement claims must (either suspend the proceedings or) treat a registered mark as valid until invalidity has been established.[34] Nevertheless, use of a sign that is identical or similar to a registered mark does not necessarily result in a finding of infringement. It first must be assessed whether the allegedly infringing sign is actually used as a mark. If the protected mark consists of the shape of the products it designates, it is likely that the average consumer only perceives the same or similar shape used by a competitor as belonging to the same species of goods, and not as indicating commercial origin.

The same reasoning was employed in a number of other conflicts involving shape marks.[35] However, the circumstances under which an infringement is excluded on that basis remain somewhat unclear. Thus, in a recent judgment the BGH rejected the finding of the Court of Appeal of Cologne that the shape of a candy bar that was closely similar to the shape of products sold under the trademark "Bounty" had not been used as a mark. The BGH argued that the Court of Appeal had failed to realize that the actual case, in which evidence had been procured to show that the shape was actually perceived by the public as indicating origin, must be distinguished from the situation in the éclair case, where the shape mark had been registered due to inherent distinctiveness. In the first scenario, the fact that the capacity of the shape to identify commercial origin has been proven is held to exclude a finding that the same or a similar shape used by a competitor is nevertheless not perceived as a mark by the relevant public.[36] No attention was paid to the fact that the competitor's product, as well as that of the trademark proprietor, was sold in packages under their own, clearly different trademarks, thus effectively excluding any likelihood of confusion at the point of sale.

2. *Assessing likelihood of confusion*

If use as a mark has been established, the general principles for assessing likelihood of confusion apply (unless the shapes are identical, in which case no further assessment is necessary).[37] Without going into much detail, the operation of those principles in case of shape marks shall be illustrated by the example of the lawsuit between the

[33] BGH Feb. 3, 2005, GRUR 414, 2005. [34] *Id.*

[35] BGH Jan. 25, 2007, GRUR 780, 2007; BGH Apr. 22, 2010, GRUR 1103, 2010 (both concerning the shape of a chocolate truffle); BGH Apr. 30, 2008, GRUR 793, 2008 (regarding suitcases with grooves similar to those of Rimowa); BGH Dec. 5, 2002, GRUR 332, 2003 (concerning the butt of a writing utensil); BGH Oct. 25, 2007, GRUR 505, 2008 (concerning the shape of salted crackers). In the last case the shape was not protected as such, but only in combination with the trademark engraved on it, with the allegedly infringing cracker showing a separate mark. The case could therefore also have been decided under the principles addressed under Section B.2.

[36] BGH Oct. 21, 2015, GRUR 197, 2016.

[37] This follows from the "double identity clause"; TMD 2015 art. 10(2)(a). Cases falling under the double identity clause are not considered in this chapter.

firms Lindt & Sprüngli and Riegelein, concerning chocolate products in the shape of a sitting bunny.[38]

Readers who are familiar with CJEU case law will recognize the "Golden Bunny" as the object of two rather important CJEU decisions, one concerning application in bad faith[39] and the second regarding registration of shape marks based on acquired distinctiveness.[40] In the latter decision the CJEU confirmed that it was not possible on the basis of the evidence adduced by Lindt & Sprüngli to register, as a Community Trade Mark (CTM), the shape of a sitting bunny wrapped in golden foil with a red bow and a bell, with the bow being made of fabric.[41] However, already before that date, Lindt & Sprüngli had secured registration of the same shape, with "Lindt & Sprüngli" being written, in small font, on one side of the bunny's flanks. Based on that registration, an infringement suit was filed against Riegelein, a competitor selling chocolate bunnies of a closely similar shape but in slightly different color and with different graphical features forming the "face" of the bunny, with the (equally red) bow painted on the foil, and the trademark "Riegelein" being printed on the flanks. The Court of Appeal of Frankfurt rejected the infringement claim, holding that, as in case of word/picture combination marks, central importance must be attributed to the word element, which is usually considered to be the dominating feature in such combinations.[42] As the respective elements were clearly different ("Lindt & Sprüngli"/"Riegelein"), the signs in their entirety were not held to be sufficiently similar to trigger likelihood of confusion. On further appeal the decision was remanded by the BGH, criticizing that the assessment scheme applied by the Court of Appeal did not take into account that the similarity of shapes can only be assessed visually, whereas the principle that word elements are regularly dominant can only apply where similarity is (also) assessed orally.[43] The case went back to the Court of Appeal, then to the BGH again and another time down to the Court of Appeal. The details of this judicial roller-coaster do not need to be discussed here. It is only important to highlight that the BGH, though assuming a rather right holder-friendly attitude in its first decision, turned the tables by pointing out in the second decision that the "natural" shape of a sitting bunny cannot be protected as such, and that also elements of the sign which, in the public's perception, primarily serve to create an aesthetically appealing product, cannot be regarded as having distinctive character. The Court of Appeal was therefore instructed that when reassessing the case (for the third time!) account must be taken of established judicial

[38] For a more detailed overview on the general principles governing the assessment of likelihood of confusion see KUR & SENFTLEBEN, *supra* note 3, at 220; *see also* the summary of criteria developed in CJEU case law in Case C-252/12, Specsavers Int'l Healthcare v. Asda Stores Ltd., 2012 E.W.C.A. Civ. 24, F.S.R. at 52.

[39] Case C-529/07, Lindt & Sprüngli v. Hauswirth, 2009 E.C.R. I-04893, EU:C:2009:361 (Golden Bunny I).

[40] Case C-98/11 P, Lindt & Sprüngli v. OHIM, 2012 EUR-Lex-62011CJ0098, EU:C:2012:307 (Golden Bunny II).

[41] Whereas at the time of decision marks registered on the EU level were called "Community Trademarks" (CTMs), the terminology has now changed to "European Union Trademarks" (EUTMs).

[42] OLG Frankfurt Jan. 29, 2004, Wettbewerb in Recht und Praxis (WRP), 638, 2004.

[43] BGH Oct. 26, 2006, GRUR 235, 2015.

practice pursuant to which the scope of protection of a mark partly consisting of non-distinctive elements "regularly does not extend to signs which, in addition to such non-distinctive elements, contain further elements that are actually distinctive, such as in particular distinctive word elements."[44] True to those instructions, the Court of Appeal arrived at the conclusion that likelihood of confusion had to be denied, considering that the respective word elements were "absolutely dissimilar."[45] This time, Lindt & Sprüngli's attempt to bring the case up again to the BGH was not successful.[46]

Reading the decisions one may wonder whether this was anything more than "much ado about nothing." After all, the Court of Appeal already held in its first decision that likelihood of confusion must be dismissed due to the dissimilarity of the word elements. However, there is a substantive distinction between an undifferentiated application of principles developed for assessing two-dimensional combinations of words and figurative elements and the rather complex considerations that the BGH (also in parts of the decisions that are not addressed above) declares as appropriate for shape marks. This is true in particular for the core message that neither the shape of a sitting bunny nor elements serving the aesthetic appeal of the product are able to enjoy trademark protection, even when wrapped into the cloak of a combination mark that also consists of distinctive features.

III. Principles of European Law

The ample reference made above to German case law must not distract from the fact that no leeway exists within the EU for national legislatures and courts to develop their own rules and principles of trademark law. The area is fully harmonized, and at least in principle, national practice must follow the authoritative rulings by the CJEU. Being aware of that, the BGH takes care to ground its decisions on maxims enunciated in CJEU judgments. However, it is not completely clear whether the decisions are always exactly on the same track, as will be explained below.

A. "Use as a mark"

For some time the question of under which circumstances use of a similar—and in particular an identical—sign falls into the ambit of trademark law was a highly disputed topic in EU trademark law. It became usual to refer to the issue under the notion of "use as a mark."[47] However, the phrase was rarely used by the CJEU itself.[48] Instead the CJEU has relied on several criteria, one of which is the statutory

[44] BGH Jul. 15, 2010, GRUR 148, 2011.

[45] OLG Frankfurt Oct. 27, 2011, GRUR-Rechtsprechungs-Report (GRUR-RR), 255, 2012.

[46] BGH Mar. 27, 2013, Beck Rechtsprechungs-Sammlung (BeckRS) 12557, 2013.

[47] *See e.g.*, contributions in JEREMY PHILLIPS & ILANAH SIMON, TRADE MARK USE (2005).

[48] It seems that phrase was only used in the CJEU, *see* Case C-63/97, BMW v. Deenik, 1999 E.C.R. I-905, ECLI:EU:C:1999:82 (the very first decision when the CJEU was confronted with the issue of

requirement of "use in relation to goods and services."[49] Different from the manner in which the "use as a mark" criterion is used in the case law of the BGH, the meaning of "use in relation to goods and services" is rather loose. It is satisfied already if the sign is used in connection with advertising of goods or services in a manner that serves the commercial interests of the alleged infringer.[50] It is no indispensable requirement that the mark is perceived as a badge of origin.[51]

In case of double identity, that rather low initial threshold is complemented by the question of whether the use jeopardizes or is likely to jeopardize the protected trademark functions.[52] Within that framework the effects on the interests of the public (whether they are actually led to believe that the product originates from the trademark holder) as well as on the interests of the trademark holder (under the aspect of the advertising and investment functions) are analyzed and evaluated. If, however, the signs or the goods or services for which they are used are only similar, no particular analysis of that kind is performed. After the threshold of "use in relation to goods and services" is cleared the Court immediately enters into assessing likelihood of confusion.[53]

It is therefore hardly possible to say that the BGH's scheme of assessment finds a clear basis in CJEU jurisprudence. The emphasis put on the "use as a mark" criterion even where signs (in particular colors or product shapes) are only similar is no established feature in the legal practice of EU courts. This makes it likewise improbable that principles corresponding to those developed by the BGH have been adopted in other EU Member States.

To some extent this is no surprise. Arguably, one important reason for the BGH's emphasis on the "use as a mark" criterion in shape (and color) mark infringement cases lies in the bifurcation system. In such cases German courts may have to decide on infringement of signs which they consider as plainly non-distinctive (such as the chocolate-covered éclair), without being able to treat them as invalid. As, with the exception of Austria, the bifurcation system does not apply in other EU Member States the courts in those countries would have no problems anyhow to dismiss

whether use of a mark in order to designate the trademark proprietor's products amounted to potentially infringing trademark use).

[49] This conforms to the wording of TMD 2015 art. 10(2) (previously TMD 1989 and TMD 2008 art. 5(1)).

[50] Thus, use of the protected mark in relation to the alleged infringer's goods or services is also found in case of comparative advertising, *see* C-533/06, O2 v. Hutchison, 2008 E.C.R. I-04231, ECLI:EU:C:2008:339, ¶¶ 36, 37; or in a case of keyword advertising, *see* Joined Cases C-236 to 238/08, Google & Google France v. Louis Vuitton, 2008 E.C.R. I-02417, ECLI:EU:C:2010:159, ¶ 72.

[51] For instance, use as a mark was assumed in CJEU, Case C-48/05, Opel v. Autec, 2007 E.C.R. I-01017 (although the relevant public perceived the protected sign, which was affixed on a toy model car, as a necessary element of faithful scale reproduction, and not as a badge of origin).

[52] The development of that scheme was a lengthy and at times confusing process. However, it has been applied in a fairly consistent manner since Case C-487/07, L'Oréal v. Bellure, 2009 E.C.R. I-05185, ECLI:EU:C:2009:378. Although it still attracts criticism due to the non-transparent and possibly far-reaching character of the CJEU's open-ended definition of the protected functions, its repercussions have remained controllable, in particular after the trademark law reform has broadened the catalogue of limitations.

[53] *See O2, supra* note 50.

such claims without taking resort to complex reasoning. That a close connection exists between the relevance of the "use as a mark" criterion and the (in)ability to evaluate validity issues together with the infringement claim is corroborated by the BGH's finding in *Bounty* that if it is clearly established that the shape of the plaintiff's product is capable of identifying commercial origin, "use as a mark" of an identical or similar sign cannot be denied.[54]

However, it would be wrong or at least premature to reduce the relevance of the principles developed by the BGH to the situation when infringement claims are based on shape (or color) marks that should not have been registered in the first place. Different from what the BGH seems to indicate in *Bounty*, applicability and relevance of the "use as a mark" criterion were confirmed in previous decisions by the same Court even when the validity of the registration was based on acquired distinctiveness. Furthermore, the same principle was applied when the distinctiveness of the plaintiff's sign could not be questioned due to the fact that a distinctive word element had been added.[55] There is a distinction, after all, between reasons to confirm the validity of a shape mark and the question whether the use of a *similar shape* by a *third party* is perceived as indicating origin. The fact that until now such considerations do not find a proper place in the assessment scheme established by CJEU jurisprudence—and that to some extent its application in German case law may be a tribute to the bifurcation principle—should not discourage such practices. On the contrary, it should be explored whether corresponding evaluations can be applied, or be reinforced, on the basis of the new limitation clause for non-distinctive signs.

B. Likelihood of confusion in case of "weak" marks

Also the second strain of case law referred to above—that similarity of signs cannot be found if the elements coinciding in two conflicting signs are not protectable as such—is not, or at least not firmly, anchored in the jurisprudence of the EU courts.[56] Some decisions even point in the opposite direction. Thus, the CJEU emphasized that the distinctiveness of the features which are common to allegedly conflicting signs is only one factor in the overall assessment and must therefore be considered in connection with the other factors, in particular with the overall similarity of the marks in their entirety.[57] Furthermore it is pointed out that the distinctiveness of a mark is not a factor which influences the perception of similarity that the consumer

[54] *Id.* [55] BGH Oct. 25, 2007, GRUR 505, 2008.

[56] Decisions on that point are usually those of the General Court of the European Union (GCEU) hearing appeals against decisions by the Boards of Appeal of the EUIPO. It is in particular the GCEU which has developed the principle that the non-distinctive character of individual elements of combination signs does not change the result if an overall similarity between the signs is found. However, the CJEU expressly endorsed at least some of these findings.

[57] Case T-434/10, Hrbek v. OHMI, 2012 EUR-Lex-62012CO0042, ECLI:EU:T:2011:663, ¶ 61 (Alpine/ALPINE PRO SPORTSWEAR).

has of the conflicting signs.[58] In other words, it is necessary to take full account also of elements which cannot be protected as such.

Until now the repercussions of that approach were primarily felt in the area of word/picture combinations. Thus, likelihood of confusion was found by the GCEU and confirmed by the CJEU between marks designating sportswear that both contain the word "Alpine" as a visually prominent element. As the graphic configuration as well as other, additional verbal features were clearly different, the finding of similarity (and likelihood of confusion) was essentially based on the common word element "Alpine" which, for products of that kind, is arguably descriptive or at least very weak.[59] Further examples[60] concern the conflict between "Star food" (word mark) and a figurative mark containing the word element "star snack," both to be used for foodstuff,[61] as well as the *Carbonell* decision regarding trademarks designating olive oil.[62] The marks consisted of clearly different word elements ("Carbonell" and "Espinosa" respectively) and figurative elements that coincided in their theme—a female figure in a typical Southern European landscape—but were different in regards to the details. Considering the highly descriptive character of the picture as alluding to the Southern European origin of the product, the finding of likelihood of confusion in that case is hard to justify.

Again it would be wrong or premature to hold that due to the supremacy of EU law as interpreted by the CJEU those principles must be given preference over the more competition-friendly approach reflected inter alia in the second Golden Bunny decision by the BGH. First, the CJEU itself endorses the principle that trademark law is founded on and must be contained by the principle of undistorted competition. Second, the position that non-distinctive elements cannot serve to sustain a finding of infringement may have gained weight due to the recent amendments of European trademark law.

IV. 'Indistinctive Signs': A Novel Kind of Limitation in EU Trademark Law

A. Background

Article 6(1)(b) TMD 2008/95/EC stipulates that the proprietor of a trademark cannot object to use of "indications concerning the kind, quality, quantity, intended purpose, value, geographical origin, the time of production of goods or of rendering of the service, or other characteristics of goods or services," provided that use is made

58 Case C-235/05, L'Oréal v. OHIM, 2006 E.C.R. I-00057, EU:C:2006:271, ¶¶ 41, 42 (Alpine/ALPINE PRO); *see also* Case C-42/12 P, Hrbek v. OHIM, 2008 E.C.R. I-04231, ECLI:EU:C:2012:765, ¶ 57.

59 *See Hrbek, supra* note 58.

60 *See also* Case C-171/06 P, T.I.M.E. ART v. OHIM, 2007 E.C.R. I-00041 (Quantum/ figurative mark containing the word element Quantième); Case C-182/14 P, MEGA Brands International v. OHIM, 2015 EUR-Lex-62014CJ0182 (Magnext/Magnet 4).

61 Case T-492/08, Wessang v. OHIM, 2010 E.C.R. II-00082.

62 Case C-498/07 P, Aceites del sur v. Koipe, 2009 E.C.R. I-07371.

"in accordance with honest practices in industrial or commercial matters." In the course of the EU trademark law reform, the provision was changed so as to refer to "signs or indications *which are not distinctive* or which concern the kind, quality . . . ."[63] Until now, little has been written about the potential effects of that rule which appears to be the first of its kind: as far as can be seen, it does not have a forerunner in any of the pre-existing trademark laws in the EU, nor does it have a clear counterpart in the United States (U.S.) or another larger non-EU legislation.[64]

The amendment was primarily based on the argument that non-distinctive and descriptive signs should not only be treated equally where they figure as obstacles to protection, but also in the context of limitations. Similar to descriptive signs which, even when they are registered after having acquired distinctiveness, still contain residues of their original descriptive character that others are free to make use of, inherently indistinctive signs as well will never become the "sole property" of the trademark holder, but must leave room for use by others that only relates to the sign in its original, non-distinctive capacity. Such use can only be found infringing if it clashes with fundamental standards of honest commercial practices.

In the following, several scenarios are pointed out in which the new limitation could become operative. A distinction is made therein between cases when the protected mark itself, though being valid, has certain deficiencies (in the following called "limping marks"), and the situation that the use made of the allegedly infringing sign is such that it is not perceived by the relevant public as an indication of origin.[65] It is not posited that both types of cases can be clearly distinguished from each other; they rather present a switch of focus than two distinct categories.

B. Potential scenarios

1. "Limping" marks

As pointed out above, establishing acquired distinctiveness of colors or shape in the entire EU presents an arduous task. The burden was however alleviated to some extent when the CJEU declared that it would be asking too much if acquired distinctiveness were to be established separately for all (currently) twenty-eight Member States.[66] While the exact implications of that holding remain unclear, it does mean that EU-wide registration may be based on acquired distinctiveness established only

[63] TMD 2015 art. 14(1)(b) (emphasis added). The same provision is found in art. 14(1)(b) of the European Union (EU) Trademark Regulation (Regulation (EU) 2017/1001 of the European Parliament and of the Council of 14 June 2017 on the EU trade mark, 2017 O.J. L154/1 (EC) [hereinafter EUTMR], repealing Council Regulation 207/2009 of 26 February 2009 on the EU trade mark, which codified and amended Council Regulation 40/94 of December 20, 1993 on the Community Trade Mark, 1994 O.J. L11/1 (EC)).

[64] The rule was first suggested in Max Planck Institute (MPI) for Intellectual Property and Competition Law, *Study on the Overall Functioning of the European Trade Mark System*, http://ec.europa.eu/internal_market/indprop/docs/tm/20110308_allensbach-study_en.pdf, 2011, ¶ 2.256.

[65] The author would like to apologize if the expression raises misgivings, and to clarify that the intention of the author was not to offend.

[66] *Lindt & Sprüngli, supra* note 40, ¶ 62.

for a (more or less) limited number of territories.[67] As a result, the sign is validly protected in the entire EU, including those Member States where no or only sparse use has been made of it. The scenario presents a clear example for operation of the new limitation: if the same or a similar color or shape is used in a Member State where the registered mark was not or only sparsely used and is therefore not recognized by the domestic public as a distinctive sign, such use by competitors must be tolerated, unless it does not comply with honest commercial practices.

A related scenario concerns the situation when a mark, after having been registered due to acquired distinctiveness, loses part of its distinctive force for factual reasons, for example due to budget-cutting in the area of advertising or a decline in other marketing efforts. Cancellation is not an option,[68] except for the rare cases where the mark becomes generic.[69] The mark therefore remains valid, but, in the terminology introduced above, it is "limping." In this context as well, the new limitation provides a remedy by allowing competitors to point to the lack of distinctiveness of the mark or, more precisely, to the (corresponding) non-distinctiveness of the identical or similar sign they are using themselves.

Further, the question arises to what extent the new limitation applies when inherently non-distinctive marks, in particular product shapes, are registered only due to a small distinctive detail being added, such as a word mark or figurative element. Such marks as well can be referred to as "limping." Consider for example the situation that a shape mark consisting of a chocolate bunny with a word element imprinted on the flanks is sought to be enforced against competing products of a similar shape, but without a word element being added. Based on the CJEU's contention that distinctiveness is not the only factor for assessing the similarity of signs in conjunction with the fact that the products are identical it may follow from a schematic assessment that likelihood of confusion exists. Nevertheless, as it is clear in this scenario that the "unmarked" bunny is not distinctive, the limitation can be invoked, with the consequence that further use of the competing shape can only be enjoined if, in view of the concrete circumstances, it clashes with fundamental principles of honest commercial practices.

Less obvious is the solution where the competitor's product also shows a (different) word element, such as the word "Riegelein" in the court case reported above. Under a strictly literal interpretation, the new limitation would not apply, as the allegedly infringing sign concerns a complex configuration combining distinctive and non-distinctive elements; different from the first example just discussed, it is not a "sign that is not distinctive." A narrow understanding of the provision would thus lead to the absurd result that a competitor who actively tries to distinguish his goods from those of the right holder by adding distinctive elements would not have access to the new defense, and would thus be in an inferior position vis-à-vis a person who

[67] It is supposed to mean that even though evidence is not adduced for each Member State separately, it is nevertheless clear that basically the same conditions apply throughout the EU. However, that kind of reasoning can hardly ever be fully conclusive.

[68] Unless it is found that the mark no longer satisfies the requirement of "genuine use"; TMD 2015 art. 19; EUTMR art. 18.

[69] *See* TMD 2015 art. 20; EUTMR art. 58(1)(b).

simply markets the shape as such. In line with the legal objectives underpinning the provision, "sign" should therefore be understood as comprising also non-distinctive elements of a sign. The result would be that the limitation becomes effective whenever similarity of signs is essentially founded on the coincidence of elements that are not distinctive (or that are descriptive) as such.[70] The final decision would again turn on the question whether use of the allegedly infringing sign clashes with honest practices.

2. *Use in a non-distinctive manner*

While in the scenarios discussed before, the accent was laid on the *allegedly infringed mark*, the focus is now turned toward the *allegedly infringing sign* and in particular to *the use which is made of it*.

Examples for situations arguably triggering such considerations can be found in the case studies presented above. For instance, in the *Bounty* case decided by the BGH the defendant could make the argument on the basis of the new limitation that notwithstanding the distinctive character of the shape used by the plaintiff, the (similar) product shape used by the defendant was neither inherently distinctive nor was it used to indicate origin, as it was sold in packages indicating the defendant's own word mark.[71] More generally speaking this would mean that, if it is accepted that product shapes can acquire distinctive character even if they are only sold in packaged form, it would be a valid objection against infringement of such signs[72] if the alleged infringer likewise sells the product inside packages which are distinctly marked by other elements than by reference to the shape.[73]

Also in litigation concerning color marks, application of the new limitation could help to achieve better calibrated results. Prohibiting the use of colors has far-reaching effects in all areas of public relations and marketing. The consequences are particularly aggravating for companies that are active in different countries, trying

[70] Such an understanding would ensure that application of the provision becomes an effective corollary to the deletion of (mandatory) disclaimers by the law reform.

[71] As may be recalled, the Court of Appeal's findings in that case had led to the same result; the Court considered that the shape was not "used as a mark."

[72] It must be pointed out here that post-sales confusion is not an established category of EU trademark law. It is true that the CJEU referred to the post-sales situation in Case C-206/01, Arsenal Football Club v. Deenik, ECLI:EU:C:2002:651, ¶ 57. However, that reference was unneccessary under legal aspects and it concerned a very peculiar situation (that the announcements put up by the defendant on his stall that the articles sold were not original). Further on this *see* Ansgar Ohly, *Post-sale confusion?*, FESTCHRIFT FÜR KARL-HEINZ FEZER 615–32 (Wolfgang Büscher, Jochen Glöckner, Axel Nordemann, Christian Osterrieth, and Rudolf Rengier eds., 2016).

[73] The issue is contested in EU trademark law. Pursuant to established practice in the United Kingdom (UK), it is a requirement for establishing acquired distinctiveness that the relevant public "relies" on the shape, which is practically impossible if it is sold in the package, *see* Joined Cases Ch/2013/0392 to 0394, Société des produits Nestlé v. Cadbury, 2014 E.W.H.C. 16 (Ch.) (opinion by Arnold J.). In other EU Member States it is sufficient that the relevant public recognizes the shape as coming from a specific enterprise, irrespective of whether this guides the decision at the point of sale. The question which of the two approaches is a correct interpretation of EU law was referred to the CJEU, *see* Case C-215/14, Nestlé v. Cadbury, EUR-Lex-62014CJ0215, ECLI:EU:C:2015:604, but the CJEU's response was not clear enough to put an end to the dispute.

to develop and maintain a clearly recognizable profile in spite of territorial diversity. "House colors" are of primary importance for such supra-national profile-building. If the selected color can no longer be used in one particular state, the strategy is disrupted: switching to a different color (provided it is still available) sets the territorial branch apart from the multinational "family" to which it belongs; however, if no particular color-coding is used, the profile of the branch may be weakened. Of course, such commercial drawbacks must be accepted to the extent that use of a particular color actually confuses consumers as to the source of the goods or services offered. However, quite often that is only a fictitious scenario; in reality, consumers are hardly at risk of confusion, in particular where the colors are only used as background tone underpinning a broad and prominent display of the parties' distinctive word marks and logos.

This is exactly the situation that the new limitation is fit to address. The starting point must be that using a color in advertisements, websites, or other elements accompanying market appearance is neutral as such. Even if the same or a similar color is protected as a mark, this does not change the fact that the color retains its basic capacity of "simply coloring," without conveying any meaning besides the conceptual and emotional message inherent in the color itself. This is not different from a descriptive word which, after acquiring distinctiveness, still has the capacity to describe, and can be used for that purpose. That double role is aptly expressed in the term "secondary meaning."[74] While a new meaning is acquired, the original, "primary" meaning is retained and justifies use by others. Here again, the limits of such use are (only) met where it clashes with honest commercial practices.

C. Honest commercial practices

Pursuant to the scheme presented above, the key issue for evaluating whether a trademark is infringed by use of a shape or color is to consider whether the use complies with "honest practices in trade and commerce." The role and extent of that catch-all clause are not entirely clear. During the law reform process misgivings were raised that a restrictive interpretation of "honest practices" could eliminate much of the effect that the limitations are meant to entail. Those reservations were fuelled by the proposal[75] to define conduct that would *not* be in compliance with honest practices by enumerating the same concerns that also account for infringement—consumer confusion, taking unfair advantage, or inflicting detriment.[76] The

[74] Different from United States (U.S.) law, "secondary meaning" is not a valid legal term in EU law which refers instead to "acquired distinctiveness"; *see* art. 4(4) TMD and art. 7(3) EUTMR.

[75] That proposal was initially made in the MPI Study, *supra* note 64, and was adopted in the Commission proposals of Mar. 2013; *see* COM/2013/0161 final (EUTMR) and COM/2013/0162 final (TMD).

[76] The proposed definition only codified what had been set forth in previous CJEU decisions; *see* Case C-100/02, Gerolsteiner Brunnen v. Putsch GmbH, 2004 E.C.R. I-00694, ECLI:EU:C:2004:11, ¶¶ 24, 26; Case C-228/03, Gillette v. LA-Laboratories, 2005 E.C.R. I-02337, ECLI:EU:C:2005:177, ¶ 49; Case C-245/02, Anheuser-Busch v. Budvar, 2004 E.C.R. I-10989, ECLI:EU:C:2004:717, ¶ 83; Case C-17/06, Céline SAR v. Céline SA, 2007 E.C.R. I-07041, ECLI:EU:C:2007:497, ¶ 34.

proposed wording could have invited the interpretation that the reasons for finding infringement would always prevail.[77]

However, even without an express definition, it is true that the final check of conduct falling within the ambit of the limitations is substantially informed by factors mirroring the infringement criteria, such as consumer confusion, free riding, and detriment.[78] It is therefore important to emphasize that instead of applying those factors in the same way as when infringement is *prima facie* established, the interpretation must proceed in a more fine-grained fashion, taking account of the countervailing interests safeguarded by the limitations. This means that the concrete manner and dimensions of the use made must be appraised for their appropriateness and proportionality in view of all circumstances. Furthermore, the principle should be established that insofar as the limitations apply, use of the mark can only be qualified, but not entirely prohibited.

V. Conclusion

If the interpretation suggested above of the new limitation for non-distinctive signs is correct, the use by others of shapes and colors registered as trademarks rests on safer ground. This could also improve the chances for a harmonious development of European court practice.

It could be criticized, however, that by granting such weight to the new limitation it would effectively reduce the legal position acquired through registration of such marks to protection against unfair competition. This is true insofar as substance and scope of the protection are concerned; as pointed out before, the crucial step in assessing infringement will regularly be whether the use made by third parties complies with honest commercial practices. On the other hand, different from pure unfair competition rules, the trademark proprietor does not have to establish that the sign meets the various requirements for protection posed under the respective (non-harmonized) national laws.

In the specific case of German law, the amendment confirms tendencies already reflected in decisions of the BGH. However, the repercussions go further than that. By transporting principles previously applied as general prerequisites for trademark infringement ("use as a mark") or as part of the infringement analysis (disregard to non-distinctive elements) to the limitations, their impact has been reinforced and deepened. It is true that by conceptualizing them as limitations the burden of pleading lies with the defendant, whereas under current German practice "use as a mark" forms part of the infringement criteria which must be established by the plaintiff. However, that is unlikely to result in negative effects for the defendant, as

[77] Martin Senftleben et al., *The Recommendation on Measures to Safeguard Freedom of Expression and Undistorted Competition: Guiding Principles for the Further Development of EU Trade Mark Law*, 37 European Intell. Prop. Rev. 337, 339 (2015).

[78] This follows from the fact that the CJEU judgments enunciating those factors (see *supra* note 76) retain their authoritative value.

the court makes its own assessment anyhow without expecting the parties to adduce specific evidence on this point. Furthermore, and quite importantly, it is clear from previous CJEU case law that in the framework of the limitations a broad analysis of compatibility with honest practices must be conducted.[79] Thus, the evaluation can, and should be, more comprehensive and robust than that carried out for assessing "use as a mark. " That way, teeth can be added to the new limitation permitting use of non-distinctive signs.

[79] *See* CJEU Case C-100/02, Gerolsteiner Brunnen v. Putsch, ECLI:EU:C:2004:11, ¶ 24. The suggestion by the referring (German) Court that application of the limitation depends on, or is influenced by, the question of whether the allegedly infringing sign is used as a mark was implicitly rejected in favor of the broader, honest practices-oriented approach.

5

Non-Traditional Trademarks and the Dilemma of Aesthetic Functionality

*Justin Hughes**

1. Introduction

The basic principles of American trademark law have allowed for its increasing application to protect "non-traditional" designators—product packaging trade dress, product design trade dress, single colors, sounds, cartoon characters, and more. The "functionality" doctrine is arguably the most important tool regulating and moderating this expansion. Traditional functionality—sometimes called "utilitarian" or "mechanical" functionality—has a stable analytic framework in U.S. law, but the same cannot be said of "aesthetic functionality," the Supreme Court-blessed notion that some product or trade dress features are so aesthetically pleasing or trigger such specific, desirable mental responses among consumers that those features should not be monopolized by any one competitor.

This chapter explores the aesthetic functionality doctrine in American trademark law in relation to non-traditional marks. Building on prior work,[1] the chapter proposes that (a) the most convincing cases for aesthetic functionality are not truly about aesthetics, but concern cognitive and psychological responses in consumers, and (b) when properly applied aesthetic functionality should only bar trademark protection for features related to specific cognitive, perceptual, or aesthetic biases that were widespread among consumers *before* the trademark owner began its own marketing efforts. This understanding of the doctrine overcomes one of the more fundamental criticisms of aesthetic functionality: that aesthetic preferences are "heterogeneous" and, therefore, not the proper subject of a functionality analysis.

* My thanks to the participants in the Singapore Management University's January 2017 Roundtable on the Protection of Non-Traditional Marks. Thanks also to Silver Kim and Julius Bodie for excellent research assistance. The remaining errors are the exclusive intellectual property of the author.

[1] Justin Hughes, *Cognitive and Aesthetic Functionality in Trademark Law*, 36 CARDOZO L. REV. 1227 (2015).

Requiring the aesthetic preference to exist *before* the trademark owner began its own marketing efforts also ensures that the doctrine does not penalize successful marketers who, in the process of establishing valuable brands, also influence consumer preferences and aesthetics.

Although American jurists have never set out these doctrinal requirements expressly, as principles for aesthetic functionality these two elements are both consistent with the bulk of the modern case law and, in conjunction with existing enquiries into "competitors' ability to compete in the relevant market,"[2] provide a stable framework for meaningful application of the aesthetic functionality doctrine going forward.

II. Utilitarian Functionality

The "functionality" doctrine in American trademark law forbids trademark protection of any aspect of a product that is essential to the use or purpose of the product, that affects the quality of the product, or that affects the cost of bringing the product to consumers. For example, if "fins" along the thin walls of a plastic product add strength and provide stability to the product, the fins would be considered functional.[3] Broadly speaking, a product feature is "functional" where exclusive use of that feature by a single producer "would put competitors at a significant non-reputation-related disadvantage."[4] As a policy lever, the functionality doctrine can be especially important when private parties attempt to use trademark law to gain or maintain market exclusivity when they cannot (or can no longer) get such exclusivity through patent or copyright law. Such scenarios are likely to arise because copyright and patent are exclusive rights "for limited times," while—to riff on a protected slogan—trademarks are forever.[5]

The U.S. Supreme Court had its first brush with the yet-unnamed functionality doctrine in just such a situation: the 1938 *Kellogg v. Nabisco* case concerning shredded wheat.[6] After the expiry of patents covering the process of making shredded wheat,

[2] Christian Louboutin S.A. v. Yves Saint Laurent Am. Holdings, 696 F.3d 206, 222 (2d Cir. 2012).

[3] *See, e.g.*, Eppendorf-Netheler-Hinz GMBH v. Ritter GMBH, 289 F.3d 351, 358 (5th Cir. 2002) (particular arrangement of fins along the side of Eppendorf's syringe product was functional because "fins of some shape, size or number are necessary to provide support for the flange and to prevent deformation of the product").

[4] Qualitex Co. v. Jacobson Prods. Co., 514 U.S. 159, 165 (1995); *see also* TrafFix Devices, Inc. v. Mktg. Displays, Inc., 532 U.S. 23, 32 (2001) (quoting *Qualitex Co.*, 514 U.S. at 165).

[5] "A Diamond is Forever" is the original DeBeers slogan that dates from 1947. *See* DeBeers, *A Diamond is Forever ... 50th Anniversary*, PR NEWSWIRE, http://www.prnewswire.co.uk/cgi/news/release?id=12285 (last visited Mar. 3, 2015). In 2000, ADVERTISING AGE magazine named "A Diamond is Forever" the best advertising slogan of the twentieth century. After many decades of use, it is now the subject of USPTO registration number 3376133, registered on Jan. 29, 2008. *See* A DIAMOND IS FOREVER, Registration No. 3376133. The plural version, "Diamonds are Forever," became the title of the seventh James Bond film (1971) and a hit theme song for the film sung by Shirley Bassey. Bassey's classic became the subject of a remix project issued in 2001 including Groove Armada, the Propellerheads, and Kurtis Mantronik. Perhaps some slogans really are forever.

[6] Kellogg Co. v. Nat'l Biscuit Co., 305 U.S. 111 (1938).

Nabisco claimed what we would now call trade dress protection in the pillow shape of the shredded wheat biscuit. The Court denied this claim, finding that the pillow shape of Nabisco's biscuit was functional because "the cost of the biscuit would be increased and its high quality lessened if some other form were substituted for the pillow-shape."[7] That same year the Restatement of Torts, in a view consonant with *Kellogg*, described the design of goods as "functional" if that design "affects their purpose, action or performance, or the facility or economy of processing, handling or using them."[8]

Utilitarian functionality doctrine percolated in American courts for the ensuing decades. In 1957, the Third Circuit found that the blue dot on Sylvania flash bulbs for cameras was functional because a change in the dot's color was used to detect defective bulbs in the manufacturing process as well as bulbs which had developed air leakage after purchase.[9] In 1975, another appellate Court denied trademark registration to the design of an aluminum fitting used to join lengths of tubing because the product's shape was what made the tubes fit tightly together.[10]

In 1982, the U.S. Supreme Court returned to the functionality doctrine in *Inwood Laboratories v. Ives Laboratories*, a case where the trial Court had found the coloring of pills to be functional.[11] While the Supreme Court's decision focused on the appellate Court overstepping appropriate appellate review, the *Inwood Labs* opinion included a footnote telling us that "[i]n general terms, a product feature is functional if it is essential to the use or purpose of the article or if it affects the cost or quality of the article."[12] With some limited, further elaboration, this became the basic formula for utilitarian functionality in American trademark law.

III. The Other Kind of Functionality

Parallel to utilitarian functionality—and sometimes being argued alongside it—courts grappled with claims of functionality arising from consumers' aesthetic preferences. But a challenge for this doctrine (even more than for *utilitarian* functionality) has been the tendency to frame the standard too broadly. The problem started at least as early as the 1938 Restatement of Torts, which included a very explicit discussion of functionality stemming from "aesthetic value":

> When goods are bought largely for their aesthetic value, their features may be functional because they definitely contribute to that value and thus aid the performance of an object for which the goods are intended .... The determination of whether or not such features are functional depends upon the question of fact whether the prohibition of imitation by others will deprive the others of something which will substantially hinder them in competition.[13]

7 *Id.* at 122. 8 Restatement (First) of Torts § 742 (1938).

9 Sylvania Elec. Prods. v. Dura Elec. Lamp Co., 247 F.2d 730, 732 (3d Cir. 1957).

10 *In re* Hollaender Mfg. Co., 511 F.2d 1186, 1189 (C.C.P.A. 1975).

11 Inwood Labs., Inc. v. Ives Labs., Inc., 456 U.S. 844 (1982).

12 *Id.* at 850 n.10 (no mention of *Morton-Norwich*).

13 3 Restatement (First) of Torts § 742, cmt. A (1938).

This provided the germ for the aesthetic functionality doctrine, which emerged in the Ninth Circuit's 1952 *Pagliero v. Wallace China Co.* decision.[14] At issue in *Pagliero* were patterns for dinnerware that the Wallace China Company marketed under the names "'Tweed', 'Hibiscus', 'Shadowleaf', and 'Magnolia' …."[15] Defendants were accused of copying both the patterns and the pattern names.[16] A skillful jurist today might dispose of the trade dress claims on grounds of an absence of secondary meaning in the china patterns,[17] but the *Pagliero* court found that "from the standpoint of the purchaser china satisfies a demand for the aesthetic as well as for the utilitarian"[18] and that the "attractiveness and eye-appeal of the design sells the [Wallace] china."[19] Based on these findings, the court concluded that the china patterns were functional and announced a test that a product feature is aesthetically functional "[i]f the particular feature is an important ingredient in the commercial success of the product," or, even more broadly, if the product feature was "related to basic consumer demand in connection with the product."[20]

A broad *Pagliero*-like approach was applied in some decisions in the 1970s and 1980s, but courts quickly realized that if aesthetic functionality boiled down to the low threshold question of whether a product feature was an "important ingredient" in that product's success, the trademarks safest from aesthetic functionality would be those that the consumer found the most unattractive, off-putting, or dissonant.[21] In short, trademark law would stand as a disincentive to original, attractive packaging and product design.

Subsequent judicial opinions narrowing the scope of aesthetic functionality frequently mentioned this point. For example, in 1981, the Third Circuit opined that trademark should not discourage the "use of a spark of originality which could transform an ordinary product into one of grace."[22] In 1987, the Tenth Circuit joined other courts in rejecting the *Pagliero* "important ingredient" standard "because it would be a disincentive to creative design"[23] and four years later a Second Circuit panel added its voice to the chorus noting "[b]y allowing the copying of an exact design without any evidence of market foreclosure, the *Pagliero* test discourages both originators and later competitors from developing pleasing designs."[24] The current test in Article 3(1)(e)(iii) of the European Union's Trade Mark Directive—barring trademark protection of any "shape which gives substantial value to the

14 Pagliero v. Wallace China Co., Ltd., 198 F.2d 339 (9th Cir. 1952).

15 *Id.* at 340.

16 *Id.* at 340–41.

17 That is, under Wal-Mart v. Samara, 529 U.S. 205 (2000) the plaintiff would have to establish secondary meaning in the product design trade dress.

18 *Pagliero*, 198 F.2d at 343.

19 *Id.* at 343–44.

20 *Id.*

21 As J. Thomas McCarthy writes, "if the theory of 'aesthetic functionality' were the law, then the uglier and more repulsive the symbol, the less 'functional' it would be." J. THOMAS MCCARTHY, MCCARTHY ON TRADEMARKS AND UNFAIR COMPETITION § 7:80, at 7-283 (4th ed. 2014) [hereinafter MCCARTHY ON TRADEMARKS]. Of course, aesthetic functionality *is* the law, but just not this unworkable version.

22 Keene Corp v. Paraflex Indus., Inc., 653 F.2d 822, 825 (3d Cir. 1981).

23 Brunswick Corp. v. Spinit Reel Co., 832 F.2d 513, 518 (10th Cir. 1987).

24 Wallace Int'l Silversmiths, Inc. v. Godinger Silver Art Co., Inc., 916 F.2d 76, 80 (2d Cir. 1990), *cert. denied*, 499 U.S. 976 (1991).

goods"[25] —seems to have the same sort of overbreadth problem, denying trademark protection to design shapes that are aesthetically pleasing in and of themselves.[26]

The typical move by American jurists to avoid *Pagliero*-like outcomes has been to focus on some "analysis of whether the 'use of [a design] feature is necessary for effective competition' ";[27] whether protection of a product feature "*significantly* undermines competitors' ability to compete in the relevant market";[28] and whether "alternative appealing designs or presentations of the product can be developed."[29] This soberer approach recognized that "the policy predicate for the entire functionality doctrine stems from the public interest in enhancing competition."[30] By the late 1980s, revision of the Restatement of Unfair Competition took the same approach. The Third Restatement observes that a "design is functional because of its aesthetic value only if it confers a significant benefit that cannot practically be duplicated by the use of alternative designs."[31]

A few years later—in 1995—the U.S. Supreme Court gave us its first and only extended discussion of aesthetic functionality in the unanimous *Qualitex v. Jacobson Products* decision.[32] Justice Breyer begins the *Qualitex* discussion of functionality by saying that the doctrine prevents any one producer from controlling "a useful product feature."[33] Justice Breyer contrasts trademark law with patent law, giving a technological example (a patented light bulb) of a useful feature that cannot be protected with trademark law; in other words, "useful" is first presented as a utilitarian, technological concept.[34] The Court then elaborates on its prior statement in *Inwood Labs*, telling us:

> "[I]n general terms, a product feature is functional," and cannot serve as a trademark, "if it is essential to the use or purpose of the article or if it affects the cost or quality of the article," that is, if exclusive use of the feature would put competitors at a significant non-reputation-related disadvantage.[35]

[25] Directive 2008/95/EC of the European Parliament and of the Council of 22 October 2008 to approximate the laws of the Member States relating to trade marks, 2008 O.J. L299/25.

[26] The Court of Justice of the European Union gave a broad reading of art. 3(1)(e)(iii) in Case C-371/06, Benetton v. G-Star, 2007 E.C.R. I-7709, appearing to conclude that a design that is initially aesthetically pleasing and thereby "gives substantial value to the goods" is barred from acquired distinctiveness, even when distinctiveness exists at the time of trademark regisitration. For criticisms of this decision, see Annette Kur, *Too Pretty to Protect? Trademark Law and the Enigma of Aesthetic Functionality*, Max Planck Institute for Intellectual Property and Competition Law Research Paper No. 11-16 (2010), 14–16. *See also* Annette Kur, *Too Common, Too Splendid, or "Just Right"? Trademark Law Protection for Product Shapes in the Light of CJEU Case*, Max Planck Institute for Intellectual Property and Competition Law Research Paper No. 14-17.

[27] Villeroy & Boch Keramische Werke K.G. v. THC Sys., Inc., 999 F.2d 619, 621 (2d Cir. 1993) (alteration in original) (quoting Wallace Int'l Silversmiths, Inc. v. Godinger Silver Art Co., Inc., 916 F.2d 76, 80 (2d Cir.1990), *cert. denied*, 499 U.S. 976 (1991)).

[28] Christian Louboutin S.A. v. Yves Saint Laurent Am. Holdings, 696 F.3d 206, 222 (2d Cir. 2012).

[29] Brunswick Corp. v. Spinit Reel Co., 832 F.2d 513, 519 (10th Cir. 1987).

[30] Keene Corp. v. Paraflex Indus., Inc., 653 F.2d 822, 827 (3d Cir. 1981). The Third Circuit panel in *Keene* said this in the context of searching for a narrower test than *Pagliero*. *See Keene Corp.*, 653 F.2d at 825–27.

[31] RESTATEMENT (THIRD) OF UNFAIR COMPETITION § 17, cmt. c (1995).

[32] Qualitex Co. v. Jacobson Prods. Co., Inc., 514 U.S. 159 (1995).

[33] *Id.*

[34] *Id.* at 165.

[35] *Id.* at 165 (quoting Inwood Labs., Inc. v. Ives Labs., Inc., 456 U.S. 844, 850 n.10 (1982)).

Up until this point, the discussion could be understood as limited to utilitarian functionality, but *Qualitex* concerned a claim over trademark rights in a single color, and the Court notes that "sometimes color plays an important role . . . in making a product more desirable . . ."[36] When the Court resumes its discussion of functionality a few paragraphs later, it makes no attempt to separate utilitarian from aesthetic functionality. Instead, the Court discusses four cases in which the color of a product was held to be functional,[37] and refers approvingly to the discussion in the Restatement (Third) of Unfair Competition that a design is "functional" when its "aesthetic value" confers "a significant benefit that cannot practically be duplicated by the use of alternative designs."[38] Justice Breyer then waxes poetic:

> The upshot is that, where a color serves a significant nontrademark function—whether to distinguish a heart pill from a digestive medicine or to satisfy the "noble instinct for giving the right touch of beauty to common and necessary things," G. CHESTERTON, SIMPLICITY AND TOLSTOY 61 (1912)—courts will examine whether its use as a mark would permit one competitor (or a group) to interfere with legitimate (nontrademark-related) competition through actual or potential exclusive use of an important product ingredient.[39]

The unanimous *Qualitex* opinion is quite express that trademark rights in the "right touch of beauty" in a product's trade dress might "interfere with legitimate (nontrademark-related) competition"[40] and when that happens, the proper inquiry for courts is "whether the recognition of trademark rights would significantly hinder competition."[41]

Qualitex stands as the Court's only meaningful exposition on aesthetic functionality, although there was a sideways glance toward aesthetics in its discussion of utilitarian functionality in the 2001 *TrafFix Devices v. Marketing Displays* decision.[42] While *Traffix* was narrowly focused on "whether the existence of an expired utility patent forecloses the possibility of the patentee's claiming trade dress protection in the product's design,"[43] the unanimous *TrafFix* decision (a) reiterated its broader view that the *Inwood* approach should be applied vis-a-vis utilitarian functionality claims, then (b) both endorsed and distinguished aesthetic functionality with the simple statement, "[i]t is proper to inquire into a 'significant non-reputation-related disadvantage' in cases of esthetic functionality, the question involved in *Qualitex*."[44]

Among lower courts, the Second, Seventh, Ninth, Tenth, and Eleventh Circuits have embraced aesthetic functionality, while the Fifth Circuit seems to reject the

[36] *Id.* at 165.

[37] *Id.* at 169–70. The cases are: Deere & Co. v. Farmhand, Inc., 560 F. Supp. 85, 98 (S.D. Iowa 1982), *aff'd*, 721 F.2d 253 (8th Cir. 1983); Brunswick Corp. v. British Seagull Ltd., 35 F.3d 1527, 1532 (Fed. Cir. 1994); Nor-Am Chemical v. O.M. Scott & Sons Co., 4 U.S.P.Q.2d 1316, 1320 (E.D. Pa. 1987), as well as its own discussion of color in *Inwood*.

[38] RESTATEMENT (THIRD) OF UNFAIR COMPETITION § 17, cmt. c (1995).

[39] *Qualitex*, 514 U.S. at 170. [40] *Id.* [41] *Id.* (internal quotation marks omitted).

[42] TrafFix Devices, Inc. v. Mktg Displays, 532 U.S. 23 (2001).

[43] *Id.* at 28. The Fifth, Seventh, and Federal Circuits had held that an expired utility patent need not foreclose trademark protection, while the Tenth Circuit held that such an expired patent precludes trade dress protection. *Id.*

[44] TrafFix Devices, Inc. v. Mktg. Displays, Inc., 532 U.S. 23, 33 (2001). The *TrafFix* Court also told us "[i]n *Qualitex* . . . esthetic functionality was the central question." *Id.*

doctrine entirely.[45] In a 2012 decision, the Sixth Circuit remained coy about the doctrine, giving an interpretation of what the "dicta" in *Qualitex* "propose[s]," but stating that they had "not yet plainly stated which test we would apply under aesthetic functionality doctrine . . . or that we have even adopted aesthetic functionality doctrine at all . . . ."[46]

While the Fifth and Sixth Circuits are, *stricto senso,* correct that the aesthetic functionality discussion in *Qualitex* was not necessary for the result, not all dicta are equal in American law. Justice Breyer's *Qualitex* opinion on behalf of a *unanimous* Court expressly discusses the aesthetic functionality doctrine in a moderately long passage, relying on and referring to cases that were briefed *both* by the *petitioner* and the *U.S. Government*; a few years later, Justice Scalia referred favorably to the *Qualitex* "esthetic appeal" considerations in the Court's 2000 *Wal-Mart* decision;[47] and the next year, Justice Kennedy, again on behalf of a *unanimous* Court in *TrafFix*, expressly states that *Qualitex* was a case about aesthetic functionality—and tells us that the approach *Qualitex* lays out is "proper."[48] The comments in *Wal-Mart* and *TrafFix* only galvanize the view that the *Qualitex* discussion is "considered dicta" that is "instructive of the Supreme Court's views" and should be followed.[49] In all this, the Second Circuit is surely correct "that the combined effect of *Qualitex* and *TrafFix* was to validate the aesthetic functionality doctrine as it had already been developed" by lower courts.[50]

45 Bd. of Supervisors for La. State Univ. Agric. & Mech. Coll. v. Smack Apparel Co., 550 F.3d 465, 487–88 (5th Cir. 2008) (arguing that the Supreme Court has recognized the aesthetic functionality doctrine only in dicta, and that therefore the Fifth Circuit's long-standing rejection of the doctrine was not abrogated by *Qualitex* and *TrafFix*).

46 Maker's Mark Distillery, Inc. v. Diageo N. Am., Inc., 679 F.3d 410, 418 (6th Cir. 2012) (citations omitted). In the particular dispute before it, the Sixth Circuit panel said they would reach the same result "[e]ven assuming we were to recognize aesthetic functionality doctrine . . . ." *Id. See also* Antioch Co. v. W. Tramming Corp., 347 F.3d 150, 155–56 (6th Cir. 2003) (questioning aesthetic functionality doctrine in the Sixth Circuit).

47 Wal-Mart Stores v. Samara Bros., 529 U.S. 205, 214 (2000) ("It is true, of course, that the person seeking to exclude new entrants would have to establish the nonfunctionality of the design feature . . . —a showing that may involve consideration of its esthetic appeal, *see Qualitex*").

48 TrafFix Devices, Inc. v. Mktg. Displays, Inc., 532 U.S. 23, 33 (2001) ("It is proper to inquire into a 'significant non-reputation-related disadvantage' in cases of esthetic functionality, the question involved in *Qualitex*. Where the design is functional under the *Inwood* formulation there is no need to proceed further to consider if there is a competitive necessity for the feature. In *Qualitex*, by contrast, esthetic functionality was the central question, there having been no indication that the green-gold color of the laundry press pad had any bearing on the use or purpose of the product or its cost or quality.").

49 Wright v. Morris, 111 F.3d 414, 419 (6th Cir. 1997) ("We believe that this [dictum] is instructive of the Supreme Court's views and cannot be dismissed out of hand . . . . Where there is no clear precedent to the contrary, we will not simply ignore the Court's dicta."). *See also* McCoy v. Mass. Inst. of Tech., 950 F.2d 13, 19 (1st Cir. 1991) ("We think that federal appellate courts are bound by the Supreme Court's considered dicta almost as firmly as by the Court's outright holdings, particularly when, as here, a dictum is of recent vintage and not enfeebled by any subsequent statement."); Nichol v. Pullman Standard, Inc., 889 F.2d 115, 120 n.8 (7th Cir. 1989) (courts of appeal "should respect considered Supreme Court dicta"); United States v. Bell, 524 F.2d 202, 206 (2d Cir. 1975) (considered dicta "must be given considerable weight and cannot be ignored in the resolution of [a] close question").

50 Christian Louboutin S.A. v. Yves Saint Laurent Am., 696 F.3d 206, 221 (2d Cir. 2012). For further discussion of the status of the Court's *Qualitex* analysis, see Hughes, *supra* note 1, at 1241–47.

IV. Making Sense of Aesthetic Functionality

Yet the Supreme Court's embrace of aesthetic functionality for American trademark law has not much tempered the doctrine's critics: the aesthetic functionality doctrine is said to have "a somewhat checkered history," to lack "coherent jurisprudence,"[51] and to be "a most controversial and ill-defined concept."[52] The leading treatise on American trademark law remains convinced that aesthetic functionality is "an oxymoron"[53] and goes to great rhetorical lengths to undermine the Supreme Court's pronouncements.[54]

Moreover, the Supreme Court's blessing does not mean that aesthetic functionality necessarily forms part of a seamless doctrinal whole with utilitarian functionality. Although aesthetic functionality is treated as part of overall functionality doctrine in the Restatement, in *Qualitex* and in *TrafFix*, one can still ask, as Graeme Dinwoodie and Mark Janis do, "is the doctrine of 'aesthetic functionality' a separate doctrine from a doctrine of 'utilitarian functionality'? Do we need different tests to determine the limits of trademark protection for 'aesthetic' as opposed to 'utilitarian' features?"[55] Mark McKenna believes that doctrinal differences between the two types of functionality arise because aesthetic functionality does not directly implicate the policy objectives of patent law—an often-stated objective in utilitarian functionality analysis.[56] In a 2014 review of the functionality doctrine, Robert Bone takes the general view that "market competition can be impaired by protecting aesthetic trade dress just as much as it can by protecting utilitarian trade dress"[57] but he recognizes that his own preferred analytic framework for functionality may have to be adjusted with aesthetic functionality, largely because of the "heterogeneity of aesthetic preference."[58]

[51] Au-Tomotive Gold, Inc. v. Volkswagen of America, Inc., 457 F.3d 1062, 1064, 1068 (9th Cir. 2006).

[52] A. Samuel Oddi, *The Function of "Functionality" in Trademark Law*, 22 Hous. L. Rev. 925, 951–62 (1985) (surveying the history of aesthetic functionality and concluding that "[f]rom the outset, 'aesthetic functionality' has proved to be a most controversial and ill-defined concept").

[53] McCarthy on Trademarks § 7:81, at 7–298 ("'Aesthetic functionality' is an oxymoron. Ornamental aesthetic designs are the antithesis of utilitarian designs." (footnote omitted)).

[54] *Id.* § 7:80, at 7–277 ("[T]he Supreme Court has never directly addressed aesthetic functionality *as a dispositive issue in a case....*" (emphasis added)); on the next page of the treatise, McCarthy dismisses Breyer's discussion and four case citations in *Qualitex* as "passing comments" that "might put some life in the fading theory of aesthetic functionality," labels Scalia's reference to *Qualitex* in the 2000 *Wal-Mart* as "cryptic[]," and says that Justice Kennedy's 2001 *TrafFix* opinion characterizing *Qualitex* as a case about aesthetic functionality only "muddied the waters of the aesthetic functionality theory." *Id.* § 7:80, at 7–278.

[55] Graeme B. Dinwoodie & Mark Janis, Trade Dress and Design Law 124 (2010).

[56] Mark P. McKenna, *(Dys)functionality*, 48 Hous. L. Rev. 823, 854 (2011) ("It makes sense to differentiate these types of functionality because they interact with patent law in different ways: features related to mechanical function implicate a concern about overlap with the utility patent system, while features needed because of consumer expectations do not.").

[57] Robert Bone, *Trademark Functionality Reexamined*, 7 J. Legal Analysis 183, 238 (2015).

[58] *Id.* at 239. Bone also identifies two other reasons aesthetic functionality may be different. He calls these "close connection between aesthetics and source-identification [devices]" the subjectivity of judgments about superior designs. I take the last point to largely overlap with heterogeneity of aesthetic preferences.

Indeed, the "heterogeneity of aesthetic preference" among consumers is probably the greatest source of discomfort with the aesthetic functionality doctrine, but the problem stems from the "aesthetic" label not from how the doctrine has operated in most of the case law. (Elsewhere I have suggested that long ago the doctrine might have been more profitably called "cognitive" or "psychological" functionality.[59])

This is not to deny that "heterogeneity" is a basic characteristic of aesthetic preferences generally, but it is considerably less characteristic of the aesthetic functionality case law. My claim is that what we have called "aesthetic functionality" can be better understood as functionality in product features arising from widely shared consumer responses to sensory inputs, whether based either on evolution or deeply rooted acculturation. The widely shared consumer responses can be called psychological, cognitive, or aesthetic. This understanding of the proper application of aesthetic functionality can be seen through two distinct clusters of aesthetic functionality case law, what we might call the "matching" cases and the "cognition" cases.

V. *Brunswick Corp.* and the "Matching" cases

The perfect case to introduce both clusters of case law is one of the cases mentioned favorably by the Supreme Court in *Qualitex*: the 1994 *Brunswick Corp. v. British Seagull Ltd.* decision[60] in which Brunswick sought registration of the color black as a trademark for outboard motors manufactured by its Mercury Marine division.

The U.S. Patent and Trademark Office's Trademark Trial and Appeals Board (TTAB) refused this registration, finding that black in relation to outboard motors for boats was functional for two distinct reasons. The first reason was "because it is a color compatible with a wider range of boat colors," that is, that "[t]he evidence show[ed] that people who buy outboard motors for boats like the colors of the motors to be harmonious with the colors of their vessels."[61] The second reason was that "objects colored black appear smaller than they do when they are painted other lighter or brighter colors" and "people who buy outboard motors for boats ... find it desirable under some circumstances to reduce the perception of the size of the motor in proportion to the boats."[62] On appeal, the Federal Circuit was coy about

[59] Hughes, *supra* note 1, at 1247. In fact, the entirety of the functionality doctrine is poorly named. Judge Posner noted that "utilitarian" should really describe all the functionality cases because "'utilitarian' is ambiguous" and "can mean anything which gives pleasure," W.T. Rogers Co., Inc. v. Keene, 778 F.2d 334, 344–45 (1985). Mark Lemley and Mark McKenna suggest we would be better off understanding "utilitarian" functionality as "mechanical" functionality. Mark A. Lemley & Mark P. McKenna, *Is Pepsi Really a Substitute for Coke? Market Definition in Antitrust and IP*, 100 Geo. L.J. 2055, 2063 (2012).

[60] Brunswick Corp. v. Brit. Seagull Ltd. & Outboard Marine Corp., 35 F.3d 1527 (Fed. Cir. 1994).

[61] Brit. Seagull Ltd. v. Brunswick Corp., 28 U.S.P.Q.2d 1197, 1199, 1993 WL 409141 (T.T.A.B. 1993).

[62] *Id.*

its embrace of "aesthetic functionality"[63] but nonetheless upheld the TTAB ruling, accepting both rationales.[64]

The first grounds for refusal could certainly sound "aesthetic": that black is "a color compatible with a wider range of boat colors," and that "[t]he evidence show[ed] that people who buy outboard motors for boats like the colors of the motors to be harmonious with the colors of their vessels."[65] Yet this concern for "color compatibility" does not lead us into a situation where "heterogeneity" of aesthetic preferences undermines aesthetic functionality as a doctrine. Instead, these "compatibility" or "matching" situations form a discrete and reasonable body of aesthetic functionality case law in which courts conclude that consumers want things to "match," particularly when it comes to accessory or replacement elements for goods in which the consumer has made a substantial investment. In *Brunswick Corp.*, the consumer has made a substantial investment in his or her boat—and reasonably wants to attach an outboard motor whose color is compatible. Giving one manufacturer exclusive control of a particular color that is uniquely compatible with different boat hull colors would confer too great a non-reputational advantage. And this is true despite the basic heterogeneity among consumers as to their preference for boat hull color.[66]

Another classic example of the "matching" fact pattern—and one that resonated with the Supreme Court—is the 1982 case *Deere & Co. v. Farmhand, Inc.*[67] The John Deere Company had been using a particular shade of green for its farm tractors since 1955[68] and a survey introduced at trial showed that 80% of respondents identified the green shade with John Deere.[69] A much smaller competitor, Farmhand, was in the business of selling front-end loaders ("loaders"), bulldozer-like hydraulic scoops that attach to the front chassis of a tractor. When Farmhand introduced models specifically designed to fit the newest Deere tractors, it painted those loaders "the exact same shade of green as John Deere . . . ."[70]

[63] Judge Rader's analysis goes directly to the conclusion that each of the two reasons shows that black is needed for effective competition. *Brunswick Corp.*, 35 F.3d at 1533 ("In this case, the Board did not improperly deny registration to Mercury merely because black served purely aesthetic functions. Color compatibility and ability to decrease apparent motor size are not in this case mere aesthetic features. Rather these non-trademark functions supply a competitive advantage. The Board properly analyzed Mercury's use of black in terms of its non-trademark functions and its effect on competition.").

[64] *Brunswick Corp.*, 35 F.3d at 1531–32. The T.T.A.B. also found that Brunswick had not established acquired distinctiveness in its Mercury division's use of the color black, partly because "[t]he Board also found that Mercury's use of black on outboard motors was not exclusive. Several of Mercury's competitors in the outboard market had engines colored black or dark colors easily perceived as black." *Id.* at 1530.

[65] *Brit. Seagull*, 28 U.S.P.Q.2d at 1199. Judge Rader was adamant that this reason was not a "purely aesthetic function." *Brunswick Corp.*, 35 F.3d at 1533.

[66] That heterogeneity is evident in the wide range of colors offered by boat manufacturers. For example, Century Boats offers ten different boat hull colors, from "red" to "aqua mist" and "ice blue." *See Optional Hull Colors*, CENTURY BOATS, http://www.centuryboats.com/optional-hull-colors/ (last visited Feb. 28, 2017); Clackacraft Boats offers fifteen colors, which can be deployed in two-tone combinations. *See Clackacraft Drift Boat Color Options*, CLACKACRAFT, https://www.clacka.com/boat-builder/ (last visited Feb. 28, 2017); *See also Gig Harbor Boat Works*, SPECIAL COLORS, http://www.ghboats.com/options/custom-boat-options/custom-colors/ (last visited Feb. 28, 2017).

[67] Deere & Co. v. Farmhand, Inc., 560 F. Supp. 85, 98 (S.D. Iowa 1982), *aff'd*, 721 F.2d 253 (8th Cir. 1983).

[68] *Id.* at 89. [69] *Id.* at 93. [70] *Id.* at 89.

The *Deere* court reviewed "abundant evidence at trial to the effect that farmers desire to 'match' their loaders to their tractors"[71] and "conclude[d] that the doctrine of aesthetic functionality should apply to the dispute" as well as "that protection of John Deere green ... would hinder Farmland in competition."[72] Notice that the consumers' aesthetic preference here is *not* for the *color green* or a particular shade of green per se; it is a consumer preference for "match" combined with the consumer having already made a substantial capital investment on one side of the color compatibility.

Such "matching" situations also occurred in a set of cases about architectural components: the Third Circuit's 1981 *Keene Corp. v. Paraflex Industries*[73] decision; a 1999 Federal Circuit decision, *L.D. Kichler Co. v. Davoil, Inc.*;[74] and the 2001 TTAB decision, *M-5 Steel Manufacturing v. O'Hagin's, Inc.*[75] In *Keene v. Paraflex*, the issue was a modernist exterior lighting fixture and the Third Circuit concluded that the fixture's overall design could not be trademarked, because "part of its function includes its architectural *compatibility* with the structure or building on which it is mounted."[76] In *Kichler*, the plaintiff claimed trademark protection for a surface treatment—an antiqued, weathered finish for lighting fixtures which it called "Olde Brick" and which was "described as 'rust-type' " and "color compatible with many interior finishes."[77] The district court granted summary judgment to the defendant, reasoning that the Olde Brick finish could not be protected because of other fixture manufacturers' need to use similar finishes to match existing building interiors.[78]

Finally, in the most blatant of this trio of cases, *M-5 Steel v. O'Hagin*, the trademark claimant sought to register the shape of its products as trademarks; these products were metal roof vent covers that mimicked "the shapes of the roof tiles made and sold by various unrelated roof tile manufacturers."[79] This meant that a home with a Spanish tile roof could have a roof vent that matched the curvature of the roof tiles (instead of being an apparent vent outlet). Testimony for the opposition focused on how a typical "customer wants the vent to match the [roof] tile,"[80] that the purpose of a curved vent cover was "to make it appear as a tile, a roof tile" and that "[o]nce it's on the roof, and it's painted, it's very difficult to identify them as either vent or tile."[81]

[71] *Id.* at 91–92 ("The farmers who testified either specifically stated that they desired their loader to match their tractor or at least recognized the visual impact of color combinations in farm machinery.").

[72] *Id.* at 98. But this apparent holding as to aesthetic functionality was actually not necessary to the result as the court, criticizing John Deere's survey evidence, concluded that it was "unwilling to find that plaintiff has established a secondary meaning for the color John Deere green." *Id.* at 99.

[73] Keene Corp. v. Paraflex Indus., Inc., 653 F.2d 822 (3d Cir. 1981).

[74] L.D. Kichler Co. v. Dacoil, Inc., 192 F.3d 1349 (Fed. Cir. 1999).

[75] M-5 Steel Mfg., Inc. v. O'Hagin's Inc., 61 U.S.P.Q.2d 1086, 2001 WL 1167788 (T.T.A.B. 2001). The three federal court cases discussed in this section are all featured in the U.S. Government's pleadings in *Qualitex*. Brief for the United States as Amicus Curiae Supporting Petitioner at 14–15, Qualitex Co. v. Jacobson Prods., Inc., 514 U.S. 159 (1995) (No. 93–1577).

[76] *Keene Corp.*, 653 F.2d at 826 (emphasis added).

[77] *L.D. Kichler Co.*, 192 F.3d at 1351.

[78] Emphasis added. While the appellate panel reversed and remanded for further determinations of fact, they recognized that "color compatibility" could produce *de jure* functionality where a claimed color "is one of a few colors that are uniquely superior for use in home decorating." *Id.* at 1353.

[79] *M-5 Steel Mfg., Inc.*, 61 U.S.P.Q.2d at 1088. [80] *Id.* [81] *Id.* at 1089.

On this record, the TTAB "agree[d] with opposer that applicant's product designs are functional in the sense that these configurations blend in or match the roof tiles with which they are used better than alternative products."[82]

In all these cases a consumer has made a capital investment in a physical good and wants to visually coordinate products to that capital investment. *Brunswick, Kichler, Keene*, and *M-5 Steel* differ from *Deere* only in that John Deere sold both the product (front loaders) *and* the capital good to which the product was being matched (tractors). But in all these cases, unless the product feature is found to be functional, the party claiming trademark rights would gain a distinct non-reputational advantage for a market or a segment of a market based on consumers' general propensity to want things to "match." Aesthetic functionality arising from "matching" might include any colors that are neutral in relation to the product or product environments on which they are used.[83] The chief examples would obviously be white, black, and gray (separate from their *cognitive* functionality discussed below). But *M-5 Steel* and *Deere* remind us that this could include colors distinctly needed to "match" in particular environments.

VI. The Perceptual Functionality of Black, Blue, and Other Features

Now, let us turn to the second basis in *Brunswick* for finding the color black to be aesthetically functional in relation to outboard motors for boats: that "objects colored black appear smaller than they do when they are painted other lighter or brighter colors." This functional effect is not really about aesthetics; it concerns how our sensory and neurological systems work. It seems to be the case that things in black (or extremely dark colors) *appear* smaller to us; as a species, we literally see them *less*. Not only are black clothes slenderizing, but studies seem to agree that black (or very dark) cars are more prone to accidents because they are less visible[84] and extreme (artificially created) black is literally invisible to us.[85]

[82] *Id.* at 1097.

[83] But we must recognize that if "matching" is broadly acceptable as a foundation for aesthetic functionality, once a girl buys one Barbie doll, she will want that doll's playmates to match; once a woman buys one Gucci bag with its distinctive red/green/beige stripe, she may want shoes and other accessories to match. *See* Hughes, *supra* note 1, at 1282–84. Matching rationales have been rejected by two important courts in the context of replacement goods. Villeroy & Boch Keramische Werke K.G. v. THC Sys., Inc., 999 F.2d 619 (2d Cir. 1993) (rejecting defendant's argument for aesthetic functionality on the grounds that if it was unable to copy the plaintiff's china patterns it would be unable to provide replacement china to institutions that had made a large initial investment in dinnerware); W.T. Rogers Co. v. Keene, 778 F.2d 334, 343 (7th Cir. 1985) (rejecting the argument that "the décor compatibility of stacked trays requires that any manufacturer of such trays be allowed to use the same shaped end panel as any other").

[84] *See, e.g.*, STUART NEWSTEAD & ANGELO D'ELIA, MONASH UNIV. ACCIDENT RES. CTR, AN INVESTIGATION INTO THE RELATIONSHIP BETWEEN CAR COLOUR AND CRASH RISK 9 (2007) (showing that cars of dark colors—black, blue, green, gray, etc.—are associated with both higher crash risk and higher risk of severe crashes); Pablo Lardelli-Claret et al., *Does Vehicle Color Influence the Risk of Being Passively Involved in a Collision?*, 13 EPIDEMIOLOGY 721 (2002) (study concluding that darker cars such as grey, black, red, and blue have a higher risk of being in a collision).

[85] Ian Johnston, *Blackiest is the Newest Black: Scientists Develop a Material so Dark that You Can't See It*, THE INDEPENDENT, July 12, 2014, http://www.independent.co.uk/news/

Legal professionals need to be cautious in the representation of scientific claims, but if the general point is that our visual and neurological system see black things as "smaller," then this is no different from our visual and neurological system seeing reflective surfaces as brighter; in other words, this part of the *Brunswick* analysis is no different than the 1963 *In re Pollak Steel Company* case in which the reflective area at the top of a farm fence post was held to be a "utilitarian coating" that was "inherently functional."[86]

We can go further and reasonably postulate that some of the responses at issue in "aesthetic" functionality cases are probably the result of evolution and some of the responses are probably the result of acculturation. In the case of the visibility of black objects, it is reasonable to believe that their low impact on our visual and cognitive awareness is the result of evolution. The same may apply to bright orange and yellow being used for extension cords, safety jackets, and hard hats: the attention-attracting power of these colors is just part of how our neurological and sensory systems evolved. In such an "ecological valence" account "color preferences exist to facilitate an organism's adaptive interactions with its environment, guiding it toward ecological objects and situations that would be likely to benefit it, and away from those that would be likely to harm it."[87] And when such a cognitive or perceptual response is the result of such adaptive mechanisms, there will presumably be little "heterogeneity" across people.

In principle, cognitive biases that result from acculturation may be subject to more heterogeneity on the edges or across populations, but they can still have enough consistency in consumer responses for a sound aesthetic functionality claim. A set of such widely shared association(s) produced by acculturation are discussed in the TTAB's 2013 *In re Florists' Transworld Delivery* decision[88] in which the Board found the color black to be aesthetically functional in relation to packaging for floral arrangements because, depending on the circumstances, it would be "associated with stylish or formal events," "in other contexts may connote grief or condolence" and in still other contexts "is a critical color in connection with Halloween displays."[89] The first two of these consumer associations seem *more* (but not completely) universal; the third is *more* (but not uniquely) American. But any one of these acculturated, widespread responses among consumers would have been enough for the TTAB to uphold the Trademark Examiner's conclusion that "there is a competitive need for

science/blackest-is-the-new-black-scientists-have-developed-a-material-so-dark-that-you-cant-see-it-9602504.html

[86] *In re* Pollak Steel Co., 131 U.S.P.Q. 482, 1961 WL 7862, at *1 (T.T.A.B. 1961), *aff'd* 314 F.2d 566 (C.C.P.A. 1963) ("It is obvious from the facts adduced herein that the reflective coating utilized by applicant is inherently functional and that its placement at the uppermost portion of the post conforms to the commonly accepted practice of applying reflecting indicia to road signs and boundary markers for safety and protection purposes. Any device, the immediate aim of which is to serve a functional mission, cannot be granted the legal protection a registration achieves. To do otherwise would enable the registrant to pre-empt others from applying a utilitarian coating in any fashion.").

[87] Karen B. Schloss & Stephen E. Palmer, *Ecological Aspects of Color Preference*, in HANDBOOK OF COLOR PSYCHOLOGY 435 (Andrew J. Eliot, Mark D. Fairchild, and Anna Franklin, eds. 2015).

[88] *In re* Florists' Transworld Delivery, Inc., 106 U.S.P.Q.2d 1784.

[89] *Id.* at 1789.

others in the industry to use the color black in connection with floral arrangements and flowers."[90]

Similarly, in the 1989 New Jersey district court case *Warner Lambert Co. v. McCrory's Corp.*,[91] the court found that in the mouthwash market particular colors are strongly associated with particular flavors: an amber colored liquid signifies a medicinal-tasting product, blue signifies peppermint, green signifies mint, and red signifies a cinnamon flavor.[92] Perhaps humans learned long ago to associate particular green tones with mint flavor, but the associations between cinnamon and red (a color which cinnamon is not) and between amber color and medicinal taste are surely more recent and more culturally contingent. The positive associations we have with the color blue may be a matter of evolution[93] as may be darker blues with nighttime (and sleep).[94] In contrast, the perception of blue as a masculine color—versus pink as a feminine color—is a nurtured and fairly recent part of our shared western psychology.[95]

Saying that the cognitive or perceptual response should be "widespread" does not mean that the response needs to be universal among relevant consumers. A cognitive or perceptual response common to a substantial composite of the relevant consumers should be enough; a response common to a quarter of them might be enough. In other words, orange flavoring for medicines that are ingested counts as a pre-existing sensory preference even if a court "cannot definitively say that orange is the most popular flavor" but only that "it certainly would appear on the short list of [the] most popular flavors"[96] that can be mimicked in medicines.

The point of all this is to see that much of what American courts and jurists have labeled "*aesthetic* functionality" involves consumer preferences and responses that manifest perceptual and cognitive biases developed over the long course of evolution and/or acculturation. In contrast, when we ask people their favorite color for

[90] *Id.* at 1791.

[91] Warner Lambert Co., McCrory's Corp., 718 F. Supp. 389 (D.N.J. 1989).

[92] *Id.* at 396.

[93] Kazuhiko Yokosawa, Karen Schloss, et al., *Ecological Effects in Cross-Cultural Differences Between U.S. and Japanese Color Preferences,* 40 Cognitive Science 1590, 1592 (2016) ("people's general liking of blues and cyans can be explained, at least in part, by their positive responses to blue and cyan objects, such as clear sky and clean water"). *See also* Chloe Taylor & Anna Franklin, *The Relationship between Color Preference and Color–Object Associations: Further Investigation of Ecological Valence Theory,* 19 Psychonomic Bulletin & Review 190–97 (2012); Stephen E. Palmer & Karen B. Schloss, *An Ecological Valence Theory of Human Color Preference,* 107 (19) Proceedings of the National Academy of Sciences 8877–82 (2010); I.C. McManus, A.L. Jones, & J. Cottrell, *The Aesthetics of Color,* 10 Perception 651–66 (1982).

[94] National Institute of General Medical Sciences, *Circadian Rhythms Fact Sheet* ("[r]esearchers have already identified genes that direct circadian rhythms in people"), https://www.nigms.nih.gov/Education/Pages/Factsheet_CircadianRhythms.aspx (last visited Apr. 4, 2017).

[95] Jo B. Paoletti, Pink and Blue: Telling the Boys from the Girls in America (2012); Susan Stamberg, *Girls Are Taught To "Think Pink," But That Wasn't Always So,* NPR (Apr. 1, 2014, 3:08 AM), http://www.npr.org/2014/04/01/297159948/girls-are-taught-to-think-pink-but-that-wasnt-always-so (describing temporary show at the Boston Museum of Fine Arts showing male use and identification with pink at different points before World War II).

[96] *In re* N.V. Organon, 79 U.S.P.Q.2d 1639, 2006 WL 1723556 at *8 (T.T.A.B. 2006).

personal clothing, the heterogeneity we associate with true aesthetic choices comes to the fore—some people prefer red, some green; for some, orange is the new black.

VII. Applying these Principles

A series of examples, both cases and hypotheticals, may be the best way to understand the proposal that aesthetic functionality should apply best when *the product feature appeals to reasonably specific cognitive, psychological, or aesthetic biases or preferences that are widespread among consumers and that exist regardless of (and prior to) anything the trademark creator or owner has done.*

Imagine that a company claimed trademark protection for some trade dress predominantly in the form of a red octagon, either as the dominant figure on paper wrapping product packaging or perhaps as the shape and color of a bottle—and that they sought this trademark for a pesticide. It's reasonable to think that red octagonal shapes are cognitively functional in relation to products that promise to *halt* or *arrest* something (weeds, termites, dandruff, lice)—because consistent road signage in the United States since the 1920s (and now globally) has conditioned people to associate red octagons with stopping something. This recognition of red octagons is widespread and would predate the efforts of any party claiming trademark rights. Similarly, if a company sought to trademark a glass slipper shape, either as a bottle for a sparkling wine or as serving glasses, it would, again, be reasonable to think the shape is aesthetically functional because of a wide-spread, pre-existing association of drinking champagne from a "slipper."

Contrast these examples with a product feature that was once mechanically functional but became purely aesthetic: the Lincoln Mark trunk "hump." From 1958 through the 1980s, Ford Motor Company marketed the Lincoln Continental "Mark" series with a distinctive "trunklid spare-tire hump," although there was no longer a spare tire underneath and the feature was purely stylistic.[97] There is no question that this was distinctive of the Lincoln Continental "Mark" cars, but it is also true that there was a market for "Continental kits,"[98] that were sold to consumers in order to retro-fit Thunderbirds, Cadillacs, and other cars with humped trunk lids—suggesting at least some aesthetic preference for humped trunk lids.

Does consumer demand for these "kits" establish that the trunk hump was "aesthetically functional"? I think the answer has to be no—on the grounds that this aesthetic preference did not exist until Ford established it. This sort of fact pattern occurred in *Truck Equipment Services Co. v. Fruehauf*[99] in which the plaintiff had

[97] *Lincoln Continental*, WIKIPEDIA, http://en.wikipedia.org/wiki/Lincoln_Continental_Mark_VI (last visited Aug. 2, 2017). My thanks to Dean Weber, archivist at Ford Motor Company for discussions on the history of the trunklid "hump" in the Continental Mark series.

[98] *Continental Mark II*, WIKIPEDIA, http://en.wikipedia.org/wiki/Continental_Mark_II (last visited Aug. 2, 2017). For car enthusiasts, there is a long history in how Ford branded and sold Lincolns versus Continentals, but Ford Motor Company's Continental division was later absorbed into its Lincoln division so that "Lincoln" became the house brand and "Continental" or "Continental Mark V" became the product brand.

[99] Truck Equip. Servs. Co. v. Fruehauf Corp., 536 F.2d 1210 (8th Cir. 1976).

created a uniquely shaped grain trailer and "[t]he appearance of the trailer was intended to be its selling point."[100] In that case, the Eighth Circuit panel considered only a utilitarian functionality analysis and easily concluded that the copied aspects of the grain trailer were not functional.[101] But if the defendant had claimed that it needed to copy the "sloping-end walls" of the plaintiff's grain trailers because grain trailer operators found that shape beautiful, the court should have reached the same result—because grain trailer operators' preferences for that shape did not pre-exist the trademark holder's efforts.

As I have said, for a sound aesthetic functionality defense the pre-existing aesthetic response among consumers must also be fairly *specific* in relation to the claimed mark. We cannot bar *beautiful* trademarks on the grounds that consumers have a general predisposition for the beautiful, no matter what the Supreme Court has said about a "touch of beauty."[102] Consider the treatment of aesthetic functionality in the 2013 *Apple v. Samsung* litigation.[103] The evidence showed that Apple had chosen the design of the iPhone for aesthetic reasons and that "the beauty of the iPhone [wa]s a factor in its success."[104] On this basis, Samsung argued—in *Pagliero* style—that the iPhone design was aesthetically functional. The court rejected this argument not on doctrinal grounds, but on the grounds that elsewhere in the case Samsung had argued just the opposite—that "few consumers are motivated by design considerations such as aesthetics."[105] On the basis of "the limited role of aesthetics in purchasing decisions," the court found that "Samsung did not need to infringe Apple's trade dress in order to compete with the iPhone."[106]

The implication is that if aesthetics played a larger role in smartphone purchasing decisions (as many of us think is true), Samsung could have "need[ed] to infringe Apple's trade dress in order to compete with the iPhone."[107] But aesthetic functionality is not concerned when some particular design is *one* of *many ways* to meet a *general* consumer aesthetic for things of beauty. Aesthetic functionality should bar protection of the iPhone shape only when we can say that before the iPhone existed consumers had a pre-existing bias *for that particular shape.*

Another example of the appropriate specificity in consumer tastes is *Maker's Mark Distillery, Inc. v. Diageo North America, Inc.*,[108] a 2012 decision concerning Jose Cuervo's imitation of Maker's Mark's distinct red dripping wax covering the cap and neck of its bourbon bottles. Maker's Mark had applied red dripping wax to its bottles since 1958 and had received a federal trademark registration in 1985 for the trade dress.[109] Accepting that Maker's Mark[110] had succeeded in making the dripping

[100] *Id.* at 1218.

[101] The court concluded "[t]he evidence is consistent with the conclusion that the sloping-end walls of the Cornhusker 800, arbitrarily designed for the purpose of identification, were no more than merely incidentally functional." *Id.*

[102] Qualitex Co. v. Jacobson Prods. Co., Inc., 514 U.S. 159, 170 (1995).

[103] Apple, Inc. v. Samsung Elecs. Co., Ltd., 920 F. Supp. 2d 1079 (N.D. Cal. 2013).

[104] *Id.* at 1096. [105] *Id.* [106] *Id.* [107] *Id.*

[108] Maker's Mark Distillery, Inc. v. Diageo N. Am., Inc., 679 F.3d 410 (6th Cir. 2012).

[109] USPTO registration 1370465; *Maker's Mark Distillery, Inc.*, 679 F.3d at 417. During the litigation with Diageo, Maker's Mark stipulated that it only sought to protect the trade dress in relation to red colored wax. *Id.*

[110] *Id.* at 414.

red wax top into "one of the most recognizable branding symbols in the world."[111] The Sixth Circuit upheld the trial court's order enjoining Cuervo "from using red dripping wax on the cap of a bottle in the sale, offering for sale, distribution or advertising of Cuervo tequila products . . . ."[112]

What is useful for us is that the *Maker's Mark* litigation points out how an aesthetic functionality problem can depend on the *breadth* of trademark protection being claimed. Sealing a bottle with wax is certainly *aesthetically attractive* and dripping wax may suggest that a product is *old, old-fashioned*, or *traditional*—and these are consumer responses that presumably predate Maker's Mark's commercial activities. But in *Maker's Mark*, the plaintiff stipulated that it only sought to protect its trade dress as *red dripping* wax. This allowed both the district court and the appellate court to rebuff Cuervo's aesthetic functionality claim on market competition grounds that "[t]here is more than one way to seal a bottle with wax to make it look appealing."[113] And the plaintiff's stipulation also distinguished between a general, pre-existing aesthetic response among consumers and the consumer response that Maker's Mark had engendered through over half a century of marketing.[114]

VIII. Conclusion

The principles for aesthetic functionality proposed in this chapter have not been explicitly announced by courts, but I would argue that these principles are consistent with and implicit in that case law. When the unanimous Court in *Qualitex* opined that their view of aesthetic would "not discourage firms from creating esthetically pleasing mark designs, for it is open to their competitors to do the same,"[115] they envisioned that trademark owners would continue to develop new aesthetic tastes and preferences among consumers: when a trademark is appealing because it relies on such *developed* aesthetics, there should be no danger to the trademark rights.

Similarly, in the Ninth Circuit's 2006 *Au-Tomotive Gold v. Volkswagen* decision,[116] the defendant was copying the VOLKSWAGEN and AUDI trademarks for automobile accessories such as license plate frames and key chains. The court recognized that these products met the broad *Pagliero* standard in that consumers purchased the products *for the trademarks*, but also understood that this was a situation in which "consumer demand is difficult to quarantine from the source identification and reputation-enhancing value of the trademarks themselves."[117] The Ninth Circuit withheld application of aesthetic functionality, noting "[i]n practice, aesthetic functionality has been limited to product features that serve an aesthetic purpose wholly

[111] *Id.* at 421 (quoting a *Business Week* article from 2002).

[112] *Id.* at 417.

[113] *Id.* at 418. The court added that "red wax is not the only pleasing color of wax . . . nor does it put competitors at a significant non-reputation related disadvantage to be prevented from using red dripping wax." *Id.* at 418–19 (alteration in original).

[114] *See* Hughes, *supra* note 1, at 1279–82.

[115] Qualitex Co. v. Jacobson Prods. Co., Inc., 514 U.S. 159, 170 (citation omitted).

[116] Au-tomotive Gold, Inc. v. Volkswagen of Am., Inc., 457 F.3d 1062 (9th Cir. 2006).

[117] *Id.* at 1073.

independent of any source-identifying function."[118] That requirement—"an aesthetic purpose *wholly independent* of any source-identifying function"—indicates that the widespread consumer preference would predate the efforts of the trademark owner (or its predecessors in interest).[119]

The observation that the best examples of aesthetic functionality are based on cognitive or psychological biases allows us to understand that the *doctrine* of "aesthetic functionality" does not suffer much from the heterogeneity of true *aesthetics*. Recognizing that aesthetic functionality should be based on consumer biases/preferences that are widespread before the trademark owner begins its commercial efforts allows us to avoid the troubling reasoning of *Pagliero* and its ilk. Both of these principles can be used in conjunction with a court's market competition analysis to reach a sounder conclusion when a defendant claims the trademark at issue is "aesthetically functional."

Thus, widespread consumer preference for pancake syrup that is golden-colored, for outboard motors that look smaller than they really are, and for roof vents that match roof tiles form the basis for sound application of aesthetic functionality. In contrast, aesthetic functionality does not properly apply to consumer tastes cultivated by trademark holders, whether for interlocking Gs on handbags, certain cartoon characters on t-shirts, or particular shapes of grain trailers or the trunks of luxury automobiles. An aesthetic response in consumers that is the result of the trademark holder's efforts is not the stuff of aesthetic functionality, but rather the stuff of modern marketing.

[118] *Id.* at 1073. [119] *Id.*

6

Should Trademark Law Protect Non-Traditional Trademarks?

A Look at How Marketing Practices Try to Capture Essences

*Deven Desai**

I. Introduction

Why not?[1] That question taunts trademark law and scholarship. That is, trademark law, by design, rarely limits the subject matter eligible for protection under trademark law.[2] Trademark law, at least in the U.S., is the handmaiden of corporate and competition law, neither of which places much limit on the behavior of traders.[3] Instead, those areas of law defer to the individual commercial enterprise[4] as the best

* I, and this chapter, have benefitted from discussions with and input from attendees at the Workshop, The Protection of Non-Traditional Trademarks: Critical Perspectives 2017, at Singapore Management University, School of Law and attendees at IP Scholars 2017 at Cardozo School of Law. In addition, I am indebted to Martin Senftleben and Irene Calboli for their guidance on the beginning of these ideas and their excellent feedback during the writing of this chapter. The views expressed herein are those of the author alone and do not necessarily reflect the view of those who helped with and supported this work.

[1] *Cf.* Qualitex Co. v. Jacobsen Products Co., 514 U.S. 159, 162 (1995) ("If a shape, a sound, and a fragrance can act as symbols why, one might ask, can a color not do the same? ... Again, one might ask, if trademark law permits a descriptive word with secondary meaning to act as a mark, why would it not permit a color, under similar circumstances, to do the same? We cannot find in the basic objectives of trademark law any obvious theoretical objection to the use of color alone as a trademark, where that color has attained 'secondary meaning' and therefore identifies and distinguishes a particular brand (and thus indicates its 'source')"); *see also* Ann Bartow, *The True Colors of Trademark Law: Greenlighting a Red Tide of Anti-Competition Blues*, 97 Ky. L. J. 263, 270 (2008–09) ("The Court framed the question as 'Why not?' "); ANNETTE KUR & MARTIN SENFTLEBEN, EUROPEAN TRADEMARK LAW § 1.29 (2017) (noting the lack of clear policy objective for expanded protection of trademarks).

[2] *See* Deven R. Desai, *The Chicago School Trap in Trademark: The Co-Evolution of Corporate, Antitrust, and Trademark Law*, 37 Cardozo L. Rev. 551 (2015); *cf.* Bartow, *supra* note 1, at 263 ("The elevation of color to stand–alone trademark status illustrates the unbounded nature of trademarks within the judicial consciousness.").

[3] *See* Desai, *supra* note 2.

[4] *Id.* Although I believe matters of the firm as conceptualized in Chicago School economics drive much of the current shape of trademark law, I use the term "enterprise" in this chapter as that term fits with non-U.S., and especially European trademark vocabulary. I thank Martin Senftleben for alerting me to this point of language.

place to determine what to do in a market, and they defer to markets to discipline the various commercial players in general.[5] As such, when enterprises, often through their marketing departments, pursue new ways of developing and selling goods and services, trademark law has been more than happy to sanction such practices with the force of law.[6] That has happened even when a given practice or outcome strays far from trademark law's alleged search costs foundation.[7] The question "Why not?" reflects this deferential posture. This chapter looks at marketing practices behind the signs that enterprises may claim as non-traditional trademarks and asks whether there are good reasons not to protect those signs as non-traditional marks under trademark law. Even if such reasons exist, given policy's practice of deference to and protection of the latest marketing practices suggests that protection will persist. If so, lawsuits and doctrinal debates will be where limits might appear, but only after great cost to enterprises and consumers.

II. The Brand Imperative, Essences, and Non-Traditional Marks

To understand a given trademark protection, we must start by understanding the branding practice that the protection covers. Design, which encompasses the subject matter of non-traditional trademarks, is an integral part of branding.[8] Non-traditional marks are in essence marks other than word marks and logos, but that definition understates the range of design practices behind what non-traditional marks encompass.[9] Packaging (aka trade dress), sound, smell, color, taste, texture, motion, and even hologram marks have been granted trademark protection and are considered examples of non-traditional trademarks.[10] It would be easy to think that as countries, via legislation, and courts, via case law, protected non-traditional marks, enterprises—via their marketers—might have had more incentive to

[5] *Id.* at 554 (arguing that Chicago School approach to law and economics vaunts "the autonomy of the firm and maximizing total welfare rather than consumer protection and wealth distribution").

[6] *See* Deven R. Desai, *From Trademark to Brands*, 64 Fla. L. Rev. 981 (2012).

[7] *See* Desai, *supra* note 2.

[8] *See e.g.*, Jordi Montaña, Francisco Guzmán, & Isa Moll, *Branding and Design Management: A Brand Design Management Model*, 23 J. Mktg. Mgmt., 829, 829 (2007) ("Design is an unequivocal source of differentiation and has become a key element for branding . . . because design may serve as the cohesive factor for all elements that configure a brand experience."); Michael B. Beverland, *Managing the Design Innovation–Brand Marketing Interface: Resolving the Tension between Artistic Creation and Commercial Imperatives*, 22 J. Prod. Innov. Mgmt. 193, 193 (2005) (noting importance of design for competitiveness and to "revitalize brands"); *cf.* Desai, *supra* note 6, at 983 ("Brands are regulated by trademark law, which fails to grasp that trademarks are merely a subset of brands and that it manages brands at all.").

[9] *See* Melissa E. Roth, *Something Old, Something Borrowed, Something Blue: A New Tradition in Nontraditional Trademark Registrations*, 27 Cardozo. L. Rev. 457, 458 n. 11 (2005); Jerome Gilson & Anne Gilson LaLonde, *Cinnamon Buns, Marching Ducks, and Cherry Scented Car Exhaust: Protecting Non-Traditional Trademarks*, 95 Trademark Rep. 773, 774 (2005); Christopher George, Shane Hardy, Casey Mangan, & Allan Poulter, The Explosion of Non-Traditional Trademarks at 6, ACC 2013 Annual Meeting (Oct. 27–30, 2013), http://www.acc.com/_cs_upload/vl/membersonly/ProgramMaterial/1355635_1.pdf.

[10] *See* Roth, *supra* note 9; Gilson & Gilson LaLonde, *supra* note 9.

pursue and develop innovations around color, smell, and shapes, and to compete and distinguish their goods and services in the marketplace. That view inverts and misunderstands the dynamic.

Enterprises have been innovating and will continue to innovate marketing and related branding techniques regardless of legal protection for those developments.[11] Design is part of branding, and enterprises use branding to compete. Branding allows enterprises to move beyond the four Ps—product, price, place, and promotion—and to develop a personality or identity that connects management, employees, consumers, and the media.[12] Thus a goal of branding is to differentiate one's offering to such an extent that the fifth P is something that competitors cannot copy.[13] Put differently, if competing based on the four Ps, an enterprise faces the problem of competing with others who are selling essentially the same goods.[14] That strategy ends up in a price war—what Michael Porter says "any fool can do"[15]—and that is the exact opposite of differentiation, which he and others espouse as smart competitive strategy.[16] The differentiation problem dates from the end of the 1800s to today.[17] And by at least the 1970s, design of products *and of packaging* became vital for enterprises trying to differentiate their offerings as a way to attract consumers.[18] As one example, Master Lock had a patent that protected its market position; but once the patent expired, new, low-cost entrants competed over making locks.[19] To combat the challenge, Master Lock used "a design-focused approach to uncover opportunities for segmentation and market differentiation."[20]

Design works in two, complementary ways. Good design or "aesthetically pleasing" design helps capture consumer attention *and* "may [also] serve as the cohesive factor for all elements that configure a brand experience."[21] Many factors and questions beyond source identification go into the end product. As one study explained, product designers must understand whether "aesthetics, ease of use, technical quality, or features are most important in the brand choice for the target group of consumers," as they decide on "product shape, colors, materials,

[11] *See e.g.*, Philip Kotler & G. Alexander Rath, *Design: A Powerful But Neglected Strategic Tool*, 5 J. Bus. Strategy 16, 16, 21 (1984) (stating the importance of design as source of competitive advantage and calling for greater emphasis on exploiting that possibility).

[12] *See* Desai, *supra* note 6, at 995.

[13] *Id.*

[14] Liz Moor, The Rise of Brands 26–27 (2007).

[15] Michael E. Porter, Competitive Advantage: Creating and Sustaining Superior Performance 501 (1985); *see also* Deven R. Desai & Spencer Waller, *Brands, Competition, and the Law*, 2010 BYU L. Rev. 1425, 1465–67 (2010) (comparing Chicago School focus on price theory to business practices and strategy views on price).

[16] Michael E. Porter, Competitive Strategy: Techniques for Analyzing Industries & Competitors 21–22, 170–71 (1980).

[17] Moor, *supra* note 14.

[18] *See* Abbie Griffin & John R. Hauser, *Integrating Marketing and R&D: A Review and Analysis of the Literature*, 13 J. Prod. Innov. Mgmt. 191, 192 (1996) (noting practice of combining research on design with marketing is not new; but has been growing since the 1970s); Celia Lury, Brands: The New Logos of the Global Economy 20–22 (2004); *see also* Marcel Danesi, Brands 60–67 (2006) (noting product and package designs' importance to the automobile, perfume, and tobacco industries).

[19] *See* Gabriella Lojacono & Gianfranco Zaccai, *The Evolution of the Design-Inspired Enterprise*, 45 MIT Sloan Mgmt. Rev. 75, 77–78 (2004).

[20] *Id.*

[21] *See* Montaña, Guzmán, & Moll, *supra* note 8, at 829.

and configuration"—the subject matter trademark law might deem non-traditional trademarks—for the offering.[22] Put simply, design and marketing work together.[23]

Design is not an afterthought; it is a core part of marketing and branding. Enterprises study what aspect of design will appeal to consumers, and enterprises seek to exploit that finding, because "design functions as a prior media to influence product and brand categorisation and to shape consumer beliefs about products and brands."[24] One literature review of "Product Appearance and Consumer Evaluation" offers that "If all the roles mentioned in the literature are considered as a whole, the following six roles of product appearance for consumers can be distinguished: (1) communication of aesthetic; (2) symbolic; (3) functional; (4) ergonomic product information; (5) attention drawing; and (6) categorization."[25] Or as one designer put it, "Designers are well aware of [] innate attitudes, and product design reflects" that awareness. [26] When possible, designers seek out designs that "seem to be innate and common to most human beings—for example, the affinity for symmetry."[27] As a specific example, color is noted as a "critical" part of driving consumer decision-making at the point of purchase.[28]

In general, companies "select features, such as shapes, forms, colours, materials, surfaces, textures, graphical elements, and logos on the basis of their 'plain' attractiveness and simply use them repeatedly to create recognition."[29] Or enterprises may look to "value-based design cues" that fit an enterprise's brand such as oval grillwork or V-shapes to build an overall brand image.[30] Thus BMW uses general aesthetics such as "strong shapes and dynamic forms" to "clearly communicate the BMW values of power and performance, equating making BMW cars to 'ultimate driving machines,' as the brand slogan has suggested."[31] In addition, some branding experts have argued that branding efforts must go further and use smell, taste, and touch to engage in "multisensory branding" that deepens the emotional connection between brand and consumer.[32] Despite all these efforts, some consumers may seek products that match the aesthetics of products they already own, and so "Consumers may like a product's appearance but may not buy it because it does not fit aesthetically with their home interior."[33]

[22] Mariëlle E.H. Creusen & Jan P.L. Schoormans, *The Different Roles of Product Appearance in Consumer Choice*, 22 J. Prod. Innov. Mgmt. 63, 77 (2005).

[23] See Beverland, *supra* note 8, at 193, 196 ("[Both] designers and marketers agree that design must be integrated with other business functions or, at the very least, guided by the brand's position").

[24] Toni-Matti Karjalainen, *It Looks Like a Toyota: Educational Approaches to Designing for Visual Brand Recognition*, 1 Int'l J. Design, 67, 67 (2007).

[25] Creusen & Schoormans, *supra* note 22, at 65.

[26] Guido Stompff, *The Forgotten Bond: Brand Identity and Product Design*, 14 Design Mgmt. J. 26, 29 (2003).

[27] *Id.*; Creusen & Schoormans, *supra* note 22.

[28] Lawrence L. Garber, Jr., Raymond Burke, & J. Morgan Jones, *The Role of Package Color in Consumer Purchase Consideration and Choice*, Mktg. Sci. Inst. (2000), http://152.33.80.122/lgarber/misc/garber-package-color-consumer-choice.pdf.

[29] Karjalainen, *supra* note 24, at 68. [30] *Id.* at 68–69. [31] *Id.* at 68.

[32] Gilson & Gilson LaLonde, *supra* note 9, at 775.

[33] Creusen & Schoormans, *supra* note 22, at 65–66.

In short, the very things that might receive protections as non-traditional trademarks can hardly be qualified as non-traditional from a marketing perspective; they are vital and the current frontier.[34] If a shape, color, material, texture, smell, taste, or combination thereof attracts and speaks to a consumer group, enterprises will pursue this insight into consumer preferences and use it strategically. Marketers have developed design ranging from product shape to packaging, smell, taste, touch, and more in an effort to differentiate products and build brands so that, in the end, consumers are connected to the offerings of a particular enterprise and less likely to switch to goods of a competitor. The very design and branding practices that have developed over the past decades correspond rather well to the various types of non-traditional marks, which trademark laws embrace and some scholars question.

III. Trademark Laws Embracing Non-Traditional Marks

The pattern of protecting the brand experience, which enterprises develop as part of attracting and retaining consumers, has deep roots in U.S. trademark law and more recently in European trademark law.[35] This section sets out the ways in which different trademark laws embrace non-traditional marks.

Although many point to the U.S. Supreme Court's decision in *Qualitex v. Jacobsen Products* as the font of expansion and perhaps dubious protection of non-traditional marks, trademark law, by its nature, is the most permissive branch of intellectual property. Hence, it does not come as a surprise that protection of non-traditional marks occurs and continues to expand.[36] Even before the Lanham Act, the U.S. Supreme Court explained:

> The protection of trade-marks is the law's recognition of the psychological function of symbols. If it is true that we live by symbols, it is no less true that we purchase goods by them. A trademark is a merchandising short-cut which induces a purchaser to select what he wants, *or what he has been led to believe he wants*. The owner of a mark exploits this human propensity by making every effort to impregnate the atmosphere of the market with the drawing power of a congenial symbol. Whatever the means employed, the aim is the same—to convey through the mark, in the minds of potential customers, the desirability of the commodity upon which it appears. Once this is attained, the trade-mark owner has something of value.[37]

[34] *See e.g.*, Gilson & Gilson LaLonde, *supra* note 9 ("Under the Lindstrom teaching, using nontraditional trademarks and other off-beat stimuli to differentiate and reinforce a brand is imperative. Brand owners must pursue multisensory ways to entice consumers and get their message across.").

[35] Desai, *supra* note 6, at 1009–26; Willajeanne F. McLean, *Protecting Unconventional Trademarks in the European Union and the United States*, *in* THE GLOBAL CHALLENGE OF INTELLECTUAL PROPERTY RIGHTS 177 (Robert C. Bird & Subhash C. Jain eds., 2008) (noting European historical hostility toward trademark law as a prop for advertising practices).

[36] *Cf.* Desai, *supra* note 2; Robert Bone, *Trademark Functionality Reexamined*, 7 J. LEGAL ANALYSIS 183, 184 (2015) ("[A]ny kind of symbol can qualify for protection as long as it is capable of identifying source, including subject matter within the domains of patent and copyright.").

[37] Mishawaka Rubber & Woolen Mfg. Co. v. S.S. Kresge Co., 316 U.S. 203, 205 (1942) (emphasis added).

The logic is clear. Symbols drive how we live, including how we purchase. Consumers are "induced" to make purchases, and marketers make "every effort to impregnate the atmosphere of the market with the drawing power of a congenial symbol." Marketers pursue all manners of creating the buying impulse, and if they succeed, trademark law is supposed to protect such efforts.

The main change has been in seeing that the way in which marketers "impregnate the atmosphere of the market" as they build "the drawing power of a congenial symbol" encompasses far more than words and logos. This understanding supports the protection of non-traditional marks even before the Lanham Act's expansive language was in place.[38] It is debatable whether, at the time the above passage was published, in 1942, non-traditional trademarks would have fared well.[39] Nonetheless just a few years later the definition of trademark enshrined in the Lanham Act had language tracking this view and that would support trademark law's embrace of non-traditional trademarks over time.

Passed in 1946, the Lanham Act defines a trademark expansively to include, "any word, name, symbol, or device, or any combination thereof."[40] Almost fifty years later, the Supreme Court echoed its view from 1942 and the legislature's in 1946, "[s]ince human beings might use as a 'symbol' or 'device' almost anything at all that is capable of carrying meaning, this language, read literally, is not restrictive."[41] As long as part of that meaning is "source-distinguishing," the type of symbol does not matter.[42] Thus it was no surprise that trademark law had protected a shape (the Coca-Cola bottle), a sound (the NBC chimes), and a scent (plumeria for thread) over the years, and so "why, one might ask, can a color not do the same?"[43] European law has converged on a somewhat similar approach to trademark protection.

In the European Union (EU), what began as skepticism and "a hostile attitude" toward trademarks as ways to support advertising has shifted to an embrace of trademarks and broad view of what can act as a trademark.[44] Current trademark legislation in EU Member States and at EU level recognizes the broad range of symbols—or in those laws' language, signs—capable of operating as a trademark. This approach corresponds with the view taken in the U.S. and the international harmonization reached in the Agreement on Trade-Related Aspects of Intellectual

[38] *See* 15 U.S.C. § 1127 ("The term 'trademark' includes any word, name, symbol, or device, or any combination thereof)"; *accord, Qualitex, supra* note 1, 162.

[39] *See, e.g.*, Lars Smith, *Trade Distinctiveness: Solving Scalia's Tertium Quid Trade Dress Conundrum*, 2005 MICH. ST. L. REV. 243; Glynn S. Lunney, Jr., *The Trade Dress Emperor's New Clothes: Why Trade Dress Does Not Belong on the Principal Register*, 51 HASTINGS L. J. 1131 (2000); but see Desai, *supra* note 6, at 1023–26 (arguing that "the history of trade dress practices as brand practices" shows that trademark law adapted to embrace and protect those practices as they grew); Bone, *supra* note 36, at 242 (arguing such protection has been present in some form for 130 years).

[40] *See supra* note 38.

[41] *Qualitex, supra* note 1, 162.

[42] *Id.* at 164 (rejecting the idea that a mark's "ontological status as color, shape, fragrance, word, or sign" dictates whether a mark works as desired by trademark law).

[43] *Id.* at 162; *but see* Michael B. Sapherstein, *The Trademark Registrability of the Harley-Davidson Roar: A Multimedia Analysis*, BC INTELL. PROP. & TECH. F. 101, 102 (1998) (as of 1998 "23 of the more than 729,000 trademarks in force in the United States are sounds. And, since 1946, there have only been 71 applications to register sounds as trademarks or service marks.").

[44] *See* McLean, *supra* note 35.

Property Rights.[45] In addition, changes in European trademark legislation indicate a shift to embracing more protection for not only non-traditional trademarks but also branding efforts in general. Nonetheless, the way in which courts have interpreted trademark protection legislation may indicate ways in which European trademark law has and will limit the ability to register non-traditional trademarks.

Sound, color, smell, touch, taste, hologram, and movement marks can technically qualify for European trademark protection. Unlike the U.S., however, there have been stronger limits on the ability to register such marks. Prior to the recent amendment of EU trademark legislation, a non-traditional mark had to be a sign, capable of graphical representation, and able to distinguish the goods or services of the claimant from the goods or services of competitors.[46]

The graphical representation requirement posed a strong barrier to some non-traditional trademark registrations. If one tried to register, for example, a smell, graphical representation and the sort of desired precision that such representation was supposed to enable, was (and currently still is) a practical impossibility.[47] This was the result of the *Sieckmann* case where the Court of Justice of the European Union (CJEU) established specific representation requirements, namely that the representation be "clear, precise, self-contained, easily accessible, intelligible, durable and objective."[48] Thus color registrations were not impossible, but had to be precise under the standards. When Cadbury submitted a registration for the color purple as "applied to the whole visible surface, or being the predominant colour applied to the whole visible surface, of the packaging of the goods," the England and Wales Court of Appeal rejected the claim as overbroad and ambiguous to such an extent that it encompassed too many purple marks and shades of purple.[49] The use of Pantone numbers and

[45] *See* Agreement on Trade-Related Aspects of Intellectual Property Rights, Apr. 15, 1994, Marrakesh Agreement Establishing the World Trade Organization, Annex 1C, 1869 U.N.T.S. 299, 33 I.L.M. 1197 (1994) art. 15(1) [hereinafter TRIPS]. The definition in the EU legislation is provided for in art. 3 of the Council Directive 2015/2436 of the European Parliament and of the Council of 16 Dec. 2015 to approximate the laws of the Member States relating to trademarks, 2015 O.J. L336/1 [hereinafter TMD 2015] and art. 4 of the Regulation (EU) 2017/1001 of the European Parliament and of the Council of 14 June 2017 on the EU trade mark, 2017 O.J. L154/1 (EC) [hereinafter EUTM Regulation 2017]. This definition reads:

> A trade mark may consist of any signs, in particular words, including personal names, or designs, letters, numerals, colours, the shape of goods or of the packaging of goods, or sounds, provided that such signs are capable of:
>
> a) distinguishing the goods or services of one undertaking from those of other undertakings; and
> b) being represented on the register in a manner which enables the competent authorities and the public to determine the clear and precise subject matter of the protection afforded to its proprietor.

[46] *See* Case C-273/00, Sieckmann v. Deutches Patent und Markenamt, 2002 E.C.R. I-11737, ¶ 45–55; accord Carmel Corocan, *Scope and Validity of Nontraditional Trademarks in the EU: Some Recent Developments*, 70(9) INTA Bull. (2015), https://www.inta.org/INTABulletin/Pages/NontraditionalTrademarksintheEU_7009.aspx; Neha Mishra, *Registration of Non-Traditional Marks*, 13 J. Intell. Prop. Rts. 43, 44 (2008) (noting the power of the graphical representation test in *Sieckmann*).

[47] *See Sieckmann, supra* note 46; Corocan, *supra* note 46.

[48] *See Sieckmann, supra* note 46, 55.

[49] Société des Produits Nestlé SA v. Cadbury UK Ltd [2013] E.W.C.A. Civ. 1174 (High Court of Justice of England and Wales—Chancery Division).

applications limited to specific packaging are, however, sufficiently precise to meet the graphical representation requirement.[50] Smell marks for things such as fresh cut grass for tennis balls, beer for dart flights, and roses for tires have been registered prior to the evolution of the aforementioned *Sieckmann* criteria, but they might not have been granted registration after the criteria were in place.[51]

As a general matter, if one follows the precision and perception requirements of the *Sieckmann* criteria, many claims for registration of non-traditional trademarks face difficulties. Proper graphical representation for taste, smell, etc. is difficult to determine. Understanding what one consumer smells as opposed to another is imprecise.[52] The same is true of color perception, taste, and texture. Even in a product packaging case where precision and perception matters should be less complex, the CJEU has stated, "Average consumers are not in the habit of making assumptions about the origin of goods based on the shape of their packaging, in the absence of any graphic or word element."[53] The CJEU has applied this logic to colors as well.[54] Together, these subjective issues muddy the waters for questions of the claimed mark's capacity to distinguish goods or services in the marketplace, the scope of the claim, and for what might be infringing. Nonetheless, recent developments indicate that European trademark law will continue to protect non-traditional trademarks.[55]

A series of cases in the late 2000s and early 2010s created some uncertainty and an opportunity to limit the reach of trademark law.[56] The case that caused much concern, *L'Oreal v. Bellure*, held that simply trying to ride on the coat tails of another's marketing efforts may amount to trademark infringement.[57] The CJEU held in L'Oréal that the exclusive rights granted in trademark law are supposed:

> to enable the trade mark proprietor to protect his specific interests as proprietor, that is, to ensure that the trade mark can fulfill its functions and that, therefore, the exercise of that right must be reserved to cases in which a third party's use of the sign affects or is liable to affect the functions of the trade mark. These functions include not only the essential function of the trade mark, which is to guarantee to consumers the origin of the goods or services, but also its

[50] Corocan, *supra* note 46 ("the Pantone Red 18.1663TP applied to the sole of high heeled shoes [Case T-631/14 Roland SE v. OHIM, 2015 EURLex 62014TJ0631]; or a description of a color or combination of colors applied to the shape of goods, for example, the color combination green and yellow applied to agricultural machinery [Case T137/ 08 BCS SpA v. OHIM, 2009 E.C.R. II 04047], does not face particular problems.").

[51] Mishra, *supra* note 46. [52] *Id.*

[53] Case C-218/01, Henkel v. DPMA, 2004 E.C.R. I-01725, ¶ 52.

[54] Case C-104/01, Libertel Groep v. Benelux-Merkenbureau, 2003 E.C.R. I-03793, ¶¶ 65–66. *See also* Martin Senftleben, *Public Domain Preservation in EU Trademark Law—A Model for Other Regions?*, 103 Trademark Rep. 775, 801–02 (2013) (explaining exclusions that work to protect the public domain in EU trademark law).

[55] *See, e.g.*, Martin Senftleben, *Trade Mark Protection—A Black Hole in the Intellectual Property Galaxy*, 42 Int'l Rev. Intell. Prop. & Competition L. 383 (2011) (illustrating that Martin Senftleben's work calling trade mark protection "A Black Hole" captures the seemingly one-way direction trademark law has been on, and I argue here that Professor Senftleben's prediction is further supported by the EU's approach to non-traditional and traditional marks).

[56] *See, e.g., id.* [57] *See* Case C-487/07, L'Oréal v. Bellure, 2009 E.C.R. I-05185, ¶ 49.

other functions, *in particular that of guaranteeing the quality of the goods or services in question and those of communication, investment or advertising.*[58]

The CJEU thus identified trademark functions beyond source identification and elevated them, including advertising, to being almost on par with source identification.[59] A later case offers that the investment function relates to the way a trademark is used "to acquire or preserve a reputation capable of attracting consumers and retaining their loyalty."[60] As Professors Annette Kur and Martin Senftleben explain, "the investment function may be concerned where not only advertising but also 'various commercial techniques' are employed when the trade mark is used to acquire or preserve a reputation."[61] In addition, functions beyond the essential function are not only advertising, investment, and communication, but also ("other functions"), which allegedly leaves the door open for further enhancements.[62] As the professors note, there is a lack of clarity as to why functions other than the "essential function" should be protected.[63] I offer that the move to protect branding explains why.

In simple terms, advertising encompasses branding.[64] Branding is about an overall image built in a variety of ways.[65] If one includes the protection of the advertising function in trademark law, protecting a specific instance of advertising and branding as manifested by a range of non-traditional marks should not be surprising; it seems almost required.[66] As the U.S. system might ask, "Why not?" In that sense it appears that European trademark law will continue to embrace greater registration and protection of non-traditional trademarks.

Indeed, at the legislative level European trademark law has moved further toward embracing non-traditional trademarks. For example, new legislation has no

[58] *Id.* ¶ 58 (emphasis added); *accord* Dev Gangjee & Robert Burrell, *Because You're Worth It: L'Oréal and the Prohibition on Free Riding*, 73 MOD. L. REV. 282, 285 (2010); Annette Kur, Lionel Bentley, & Ansgar Ohly, *Sweet Smells and a Sour Taste–The ECJ's L'Oreal Decision*, MAX PLANCK INST. INTELL. PROP., COMPETITION & TAX L. RES. PAPER SERIES No. 09-12, http://ssrn.com/abstract=1492032; Martin Senftleben, *Function Theory and International Exhaustion–Why it is Wise to Confine the Double Identity Rule to Cases Affecting the Origin Function*, 36 EUR. INTELL. PROP. REV. 518 (2013).

[59] *Accord* Gangjee & Burrell, *supra* note 58, at 286.

[60] Case C-323/09, Interflora v. Marks & Spencer, 2011 E.C.R. I-08625, ¶ 60.

[61] ANNETTE KUR & MARTIN SENFTLEBEN, EUROPEAN TRADEMARK LAW § 1.24 (2017) (quoting CJEU, *Interflora, supra* note 60, ¶ 60). Nonetheless, there are signs that European courts wish to limit the potentially runaway nature of the functions approach to trademarks. In one case, the functions approach appears to have limited trademark expansion by holding that the advertising function alone was not enough to sustain a claim of infringement (Case *Interflora, supra* note 60, ¶ 54–66). That case is, however, quite limited to one context, online keyword advertising (*Id.*), and it appears that one has to show no harm to any of the functions to defeat a functions claim (*Id.* at Ruling 1); *accord* KUR AND SENFTLEBEN, *supra* note 61, § 1.26 (if "no adverse effect *on a protected function* could be found, the CJEU employed the function analysis as a tool to dismiss trade mark claims in keyword advertising cases") (emphasis added).

[62] KUR & SENFTLEBEN, *supra* note 61, § 1.25.

[63] *Id.* § 1.29.

[64] *Cf.* Senftleben, *supra* note 58, at 521. ("A strong brand is capable of conveying lifestyle messages that are the result of substantial investment in advertising.").

[65] Desai, *supra* note 6, at 992–99 (discussing ways in which corporations build brands).

[66] *Cf.* Senftleben, *supra* note 58, at 521 ("Protection of communication, investment, and advertising functions is thus protection of the investment in the creation of a favourable brand image and the brand communication based on this image.").

language requiring that non-traditional marks have a graphical representation and instead requires only that the claimed sign be capable of representation "in a manner which enables the competent authorities and the public to determine the clear and precise subject matter of the protection afforded to its proprietor."[67] If one thinks the statutory language might still require graphical representation, the recitals indicate that is not so. Paragraph 10 of the recitals states that a claimed sign can be represented by "in any appropriate form using generally available technology, and thus not necessarily by graphic means."[68] Paragraph 10 nonetheless retains precision ideals in line with the *Sieckmann* decision of the CJEU, by stating that the trademark "representation [must be] clear, precise, self-contained, easily accessible, intelligible, durable and objective."[69] This new language could work to retain some of the practical barriers to non-traditional trademark registration that the graphic representation requirement had.

Yet, questions about how to be clear, what is precise, what is "easily accessible," and objective could work together to expand the approach in place for color marks. Recall that registrations for colors are to be limited by a standard for shades of color as well as being tied to packaging context. One can imagine that registrations for other non-traditional trademarks would face difficulty, or at least much litigation, because it remains an open question what levels of precision, self-containability, accessibility, objectivity, etc. are necessary regardless of dropping the graphical representation requirement. Thus the change may be seen as simply a nod to the way marketers are using techniques that are not easily reduced to graphical representation.[70] That acknowledgement is seemingly neutral, but it also shows a willingness to open the door to more protection and a willingness to sort exactly how to manage types of non-traditional marks on a category-by-category basis.

Other jurisdictions that have also embraced non-traditional marks will likely face problems with administering them, but follow the "Why not" path of more protection rather than less. New Zealand explicitly recognizes some non-traditional marks in its definition of signs eligible for trademark protection as including a brand, color, device, heading, label, letter, name, numeral, shape, signature, smell, sound, taste, ticket, or word; and any combination of signs.[71] This broad concept has also been questioned based on issues of scope and variances in consumer perceptions of things like color and sound.[72] India's trademark law requires graphical representation and so appears likely to track the limits and problems which EU trademark law had under its graphical representation approach.[73] A 2013 survey of more than sixty-five countries showed that many non-EU countries protect some non-traditional marks

[67] EUTM Regulation 2017 art. 4(b). [68] EUTM Regulation 2017, ¶ 10. [69] *Id.*

[70] *Id.* ("A sign should be permitted to be represented in any appropriate form using generally available technology, and thus not necessarily by graphic means . . .").

[71] Trademarks Act of 2002 § 5(1) reprint as at Mar. 1, 2017 (N.Z.).

[72] *See e.g.*, Jacey K. McGrath, *The New Breed of Trade Marks: Sounds, Smells and Tastes*, 32 Victoria Univ. Wellington L. Rev. 277 (2001), http://www.austlii.edu.au/nz/journals/VUWLawRw/2001/11.html.

[73] Mishra, *supra* note 46, at 48–49.

although more than fifteen had little to no protection of such marks.[74] Canada will protect such marks once its trademark law amendment comes into effect.[75] As of 2015, Japan allows non-traditional marks to be registered.[76] From the start the number of applications was high, and at least in the first six months, the rate of applications stayed at levels on par with the U.S. and EU.[77]

It may seem that there are few objections to the protection of non-traditional trademarks, but that is not so. There are answers to "Why not," but whether they can turn the tide of the broad view of trademarks is a different matter.

IV. Current Doctrines Struggle to Unravel What Should or Shouldn't Be Protected

Objections to trademark protection for non-traditional marks take many forms. In the U.S. context, the criticism about protection for colors shows the problems for non-traditional trademark protection in general.[78] Ann Bartow has argued that color protection should not be allowed because of "aesthetic functionality, the related concept of communicative functionality, uncertainty about scope, and color exhaustion" problems.[79] Scope and color exhaustion are practical problems. As one study points out, clearance of color marks for "client use or registration is not easy."[80] Exactly what color is claimed poses problems, because, in contrast to the standard applied in the EU, in the U.S. there is not a required, uniform language for claiming color or a standard, such as the Pantone system, that might at least give some precision as to what color is claimed.[81] Of course, just because two competing enterprises use close, but different Pantones does not mean protecting color will be simple. Whether a color is merely a nice design flourish or operates to identify source will be a continuous source of questions and cause for litigation.[82] Questions

[74] Christopher George, Shane Hardy, Casey Mangan, & Allan Poulter, *The Explosion of Non-Traditional Trademarks: Anon-Traditional Marks: A Country Guide*, at 29 ACC 2013 Annual Meeting (Oct. 27–30, 2013), http://www.acc.com/_cs_upload/vl/membersonly/ProgramMaterial/1355635_1.pdf.

[75] *See* Trademarks Act, R.S.C., 1985, c. T-13, Amendments Not in Force, at 136 (current to Oct. 25, 2017, last amended Sept. 21, 2017) ("'sign' includes a word, a personal name, a design, a letter, a numeral, a colour, a figurative element, a three-dimensional shape, a hologram, a moving image, a mode of packaging goods, a sound, a scent, a taste, a texture and the positioning of a sign (*signe*)"), http://laws-lois.justice.gc.ca/PDF/T-13.pdf (last visited Nov. 11, 2017). I thank Ariel Katz and Carys Craig for their help in understanding the status of this law.

[76] *See* The Act on the Partial Revision of the Patent Act and Other Acts, Act No. 36 of May 14, 2014, https://www.jpo.go.jp/torikumi_e/hiroba_e/hourei_e/patent260514.htm; Outline of the Partial Revision Act (listing expansion of protection to include non-traditional including color and sound), https://www.jpo.go.jp/torikumi_e/hiroba_e/hourei_e/pdf/patent260514/outline.pdf; *accord* John A. Tessensohn, *Non-traditional Trademarks Thriving in Japan*, 11 J. Intell. Prop. L. & Prac. 413 (2014).

[77] Tessensohn, *supra* note 76.

[78] *Cf.* Roth, *supra* note 9, at 784 (arguing *Qualitex* "stands at the apogee of nontraditional trademark protection in the United States" and "will no doubt have a lasting impact on ... nontraditional marks ... for years to come").

[79] *See* Bartow, *supra* note 1, at 264.

[80] Gilson & Gilson LaLonde, *supra* note 9, at 784.

[81] *See* Roth, *supra* note 9, at 476–79; *accord* Gilson & Gilson LaLonde, *supra* note 9, at 784.

[82] Gilson & Gilson LaLonde, *supra* note 9, at 780.

of distinctiveness will run into the same problems.[83] One can imagine two enterprises having color marks for similar, but technically different, shades of pink. The precision of the claims for hypothetically granted marks will not solve whether consumers can tell the difference between the two Pantones such that each functions as source-identifying.

But given the trend to embrace non-traditional marks and the implicit belief that sufficient precision will address practical issues, the practical arguments against protecting non-traditional marks have less traction right now. In U.S. law that leaves aesthetic functionality and communicative functionality as possible objections to protecting non-traditional marks.

Aesthetic functionality, and its related doctrine of functionality, is considered a mess and has a curious history, but the debate can be understood as revolving around whether to protect non-traditional trademarks.[84] The simplest version of the doctrine is that "[i]n general terms, a product feature is functional, and cannot serve as a trademark, if it is essential to the use or purpose of the article or if it affects the cost or quality of the article, that is, if exclusive use of the feature would put competitors at a significant non-reputation-related disadvantage."[85] The rule applies to both utilitarian features and aesthetic ones.[86] Aesthetic issues arise when a claimed trademark "serves a significant non-trademark function—whether to distinguish a heart pill from a digestive medicine or to satisfy the noble instinct for giving the right touch of beauty to common and necessary things, courts will examine whether its use as a mark would permit one competitor (or a group) to interfere with legitimate (not trademark-related) competition."[87] In short, if a feature is deemed aesthetically functional, it will not be granted trademark protection.

And yet there is still the problem of what exactly will be deemed aesthetically functional. Determining whether something should not be protected based on aesthetic functionality poses problems similar to those in determining how to limit the scope of, or whether to, protect colors and other non-traditional trademarks. Returning to protecting color as a trademark, we can see the problems. Ann Bartow has argued that protecting color alone as a trademark poses problems of aesthetic functionality and communicative functionality, and restricts the ability "to communicate social meanings."[88] The specifics of her critique revolve around "uncertainty for competitors," because knowing whether a color will appear the same and be infringing varies, and "the supply of commercially useful colors is fairly limited."[89] The objection to color-alone marks seems, however, to leave open protection for colors

[83] *Id.*

[84] *See e.g.*, Justin Hughes, *Cognitive and Aesthetic Functionality in Trademark Law*, 36 CARDOZO L. REV. 1227, 1229 (2015) (noting criticisms of utilitarian and aesthetic functionality doctrines as "a mess" and "ill-defined") (citations omitted).

[85] *Qualitex, supra* note 1, 165 (1995) (citations omitted); *see also* Case C-205/13, Hauck v. Stokke, 2014 EURLex 62013CJ0205, ¶ 18 (explaining the nature of ban on registering a shape as a mark when the claimed shape is "necessary to obtain a technical result").

[86] *Qualitex, supra* note 1,169–70; *see also* Hughes, *supra* note 84, at 1241–42 (2015) (discussing Justice Breyer's examination of useful or "mechanical" interests as compared to aesthetic issues).

[87] *Qualitex, supra* note 1,170 (citations omitted).

[88] *See* Bartow, *supra* note 1, at 283, 289–90.

[89] *Id.* at 290.

in combination with other things, but combinations still pose problems for what should or should not be given trademark protection.

A recent case in European trademark law tries to unravel what should or should not be protected when protecting non-traditional marks that have multiple elements. In *Hauck v. Stokke* the shape of a child's high chair had been claimed as a trademark.[90] Under EU law one cannot register a sign that consists exclusively of a "shape, or another characteristic, which results from the nature of the goods themselves."[91] At the time of the case, the statute was less broad and applied only to shapes, but the logic applies to the current, broader language.[92] The Court explained that the exclusion must include denying registration when the claimed mark is "a sign which consists exclusively of the shape of a product with one or more essential characteristics which are inherent to the generic function or functions of that product and which consumers may be looking for in the products of competitors."[93] In understanding whether the claim comes under the "nature of the goods analysis," one must "identify the essential characteristics ... on a case-by-case basis" by either looking at the "overall impression produced" or "an examination of each of the components" of the claimed sign.[94] If the claimed shape has "another element, such as a decorative or imaginative element, which is not inherent to the generic function of the goods, [that] plays an important or essential role" rejection based on "nature of the goods analysis" is not proper.[95] This analysis parallels technical or functional necessity concerns in U.S. law.

Another ground for prohibiting registration is that the claimed sign exclusively consists of "the shape, or another characteristic, which gives substantial value to the goods."[96] This inquiry relates to the aesthetic value that may be part of the claimed mark.[97] Because there can be parts that contribute to the claimed shape's value, analysis must look at all the "characteristics" lest essential functional value, for example "safety, comfort and reliability," be captured along with aesthetic value.[98] Thus registration may be denied "to a sign which consists exclusively of the shape of a product with several characteristics each of which may give that product substantial value."[99] Perhaps most important for defeating claims that the advertising, marketing, or communication functions should drive the analysis, the Court further explained that consumer perception "of the shape of that product is only one of the assessment criteria which may be used to determine whether that ground for refusal is applicable."[100]

Although the case offers guidance about what to analyze when determining whether to protect a claim for a non-traditional trademark, exactly how to parse those elements must still be answered. Thus figuring out what are essential elements in this analysis is important.

[90] *Hauck, supra* note 85. [91] EUTM Regulation (EU) art. 7(e)(i).

[92] *Hauck, supra* note 85, ¶ 3. I thank Martin Senftleben for pointing me to the change in the statute.

[93] *Id.* [94] *Id.* ¶ 21. [95] *Id.* ¶ 22.

[96] EUTM Regulation 2017 art. 7(e)(iii); *cf. Hauck, supra* note 85, ¶ 3 (applying old version of the statute).

[97] *Hauck, supra* note 85, ¶ 29. [98] *Id.* ¶ 29–32. [99] *Id.* ¶ 36. [100] *Id.*

Justin Hughes has tried to provide a way to discern when protection should or should not be offered for non-traditional marks. Hughes's approach is in the context of U.S. law. But because it looks at core questions about what is essential, what work by an enterprise should be protected, and the need to balance competitive need, the approach helps illustrate issues for European and other jurisdictions. Hughes has argued that aesthetic functionality should turn on whether "the product feature at issue triggers a positive cognitive, psychological, or aesthetic response among a substantial composite of the relevant consumers *and* that response predates the trademark owner's activities."[101] Such predating can be a matter of evolution or in some cases "undoubtedly the result of acculturation."[102] For Hughes, those cases merit asking whether protecting the claimed trademark "would significantly hinder competition."[103] Hughes, however, believes there are cases where "aesthetic appeal is actually the achievement of the trademark holder or its predecessors," and in such cases "courts should be hesitant to use aesthetic functionality to deny trademark rights—precisely because building such aesthetic appeal is endemic to modern marketing, building brands, and, yes, the emergence of trademarks as valuable in and of themselves."[104] Hughes's view tracks the idea that protecting brand practices is what trademark law does,[105] is likely to persist and grow, and so the question becomes how to manage trademarks in such a world.[106]

The assumptions behind Hughes's analysis reveal some problems with the approach's ability to address when or when not to deem a claimed mark aesthetically functional, and they also show a clear preference for protecting marketing practices. Hughes points to an octagon for indicating stop, brown and yellow for maple syrup, blue for nighttime, baroque designs on silverware, purple for batwing capes, Abercrombie & Fitch's use of the combination of the words "performance," "genuine brand," "authentic," with "primary color combinations ... in connection with solid, plaid and stripe designs" and "symbols like lacrosse sticks and the ski patrol cross," as examples of symbols that have preexisting consumer bias[107] and contrasts those examples with the Lincoln Hump[108] and Maker's Mark's dripping red wax as examples where marketing and branding did work to create the desire and so should be protected.[109] The assumption is that we can detect what is a preexisting preference for most consumers so that we would say a mark holder should not get the mark.[110] The logic is similar to the U.S. legal test for genericism, for one has to determine whether enough of the populace thinks of the feature in a general or "preexisting" manner, whether the feature had meaning from a culture

[101] Hughes, *supra* note 84, at 1230. [102] *Id.* at 1253. [103] *Id.* at 1273.

[104] *Id.* [105] *Cf.* Desai, *supra* note 6.

[106] *Cf.* Desai *supra* note 2, at 612–19 (explaining theoretical limits in the search costs approach to trademark law and arguing clear arguments about how and why to limit trademark law are needed if change is possible).

[107] Hughes, *supra* note 84, at 1274, 1277–78, 1281. [108] *Id.* at 1274.

[109] *Id.* at 1279–80.

[110] *Id.* at 1278 ("when we speak of a preexisting aesthetic response, we have to mean a fairly specific aesthetic, cognitive, or psychological response *in a broad range of the relevant (consumer) group*") (emphasis in original).

generally, or whether the feature's salience comes from a trademark claimant.[111] As with genericism analysis, courts may try to find a moment of genericness and say once generic always generic, yet that still requires identifying some type of essence or time at which meaning was stable.[112] With word marks that determination is not so simple; with colors, shapes, sounds, and smells the problems will likely be worse.

The idea that consumers have a pre-existing idea of baroque patterns for silverware or purple for batwing capes shows a bias for a certain level of knowledge or at least shows a problem in figuring out what is preexisting. When explaining the sort of "preexisting aesthetic disposition" that should count, Hughes offers that the preference "in some people for Baroque architecture ... is not the sort of aesthetic functionality that should count. When we speak of utilitarian or mechanical functionality, we are concerned with a level of universal, general effects—and we should require the same for aesthetic functionality."[113] Yet in explaining why a claim for baroque patterns on silverware meant a trademark for such patterns could not be allowed, the explanation was "because there was a substantial, acculturated, preexisting response among consumers for ornate, baroque decorative styles."[114] One does not need "all consumers" but only "a substantial group" to justify denying the trademark right.[115] It seems that under this assessment standard, the test of "universal" response becomes a special subset of "universal" response for silverware consumers. Regardless of where one thinks the line is, the main problem is figuring out what is pre-existing and for whom.

The examples of the Lincoln Hump and Maker's Mark's dripping red wax face similar problems. Although Lincoln may have developed the hump and continued its use as an aesthetic flourish, Lincoln was not the first to develop ways to cover a spare tire at the back of the car.[116] For Hughes, the argument is that because Lincoln stayed with the hump for nonfunctional reasons, and consumers started using kits to create humps for other cars, Ford, the maker of Lincoln, "established" the aesthetic.[117] For Maker's Mark, the argument is that although sealing a bottle with wax is no longer "efficient and functional packaging technique, it is certainly still *aesthetically attractive.*"[118] Hughes cedes that dripping wax may trigger his test for pre-existing biases, because dripping wax may indicate that something is old or traditional.[119] Nonetheless, because Maker's Mark only wanted to protect red dripping wax, a symbol it had developed over the years, the preference for red dripping wax came from Maker's Mark and should be protected.[120]

[111] *See, e.g.*, Deven R. Desai & Sandy L. Rierson, *Confronting the Genericism Conundrum*, 28 Cardozo L. Rev. 1789, 1809–10, 1820–25 (2007) (explaining generic marks and the primary significance test).

[112] *Id.* at 1830–33 (discussing the doctrine that a word that was at one time the generic term for a given thing cannot be transformed into "a registrable trademark").

[113] Hughes, *supra* note 84, at 1278. [114] *Id.* at 1281. [115] *Id.*

[116] *See* Jim Donnelly, *A Classy Rear, Continental Kits Mean Elegance is Both Coming and Going*, Hemmings Motor News, Nov. 2006, https://www.hemmings.com/magazine/hmn/2006/11/A-Classy-Rear/1369500.html (last visited Sept. 27, 2017).

[117] Hughes, *supra* note 84, at 1275. [118] *Id.* at 1280. [119] *Id.*

[120] *Id.* ("the stipulation helped distinguish a general, preexisting aesthetic response from the consumer response that Maker's Mark had engendered through over half a century of marketing").

Part of Hughes's analysis revolves around whether over-claiming is a problem. Rather than, or perhaps on top of, concerns about pre-existing desires for baroque silverware, Hughes also notes that the claimant for baroque silverware patterns seems to have over-claimed and reached for the general idea of baroque patterns.[121] The problem of what is narrowed and/or pre-existing is highlighted by the Abercrombie example. Why Marker's Mark can claim red, dripping wax and not have over-claimed, and yet Abercrombie could not claim "the *combination*" of many things along with its A&F marks into one trade dress is unclear.[122] Perhaps Abercrombie was indeed too broad in claims about primary colors and certain general words associated with athletic gear, but Abercrombie seemed to have a claim as narrowed or specific as Marker's Mark. The goal here is not to dissect and justify the different outcomes to the end of times. Rather the point is that a narrowed claim will have to sort how narrow is narrow enough and again what is or is not pre-existing.[123]

In other words, what exactly does a mark need to do to show that its efforts should win the day? Did Ford via its Lincoln line say "Buy the car with the hump?" or did people happen to like that flourish? Should that matter? With word marks, the amount spent to deploy a mark matters and is a way to show that a descriptive term has secondary meaning.

Perhaps that is the same metric for features, but such a metric has problems. Is there some pre-existing preference for circles? There was a preference for circles in ancient and medieval times with the circle being seen as a perfect form.[124] Does that matter? Do people know about this aesthetic? Is knowledge of it the best way to show trademark salience? Given that European trademark looks at consumer perception as one factor in analyzing registration of a sign, similar questions could arise under that law too.

Examining color, patterns, and colors and patterns in combination further illustrates the problems. What about red dripping wax? A search for the traditional color of a wax seal shows that vermillion—a pigment that was made from cinnabar and was a brilliant red or scarlet color—was common.[125] Although other colors came into use, a search for "what color is sealing wax" led to pages that often used pictures of red wax as the example of such wax.[126] And there appears to be a changing etiquette for using red wax from an era when only men should use it to red being for

[121] *Id.* at 1281.

[122] Abercrombie & Fitch v. American Eagle Outfitters, 280 F. 3d 619, 644 (6th Cir. 2002).

[123] Hughes, *supra* note 84, at 1281.

[124] *See e.g.*, Joshua Korenblat, *Perfect Circles*, SMITHSONIAN.COM, May 23, 2007, http://www.smithsonianmag.com/arts-culture/perfect-circles-180940946/ (last visited Sept. 27, 2017) (discussing quest to be able to draw perfect circles and stories of great artists who drew prefect circles to show their virtuosity); *Perfection*, WIKIPEDIA, https://en.wikipedia.org/wiki/Perfection#Aesthetics (last visited Sept. 27, 2017) ("Another early idea—one that was to be espoused by many illustrious writers and artists of various periods—found perfection in the circle and the sphere.").

[125] *Sealing Wax*, WIKIPEDIA, https://en.wikipedia.org/wiki/Sealing_wax; https://en.wikisource.org/w/index.php?title=1911_Encyclop%C3%A6dia_Britannica/Sealing_Wax&oldid=5208980 (last visited Sept. 27, 2017).

[126] *See e.g., id.* (default wax sticks are red); Brett McKay & Kate McKay, *Wax Seals: A History & How-To*, Feb. 13, 2013, http://www.artofmanliness.com/2013/02/13/wax-seals-a-history-and-how-to/ (last visited Sept. 27, 2017).

business seals.[127] In addition there was an issue about whether a runny wax was high or low quality.[128] Some official seals were attached in a pendant style—with strings and tassels flowing free below the seal.[129] Perhaps dripping wax is similar to the eye as those seals. For someone who watched films about or knew about European royalty, red wax with some dripping may be the full aesthetic desired.[130] To say Maker's Mark chose red, but there are plenty of other colors for dripping wax, does not address why red matters, why Marker's Mark chose red, and it does not address whether "an aesthetic response" to dripping wax or red or the combination "predates Maker's Mark's commercial activities."[131]

The fights red-soled shoes raise have the same issues. Christian Louboutin admitted that the red sole of his show was chosen "to give his shoe styles 'energy,' [] because [red] is 'engaging,' red is 'sexy' and 'attracts men to the women who wear my shoes.' "[132] Yves Saint Laurent claimed it wanted "to evoke Chinese design elements" or use "monochromatic style that it [claims] is part of the brand's history" and to "coordinate with clothing items offered in the same collection."[133] All these claims about the use of red have large "preexisting elements."

Regardless of whether you begin with a claim that a feature is pre-existing or that a mark claimant developed something beyond that pre-existing bias, you must delve into questions that are messier than wanted. That will boil down to what a judge (or scholar) thinks people know to start,[134] as she tries to parse what is or isn't essential. But there are deeper problems with this approach.

V. How Marketers and Brand Builders Seek to Use and Claim Innate and Cultural Signals and Meaning

The idea that when marketers develop an aesthetic they should get rights to that development misses the way marketing and branding operate. It also appears to concede that trademark law protects brand building and a labor theory approach to trademark law rather than adhering to search costs analysis as the lodestar for trademark rights justification.[135] Remember marketers and designers are quite aware of

[127] *Unfolding the Mysteries of Sealing Wax & Wafers*, Victorian Passage into Time, http://www.victorianpassage.com/2009/07/unfolding_the_mysteries_of_sea.php (last visited Sept. 27, 2017).

[128] *Id.* [129] McKay & McKay, *supra* note 126.

[130] As anecdote, I recall scenes in the television adaptation of *The Scarlet Pimpernel* where red wax seals with some messy edges were important. Thus red wax for me has a connotation of importance and an older era, both of which matter for aged alcohol.

[131] Hughes, *supra* note 84, at 1280; *but see id.* at 1255 (acknowledging why a color may have an effect can be unclear).

[132] Christian Louboutin v. Yves Saint Laurent America, 778 F. Supp. 2d 445, 453 (S.D.N.Y. 2011).

[133] *Id.*

[134] *See* Bone, *supra* note 36, at 220–21 (arguing that the issue is really about copying and public policy issue that should turn on the errors costs that go with granting such rights).

[135] *Cf.* Lunney, *supra* note 39, at 1163–66 (arguing that trade dress does not necessarily serve a source-identifying function, there are other ways to identify source, and protecting trade dress leads to property rather than deception-based analysis which in turn encourages enforcement against "trivial infractions"; Kur and Senftleben, *supra* note 61, § 1.36 (discussing problems with a Lockean labor basis for trademark rights).

the need to use design to aid in brand building and they look to pre-existing or innate design cues to create their brands.[136] The explanations of both the plaintiff and defendant in the *Louboutin* case show that sensitivity. So yes, "building such aesthetic appeal is endemic to modern marketing, building brands, and, yes, the emergence of trademarks as valuable in and of themselves,"[137] but the way that happens is not divorced from drawing on and exploiting pre-existing aesthetic features. Instead it involves studying those essential features for incorporation into the design and brand.

A review of design and consumer choice studies shows that the designer (and by extension the mark claimant) draws on pre-existing culture and calls into question how to discern what is unique to a marketer or trademark claimant and what is already in place. The review lists "six roles of product appearance for consumers," and starts with "communication of aesthetic."[138] That area draws on "innate preferences" such as "unity," "proportion and symmetry," the inversion of "U-shaped relation," and "color" as well as "prototypicality," that is "the degree to which something is representative of a category."[139] But "an optimal combination of prototypicality and novelty are preferred aesthetically."[140] For symbolic design elements, designers know that "linking of brand meaning to elements of the product appearance will be easier when the associations these elements engender by themselves (e.g., because they are innate or are determined by culture) correspond to the desired brand image."[141] Studies have shown that "bright colors and a large size, which is associated with aggression will make it easier to position a car brand as aggressive."[142] Despite variances based on individuals or eras, marketing scholars point to "certain associations that seem to be relatively constant" such as "angular forms [being] associated with dynamism and masculinity, while roundness evok[ing] softness and femininity."[143]

Thus use of red, circular, symmetrical, and certain sizes draws on innate or perhaps "preexisting" biases while also needing some novelty to stand out. This analysis suggests that Lincoln's Hump draws on innate preferences for shapes and symmetry, and yet may also have something new. Did Lincoln want to be feminine too? For red dripping wax and shoe soles, if red is used in combination to narrow a claim for just a color, the designers and brand builders still have drawn on some idea of innate to achieve their goal.

Functional and ergonomic concerns also involve choices to signal general matters to consumers. Functional design choices may turn on using largeness to indicate power of a hairdryer or making sure "the appearance as a whole [] communicate quality by looking reliable or solid."[144] Thus the practical function is the power of the hairdryer, which may not need to be a large product and still generate large amounts of power, but the aesthetic of size means a larger hair dryer is a strong design need. Even ergonomic issues require some extra thought about appearance. "In order to influence consumer preference positively, it is not sufficient that a product

[136] *See supra* Section II. [137] Hughes, *supra* note 84, at 1273.
[138] Creusen & Schoormans, *supra* note 22, at 65. [139] *Id.* [140] *Id.*
[141] *Id.* at 66. [142] *Id.* [143] *Id.* [144] *Id.* at 67.

be simply easy to use."[145] Appearance influences whether a consumer will think that a product operates in an ergonomic way. Thus a product designed "in such a way that it cannot fall over in normal use," may still find that consumers reject the product based on the way it looks.[146] Or simply having "a small number of controls (such as buttons) makes a product look easy to use." [147]

Product designers are quite aware of the need to draw attention to a product. Attention drawing "can be enhanced by increasing its size and by using bright colors."[148] Furthermore, "people attend to stimuli that contrast with their background and are novel (unusual or unexpected)."[149] Thus Louboutin may have simply drawn on design principles for colors and contrast. Its combination may have been the first, and one might say limiting the red and placement claim is enough. Yet again we should recall why the precise bright color, red, and the place of contrast—the sole of the shoe—are at stake. Both are general parts of design. If so, the choice of red seems like it should be open to all. And if one wants to gain contrast on a shoe, the sole is an excellent spot for that. Thus a claim to the red sole of a shoe is quite a powerful claim against competitors in the shoe market.

Last, design can affect product categorization—the way a consumer chooses products as fitting within a product market—and that perception can drive consumer choice too.[150] The goal is to have a "product [that] resembles other products in the same category, that is, when it is more prototypical of the category" and "[w]ith respect to product appearance, this means that it should be more visually typical."[151] Visual typicality has been defined as "the look or appearance that most consumers would associate with a product category, and by which they identify brands that belong to the category."[152] Product categorization matters, because when consumers cannot put a product into a category or find it "difficult" to do so, "consumers may not regard the product as a purchase alternative."[153]

The trade dress issues in *Apple, Inc. v. Samsung Electronics Co., Ltd.*[154] highlight the intersecting and overlapping issues of design choices. Apple's iPhone broke open the smart phone market, and the race to compete has been strong. As expected with a new, lucrative market, Samsung and others have tried to take some of the market if not unseat Apple. Apple cared about design and claimed design features as its unregistered trade dress. Specifically Apple asserted trade dress in:

> a rectangular product with four evenly rounded corners; a flat, clear surface covering the front of the product; a display screen under the clear surface; substantial black borders above and below the display screen and narrower black borders on either side of the screen; and when the device is on, a row of small dots on the display screen, a matrix of colorful square icons with evenly rounded corners within the display screen, and an unchanging bottom dock of colorful square icons with evenly rounded corners set off from the display's other icons.[155]

[145] *Id.* at 68. [146] *Id.* [147] *Id.* [148] Hughes, *supra* note 84, at 68.
[149] Creusen & Schoormans, *supra* note 22, at 68. [150] *Id.* [151] *Id.* [152] *Id.*
[153] *Id.* For a discussion of the way U.S. courts mistake alternative design analysis as competitive rather than rivalrous in the economic sense *see* Lunney, *supra* note 39, at 1170–71.
[154] Apple, Inc. v. Samsung Electronics Co., Ltd., 920 F. Supp. 2d 1079 (2013).
[155] Apple, Inc. v. Samsung Electronics Co., Ltd., 786 F.3d 983, 992 (2015).

The Federal Circuit looked to utilitarian issues and found the unregistered trade dress functional, because it improved "usability."[156]

And yet the aesthetic aspects indicate that aesthetic functionality should prevent the ability to register trade dress here too. As designers and marketers know, practical design issues such as ease of use matter for even old-school desktop phones where the *way buttons look* and whether the phone is easy to hold matters.[157] Even with old desktop answering machines, aesthetics, as in attractive appearance, mattered to 65% of a consumer study group.[158] In addition, shapes and sizes matter for the overall success of the product. Sometimes largeness, smallness, or sleekness will matter as well as the colors that signal the type of technology. Color and contrasting colors matter. Perhaps most important, these factors can affect categorization, the way consumers decide whether an offering is "a purchase alternative."[159]

Apple's claimed trade dress touches on almost all the roles of design in consumer decision-making—rounded corners, displays that are easy to read, contrasting colors between borders and the screen, icons (or back in the day buttons) that are arranged to be easy to see and use, and rounded shapes for the phone and the icons—speak to a savvy consumer about design. Apple, as the leader in smart phones, drew on many pre-existing or innate biases in consumers, but that does not mean it should have exclusive rights to those designs. Recall that consumers perceive features as indicative of a category, and so competitors need to make smart phones that fit the category. Giving Apple or any design-driven enterprise the chance to claim innate aspects of design fosters a race to claim rights and litigate simply to keep competitors out of the market.

In sum, designers, marketers, and brand builders are well aware of pre-existing biases and use them to create their offerings. Depending on the consumer market, each, or a combination, of the roles matters for design.[160] Something that has attractive packaging may not be something that a consumer wants to stand out in his or her home.[161] As with hybrid word marks that "perform a variety of informational functions—ranging from the provision of pure commercial or source-related information to the provision of pure generic or product-category information—at the same time," design roles can and do overlap for designers and marketers as they choose what to do and for consumers as they evaluate a product.[162]

The point is that marketing and branding draw on design principles and strategies that explicitly seek to connect to innate consumer preferences, speak to non-verbal

[156] *Id.* at 994. [157] Creusen & Schoormans, *supra* note 22, at 61. [158] *Id.* at 71.

[159] *See* Lunney, *supra* note 39, at 1170–71 (explaining alternative designs foster differentiation or rivalry, which means that a consumer is less likely to switch products without steep price discounts. Competition means that consumer sees the products as essentially interchangeable and small price variances encourage switching); *Id.* at 1171 (protecting a design such as round for a grill or phone edge thus allows one company the ability to charge supracompetitive prices).

[160] Creusen & Schoormans, *supra* note 22, at 77.

[161] *Id.* at 74 (noting that some wanted an answering machine to blend into décor but "Females significantly more often mention attention drawing as a choice reason than males.").

[162] Ralph H. Folsom & Larry L. Teply, *Trademarked Generic Words*, 89 YALE L. J. 1323, 1339 (1980); Creusen & Schoormans, *supra* note 22, at 71–75 (discussing variances in consumer understandings of design and overlaps in for example symbolic and aesthetic values).

cues, create brands and create social meaning, and to compete in general. The questions about exactly why trademark law should protect these practices and, if so, how to protect those practices so that protection is not overbroad, run into each other and provide an answer as to whether trademark law should protect marketing.

VI. Conclusion: Practical and Ideal Realities

Trademark law in the U.S. pretends not to be about protecting brand building. Non-U.S. trademark law, by contrast, seems more willing to embrace that it is protecting branding. In both scenarios the practical reality is that marketing practices that relate to non-traditional trademarks will be afforded trademark protection. The reasons offered and scholarship around protection of U.S. non-traditional trademarks shows the trend to accept this approach. If one takes seriously that trademark law is not about incentives[163] and should be anchored in search cost rationales instead, aesthetic functionality might merit a per se bar in general, not just for "aesthetic features that are central to the consumption value of a product."[164]

In simplest terms, attention to design as part of packaging and more has been around for at least a hundred years. Marketers and brand managers have been and are paying attention to design at many levels. They will continue to do so, and they will adapt to the legal landscape. More than fifteen years ago, Glynn Lunney argued that absent protection for trade dress, producers would still rely on word marks and labels to convey information about products, and consumers could and would tell the difference amongst trade dresses.[165] Following a similar logic, Robert Bone has argued that we could abolish trade dress protection and producers would be "likely to respond to the denial of trade dress protection by investing more in promoting and advertising word marks and catchy logos."[166] Consumers would "learn that products with the same distinctive trade dress do not necessarily come from the same source," which would lead to producers relying on other identifiers to reach consumers about the source of goods.[167] Thus one can, and I do, extend Lunney and Bone's points to non-traditional trademarks in general. Nonetheless, the fact of current and expanding protection for trade dress and non-traditional trademarks remains. We may wish that were not so, but wishing does not change the reality.[168]

[163] Bone, *supra* note 36, at 242 ("trademark law would no longer be available to encourage the creation of attractive product designs, but incentivizing creativity is not a core trademark goal."); Hughes, *supra* note 84, at 1241 ("Judicial opinions narrowing the scope of aesthetic functionality frequently mention creativity incentives/disincentives ... While it is sensible to say that trademark law should not be a disincentive to creative or pleasing designs, obviously we must be cautious not to cast trademark law too much in copyright's constitutional role of encouraging creativity."); KUR & SENFTLEBEN, *supra* note 61, § 1.39 ("[T]he incentive argument and the reward argument [] hardly provide a sufficient basis for the protection of a trade mark's accessory functions which reflect the creation and exploitation of a brand image.").

[164] Bone, *supra* note 36, at 239.

[165] Lunney *supra* note 39, at 1164–65, 1167.

[166] Bone, *supra* note 36, at 241.

[167] *Id.* at 241–42.

[168] *Cf.* Desai *supra* note 2, at 612–19.

Efforts to explain why specific categories of non-traditional trademark protection should not receive protection and to offer ways to try and to cabin the way protection for non-traditional trademarks operates are to be lauded, but there may be simpler lessons too. The U.S. should learn from the EU and other jurisdictions and demand much greater precision about what is claimed. The current EU language—"representation [must be] clear, precise, self-contained, easily accessible, intelligible, durable and objective" and claims must use "any appropriate form [of representation] using generally available technology," including but "not necessarily by graphic means"—would help address the scope and indeterminacy problems non-traditional marks present.[169] That approach, however, seems to move trademark law closer to patent law. As a result, issues about claiming and scope known from the patent arena may invade trademark law. If trademark law is indeed now about trademark rights in gross and implicitly has taken a property approach, moving to the way other areas of intellectual property law manage rights may make sense or be inevitable.[170] Short of that, although I have critiqued Hughes's proposal, I should be clear that his project as I see it—to develop a map of how to understand non-traditional trademarks that parallels current U.S. law for word marks—is probably a plausible way forward, because stopping protection for non-traditional trademarks is unlikely. In that sense, my critique is a note of caution that the problems for such a map are significant. In addition, given how poorly trademark law has cabined word marks, we should not expect much to limit what can be, and the reach of, non-traditional marks going forward.

Should trademark law protect non-traditional trademarks? No. Will it? It does and will continue to do so. The challenge is to dive into the practices in question and fashion limits as much as possible. What the law sees as separable aspects of non-traditional marks, businesses see as a whole. Thus this chapter has looked at the way designers, marketers, and brand builders understand, and seek to use, aesthetics to capture essences. As such this chapter hopes to have at least opened the door to arguments about when not to grant protection to whole categories of non-traditional trademarks and how to show that any given claimed non-traditional mark is likely aesthetically functional and thus should not receive trademark protection.

[169] EUTM Regulation ¶ 10.

[170] *Cf.* Desai *supra* note 2, at 617–18 (arguing that trademark law functions closer to copyright law than admitted and so embracing a property approach may be better than ignoring this reality).

7

Absolute Bans on the Registration of Product Shape Marks

A Breach of International Law?

Ng-Loy Wee Loon

I. Introduction

Amongst three-dimensional shape marks, there is one subcategory that can be especially controversial when protection is sought therefor under trademark law: marks comprising the three-dimensional shape of the product itself. The nature of the controversy is encapsulated in this question posed by Lord Justice Jacob in a passing off case involving the three-dimensional shape of a cushion: "[There can be] an intractable problem: how do you distinguish between a capricious addition and the article itself?"[1]

His point is that a mark is a "capricious addition"[2] to the article, rather than the article itself, and if this distinction is not rigorously maintained, there is a risk that trademark protection will extend beyond the mark to the article itself or to the functional or aesthetically pleasing design features of the article; if there should be any protection for the article or these functional or aesthetically pleasing features, this protection more properly lies in the patents or designs regime where the rights conferred are of limited duration.[3]

Some countries have responded to this risk by enacting absolute bans on the registration of certain types of product shape marks. For example, Section 7(3) of Singapore's Trade Marks Act provides as follows:

[1] Hodgkinson Corby Ltd. v. Wards Mobility Servs. Ltd. [1995] F.S.R. 169, 177 (Ch. D). The shape of this cushion was designed to prevent the onset of decubitus ulcers (pressure sores). The cushion was typically used on wheelchairs by the permanently immobile. The passing off action failed in this case.

[2] This term "capricious addition" originated from J.B. Williams Co. v. H. Bronnley & Co. Ltd. (1909) 26 R.P.C. 765, 773 (C.A.). This case sets out the proposition that the common-law action for passing off may assist a plaintiff seeking to protect a distinctive "get-up" of his article. Fletcher Moulton LJ in this case defined "get-up" to mean a capricious addition "to the article itself," such as the colour or the shape of the article. *Id.* at 773.

[3] See further Chapters 3, 4, 5, and 6 in this volume.

Absolute Bans on the Registration of Product Shape Marks – A Breach of International Law? Ng-Loy Wee Loon.

A sign shall not be registered as a trade mark if it consists exclusively of—
(a) the shape which results from the nature of the goods themselves;
(b) the shape of goods which is necessary to obtain a technical result; or
(c) the shape which gives substantial value to the goods.[4]

The three grounds set out in (a), (b), and (c) shall be referred to in this chapter as "the Natural Shape Ban," "the Functional Shape Ban," and "the Aesthetic Shape Ban," respectively.

Other jurisdictions that have enacted identical or similar bans in their trademark legislation include the following:[5] China, the European Union (EU) and its Member States, Hong Kong, India, Japan, Korea, and South Africa. These bans were successfully activated as grounds to refuse or invalidate the registration of the shape of a chair,[6] the shape of the head of a shaver,[7] the shape of the LEGO brick,[8] the shape of the KIT KAT bar of chocolate,[9] the shape of a pharmaceutical tablet,[10] and the shape of an automobile.[11]

The *absolute* nature of these legislative bans on registration merits another mention: a product shape mark that offends any of these bans cannot be registered, regardless of whether this shape mark has acquired distinctiveness as a result of prior use by its proprietor. It is precisely this absolute nature that has spawned criticism of these legislative bans.[12] Why not leave the issue of registration of a product shape mark to be determined by the distinctiveness requirement? After all, distinctiveness is *the* critical criterion in the international definition of "trademark" found in Article 15(1) of the Agreement for Trade-Related Aspects of Intellectual Property Rights (the TRIPS Agreement).[13] These critics argue that, if a product shape mark has been

[4] Trade Marks Act, Rev. ed. 2005 Cap. 332, § 7(3) (2005) (Sing.).

[5] The relevant articles/sections in these countries' trademark legislation are as follows: China [art. 12]; Hong Kong [§ 11(3)]; India [§ 9(3)]; Japan [art. 4(i)(xviii)]; Korea [art. 7(13)]; and South Africa [§ 10(5), (11)]. In the case of the EU Member States, see art. 3(1)(e) of the former EU Trade Marks Directive (2008/95/EC) and art. 4(1) the current EU Trade Marks Directive (2015/2436 of December 16, 2016), and art. 7(1)(e) of the Community Trademark Regulation (No. 207/2009), as amended by Regulation (2015/2424 of December 16, 2016).

[6] Hauck GmbH & Co. KG v. Stokke A/S [2014] E.T.M.R. 60. In this case from the Netherlands, the shape of the chair (specifically, a high chair for children) was found to offend the Natural Shape Ban.

[7] Philips Electronics NV v. Remington Consumer Products Ltd. [2003] R.P.C. 2. In this case from the UK, the shape of the head of shaver (which was the subject of a patent) was found to offend the Functional Shape Ban.

[8] Lego Juris A/S v. OHIM [2010] E.T.M.R. 63. In this case from the Office for the Harmonisation in the Internal Market (now known as the "European Union Intellectual Property Office"), the shape of the LEGO toy brick (which was the subject of a patent) was found to offend the Functional Shape Ban.

[9] Société des Produits Nestlé v. Petra Foods Ltd., [2017] 1 S.L.R. 35. In this case from Singapore, the shape of the KIT KAT bar of chocolates (a rectangular box shape with grooves arranged along the length of the rectangle) was found to offend the Functional Shape Ban.

[10] Triomed (Pty) Ltd v. Beecham Group Plc [2003] F.S.R. 27. In this case from South Africa, the shape of the pharmaceutical tablet (which allowed the tablet to be swallowed more easily) was found to offend the Functional Shape Ban. The shape was also refused registration because it was "likely to limit the development of the relevant art" (the equivalent to the Aesthetic Shape Ban).

[11] London Taxi Corp Ltd. v. Frazer-Nash Research Ltd. [2016] F.S.R. 20. In this case from the UK, the shape of the automobile (a taxi) was found to offend the Aesthetic Shape Ban.

[12] *See* Section II *infra* for details of this critique.

[13] The pertinent part of art. 15(1) is the following: "Any sign, or any combination of signs, capable of distinguishing the goods or services of one undertaking from those of other undertaking, shall be

used and promoted to the extent that it has truly become distinctive of the goods of the trademark applicant—and we can impose an exacting standard of proof in this regard[14]—there seems to be no good reason to refuse registration and protection of this product shape mark.[15]

This chapter is concerned with a different objection to these absolute bans, namely, they are inconsistent with international law. Specifically, two provisions in international agreements have been cited. Section II examines the objection based on Article 6*quinquies* of the Paris Convention for the Protection of Industrial Property (the Paris Convention). Section III of this chapter examines the objection based on Article 15 of the TRIPS Agreement.

II. Article 6*quinquies* of the Paris Convention (1967)

Article 6*quinquies* A(1) of the Paris Convention (the Stockholm Act 1967) obliges a Paris Union member to accept for registration and protection "as is" (or, in French, "*telle quelle*") a trademark that has been duly registered in the country of origin of its proprietor. This *telle quelle* principle is subject to the four (and only four) cases of exceptions set out in Article 6*quinquies* B, namely:

- where this trademark conflicts with an earlier trademark or right of a third party in the country where registration is sought;
- where this trademark lacks distinctiveness;
- where this trademark is contrary to morality or public order; and
- where Article 10*bis* of the Paris Convention (to give effective protection against unfair competition) applies.

It is further provided in Article 6*quinquies* C that, when determining whether a mark is eligible for registration, all factual circumstances must be taken into consideration, particularly the length of time the mark has been in use. The impact of this mandate is that a mark that is found to have acquired distinctiveness as a result of its use by its proprietor cannot be refused registration on the ground that it lacks distinctiveness (the second exception).

Some critics of the Natural Shape Ban, the Functional Shape Ban, and the Aesthetic Shape Ban have argued that a Paris Union member that enacts these bans

capable of constituting a trademark. . . . Where signs are not inherently capable of distinguishing the relevant goods or services, Members may make registrability depend on distinctiveness acquired through use." Agreement on Trade-Related Aspects of Intellectual Property Rights, Apr. 15, 1994, Marrakesh Agreement Establishing the World Trade Organization, Annex 1C, 1869 U.N.T.S. 299 [hereinafter TRIPS Agreement]. There will be more discussion of art. 15(1) in Section III of this chapter.

[14] A more exacting standard of proof would require evidence that the relevant public *relies* exclusively on the shape of the product to locate the trademark applicant's goods. This is the standard of distinctiveness adopted in Singapore. *See Société des Produits Nestlé*, supra note 9; *see also* Chapter 15 in this volume.

[15] *See* Section II *infra* for details of this critique.

is in breach of the *telle quelle* principle.[16] More specifically, they argue that these bans are inconsistent with the second exception relating to lack of distinctiveness because the absolute nature of these bans means that a product shape mark that offends one of these bans shall be denied registration even if it is found to have achieved distinctiveness as a result of prior use. This outcome conflicts with the mandate in Article 6*quinquies* C to have regard to prior use of the mark when determining whether the mark is eligible for registration.

Others have argued that there is no inconsistency with the *telle quelle* principle because these bans may be justified under the third exception relating to public order, especially in the case of the Functional Shape Ban, because registration and protection of purely functional shape marks as trademarks raises very serious competition concerns.[17]

I am also of the view that there is no inconsistency—but for a different reason. In my view, there is no need to resort to any of the four exceptions recognized by Article 6*quinquies* B to justify the enactment of those absolute bans. My argument is simply this: the Paris Convention in its entirety has no application whatsoever to product shape marks or, for that matter, to other types of non-traditional trademarks such as sound marks and smell marks. This proposition finds support in the *travaux préparatoires* of the Paris Convention,[18] specifically those relating to the proceedings in the diplomatic conferences in Paris (1800–1883), Brussels (1897–1900), Washington (1911), and Lisbon (1958). These *travaux préparatoires* reveal that it was a big challenge to find a definition of a "trademark" that was acceptable to all the countries involved in the negotiations. In fact, it was an unsurmountable challenge. Objections were raised by various countries whenever there was a suggestion that the notion of a trademark included sound marks, smell marks, or three-dimensional marks such as the container for the product. The failure to reach a consensus on this issue means that every Paris Union member is free to determine for itself what type of sign is capable of constituting a trademark. When a Paris Union member enacts the Natural Shape Ban, the Functional Shape Ban, or the Aesthetic Shape Ban in its trademark legislation, it is merely exercising this freedom to declare that certain product shape marks do *not* qualify as trademarks. To put it in another way, these bans operate as a *negative* definition of a "trademark" in this Paris Union member.

The documents also reveal that the *telle quelle* principle in Article 6*quinquies* A(1) has a very limited application: to prevent countries from rejecting a mark on the ground that the mark is not represented in a particular script. For example, if China refuses to register a word mark represented in Latin script because of a requirement in its trademark law that the mark must be represented in *kanji* characters, that

[16] Qian Zhan, *The International Registration of Non-Traditional Trademarks: Compliance with the TRIPS Agreement and the Paris Convention*, 16 World Trade Rev. 111 (2017).

[17] Annette Kur, *Marks for Goods or Services (Trademarks)*, *in* Research Handbook on the Protection of Intellectual Property under WTO Rules 408, 416–17 & n.37 (Carlos M. Correa ed., 2010); Martin Senftleben, *Public Domain Preservation in EU Trademark Law—A Model for Other Regions?*, 103 Trademark Rep. 775, 785 (2013).

[18] Recourse to *travaux préparatoires* to interpret an article in an international treaty may be justified by the Vienna Convention on the Law of Treaties art. 32, May 23, 1969, 1155 U.N.T.S. 331, 340.

would be a breach of the *telle quelle* principle. In this sense, the *telle quelle* principle is said to concern only the "form" of the mark. The "form" of the mark does *not* encompass the shape of the product. As noted above, the Paris Convention in its entirety has no application whatsoever to product shape marks. The absolute bans, being a negative definition of a "trademark," relate to matters of substance, and such matters fall outside the ambit of Article 6*quinquies* A(1). Thus, there is no question of having to justify these bans under the exceptions recognized by Article 6*quinquies* B.

I will first refer to the parts of the *travaux préparatoires* of the Paris Convention, which provide the basis for my arguments. Thereafter, I will briefly refer to a WTO ruling on Article 6*quinquies*, which affirmed that the application of the *telle quelle* principle is limited to the "form" of the mark.

A. The Paris Conference 1880–1883

The problem that the *telle quelle* principle was intended to resolve was raised by France during the first meeting of the diplomatic conference in Paris in November 1880. France alerted the conference to the differences in national laws governing the registration of signs and emblems, and how this divergence resulted in some countries rejecting marks that had been registered in France.[19] For example, Russia's trademark legislation only registered marks that were denoted in Russian characters and hence no French trademark could be registered in Russia. This necessitated the two countries to enter into a treaty where it was agreed that marks duly deposited in France would be registered "*telle quelle*" and protected in Russia, even when these marks were denoted in French characters.[20] Clearly, France wished for such bilateral agreements to be replaced by the international agreement that the diplomatic conference was convened to adopt. A draft of the article (designated as Article 5) was put up for consideration:

1. The character ... of trademarks will be assessed in all the contracting parties of the Union according to the law of the country of origin.
2. The country in which the applicant is domiciled or has his principal establishment shall be considered as the country of origin.
3. The application can be refused if the subject-matter of the application is contrary to morality or public order.[21]

However, the effect of this draft article was that a Contracting Party would be giving up the freedom to determine for itself what type of signs could qualify as trademarks. This idea was rejected by various countries. For example, Austria noted that it did

[19] *See* CONFÉRENCE INTERNATIONALE POUR LA PROTECTION DE LA PROPRIÉTÉ INDUSTRIELLE 70 (1880) [hereinafter PARIS CONFERENCE 1880] (minutes from the fourth session of the first meeting of the Paris Conference, held on Nov. 9, 1880).

[20] *See id.* at 140 (minutes from the tenth session from the first meeting of the Paris Conference, held on Nov. 18, 1880).

[21] *See id.* at 132 (minutes from the ninth session of the first meeting of the Paris Conference, held on Nov. 17, 1880). This is the author's translation of the French version of this draft article. Note also that the paragraphing is added by the author.

not—and it would not—register numerical figures as trademarks, as was done in France.[22] At one point, Belgium proposed that one of the future conferences should undertake the task of determining the signs that could be used as trademarks in all the states of the Union, a task that Belgium was optimistic would be resolved "*sans peine*" ("easily" or "without difficulty").[23] But as we shall see, Belgium's proposition never materialized within the context of the Paris Convention.

In the meantime, the focus shifted to finding a solution to a more specific problem, namely, the requirement in some countries that the mark must be represented in a particular way or script. Eventually at the conclusion of the first meeting of the Paris Conference, all the countries present were able to agree on the following wording of the solution (designated as Article 6):

Article 6 (Paris text)

1. Every trademark duly filed in the country of origin shall be accepted for filing and protected *as is* [*tele quelle*] in all the other countries of the Union.
2. ...
3. ...
4. The filing may be refused if the subject-matter of this filing is considered as contrary to morality or public order.[24]

Thus, the "*telle quelle*" ("as is") principle started off life in the Paris Convention as Article 6(1). The origins of the phrase "*telle quelle*" can be traced to the bilateral treaty between France and Russia. The choice of this phrase is unfortunate because a literal interpretation of Article 6(1) could extend the application of Article 6(1) beyond the very limited purpose for which it was conceived. It is for this reason that the article became the subject of revisions and attempted revisions in subsequent diplomatic conferences in Brussels (1897–1900), Washington (1911), and Lisbon (1958).

In fact, the ambiguity caused by the phrase "*telle quelle*" almost threatened the adoption of Article 6 at the second (and final) meeting of the Paris Conference in March 1883. At this second meeting, Spain (who was not present at the first meeting in 1880) objected to Article 6(1). Spain was made aware of the debates surrounding Article 6(1) in the first meeting of the Paris Conference in 1880, and the limited application of Article 6(1). Nevertheless, Spain noted that there was the possibility that one might insist on the literal interpretation of Article 6(1)—an interpretation which Spain could not accept.[25] It wanted the true intent of Article 6(1) to be explicitly reflected in the text itself.

[22] *See id.* at 70 (minutes from the fourth session of the first meeting of the Paris Conference, held on Nov. 9, 1880); *id.* at 133 (minutes from the ninth session of the first meeting of the Paris Conference, held on Nov. 17, 1880).

[23] *See id.* at 142 (minutes from the tenth session of the first meeting of the Paris Conference, held on Nov. 18, 1880).

[24] *See id.* at 164 (emphasis added) (minutes from the eleventh and last session of the first meeting of the Paris Conference, held on Nov. 20, 1880). Note that the sub-paragraphing within art. 6 is added by the author.

[25] *See* CONFÉRENCE INTERNATIONALE POUR LA PROTECTION DE LA PROPRIÉTÉ INDUSTRIELLE 24–25 (1883) (minutes from the second meeting of the Paris Conference).

Any amendment to Article 6(1) at this stage would have meant a resubmission of the Article to each and every one of the governments of countries represented at the Paris Conference for their consideration and approval. To avoid the delay an amendment would have caused and as a compromise, it was proposed that the true intent of Article 6(1) be inserted into the Final Protocol that would accompany the Paris Convention, which would be used in the interpretation of the articles of the Paris Convention. This proposal was acceptable to Spain. The end result was the adoption of the text of Article 6 without any modification, but with its ambit clarified by the following paragraph (designated as Paragraph 4) in the Final Protocol:

Paragraph 4 (Final Protocol):

1. Paragraph 1 of Article 6 should be understood in the sense that no trade mark may be excluded from protection in one of the States of the Union for the sole reason that it does not comply, with regard to the signs for which it is composed, with the conditions of the laws of that State; provided it complies on this point with the laws of the country of origin and that it has been properly filed there. Subject to this exception, which *only concerns the form of the mark*, and subject to the provisions of the other Articles of the Convention, each State shall apply its domestic law.
2. To avoid any misinterpretation, it is agreed that the use of public armorial bearings and decorations may be considered as contrary to morality or public order in the sense of the last paragraph of Article 6.[26]

The Final Protocol was made an integral part of the Paris Convention,[27] and it was in this way that the *telle quelle* principle set out in Article 6(1) was explicitly limited by Paragraph 4(1) to "the form of the mark," that is, the way in which the mark was represented. The *telle quelle* principle prohibited a Contracting Party from rejecting a mark duly registered in the country of origin on the ground that the mark was not represented in a particular format or script such as the Russian script or the *Hiragana* script or the Sanskrit script. That is the extent of the *telle quelle* principle.

The last sentence of Paragraph 4(1) of the Final Protocol had another objective when it explicitly stipulated that, in all other matters, "each State shall apply its domestic law." This sentence addressed the concern that a Contracting Party had about giving up the freedom to determine for itself the *substantive* conditions for registration including the question of whether the subject matter of the application was a "trademark." Thus, Paragraph 4(1) of the Final Protocol made it unequivocally clear that, while matters relating to the *form* of the mark were determined by the law of the applicant's country of origin, matters relating to the *substance* of the mark were determined solely by the country where registration was sought. As we will see later, the desire to retain the freedom to determine the substantive conditions for registration was so important to Paris Union members that, at the diplomatic

[26] *See Protocole de Clôture*, CONVENTION DE PARIS POUR LA PROTECTION DE LA PROPRIÉTÉ INDUSTRIELLE 38 (1883) [hereinafter Final Protocol] (this is the author's translation of the French text and both the sub-paragraphing within ¶ 4 and the emphasis are added by the author).

[27] *See* Final Protocol, *id.* art. 7.

conference in Lisbon (1958), this freedom was enshrined in a proper article in the Paris Convention.[28]

B. The Brussels Conference 1897–1900

The Brussels diplomatic conference set out to revise Article 6 to provide the "unity and clarity" that the article presently lacked.[29] The objective of the revision was to integrate Paragraph 4(1) of the Final Protocol into Article 6(1) so that the limitation of the *telle quelle* principle to "the form of the mark" would be made explicit in Article 6(1) itself. A draft of the revised text of Article 6(1) was circulated before the conference. For our purposes, the critical aspect of this draft provided that a contracting country must apply the *telle quelle* principle "even if the form of the mark does not comply with the conditions prescribed by the domestic law of that country."[30] With this integration, Paragraph 4(1) would be deleted from the Final Protocol.

At the first meeting of the Brussels Conference in December 1897, Great Britain officially put forward another draft to revise Article 6. In this proposal, there would be no change to the text of Article 6(1) nor would Paragraph 4(1) of the Final Protocol be deleted. Instead, the British proposal sought to limit the application of the *telle quelle* principle in Article 6(1) by creating more exceptions than what was permitted in Article 6(4). The latter recognized only one exception: a contracting country could opt out of applying the *telle quelle* principle if the mark was contrary to morality or public order. The essence of the British proposal was to expand Article 6(4) to permit non-application of the *telle quelle* principle for the following marks:

- names of persons or societies that were not presented in a distinctive manner as in a signature;
- descriptive marks and geographical names; and
- public armorial bearings and decorations.[31]

The proposal to make an exception for public armorial bearings and decorations was uncontroversial because Paragraph 4(2) of the Final Protocol already provided that the use of public armorial bearings and decorations was contrary to morality or public order.

It was the first two cases—descriptive marks and other non-distinctive marks—that baffled some countries. Austria reminded the conference that the *telle quelle* principle in Article 6(1) concerned only "the *form* and not the *substance* of the mark."[32] In its view, a Paris Union member was not obliged by the *telle quelle*

[28] *See infra* note 58 and the accompanying main text.

[29] *See* ACTES DE LA CONFÉRENCE DE BRUXELLES: PREMIÈRE ET DEUXIÈME SESSIONS 1898 ET 1900, 43 (BIRPI 1901) [hereinafter CONFÉRENCE DE BRUXELLES] (This is the author's translation of the French phrase "l'unité et la clarté.").

[30] *Id.* (This is the author's translation of the French sentence "même si elle ne répond pas, par sa forme, aux conditions prescrites par la législation intérieure de ces États.").

[31] *See id.* at 281.

[32] *Id.* at 282 (This is the author's translation of the French sentence "*telle quelle* ne se rapporte qu'à la *forme* et nullement au *contenu* de la marque.").

principle in Article 6(1) to register a non-distinctive mark since lack of distinctiveness was a matter that related to the substance of the mark and not to its form. Therefore, Austria did not see the need to carve out non-distinctive marks as exceptions to the *telle quelle* principle when this principle had no application to such marks in the first place. At the same time, Austria did not object to the British proposal because the British proposal made no difference; with or without the revision, a contracting country could refuse to register non-distinctive marks. In this sense, the British proposal was not contrary to Article 6(1) or Paragraph 4(1) of the Final Protocol. However, other countries thought differently. For example, Sweden took the position that the fact that the British proposal was not contrary to Article 6 was precisely why there was no good reason to proceed with this proposal. Sweden wanted to maintain the status quo, that is, retain the original text of Article 6(1) as well as Paragraph 4(1) of the Final Protocol.[33]

There was no unanimous support for the British proposal at the conclusion of the first meeting of the Brussels Conference in December 1897.[34] The decision was to re-examine the issue at the second meeting of the conference together with the other unresolved issues. Meanwhile, Belgium (the host of the conference) was entrusted with the task of continuing diplomatic negotiations to pave the way for a unanimous agreement on all unresolved issues.

The further diplomatic negotiations facilitated by Belgium resulted in Great Britain agreeing to withdraw its proposal to revise Article 6.[35] Critical to this concession by the British was Belgium's assurance that the discussions at the first meeting in 1897 had clarified that Paris Union members were already permitted under the original text of Article 6 and Paragraph 4(1) of the Final Protocol to refuse registration of non-distinctive marks. Belgium even revealed that some delegates at the first meeting had remarked amongst themselves that the British proposal was "superfluous and an over-abundant commentary."[36] In light of this clarification of the ambit of Article 6, would Great Britain consider maintaining the original text of Article 6? The British response to this suggestion from Belgium was the following:

> Her Majesty's Government would be disposed in view of the exchange of opinion which took place at Brussels in 1897, to look upon favourably on the maintenance of the existing text of Article 6 of the Convention, and the paragraph relating to it in the Final Protocol, *provided that it be clearly understood that Great Britain is at liberty to maintain her existing municipal law as touching this point.*[37]

[33] *See id.* at 286.

[34] There were eight countries (excluding Britain) that were in favor of the Britain proposal, five countries that were against this proposal, and one abstention. *See id.*

[35] These diplomatic negotiations between the two governments were made via exchange of letters. To find these letters, as well as letters amongst the different agencies in the British government concerned with intellectual property (such as the Board of Trade), see PAPERS AND CORRESPONDENCE RELATIVE TO THE RECENT MEETING AT BRUSSELS OF THE ADJOURNED CONFERENCE OF THE UNION FOR THE PROTECTION OF INDUSTRIAL PROPERTY, 1901, [Cd. 603], at 27 (Gr. Brit.).

[36] *See id.* at 10 (letter dated Apr. 19, 1898 from the Belgian Government to the British Government).

[37] *See id.* at 27–28 (emphasis added) (letter dated Aug. 20, 1898 from the British Foreign Office to the Board of Trade, and the latter's reply dated Aug. 31, 1898); *see also id.* at 35 (letter dated May 6, 1899 from the Belgian Government to the British Government thanking the latter for not insisting on its

It should be noted that the governing trademark legislation in Great Britain at that time (the Patents, Designs, and Trade Marks Act 1883, as amended in 1888[38]) did not accept for registration product shape marks or, for that matter, other types of non-traditional marks like sound marks and smell marks.[39]

Belgium communicated to the other Paris Union members the terms of the British agreement to withdraw its proposal to revise Article 6,[40] and it was on this basis that Article 6 was dropped from the agenda of the second (and final) meeting of the Brussels Conference in 1900. The result was that Article 6 and Paragraph 4(1) of the Final Protocol were left intact.

C. The Washington Conference 1911

At the Washington Diplomatic Conference in 1911, there was another attempt to revise Article 6(1) by integrating the text of Paragraph 4(1) of the Final Protocol into the Article itself. As at the Brussels Conference, this second attempt failed. Concerns were expressed that this integration would only perpetuate the confusion generated by the *telle quelle* formula.[41]

Accordingly, the goal of integration was abandoned. Instead, the countries participating in the Washington Conference considered another way of revising Article 6(1), namely, by expanding the range of exceptions (beyond the exception relating to morality and public order) to two other cases:

- where the trademark conflicted with an earlier trademark or right of a third party in the country where registration is sought; and
- where the trademark lacked distinctiveness.[42]

It should come as no surprise that these exceptions were proposed by Great Britain (along with Germany). The proposal was met with less resistance this time around—except that France would only agree to these two exceptions on the condition that Paragraph 4(1) of the Final Protocol be deleted.[43] This suggestion alarmed the delegates from some other countries; these delegates were concerned that, because the original text of Article 6(1) would remain unchanged, the deletion of Paragraph 4(1)—and with it, the disappearance of the limitation of the *telle quelle* principle to the "form" of the mark—could be interpreted in a way to require them to accept

proposal to revise art. 6, and advising that it would inform the other Paris Union members of the terms of the British agreement to withdraw its proposal).

[38] *See* Patents, Designs, and Trade Marks Act 1883, 46 & 47 Vict. c. 57 (Gr. Brit.).

[39] Only the following signs qualified as "trademarks": (a) the names of persons or firms printed in a distinctive manner; (b) the signatures of the trademark applicant; (c) distinctive devices; (d) invented words; and (e) words, other than geographical names, which have no reference to the character or quality of the goods. *See id.* § 64 (as amended in 1888).

[40] *See* CONFÉRENCE DE BRUXELLES, *supra* note 29, at 356.

[41] *See* UNION INTERNATIONALE POUR LA PROTECTION DE LA PROPRIÉTÉ INDUSTRIELLE: CONFÉRENCE DE WASHINGTON DU 15 MAI AU 2 JUIN 1911, 296 (BIRPI 1911) [hereinafter CONFÉRENCE DE WASHINGTON].

[42] *See id.* at 252.

[43] *See id.* at 229–30.

for registration certain objects, such as a bottle or a living animal, that could not be regarded as trademarks in their domestic law.[44] For this reason, these countries wanted to retain Paragraph 4(1). Naturally, one of these countries was Great Britain.

Eventually, France got its way. However, Great Britain made a declaration that its vote in favor of deleting Paragraph 4(1) of the Final Protocol was on the condition that "one cannot ignore that there may exist in different countries of the Union divergences in the interpretation of the term 'trademark.' "[45]

The United States and Portugal made similar declarations.[46] This reservation suggests that these countries did not see the deletion of Paragraph 4(1) as restricting their freedom to interpret the term "trademark" as they wished. In fact, this suggestion finds support in the report of the British delegate to his government after the Washington Conference where he explained the reason for making the reservation:

> The old "Protocole de Clôture" [Final Protocol], which in effect confined the meaning of "telle quelle" to the form of the mark was omitted after considerable debate. At the earlier stages of the Conference we felt it necessary to support the retention of this clause, in view of the opinion held by France, and apparently some other countries, that a Trade Mark may consist not only in some sign or trade mark affixed to goods or merchandise, but in *the actual form or shape of the merchandise or article itself.* It was not made clear how far this opinion was in fact adopted by the Courts or the legislation of France and other countries, but it constituted a certain difficulty in our accepting the Article [Article 6], even with the amendments already mentioned. We felt that it would not be possible to take upon ourselves any obligation to accept marks of such a character. Our views upon this point were clearly expressed in Committee, but it was pointed out in answer that *it would obviously be open to every country to decide for itself what may or may not be admitted as a trade mark.* We finally agreed to the excision of [Article 4] in the "Protocole de Clôture" as otherwise the new revision of [Article 6] would have been imperilled through the opposition of France. We felt it necessary however in agreeing to the proposal in the séance plénière to draw attention to the difference of view which might be held upon the interpretation of the expression "marque de fabrique."[47]

It bears repeating the assurance that Great Britain received during the proceedings: if Paragraph 4(1) of the Final Protocol was deleted, "it would obviously be open to every country to decide for itself what may or may not be admitted as a trade mark."[48] This assurance is yet another confirmation of the agreement reached during the Paris Conference, namely, that the *telle quelle* principle in Article 6(1) was intended to apply only to the form of the mark, and the addition of Paragraph 4(1) into the Final Protocol did not add to or subtract from this intent. (The

[44] *See id.* at 308–09.

[45] *See id.* at 252 (This is the author's translation of the French sentence "on n'ignore pas qu'il peut exister dans les différents pays de l'Union des divergences dans linterprétation de l'expression 'marque de fabrique'.").

[46] *See id.* at 252–53.

[47] *See* PAPERS AND CORRESPONDENCE RELATIVE TO THE RECENT CONFERENCE AT WASHINGTON FOR THE REVISION OF THE INTERNATIONAL CONVENTION FOR THE PROTECTION OF INDUSTRIAL PROPERTY AND THE ARRANGEMENT FOR THE PREVENTION OF FALSE INDICATIONS OF ORIGIN ON GOODS, 1911, [Cd. 5842] , at 98 (UK) (emphasis added).

[48] *Id.*

reader will recall that Paragraph 4(1) was inserted into the Final Protocol to address Spain's concern that this intent was not clear enough.) In short, the deletion of Paragraph 4(1) from the Final Protocol did not change the position. Thus, it remained open for Great Britain and any other Paris Union member to refuse to register a sign which its domestic law did not recognize as a trademark such as "the actual form or shape of the merchandise or article itself."[49]

The material parts of the revised text of Article 6 adopted at the conclusion of the Washington Conference were the following:

1. Every trademark duly registered[50] in the country of origin shall be accepted for filing and protected as is [*telle quelle*] in the other countries of the Union.
2. However, the following may be refused or invalidated:
   (i) Marks which are of such a nature as to infringe rights acquired by third parties in the country where protection is claimed.
   (ii) Marks which are devoid of any distinctive character, or consist exclusively of signs or indications which may serve in trade to designate the kind, quality, quantity, intended purpose, value, or place of origin, of the goods or time of production, or have become customary in the current language or in the bona fide and established practices of the trade of the country where protection is claimed.

   In determining the distinctive character of a mark, all the factual circumstances must be taken into consideration, particularly the length of time the mark has been in use.

   (iii) Marks which are contrary to morality or public order.
3. ...
4. ...[51]

D. The Lisbon Conference 1958

There were further revisions to Article 6 at the Hague Conference in 1925 and at the London Conference in 1934, but these revisions are not material for our purposes. The important revision to Article 6 is the one made at the Lisbon Conference in 1958.

The proposal to revise Article 6 at the Lisbon Conference was accompanied by a very useful account of the background and history of the article.[52] Two particular points in this account should be noted. First, it acknowledged that the *telle quelle* formula in Article 6(1) was a compromised solution to the problem of national laws

[49] *Id.*

[50] *Cf.* the Paris text of art. 6(1), which mandated the application of the *telle quelle* principle if the trademark was "duly filed" in the country of origin.

[51] *See* CONFÉRENCE DE WASHINGTON, *supra* note 41, at 300.

[52] *See* UNION INTERNATIONALE POUR LA PROTECTION DE LA PROPRIÉTÉ INDUSTRIELLE: ACTES DE LA CONFÉRENCE RÉUNIE A LISBONNE DU 6 AU 31 OCTOBRE 1958, 545–73 (BIRPI 1963) [hereinafter CONFÉRENCE DE LISBONNE].

having different definitions as to what types of signs could constitute trademarks. Regret was expressed that the Paris Conference settled on the *telle quelle* formula—this was described as an "extremely bad choice"[53]—instead of pursuing the suggestion made by Belgium at the Paris Conference to work toward an international definition of a trademark.[54] Even more importantly, it noted that such a definition was still missing.

Second, the account repeatedly noted that the *telle quelle* principle was concerned only with the form of the mark. There was a reminder that Great Britain was given the assurance at the Brussels Conference that there was no obligation to register a non-distinctive mark, as this was a matter concerning the substance of the mark. It also emphasized that this limitation to the form of the mark was inherent within the *telle quelle* principle itself and was not added by Paragraph 4(1) of the Final Protocol. Therefore, the deletion of Paragraph 4(1) at the Washington Conference was not meant to extend the ambit of the *telle quelle* principle. The latter point must surely lay to rest any remaining doubt that the reader may have about the effect of the deletion of Paragraph 4(1).

The Lisbon Conference set for itself the aim of revising the *telle quelle* formula in Article 6(1) to achieve the much-needed clarity. In the proposal put forward at this conference, the question of whether a sign constituted a trademark would be determined by the law of the applicant's country of origin.[55] This proposal was met with objections from some countries, which pointed out that it would mean that they had to register sound marks, smell marks, and moving image marks.[56] Eventually, the majority voted against this proposal.[57] This outcome clearly demonstrates that there was still no consensus in 1958 as to what signs could constitute trademarks. This is a matter relating to substantive conditions for registration, and not merely the form of the mark (how the mark is represented).

It should also be noted that the Lisbon Conference inserted a new article into the Paris Convention, one that governs the registration of "ordinary trademarks," that is, trademarks that had not been duly registered in the applicant's country of origin. For these "ordinary trademarks," the new article declares that the conditions for filing and registration shall be determined by the country where registration is sought. In actual fact, this declaration is not new; it existed from the inception of the Paris Convention in 1883 in the last sentence of Paragraph 4(1) of the Final Protocol. The reader will recall that this last sentence stipulated that, in all matters not governed by the *telle quelle* principle, "each State shall apply its domestic law."[58] Thus, we see that whilst Paragraph 4(1) was deleted during the Washington Conference, its last sentence was deemed so important that it was resurrected by the Lisbon Conference—this time, seated within the Paris Convention itself in an

[53] *Id.* at 567 ("*fort mal choisie*"). [54] *See supra* note 23 and the accompanying main text.

[55] *See* CONFÉRENCE DE LISBONNE, *supra* note 52, at 580.

[56] These countries were Denmark, Finland, Japan, Norway, and Sweden. *See id.* at 586–93.

[57] The results of the vote: twenty-two against this proposal, seven for this proposal, and six abstinence. *See id.* at 601.

[58] *See supra* note 28 and the accompanying main text.

independent article. This was how important the Paris Union members saw their freedom to decide on substantive conditions for registration.

This new article was designated as Article 6, and the *telle quelle* principle was re-designated as Article 6*quinquies*. This remained unchanged in the Stockholm Act of the Paris Convention (1967). The material parts of these two articles are set forth below:

Article 6 (Lisbon text and Stockholm text)[59]

(1) The conditions for the filing and registration of trademarks shall be determined in each country of the Union by its domestic legislation.
(2) …
(3) …

Article 6*quinquies* (Lisbon text and Stockholm text)[60]

A. (1) Every trademark duly registered in the country of origin shall be accepted for filing and protected as is in the other countries of the Union, subject to the reservations indicated in this Article. …

(2) …

B. Trademarks covered by this Article may be neither denied registration nor invalidated except in the following cases:

(i) when they are of such a nature as to infringe rights acquired by third parties in the country where protection is claimed;

(ii) when they are devoid of any distinctive character, or consist exclusively of signs or indications which may serve, in trade, to designate the kind, quality, quantity, intended purpose, value, place of origin, of the goods, or the time of production, or have become customary in the current language or in the bona fide and established practices of the trade of the country where protection is claimed;

(iii) when they are contrary to morality or public order and, in particular, of such a nature as to deceive the public. It is understood that a mark may not be considered contrary to public order for the sole reason that it does not conform to a provision of the legislation on marks, except if such provision itself relates to public order.

This provision is subject, however, to the application of Article 10*bis*.[61]

C. …

D. …

[59] *See* CONFÉRENCE DE LISBONNE, *supra* note 52, at 989, and the Paris Convention (Stockholm Act) 1967 at 1336.

[60] *See* CONFÉRENCE DE LISBONNE, *supra* note 52, at 989, and the Paris Convention (Stockholm Act) 1967 at 1340.

[61] *Cf.* the Washington text of art. 6(1)(B), which had only three exceptions. The fourth exception relating to art. 10*bis* (to give effective protection against unfair competition) was added at the Lisbon Conference.

E. ...

F. ...

E. World Trade Organization jurisprudence

There is jurisprudence from the World Trade Organization (WTO) Dispute Settlement Body affirming that the *telle quelle* principle in Article 6*quinquies* of the Paris Convention is limited to the form of the mark. This WTO ruling arose in the context of Article 2(1) of the TRIPS Agreement, which requires all WTO members to comply with Articles 1 through 12 and Article 19 of the Paris Convention (the Stockholm Act 1967).

The subject of the complaint in *United States—Section 211 Omnibus Appropriations Act of 1998* was Section 211 of the U.S. Omnibus Appropriate Act 1998. The effect of this U.S. provision was that a trademark that had been confiscated by the Cuban government could not be registered or renewed in the U.S. without the express consent of the original owner of the trademark (the victim of the confiscation). One of these confiscated trademarks was HAVANA CLUB (for rum), which was subsequently assigned by the Cuban government to a French company. The inability of this French company to get trademark protection for the mark HAVANA CLUB in the U.S. prompted the European Communities to bring a complaint against the U.S. on the ground that Section 211 was inconsistent with Article 6*quinquies* of the Paris Convention, and accordingly, Article 2(1) of the TRIPS Agreement.[62] The complaint was dismissed by the WTO Panel,[63] and this decision was upheld by the WTO Appellate Body.[64] The WTO Appellate Body ruled that the *telle quelle* principle related only to the "form" of the trademark as registered in the applicant's country of origin. Section 211 was not concerned with the "form" of the confiscated trademarks, but rather with the question of rightful ownership of these trademarks. Therefore, the *telle quelle* principle in Article 6*quinquies* A(1) had no application, and it was immaterial that Section 211 was outside the exceptions recognized in Article 6*quinquies* B.

Two reasons were given for this interpretation of the *telle quelle* principle. First, the WTO Appellate Body referred to Paragraph 4(1) of the Final Protocol. The WTO Appellate Body noted that, while this paragraph was omitted at the Washington Conference in 1911, "no delegation to that conference expressed the view at that time that this omission should change the meaning of [the *telle quelle* principle]."[65] I would add that this was explicitly acknowledged at the Lisbon Conference when the point was repeatedly made that the role of Paragraph 4(1) was merely to clarify

[62] The European Communities also relied on other articles in the TRIPS Agreement, including art. 15. *See infra* Section III, note 69 the accompanying main text.

[63] *See* Panel Report, *United States—Section 211 Omnibus Appropriation Act of 1998*, WTO Doc. WT/DS176/R (Aug. 6, 2001).

[64] *See* Appellate Body Report, *United States—Section 211 Omnibus Appropriation Act of 1998*, ¶ 139, WTO Doc. WT/DS176/AB/R (Jan. 2, 2002) [hereinafter Appellate Body Report].

[65] *See id.* ¶ 146.

what was inherent within the *telle quelle* principle, and hence its deletion at the Washington Conference did not extend the ambit of this principle.

Second, the WTO Appellate Body relied on Article 6(1):

> We find that there is considerable contextual support for the view that the requirement to register a trademark "as is" under Article 6*quinquies* A(1) does *not* encompass all the features and aspects of that trademark.... Article 6(1) of the Paris Convention (1967) reserves to the countries of the Paris Union the right to determine the *conditions* for filing and registration of trademarks by their domestic legislation. Article 6(1) confirms that the countries of the Paris Union did not relinquish their right to determine the conditions for filing and registration of trademarks by entering into the Paris Convention (1967) – subject, of course, to the other obligations of Paris Union countries under the Paris Convention (1967). Clearly, if Article 6*quinquies* A(1) were interpreted too broadly, the legislative discretion reserved for Members under Article 6(1) would be significantly undermined.[66]

I would add that many delegations made it very clear at the Paris Conference, at the Brussels Conference, and at the Washington Conference that they were not giving up their freedom to determine for themselves the substantive conditions for registration, in particular the question of whether signs such as smell marks, sound marks, moving image marks, and three-dimensional shapes of products could constitute trademarks. To them, this was a matter concerning the substance of the mark and not merely its form. And on this matter of substance, there was no consensus. At the time of the Lisbon Conference in 1958, regret was expressed that an international definition of "trademark" was still missing. The conclusion must be that non-traditional trademarks, particularly product shape marks, are outside the purview of the *telle quelle* principle and more generally the entire Paris Convention.

III. Article 15 of the TRIPS Agreement

The material parts of Article 15 of the TRIPS Agreement are set out below:

Article 15: Protectable Subject Matter

1. Any sign, or any combination of signs, capable of distinguishing the goods or services of one undertaking from those of other undertakings, shall be capable of constituting a trademark. Such signs, in particular words including personal names, letters, numerals, figurative elements and combinations of colours as well as any combination of such signs, shall be eligible for registration as trademarks. Where signs are not inherently capable of distinguishing the relevant goods or services, Members may make registrability depend on distinctiveness acquired through use. Members may require, as a condition of registration, that signs be visually perceptible.
2. Paragraph 1 shall not be understood to prevent a Member from denying registration of a trademark on other grounds, provided that they do not derogate from the provisions of the Paris Convention (1967).
3. ...[67]

[66] *See id.* ¶ 139. [67] TRIPS Agreement art. 15, *supra* note 13.

The argument that absolute bans on the registration of certain product shape marks are inconsistent with Article 15 may be summarized as follows. The scene has changed since the Paris Convention, and there is now an international definition of "trademark," which exists in the form of Article 15(1) of the TRIPS Agreement. Article 15(1) explicitly preserves the freedom of WTO members to decide whether to register non-visually perceptible signs (e.g., sound marks and smell marks). However, when the sign is visually perceptible—as is the case for product shape marks—Article 15(1) provides that it is capable of constituting a trademark and shall be eligible for registration so long as it satisfies one and only one criterion, namely, it is "capable of distinguishing" the goods or services of one party from those of other parties. Because absolute bans on registration of certain product shape marks apply without regard to whether the product shape mark has such capacity to distinguish, they are inconsistent with Article 15(1).

One difficulty with this argument is that it runs counter to the ruling of the WTO Appellate Body in *United States—Section 211 Omnibus Appropriations Act of 1998*.[68] It has been mentioned that in its complaint against the U.S., the European Communities cited Article 2(1) of the TRIPS Agreement.[69] They also relied on Article 15(1) of the TRIPS Agreement, arguing that the effect of Article 15(1) was to oblige WTO countries to register any sign that fits the description set out in this article. The Appellate Body ruled against this interpretation, reasoning that:

> Identifying certain signs that are *capable of* registration and imposing on WTO Members an obligation to make those signs *eligible for* registration in their domestic legislation is not the same as imposing on those Members an obligation to register *automatically* each and every sign or combination of signs that are *capable of* and *eligible for* registration under Article 15.1. This Article describes which trademarks are "capable of" registration. It does not say that all trademarks that are capable of registration "shall be registered." This Article states that such signs or combinations of signs "shall be *eligible* for registration" as trademarks. It does not say that they "shall be registered[.]" To us, these are distinctions with a difference. And, as we have said, supporting these distinctions is the fact that the title of [Article 15] [*viz.* "Protectable Subject Matter"] ... expresses the notion that the subject matter covered by the provision is subject matter that *qualifies* for, but is not necessarily *entitled to*, protection.[70]

There is also Article 15(2), which, the WTO Appellate Body noted, allows a WTO member to impose other conditions for registration, provided these other conditions do not derogate from the provisions of the Paris Convention.[71] WTO members like Singapore, which have the Natural Shape Ban, the Functional Shape Ban, or the Aesthetic Shape Ban in their trademark legislation, are exercising their discretion under Article 15(2).[72] These bans do not derogate from the provisions of the

[68] *See* Appellate Body Report, *supra* note 64.

[69] *See supra* note 62 and the accompanying main text.

[70] *See* Appellate Body Report, *supra* note 64 ¶ 155.

[71] *See* Appellate Body Report, *supra* note 64 ¶¶ 157–59. *See also* ¶¶ 171–77 (The WTO Appellate Body opined that a condition for registration need not be expressly mentioned in the Paris Convention in order not to "derogate" from it.).

[72] Commentators on the TRIPS Agreement who take the position that such bans are permitted by art. 15(2) include Carlos Correa. *See* CARLOS M. CORREA, TRADE RELATED ASPECTS OF INTELLECTUAL PROPERTY RIGHTS: A COMMENTARY ON THE TRIPS AGREEMENT 177 (2007).

Paris Convention because, as I have argued in Section II above, product shape marks are outside of the purview of the Paris Convention.

There may be another reason why these absolute bans are not inconsistent with Article 15. Although WTO members settled on an international definition of "trademark" as set out in Article 15(1), it is conceivable that they did not agree that product shape marks would come within this definition. This possibility exists because the list of signs in an earlier draft of Article 15(1) included "the shape of goods,"[73] but this was dropped from the list in the final draft of Article 15(1) that was adopted by the WTO members. Some will argue that this omission is immaterial given that this final list is clearly only illustrative and not exhaustive. However, the fact of the matter, as one commentator has put it, is that this final list "reflects only those examples on which negotiators reached a consensus."[74]

IV. Conclusion

Various countries have enacted absolute bans on the registration of product shape marks along the lines of the Natural Shape Ban, the Functional Shape Ban, or the Aesthetic Shape Ban, found in Singapore's trademark legislation. This chapter is concerned with the proposition that these bans are inconsistent with international law, more specifically Article 6*quinquies* of the Paris Convention and Article 15 of the TRIPS Agreement.

I argue against this proposition. My argument is simply this: product shape marks are outside the purview of the Paris Convention. The *travaux préparatoires* of the Paris Convention reveal a total lack of consensus on the definition of a "trademark," particularly, whether non-traditional marks such as smell marks, sound marks, moving image marks, and product shape marks could constitute trademarks. While it can be said that the TRIPS Agreement achieved what eluded the Paris Convention and an international definition of "trademark" is now provided by Article 15(1) of the TRIPS Agreement, there remains a real possibility that this definition does not extend to product shape marks.

Whether these bans are necessary or even desirable is a different question. That is the subject of discussion in the other chapters in this book.[75]

[73] *See* art. 1A.1 of § 2 (Trademarks) in the draft text annexed to Chairman's Report, *Negotiating Group on Trade-Related Aspects of Intellectual Property Rights, Including Trade in Counterfeit Goods*, GATT Doc. MTN.GNG/NG11/W/76 (July 23, 1990).

[74] NUNO PIRES DE CARVALHO, THE TRIPS REGIME OF TRADEMARKS AND DESIGNS § 15.37 (3d ed., 2014); *see also* DANIEL GERVAIS, THE TRIPS AGREEMENT: DRAFTING HISTORY AND ANALYSIS § 2.151 (4th ed. 2012) (noting that "[i]t was difficult to agree on a common list, . . ., as each participant agreed on some of the terms but not all of them").

[75] *See, e.g.*, Chapter 5 in this volume.

8

What Should Constitute Infringement of a Non-Traditional Mark?

The Role of "Trademark Use"

*Michael Handler**

I. Introduction: Why We Need to Focus More on Infringement of Non-Traditional Marks

When thinking about non-traditional marks it is fair to say that, at least outside the United States (U.S.), most attention is paid to questions of whether, and in what circumstances, such marks should be allowed on to the register. At a threshold level, there is the difficult question of what constitutes an adequate representation of a non-traditional sign. This is an issue that goes beyond applications for registration of "non-visual" marks, such as sounds, scents, and tastes,[1] and extends to applications for shape and/or color marks, where vague representations can give rise to uncertainties over what the mark actually is and the scope of what is being claimed.[2] An even larger set of challenges involves applying the tests for inherent and acquired distinctiveness to non-traditional marks. This is especially the case given that consumers are, in many cases, not readily in the habit of ascribing source significance to product or

* My thanks go to Robert Burrell, Dev Gangjee, and Megan Jones, and to Irene Calboli and Martin Senftleben for their editorial assistance. This chapter draws on and develops material first published in Michael Handler, *Disentangling Functionality, Distinctiveness and Use in Australian Trade Mark Law*, 42 Melb. U. L. Rev. 55 (2018).

[1] For example, in the European Union (EU), under the original Trade Marks Directive and Community Trade Mark Regulation, the Court of Justice set up criteria for "adequate" representations that meant that scent marks, and many sound marks, were never able to meet the requirement that a trademark be able to be graphically represented. *See* Case C-273/00, Sieckmann v. Deutsches Patent- und Markenamt, 2002 E.C.R. I-11737 (olfactory marks); Case C-283/01, Shield Mark BV v. Kist, 2003 E.C.R. I-14313 (sound marks). *See generally* Robert Burrell & Michael Handler, *Making Sense of Trade Mark Law*, 2003 Intell. Prop. Q. 388.

[2] For recent UK examples where applications for color marks were rejected on the basis of imprecise descriptions, *see* Société Des Produits Nestlé SA v. Cadbury UK Ltd., [2014] R.P.C. 7 (C.A.); Glaxo Wellcome UK Ltd. v. Sandoz Ltd., [2017] F.S.R. 33 (C.A.).

packaging features, such as shape or color.[3] And even when traders attempt to use such signs as indicators of origin, this is often in conjunction with other forms of branding, such as word marks and logos, which greatly complicates the distinctiveness inquiry.[4] In addition, most jurisdictions need to deal with a third issue: whether non-traditional marks ought to be prevented from registration because they serve a functional purpose. Although the primary policy goal of a functionality bar—to ensure that competition is not unduly hindered by allowing single undertakings to monopolize certain technical (and possibly aesthetic) product features by way of potentially perpetual trademark rights[5]—is clear, the various legislative and judicial tests that have been developed to screen out functional marks from registration are anything but.[6]

Issues of graphical representation, distinctiveness, and functionality are clearly worthy of sustained attention. It is vitally important that these legal requirements are carefully calibrated, to ensure that only those non-traditional signs that *are* in fact functioning as trademarks, and that do not give rise to compelling competition concerns, are entered onto registers. However, this focus on barriers to registration should not come at the expense of a critical inquiry into a related issue that is somewhat underdeveloped in legal scholarship outside the U.S.: what should constitute *infringement* of a registered non-traditional mark? There is something of a danger in focusing all of our energies on the legal techniques for filtering out problematic non-traditional signs at the pre-registration stage. This is because it might create the impression that what amounts to infringement of non-traditional marks (keeping in mind that such marks have already surmounted various obstacles to registration) should be relatively straightforward. By saying this, I do not mean to suggest that the legal tests that apply at the infringement stage, such as the tests for determining when two marks or sets of goods/services are sufficiently similar, or for determining a likelihood of confusion, are simple or easy to apply. Rather, my concern is that there is a danger in assuming that, since problematic signs ought to have been weeded out in the registration process, the *only* relevant issue at the infringement stage should involve a comparison between the registered mark and the product feature used by the defendant.

There are a number of problems in thinking that infringement ought to play such a straightforward role in cases involving non-traditional marks. One problem is that it is simply not the case that all problematic marks can be identified *ex ante* and kept off the register. This is not just because any registration system will invariably throw up false positives,[7] raising the question of whether actions to invalidate registrations

[3] This point has been explicitly recognized in EU law: *see, e.g.*, Case C-104/01, Libertel Groep BV v. Benelux-Merkenbureau, 2003 E.C.R. I-3793, ¶ 65; Case C-218/01, Henkel KGaA v. Deutsches Patent- und Markenamt, 2004 E.C.R. I-1725, ¶ 52.

[4] For detailed consideration, *see* Chapter 15 in this volume.

[5] A related goal is to ensure a degree of consistency between intellectual property regimes, to ensure that the limited terms of protection afforded by patent and design laws over functional products are not circumvented by the grant of potentially perpetual trademark rights.

[6] For detailed consideration of "aesthetic functionality" in particular, *see* Chapter 5 in this volume.

[7] For example, this might be because a registry will accept a non-traditional mark for registration too readily on the basis of attenuated evidence of acquired distinctiveness, and no third party will seek to oppose registration. On the problems of false positives in registration systems, *see* Robert Burrell,

provide sufficient protection for defendants using such marks or whether certain additional protections need be built into the infringement test. It is also because there are limits to what pre-registration screening techniques can achieve. This is particularly so where applicants seek to register "hybrid" marks that consist of features of shape and/or color combined with an inherently distinctive word or logo. In many cases the presence of the inherently distinctive element will be enough to ensure that the registry will not raise distinctiveness or functionality objections to the mark as a whole. But if such hybrid marks are to be readily accepted for registration, we need to think carefully about the scope of rights that should be afforded to such marks.[8] Infringement tests that focus only, or even primarily, on a comparison between the registered mark and the defendant's sign might not be enough to protect defendants that wish to make use of the non-distinctive or functional elements of the registered mark.

The final point above is indicative of the second, broader problem in dealing with the question of what should constitute infringement of non-traditional marks. It is fundamentally important in any registration system to identify a range of situations where we want to leave room for third parties to be able to make use of registered non-traditional marks, or confusingly similar variants. While there will always be disagreement over exactly how much room should be kept available, two obvious situations present themselves in this context. One is where defendants wish to make use of functional product and packaging elements. Another is where defendants wish to make "decorative" or "descriptive" use of product and packaging features, essentially to access what we might call the common meanings of such features. This second situation is particularly noteworthy, since it raises a fundamental tension in working out the scope of protection that ought to be afforded to non-traditional marks. On the one hand, we can readily accept that traders might be able to demonstrate, through evidence of extensive use and consumer recognition, that a design or packaging feature has come to function as a source identifier. On the other hand, this does not mean that another trader's adoption of the same or similar feature will be seen as anything other than the use of that feature for decorative, rather than source-identifying, purposes. In the same way that we can recognize that a prima facie descriptive word can both acquire secondary meaning when used by one trader, but also retain its descriptive properties when used by another trader, much the same issue arises with almost *any* non-traditional mark. But while we might want to carve out space in the infringement inquiry to allow third parties to access meanings conveyed by particular shapes and colors, or to use attractive design elements in a primarily non-source identifying manner, some care is needed to limit this space so that the rights given to owners of registered non-traditional marks are not entirely eviscerated.

Trade Mark Bureaucracies, *in* TRADEMARK LAW AND THEORY: A HANDBOOK OF CONTEMPORARY RESEARCH (Graeme B. Dinwoodie & Mark D. Janis eds., 2008).

[8] For further consideration, *see infra* Section IV and Chapter 3 in this volume.

There are a number of "defensive doctrines"[9] that could be employed in domestic laws to create such breathing room for defendants wishing to make legitimate use of features of registered non-traditional marks. These doctrines might be worked into the test for infringement, for example through a requirement that even if the marks are sufficiently similar, only those uses that impact on certain "trademark functions" will infringe.[10] Where the test for prima facie infringement operates in a more straightforward, comparison-based manner, such a doctrine could operate as a bespoke defense to infringement, for example permitting "descriptive use," or the use of parts of a registered mark that are functional or not distinctive.[11] Rather than seeking to analyze all of the potentially applicable defensive doctrines across jurisdictions, or make claims about the relative merits of them,[12] in this chapter I wish to explore one particular doctrine in detail—a requirement that infringing use be "use as a trademark," or "trademark use."

Trademark use forms part of the current statutory tests for infringement of a registered mark in countries such as Australia,[13] New Zealand,[14] and Malaysia,[15] and has been read into the test in other countries, including Singapore[16] and South Africa.[17] It is a doctrine that has some similarities with the developing requirement in EU law that an infringing use (at least in cases where there is "double identity" between the respective marks and respective goods/services) must damage one of the functions of the registered mark, including the origin function—such damage has been found not to have existed in cases where defendants have made descriptive or decorative use of word or device marks.[18] In addition, the concept of trademark

[9] *See* Graeme B. Dinwoodie, *Developing Defenses in Trademark Law*, 13 Lewis & Clark L. Rev. 99 (2009) (using this terminology to refer both to defenses to infringement and to elements within the test for infringement that perform similar work).

[10] *See infra* note 18.

[11] For detailed consideration in the context of EU law, *see* Chapter 4 in this volume.

[12] This is a fraught task, since the role that a particular doctrine plays in a country's law is likely to depend on its relationship to the barriers to registrability, and to other techniques that are employed at the infringement stage: *see infra* Section III. A further complication is that in some countries, the test for infringement of a registered mark will take account of the full context of the defendant's use in the marketplace, whereas in others it will be based on a more abstract comparison between the registered mark and the defendant's sign. For an attempt to provide a global overview of trademark limitations, showing the difficulties in comparing defensive doctrines across jurisdictions, *see* Study Committee of the Association Internationale pour la Protection de la Propriété Intellectuelle (AIPPI), Q195 Limitations of the Trademark Protection (2007), http://aippi.org/committee/limitations-of-the-trademark-protection-2/.

[13] Trade Marks Act 1995 (Austl.) § 120(1)–(3).

[14] Trade Marks Act 2002 (N.Z.) § 89(2).

[15] Trade Marks Act 1976 (Malaysia) § 38(1)(a).

[16] *See* City Chain Stores (S) Pte Ltd. v. Louis Vuitton Malletier [2010] 1 S.L.R. 382, ¶¶ 14–36. For comment, *see* Wee Loon Ng-Loy, *The Conundrum of "Trade Mark Use"*, 23 Sing. Academy L.J. 640 (2011).

[17] *See* Verimark (Pty.) Ltd. v. Bayerische Motoren Werke AktienGesellschaft, 2007 (6) S.A. 263, ¶¶ 5–7. For comment, *see* Wim Alberts, *Origin of the Species II: The* Verimark *Case and Trade Mark Infringement*, 124 S. African L.J. 702 (2007).

[18] *See* Lionel Bently, et al., Intellectual Property Law 1118 (5th ed. 2018) (discussing the Court of Justice's decisions in Case C-2/00, Hölterhoff v. Freiesleben, 2002 E.C.R. I-4187 and Case C-48/05, Adam Opel A.G. v. Autec A.G., 2007 E.C.R. I-1017). Admittedly, EU law has developed since these cases, such that a "descriptive" use that damages other functions, such as the advertising, investment or communication function, will infringe (*see*, most notably, Case C-487/07,

use has sometimes been floated in other jurisdictions with confusion-centered tests for infringement as a limiting doctrine that might help rein in the over-expansive scope of owners' rights.[19] For these reasons alone, trademark use is worth exploring. But such an exploration is also illuminating in showing that the doctrine as it has been developed over many decades in countries such as Australia and New Zealand is far more complex than is often appreciated. Understanding the various roles the doctrine has been called upon to play, and the policies it is designed to serve, is vital in assessing how well it has operated to create space for third parties seeking to use various product features for functional or decorative/descriptive purposes. An exploration of trademark use in the context of non-traditional marks also shows up the limits of the doctrine, and thus serves as something of a corrective to the idea that trademark use is a panacea that can cure the problems of over-expansive infringement provisions.

After a short introduction to the history and general concept of trademark use in Section II, I turn to assess how the doctrine has applied in Australian and New Zealand cases involving allegations of infringement of non-traditional marks, focusing on cases involving use of functional product features and cases arguably involving decorative use. This analysis explains how and why the doctrine of trademark use in these countries has (i) at times been stretched to accommodate worthy policy considerations, but in a manner that has created tensions with other aspects of the registration system (Section III), and (ii) at other times been applied far too restrictively, in a manner that unduly restricts the scope of permissible third party use of product features (Section IV). In doing so, I offer some suggestions as to how the trademark use requirement might be recalibrated to manage the full range of concerns raised by non-traditional marks, in a manner that both affords owners an adequate scope of protection, while leaving sufficient breathing room for third party traders—a model that might, in turn, be of interest to other countries that do not currently have a trademark use requirement in their domestic laws.

II. A Primer on Trademark Use in the British Commonwealth

The requirement that infringing use be use "as a trademark" started to take shape in the UK in the 1920s, as English courts grappled with the question of how far an

L'Oréal S.A. v Bellure N.V., 2009 E.C.R. I-5185, ¶ 58). However, it must be the case, as Bently et al. suggest, that there will be some cases involving "descriptive" and "decorative" use that will not impact on any of these other functions and therefore be non-infringing. See also Annette Kur, *Trade Marks Function, Don't They? CJEU Jurisprudence and Unfair Competition Principles*, 45 INT'L. REV. INTELL. PROP. & COMPETITION L. 434, 446–47 (2014) (noting that national courts are left with some scope to determine whether a use impacts on a protected function, and that "[n]o judge is compelled by the functions doctrine to grant overly broad protection").

[19] In the U.S., *see, e.g.*, Stacey L. Dogan & Mark A. Lemley, *Grounding Trademark Law Through Trademark Use*, 92 IOWA L. REV. 1669 (2007); Margreth Barrett, *Finding Trademark Use: The Historical Foundation for Limiting Infringement Liability to Uses "In the Manner of a Mark"*, 43 WAKE FOREST L. REV. 893 (2009).

owner's exclusive rights should extend, in the absence of explicit guidance in the Trade Marks Act 1905.[20] The doctrine was firmly entrenched by the House of Lords in its 1934 decision in *Irving's Yeast-Vite Ltd. v. Horsenail*, where it was found that the use of a registered mark in a comparative advertisement (where the defendant described its goods as a "substitute for" the registered mark) did not infringe because it was not trademark use.[21] The requirement was embraced by courts, and subsequently became an explicit part of the statutory test for infringement, in a number of British Commonwealth countries.[22]

The underlying principle of trademark use as it has come to be reflected in the current laws of Australia and New Zealand is simple enough to state. As the High Court of Australia confirmed in *The Shell Co. of Australia Ltd. v. Esso Standard Oil (Australia) Ltd.*, it is only use of a sign by the defendant as a badge of origin that will infringe.[23] That is, the use must indicate "a connection in the course of trade between goods and the person who applies the mark to the goods."[24] This is to be judged objectively, by reference to likely consumer reaction, taking into account the particular manner and context of the defendant's use.[25] The converse of the trademark use requirement is that other types of use, such as nominative, descriptive, or decorative use, will not infringe.[26]

The effect of making trademark use a condition of infringement is to limit the scope of protection afforded to prima facie descriptive marks that are registered on the basis of acquired distinctiveness. A clear illustration of this in Australian law is *Pepsico Australia Pty. Ltd. v. The Kettle Chip Co. Pty. Ltd.*,[27] which involved the registered mark KETTLE for potato chips. The Full Court of the Federal Court held that the defendant's use of the phrase "Kettle cooked potato chips" on its packaging, in conjunction with its primary brand "Thins," was not a use of "Kettle" as a trademark;

[20] An early example is Edward Young & Co. Ltd. v. Grierson, Oldham & Co. Ltd., (1924) 41 R.P.C. 548, 577 (C.A., Serjeant L.J.) ("the [proprietor's] right . . . is only infringed if the registered mark is used as a trade mark").

[21] Irving's Yeast-Vite Ltd. v. Horsenail, (1934) 51 R.P.C. 110 (H.L.).

[22] It is worth noting that some of these countries extended their infringement provisions to catch conduct that fell outside the scope of trademark use, such as comparative advertising: *see, e.g.*, Trade Marks Act 1938 (U.K.) § 4(3)(b); Trade Marks Act 1953 (N.Z.) § 8(1). However, the essential contours of the doctrine remained broadly consistent among these countries.

[23] The Shell Co. of Australia Ltd. v. Esso Standard Oil (Australia) Ltd., (1963) 109 C.L.R. 407, 422 (Kitto J.).

[24] Coca-Cola Co. v. All-Fect Distributors Ltd., (1999) 96 F.C.R. 107, 115 (Full Fed. Ct.). This reasoning was approved by the High Court of Australia in E & J Gallo Winery v. Lion Nathan Australia Pty. Ltd., (2010) 241 C.L.R. 144, 163 (French C.J., Gummow, Crennan, and Bell J.J.), 175 (Heydon J.).

[25] For a recent re-articulation of the principles, *see* Nature's Blend Pty. Ltd. v. Nestlé Australia Ltd., (2010) 87 I.P.R. 464, 468 (Full Fed. Ct.). On the relevance of Australian authorities in interpreting "trademark use" under New Zealand law, *see* Tasman Insulation New Zealand Ltd. v. Knauf Insulation Ltd., [2016] 3 N.Z.L.R. 145, 184 (N.Z.C.A.); Paul Sumpter, *Some Observations on Trans-Tasman Trade Mark Law*, 27 Austl. Intell. Prop. J. 88, 90–93 (2017).

[26] It is worth emphasizing here that although both Australian and New Zealand law provide a layer of protection for "well-known" marks (which, in the case of New Zealand, extends to preventing use that takes unfair advantage of the distinctive character or repute of the mark), such protection is still conditional on the defendant making trademark use of the well-known mark. *See* Trade Marks Act 1995 (Austl.) § 120(3); Trade Marks Act 2002 (N.Z.) §§ 89(1)(d) and (2).

[27] Pepsico Australia Pty. Ltd. v. The Kettle Chip Co. Pty. Ltd., (1996) 33 I.P.R. 161 (Full Fed. Ct.).

rather, in the circumstances, it was merely descriptive of the defendant's cooking process. As the Court explained, the trademark use requirement means that even where a term has acquired distinctiveness, another party's use of that term in its original descriptive sense cannot be restrained by the owner.[28] However, much depends on the context of the defendant's use. For example, in *Mainland Products Ltd. v. Bonlac Foods (NZ) Ltd.*,[29] the New Zealand Court of Appeal held that the defendant's prominent and repeated use of the word "Vintage" on the packaging of its cheese "would be taken by at least a substantial number of prospective buyers . . . as a means for distinguishing the particular cheese from the equivalent types of cheese supplied by others as opposed to a mere description of the cheese,"[30] thus constituting trademark use of the plaintiff's registered VINTAGE mark.[31]

Although the principles of trademark use are largely uncontroversial, applying them in practice is not straightforward. This is partly because consumer reaction is rarely uniform (i.e., some consumers will understand a defendant's use to be as a badge of origin when others will not) and partly because a variety of different policy considerations have been built into the trademark use enquiry over time. Historically, the doctrine was developed not only to permit comparative advertisements involving references to registered marks, but also to allow the importation and sale of legitimate goods to which registered marks had been applied—such acts of importation and sale were deemed not to involve trademark use.[32] More recently, we can see cases where the doctrine has been relied on to promote free speech interests, for example by preserving the ability of defendants to make commercial use of titles of public domain literary works that have been registered as trademarks.[33] The effect of some of these decisions has been to create a degree of internal inconsistency in the law.[34] However, it can be argued that this is a small price to pay for having a threshold requirement for infringement that can operate in a flexible, forward-looking manner to preserve valuable third party uses of signs for a range of policy

[28] *Id.* at 162 (Lockhart J.).

[29] Mainland Products Ltd. v. Bonlac Foods (NZ) Ltd. [1998] 3 N.Z.L.R. 341.

[30] *Id.* at 351.

[31] This is consistent with Australian cases where it has been held that a descriptive term can be used as a badge of origin: *see* Anheuser-Busch Inc. v. Budějovický Budvar, Národní Podnik, (2002) 56 I.P.R. 182, 228 (Fed. Ct., Allsop J.).

[32] *See* Champagne Heidsieck et Cie Monopole Société Anonyme v. Buxton, [1930] 1 Ch. 330 (Ch.). For discussion of the line of Australian cases following *Champagne Heidsieck*, *see* Robert Burrell & Michael Handler, *A Requiem for* Champagne Heidsieck: *Trade Mark Use and Parallel Importation*, 26 Austl. Intell. Prop. J. 110, 112–14 (2016). On the different approach taken in New Zealand, *see* Rob Batty, *Parallel Importing and Trade Mark Use: A Tale of Two Uses*, 25 N.Z. U. L. Rev. 467 (2013).

[33] *See, e.g.*, Christodoulou v. Disney Enterprises Inc., (2005) 156 F.C.R. 344 (Fed. Ct.) (Disney's use of "The Hunchback of Notre Dame" as a film title did not infringe the plaintiff's registered trademark for THE HUNCHBACK OF NOTRE DAME for entertainment services).

[34] *See, e.g.*, Mark Davison, *Parallel Importation: Unlawful Use of Trade Marks*, 19 Fed. L. Rev. 420 (1990) (noting the logical difficulty in excluding the acts of importation and sale of legitimate branded goods from the rubric of trademark use, when the same acts involving goods bearing counterfeit marks would be held to involve trademark use, and thus infringe).

purposes, often in situations where it is difficult to conceive of a defense to infringement that could do the same work.[35]

These elements of the trademark use doctrine need to be kept in mind when considering how the doctrine has applied in cases involving allegations of infringement of registered non-traditional marks. This is an issue that has not received a significant amount of attention in Australia and New Zealand, arguably because the results in most of the cases appear to be reasonable. That is, judged only in terms of outcomes, the cases addressed below might appear to suggest that the law is well adapted to safeguard the interests of defendants seeking to make use of product and packaging features for either functional or decorative purposes. However, a closer analysis of the cases reveals a range of problems with the way the trademark use doctrine has been developed and applied by the courts, and that the law is pulling in different directions depending on the types of non-traditional marks involved, and the nature of the use that defendants wish to make of such marks.

III. Trademark Use and Functional Marks

Over the past twenty years, trademark use has played an important role in Australian cases involving the use of functional product features by defendants. The key case in this context is *Koninklijke Philips Electronics NV v. Remington Products Australia Pty. Ltd.*[36] Unlike in related litigation between these parties in other jurisdictions in the late 1990s and early 2000s, where attention was focused on the registrability of the shape of Philips' three-headed rotary shaver,[37] the Australian Federal Court litigation turned solely on the question of infringement. Specifically, the main issue was whether Philips' registered mark, which consisted of a two-dimensional representation of the shape of its shaver, had been infringed by Remington's marketing and sale of its similarly-shaped three-headed rotary shaver.[38] These are shown in Figure 8.1.

At trial, Lehane J found that Remington was not using its shape as a badge of origin. Applying the orthodox test of trademark use—that is, looking to the context of the defendant's use of the sign to ask whether it was being presented as an indication of the origin of its goods—Lehane J considered that the specifics of Remington's marketing of its shaver, especially the way the "Remington" brand

[35] *See* Burrell & Handler, *A Requiem, supra* note 32, at 128–30 (showing the difficulties involved in attempting to draft an adequate defense to permit parallel importation of legitimate goods, and arguing that "trademark use" represents the best possible vehicle to address this issue).

[36] Koninklijke Philips Electronics NV v. Remington Products Australia Pty. Ltd., (1999) 91 F.C.R. 167 (Fed. Ct.), *aff'd* (2000) 100 F.C.R. 90 (Full Fed. Ct.).

[37] *See, e.g.*, Koninklijke Philips Electronics NV v. Remington Consumer Products Ltd., [2006] F.S.R. 30, ¶ 8 (C.A.) (describing litigation in six EU countries).

[38] Philips' mark had been registered under the Trade Marks Act 1955 (Austl.) and remained valid under the Trade Marks Act 1995 (Austl.). Remington did not seek to argue that the mere passage of the 1995 Act could not have served to enlarge the rights given to Philips in its two-dimensional device mark, without Philips separately establishing that it could now register the three-dimensional version of its device as a shape mark under the new Act. Such an argument later found favour in Nation Fittings (M) Sdn Bhd v. Oystertec Plc, [2006] 1 S.L.R. 712 (Sing. High Ct.), thus substantially limiting the scope of rights in two-dimensional representations of shapes under Singaporean law.

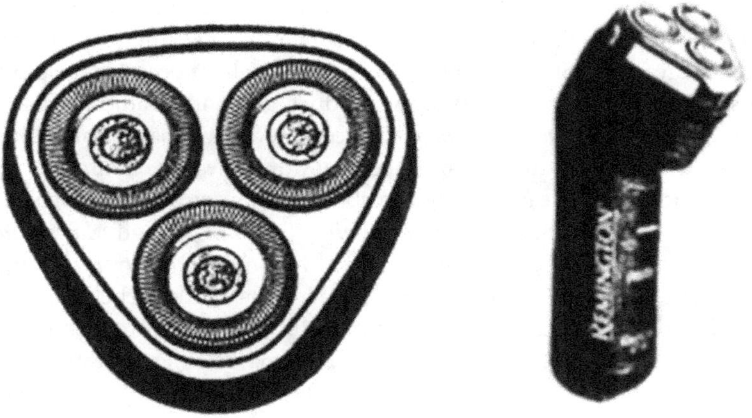

Figure 8.1 Philips' Australian registered trade mark 309250 & Remington's RR DT55 shaver

name was emphasized, meant that it was not using the shape as a mark and therefore had not infringed.[39]

On appeal, the Full Court of the Federal Court agreed with this outcome, but based on different reasoning. Burchett J, writing for the Court, was troubled by the prospect of Philips being able to secure a perpetual monopoly over functional product features that would put it in a better position than a patentee or design owner, and would put its competitors at a commercial disadvantage.[40] This strongly influenced his approach to the question of trademark use. Burchett J considered that even though the definition of "sign" in the Trade Marks Act 1995 encompassed "shape," the position under the former Act, where a "mark" needed to have a separate identity from the marked goods, remained unchanged. Thus, it was held that Remington's manufacture and sale of goods with a functional shape did not involve a use of the shape in a trademark sense, because there was nothing "added" to or severable from Remington's goods that could be considered to be a "trademark" at all.[41]

The Full Court's decision in *Philips v. Remington* has been embraced in subsequent Federal Court cases involving allegations of infringement of three-dimensional marks. *Mayne Industries Pty. Ltd. v. Advanced Engineering Group Pty. Ltd.* provides the best example.[42] The registered mark consisted of the three-dimensional shape of a fence dropper (a device that clips to a wire fence to maintain its integrity). The fence dropper had been the subject of a patent that had expired in 1984; the application for registration of the shape as a trademark was made in 2001. After that time the defendant copied the shape of the product and marketed it under a different brand name ("ezy-lock"). Given the technically functional nature of the fence dropper, Greenwood J had little difficulty applying *Philips v. Remington* in

[39] *See* Koninklijke Philips Electronics NV v. Remington Products Australia Pty. Ltd., (1999) 91 F.C.R. 167, 183–84.

[40] *See* Koninklijke Philips Electronics NV v. Remington Products Australia Pty. Ltd., (2000) 100 F.C.R. 90, 93.

[41] *Id.* at 101–02, 105.

[42] Mayne Industries Pty. Ltd. v. Advanced Engineering Group Pty. Ltd. (2008) 166 F.C.R. 312.

finding that the defendant had not engaged in trademark use in selling its competing product.[43] Even though the defendant had sought to draw attention to the shape of its fence dropper in its marketing, this was held to have been for the purpose of advertising the functional features of the product, and not to indicate trade origin. Like Burchett J in *Philips v. Remington*, Greenwood J was particularly concerned about what a finding of trademark infringement would mean in circumstances where patent law had limited the monopoly available to the inventor of functional goods.[44]

The interpretation of trademark use in *Philips v. Remington* and *Mayne Industries* is now entrenched.[45] In *Sebel Furniture Ltd. v. Acoustic & Felts Pty. Ltd.*,[46] the most recent Federal Court case to have considered functional marks, Sebel, the owner of a registered mark for the shape of an ergonomic chair, sought an interlocutory injunction to restrain the sale of a similar-looking chair, marketed under the brand name "Titan." In rejecting Sebel's application, Foster J considered that there was not even a serious question to be tried as to whether the defendant had engaged in trademark use of the shape of its chair, stating that:

> [a] shape which is dictated by the nature of the goods or by the need to achieve some particular technical result or functional outcome cannot operate as a trade mark. In order to function as a trade mark, the shape must be something which is extra or which is added to the inherent form of the particular goods as something distinct which can denote origin. A shape cannot function as a trade mark if it is something that other traders may legitimately wish to use either because it is inherent to the particular goods ... or because it provides some technical or functional benefit to the goods.[47]

At this point it is worth pausing to note a quirk of Australian law. Unlike almost every other jurisdiction, Australia does not have an explicit statutory bar to the registration of functional marks. Having said this, the Full Court of the Federal Court asserted in obiter dicta in two early decisions under the Trade Marks Act 1995 that technically functional marks would never be able to be registered, either because such signs would not meet the statutory definition of a "trade mark,"[48] or because such marks could never be distinctive.[49] However, these assertions were made without careful reference to the wording of the grounds of refusal contained in the Act,[50] they have

[43] *Id.* at 338–39. [44] *Id.* at 340.

[45] *See also* Polo/Lauren Co. LP v. Ziliani Holdings Pty. Ltd., (2008) 173 F.C.R. 266, 272 (Full Fed. Ct.) (expressing support, in obiter dicta, for the Full Court's approach in *Philips v. Remington*).

[46] Sebel Furniture Ltd. v. Acoustic & Felts Pty. Ltd., (2009) 80 I.P.R. 244.

[47] *Id.* at 272.

[48] *See* Koninklijke Philips Electronics NV v. Remington Products Australia Pty. Ltd., (2000) 100 F.C.R. 90, 103 (Full Fed. Ct., Burchett J.).

[49] *See* Kenman Kandy Australia Pty. Ltd. v. Registrar of Trade Marks, (2002) 122 F.C.R. 494, 529–30 (Full Fed. Ct., Stone J.).

[50] For criticism of *Kenman Kandy* in particular, *see, e.g.*, Julia Baird, *The Registrability of Functional Shape Marks*, 13 Austl. Intell. Prop. J. 218, 225–26 (2002); Jani McCutcheon, *Monopolised Product Shapes and Factual Distinctiveness under s 41(6) of the Trade Marks Act 1995 (Cth)*, 15 Austl. Intell. Prop. J. 18 (2004); Mark Davison, *Shape Trade Marks: The Role and Relevance of Functionality and Aesthetics in Determining Their Registrability*, 15 Austl. Intell. Prop. J. 106, 108–09 (2004); Craig Smith, *Trade Mark Protection for Product Shape—Where Does the Public Interest Lie?*, 63 Intell. Prop. F. 32, 41 (2005).

been sidestepped in a subsequent case involving color marks,[51] and, most tellingly, they have not been adopted by the Trade Marks Office in its examination practices involving non-traditional marks.[52] The current position in Australia appears to be that if an applicant for registration of a functional shape or color mark can demonstrate that the mark has acquired distinctiveness, it will be accepted for registration. Although this has proven to be a difficult test to satisfy, given that the Office demands robust evidence that the shape or color has come to be relied on by consumers as a badge of origin,[53] it is by no means impossible. An analysis of the Australian register reveals that a substantial number of functional non-traditional marks (including the fence-dropper shape in *Mayne Industries*, and the chair shape in *Sebel*) have been registered since the new Act came into force. Much the same position has been reached in New Zealand, which also lacks a functionality bar to registration.[54]

What this means is that the requirement that infringing use be "trademark use" is the *only* mechanism in Australian and New Zealand trademark law that can potentially ensure that third parties remain free to use functional features of product packaging and product design. In this regard—and keeping in mind the point made above that trademark use at the infringement stage has long been interpreted flexibly, in order to secure valuable policy objectives—it is unsurprising that Australian courts have found that the use of functional features of registered marks categorically falls outside the scope of the doctrine. This categorical exclusion is to be welcomed from a policy perspective. Indeed, the Federal Court's approach has helped ensure that market space is created for competitors who wish to copy the functional features of the mark owner's goods, even if technical alternatives of dissimilar appearance are available to those competitors.[55] However, the reasoning in *Philips v. Remington* and subsequent cases has two key problems, and has created something of an internal tension as to how the concept of "use" operates at different stages within the registration system.[56]

The first problem relates to the ongoing reliance on the idea developed under former legislation that a "mark" needs to have a separate identity from the marked goods—something known as the severability doctrine. Put simply, the applicability of the severability doctrine depends entirely on the level of abstraction at which the

[51] *See* Philmac Pty. Ltd. v. Registrar of Trade Marks, (2002) 126 F.C.R. 525, 544–46 (Mansfield J.) (recognizing that colors might serve a number of functional purposes, but finding these to be relevant only to the question of whether a color mark is inherently distinctive).

[52] On Office practice, *see* IP AUSTRALIA, TRADE MARKS OFFICE MANUAL OF PRACTICE AND PROCEDURE pt 19A.2.6 (2018), http://manuals.ipaustralia.gov.au/trademarks/Part_19A_Use_of_a_Trade_Mark/19A.2_Use__as_a_trade_mark_.htm ("Functional features (e.g. on a shape trade mark) make it less likely (though not impossible) that a sign is acting as a badge of origin"). *See also* Michael Arblaster, *Shape as a Trade Mark*, 40 INTELL. PROP. F. 30, 34–35 (2000).

[53] *See generally* ROBERT BURRELL & MICHAEL HANDLER, AUSTRALIAN TRADE MARK LAW 147–51 (2d ed. 2016).

[54] *See* Fredco Trading Ltd. v. Miller, [2006] N.Z.C.A. 151. For comment, *see* Rob Batty, *Is New Zealand's Trade Marks Law Out of Shape?*, 33 EUR. INTELL. PROP. REV. 281 (2011).

[55] For extensive discussion of the consideration of the "right to copy" and the "need to copy" in the utilitarian functionality doctrine under U.S. law, *see* Mark P. McKenna, *(Dys)functionality*, 48 HOUS. L. REV. 824 (2011); Robert G. Bone, *Trademark Functionality Reexamined*, 7 J. LEGAL AFF. 183 (2015).

[56] My discussion of these problems draws on BURRELL & HANDLER, *supra* note 53, at 77–78, 135–36.

"goods" are defined. It is only if the inherent form of goods is defined as being coterminous with the functional shape or other functional feature that it makes any real sense to say that they are inseparable (such that there can be no use of any "mark" for the purposes of the trademark use inquiry). But once that inherent form is defined at a higher level of abstraction, a distinction can more readily be drawn between that form and the product feature in question. Thus, in *Philips v. Remington*, the only way it could be said that Remington's shape was inseparable from its goods is if the goods were categorized as "electric shavers with three rotary shaving heads arranged in an equilateral triangle". But if the goods were classified generically, as "shavers" or even "electric shavers," it must be possible to say that a particular configuration of the shaving head is different or severable from the goods. In such a case, the shape could therefore be a sign "used in relation to the goods," and potentially used "as a trademark."[57] The retention of the severability doctrine to avoid a finding of trademark use seems to involve little more than the assertion of a desirable policy outcome.

The second, related problem with *Philips v. Remington* and the subsequent infringement cases is that they pay insufficient attention to what the finding that a functional product feature can never be "used" as a trademark means for the distinctiveness inquiry. The essence of the acquired distinctiveness test is whether a sign has been presented to consumers in such a way that, over time, they have come to associate the sign exclusively with the applicant for registration and rely on it as a source indicator. There are complex issues here about the desirability of, say, allowing a former patentee or design owner to be able to point to a period of monopoly use of the product under the patent or design as evidence that can go toward establishing acquired distinctiveness in the configuration of the product.[58] But the key point is that a sign is clearly being used as a trademark if consumers come to rely on the sign as an indicator of trade origin. This can even be seen in *Philips v. Remington* itself: the evidence presented by Philips, in the context of its separate argument that Remington had engaged in passing off, indicated that consumers had come to associate the equilateral triangle shaver head shape with Philips—this being strong evidence of use of its shaver configuration as a trademark.[59] All of this points toward something that in most other jurisdictions has been recognized as uncontroversial: because functional marks *can* be used so that they acquire distinctiveness, then if it is thought desirable to prevent such marks from registration on competition-based policy grounds a separate bar to registration is needed. A functional mark cannot be kept off the register on the basis that it can never be used as a mark. Yet in neither the Full Court's decision in *Philips v. Remington* nor any of the subsequent Australian cases is there any recognition of this point, or its implications. None of the judges looked to the grounds of refusal in the EU, the U.S. or any other country that had adopted a functionality bar to registration—such grounds having been structured

[57] *See also Kenman Kandy, supra* note 49, 525 (Full Fed. Ct., Lindgren J.).

[58] *See, e.g.*, Justin Hughes, *Cognitive and Aesthetic Functionality in Trademark Law*, 36 Cardozo L. Rev. 1227, 1270–73 (2015); McCutcheon, *supra* note 50.

[59] *See Koninklijke Philips Electronics NV, supra* note 39, 204, 207 (Lehane J.).

around the possibility that a functional mark could acquire distinctiveness—and considered how those grounds might, in turn, indicate that third parties could also potentially use functional signs as trademarks, and infringe a registered mark by doing so.[60]

What is perhaps striking about *Philips v. Remington* on appeal, *Mayne Industries*, and *Sebel* is that the courts could have arrived at the same results through a much more orthodox interpretation of trademark use.[61] In each case there was no evidence to suggest that the defendants were doing anything in the promotion of their goods to suggest their shapes were operating as badges of origin. Further, in each case the defendants were using clear, primary branding on their goods ("Remington" on the shaver; "ezy-lock" on a swing tag attached to the fence dropper; "Titan" branded chairs), which, for reasons that will be explored in more detail in the next section, must have counted against the shapes playing a source-identifying role in the minds of consumers. Instead, by attempting categorically to exclude functional signs from the rubric of "trademark use," the Federal Court has created a somewhat unstable doctrine that has caused tensions between understandings of "use" at the distinctiveness and infringement stages.[62] While this approach is consistent with the protean, policy-oriented role that the doctrine has long played specifically at the infringement stage in British Commonwealth law, the tensions created by this approach reveal that the problems raised by functional marks are better addressed at a threshold level, by attempting to filter out such marks through a standalone bar to registration.[63]

There is, however, a more unexpected, and more significant, problem with the way the Australian courts have embedded functionality concerns within the trademark use inquiry. It relates to the way the courts have come to interpret trademark use in cases involving *non-functional*, non-traditional marks. As will be seen in the following section, both Australian and New Zealand courts have approached this

[60] That a product feature may serve a functional purpose and also serve as a trademark has been recognized by the High Court of New Zealand, in obiter dicta: *see* Coca-Cola Co. v. Frucor Soft Drinks Ltd., (2013) 104 I.P.R. 432, 461 (Wylie J.).

[61] *See supra* note 39 and accompanying text.

[62] A point made by Batty, *Is New Zealand's Trade Marks Law Out of Shape?*, *supra* note 54, at 286.

[63] There are additional costs in allowing functional marks on the register, even if the problems with many of them are addressed at the infringement stage. If we take seriously that a primary justification for having a register is that it provides valuable information, verified by a bureaucratic process, as to the signs that third parties should and should not be able to use, then it must be the case that some traders will understand that a registration is a clear signal to steer clear of the use of that mark or a similar variant. A well-advised trader might be told that if it chooses to adopt a functional sign that is closely similar to a registered but functional mark the chances of a successful infringement action being brought against it are small. But even a well-advised trader might not wish to take such a risk. This is not only because of the difficulty of determining whether or not a registered mark is truly functional, or whether the trader might be liable if it copies both functional and non-functional elements of a registered mark. It is also because the costs of adopting a different functional product and suffering any associated commercial disadvantage in so doing might seem to be better able to be absorbed than the costs and inconvenience involved in successfully defending Federal Court infringement proceedings. In other words, even if the law seems to be clearly on the side of parties seeking to make use of functional trademarked product features, the chilling effects of registration, and the potentially negative impact on competition that might result, still need to be taken seriously: *see generally* Robert G. Bone, *Notice Failure and Defenses in Trademark Law*, 96 B.U. L. Rev. 1245 (2016).

issue in a worrying manner, the consequence of which is that third party traders are unduly restricted in their ability to make decorative or descriptive use of features of shape and color contained in registered marks.

IV. Trademark Use and Non-Functional Marks

Understanding the way Australian courts have treated non-functional, non-traditional marks at the infringement stage first requires an appreciation of the surprising way they have come to assess the distinctiveness of such marks. The key authority here is the 2002 decision of the Full Court of the Federal Court in *Kenman Kandy Australia Pty. Ltd. v. Registrar of Trade Marks*.[64] That case concerned the distinctiveness of an imaginary, six-legged "bug shape" for confectionery, represented below in Figure 8.2.

Notwithstanding that the bug shape was not technically functional, the two majority judges considered functionality and the Full Court's reasoning in *Philips v. Remington* in detail. In doing so, they seemed to believe that only technically functional shape marks give rise to sufficient competition concerns that would justify the distinctiveness test being interpreted strictly, so that it might operate as a barrier to the registration of such marks.[65] But when the judges turned their attention to the distinctiveness of the shape before them, they considered that because it could be described as being "invented"[66] or "concocted"[67] it should be treated as if it were an invented or concocted word. On that basis, the majority found the shape mark to be inherently distinctive.

Other commentators and I have argued elsewhere that *Kenman Kandy* is a troubling decision that draws a false ontological equivalence between invented words and invented shapes, and puts the Australian law of distinctiveness badly out of step with other jurisdictions,[68] most notably the U.S.[69] The key problem with the decision for present purposes is that by seeing the functionality of a shape as a factor that makes it non-distinctive, the Court mistakenly assumed the obverse of this proposition: that non-functional, sufficiently striking features of a shape must therefore make it inherently distinctive. In doing so, *Kenman Kandy* has significantly lowered the threshold for what makes a non-functional shape mark distinctive, riding roughshod over competition concerns in the process.[70]

The Federal Court's approach to non-functional shape marks in *Kenman Kandy* has, unfortunately, influenced the way it has come to assess such marks at the infringement stage. The clearest illustration of the Court's problematic approach is

[64] *Kenman Kandy, supra* note 49.

[65] *See supra* note 50 for criticism of this reasoning.

[66] *Kenman Kandy, supra* note 49, 535 (Stone J.).

[67] *Id.* at 536–37. A similar approach was taken by French J.: *id.* at 510–11.

[68] BURRELL & HANDLER, *supra* note 53, at 136–38; Davison, *Shape Trade Marks, supra* note 50, at 109–10.

[69] *See* Wal-Mart Stores, Inc. v. Samara Bros., Inc., 529 U.S. 205 (2000) (holding that product configuration can never be inherently distinctive).

[70] That is, the effect of the decision is that it allows a first mover in a market to secure potentially perpetual trademark rights over a new product design even before it commences use of the design, denying future competitors the ability to compete in the market for similarly shaped goods by using that or a similar design.

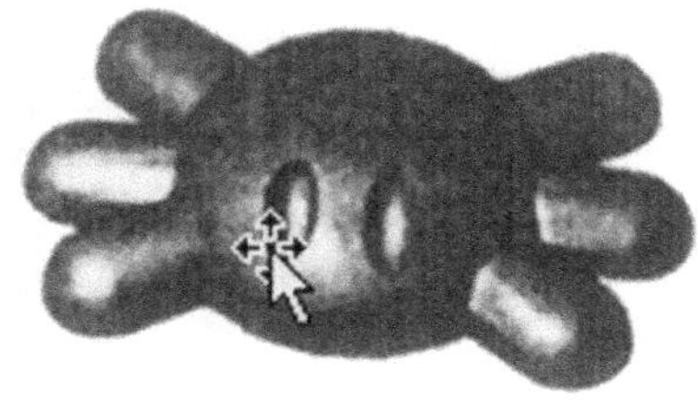

Figure 8.2 Australian registered trade mark 783465

Global Brand Marketing Inc. v. YD Pty. Ltd.[71] The two registered marks in question consisted of the configuration of a shoe and the sole of a shoe, both represented below in Figure 8.3. These marks had been registered on the basis of inherent distinctiveness, but arguably only because both shapes bore the owner's prominent stylized "D" logo (which would have been inherently distinctive in its own right).[72] With no requirement under Australian law for a mark that consists of both distinctive and non-distinctive elements to be registered subject to a disclaimer over the exclusive use of the non-distinctive elements,[73] the two marks were registered without the owner needing to show that the shoe configuration or the sole pattern bore any source significance in isolation. The defendant sold shoes with an allegedly similar sole pattern and overall appearance, albeit marked with its "yd" logo and not the trademark owner's stylized "D" logo.

In considering the threshold question of whether the defendant's use of its sole and its shoe configuration involved trademark use, Sundberg J drew a distinction between functional features of goods on the one hand, and those features that might be "striking" or "make goods more arresting of appearance and more attractive" on the other hand. The latter were thought to be likely to be used as trademarks.[74] The defendant's shoe configuration was seen as presenting something of a challenge, in that it consisted of a mix of functional/common features (stripes on the side, a square toe cap, a facing, and a padded collar) and non-functional features (a piece on the heel, a flat sole, a rubber panel on the instep, the pattern on the sole, and the "yd" label). Sundberg J ultimately concluded that the non-functional elements

[71] Global Brand Marketing Inc. v. YD Pty. Ltd., (2008) 76 I.P.R. 161.

[72] The "D" logo had, in fact, been registered in Australia on the basis of inherent distinctiveness: Australian registered trademark 740924.

[73] The lack of such a requirement has been recognized as a problem in a number of recent Australian law reform inquiries: *see, e.g.*, ADVISORY COUNCIL ON INTELLECTUAL PROPERTY, REVIEW OF TRADE MARK ENFORCEMENT: FINAL REPORT 14–15 (2004), https://www.ipaustralia.gov.au/sites/g/files/net856/f/acip_final_report_review_of_trade_mark_enforcement.pdf; PRODUCTIVITY COMMISSION, INTELLECTUAL PROPERTY ARRANGEMENTS: DRAFT REPORT 335–36 (2016), http://www.pc.gov.au/inquiries/completed/intellectual-property/draft/intellectual-property-draft.pdf.

[74] *Global Brand*, *supra* note 71, 175, referring to *Coca-Cola Co. v. All-Fect Distributors Ltd.*, *supra* note 24, 118 (Full Fed. Ct.).

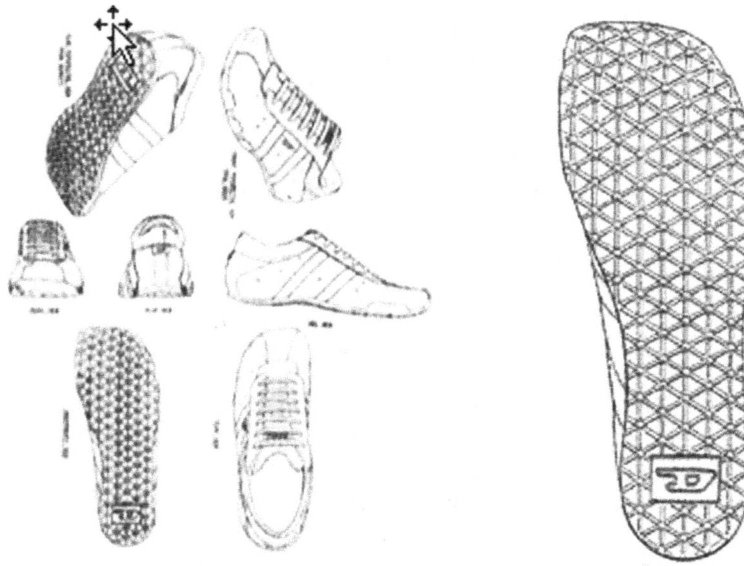

Figure 8.3 Diesel SpA's Australian registered trademarks 986713 & 986709

"overwhelmed" the functional elements, such that the *entire* configuration was being used as a trademark.[75] As for the defendant's sole, which Sundberg J emphasized was not technically functional, it was held that because the pattern was "distinctive" and would be noticed by shoppers, it was also being used as a trademark.[76] Ultimately, the defendant was able to avoid liability, but only on the basis that its sole and shoe designs were not sufficiently similar to the registered marks.

Global Brand suffers from a similar problem to *Kenman Kandy* in its assumption that features of a shape that are not technically functional will almost invariably serve a trademark purpose. By setting up this false dichotomy, the Court ended up taking the wrong approach in assessing whether non-functional product design features are being used in a trademark sense. It simply cannot be decisive that such features are "attractive" or "arresting of appearance," because this could equally support a finding that the features are being used in a purely ornamental or decorative (and non-trademark) manner. The Court ended up glossing over the factors that would help in a determination of whether features of shape are being used as trademarks, rather than as mere decoration. For example, there was little evidence in the case that the defendant had marketed its shoes in a manner that sought to present them, or the sole pattern in particular, as having source significance. Equally, there was little to suggest that consumers did in fact recognize these features as indicating the origin of the defendant's shoes—the limited evidence that consumers might have *noticed* the overall appearance and sole pattern of the defendant's shoes before purchase was clearly insufficient in this regard. Even more significantly, there was no consideration of the fact that the registered owner had not established that the configuration and sole pattern of its shoes, apart from its "D" logo, were distinctive, which would

[75] *Global Brand, supra* note 71, 177. [76] *Id.* at 176.

seem to be relevant to the question of whether consumers might ascribe source significance to such features when used by competitors. The reasoning in the case is problematic, and significantly limits the ability of traders to use aspects of registered shape and color marks in an ornamental manner.

Three other Australian and New Zealand cases—all involving allegations of infringement of Coca-Cola's registered "contour" bottle shape—also help to show some of the problems with the prevailing interpretation of trademark use as it applies to non-functional signs. Perhaps more importantly, these cases provide useful case studies of the *potential* for trademark use to be interpreted in a manner that gives owners of non-traditional marks an adequate degree of protection, while still ensuring that sufficient space is left for defendants seeking to make decorative use of features of shape and color.

In the earliest of these cases, *Coca-Cola Co. v. All-Fect Distributors Ltd.*,[77] the defendant's sale of cola-flavoured confectionery in the form of a flattened bottle shape reminiscent of Coca-Cola's contour bottle was held to involve trademark use of the shape. In its decision, the Full Court of the Federal Court focused on what it called the "non-descriptive" features of the defendant's bottle shape, being the silhouette, the fluting at the top and bottom, and the label band, which it considered to be "put there to make the goods more arresting of appearance and more attractive."[78] A broadly similar finding was made by the High Court of New Zealand in *Coca-Cola Co. v. Frucor Soft Drinks Ltd.*[79] and by the Federal Court of Australia in *Coca-Cola Co. v. PepsiCo Inc. (No. 2)*.[80] Both cases involved PepsiCo's use of an allegedly similar bottle to Coca-Cola's registered contour bottle. And in both cases, it was held that PepsiCo had made trademark use of its bottle shape. The Australian judge considered that the shape was "distinctive and [that] consumers would associate it with the Pepsi brand."[81] The New Zealand judge emphasized how PepsiCo's bottle was presented to the market: "as a 'unique, cool and trendy looking', 'easy to recognise' bottle with 'a great look', and a 'classic soda bottle shape'."[82] PepsiCo escaped liability in both jurisdictions only on the basis that its bottle shape was not deceptively similar to Coca-Cola's contour bottle.

On one level, the criticisms that can be levelled against the *Global Brand* decision apply with equal force to the three Coke bottle decisions—to concentrate on whether the defendant's sign is "striking" or "attractive" or "recognisable" cannot provide the answer as to whether the sign is being used as a trademark, rather than merely ornamentally. However, the cases are instructive in showing that shapes, as sub-brands, often perform different roles depending on the other signs that are used in conjunction with them, and that the trademark use doctrine *could* be used in a more sophisticated way to differentiate between permissible decorative use and use that ought to attract liability.[83]

77 *All-Fect Distributors Ltd., supra* note 24.

78 *Id.* at 118.

79 *Frucor, supra* note 60.

80 Coca-Cola Co. v. PepsiCo Inc. (No. 2), (2014) 109 I.P.R. 429.

81 *Id.* at 468 (Besanko J.).

82 *Frucor, supra* note 60, 462 (Wylie J.).

83 The following draws on ideas explored in BURRELL & HANDLER, *supra* note 53, at 381–82.

In many cases, shapes will be used where there is clearly a "competitive" relationship between the plaintiff's and defendant's goods, where such goods are marked with a word and/or device that acts as the primary indicator of source. Even if consumers learn that the plaintiff's shape can be used to determine the origin of the goods, and even where that shape is used for identical goods, consumers will rarely be confused if the principal brands are obviously different. For this reason, the findings in the related *PepsiCo* and *Frucor* decisions remain problematic. The fact that PepsiCo's bottle was prominently marked PEPSI must have served to push out any source identification function the shape of the bottle might otherwise have performed. In other words, the very presence of the word "Pepsi" must have prevented, or at least inhibited, consumers from perceiving the defendant's shape as a trademark.[84] Indeed, this is a further criticism that can be made of *Global Brand*—the presence of the "yd" logo on the defendant's competing shoes ought to have been seen as a strong visual cue that meant that consumers would not have ascribed source significance to the defendant's overall shoe configuration and sole pattern.

The situation might be different, however, in circumstances where there might be a "complementary" rather than a competitive relationship between brands. For example, imagine a pre-mixed vodka and cola drink being sold in a "contour" shaped bottle. Even if this bottle were to bear the mark of a well-known manufacturer of alcoholic beverages, say SMIRNOFF, the bottle shape might convey a very different meaning from the Pepsi example above. Some consumers might well conclude that the pre-mixed drink had been made using Coke (and not cola produced by some other manufacturer). Admittedly, this would not be enough to dispose of the question of whether this constituted use of the contour bottle shape as a trademark. If, instead of using the contour bottle, Smirnoff were to run an advertising campaign in which it was stated that "unlike other manufacturers, we make our pre-mixed drinks using Coca-Cola" then there would be an excellent argument that, in this context, use of the word "Coca-Cola" would be a form of nominative use that has not typically been regarded as trademark use in Australia.[85] However, in the case of the use of the contour bottle by Smirnoff, the meaning this would convey to consumers would be uncertain, and some consumers might well conclude not only that the pre-mixed drink must contain Coke but also that there must be some form of direct commercial relationship between the Coca-Cola Co. and Smirnoff. This uncertainty would be sufficient to categorize the use of the bottle shape as trademark use. It is for this reason that the *outcome* in *All-Fect* seems to be correct, even if the reasoning used by the Court to reach that outcome is flawed. In that case, the defendant's use of a similar contour bottle shape as the shape of its cola-flavoured confectionery may have created real uncertainty about

[84] It should be recalled that neither Australian nor New Zealand law prevent the taking of "unfair advantage" of well-known marks, in the absence of trademark use by defendants: *supra* note 26. A different outcome might be reached under EU law.

[85] *See* BURRELL & HANDLER, *supra* note 53, at 382–85.

the extent of a complementary trade relationship between the Coca-Cola Co. and the defendant, justifying a finding of infringement.

V. Conclusion

Historically, the requirement in many British Commonwealth countries that infringing use must be "trademark use" has proven to be a powerful mechanism for safeguarding various speech and competition concerns. In particular, it has helped ensure that even where registration of a mark is validly obtained, third party traders remain free to use descriptive language for descriptive purposes, or to use slogans and other insignia in a decorative manner. However, the trademark use doctrine has played a somewhat uncertain role in contemporary Australian and New Zealand law in dealing with the challenges thrown up by non-traditional marks. While it has been usefully employed to ensure that defendants remain free to use functional features of registered shape marks, the reasoning in some of the Australian cases tends to rest on a largely unarticulated distinction between "use" at the infringement and distinctiveness stages,[86] and seems designed to compensate for the absence of a functionality bar to registration. Further, the courts' focus on functionality in assessing infringement has had a highly unfortunate side effect: courts have too readily accepted that a defendant's use of *non-functional* features of shape constitutes trademark use. The longstanding care taken by courts to ensure that defendants can make descriptive or ornamental use of registered word and device marks is barely to be seen in the modern Australian and New Zealand cases involving descriptive or ornamental use of non-functional, non-traditional marks.

These problems do not, however, indicate fundamental weaknesses in the doctrine. Trademark use could easily be reshaped by the courts in cases involving non-traditional marks. In particular, courts need to look beyond whether a defendant has adopted a "striking" or "attractive" product feature, and demand cogent evidence, based on the specifics of the defendant's conduct, that demonstrates that the defendant is using a feature of shape or color as *its* source identifier. In doing so, courts should scrutinize whether the defendant's use is in a clearly competing context, such that the presence of a primary, distinguishing brand is more likely to ensure that the feature of shape or color is not playing a source identifying role, or whether the defendant's use of such a feature gives rise to real doubt about whether there is a complementary trade relationship between it and the mark owner. In calling for this recalibration of trademark use—a model which might potentially be of interest to other jurisdictions—it is worth emphasizing that this would ensure that owners of

[86] It is also a distinction the Federal Court might potentially revisit, given the way it has (problematically) read out the *Champagne Heidsieck* principle from the modern Australian test of trademark use, in developing a more unitary conception of "use": *see* Burrell & Handler, *A Requiem, supra* note 32, 115–18; Scandinavian Tobacco Group Eersel BV v. Trojan Trading Co. Pty. Ltd., (2016) 243 F.C.R. 152 (Full Fed. Ct.).

non-traditional marks only have a narrow sphere of protection. Yet this is to be welcomed: non-traditional marks should, in general terms, be both difficult to register *and* difficult to infringe, given the serious competition problems that would result from affording over-broad protection to such subject matter. Trademark use, despite its complexities and problems in application, remains an important means of ensuring that the scope of protection given to such marks remains in check.

9

Protecting Non-Traditional Trademarks in China

New Opportunities and Challenges

Haochen Sun

I. Introduction

China has become the world's second largest consumer market.[1] Chinese consumers purchased an estimated US $10.2 billion worth of luxury goods in 2013 alone, amounting to approximately 47% of the luxury sector's total global sales.[2] In addition, the country's consumers now purchase more non-luxury goods and services than their counterparts anywhere else in the world. For example, China is now the world's largest car market.[3] Given Chinese consumers' general preference for foreign branded products and services, China has become the most significant market for many transnational companies.

Non-traditional trademarks have become an important tool for transnational companies looking to market their goods and services in China. They offer new ways to attract consumers, as they differ from the words, logos, letters, and numbers that are traditionally used as trademarks. Today, they are increasingly being used in the marketplace thanks to the expansion of the Internet and rising use of new technologies.

This chapter addresses the scope of non-traditional trademarks in the context of China. That scope encompasses not only color, motion, sound, and three-dimensional marks, but also marks that have been adapted into Chinese-language versions. Transnational companies need to localize their marketing strategies in ways that suit the cognitive abilities of Chinese consumers. One such strategy is the use

[1] Jeff Walters et al., *Five Profiles That Explain China's Consumer Economy*, THE BOSTON CONSULTING GROUP, June 2017, http://image-src.bcg.com/Images/BCG-Five-Profiles-That-Explain-Chinas-Consumer-Economy-June-2017_2_tcm52-162981.pdf. ("China's consumer market, both currently and as projected for 2021, is the world's second largest, behind only the US.")

[2] Lian Liu, *Is the Shine Gone from Luxury Goods?*, China Daily Asia, Feb. 19, 2014, http://www.chinadailyasia.com/business/2014-02/19/content_15119218.html.

[3] Tian Ying, *China Ends U.S.'s Reign as Largest Auto Market*, Bloomberg News, Jan. 11, 2010, http://www.bloomberg.com/apps/news?pid=newsarchive&sid=aE.x_r_l9NZE.

Protecting Non-Traditional Trademarks in China: New Opportunities and Challenges. Haochen Sun.

in China of a Chinese version of a company's trademark, which will of course look quite unfamiliar, and even strange, to people in other parts of the world who do not know the Chinese language.[4] From this perspective, the Chinese version of a trademark can be regarded as a non-traditional trademark.

Drawing on a series of cases that Hermès has litigated in China, the chapter discusses how transnational companies should tap into the potential of non-traditional trademarks to promote their businesses in China. Section I of the chapter provides an overview of the most important requirements for registering such trademarks in China. It considers why the Chinese courts rejected Hermès' bid to register the shape of its Kelly bag as a three-dimensional trademark in China. Through the lens of several trademark cases that the French high-fashion luxury brand litigated in China, Sections II and III offer nuanced analysis of how companies can protect their trademarks in the Chinese first-to-file registration system and how to determine the well-known-trademark status in the country. Sections IV and V further examine the lessons that can be learnt from the Hermès cases about securing anti-confusion and anti-dilution protection of non-traditional trademarks in China.

II. Registration of Non-Traditional Trademarks

A. Registrable subject matter

The Chinese Trademark Law was first enacted in 1982 and has been revised several times since then. Article 7 of the 1982 Trademark Law prescribes that "[a]ny word or design, or combination thereof, used as a trademark, shall have distinctive characteristics so as to facilitate identification."[5] Therefore, the law allows the registration of Chinese versions of foreign marks. However, it remains ambiguous concerning whether other forms of non-traditional marks are registrable in China.

China joined the World Trade Organization in December 2001, which made it a member state of the Agreement on Trade-Related Aspects of Intellectual Property Rights (the TRIPS Agreement). Accordingly, it revised the 1982 Trademark Law (including Article 7) in 2001 to bring it into line with the minimum standards of protection in the TRIPS Agreement. Article 8 of the 2001 Trademark Law specifies the scope of registrable marks in China as follows:

> Any visible sign that can serve to distinguish the goods of a natural person, legal person, or other organization from those of another, including any word, design, letter of the alphabet, numeral, three-dimensional symbol and color combination, or any combination of the above, may be made a trademark for application for registration.[6]

[4] LOKE-KHOON TAN, TRADEMARK LAW IN CHINA—PIRATES IN THE MIDDLE KINGDOM: THE NEW FRONTIER 21–32 (2017) (discussing how to use the Chinese version of trademarks to do business successfully in China).

[5] Shangbiao Fa (商标法) [Trademark Law] (promulgated by the Standing Comm. Nat'l People's Cong., Aug. 23, 1982, effective Mar. 1, 1983), http://en.pkulaw.cn/display.aspx?cgid=44439&lib=law.

[6] Shangbiao Fa (商标法) [Trademark Law] (promulgated by the Standing Comm. Nat'l People's Cong., Aug. 23, 1982, effective Mar. 1, 1983, amended by the Standing Comm. Nat'l People's Cong., Oct. 27, 2001), http://www.wipo.int/wipolex/en/text.jsp?file_id=131395.

Article 8 clarifies two aspects of non-traditional trademark registration. First, it allows the registration of such non-traditional marks as those in three-dimensional form and those consisting of colors. Second, as it expressly requires that registrable signs be visible, it excludes sound and smell marks from the scope of registrable marks.

In 2013, China revised the Trademark Law[7] again, with the revised Article 8 further expanding the scope of registrable marks:

> Any signs, including words, graphs, letters, numbers, three-dimensional symbols, color combinations, sound or any combination thereof, that are capable of distinguishing the goods of a natural person, legal person or other organization from those of others may be applied for registration as trademarks.

By removing the visibility requirement, the 2013 Trademark Law permits the registration of sound marks, but the revision made no attempt to render other types of non-traditional trademarks, including smell, taste, and motion marks, registrable in China.[8] The draft revision proposed allowing the registration of single-color marks if they had acquired distinctiveness through use, but the proposal was not adopted.[9] Therefore, single-color marks remain unregistrable in China.[10]

B. Distinctiveness and functionality

Distinctiveness is a core requirement for registering trademarks, including non-traditional trademarks, in China. Article 9 of the 2013 Trademark Law states that "[a] trademark submitted for registration shall bear noticeable characteristics and be readily distinguishable . . . ."

The distinctiveness requirement under Chinese trademark law has two layers: inherent distinctiveness and acquired distinctiveness. On the one hand, Article 9 of the 2013 Trademark Law allows a sign that has inherent distinctiveness to be registered as a trademark. On the other, Article 11 permits a descriptive or generic sign that lacks inherent distinctiveness to become registrable if it has acquired distinctiveness through use.[11]

[7] Shangbiao Fa (商标法) [Trademark Law] (promulgated by the Standing Comm. Nat'l People's Cong., Aug. 23, 1982, effective Mar. 1, 1983, amended by the Standing Comm. Nat'l People's Cong., Aug. 30, 2013), http://www.wipo.int/wipolex/en/text.jsp?file_id=425554 [hereinafter 2013 Trademark Law].

[8] Peizhen Wu, *The Colourful Challenge of Non-Traditional Trademarks in China*, World Trademark Rev., Aug.–Sep. 2011, at 104, http://www.worldtrademarkreview.com/Magazine/Issue/32/Country-correspondents/China-Kangxin-Partners-PC.

[9] *See e.g.*, King & Wood Mallesons' Trademark Group, *Eight Key Points about the Third Amendment to the PRC Trademark Law*, King & Wood Mallesons, Sep. 6, 2013, http://www.chinalawinsight.com/2013/09/articles/trademark/eight-key-points-about-the-third-amendment-to-the-prc-trademark-law/.

[10] John Froemming et al., *Lending Color to Trademarks: Protection and Enforcement of Color Marks in the U.S., EU, China and Japan*, INTA Bulletin (July 1, 2015), https://www.inta.org/INTABulletin/Pages/ColorMarks_in_US_EU_China_Japan_7012.aspx.

[11] Article 11 of the 2013 Trademark Law stipulates as follows:

Among all non-traditional trademarks, it is most difficult for an applicant to demonstrate the distinctiveness of a sound mark. This is because average consumers do not necessarily treat sound as an indicator of source of goods. Rather, they may perceive sound merely as background music in an advertisement or as an emission generated by a product when it is used. In 2014, Tencent applied to register the "Di Di Di Di Di Di" sound mark, which was a notification sound used in its QQ instant messaging software. The Chinese Trademark Office rejected the application on the grounds that the sound lacks distinctiveness. Given that the sound is simple and not creative, consumers would not associate the instant messaging software with Tencent.[12]

However, a sound mark could still acquire distinctiveness through long-term use. The first successful registration of a sound mark in China was achieved by the Chinese Radio International (CRI) in 2016. The sound mark consists of forty-seconds of music with a human voice pronouncing the full Chinese name of CRI. Owing to CRI's consistent use of this sound mark at the beginning of its broadcasting programs since 1998, listeners have become able to associate the mark with CRI.[13]

In addition to distinctiveness, the 2013 Trademark Law has a special requirement for three-dimensional trademarks. To be registered as a trademark, a three-dimensional sign must be non-functional. Article 12 of the 2013 Trademark Law stipulates this requirement as follows.

> No application for registration of a three-dimensional symbol as a trademark may be granted, where the sign merely indicates the shape inherent in the nature of the goods concerned, or it is only dictated by the need to achieve technical effects or the need to give the goods substantive value.

The Chinese Supreme Court's ruling in a case brought by Hermès sheds important light on how the distinctiveness and non-functionality requirements should be applied to assess the registrability of three-dimensional marks. The case concerned Hermès' attempt to register the shape of its Kelly bag as a three-dimensional trademark, which the Chinese Trademark Office refused. That refusal prompted Hermès to litigate in the Beijing First Intermediate Court and High Court, both of which upheld the decision made by the Chinese Trademark Office. Hermès then petitioned the Chinese Supreme Court, requesting that it review the lower court decisions. The Supreme Court handed down a decision against Hermès, ruling that the shape of its Kelly bag could not be registered as a three-dimensional trademark in China.

None of the following marks may be registered as trademarks:

(1) Where the mark bears only the generic name, design, or model number of the goods concerned; (2) Where it only directly indicates the quality, principal raw materials, function, use, weight, quantity or other features of the goods; and (3) Signs that otherwise lack any distinctive character. Any mark mentioned in the preceding paragraph may be registered as a trademark if it has acquired distinctive features through use and is readily distinguishable.

[12] *Tencent QQ Sues Chinese Government for Denying Signature Sound's Trademark*, CHINA DAILY, Dec. 9, 2016, http://www.chinadaily.com.cn/china/2016-12/09/content_27620932.htm.

[13] Ai-Leen Lim, *The Trademarking of Sounds—China Witnesses a Cacophony of Applications*, CONVENTUS LAW, Apr. 22, 2017, http://www.conventuslaw.com/report/the-trademarking-of-sounds-china-witnesses-a/.

On the one hand, the Chinese Supreme Court explained why functionality is a bar to registering a three-dimensional mark as a trademark. Because the three-dimensional shape of a product is inseparable from the product itself, the public will normally view a three-dimensional mark as an integral part of the product concerned, thus rendering it unsuitable for registration as a trademark.

On the other hand, the Supreme Court also pointed out that a three-dimensional product shape can be registered as a trademark if it has inherent or acquired distinctiveness. A three-dimensional such shape has inherent source-identifying distinctiveness if it contains distinctive features allowing it to be differentiated from the shape of similar products. Alternatively, it can acquire distinctiveness through repeated use in the marketplace. Acquired distinctiveness through use enables the consuming public to associate the shape with the product's manufacturer.

Hence, the Supreme Court decided the case on the basis of whether the shape of the Hermès Kelly bag had inherent or acquired distinctiveness. With respect to the former, it opined that the main features of the Kelly bag design, such as its upper cover, belt, and metal lock, were common elements of other bag designs. Given that the combination of those features did not render the Kelly bag distinguishable from numerous other bags on the market, its three-dimensional shape could not be deemed inherently distinctive. With respect to the latter, the Supreme Court further ruled that the evidence submitted by Hermès did not demonstrate that the bag's three-dimensional shape had acquired distinctiveness through use for two reasons. First, in the Court's opinion, Hermès had presented a paucity of evidence of advertising in mainland China. Furthermore, the promotional materials it offered had nothing to do with the three-dimensional shape of the Kelly bag, but primarily concerned the company's historical developments and commercial operations. Second, the consumer survey report that Hermès submitted to the Court failed to prove that any association between the Kelly bag shape and Hermès had been created in the minds of the relevant sector of consumers. Instead, the report exhibited only consumers' interest in the three-dimensional shape of the bag itself. It remained unclear whether consumers considered the three-dimensional mark to have acquired a source-identifying function.

Based on its analysis of the distinctiveness requirement under Chinese trademark law, the Supreme Court ruled out the possibility of the three-dimensional shape of the Kelly bag being registered as a trademark. However, that ruling does not necessarily mean that it is exceedingly difficult, or even impossible, to prove the distinctiveness of a three-dimensional mark to the satisfaction of the Chinese Trademark Office or the Chinese courts. After all, recent years have seen an increasing number of registrations of three-dimensional trademarks in China, including, for example, the Coca-Cola bottle, Zippo lighter, Toblerone chocolate bar, Rolls Royce's Spirit of Ecstasy hood ornament, [14] and Ferrero Rocher's golden paper-wrapped chocolate packaging.[15]

[14] Brandy E. Baker, *The Gradual Expansion of Non-traditional Trademark Registration in China*, Kangxin Partners Jan. 21, 2014, http://www.kangxin.com/en/index.php?optionid=992&auto_id=590.

[15] Gang Hu, *Registrability on 3D Trademark Recognized by Chinese Court*, CCPIT Patent And Trademark Law Office, Sep. 4, 2008, http://www.ccpit-patent.com.cn/node/2815.

As long as a non-traditional mark meets the requirements for registration (the distinctiveness requirement in particular), it can be registered in China and will be protected. For example, the Chinese Court ruled that Ferrero Rocher's mark consisting of the three-dimensional shape of a ball-shaped praline wrapped in gold-colored creased paper set in a brown and gold base with ripple patterns was sufficiently distinctive for trademark registration. Because those colors and the layout of the mark are not commonly used in the industry for chocolates, the unique creativity of the mark makes it a symbolic design for Ferrero Rocher's chocolates. In this context, consumers could associate chocolates bearing such a mark with Ferrero Rocher.[16]

III. The First-to-File Rule

The Chinese Trademark Office closely adheres to the "first-to-file" rule in assessing the registrability of a trademark.[17] Under this procedural rule, a trademark registration will be granted to the first person or company to file the mark with the Chinese Trademark Office, provided that it meets the substantive requirements for registration. Although the first-to-file rule seems a simple procedure on its face, it actually poses an enormous challenge for transnational companies looking to register and protect non-traditional marks in China.[18] Trademark squatters may come up with words or logos that sound or look similar in Chinese in ways that transnational companies could not foresee owing to cultural gaps and their limited Chinese-language ability. Many such squatters attempt to register those words or logos as trademarks without any intention of using them commercially but simply to be able to demand payouts and threaten litigation against companies using similar—very often legitimate—marks in China.

The legal battle between Hermès and Chinese company Dafeng epitomizes the urgency for transnational companies to take the first-to-file rule seriously and adopt proper registration strategies for their non-traditional trademarks. Hermès registered the Hermès mark and its logo in China in 1977, but did not register any Chinese transliteration of "Hermès" as a trademark. In 1995, Dafeng applied to the Chinese Trademark Office to register a Chinese word mark reading "Ai Ma Shi" for its clothing products. The application passed the preliminary review. Then, in 1997, Hermès brought an action to the Chinese Trademark Office opposing the preliminary approval of Dafeng's trademark registration. The company

[16] Feilieluo Youxian Gongsi Su Guojia Gongshang Xingzheng Guanli Zongju Shangbiao Pingshen Weiyuanhui (费列罗有限公司诉国家工商行政管理总局商标评审委员会) [Ferrero SpA v. Trademark Appeal Board of the State Administration for Industry & Commerce of the People's Republic of China], 9 C.T.M.R. 105 (Beijing First Interm. People's Ct. Nov. 12, 2007).

[17] Sunny Chang, *Combating Trademark Squatting in China: New Developments in Chinese Trademark Law and Suggestions for the Future*, 34 Nw. J. Int'l L. & Bus. 337, 345 (2014) ("China follows a first-to-file system for trademark.").

[18] *Id.* at 346.

contended that Dafeng's trademark was too similar to the Chinese transliteration of its own registered trademark (also pronounced "Ai Ma Shi" in Chinese). The Trademark Office rejected Hermès' appeal and officially approved Dafeng's registration in 2001, prompting Hermès to take its appeal to the Beijing First Intermediate Court.[19]

Hermès' grounds for appeal were twofold. First, it asserted that the Chinese transliteration of "Hermès" did not have a fixed Chinese translation, and it was naturally first developed and utilized by Hermès itself. Further, the Hermès trademark and its Chinese transliteration were highly reputable within China. Thanks to the considerable amount it had spent on advertising, the company argued, the Hermès trademark and its Chinese transliteration were strongly and clearly differentiated in the minds of Chinese consumers. Second, Hermès alleged that Dafeng had acted in bad faith in registering its mark, because it obviously knew that its mark would cause confusion among consumers. Hermès provided evidence regarding the fame and recognition of its trademark, as well as evidence suggesting that Dafeng's registered trademark constituted an imitation of the Hermès trademark for exploitative purposes. However, the Beijing First Intermediate Court upheld the Trademark Office's decision, prompting Hermès to further appeal to the Beijing High Court in 2012.[20]

The Beijing High Court, too, ruled against Hermès, determining that Dafeng had legally registered its Chinese trademark. It held that allowing Hermès to register Dafeng's Chinese trademark would run counter to Article 28 of the 2010 Trademark Law on several grounds: (1) Dafeng had registered its mark prior to Hermès; (2) both marks come under the "clothing" category; (3) the two marks bear striking similarities; and (4) Hermès could not satisfactorily prove that its mark would not sow public confusion. Central to the High Court's decision was its adherence to the first-to-file rule. Because Hermès had not attempted to register the Chinese transliteration of its mark before Dafeng, it was not entitled to that transliteration despite having registered the Hermès mark in China and having an international reputation.

Moreover, as later cases revealed, not only had the Chinese transliteration of the Hermès mark been registered as a trademark, but so too had been a wide range of surprisingly strange variations of the Hermès mark and logo, including "HermesEpitek," "HERM," and "Aimas." Therefore, it is clearly not feasible for transnational companies to foretell all possible scenarios and then register every Chinese transliteration or logo that may sound and appear similar to their registered trademarks. The range of cases associated with the Hermès mark suggests that the problem of the "trademark troll" stems from the Chinese trademark system's first-to-file rule. The French firm is not alone in suffering such a fate, with the number of trademark troll cases growing rapidly in recent years. Trademark squatters typically

[19] Hermès Int'l S.A. v. Trademark Appeal Board of the State Admin. for Indus. & Commerce of the People's Republic of China (Third party: Dafeng Garment Factory), 2013 Gaoxingzhong No. 615 (Beijing First Intermediate Ct. Apr. 28, 2013).

[20] *Id.*

target transnational companies, causing severe damage to their businesses and reputations.[21] For example, in April 2012, a Chinese Court ordered Castel Freres SAS, a French wine manufacturer, to pay over US$5 million in compensation for infringing the "Ka Si Te" trademark, which is the Chinese transliteration of "Castel."[22] Moreover, in August 2014, Tesla Motors Inc. had to resolve a trademark squatting dispute with a Chinese businessman before the U.S. electric car maker could finally market its brand in China.[23]

As a response to the increasingly serious problem of trademark trolls, the 2013 revision of the Chinese Trademark Law was intended to prevent abusive exploitation of the first-to-file rule. First, the 2013 revision establishes the principle of good faith as the legal basis for filing trademark cancellation requests.[24] The new Article 7 provides that an application for trademark registration and the use of a trademark be based on the principle of good faith and that the principle constitutes a solid ground for trademark cancellation.[25] The new Article 45 also addresses the consequences of malicious registration, stipulating that trademarks so registered may be canceled even after the five-year limit. Moreover, the 2013 Trademark Law also takes into account the liability of trademark agencies, which are now required to act in good faith and abide by relevant laws and regulations,[26] and are civilly liable in the case of any violation.[27] The incorporation of the principle of good faith in the 2013 Trademark Law, together with the corresponding statutory provisions, requires the Chinese Trademark Office and the courts to examine trademark registration applications more rigorously. Therefore, the owners of registered non-traditional marks are now in a better position to guard against malicious attempts to register signs that look identical or similar to those marks, whether they are registered in China or elsewhere in the world.

IV. Recognition of Well-Known Trademarks

Compared with ordinary trademarks, well-known trademarks receive a higher level of protection in China. For instance, while unregistered ordinary marks are not protected at all, unregistered well-known marks are protected against unauthorized

[21] Paolo Beconcini, *China: An End to Trademark Grabbing in China?*, MONDAQ, Dec. 11, 2013, http://www.mondaq.com/x/272936/Trademark/Enforcement+Of+Trademark+Rights+In+China+In+Light+Of+The+New+Trademark+Law+Does+The+New+Law+Properly+Address+The+Issue+Of+Trademark+Grabbing.

[22] Paolo Beconcini & Kelly Liu, *$5M Case Highlights Risk From Chinese Trademark Trolls*, LAW360, Oct. 17, 2012, http://www.law360.com/articles/386205/5m-case-highlights-risk-from-chinese-trademark-trolls.

[23] Stephen Edelstein, *Tesla Motors Resolves Dispute with Chinese "Trademark Troll"*, MONITOR, Aug. 7, 2014, http://www.csmonitor.com/Business/In-Gear/2014/0807/Tesla-Motors-resolves-dispute-with-Chinese-trademark-troll.

[24] 2013 Trademark Law, *supra* note 7, art. 7.

[25] Guangming Liu & Richard Yao, *In Good Faith: Reflections on the Freudenberg Case and China's Trademark Law*, FUJAE PARTNERS, Sep. 18, 2014, http://fujaelaw.com/news/in-good-faith-reflections-on-the-freudenberg-case-and-chinas-trademark-law.

[26] 2013 Trademark Law, *supra* note 7, art. 19.

[27] *Id.* art. 68.

uses that would lead to consumer confusion.[28] The protection of registered well-known trademarks covers all classes of goods and services.[29] Moreover, under Chinese trademark law, only well-known trademarks are entitled to anti-dilution protection, which is a form of protection divorced from the anti-confusion protection covering all kinds of registered trademarks. Hence, gaining well-known-trademark status is of critical importance to the protection of non-traditional marks. By examining the *Hermès v. Dafeng* ruling and a number of other cases involving Hermès, this section considers the crucial factors for determining whether a non-traditional trademark can achieve such status in China.

China operates a passive system for recognizing well-known trademarks. Only when a trademark dispute arises can a trademark owner apply to the court and administrative organs to confer well-known status upon that mark.[30] Under Article 14 of the 2013 Trademark Law, there are four major factors determining whether a mark is a well-known trademark: (1) the degree of recognition of the mark among the relevant public sector in its trading areas; (2) how long the mark has been in use; (3) the duration and extent of advertising and publicity of the mark and the geographical extent of the trading areas in which it is used; and (4) the mark's record of being protected as a well-known trademark.[31]

In *Hermès v. Dafeng*, the Beijing High Court had to decide whether Hermès and its unregistered Chinese version had achieved well-known-trademark status by the time the defendant, Dafeng, registered its trademark in 1995. The High Court's analysis focused on the first three standards in Article 14 of the 2013 Trademark Law. First, the Court held that the first factor in Article 14 means that only when a mark is recognized by the relevant consuming public in mainland China can it potentially be regarded as a well-known trademark. Hermès submitted evidence of media coverage of its marketing efforts by such Hong Kong newspapers as *Ta Kung Pao, Ming Pao*, and the *Hong Kong Economic Journal*. In the High Court's opinion, however, Hermès had proved wide media coverage only in Hong Kong, not, as required by Chinese trademark law, in mainland China. By the same token, the Taiwan Court's recognition of Hermès as a well-known trademark in Taiwan would not lend support to Hermès' case. Therefore, in terms of public recognition in mainland China, the High Court did not rule in Hermès' favor. Second, the High Court held that the evidence submitted by Hermès did not meet the second and third factors listed in Article 14 of the 2013 Trademark Law. Although the company submitted media coverage by such mainland Chinese magazines as the *Shopping Guide to Quality Goods*, the High Court pointed out that it did not show the total number

[28] *Id.* art. 13.2. [29] *Id.* art. 13.3.

[30] Jing "Brad" Luo & Shubha Ghosh, *Protection and Enforcement of Well-Known Mark Rights in China: History, Theory and Future*, 7(2) Nw. J. Tech. & Intell. Prop. 119, 121–22 (2014).

[31] 2013 Trademark Law, *supra* note 7, art. 14.1; Kaiyu Xiao, Claus Barrett Christiansen, & Matthew J. Elsmore, *The New Legal Framework for Acquiring "Well-Known" Status in China: Signalling a More Coherent Phase of Enhanced Trade Mark Protection?*, 48(3) Int'l Rev. Intell. Prop & comp. 305, 324–26 (2017).

of magazines circulated to the public, the geographic scope of magazine circulation, or the duration of media coverage.[32]

By contrast, the Beijing High Court did recognize Hermès as a well-known trademark in *Hermès v. HermèsEpitek*, a case it decided in 2013, just one year after the *Hermès v. Dafeng* decision. Judging from the evidence submitted by Hermès in the 2013 case, the High Court held that the company had extensively and persistently promoted its brand and goods in China for a relatively long time and with a wide geographic reach before the date on which HermesEpitek submitted its trademark registration to the Chinese Trademark Office in 2004. For example, Hermès advertisements had featured prominently in mainland Chinese newspapers, magazines, and websites, and the company had opened stores in Beijing, Guangzhou, Shanghai, and elsewhere in China. Therefore, the High Court ruled that Hermès' promotional efforts had brought it sufficient fame among the relevant consuming public in mainland China.[33]

Why did the High Court reach two entirely different decisions regarding Hermès' well-known-trademark status in China? First and foremost among its reasons was the date on which Hermès was claiming recognition as a well-known trademark in China. As noted at the beginning of this section, under Chinese trademark law, the procedure for recognizing a trademark as well-known is triggered only in the event of a trademark dispute. If a senior mark owner wishes to have its mark recognized as a well-known mark and to rely on that status in a request to cancel the registration of a junior mark, then its application for well-known mark recognition must be evaluated before the junior mark's owner filed the registration of its mark. Put differently, the senior mark owner must prove that its mark had acquired well-known-trademark status before the date on which the junior mark owner submitted its trademark registration to the Trademark Office.

Therefore, to understand the two contrasting court decisions, it is necessary to examine the timing of the well-known-trademark recognition requests Hermès submitted to the Beijing High Court. In *Hermès v. Dafeng*, Dafeng filed its registration

[32] *See* Aiermeisi Guoji Su Guojia Gongshang Xingzheng Guanli Zongju Shangbiao Pingshen Weiyuanhui (Di San Ren Dafeng Zhi Yi Chang) (埃尔梅斯国际诉中华人民共和国国家工商行政管理总局商标评审委员会（第三人达丰制衣厂）[Hermès International S.A. v. Trademark Appeal Board of the State Administration for Industry & Commerce of the People's Republic of China (Third party: Dafeng Garment Factory)], 2012 Gaoxingzhong No. 705 (Beijing High People's Ct. Dec. 20, 2013), http://www.cnipr.net/article_show.asp?article_id=23398&keyword=%B4%EF%B7%E1%D6%C6%D2%C2; Aiermeisi Guoji Su Guojia Gongshang Xingzheng Guanli Zongju Shangbiao Pingshen Weiyuanhui (Di San Ren Dafeng Zhi Yi Chang) (埃尔梅斯国际诉中华人民共和国国家工商行政管理总局商标评审委员会（第三人达丰制衣厂）[Hermès International S.A. v. Trademark Appeal Board of the State Administration for Industry & Commerce of the People's Republic of China (Third party: Dafeng Garment Factory)], 2012 Gaoxingzhong No. 710 (Beijing High People's Ct. Dec. 20, 2013), http://www.cnipr.net/article_show.asp?article_id=21849&keyword=%B4%EF%B7%E1%D6%C6%D2%C2.

[33] *See* Aiermeisi Guo, Ji Su Guojia, Gongshang Xingzheng, Guanli Zongju, Shangbiao Pingshen Weiyuanhui (Di San Ren Hanmin, Keji Gufen, Youxian Gongsi) (埃尔梅斯国际与中华人民共和国国家工商行政管理总局商标评审委员会(第三人汉民科技股份有限公司)) [Hermès Int'l S.A. v. Trademark Appeal Board of the State Admin. for Indus. & Commerce of the People's Republic of China (Third Party: HermesEpitek Corp.)], 2013 Gaoxingzhong No. 1992 (Beijing High People's Ct. Apr. 11, 2014), http://www.cnipr.net/article_show.asp?article_id=22941.

application on September 5, 1995, which means that Hermès had to prove that its mark had achieved well-known-trademark status before that date.[34] Similarly, as HermesEpitek had filed for trademark registration on April 22, 2004, Hermès had to prove that such status had been achieved before that date.[35] Therefore, the dividing line between the two cases was a matter of two different dates, and hence Hermès bore a different burden of proof in each. In September 5, 1995, China's luxury goods market was barely functional. There was little, if any, demand for luxury goods (such as very expensive Hermès handbags) because very few people could afford them. It is thus entirely understandable that Hermès would not have actively advertised its brand and goods in China in those early years. Without effective promotional efforts, however, it was not possible for Hermès to have been recognized as a well-known trademark before September 5, 1995, the date on which Dafeng filed for trademark registration. From this perspective, the Court ruled correctly in *Hermès v. Dafeng*, holding that neither the registered Hermès trademark nor its unregistered Chinese version were well-known trademarks before that date.

The situation since 1995 has been entirely different. China's economy has boomed, and increasing numbers of people have acquired wealth and the desire to change their lifestyles in accordance with it. Consequently, the luxury goods market has grown rapidly in response to increased demand.[36] Therefore, it is no surprise that Hermès began more actively promoting its brand and products in a wealthier China. As *Hermès v. HermesEpitek* revealed, Hermès had actually launched substantive advertising efforts and opened stores in mainland China before 2004, the year in which HermesEpitek filed its trademark registration.

In addition to the issue of timing, the two cases also demonstrate that the legal standards for conferring well-known-trademark status require applicants to furnish evidence sufficient to convince the courts. In determining whether a mark is deserving of such status, the courts focus primarily on its degree of public recognition and the duration and extent of the advertising and publicity surrounding it. The courts place emphasis on the strength of the trademark owner's evidence in the form of advertisements, media coverage, and consumer surveys to assess whether those efforts were effective in achieving fame for its trademark in mainland China.[37] As discussed previously, in *Hermès v. HermesEpitek*, Hermès' reliance on evidence showing that it had carried out extensive promotional activities in the country proved successful in demonstrating its well-known-trademark status to the Court's satisfaction.

[34] *See* Hermès Int'l S.A. v. Trademark Appeal Board of the State Admin. for Indus. & Commerce of the People's Republic of China (Third party: Dafeng Garment Factory)], 2012 Gaoxingzhong No. 705; Hermès Int'l S.A. v. Trademark Appeal Board of the State Admin. for Indus. & Commerce of the People's Republic of China (Third party: Dafeng Garment Factory)], 2012 Gaoxingzhong No. 710.

[35] *See* Hermès Int'l S.A. v. Trademark Appeal Board of the State Admin. for Indus. & Commerce of the People's Republic of China (Third Party: HermesEpitek Corp.), 2013 Gaoxingzhong No. 1992.

[36] L. Alan Winters & Shahid Yusuf, *Introduction: Dancing with Giants*, *in* DANCING WITH GIANTS: CHINA, INDIA, AND THE GLOBAL ECONOMY (L. Alan Winters & Shahid Yusuf eds., 2007), http://documents.worldbank.org/curated/en/344901468004169716/pdf/383390Dancing0with0giants01PUBLIC1.pdf (pointing out that China's economy grew at 15.1% over 1995–2004).

[37] TAN, *supra* note 4, at 43.

The foregoing discussion of these two important Hermès cases shows that companies must be proactive in designing and implementing marketing and advertising plans if they wish to have their non-traditional trademarks recognized as well known in China. The mere act of registering trademarks in China is far from sufficient to achieve effective branding strategies. As shown by *Hermès v. Dafeng*, the near absence of promotional efforts in mainland China in the relevant period made it impossible for Hermès' mark to be recognized as a well-known trademark by the Chinese courts. Hence, Hermès lost the case to Dafeng, legally allowing Dafeng to continue using the Chinese transliteration of "Hermès" as a trademark for its clothing products.

V. Anti-Confusion Protection

One of the core functions of trademark law is to prohibit the unauthorized use of a trademark, which could mislead the relevant sector of consumers. Thus, such unauthorized use causing likely confusion over the source of goods or services amounts to an infringement of the exclusive right to use a trademark. The cases that Hermès has litigated have profound implications for whether the owners of non-traditional marks can effectively secure anti-confusion protection in China.

Article 57.2 of the 2013 Trademark Law constitutes the primary provision conferring such protection upon all registered marks. It provides that the following act infringes the exclusive right to use a registered trademark:

> Using a trademark that is similar to a registered trademark in connection with the same goods, or that is identical with or similar to a registered trademark in connection with the same or similar goods, without the authorization of the owner of the registered trademark, which may cause public confusion.

In addition to the above anti-confusion provision, the Trademark Law also extends the scope of anti-confusion protection for well-known trademarks. Article 13.3 of the 2013 Trademark Law stipulates that the registration and use of marks in all classes of goods or services are prohibited if they would "mislead the public so that the interests of the owner of the registered well-known trademark are likely to be impaired."[38] Similarly, Article 1 of the Chinese Supreme Court's Well-Known Trademark Interpretation states that "copying, imitating or translating the registered well-known trademark … for the purpose of misleading the general public" constitutes trademark infringement.

Most of the cases that Hermès has litigated in China have concerned anti-confusion protection, but the outcomes of their judicial rulings have varied. First, in some cases, it seems that the class of the goods or services concerned was the leading factor in determining the case outcome. In *Hermès v. France Ai Ma Shi*, for example, the defendant, a Chinese company called France Ai Ma Shi Limited, had applied for registration of the "Aimas" mark in Class 12, which includes automobile

[38] 2013 Trademark Law, *supra* note 7, art. 13.3.

and luggage racks. Hermès opposed the registration on the grounds that "Aimas" sounds confusingly similar to the pronunciation of the Chinese transliteration of "Hermès." Although the Beijing First Intermediate Court held that the Hermès mark had obtained high repute, it did not address the question of whether that mark should be recognized as a well-known trademark. The Court further ruled that the "Aimas" mark was unlikely to cause confusion, as Hermès had registered its trademark in the class of "apparel, luggage and leather products, and scarves," a class of goods quite different from Class 12 in terms of function, place of production, and distribution channels. As a result, the relevant public was unlikely to connect the two marks in terms of the goods' sources.

Second, well-known-trademark status has also affected the outcome of confusion-based cases. In *Hermès v. HermesEpitek*, the defendant had registered the HermesEpitek mark for Class 9, which covers semiconductor goods. As discussed in Section III, the Beijing High Court recognized the Hermès mark as a well-known trademark. It also noted that Class 9 goods obviously differed from the class of goods (i.e., "apparel, luggage and leather products, and scarves") for which the Hermès mark was registered. According to Article 13.3 of the Trademark Law, the well-known Hermès mark should enjoy anti-confusion protection over all classes of goods and services, and the Court therefore emphasized that well-known trademarks are subject to broader protection in China. Given that "Epitek" was an unknown word and that the two marks shared the word "Hermes," the Court held that the use of the HermesEpitek mark would likely cause confusion.[39]

Third, several other cases demonstrate that the way in which trademarks under dispute are similar in terms of their visual effect can also be a key factor in determining whether confusion-based trademark infringement has occurred. In 2010 litigation, for example, Hermès lost its case to the registrant of the HERM trademark, even though the two marks were registered in a similar class of goods, because the "visual effects" of the two marks are sufficiently distinct that consumers were unlikely to be confused (the Court did not discuss the strong similarity between the sounds of the two brands, with "HERM" pronounced the same as the first syllable of "Hermès"). Two years later, Hermès sued the Chinese stationery brand LOYAL-DINO. The defendant in the 2012 case was using a logo that was very similar to the Hermès horse logo, featuring a man and a horse-pulled cart. However, the Court ruled that the two logos were not similar enough to cause the likelihood of confusion.[40]

It seems that the courts in the foregoing cases adopted a subjective approach to evaluating various elements of the trademarks concerned, including spelling, level of fame, visual effects and design, and/or classes of goods, in determining the

[39] Hermès Int'l S.A. v. Trademark Appeal Board of the State Admin. for Indus. & Commerce of the People's Republic of China (Third Party: HermesEpitek Corp.)], 2013 Gaoxingzhong No. 1992.

[40] Aiermeisi Guo, Ji Su Guo, Jia Gong, Su Xing Zheng, Guan Li Zong, Ju Shang Biao, Ping Shen, Wei Yuan Hui (Di San Ren Nanjing Youqishi Gong Si) (埃尔梅斯国际与中华人民共和国国家工商行政管理总局商标评审委员会(第三人南京有奇氏公司)) [Hermès Int'l S.A. v. Trademark Appeal Board of the State Admin. for Indus. & Commerce of the People's Republic of China (Third Party: Nanjing Youqishi Co.)], 2012 Zhixingchu No. 1387 (Beijing First Interm. People's Ct. Aug. 30, 2012), http://bjgy.chinacourt.org/paper/detail/2012/12/id/951584.shtml.

likelihood of confusion. However, the use of subjective judgment in the decision-making process means that court rulings may not reflect the true view of the relevant public, possibly resulting in unfairness to trademarks that are moderately similar to disputed marks. Hence, it would be better for the courts to use objective judgment based on expert and survey evidence in deciding confusion-based cases.

VI. Anti-Dilution Protection

Last but not least, the cases that Hermès has litigated in China also suggest that companies doing business in the country should seek not only anti-confusion protection but also anti-dilution protection for their non-traditional trademarks. Although Hermès did not claim anti-dilution protection in *Hermès v. Dafeng*, it asserted that its trademark had been diluted in several other cases.

In the absence of consumer confusion, anti-dilution protection safeguards a well-known trademark against acts that blur its distinctiveness or tarnish its reputation. However, the Chinese Trademark Law contains no provisions that explicitly protect a trademark owner's anti-dilution right,[41] although Article 13, the well-known-mark protection provision, prescribes that the registration and use of a mark be prohibited if the mark "may mislead the public and cause injury to the interests of the registrant of the well-known trademark."[42] Further, the 2009 Judicial Interpretation Concerning the Trial of Civil Cases of Protection of Well-Known Marks issued by the Chinese Supreme Court provides some clarification concerning whether and how the anti-dilution right is protected in China. This interpretation stipulates that Article 13 of the Trademark Law ought to protect well-known-trademark owners in situations "where the relevant general public would believe that the trademark on trial is associated with the well-known trademark, and as a result detriment is caused to the distinctiveness of the well-known trademark and the market reputation of the well-known trademark is derogated or unfairly utilized."[43]

Prior to the Supreme Court's issuance of this judicial interpretation, which has binding power on the lower courts, the Chinese courts applied the concept of trademark dilution in deciding cases. A survey reviewing the one hundred trademark-related judicial decisions made by the Chinese courts up to 2009 reveals that thirty-one referred specifically to trademark dilution.[44] For example, Dong Zhi Tong's trademark registration for medicines for humans was canceled by the Trademark Office upon a request from Toshiba Corporation on the grounds that the Dong Zhi Tong mark (meaning "Toshiba Hall" in English) would dilute both the well-known Toshiba trademark and its Chinese mark "Dong Zhi." Similarly, both the Beijing Intermediate Court and High Court invalidated the trademark

[41] Luo & Ghosh, *supra* note 30, at 155. [42] 2013 Trademark Law, *supra* note 7, art. 13.

[43] Interpretation of the Supreme People's Court on Several Issues Concerning the Application of Law to the Trial of Cases of Civil Disputes over the Protection of Well-Known Trademarks art. 9, (Adopted on Apr. 22, 2009, entered into force May 1, 2009).

[44] Luckie Hong, *China's Dilution of the Dilution Doctrine*, 18 World Trademark Rev., 24, 27 (2009).

registration of Yili for bathroom sanitary devices on the grounds that it would dilute the well-known trademark Yili for dairy products.[45]

Hermès could not invoke the anti-dilution right in *Hermès v. Dafeng* because Hermès was not recognized as a well-known trademark, which is a core precondition for anti-dilution protection. However, the company did assert such protection in several other cases. In *Hermès v. Hermes Epitek*, for example, as we saw in Section III, the defendant had registered the HermesEpitek mark for Class 9 semiconductor goods. The Beijing High Court upheld Hermès' anti-dilution claim, ruling that the HermesEpitek mark blurred the distinctiveness of the well-known Hermès trademark. Although the dilution component of the ruling was very brief, it still sheds light on how anti-dilution claims are dealt with by the Chinese courts.

First, the Beijing High Court conditioned anti-dilution protection upon whether a mark can be deemed a well-known trademark. In *Hermès v. Hermes Epitek*, it first analyzed whether the Hermès mark could be recognized as such a trademark and then, after confirming its well-known-trademark status, moved on to consider whether the defendant's action had served to dilute the mark.[46]

Second, the Beijing High Court implied that to enjoy anti-dilution protection, a trademark ought to have a high degree of fame in the marketplace. In its anti-dilution protection analysis, the High Court confirmed that the Hermès mark enjoyed a very strong reputation. However, it did not delve into the issue of whether a trademark must have nationwide fame to receive anti-dilution protection, which is the fame standard adopted by U.S. anti-dilution law.[47] Nor did the Court consider whether a trademark with only niche fame, that is, fame among only a certain sector of the consuming public, warranted such protection. The niche fame standard is applied under EU anti-dilution law.[48] With respect to the fame requirement in China, the Provisions on the Recognition and Protection of Well-Known Trademarks have failed to clarify the issue.[49] Before their revision in 2013, these provisions required that a well-known trademark be "generally known by the relevant public in China and enjoying relatively high reputation."[50] Afterward, a well-known trademark was defined as "deeply known by the relevant public in China."[51] Therefore, Chinese trademark law has kept the door open to affording well-known trademarks niche fame anti-dilution protection.

[45] Melanie Zhu & Cecilia Zhou, *Anti-Dilution: A Power Tool for Well-Known Mark Protection in China*, China Law & Practice, Mar. 16, 2011, http://www.niuyie.com/anti-dilution-a-powerful-tool-for-well-known-mark-protection-in-china/.

[46] Hermès Int'l S.A. v. Trademark Appeal Board of the State Admin. for Indus. & Commerce of the People's Republic of China (Third Party: HermesEpitek Corp.)], 2013 Gaoxingzhong No. 1992.

[47] Case C-375/97, General Motors Corp. v. Yplon S.A., 1999 E.C.R. 122.

[48] Top Tobacco, L.P. v. N. Atl. Operating Co., 509 F.3d 380, 384 (7th Cir. 2007) (noting that the general public requirement "eliminated any possibility of 'niche fame,' which some courts had recognized before the amendment").

[49] 2013 Trademark Law, *supra* note 7, art. 13.1.

[50] Recognition and Protection of Well-known Trademarks Provisions art. 2 (promulgated by the State Administration for Industry & Commerce (2009)) (before the 2013 Amendment).

[51] *Id.*

Finally, the Beijing High Court did not elaborate upon the standards for determining whether trademark dilution had occurred in *Hermès v. Hermes Epitek*. It only briefly ruled that the use of "Hermes" as part of the HermesEpitek mark in Class 9 semiconductor goods had blurred the distinctiveness of the Hermès trademark. In fact, in the other Hermès cases discussed herein, the defendants could have been sued on dilution grounds if Hermès had proved that their use of the trademarks was intended to create an association with the Hermès mark. Similarly, they could also have been sued on the basis of dilution by tarnishment because their trademark use had tarnished the reputation of the Hermès mark.

VII. Conclusion

China is currently the world's second largest consumer market, and Chinese consumers are anticipated to spend even more on goods and services at home and abroad in the years to come.[52] Therefore, securing adequate legal protection for non-traditional trademarks in China is of vital importance to companies, given that those trademarks are playing an increasingly important role in the merchandizing of goods and services.

This chapter has reviewed the expanded scope of registrable non-traditional trademarks under Chinese trademark law. It has also examined the core substantive standards that have been applied in considering whether a non-traditional trademark is registrable with a particular focus on *Hermès v. Dafeng* and the other trademark-related cases that the French luxury brand Hermès has litigated in China. These case studies illustrate the need for companies to capitalize on the first-to-file rule, well-known-trademark recognition standards, and anti-confusion and anti-dilution rules to achieve adequate protection for their non-traditional trademarks in this burgeoning market.

[52] *Doing It Their Way*, THE ECONOMIST, Jan. 25, 2014, http://www.economist.com/news/briefing/21595019-market-growing-furiously-getting-tougher-foreign-firms-doing-it-their-way ("Now China seems poised to become the next consumption superpower.").

PART II

ASSESSING THE IMPACT ON COMPETITION AND CULTURE

10

The Protection of (Three-Dimensional) Shape Trademarks and Its Implications for the Protection of Competition

Gustavo Ghidini

> *There are other factors, emotive as much as rational, which still today divide attitudes towards the legal protection of trade marks. Pro-branders argue for generous extensive support, branding-sceptics for limited and controlled assistance. I shall label the former green-lighters and the latter red-lighters. I declare at once that my own inclination has long been to see red, rather than green.*
>
> *W.R. Cornish*[1]

I. Introduction

"Shape trademarks" raise serious concerns. The exercise of trademark rights relating to shapes may have a negative impact on competition in relevant markets.[2] The materialization of this impact, and hence the conflict with the essentially pro-competitive vocation of a trademark's fundamental distinctive function, does not typically relate to every shape. This conflict especially (albeit not exclusively) relates to three-dimensional shapes, in particular those "intrinsic" to the finished product itself,[3] or

[1] WILLIAM CORNISH, INTELLECTUAL PROPERTY: OMNIPRESENT, DISTRACTING, IRRELEVANT? 77 (2004).

[2] GIUSEPPE SENA, IL DIRITTO DEI MARCHI. MARCHIO NAZIONALE E MARCHIO COMUNITARIO 80 (2007) (pointing out there may well be two-dimensional marks intrinsically connected to a product); Smith, Kline and French Laboratories Ltd v. Sterling-Winthrop Group Ltd, (1976) R.P.C. 511 (H.L.) (illustrating through a famous example from the United Kingdom (UK) concerning a polychrome coating that was applied to the surface of the product (a sign). The coating was correctly held to qualify for registration); Case T-234/01, Stihl v. OHIM, 2003 E.C.R. II-2867) (illustrating that on the other hand, two-dimensional marks, and even just chromatic ones at times, have been held to have a functional character (*e.g.*, the color orange as a sign of danger)).

[3] Thus, the concerns for competition tend to disappear vis-à-vis three-dimensional shapes that include an *additional* distinguishing element *extrinsic* to the finished product: *e.g.*, a statuette placed on a lamp's base. In the words of Lord Aldous in the *Philips* case (Philips Electronics v. Remington Consumer Products, [1999] 116 Reports of Patents, Designs and Trademark Cases, 809 (H.L.) in *Trademark and*

The Protection of (Three-Dimensional) Shape Trademarks and Its Implications for the Protection of Competition. Gustavo Ghidini. Published 2018 by Oxford University Press.

the form of its packaging when the product does not or cannot have a three-dimensional shape, as in the case of liquids.[4]

Section II of this chapter analyzes the competition-related issues arising from the registrability of three-dimensional shapes of industrial products. Section III examines the European legal framework, and the systemic dystopias and over-protectionist consequences stemming from the impasse resulting from the coexistence of trademark and registered design protection. An interpretative solution capable of overcoming such impasse in a pro-competitive perspective is presented. Such perspective is further explored in Section IV, rejecting the alleged "investment function" of trademarks as a proxy to make trademark protection the source of rent-seeking positions—*and* for a potentially unlimited period of time. Section V concludes and argues that the limits to registrability stemming from a rigorous interpretation of the European Directives and Regulations do not necessarily weaken the distinctive character of the overall appearance ("trade dress") of industrial products.

II. Competition-Related Concerns

The manufacture of "intrinsic" three-dimensional shapes of products and containers effectively allows a variety of alternatives that is far more restricted than that afforded by two-dimensional shapes, for self-evident physical, functional, and economic reasons. Thus, with regard to said marks, the interest of competitors and consumers alike to "keep free" (*Freihaltebedürfnis*) the use of these shapes conflicts with that of the trademark holders in appropriating them.[5]

It was precisely this basic competition-related concern that induced a long-lasting ostracism against the registration of three-dimensional shapes as trademarks in legal

Unfair Competition Law: "Philips", 31 Int'l Rev. Intell. Prop. & Competition L. 452, 454 (2000)) "a shape of an article cannot be registered in respect of goods of that shape unless it contains *some addition* to the shape of the article which [adds] trade mark significance" (emphasis added). On the opposite side, the shape of vehicle spare parts is excluded from registration as a trademark under art. 3(1)(e) of Directive 2008/95/EG and art. 7(l)(e) of Community Trade Mark Regulation No. 40/94. This is because the shape of spare parts is defined by their replacement function, and their commercial value derives from perfect substitutability with the original part (see also Bundespatentgericht, Oct. 20, 2004, MarkenR 2005, 56 (BMW-Motorhaube), cited also by Annette Kur, *Cumulation of IP Rights Pertaining to Product Shapes—An Illegitimate Offspring of IP Law? in* Intellectual Property and Market Power: ATRIP Papers 2006–2007 613, 627 (Luigi M. Genovesi & Gustavo Ghidini eds., 2007). The exclusion is furthermore consistent, as concerns "internal" spare parts, with the provisions of art. 4(2) of the Community Design Regulation No. 6/2002, according to which a design, including a component incorporated into the complex product, can only be registered if it remains visible during normal use. *See* Ulrike Koschtial, *Design Law: Individual Character, Visibility and Functionality*, 36 Int'l Rev. Intell. Prop. & Competition L. 310 (2005).

4 *See* Coca Cola T.M., [1986] R.P.C. (H.L.) 421, 425, 449 (stating that in the case of liquids the form of the container must necessarily be deemed to be that of the product).

5 *See* Case C-102/07, Adidas v. Marca Mode, 2008 E.C.R. I-2439, ¶ 33 (especially the conclusions of Advocate General Dàmaso Ruiz-Jarabo Colomber); Karl-Heinze Fezer, Markenrecht 308 (1999). *See also* Jeremy Phillips, *Trade Mark Law and the Need to Keep Free*, 36 Int'l Rev. Intell. Prop. & Competition L. 389 (2005) (explaining the doctrine of *Freihaltebedürfnis,* originally conceived for descriptive signs).

systems sensitive to preserving competition. This was openly emphasized by the European Commission itself in the 1980 *Explanatory Memorandum* which accompanied the Proposal for a "Harmonisation Directive" on trademarks.[6] In the UK, in particular, this ostracism—well expressed by the [petition of] principle whereby "the thing itself could not be a mark of itself"[7]—lasted into the 1980s,[8] and even beyond the adoption of the Trade Mark Act of 1994.[9] Germany shared the same reluctance up to the replacement of the previous *Warenzeichengesetz* (Trademark Law) by the current trademark law, the *Markengesetz* of 1994.[10] Italy, too, denied registration of the "shape mark" beyond the second half of the past century, on the ground that (in the words of a leading scholar, Tullio Ascarelli) "the protection might be equivalent to a model patent with no [predetermined] time limit."[11]

On the opposite front, pressures from business interests demanded, in the framework of an "ongoing battle against lookalikes," trademark protection for "original" shapes of finished products.[12] This, self-evidently, was in order to overcome the limits of the short protection of registered industrial models. These pressures were bowed to for the first time in the early 1970s, namely when the Benelux uniform laws on trademarks entered into force in 1971.[13]

The principle of registrability enshrined in Article 1(2) of the Benelux law was successively adopted by the European legal regime (Article 3(e) of Directive 89/104/EEC[14] and Article 7(e) of Council Regulation (EC) No. 40/94). The principle

[6] E.C. Bull. Supp. 5, New Trademark System for the Community, at 57, 1980 ("The shape of goods will not be refused registration unless the fact of registration would make it possible for an undertaking to monopolize that shape to the detriment of its competitors and or consumers"); *see* Alison Firth, Ellen Gredley, & Spyros M. Maniatis, *Shapes as Trademarks: Public Policy, Functional Considerations and Consumer Perceptions*, 23(2) Eur. Intell. Prop. Rev. 86 (2001) (demonstrating this concern); Irene Calboli, *Overlapping Rights: the Negative Effects of Trademarking Creative Works, in* The Evolution and Equilibrium of Copyright in the Digital Age 52 (Susy Frankel & Daniel J. Gervais eds., 2014) (illustrating the parallel concern about the overlapping of trademark protection and copyright is expressed in artistic works); *see also* Estelle Derclaye, *Overlapping Rights, in* The Oxford Handbook of Intellectual Property Rights (2017) (forthcoming, now at: https://ssrn.com/abstract=2930841).

[7] *See* Lord Templeman in *Coca-Cola, supra* note 4; Jens Schovsbo & Thomas Riis, *Design Law: Caught Between Chairs?, in* Kritka—Essays on Intellectual Property, vol. II, 88 (Gustavo Ghidini, Hanns Ullrich, & Peter Drahos eds., 2017) (reminding that Lord Templeman also referenced a British decision of a century before, Lindley L.J., *In re* James' Trade-Mark, [1886] W.N. 152 (C.A.)).

[8] *Coca Cola, supra* note 4 (referring to the 1986 decision of the House of Lords on the shape of the Coca Cola bottle).

[9] *See* Philips Electronics v. Remington Consumer Products, [1998] R.P.C. 283 (first instance, Jacob J.); Philips Electronics v. Remington Consumer Products, [1999] R.P.C. 809 (second instance); Procter and Gamble's Trademark Applications, [1999] R.P.C. 673; Whirlpool Corporation and Others v. Kenwood Ltd, [2008] E.W.I.T.C. 1930 (Ch.) (illustrating that UK courts have expressed longstanding reluctance to admit that the mere three-dimensional presentation of a product could constitute a valid trademark).

[10] Kur, *supra* note 3, at 619.

[11] Tullio Ascarelli, Teoria della Concorrenza e dei Beni Immateriali 483 (1960).

[12] Jenny Bergquist & Duncan Curley, *Shape Trade Marks and Fast-moving Consumer Goods*, 30(1) Eur. Intell. Prop. Rev. 17 (2008).

[13] *See* Ruth Annand & Helen Norman, Blackstone's Guide to the Trade Marks Act 1994 65 (1994) (on the influence of these Benelux laws (notorious pioneers of protectionist tendencies)); Kur, *supra* note 3, at 619.

[14] First Council Directive 89/104/EEC to approximate the laws of the Member States relating to trademarks, 1989 O.J. L40/1 (EC) [hereinafter TMD 1989]. In 2015, a Recast of the European

was restated, as known, in the subsequent Directive 95/08 and Regulation 207/09, both in turn revised by the 2015 "Trade Mark Reform Package" (Directive 2436/015, and Regulation 2424/2015, modifying Regulation 207/09—now in codified version in Regulation 1001/2017. National laws followed suit.

III. The European Framework: A Dual Proposal for a Systemic Reconstruction

As mentioned above, and generally known, the European Union (EU) legislation enables the registration of three-dimensional product shapes while excluding, under the provision related to "absolute grounds for refusal or invalidity," the registrability of signs which consist exclusively of the shape resulting from the nature of the goods themselves, or "the shape necessary [even if not 'inderogable,' as the European Court of Justice (ECJ) held in *Lego* C-48/09], to obtain a technical result"[15] or a shape which "gives substantial value [essentially thanks to an aesthetic quality, according to the prevailing opinion] to the goods."[16] These limits to trademark registration have then been confirmed in the revised text of EU trademark laws recently adopted as Regulation (EU) 2015/2424 (Article 4(e)(i)(ii)(iii) (see also the codified version 2017/1001) and Directive (EU) 2015/2436 (TMR 2015), see *supra* Section II.

Thus, the EU legislation (and the ensuing national ones) reflects a compromise that allows registration, but within limits aimed at avoiding both the creation of natural monopolies (first limit) and a contradiction with the system of other exclusive rights of a fixed duration, in particular patents granted with regard to shapes which have a technical effect and industrial designs granted with regard to shapes which have aesthetic value (second and third limits).

This is a wishful compromise solution, which—in its literal expression—seems vitiated by a nominalism that renders it hard to reconcile the text of the law with market reality. In fact, it seems indeed unrealistic, or in any case marginal, to suppose that a firm may adopt an *exclusively* functional or *exclusively* aesthetic shape for products intended for the market. In modern reality, marketable goods—are generally conceived with regard to both function and aesthetics: not only those for private consumption, but even instrumental ones. A lawnmower, for example, is not "totally technical," but also results from an aesthetic concern. Vice versa, a private consumption good, for example, a suit, is typically selected for predominantly aesthetic

Trademark Division (TMD) was enacted (Council Directive 2015/2436 of the European Parliament and of the Council of 16 December 2015 to approximate the laws of the Member States relating to trade marks, 2015 O.J. L336/1 [hereinafter TMD 2015]).

[15] Case C-48/09, Lego v. OHIM, 2010 E.C.R. I-08403; Case C-299/99, Philips Electronics v. Remington Consumer Prods., 2002 E.C.R. 1-05475, ¶ 78 (where the ECJ identified the rationale of European regulation as the need "to prevent trade mark protection from granting its proprietor a monopoly on technical solutions or functional characteristics of a product"); see also Joined Cases C-53 to 55/01, Linde and Others, 2003 E.C.R. 1-3161, ¶ 72.

[16] *See* Firth et al., *supra* note 6.

reasons, but also practical/functional elements enter frequently into consideration, such as the quality of the cloth, the comfort, weight, resistance to the elements, etc.

Hence it seems that a sign is unlikely to be "exclusively" functional or "exclusively" aesthetic in a literal sense. Therefore, it is necessary to elaborate a corrective exegesis of the idea of "[signs which consist] *exclusively*." Following the blueprint of the decision of the European Court of Justice (ECJ) in *Lego v. OHIM*,[17] and the General Court of the EU in *Bang & Olufsen*,[18] the adverb is thus to be understood as concerning not the object in itself but rather the material reference of the *predominant appeal* to consumers for its acquisition. Accordingly, in relation to the three-dimensional shapes of industrial products, the words "consist exclusively" are to be understood as meaning "satisfy a purchasing interest to a predominant extent referable to either the functional or the aesthetic character." Conversely, this interpretation allows room for the registration of product shapes sought and bought predominantly for their "originality"—as once was well said, their "capriciousness and arbitrariness."[19]

The EU legislative compromise solution is also vitiated by a seemingly systemic contradiction, namely with the protection for goods embodying designs granted by Council Directive 98/71[20] on works of industrial design. Said Directive grants an exclusive protection of up to twenty-five years to shapes with "individual character."[21] Now—verbal acrobatics aside—doesn't the notion of "individual character" substantially coincide with that of "distinctive character"? In my view, rather than differentiating from the general notion of distinctiveness, the concept/category of the "informed user" expresses a natural evolution thereof in the modern age in which the traditional yardstick of the not-so-smart "average consumer" shifts to that of "informed user" (with regard to the type/class of products involved). Now, purchasers of designer products are customers that typically pay specific attention to trends in tastes and aesthetics.[22]

Thus one could argue that the overall legal framework of EU trademark and design law, under the same basic postulate of distinctiveness/individuality, regulates the same substantive subject matter by means of two different regimes, one more pro-monopolistic and one more pro-competitive. Now, ignoring this systemic contradiction inevitably leads to the *cumulation/overlapping* of protections, in the sense

[17] *Lego, supra* note 15.

[18] Case T-508/08, Bang & Olufsen v. OHIM, 2011 E.C.R. II-06975.

[19] *Lego,* , *supra* note 15, ¶¶ 15, 17.

[20] Council Directive 98/71/EC on the legal protection of designs, 1998 O.J. L289/28 [hereinafter Design Directive 1998].

[21] *Id.* art. 5.

[22] Council Directive 29/2005/EC, 2005 SEC 744 (confirming the foregoing assumption on unfair commercial practices); Council Directive 29/2005/EC rec. 18, (adopting the concept previously expressed by the Court of Justice for the European Union (CJEU), *e.g.*, in *Linde, Winward Indus.*, *supra* note 15. More recently in *Calvados* (Case C-75/15, Viiniveria Oy v. Sosiaali, 2016 EURLex 62015CJ0075) the Court referred to a consumer "reasonably well informed and reasonably observant and circumspect" (a benchmark, may I add, that should be derogated from only in special cases where a weak category of consumers, such as children, is involved). See also Case T-691/17, decision of June 29, 2018, Hoechstmass Balzer, at n.32.

that once the "short" exclusive design protection expires, the trademark registration would step in, providing exclusive protection ... from here to eternity.[23]

This disgraceful consequence of a dual protection for shapes as trademarks and designs can hardly be accepted as it represents a systemic contradiction, *and* the green light to a seriously anti-competitive situation. To avoid this situation, one might be tempted to invoke the principle of "implicit abrogation" which is adopted in many legal systems in regard to the temporal succession of laws. In Italy, for example, Article 15.1 of the Civil Code states that "Laws are only abrogated by subsequent laws upon explicit legislative statement, or for incompatibility between the new regulation and the preceding or because the new law regulates the entire subject-matter regulated by the preceding law."[24] According to this principle, then, the subsequent regulation of registered design prevails on the shape-marks regime[25] as it applies to the same subject matter and is founded on the same basic criterion of access to legal protection (shape possessing "distinctive/individual character") while adopting a normative solution acutely different: granting exclusive rights for a moderately limited fixed term, instead of a potentially perpetual period.[26]

Tempting as this cut of the Gordian knot might be, it is not quite certain even after the *Silos* judgment that EU law definitely recognizes the concept of implicit abrogation.[27]

Hence, I submit another tentative solution, which seems workable from an interpretative standpoint. Let us start by recalling that, on the one side, a valid trademark registration postulates that the distinctive appeal of the shape appears as "predominant" over the functional and/or the aesthetic aspect of the product concerned. This is, as recalled above, the reasonable approach which was developed in the *Lego* and *Bang Olufsen* cases.[28] Now, this is *not* the case with design law, which does not set absolute impediments to the registration based on the relevance of the design's technical or aesthetic features. In adherence to what typically happens in the real world of the industrial design market, where, typically, buyers are predominantly attracted by the aesthetic and/or functional profiles (usually merged in one), the design registration regime just requires—and is "satisfied" on the condition—that the shape *also* exhibits an individual/distinctive character—whereas registration is only excluded if the shape is "*solely* dictated by its technical function": see Article 7.1 (see also 7.2) Directive 98/71/EC (emphasis added).[29]

[23] *See* Paul Torremans, *Three Dimensional Trade Marks and Designs for Packaging, in* INTELLECTUAL PROPERTY AND MARKET POWER: ATRIP PAPERS 2006–2007 745 (Luigi M. Genovesi & Gustavo Ghidini, eds., 2007) (accepting cumulation *de lege lata,* but sharply criticizing its monopolistic effects).

[24] Art. 15.1 Civil Code (It.).

[25] The formal reproposition of the prevision shape marks regime in the TMD 2015 and TMR 2015 does not alter the substantive order of succession of the two regimes.

[26] Design Directive 71/98 EC art. 10.1.

[27] Case C-228/99, Silos e Mangimi Martini v. Ministero delle Finanze, 2001 E.C.R. I-8401.

[28] *Lego, supra* note 15; *Bang & Olufsen, supra* note 18.

[29] *Note*: this "solely" must be literally interpreted, i.e., as "exclusively," not as "predominantly" (as vice versa the "exclusively" in the Trademark Regulation: above, text accompanying notes 18–20). This is not an exegetic subterfuge: indeed, whereas a "sign" can be predominantly "arbitrary/capricious" (hence predominantly "distinctive"), the shape of an industrially mass-produced consumption or instrumental good must first of all fulfill a utilitarian purpose, so that its "individuality" (distinctiveness) simply coexists, in practice, with an essential functional character.

On this basis, one can reasonably construe a peaceful coexistence of the two legal regimes, the protection of trademarks and the protection of industrial designs. Thus, the three-dimensional trademarks' registration should be limited to those shapes whose functional and/or aesthetic profile is secondary, however not predominant, vis-à-vis their "originality" (capriciousness or arbitrariness). Design protection should apply in the contrary case, that is to forms that attract customers for predominantly functional and/or aesthetic reasons (just excluding, as reminded, the shapes *solely* dictated by the function). According to this solution, the needle's eye for shape's registration as trademarks remains open but narrow, as it should be. And happily, the prevailing EU case law confirms that when a shape presents relevant functional features, a restrictive approach prevails in acknowledging distinctive character. Thus, declarations of invalidity outnumber the green lights.[30] This is good news for competition.

The good news is comforted by two specific, logically intertwined, normative tenets: one (A) based on legislative data, the other (B) stemming from jurisprudential intepretation.

In the first tenet, (A), the predominance of technical (or aesthetic) features as driving factors of consumers' choices constitutes, as reminded, a legal *absolute impediment* to a valid registration. Hence, the assessment of such predominance is preliminary[31] to, and possibly absorbing of, that of the distinctive character of the shape. In other words, when functional features of the shape emerge as the dominant basis for consumers' choice, their consideration outweighs—nay, preempts—the finding of distinctive character. Now, in consistency with this normative line, the prevailing European jurisprudence also reveals a pro-competitive bias in assessing/comparing the dominance of the functional versus the distinctive elements as prevailing drivers of consumers' choices. See in particular the recent decision of the General Court, in *Flamagas*, which expressly downplays the relevance of the non-functional word element of the overall mark, hence substantially privileging the "imperative of availability" of the shape's functional features.[32]

The second tenet (B) is based on the prevailing European jurisprudence. Quite correctly, this jurisprudence has so far held firm on the approach evoked under tenet (A) even when the shape marks concerned are "well known." In other words, the EU judges confirm that the acquisition of notoriety cannot outweigh the "need to keep free" intrinsically functional or aesthetic features. In *Flamagas*, the General Court (also citing in support *Bang & Olufsen* and case law cited herein) pointed out

[30] *See* Case T-580/15, Flamagas v. EUIPO, 2017 EURLex 62015TJ0580; Case T-601/17, Rubik's Brand v. EUIPO, contested decision R 452/2017-1; Case C-445/13, Voss of Norway v. OHIM, 2015 EURLex 2013CJ0445; Case C-205/13, Hauke v. Stokke, 2014 EURLex 62013CJ0205; Case C-215/14, Nestle v. Cadbury, 2015 EURLex 62014CJ0215; Case T-411/14, Coca Cola v. OHIM, 2016 EURLex 62014TJ0411; Case C-98/11, Lindt & Sprungli v. OHIM, 2012 EURLex 62011CJ0098 (illustrating that no impediment to valid registrability, (as distinctive character was acknowledged) was asserted by the EU Trib., *see* Joined Cases T-395 to 396/14, Best Lock v. OHIM, 2015 EURLex 62014TJ0395 (Lego) (referencing manifestly non-functional figures of small toys, where the earlier *Lego* case (*supra* note 17) concerned the manifestly functional shape of the classic Lego "bricks").

[31] *Flamagas, supra* note 30, n.20.

[32] *Id.*, ¶¶ 31, 34, 37, 38, 40.

that, "in so far as the applicant emphasizes that the shape of the lighter concerned has been in use for 45 years, and that a reputation has been acquired by the mark at issue, . . . a sign that consists exclusively[33] of the shape of the product can *never* acquire a distinctive character through the use made of it."[34] This is also in line with the parallel exclusion of the acquisition of "secondary meaning" by generic expressions, as this might foreclose competitors from using the descriptive sign.[35] (Hence, the protection of the "rehabilitated" trademark focuses only on the distinctive, "capricious," variations.)

IV. Intermezzo: Possible Interference of the "Theory" of Trademark "Investment Function"?

The "reductionist" (hence) pro-competitive line supported here might run in contradiction with some well-known dicta[36] of the European Court of Justice (CJEU, formerly ECJ) asserting a legal "function of investment" of trademarks—an assertion that often (tautologically) overlaps with that of an "advertising function,"[37] *and* manifestly supports an "expansionist" approach to trademarks' scope of protection. This function is implicitly but clearly assumed as separate and independent from the distinctive.

Authoritative as the CJEU cases are, this assertion lacks, in my view, a serious legal foundation.

Before proceeding in arguing my position, let me clarify that the very notion of "legal function" properly refers to a normative datum that defines, or concurs to define, either the conditions or the scope (or both) of a given legal regime, in this case that of trademark law. In other words, a "legal function" is definitely not the jurispolitical motivation, that is the (economic/social/political) rationale underlying a certain regime.[38]

[33] *Id.* ¶¶ 2, 38 (illustrating the reasonable normative meaning of the adverb, *see* ¶ 2. By the way, the overall trademark of the lighter for which registration had been sought consisted also of a fantasy word ("Clipper"), assessed by the Tribunal "of minor and secondary importance" at ¶ 38).

[34] *Id.* ¶ 60 (emphasis added).

[35] *See* Case C-408/01, Adidas v. Fitnessworld Trading, 2003 E.C.R. I-12537 (illustrating that since the opposite would grant the trademark owner a monopoly on the product, not only on the sign).

[36] *See* in particular Case C-323/09, Interflora v. Interflora British Unit, 2011 E.C.R. I-08625, (and other court law cited therein). According to the Court, the use of the trademark as described above adversely affects the trademark's investment function "if it substantially interferes with the proprietor's use of its trade mark to acquire or preserve a reputation capable of attracting consumers and retaining their loyalty." On trademarks' alleged "other" functions *see also* the CJEU's decision *in* Case C-65/12, Leidseplein Beheer BV v. Red Bull, 2014 EURLex 62012CJ0065, and the CJEU's decision *in* Case C-661/11, Martin Y Paz, 2013 EURLex 62011CJ0661.

[37] *See* Michel Vivant, *Revisiting Trade Marks*, 3 Queen Mary Intell. Prop. J., 307 (2013). We say "tautologically" since, as a matter of fact, the two asserted "functions" are Siamese twins: the "investment" in enhancing a trademark's reputation is essentially an investment in advertising.

[38] Enrico Bonadio, *Patents as Tools to Encourage the Production of Healthier Food*, *in* The New Intellectual Property—Beyond Plain Packaging 305 (Alberto Alemanno & Enrico Bonadio eds., 2016) (taking, on the one hand, the proposals to patent foodstuff to encourage investments in the production of healthier food); Andrew D. Mitchell, *Tobacco Packaging Measures Affecting Intellectual Property Protection Under International Investment Law: The Claim Against Uruguay and*

Nor does it represent the economic/social/political effect stemming from that regime. It is, repeat, a normative tenet "built in" the discipline, one that permanently "shapes" it.

Now, this is also the case of trademark law. Either as concerns the traditional protection, which is juridically conditioned by the mark's distinctive character and the occurrence of confusing activities, or even as concerns the "enlarged" (extramural) protection accorded to "famous" marks. Indeed, no matter what investment might have been made, in the current normative framework the protection is not available if the trademark has not (first of all) objectively attained "distinctive character," or it has not objectively acquired adequate "reputation," or the unauthorized use of a similar trademark by third parties has not caused either an actual prejudice to the famous mark's reputation or distinctiveness, or an actual unfair advantage to the third user.[39]

From a systemic point of view, my critical position about the alleged "investment function" is first of all based on a fundamental tenet of the intellectual property system: exclusive protection is only granted to objective *achievements* (*dixit*, in a conversation, Josef Drexl) of specific general interests. In essence, this statement reflects the trade-off, so poignantly sculpted by the U.S. Constitution (Article 1.8.8) between a private "monopoly" and the creation of a socially useful effect. Take patents and copyright: only new intellectual works, and new technological solutions, qualifying as contributions to the advancement of "science and the useful arts" justify the exclusive protection against (economically significant) free riding. And of course, for the trade-off to be effective, the contribution must be embodied in an *objective result* of intellectual effort possessing the requisites requested by the law in order to fulfill the social function.

Now, "investments" per se do not enter the legal landscape. By means of a patent the legal system protects new and non-obvious invention, no matter what investment, huge or otherwise, may have been spent on the aborted research, or even on an invention not first-filed. Likewise, copyright rewards an expressive result, whose *auctor* (from latin *augere* = to increase) enriches the cultural heritage: again, no protection is afforded, whatever the investment may have been,[40] to the efforts

Australia, *in* THE NEW INTELLECTUAL PROPERTY—BEYOND PLAIN PACKAGING 213 (Alberto Alemanno & Enrico Bonadio eds., 2016) (arguing on the other hand, the claims brought by leading tobacco industries against regulations affecting the branding, labeling, and packaging of tobacco, allegedly "punitive" of investments embodied in intellectual property, and the ensuing WTO arbitration procedures).

[39] *See* Vincenzo Di Cataldo, *The Development of Trade Marks into Common Names of Products: A Strong Push Towards a Purely Objective View of Language Evolution*, *in* KRITIKA: ESSAYS ON INTELLECTUAL PROPERTY, VOL. II 119 (Gustavo Ghidini, Hanns Ullrich, & Peter Drahos eds., 2017) (analogizing that if a once distinctive sign objectively becomes a generic term in the trade parlance, the owner would lose the entitlement through "vulgarization," no matter how much money she had poured into defending and promoting the sign).

[40] As concerns copyright, Ulrich Loewenheim recently wrote that "Das Urheberrecht schützt die geistige Leistung und nicht die Investition" *in* ULRICH LOEWENHEIM, ZEITSCHRIFT FÜR GEISTIGES EIGENTUM 568, 571 (2016) (reviewing MARCEL BISGES, KLEINE MÜNZE IM URHEBERRECHT—ANALYSE DES ÖKONOMISCHE ASPECTS DES WERKBEGRIFFS (2014)).

and attempts that never led to a publishable work. Undisputedly, neither patents or copyrights are there to protect the author's ability and investments to promote their commercial reputation.

So it is also the case, even allowing for all due differences, for trademarks. What is their socially useful function (indispensable function, in a market characterized by a potentially indefinite plurality of industrial and commercial offers) if not to ensure "distinguishing information," that is market transparency about the origin of the goods? Can we reasonably define as of general utility—and as such worthy of a monopolistic exception potentially unlimited in time—the diffusion of advertising suggestions that exalt the brand image?! Sure: it is unquestionable that such advertising and marketing efforts, aimed at enhancing the fame of the trademark, do require strong investments. But as investments *per se* do not constitute a legal condition/requisite for patent and/or copyright protection, I see no reason for claiming that the opposite should be true for trademarks.

On the less decisive but not insignificant exegetic perspective, no mention of an "investment" (or "advertising" etc.) function can be found either in the Directive or the Regulation, even in the 2015 versions. As a matter of fact, in defining the scope of protection of the Community trademark (or EU trademark under the 2015 "package," and the 2017 codified version of the Regulation), these legislations make sole express reference to the defense against confusion, including by "association."[41] The sole express reference, thus, is to the distinctive function as legal function of trademark protection, as indicated in recital 16 of TMD 2015.[42] It is true that the overall wording has some margin of ambiguity, as these recitals hint to the distinction as the "central/fundamental" function—not as "the" only function across the board. But if the European legislator had really meant to engage in expanding the legally protected functions of trademarks, one can reasonably suppose, surely, that it would have mentioned it! Anyway, it is certain that there is *no legislative recognition of such "function."* Above all, again, it is certain that "investment" does not define or concur to define either a condition or the scope of the legal protection of trademarks.

In conclusion, the evocation of the "investment function" as a separate *legal* function in addition to the distinctive function, appears as a systemic nonsense, since—in the words of Felix Cohen about the false "if value, then right" doctrine—it "purports to base legal protection upon economic value, when, as a matter of fact, the economic value of a sale device depends upon the extent to which it will be legally protected." [43]

In sum, the assertion of the EU Court of Justice (mis)identifies the *de facto* enhancement of an economic projection (effect) with its legal expression—and foundation. In other words, this (mis)identification blurs the distinction

[41] Council Directive 95/08, Rec. 11; Council Regulation 207/209, Rec. 8; Council Directive Dec. 16, 2015, O.J. L2015/2436, Rec. 16.

[42] *See* Rec. 16 of TMD 2015 (and Rec. 11 of Directive 95/08), Rec. 8 of Regulation 207/2009.

[43] Felix Cohen, *Transcendental Nonsense and the Functional Approach*, 35 Colum. L. Rev. 809, 815 (1935); *see also* Gustavo Ghidini, Hans Ullrich, & Peter Drahos, *Editorial, in* kritika—essays on intellectual property, vol. ii, xiii (2017).

between *economic assessment* and *legal conditions and limitations* of trademark protection.[44]

Now, this *quid pro quo* is no innocuous lapse: it carries a systemically improper corollary of substantive anti-competitive momentum. Affirming that the "investment function" is a legal function—that is that the factor "investment as such impacts on the legal protection—corresponds, from a systemic perspective, to surreptitiously bypass the cardinal principle that expresses the primacy of freedom of competition: the principle of the legislatively circumscribed, "closed' number (*numerus clausus*) of exclusive IP rights.

In turn, this bypass can open a Pandora's box of substantive consequences of strongly "protectionist" (i.e., anti-competitive) flavor. First and foremost, it provides the justification for affirming that goodwill must be protected as such, in contradiction with the golden rule that it can only be defended against tortious activities, such as counterfeiting and acts of unfair competition (first and foremost passing off and slandering of goods). In logical sequence, this can straightforwardly lead to an expansive (protectionist, as said) approach to the protection of "famous" trademarks: even in the sense of granting them protection just on the basis of a mere iconic similarity or coincidence, even in default of any reasonable appearance of a business "connection," as in the TRIPS Agreement (Article 16.3 of TRIPS), between the rights holder and third parties acting in distant industrial or commercial sectors.[45] This is a result that serves primarily the interests of dominant business circles,[46] and much less the cause of freedom of enterprise—as the freedom to use signs (including words,

[44] The support of investments is merely a *factual economic consequence* of the extramural reach of the protection of renowned marks; just as protection of the distinctive function itself *de facto* enhances the investments used to elaborate and support a sign and to extoll its distinguishing capacity. In analogous terms, the legal recognition of the "rehabilitating" effect of the acquisition of a distinctive character (secondary meaning) by an originally "generic," hence, null trademark, *de facto* protects the investments in advertising that created that "new" meaning. But this is a *de facto* economic projection of the legal protection, not the object nor a condition thereof, nor does it define the scope of the legal protection. The double-check: if, notwithstanding intense investments, a descriptive sign would not acquire a sufficient distinctive character or "secondary meaning," the consequent "rehabilitating" effect, would not take place. Thus, in the same terms, investments in advertising and marketing made in support of a trademark whose object is a shape that is exclusively or predominantly functional cannot be registered or validated (*see* Regulation (EU) 2017/1001 art. 7(1)(e)(i), (ii); Directive 2015/2436 art. 4(e)(i), (ii)).

[45] TRIPS art. 16.3. *See also* Opinion of Advocate General Sharpston *in* Case C-202/07, France Telecom v. Commission, 2009 E.C.R. I-02369 (interpreting the concept of "link" as "something more than a vague, ephemeral, indefinable feeling or subliminal influence").

[46] Significantly, the assertion of the "investment function" also works as an instrument to support the dominant industrial circles' battle against "lookalikes," i.e., even non-confusing imitations of branded goods (*see in particular Davidoff* and *Adidas II*). A line *seemingly* confirmed by the 2015 "package" (art. 10(2)(c) Directive and art. 9(2)(c) Regulation) that grants an extended protection to famous trademarks, not only outside *but also* within the sector of registration and similar ones. "Seemingly," repeat: in truth (the *normative* truth), even vis-à-vis identical or similar products, the protection of the mark's "notoriety" can only take place when in the specific case, and in the light of all the circumstances thereof, the use of an identical or similar sign objectively causes [effectively, not potentially: see aforesaid norms] either 'an "unfair advantage" to the third user or a "detriment" to the distinctive character or the repute of the renowned mark. Now, this can happen if and when the public is led to reasonably assume the existence of an objective business "connection" (art. 16(3)TRIPS) between the third user and the owner's firm (*note*: not just between the signs as such, on the basis of a merely iconic resemblance): thus, ultimately, in the presence of a substantively confusing "association." Obviously, the closer the affinity,

colors, shapes, and so forth) to identify one's products is indeed (also) part of the general freedom of enterprise.[47]

The evocation of the "investment function" appears to be a refreshed version of the so called "misappropriation doctrine" that the United States spelled out in *International News Service v. Associated Press*, and which in Europe received some support, starting in the early twentieth century.[48] This doctrine evoked the right to "the fruits of labor achieved by toils and expenses," with the aim of protecting goodwill as a "quasi-property," stretching beyond the boundaries of confusion (referred to as palming off/passing off).[49] This is, however, a scientifically discredited thesis, systemically inconsistent with the general framework of IP law, as well as deeply anti-competitive. Thus, the helm should be firmly kept on the sacrosanct principle, of British coin, that "[n]either the market nor the customer are the plaintiff's to own. There is no tort of making use of another's goodwill as such," as Jacob J affirmed.[50]

In sum, the theory that *investissement vaut titre* ("investment builds entitlement") has no "right of citizenship" within IP law, nor in respect of trademark law.[51,52] Hence, this theory cannot be used to make the private interest in protection of functional shapes prevail over the collective interest. Instead, the imperative should prevail that these shapes must be "kept free" in order to avoid monopolistic consequences for the market and competition.

up to the identity, between the branded products, the higher is the likelihood that either the "unfair advantage" or the "detriment" occurs.

[47] *See* Mark A. Lemley & Eugene Volokh, *Freedom of Speech and Injunctions in Intellectual Property Cases*, in 48 DUKE L.J. 147 (1998).

[48] Int'l News Service v. Associated Press, 248 U.S. 215 (1918). See the critical reconstruction and assessment of this doctrine, starting from the German *Odol* case (1924), by Barton Beebe, *The Suppressed Misappropriation Origins of Trademark Antidilution Law: The Landgericht Elberfeld's Odol Opinion and Frank Schechter's "The Rational Basis of Trademark Protetection,"* in INTELLECTUAL PROPERTY AT THE EDGE: THE CONTESTED CONTOURS OF IP 59 (Rochelle Cooper Dreyfuss & Jane C. Ginsburg eds., 2014).

[49] Case C-202/07, France Telecom v. Commission, 2009 E.C.R. I-02369.

[50] *Hodgkinson & Corby v. Ward*, [1997] F.S.A. 178.

[51] Paraphrasis of the classical principle, reaffirmed by the Napoleonic Code concerning the transfer of the possession of movable goods from a non-owner to third parties: if the latter are in good faith "possession entitles," i.e., they acquire the property "*en fait de meubles, la possession vaut titre*." There is one single normative (*seeming*) exception to the assertion that investments is not relevant for entitlement: the *sui generis right* (famously defined as "a legal monstrosity" by Jerome H. Reichman) on the information stored in databases (Council Directive 96/9/EC arts. 7–11 1996 O.J. L77/20): *see* J. Drexl, *Intellectual Property Rights as Constituent Elements of a Competition—based Market Economy in Intellectual Property and Market Power*, ATRIP Papers 2006–2007, 167. Apparent exception, indeed: such right is not an IPR right in the proper sense as it cannot be enforced in absolute terms—here meaning: even against partial infringements *irrespectively* of the measure thereof—but only depending on the assessment of a qualitative or quantitative degree ("substantial") of the investment as well as of the unauthorized data appropriation (Council Directive 96/9/EC art. 7.1). Thus, in fact, the *sui generis* right embodies the (one and only) normative recognition of "parasitism," i.e., the (one and only) normatively affirmed exception—not to the IPR regime but—to the principle overarching unfair competition law whereby there is "no misappropriation without misrepresentation."

[52] And beware the risk that this fake theory moves further on from the sector of trademarks, empoisoning the whole field of IP law (Gustavo Ghidini, Peter Drahos, & Hanns Ullrich, *Editorial*, in KRITIKA—ESSAYS ON IP, VOL. II xiii (2017)), thus also ignoring, as Peter Yu observed, the "primary justification for intellectual property protection—that is, to provide incentives for creativity and innovation" (Peter K. Yu, *Investment-Related Aspects of Intellectual Property Rights*, AMERICAN UNIVERSITY L. REV. 829, 842 (2017)).

V. Conclusion: Risk of Confusing Effects?

Let us now resume, and try to bring to conclusion, the discussion of the main theme, after the short excursion into the "investment function."

The approach advocated here might be criticized for sacrificing the use of the distinctive character that an original shape might well present. But even before such (more serious) objection, the position submitted above, in Section III, must be held firm.

I will not simply invoke the primacy of the public interest in maintaining competition over the individual interests of trademark holders—a primacy that even the CJEU has, to date, upheld, albeit to a limited extent, as in the *Dior v. Evora* case.[53]

I would rather observe that, in economic reality the solution advocated here sacrifices very little of the distinguishing appeal as *overall* pursued and achieved by trademark holders themselves. Let us recall, first of all, that the "shape mark"—which is by no coincidence a recent *parvenu* in the family of trademarks (and is not even mentioned in Article 15 of TRIPS)—substantially constitutes a typical "secondary" sign.[54] A "secondary" sign is one that, as confirmed in leading cases by the CJEU, as well as the United States (U.S.) and German Supreme Courts is not normally perceived by consumers as being a trademark, at least not as a "primary" one: so much so that its owners invariably attach to it the product's brand, whether denominative or figurative, that is the producer's "general" trademark.[55] Has anyone ever seen a bottle of Coca-Cola on which the famous mark was not

[53] Case C-337/95, Parfum Christian Dior v. Evora, 1997 E.C.R. I-6013 (where the European Commission accepts sacrifice of the "attractive" function (rather than the "distinguishing") linked to the commercial image of a famous trademark, where the protection of this function might irremediably clash with the free movement of goods and free intrabrand competition. In particular, according to the Court, "a proper interpretation of Articles 5 and 7 of Directive 89/10 ... the proprietor of a trademark may not rely on Article 7 (2) of Directive 89/104 to oppose the use of the trademark *by* a reseller who habitually markets articles of the same kind, but not necessarily of the same quality, as the trade marked goods, in ways customary in the reseller's sector of trade, for the purpose of bringing to the public's attention the further commercialisation of those goods, unless it is established that, given the specific circumstances of the case, the use of the trademark for this purpose seriously damages the reputation of the trademark").

[54] See the recent Case T-691/17, *supra* note 22, at n.27, where further adhesive jurisprudence is cited.

[55] *See* Bundesgerichtshof Dec. 5, 2002, Case I ZR 91100 *Abschlusstück (*Parker case); cited and approved by Jochen Pagenberg, *Trade Dress and the Three-Dimensional Mark—The Neglected Children of Trademark Law*, 35 Int'l Rev. Intell. Prop. & Competition L. 831, 838 (2004) (and n.17 therein) (also following the authority of W.H. Cornish). Community case law has also emphasized that although the criteria for assessing the validity of three-dimensional trademarks are not any different from those applicable to other categories of marks (principle of "equal treatment") nonetheless, the public concerned is not used to deducing the origin of products from the product shape or packaging without graphic elements or words. In this regard see Joined Cases C-456/01, P & C-457/01, P Henkel v OHIM, 2004 E.C.R. I-5089, ¶¶ 38, 39, 53; *see also* Case C-24/05, P Storck v OHIM, 2004 E.C.R. I-5677; Case C-25/05, P Storck v. OHIM, 2004 E.C.R. I-5719; Case T-129/04, Develey v. OHIM, 2006 E.C.R. II-611; Case T-88/00, Mag Instrument v. OHIM, 2002 E.C.R. II-467; Wal-Mart v. Samara, 120 S. Ct. 1339, (2000) (stressing that consumers are aware of the reality that *even the most unusual of products design*—such as a cocktail shaker shaped like a penguin *is intended not to identify the source,* but to render the product itself as more useful or appealing).

clearly visible? It is written even on the cap.[56] This is indeed "the" tendency of today: to exhibit the "brand" (in particular the "general" trademark) as ostensibly as possible on any kind of items. Indeed, even products, like clothes—even underwear!—that traditionally bore their brand label "inside," now place it outside, as an advertisement: in violation, yes, of the supreme principle of understatement required by true elegance, but in compliance with the dominant mass-driven pervasive splashy tastes.

Deprecable as it is, this tendency should however make it even easier for producers to accept that the principle of "fairness" in competition implies a specific obligation on whoever lawfully imitates a shape after the expiry of design protection to clearly place on the product or the packaging her different "product" and—especially—"general" trademark.

Thus, in conclusion, denying trademark registration of "intrinsic" three-dimensional shapes implies a denial that the same can be relied upon for distinguishing final products based on their *overall market appearance.* In other words, within the framework of a general assessment of unfair competition (including the tort of passing off), the evidence of *other* clearly distinctive formal elements, and above all a radically different "general" trademark (especially if these marks are famous) could perhaps persuade the courts that the reproduction of the shape does not entail any concrete risk of confusion for the consumer, particularly of an "informed and circumspect" one.[57]

[56] Applying the views expounded here to a hypothesis, suppose that in twenty-five years' time an equally famous company, *e.g.*, Perrier, adopts a very similar shape for the containers of its mineral water, bearing the name Perrier in a quite clearly visible fashion. Would consumers be confused as to the origin of the product? I believe not. Essentially, they might have the impression that its shape has been licensed for use. But that impression (a) could not obviously be labeled as "confusing" in a proper sense, because it would not cause any mistake as to the identity of the original producer; and (b) it would be, in any case, destined to rapidly fade away with a social awareness of the legal regulation according to which the protection of the shape of industrial products cannot be the subject of a perpetual exclusive right. Just think how commonly well known the (legal) fact is that one can imitate an expired patent and hence reproduce the invention's conceptual content, allowing the coexistence of the various manufacturers if well distinguished by their respective "general" trademarks, as is the case of generic drugs. Why should an analogous knowledge not take root, with a consequent absence of any relevant risk of confusion, in the face of a clear legal framework that allows the coexistence after expiration of the design protection for the shape of products well distinguished by their "origin" trademarks?

[57] *See e.g.*, Oberlandesgericht [Munich Court of Appeal] Jun. 23, 2000, Case 29 U 5077/99 http://www.urteilemet/Y2/13646.html, *Schokoladenverpackung; also* Jorg Hager, *Infringement of Shape Trademarks*, 33 Int'l Rev. Intell. Prop. & Competition L. 403, 408 (2003); Bundesgerichtshof, Nov. 28, 2002, 2003 GRUR 712, Case I ZR 204/00 (affirming the Munich Court of Appeal). In Italian case law, see Tribunal of Torino, June 28, 2004, n.4823 *Giurisprudenza annotata di dirittto industriale*, 2005.

11

Non-Traditional Trademarks

The Error Costs of Making an Exception the Rule

Glynn S. Lunney, Jr.

I. Introduction

In the United States over the last sixty years, courts have engaged in an ill-advised expansion of trademark subject matter. Where once only words or emblems affixed to a product or its packaging could receive protection as a trademark, today a product's design or packaging itself may receive such protection. Although there are undoubtedly cases where a product's design or packaging is serving the same function as a trademark and could be protected without reducing, to any extent, competition in the marketplace or otherwise harming consumers, such cases are the exception, not the rule. For that reason, Congress, in enacting the Trademark Act of 1946 (commonly known as the Lanham Act), expressly excluded product packaging and design from substantive trademark protection.

Would-be trade dress owners did not, however, graciously accept this outcome. Instead, they repeatedly petitioned the United States Patent and Trademark Office (USPTO) and courts to overrule Congress and to protect trade dress under the Lanham Act. Unlike Congress, the USPTO and courts are institutionally incapable of examining the economy generally. Instead, courts and the USPTO have a much narrower focus directed at the facts of the precise case before them. As a result, in a classic example of hard facts making bad law, they turned the exceptional case into the rule. Facing that rare instance where a product's design or packaging may have served as a source of brand-specific information, the USPTO and courts threw open the doors of trademark protection to product design and packaging generally.

This was a mistake. By making the exception into the rule, courts and the USPTO may have ensured protection for the rare trade dress case that warrants such protection. But they established a legal framework that has invited abuse. Instead of suing only when imitation yields material consumer confusion, companies routinely use the threat of trade dress litigation to stifle imitation that produces only competition.

Courts and the USPTO tried to reduce the costs of their mistake by requiring proof of secondary meaning for product design and by prohibiting protection for functional features. But these after-the-fact efforts have proven to be too little and

Non-Traditional Trademarks: The Error Costs of Making an Exception the Rule. Glynn S. Lunney, Jr.

have come too late. Today, a plaintiff may assert a triable claim of trade dress infringement by showing that: (i) its product was popular; and (ii) the defendant imitated the popular product. Yet, these same two facts also establish that the product at issue is precisely the product that, from a consumer or social welfare perspective, should be imitated. As a result, too often today, parties assert claims of trade dress infringement not to forestall unfair competition, but to forestall fair competition, where I define competition as fair or unfair depending on whether it increases or decreases social welfare.

From a plaintiff's perspective, this misuse of trade dress protection makes perfect sense. When a company loses sales as a result of competition, it does not matter to the company whether that competition is fair or unfair. In either case, the potential prize successful trade dress litigation or a successful threat of such litigation offers is the same: the potential rents from eliminating or forcing further differentiation on a would-be competitor's product or service. As long as a company can state a plausible trade dress claim, even if there is no serious risk of confusion, they have an incentive to do so. Moreover, the stakes in trade dress litigation are often sharply asymmetric. If a plaintiff prevails, it captures the resulting monopoly profits that flow from eliminating or forcing further differentiation on a competitor. Perhaps the result is only a little more market power (a small monopoly, if there were such a thing), but the resulting rents must be real or the company would not have invested in a lawsuit to capture them. If a defendant prevails, on the other hand, and establishes its right to add the chocolate flavor to its medicine,[1] or to sell its shredded wheat in a pillow shape,[2] for example, it gains not monopoly, not even a small one, but competition. In some cases and for some defendants, their market share, economies of scale, or task-specific human capital may offer potential rents sufficient to justify the expense of defending a trade dress lawsuit. But often, they will not. In many cases where a successful trade dress defense would increase social welfare, even sharply, most of the resulting welfare increase would flow to consumers in the form of lower prices and greater choices, and not to any one (or even all) of the potential trade dress defendants.

In such cases, would-be defendants may capture too little of the resulting welfare gains to cover the expense and risk of litigation. As a result, a potential trade dress defendant, if threatened, will too often concede, rather than fight. Indeed even without an explicit threat, potential defendants will too often modify their behavior to minimize the risk of potential litigation. They will refrain from imitating popular products, even when imitation would increase welfare. Where they decide to risk entry, they will differentiate their product or service offerings more than they otherwise would have, again even when less differentiation would increase welfare. In many cases, potential defendants have too little to gain to make litigation, or even a slight risk of litigation, worthwhile.

As a general matter, the economic rents that are available to potential trade dress plaintiffs, and largely unavailable to potential trade dress defendants, create

[1] William R. Warner & Co. v. Eli Lilly & Co., 265 U.S. 526, 531 (1924).

[2] Kellogg Co. v. National Biscuit Co., 305 U.S. 111, 120–22 (1938).

asymmetric stakes that drive: (i) trade dress plaintiffs to over-enforce, and (ii) trade dress defendants to under-defend, whatever legal rights we establish. As a result, we should not adopt legal rules that attempt to mimic the degree or kind of competition we want to have in the marketplace. The legal rules provide only a starting point. The effective degree of competition in the market will depend not only on the legal rules, but on the parties' incentives to vindicate their respective interests under the legal rules. If trade dress plaintiffs systematically over-enforce and trade dress defendants systematically under-defend, then the resulting degree of competition we will observe in the marketplace will be less, perhaps far less, than the legal rules may appear to formally provide.

In such a situation, where parties on one side will systematically over-enforce, and parties on the other side will systematically under-defend, achieving the optimal level of rights enforcement in the marketplace requires us to under-define the rights that the law provides. If asymmetric stakes will lead to systematic over-enforcement of whatever rights we provide in the trade dress context, then efficient legal rules must under-protect trade dress. As a result, rather than tinker further with the secondary meaning and functionality doctrines, we should return to the rule that Congress adopted in 1946 and bar product design and packaging from receiving trademark protection altogether. This may mean that some meritorious trade dress claims fail, but that is a small price to pay to eliminate the vast array of anticompetitive strike suits that constitute the bulk of trade dress litigation today.

To explore these issues, I will begin in Section II with a brief exploration of how the USPTO and the courts came to overrule Congress and extend trademark protection under the Lanham Act to product packaging and design. In Section III, I will examine the error costs of making an exception into the rule. As part of this discussion, I will also examine the parties' incentives to litigate or avoid litigation over product design similarities and show that the asymmetric stakes facing the parties are likely to lead to over-enforcement of trade dress rights. Because of this systematic over-enforcement, if we want to achieve a given degree of competition in the marketplace, we cannot adopt legal rules that mimic the degree of competition we would like to see. Instead, we must sharply under-define trade dress rights in order to ensure the degree and the kind of competition we desire within the marketplace. In Section IV, I will conclude.

II. How the USPTO and Courts Overruled Congress on Trade Dress

Before the enactment of the Lanham Act in 1946, trademark protection was available only for words, emblems, or symbols, affixed to, or emblazoned on, products.[3] The shape or configuration of a product could not qualify as a trademark. At best,

[3] Today, this is often referred to as the "technical" trademark limitation.

imitation of the configuration of a product or its packaging could give rise to a claim for unfair competition.[4]

This distinction between technical trademark protection and unfair competition was not mere semantics, but critical substance. While both trademark and unfair competition claims focus on whether a defendant's actions are likely to trick or deceive consumers as to the source of the goods they are buying, for a trademark claim, both secondary meaning and a likelihood of confusion can be inferred from the nature and similarity of the marks alone. In contrast, for unfair competition, the deception had to be shown.[5] It was not enough to show that a defendant had imitated a popular product.[6] Proving unfair competition required something more.[7]

[4] *See, e.g.*, Coats v. Merrick Thread Co., 149 U.S. 562, 566 (1893); Lucien Lelong, Inc. v. Lenal, Inc., 181 F.2d 3, 4–5 (5th Cir. 1950) ("It is elementary that a color or container cannot be a trade-mark.... [T]here can be no trade-mark in a package, the shape of a bottle, or a letter of the alphabet."); Philadelphia Novelty Mfg. Co. v. Rouss, 40 F. 585, 587 (C.C.S.D.N.Y. 1889) ("[I]n ordinary circumstances, the adoption of packages of peculiar form and color alone, unaccompanied by any distinguishing symbol, letter, sign, or seal, is not sufficient to constitute a trade-mark."); Adams v. Heisel, 31 F. 279, 280 (C.C.N.D. Ohio 1887); WILLIAM HENRY BROWNE, TRADEMARKS §§ 89b, 89c, at 137–38 (2d ed. 1885) ("There are decisions which, at the first glance, seem to hold that the *mere form* of a vendible article may constitute a technical trademark. Careful analyses cannot fail to induce the conclusion, that the principles of unfair competition, rather than those appertaining to trade-marks, were the bases of judgment."); Societe Anonyme de la Distillerie de la Liqueur Benedictine de L'Abbaye de Fecamp v. Puziello, 250 F. 928, 928 (E.D.N.Y. 1918) (granting relief for imitation of packaging under theory of unfair competition) ("The statute of February 20, 1905, allowing the registration of a trade-mark in use for more than 10 years, does not alter the fundamental proposition, that a trade-mark is a design or mark rather than a container or package."); JAMES LOVE HOPKINS, THE LAW OF TRADEMARKS, TRADENAMES, AND UNFAIR COMPETITION §§ 53, 54, 57 (4th ed. 1924).

[5] *See* Zangerle & Peterson Co. v. Venice Furniture Novelty Mfg. Co., 133 F.2d 266, 269–70 (7th Cir. 1943) ("The essence of unfair competition is fraud. And like fraud, it is never presumed, and its existence must be established by a clear preponderance of the evidence.") (citations omitted).

[6] *Kellogg Co.*, supra note 2, 120–22 (1938); *William R. Warner & Co.*, *supra* note 1, 531 ("The petitioner or anyone else is at liberty under the law to manufacture and market an exactly similar preparation ... [,b]ut the imitator of another's goods must sell them as his own production."); Feathercombs, Inc. v. Solo Prods. Corp., 306 F.2d 251, 257 (2d Cir.), *cert. denied*, 371 U.S. 910 (1962); Modem Aids, Inc. v. R.H. Macy & Co., 264 F.2d 93, 94 (2d Cir. 1959) (*per curiam*) ("Even [where a plaintiff is entitled to relief under unfair competition against an imitator], however, the relief would go no further than to require the defendant to make plain to buyers that the plaintiff was not the source of the machines sold by it."); Paramount Indus., Inc. v. Solar Prods. Corp., 186 F.2d 999, 1001–02 (2d Cir. 1951); Elizabeth Arden, Inc. v. Frances Denney, Inc., 99 F.2d 272, 273 (3d Cir. 1938) (*per curiam*); Vogue Ring Creations, Inc. v. Hardman, 410 F. Supp. 609, 613 (D.R.I. 1976) ("It is well established that copying another's article is not, standing alone, unfair competition. It must be shown that the defendant so confusingly presented his product through packaging, labeling or otherwise as to lead purchasers to believe that they were buying the plaintiff's article."); Remco Indus., Inc. v. Toyomenka, Inc., 286 F. Supp. 948, 952, 955 (S.D.N.Y. 1968); Key West Hand Print Fabrics, Inc. v. Serbin, Inc., 244 F. Supp. 287, 292 (S.D. Fla. 1965). For other differences, see Milton Handler & Charles Pickett, *Trade Marks and Trade Names—An Analysis and Synthesis: I*, 30 COLUM. L. REV. 168 (1930) (describing greater requirements for and narrower scope of protection for trade names under doctrine of unfair competition as compared to protection of and for trademarks).

[7] *See* Crescent Tool Co. v. Kilborn & Bishop Co., 247 F. 299, 301 (2d Cir. 1917) (noting that so long as defendant was careful to identify goods as its own, the defendant was fully entitled to "copy the plaintiff's goods slavishly down to the minutest detail"); *see also William R. Warner & Co., supra* note 1, 532; Day-Brite Lighting, Inc. v. Sandee Mfg. Co., 286 F.2d 596, 600 (7th Cir. 1960); West Point Mfg. Co. v. Detroit Stamping Co., 222 F.2d 581, 586, 589, 595 (6th Cir. 1955); Gum, Inc. v. Gumakers of Am., Inc., 136 F.2d 957, 960 (3d Cir. 1943); *Zangerle & Peterson Co., supra* note 5, 269; Sinko v. Snow-Craggs Corp., 105 F.2d 450, 452 (7th Cir. 1939); Remington-Rand, Inc. v. Mastercraft Corp., 67 F.2d 218, 220 (6th Cir. 1933); Meccano, Ltd. v. Wanamaker, 250 F. 450, 452–53 (2d Cir. 1918), *aff'd*, 253

Moreover, even where deception was shown, relief was usually limited to a requirement of proper labeling.[8]

In enacting the Lanham Act, Congress retained this traditional approach. While Congress expressly expanded the definition of a technical trademark to encompass descriptive word marks, at the same time, it expressly barred the registration of trade dress on the principal register or its protection under section 43(a). Congress expressly allowed registration of trade dress on the supplemental register in order to facilitate registration of domestic companies' trade dress in those foreign jurisdictions that chose to recognize it.[9] But the supplemental register provided then, and still provides today, no substantive, domestic rights. Within the United States, a mark registered on the supplemental register is entitled only to the protection that it would otherwise receive under state or common law.[10]

During the legislative debates leading to the enactment of the Lanham Act, no one expressed support for changing the pre-existing common law framework in a way that would allow the registration or protection of trade dress as a technical trademark. Nevertheless, the Department of Justice expressed concern that the use of the word "mark" in section 2(f) might allow cross-over registration.[11] Taking advantage

U.S. 136 (1920); John H. Rice & Co. v. Redlich Mfg. Co., 202 F. 155, 158–60 (3d Cir. 1913); Marvel Co. v. Pearl, 133 F. 160, 161 (2d Cir. 1904) ("Unfair competition is not established by proof of similarity in form, dimensions, or general appearance alone."); Globe-Wemicke Co. v. Fred Macey Co., 119 F. 696,704 (6th Cir. 1902).

[8] *See, e.g., William R. Warner & Co., supra* note 1, 532–33 (holding injunction may properly prohibit defendant and its agents from suggesting to its customers feasibility of substituting its product for that of the plaintiff, and may even require the defendant to attach a label to its products stating that its product is not to be sold or dispensed in response to a request for the plaintiff's product, but a prohibition on the use of the product feature at issue, chocolate, "goes too far" and was improper); Bose Corp. v. Linear Design Labs., Inc., 467 F.2d 304, 310 (2d Cir. 1972) (finding no unfair competition despite similarity between original and imitator given that defendant had plainly labeled its product as its own); *Modem Aids, Inc., supra* note 6, 94 (2d Cir. 1959) (*per curiam*) (noting that even if plaintiff can show consumer deception as a result of defendant's imitation, relief is limited to requirement of proper labeling); *West Point Mfg. Co., supra* note 7, 588, 589 (6th Cir. 1955); *J.C. Penney Co.,* 120 F.2d at 955–56 (ruling that "[l]abeling is the usual and accepted method of distinguishing the goods of one manufacturer from those of another in the market" and limiting relief to requirement of proper labeling and accuracy in statements made concerning defendant's products).

[9] *See* Glynn S. Lunney, Jr., *The Trade Dress Emperor's New Clothes: Why Trade Dress Does Not Belong on the Principal Register*, 51 Hastings L.J. 1131, 1150–52 (2000).

[10] For example, § 33(a) of the Act provides that registration of a mark on the principal register shall constitute "prima facie evidence of the validity of the registered mark and of the registration of the mark, of the registrant's ownership of the mark, and of the registrant's exclusive right to use the registered mark in commerce on or in connection with the goods or services specified in the registration." 15 U.S.C. § 1115(a) (2016); *see also* 15 U.S.C. § 1057(b) (2016) (same). No similar evidentiary presumption attaches for the registration of a mark on the supplemental register. Similarly, only principal register registrations may become incontestable, 15 U.S.C. § 1065 (2016), and provide constructive nationwide use and notice. 15 U.S.C. §§ 1057(c), 1072 (2016).

[11] *See Trade-Marks: Hearings Before the Subcomm. of the Senate Comm. on Patents*, 78th Cong. 62 (1944) 62 (Report of Department of Justice) ("Section 23 provides for a supplemental register for almost any conceivable mark.... [After citing the definition of a "mark" from section 23, the Report continued:] This broad authorization would appear to extend to functional packages and shapes of products, unpatentable designs, and to even include combination packages identified by tying two or more products together ... [and] by transfer to the principal register [such "marks" may] become the exclusive property of a registrant. This result would not only bypass the patent laws in establishing exclusive rights in the shape and design of articles and packages, but might well create widespread commercial

of the broad definition of a "mark" eligible for registration on the supplemental register, an applicant could register a product's design or packaging on the supplemental register. Then, once it had acquired secondary meaning, the registration could argue for cross-over registration on the principal register under section 2(f). Proponents of the bill denied any intention to enable or allow such cross-over registration.[12] Nevertheless, Congress *inter alia* expressly amended the definition of trademarks eligible for registration on the principal register to foreclose such a possibility. At the behest of the Department of Justice, Congress amended the bill to limit the subject matter of "trademarks" and "service marks" eligible for registration on the principal register and for protection under section 43(a) to "any word, name, symbol, or device, or any combination thereof."[13] Congress took this language from the Court's nineteenth-century definition of a trademark in *McLean v. Fleming*[14] and thereby expressly embraced the traditional categorical limitations of the common law's technical trademark doctrine.

Five principles of statutory construction establish that Congress intended to preclude registration and substantive protection for trade dress by this amendment. First, terms of art in a statute are to be given their technical meaning within their field, rather than their ordinary meaning.[15] The word "symbol" in the statute should, thus, not be given its broad ordinary language meaning, but the narrower meaning of "emblem" that it carried as part of the definition of a technical trademark. Similarly, the word "device" did not refer to a mechanical device, but to a coat of arms or other heraldry. Second, when Congress expressly amends a bill's language during the legislative process, that amendment should be given effect and not ignored.[16]

confusion by imposing on producers the necessity of avoiding the use of functional designs, shapes, and packages . . . .").

[12] *See Hearings on H.R. 4744 Before the Subcomm. on Trade-marks of the House Comm. on Patents*, 76th Cong. 127 (1939) (statement of Edward S. Rogers, Chairman of the Patent and Trade Mark Association of the American Bar Association and principal draftsman of the bill); *Trade-marks: Hearings on H.R. 9041 Before the Subcomm. on Trade-marks of the House Comm. on Patents*, 75th Cong. 180 (1938) (statement of Mr. Rogers); *Hearing on S. 4811 Before the Senate Comm. on Patents*, 69th Cong. 29–30 (1927) (statement of Mr. Rogers).

[13] Trademark Act of 1946 § 45, *codified as amended at* 15 U.S.C. § 1127 (2016) ("The term 'trade-mark' includes any word, name, symbol, or device, or any combination thereof . . ., used by a person . . . to identify and distinguish his or her goods . . . from those manufactured or sold by others. . . ."). For a more detailed discussion of these issues, please see Lunney, *supra* note 9, at 1148–50.

[14] 96 U.S. 245, 254 (1877) ("Subject to the qualification before explained, a trade-mark may consist of a name, symbol, figure, letter, form, or device, if adopted and used by a manufacturer or merchant in order to designate the goods he manufactures or sells to distinguish the same from those manufactured or sold by another, to the end that the goods may be known in the market as his, and to enable him to secure such profits as result from his reputation for skill, industry, and fidelity.").

[15] *See* McDermott Int'l, Inc. v. Wilander, 498 U.S. 337, 342 (1991); Morissette v. United States, 342 U.S. 246, 263 (1952) ("And where Congress borrows terms of art in which are accumulated the legal tradition and meaning of centuries of practice, it presumably knows and adopts the cluster of ideas that were attached to each borrowed word in the body of learning from which it was taken . . . ."); Woods v. Lawrence County, 66 U.S. 386,399 (1861) ("[T]erms of art are to be understood in their technical sense when used in a statute.").

[16] *See, e.g., Cardoza-Fonseca,* 480 U.S. at 442–43 ("Few principles of statutory construction are more compelling than the proposition that Congress does not intend *sub silentio* to enact statutory language that it has earlier discarded in favor of other language.") (quoting Nachman Corp. v. Pension Benefit Guaranty Corp., 446 U.S. 359, 392–93 (1980) (Stewart J., dissenting)); *see also* Stone v. INS, 514 U.S.

Before the 1943 amendment, the bill defined a trademark broadly, without categorical limitations and focused solely on distinctiveness. For example, S. 2679, introduced in 1924, and H.R. 9041, introduced in 1938, both defined trademarks registrable on the principal register as follows: "The term 'trade-mark' includes any mark so used as to distinguish the source or origin of the user's goods . . . ."[17] The 1943 amendment rewrote this language and limited trademarks eligible for registration on the principal register and substantive protection under section 43(a) to those that fell within the ontological categories "word, name, symbol, or device." Third, every word in a statute should be given effect. Interpretations that render statutory language superfluous or redundant are disfavored.[18] Interpreting "symbol" as "emblem" leaves room for the other statutory categories, "words" and "names."[19] Interpreting "symbol" as "anything at all that is capable of carrying meaning" does not. Fourth, when Congress uses different language in different sections of an Act, those sections should be given correspondingly different meanings.[20] Congress intentionally included language in defining "marks" eligible for registration on the supplemental register much broader than the language it used to define "trademarks" eligible for registration on the principal register or for protection under section 43(a). It specifically included "package" and "configuration of goods" in the definition of "marks" eligible for registration on the supplemental register. It specifically excluded this language in defining "trademarks" eligible for the principal register and section 43(a) protection. Again, interpreting "symbol" as "emblem" gives effect to this difference; interpreting "symbol" broadly does not. Fifth, if it were necessary, in the legislative history, Congress explained that it was adopting the 1943 amendment specifically to bar trade dress protection.[21]

Following the bill's enactment in 1946, for twelve years, the USPTO followed Congress' stated intentions. Applicants repeatedly tried to register various forms of trade dress, and the USPTO consistently rejected the applications.[22] In 1952,

386, 397 (1995) ("When Congress acts to amend a statute, we presume it intends its amendment to have real and substantial effect.").

[17] S. 2679, 68th Cong., 1st Sess. § 31 (1924); H.R. 9041, 75th Cong., 3d Sess. § 43 (1938), *reprinted in Trade-marks: Hearings on H.R. 9041 Before the Subcomm. on Trade-marks of the House Comm. on Patents*, 75th Cong., 3d Sess. 9 (1938) [hereinafter *1938 Trade-mark Hearings*].

[18] *See, e.g.*, Ratzlaf v. United States, 510 U.S. 135, 140–41 (1994) (noting that courts must construe statutes to give effect, if possible, to every provision); Moskal v. United States, 498 U.S. 103, 109–11 (1990) (same); Reiter v. Sonotone Corp., 442 U.S. 330, 339 (1979) (same); Market Co. v. Hoffman, 101 U.S. 112, 115 (1879) ("It is a cardinal rule of statutory construction that significance and effect shall, if possible, be accorded to every word.").

[19] "It is the duty of the Court to give effect, if possible, to every clause and word of a statute." Tabor v. Ulloa, 323 F.2d 823, 824 (9th Cir. 1963); *see also* Market Co. v. Hoffman, 101 U.S. 112, 115 (Oct. term 1879); Platt v. Union Pacific R.R., 99 U.S. 48, 58 (1878); *In re* Nantucket, Inc., 677 F.2d 95 (C.C.P.A. 1982).

[20] *See, e.g.*, Keene Corp. v. United States, 508 U.S. 200, 208 (1993); INS v. Cardoza-Fonseca, 480 U.S. 421, 432 (1987) ("[W]here Congress includes particular language in one section of a statute but omits it in another section of the same Act, it is generally presumed that Congress acts intentionally and purposely in the disparate inclusion or exclusion.") (quoting Russello v. United States, 464 U.S. 16, 23 (1983)).

[21] *See* Lunney, *supra* note 9, at 1150–52.

[22] *See, e.g.*, *Ex parte* Babson Bros. Co., 103 U.S.P.Q. (BNA) 115, 116 (Chief Exam'r 1954) ("What applicant is attempting to register is a 'configuration of goods' and it has been held in a number of

for example, Minnesota Mining & Manufacturing (or "3M") sought to register the now-classic shape of a cellophane tape dispenser on the principal register.[23] But the USPTO refused. In doing so, the Chief Examiner specifically rejected the argument that Congress intended "symbol or device" to be interpreted broadly. As the Chief Examiner explained with respect to the word "device," for example:

> The word "device" appearing in the definition of trademark cannot aid applicant. The word "device," which also appears in the older definitions, is not used as referring to a mechanical or structural device but is used in the sense of one of the definitions of the word; "an artistic figure or design used as a heraldic bearing or as an emblem, badge, trade mark, or the like," rather than in one of the other meanings of the word.[24]

Rather than refer to a mechanical device, Congress intended the word "device" to carry its technical meaning as a term of art within trademark law, as a coat of arms or other form of heraldry.

But would-be trade dress owners did not give up. The potential rents trade dress protection offered were too lucrative. As such, they kept attempting to register product, packaging, and designs until finally, in 1958, they found a sympathetic administrative ear. And with a stroke of her administrative pen, the new Commissioner of Trademarks, Daphne Robert Leeds, overturned Congress' decision on the issue and allowed trade dress on the principal register.[25]

Once the USPTO started the federal trade dress ball rolling, the Court of Customs and Patent Appeals was eager to lend a hand. Over the next forty years, it repeatedly rebuffed the USPTO's efforts to constrain the scope of registrable trade dress.[26]

cases that such configuration, if registrable, cannot be registered on the Principal Register but only the Supplemental Register."); *Ex parte* Boye Needle Co., 100 U.S.P.Q. (BNA) 124, 124 (Chief Exam'r 1953); Burgess Battery Co. v. Marzall, 92 U.S.P.Q. (BNA) 90, 91–92 (D.D.C. 1951) ("The omission of reference to labels or dress of goods in connection with the principal register and the inclusion thereof on the supplemental register would seem to indicate an intention to confine such matters to the supplemental register."); *Ex parte* American Enka Corp., 81 U.S.P.Q. (BNA) 476,478 (Comm'r Pat. 1949) ("While applicant apparently regards the definition in section 45 of the Act of 1946 as a new standard for determining what may be a trade mark, it is to be noted that this definition was apparently taken, directly, or indirectly from that contained in the treatise on the 'Law of Trade-Marks,' by Francis H. Upton, published in 1860, prior to the enactment of any provision in Federal law for the registration of trade marks.").

[23] *Ex parte* Minnesota Mining & Mfg. Co., 92 U.S.P.Q. (BNA) 74, 76 (Chief Exam'r 1952).

[24] *See id.* at 76.

[25] *See Ex parte* Haig & Haig Ltd., 118 U.S.P.Q. (BNA) 229 (Comm'r Pat. 1958).

[26] *See In re* Kotzin, 276 F.2d 411, 414–15 (C.C.P.A. 1960) (overruling the USPTO's refusal to register the placement and shape of a clothing tag, on its own, without the associated words or symbols that appeared on the tag, so long as the applicant could show secondary meaning); *In re Mogen David Wine Corp.*, 328 F.2d 925 (C.C.P.A. 1964) (reversing USPTO's refusal to protect shape of wine bottle protected by design patent); *In re* Honeywell, Inc., 497 F.2d 1344 (C.C.P.A. 1974) (reversing USPTO's refusal to register the shape of a home thermostat as a trademark where a design patent protected the shape and the shape was the product itself); *In re Morton-Norwich Products*, 671 F.2d 1332 (C.C.P.A. 1982) (reversing the USPTO's refusal to register the shape of a bottle for glass cleaner and sharply narrowing the definition of functionality); *In re Owens-Corning Fiberglas Corp.*, 774 F.2d 1116 (Fed. Cir. 1985) (reversing the USPTO's rejection of a single color uniformly applied to a product as a trademark). Given that the PTO initially rejected the notion that a uniform color could serve as a trademark and only changed its position when the Federal Circuit forced it to, it is more than a little curious that Justice Breyer in his *Qualitex* opinion relies on the PTO's position as support for the Court's conclusion

The other federal appellate courts, although a bit late to the game, soon joined in. In 1976, the Eighth Circuit became the first federal appellate court to protect trade dress under section 43(a).[27] But other circuits were not far behind.[28] Strikingly, in all of these decisions, the fact that Congress specifically amended the language of section 43(a) during the legislative process to preclude trade dress protection was not even raised. As the circuit courts gleefully jumped on the trade dress express, the Court was eventually presented with the opportunity to do its job and fix the lower courts' mistake. However, rather than do its job, the Court in its 1992 *Two Pesos v. Taco Cabana* decision joined the parade. And in a truly embarrassing opinion,[29] the Court further loosened the standards for protecting trade dress by holding that trade dress could be inherently distinctive and thus receive protection without proof of secondary meaning.[30] In its opinion, the Court offered no explanation or basis for rewriting section 43(a) to encompass trade dress protection, but simply took it for granted that Congress must have intended such protection all along. Just three years later in *Qualitex Corp. v. Jacobsen Prods.*, the Court had a second chance to correct the lower courts' mistaken expansion of the subject matter eligible for trademark protection. Instead, it chose again to rubber stamp those mistakes. Indeed, it went a step further and tried to justify the judicial recognition of trade dress protection by pointing to the broad ordinary language meaning of the phrase "symbol or device" in the statute. In doing so, the Court interpreted the language not merely incorrectly, but in precisely the opposite manner from the one Congress had intended. Congress had specifically added the "word, name, symbol or device" language to foreclose trade dress protection; the *Qualitex* Court interpreted it to encompass trade dress protection.

that a uniform color could serve as a trademark. *See* Qualitex Co. v. Jacobson Prods. Co., 514 U.S. 159, 172 (1995) (noting that "the Patent and Trademark Office had adopted a clear policy (which it still maintains) permitting registration of color as a trademark").

[27] Truck Equip. Serv. Co. v. Fruehauf Corp., 536 F.2d 1210 (8th Cir.), *cert. denied*, 429 U.S. 86 (1976).

[28] *See, e.g.*, Keene Corp. v. Paraflex Indus., Inc., 653 F.2d 822 (3d Cir. 1981).

[29] Although there are a number of aspects of the decision that are embarrassing, two are particularly so. First, the Court insisted that there was no textual basis for treating traditional trademarks and trade dress differently. *See* Two Pesos, Inc. v. Taco Cabana, Inc., 505 U.S. 763, 774 (1992) ("It would be a different matter if there were textual basis in section 43(a) for treating inherently distinctive verbal or symbolic trademarks from inherently distinctive trade dress."). Contrary to the Court's insistence, however, Congress added the "word, name, symbol, or device" language to § 43(a) specifically to preclude trade dress protection. There is therefore a quite clear and express statutory basis for treating traditional trademarks and trade dress differently. Second, the Court further insisted that it cannot "engraft, onto section 43(a), a requirement of secondary meaning" not otherwise found in the statutory language. *Id.* Yet at the same time, the Court had no trouble "engrafting" onto the statute a functionality limitation. *Id.* (noting that "[o]nly nonfunctional, distinctive trade dress is protected under § 43(a)"). Of course, there was no functionality limitation in the statute in 1992. Because Congress intended to preclude trade dress protection altogether in 1946, there was no need for a functionality limitation in the statute, and Congress did not add such a limitation until the courts forced its hand in 1998 and 1999. *See* Trademark Law Treaty Implementation Act, Pub. L. No. 330, 105th Cong., 2d Sess., § 201(a)(2)(A)(ii), 112 Stat. 3064, 3069 (1998), *codified at* 15 U.S.C. § 1052(e)(5) (2016); Trademark Amendments Act of 1999, Pub. L. No. 43, 106th Cong., 1st Sess., § 5, 113 Stat. 218, 220, *codified at* 15 U.S.C. § 1125(a)(3) (2016).

[30] *Two Pesos, Inc., supra* note 29, 776.

While they were busy formally recognizing product design and packaging as a type of trademark, despite Congress' expressly stated intention to the contrary, courts also watered down the requirements for, and broadened the scope of, the protection available against product imitation. Where the common law once required actual proof of secondary meaning, the *Two Pesos* decision eliminated that requirement for non-generic, non-descriptive product packaging.[31] Even where courts required proof of secondary meaning, they allowed the trier of fact to infer it from the uniqueness of a design, the extent of sales or advertising, or from the fact of imitation itself.[32] Where the common law once defined a product feature as functional, so long as it served "a substantial and desirable use,"[33] courts redefined the functionality to encompass only those features that were "essential to the use or purpose of the article or ... affect[ed] the cost or quality of the article."[34] Where the common law once required deceptive acts in addition to mere product similarity, courts held that similarity alone was sufficient to support an infringement finding.[35] Where the common law once limited relief to a requirement of proper labeling, courts held that proper labeling was no longer sufficient to avoid an infringement finding, and courts would prohibit the imitation of

[31] *See Two Pesos, Inc.* supra note 29. *But see* Wal-Mart Stores, Inc. v. Samara Bros., 529 U.S. 205 (2000) (restricting the *Two Pesos* analysis to product packaging and requiring proof of secondary meaning for product design claimed as trade dress).

[32] *Cf.* A.C. Gilbert Co. v. Shemitz, 45 F.2d 98, 99 (2d Cir. 1930) (ruling that similarity resulting from imitation and "many sales and much advertising" did not establish secondary meaning in design of article), *and* General Time Instruments Corp. v. United States Time Corp., 165 F.2d 853, 854–55 (2d Cir.) (ruling that sale of 3,000,000 clocks and expenditure of $2 million in advertising from 1939 to 1946 insufficient to establish secondary meaning), *cert. denied,* 334 U.S. 846 (1948), *with* Clamp Mfg. Co. v. Enco Mfg. Co., Inc., 870 F.2d 512, 517 (9th Cir.) (finding secondary meaning based upon sales and advertising expenditures alone), *cert. denied,* 493 U.S. 872 (1989).

[33] *William R. Warner & Co., supra* note 1, 531 (finding that defendant could imitate the exact chocolate flavoring of medication because it "serves a substantial and desirable use"). *See also* Norwich Pharmacal Co. v. Sterling Drug, Inc., 271 F.2d 569, 572 (2d Cir. 1959) (finding color pink for a stomach remedy was functional because it was "designed to present a pleasing appearance to the customer and to the sufferer"); Pagliero v. Wallace China Co., 198 F.2d 339, 343 (9th Cir. 1952); J.C. Penney Co. v. H.D. Lee Mercantile Co., 120 F.2d 949, 954 (8th Cir. 1941) ("A feature of goods is functional ... if it affects their purpose, action or performance; or the facility or economy of processing, handling or using them.") (*quoting* RESTATEMENT (FIRST) OF TORTS § 742 (1938)); *Crescent Tool Co., supra* note 7, 300; Smith v. Krause, 160 F. 270, 271 (C.C.S.D.N.Y. 1908) (refusing to protect the words "Merrie Christmas," woven into a ribbon as a trademark because "the fact that it has 'Merrie Christmas' inscribed upon it adds a value to it over the value of a plain ribbon").

[34] Inwood Labs., Inc. v. Ives Labs., Inc., 456 U.S. 844, 850 n.10 (1982).

[35] The evidence of confusion in the *Sears and Compco* cases has become entirely typical of the type of evidence sufficient to establish infringement. *See* Sears, Roebuck & Co. v. Stiffel Co., 376 U.S. 225, 226 (1964) (holding evidence of confusion consisted of similar appearance plus: (1) labels were not attached to showroom lamps; (2) customers had asked manufacturer of higher priced lamp about the difference in the lamps; and (3) two customers, who purchased the more expensive lamp, complained to the manufacturer of the more expensive lamps when they learned that "substantially identical lamps" were available at a "much lower price"); Compco Corp. v. Day-Brite Lighting, Inc., 376 U.S. 234, 236–37 (1964) (explaining evidence of confusion consisted of similar appearance plus request by a single plant manager that Day-Brite service what turned out to be Compco fixtures); *see also* American Safety Table Co. v. Schreiber, 269 F.2d 255, 270 (2d Cir. 1959) (finding unfair competition from product simulation even though court recognized that "[t]here is some but not much evidence of actual confusion").

desired product features even where a defendant was careful to identify the imitation as its own.[36]

This brings us to where we are today, where simply copying a popular and successful product can establish a triable claim of actionable trade dress infringement.

III. The Costs of Making an Exception the Rule

The judicial recognition of product packaging and product design as technical trademarks was, and is, a mistake. It was not the result of judicial wisdom or foresight where courts recognized that markets have changed and adapted the legal rules accordingly. Despite some early wishful thinking in the field of law and economics,[37] courts are institutionally incapable of recognizing changes in markets and identifying how legal rules should change as a result. Instead, courts focus on the parties and the facts before them. In trademark law generally, and in trade dress protection specifically, this myopia has led courts badly astray.

If we start from the general proposition that the purpose of trademark and unfair competition law is to promote competition,[38] trademark and unfair competition law must strive to ensure: (i) that consumers have perfect information about the goods and services available; and (ii) that those goods and services have perfect substitutes available. As a general matter, words, symbols, product packaging, and product design can play a mixture of roles for consumers. They may convey brand-specific information. The word "Apple" on a laptop immediately signals the company that made the computer. Words may also or alternatively convey information that is not brand-specific. The word "ale," for example, on a bottle of ale informs consumers of the nature of the product irrespective of who made it. Similarly, with respect to substitutability, consumers may accept products with different words, symbols, product designs, or packaging as substitutes for each other, or they may not.

[36] Indeed, some courts have gone so far as to say that proper labeling is itself a wrong. *See, e.g., Truck Equipment Serv. Co., supra* note 27, 1220–21 ("Fruehauf's reliance upon the fact that its trailer was labeled as its own product and sold through its own channels of distribution is not only misplaced, but also self-defeating.... [S]uch a marketing practice by a dominant figure in the market tends to promote rather than ensure against confusion.") (citation omitted).

[37] *See, e.g.*, Paul H. Rubin, *Why is the Common Law Efficient?*, 6 J. LEG. STUD. 51 (1977); Robert Cooter & Lewis Kornhauser, *Can Litigation Improve the Law Without the Help of Judges?*, 9 J. LEGAL STUD. 139, 145 (1980) (showing that if every rule but the best rule is challenged, then eventually the legal system tends toward a stable state in which the best rule always prevails).

[38] For purposes of this chapter, I will simply assume that this is true, but I would note that economists have formally proven that perfect competition yields a Pareto optimal allocation of resources. In making this assumption, I reject the view that the sole or primary function is to reduce search costs. *Cf.* Ty, Inc. v. Perryman, 306 F.3d 509, 510 (7th Cir. 2002) ("The fundamental purpose of a trademark is to reduce consumer search costs by providing a concise and unequivocal identifier of the particular source of particular goods."). If our sole goal is to reduce search costs, we should simply prohibit competition altogether. If there is only one manufacturer of jeans, bread, or beer, then consumers will never buy the wrong brand by mistake. Rather than merely reduce search costs, trademark law seeks to reduce search costs without impairing the availability of substitutes in the market. Moreover, this goal of promoting competition is an intrinsic part of trademark law and is not imposed by some external body of law, such as antitrust, though the procompetitive purposes of the two may coincide.

To promote competition, trademark and unfair competition law should readily protect something that conveys only brand-specific information if extending protection would not impair the availability of substitutes in the market. Such protection is procompetitive. It improves the information available to consumers, without impairing the substitutes available in the market. On the other hand, trademark and unfair competition law should not protect something that conveys no information, conveys information that is not brand-specific, or conveys a mixture of brand-specific and non-brand information, nor should it protect something if protection would impair the availability of substitutes in the market.[39] Such protection would be anticompetitive. It would not improve, and may well reduce, the information available to consumers, and it may reduce the availability of substitutes in the market.

From this framework, we can place things claimed as trademarks along a spectrum: from cases where granting protection would be purely anticompetitive at one end to cases where granting protection would be purely procompetitive at the other. Now, any given thing claimed as a trademark, whether word or product design, might fall anywhere along this spectrum. But categories of things are likely to fall closer to one end or the other. For example, arbitrary or fanciful words used on a product, in the location where consumers expect to find a brand, generally convey only brand-specific information. By definition, fanciful marks have no other meaning, and arbitrary marks convey no other, non-brand-specific information about the product at issue. At the same time, protecting arbitrary and fanciful words as marks in no way limits the ability of would-be competitors to offer substitutes. As long as there are other words that can be made up or that convey no information regarding the product at issue, a competitor can offer their product with a different brand name. For these reasons, the protection of arbitrary and fanciful words as trademarks will almost always prove procompetitive. A corresponding default set of rules, allowing protection from the moment of use as a trademark and with strong presumptions regarding infringement, is therefore appropriate.

Protecting product design and packaging, on the other hand, will almost always prove anticompetitive. As the Court has recognized, consumers are likely to perceive product features or packaging as features of the product, rather than as a means to convey brand-specific information about the product.[40] Moreover, given the availability of word marks, even product features or packaging that serve as a brand-specific information source, serve a secondary and subsidiary role.[41] If consumers

[39] I understand that even fanciful word marks may generate market power and thus render products, such as Coke and Pepsi, imperfect substitutes for each other. That is not my point here, but I have addressed it elsewhere. *See* Glynn S. Lunney, Jr., *Trademark Monopolies*, 48 Emory L.J. 367 (1999); *see also* Mark A. Lemley & Mark P. McKenna, *Owning Mark(et)s*, 109 Mich. L. Rev. 137 (2010).

[40] *Wal-Mart Stores, Inc.*, *supra* note 31, 213 ("Consumers are aware of the reality that, almost invariably, even the most unusual of product designs—such as a cocktail shaker shaped like a penguin—is intended not to identify the source, but to render the product itself more useful or more appealing."); *see also* Restatement (Third) of Unfair Competition § 16 cmt. b (1995) (making the same point).

[41] *See Gum, Inc.*, *supra* note 7, 960 (noting that the parties had both printed their respective corporate names on their packaging); Turner & Seymour Mfg. Co. v. A & J Mfg. Co., 20 F.2d 298, 301 (2d Cir. 1927) (denying claim for unfair competition as a result of defendant's imitation of plaintiff's coloring scheme based upon defendant's proper labeling of its products, and stating: "Where attention by

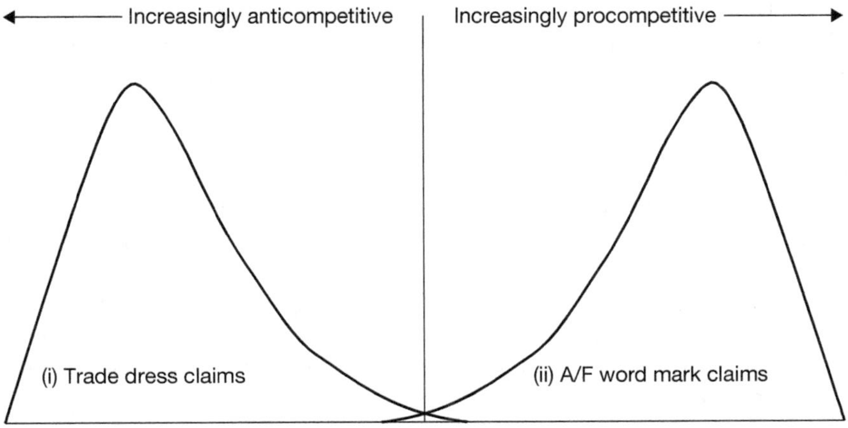

Figure 11.1 Distribution of: (i) potential trade dress claims; and (ii) potential arbitrary and fanciful word mark claims

really want to know a product's source, they can always check the label. At the same time, because product features and packaging often make the product at issue more desirable directly, protecting them is more likely to limit the ability of competitors to offer products that consumers will recognize and accept as substitutes. Furthermore, if a would-be competitor mis-estimates the boundaries of fair competition for a word mark, it can simply rebrand its product with a different word on the next production run. If it mis-estimates those boundaries for a restaurant's design or décor, to take a litigated example, "rebranding" may prove ruinously expensive.[42]

For these reasons, while any given word or product feature claimed as a trademark might fall anywhere on the spectrum, the distribution of potential trademark claims based upon arbitrary or fanciful words is likely to fall decidedly toward the end of the spectrum where protection is procompetitive. The distribution of potential trade dress claims, on the other hand, is likely to skew toward the anticompetitive end of the spectrum, as shown in Figure 11.1.

As noted, the fact that distribution of potential arbitrary and fanciful word mark claims falls decidedly on the procompetitive side of the spectrum is precisely why the common law has long protected such as technical trademarks. Because such protection is generally procompetitive, presumptions that brand significance arises at the moment use begins, and that the use of the same mark on similar goods constitutes infringement, make sense. At the same time, that the distribution of potential trade dress claims falls decidedly on the anticompetitive side of the spectrum is precisely why the common law traditionally, and Congress in enacting the Lanham Act in

the purchaser of the article will enable him to at once distinguish one from the other, a court of equity will not interfere."); *see also* Lunney, *supra* note 9, at 1164–65.

[42] Thus, when the Court found that Two Pesos had infringed Taco Cabana's trade dress in its restaurant design and décor, Two Pesos went out of business and sold its restaurants to Taco Cabana. *See, e.g.*, Greg Hassell, *Houston Chronicle Marketing Column*, Houston Chronicle, July 22, 1998.

1946, relegated such claims to the realm of unfair competition and denied them technical trademark status. While there may be exceptional cases where trade dress deserves protection, such cases are the exception, not the rule. Denying trade dress claims formal or technical trademark status, and relegating them to the realm of unfair competition, properly recognizes which case is the exception and which the rule. By requiring plaintiffs to prove affirmatively that deception is occurring and by limiting their relief to proper labeling, unfair competition provides protection for that exceptional case. Moreover, it is not just the difference in doctrinal elements that make unfair competition a better fit for claims regarding imitation of product design and packaging. The very name "unfair competition" reminds the court that the issue is regulatory, regarding the kind and nature of competition permissible in the marketplace. In doing so, it frames the dispute not merely as a question of trespass as between the parties, as the more property-like trademark claim might, but as a claim that necessarily involves the best interests of consumers who are the principal beneficiaries of competition. As a result, relegating claims based on imitation of, or similarities in, product design or packaging to unfair competition frames the question presented in a way that tends to limit the potential for that protection to become anticompetitive.

Equally important, providing broader protection to technical trademarks and lesser protection to other potential brand indicators serves a critical channeling function. It encourages companies to focus their efforts and investments in conveying brand-specific information to consumers through arbitrary and fanciful word marks. Even strong proponents of trade dress protection must concede that the protection of arbitrary and fanciful word marks will almost certainly have less tendency to reduce the ability of competitors to offer substitutes than the protection of product features or packaging. If companies desire to convey brand-specific information, the law should encourage them to convey that information through the lowest cost mechanism available. This generally means encouraging companies to tie their investments in brand-specific information to their word marks. For example, if there is any chance that some consumers desire goldfish-shaped crackers for their own sake, rather than for what brand-specific information that shape may convey, then we should design trademark and unfair competition law to encourage Pepperidge Farms to link the brand-specific desirability of its product to its arbitrary and fanciful word marks, not to the product shape.[43] Otherwise, if trademark and unfair competition law protects the product shape as a trademark because it conveys brand-specific information, even though there are other means to convey that same brand-specific information to consumers at a lower cost to competition, trademark law will restrict competition unnecessarily.

Unfortunately, courts and administrative agencies acting as courts are institutionally incapable of seeing the full distribution of potential trade dress claims. They see, and are supposed to see, only the facts of the case before them. As mentioned, there

[43] This example is based upon Nabisco, Inc. v. PF Brands, Inc., 191 F.3d 208 (2d Cir. 1999) (extending dilution protection to shape of goldfish crackers and enjoining potential competitor from offering goldfish-shaped crackers).

are undoubtedly instances where a product's design or packaging serves to convey only brand-specific information and where protection of that design or packaging would not in any way impair the availability of substitutes in the market. Perhaps, the pinch whiskey bottle that Commissioner Leeds allowed on the principal register in 1958 might be an example of such a case.[44] Failing to recognize these specific cases as exceptions, courts and the USPTO made trade dress protection the rule. By doing so, they inappropriately extended to product design and packaging many of the strong, property-like presumptions traditionally, historically, and properly available only to technical trademarks.[45]

I understand the impulse. Presented with a trademark claim to the shape of the Coca-Cola bottle and focusing on that claim alone, I sympathize with the desire to extend protection. Unfortunately, it turns out that protecting the shape of the Coca-Cola bottle as a trademark also means protection for such bland and utilitarian product packaging as the Glass-plus bottle.[46] The hope that courts could protect the first as a trademark while refusing to protect the second has proven false.[47] That leaves us with either protecting both or refusing to protect either. There may be some, albeit small welfare gains from protecting the shape of the Coke bottle, but any such gains are likely far outweighed by the welfare losses from protecting the shape of the Glass-plus bottle. Moreover, it is not a one-to-one welfare comparison. For every one case involving something like the Coke bottle, the parties' asymmetric stakes ensure that there are a hundred cases or threatened cases involving something like the Glass-plus bottle.

By protecting product design and packaging as trademarks, courts and the USPTO have fashioned trade dress protection into an anticompetitive weapon that the creators of new and popular products use to scare off competitive entry. Courts and the USPTO have tried to use the secondary meaning requirement and functionality to constrain the anticompetitive potential of trade dress litigation. Again, however, they have failed to see the whole picture. With respect to functionality, for example, they have tried to define the legal doctrine in terms of the line between fair and unfair competition that they would like to see in the marketplace.[48]

[44] Or perhaps Commissioner Leeds already knew that Haig & Haig would become one of her first clients when she stepped down as trademark commissioner. *See* Haig & Haig Ltd. v. Maradel Prods., Inc., 249 F. Supp. 575, 576 (S.D.N.Y. 1966) (listing "Daphne Robert Leeds" as "of counsel" for plaintiff in a case in which Haig & Haig sought to enforce the registration that Ms. Leeds had awarded Haig & Haig when she was Assistant Commissioner). In any event, it is less clear what possible justification the Eighth Circuit had for reaching out and protecting a grain hauler's shape as a trademark in *Truck Equipment Co., supra* note 27.

[45] *See* Lunney, *supra* note 9, at 1165–66.

[46] *In re* Morton-Norwich Prods., Inc., 671 F.2d 1332 (C.C.P.A. 1982).

[47] *Id.* at 1341–43 (holding that bottle shape was not functional and remanding for determination of distinctiveness).

[48] *See, e.g., Qualitex, supra* note 26, 165 (1995) (holding that "'[i]n general terms, a product feature is functional,' and cannot serve as a trademark, 'if it is essential to the use or purpose of the article or if it affects the cost or quality of the article,' that is, if exclusive use of the feature would put competitors at a significant non-reputation-related disadvantage") (*quoting Inwood Labs., Inc., supra* note 34, 850, n.10 (1982)).

What they have failed to recognize is that whatever doctrinal lines they draw are not the lines we will in fact see in the marketplace. Trade dress plaintiffs have a strong incentive to over-enforce whatever legal rights we recognize.[49] Trade dress defendants, on the other hand, tend to under-defend their rights to compete. The reason for this is simple: if a plaintiff wins a trade dress lawsuit, it captures the resulting rents from whatever monopoly its victory, and the resulting exclusivity in a product design or packaging, offers. If a defendant wins, on the other hand, it wins not monopoly, not even a small one, but competition. If a defendant successfully establishes, for example, that the chocolate flavor in medicine,[50] the pillow-shape of a shredded wheat cereal,[51] or the design of a crescent wrench is functional or otherwise unprotected,[52] then not only may that defendant copy that product feature, but as a result of non-mutual collateral estoppel, so may any other would-be competitor as well.[53]

Because the rents from a more competitive market are usually less than the rents available in a less competitive market, trade dress defendants usually have far less to gain from winning a trade dress lawsuit. Because they do, potential trade dress defendants will tend to stay well back from the lines that the law draws.[54] Potential trade dress defendants will avoid conduct that may lead not only to successful claims of trade dress infringement, but also to merely plausible claims. As potential competitors' behavior changes, so too will markets and consumer expectations from those markets. All of these changes will make it appear that overbroad trade dress protection is desirable even when it is not. These changes result not from courts getting it right, but instead simply from would-be competitors' inadequate incentive to challenge inefficient and overbroad trade dress protection.[55]

Given these asymmetric stakes, there are two possible solutions. First, we can alter the stakes in litigation to reduce the asymmetry. The law has embraced this approach in antitrust law, with treble damages and mandatory awards of attorneys' fees for prevailing plaintiffs,[56] and in patent law, by establishing a 180-day period of

[49] One example that my colleague Irene Calboli has pointed out is Christian Louboutin S.A.'s efforts to claim the exclusive right to a red sole even on a uniformly red shoe. *See* Christian Louboutin S.A. v. Yves Saint Laurent America Holdings, Inc., 696 F.3d 206, 228 (2d Cir. 2012) (holding that Louboutin's trade dress "extends only to the use of a lacquered red outsole that contrasts with the adjoining portion of the shoe"). As consumers, we are fortunate that Yves Saint Laurent generated sufficient rents from its own shoe sales to justify vindicating the right to red shoes for all.

[50] *William R. Warner & Co., supra* note 1, 531.

[51] *Kellogg Co., supra* note 2, 120–22 (1938).

[52] *Crescent Tool Co., supra* note 7, 300.

[53] *See* Blonder-Tongue Labs., Inc. v. Univ. of Ill. Found., 402 U.S. 313, 350 (1971) (recognizing non-mutual collateral estoppel in patent litigation and holding that a patentee is estopped from asserting a patent against a defendant after a court has found the patent invalid in litigation involving another defendant).

[54] Gillian K. Hadfield, *Bias in the Evolution of Legal Rules*, 80 Geo. L.J. 583 (1992) (identifying the activity bias that legal rules create).

[55] *See* Glynn S. Lunney, Jr., *Trademark's De-Evolution: Why Courts Get Trademark Cases Wrong Repeatedly*, 106 Calif. L. Rev. [] (forthcoming 2018).

[56] *See* Zenith Radio Corp. v. Hazeltine Research, Inc., 395 U.S. 100, 130–31 (1969) ("[T]he purpose of giving private parties treble-damage and injunctive remedies was not merely to provide private relief, but was to serve as well the high purpose of enforcing the antitrust laws."); Funeral Consumers Alliance, Inc. v. Service Corp. Int'l, 695 F.3d 330, 338 (5th Cir. 2012) ("These attorneys' fees and costs are mandatory, Congress decided, in order to encourage individuals to bring suits to enforce the

duopoly for generic drug manufacturers that successfully challenge pharmaceutical patents.[57] I have proposed using a similar approach in trademark law elsewhere.[58]

In this chapter, however, I will propose a second approach: if trade dress rights will generally[59] be over-enforced, then they must be under-defined. If potential trade dress defendants are going to stay well back from the line that the law draws, at least on average, then to get the degree and kind of competition that we desire in the marketplace, the law must draw the line between fair and unfair competition, not at the exact place where competition becomes unfair. Rather, the law must draw the line between lawful and unlawful competition to leave room for some unfair behavior. Only by doing so will we see the kind of vigorous and fair competition we desire in the marketplace. Otherwise, if we attempt to draw the line precisely at the boundary of fair and unfair competition, we risk chilling the very competition we desire and that the law might seem formally to allow. Because of the asymmetric stakes, trade dress plaintiffs will strategically assert claims against behavior on the legally fair side of the line. They will do so both to throw sand in their would-be competitor's gears and in an attempt to persuade courts to shift the line to define more and more competition as unfair. At the same time, potential trade dress defendants will stay well back from the formal line because they have little to gain from winning the right to compete. As a result, to achieve the desired competition in the market, the law must prohibit only the most pernicious and egregious forms of unfair competition and should leave less pernicious forms, even if still recognizably unfair, alone. Leaving less pernicious forms of unfair competition formally legal does not mean that we will actually see much of such forms of unfair competition in the marketplace, however.[60] Because of the generally asymmetric stakes, competitors will not engage in forms of competition right up to the "formally legal" side of the line. Whatever line we draw in this area will cast a strong and one-directional shadow that will tend to inhibit nearby and often procompetitive conduct.

antitrust laws and to discourage potential defendants from violating antitrust laws."); *see also* Pfizer, Inc. v. Gov't of India, 434 U.S. 308, 314 (1978) (making the same point for treble damages).

57 There is an extensive literature on this issue. For an introduction, see FTC, PAY-FOR-DELAY: HOW DRUG COMPANY PAYOFFS COST CONSUMERS BILLIONS 8 (2010); Glynn S. Lunney, Jr., FTC v. Actavis: *The Patent-Antitrust Intersection Revisited*, 93 N. CAR. L. REV. 375, 387–88 (2015); John R. Thomas, *Collusion and Collective Action in the Patent System: A Proposal for Patent Bounties*, 2001 U. ILL. L. REV. 305, 333–34 [hereinafter Thomas, *Patent Bounties*]; Joseph Farrell and Robert P. Merges, *Incentives to Challenge and Defend Patents: Why Litigation Won't Reliably Fix Patent Office Errors and Why Administrative Patent Review Might Help*, 19 BERKELEY TECH. L.J. 943 (2004); *see also* Alex Stein & Gideon Parchomovsky, *Intellectual Property Defenses*, 113 COLUM. L. REV. 1483 (2013) (recognizing that this problem may apply to intellectual property cases more generally).

58 *See* Lunney, *supra* note 55.

59 The key point here is "generally." There will of course be instances where particular trade dress plaintiffs will under-enforce their rights.

60 We will undoubtedly see some exceptional cases however, and courts must steel themselves to allow conduct in the exceptional case that strikes them as unfair in order to leave room for vigorous competition in the usual case—a case that courts will likely never see. Courts should also recognize that trademark law's prohibition on counterfeiting itself provides the incentive to engage in counterfeiting, just as prohibition in the 1920s provided an incentive for bootlegging. The stronger the prohibition on counterfeiting, the greater the incentive to engage in it.

Unfortunately, courts and administrative agencies acting as courts have not seen this either. They have therefore tended to define doctrines, such as functionality, in terms of the precise boundary between fair and unfair competition that they would like to see in the market. However, even if they defined these doctrines to embody perfectly the kind and degree of competition we want to see in the marketplace, the asymmetric stakes generally present in trade dress cases mean that such perfectly defined rules would not yield the kind and degree of competition we want in the marketplace. Instead, we would, and do see, far less competition than the legal doctrine formally would, and does, allow.

IV. Conclusion: It's Never Too Late to Fix a Mistake

Procompetitive trade dress claims are the exception and not the rule. Trade dress claims should not therefore receive the same favorable presumptions and strong protection we afford technical trademarks. Moreover, given the asymmetric stakes generally present in trade dress litigation, to see the kind and degree of competition we want in the marketplace, we must substantially under-define trade dress rights. For these reasons, courts and the USPTO should correct the mistake they first made in 1958. They should bar product design and packaging from the principal register and from substantive protection under section 43(a). They should once again relegate trade dress claims to the realm of state law, unfair competition. In short, they should restore the rules that Congress expressly adopted in enacting the Lanham Act in 1946.

By doing so, courts will formally under-protect trade dress. However, the asymmetric stakes generally present in trade dress litigation will ensure that, in practice, the effective scope of trade dress protection becomes just right.

12

Assessing the Impact of Registering Non-Traditional Marks

A European Union Competition Law Analysis

*Lavinia Brancusi**

I. Introduction

The registration of non-traditional trademarks (NTTMs) frequently raises concern over the capability of these signs to perform the basic function of a trademark—that is to identify the source of goods or services. It also raises concerns over a possible negative impact on competition in the market, as these trademarks often comprise features of a product or even constitute the product itself. Looking at the issue from the perspective of European Union (EU) trademark law, it is possible to identify specific legal provisions that seek to strike a balance between the rights of NTTM owners on one hand, and the rights and interests of third parties on the other. These provisions fall within the traditional paradigm of limitations and exceptions to the exclusionary effects of intellectual property rights (IPRs), and the freedom of access to use protected information and information products. In particular, EU trademark law provides for several absolute grounds for refusal, which serve as a vehicle to prevent the registration of a trademark when other market participants are put at a significant competitive disadvantage.[1] Such grounds relate to (1) a sign's lack of distinctiveness, that is, when a sign is non-distinctive, descriptive, or generic; and (2) a sign's functional nature, that is, when a sign consists of characteristics following from

* The author would like to express her gratitude to Irene Calboli and Martin Senftleben for helpful comments and generous editorial help. A separate acknowledgement is reserved to Irene Calboli for her support and encouragement in addressing this topic.

[1] *See* ANDREW GRIFFITHS, AN ECONOMIC PERSPECTIVE ON TRADE MARK LAW 234–48 (2011) (using this term referring both to the economic interests of consumers and of producers having registration denied to signs generating an increase of consumers' search costs—because of their inability to differentiate products properly—as well as imposing significant costs on producers—due to lack of free access to symbols carrying an important communication value in a given market). For critical views on trademark protection of intrinsic shapes, considered also in interaction with European Union (EU) design law, as well as of generic signs, *see* GUSTAVO GHIDINI, INNOVATION, COMPETITION AND CONSUMER WELFARE IN INTELLECTUAL PROPERTY LAW 161–77, 188 (2010).

the nature of the goods, necessary to obtain a technical result, or giving substantial value to the goods. The application of these rules, and thus the refusal of registration, frequently requires an interpretation that balances the public interest against private interests. In this context, the public interest is the interest in achieving an optimal level of competition in a market. Previous chapters of this book contain an in-depth analysis of legal concerns arising from NTTMs under this perspective.

However, there is another perspective; namely, the perspective focused on a potential distortion of competition that may result from the registration of NTTMs. This perspective goes beyond the trademark system, and takes competition law into consideration. As such an approach may raise doubts about its legitimacy and objective, the following remarks describe the particular aim of the present study. They serve as caveats.

In line with the prevailing view, the goals of competition and intellectual property law are compatible and complementary. However, the continuous expansion of IPRs (reaching increasingly higher levels of protection) causes a tension between the need to align the exercise of IPRs and the fundamental EU objective of ensuring undistorted competition in an integrated internal market. To this end, it remains paramount to keep competition free in order to increase market and consumer welfare.[2] Accordingly, there is consensus in EU law on the hierarchy of norms; the fundamental guarantee of undistorted competition in the internal market prevails over IPRs. This means that no IPR is per se immune against an intervention based on competition law, although the courts have carefully crafted the conditions of such an intervention over time in the light of the evolution of the political and economic environment.[3]

This specific topic of the chapter, first, raises the question whether the exercise of a trademark right may constitute a violation of competition law. This should be assessed under the premise that an IPR need not always generate market dominance and pose a threat to effective market competition—alternatively, it may have a consolidating effect. A simple positive answer is thus difficult (will a given trademark right consolidate or threaten market competition?). Existing judicial precedents provide useful case law that sheds light on potential issues arising from NTTM registrations and the exercise of NTTM rights. In this chapter, I review these precedents.

A second competition law issue is availability of substitutable products. This question is quintessential to the analysis of an undue market impairment in a given field. The analysis includes the issue of market definition, which may lead to further query about possible *mutatis mutandis* application for the assessment of absolute grounds

[2] *See* THORSTEN KÄSEBERG, INTELLECTUAL PROPERTY, ANTITRUST AND CUMULATIVE INNOVATION IN THE EU AND THE US 8–67 (2012). For a critical study on different objectives of the EU competition law, *see* Ioannis Lianos, *Some Reflections on the Question of the Goals of EU Competition Law*, CLES Working Paper Series, March, 2013, https://ssrn.com/abstract=2235875.

[3] For a recent analysis of the "external corrective role" of the EU competition law, see Steven Anderman, *Overplaying the Innovation Card: The Stronger Intellectual Property Rights and Competition Law*, *in* KRITIKA: ESSAYS ON INTELLECTUAL PROPERTY, VOL. I, 17 (Peter Drahos, Gustavo Ghidini, & Hanns Ullrich eds., 2015).

of refusing the registration of NTTMs, namely those in the functional exclusions category. This is an important aspect of the analysis concerning the function of certain types of trademarks, and the so-called "non-switching effect"—customers' unwillingness to choose among alternative goods. This effect is the result of (effective) branding strategies seeking to enhance the appeal and meaning of a given trade symbol—branding efforts that can render a trademark so unique that consumers are unlikely to consider alternative products. As they lead to trademark magnetism, these types of branding strategies may have a direct impact on consumers' preferences and behavior in the market. In turn, this raises anticompetitive concerns about how thin the line is between selling power and monopoly power of such strategies and resulting trademarks.

Still, the purpose of this chapter is not to disqualify any NTTM from the outset by finding it unable to fulfill procompetitive economic goals usually assigned to trademarks. Instead, this chapter seeks to advocate for a more precautionary approach regarding the examination and registration of NTTMs. This approach is justified in light of the risk of practices violating competition law, and by the objective of preventing future problems that may result from the exercise of NTTM rights. This chapter focuses on EU law and practice, with reference to United States (U.S.) antitrust experiences where the comparative analysis is helpful to clarify the topics addressed.

II. Trademarks from the Perspective of Competition Law

EU law sets forth competition rules in the Treaty on the Functioning of the European Union (TFEU). In particular, Article 101 of the TFEU addresses anticompetitive agreements, and Article 102 of the TFEU prohibits the abuse of a dominant position.[4] Additional provisions follow from several EU Commission guidelines, especially those concerning agreements in the field of IPRs. These guidelines introduce certain exemptions with respect to the application of Article 101(1) of the TFEU.[5] However, there is no legal exemption from Article 102 of the TFEU, the prohibition of abuse of a dominant position in the marketplace.

In the following, I discuss the protection of trademarks in EU jurisprudence and practice, particularly taking into account aspects of competition law that may pertain to the abuse of a dominant position created by certain types of marks in certain contexts. I additionally examine vertical agreements or merger cases with the objective to infer considerations from competition case law on the economic rationale of trademark law and protection of NTTMs.

[4] Treaty on the Functioning of the European Union, Dec. 13, 2007, 2007 O.J. C306/1 [hereinafter TFEU]; Previous versions of the TFEU had art. 101 numbered as 81 (also 85) and art. 102 as 82 (also 86).

[5] *See* EC Regulation No. 316/2014, O.J. L93/17 of Mar. 28, 2004 concerning technology transfer block exemptions [hereinafter TTBER] and replacing Commission Regulation No. 772/2004 (EC), O.J. L123/11 of Apr. 27, 2004.

A. What does EU competition case law tell us about trademarks?

Before the adoption of harmonized rules on trademark law in the EU Trade Mark Directive and Trade Mark Regulation, the difference in national legislations had a high potential to impede free movement of goods and distort competition in the EU internal market.[6] This was shown by the early case law of the European Court of Justice (ECJ, later renamed Court of Justice of the European Union, CJEU) on agreements seeking to prevent parallel imports. In one case, an exclusive distribution contract enabled a distributor in France to register a trademark of a German manufacturer for the purpose of blocking unauthorized sales.[7] The ECJ found the agreement unlawful, emphasizing that the order did not affect the grant of the national trademark right, but only limited its exercise to the extent encompassed by the prohibition of Article 85 (now Article 101 of TFEU). Such statements paved the way for the ECJ's introduction of a distinction between the existence and the exercise of an IPR—according to which, the former remains within the competence of national law.[8] Similarly, in a case involving trademark assignments to users in different EU Member States that effectively prevented parallel imports between assignees, the ECJ held that it was not the existence of a trademark right, but its exercise, that fell within the scope of the prohibition. The reason for this distinction was that here the exercise of trademark rights amounted to a continuing practice that could affect trade to an appreciable extent and, in turn, restrict competition within the internal market.[9]

The ECJ also reviewed a separate claim concerning the abuse of a dominant position.[10] Here, the ECJ held it was not a trademark right to exclude an unauthorized use giving the proprietor a dominant position. Instead, the ECJ stated that for an abuse to occur, the trademark proprietor would have to obtain power to impede the maintenance of effective competition over a considerable part of the relevant market—a market where a particularly high and objectively unjustified price of a product might be a determining factor. To this day, this argument sustains the

[6] First Council Directive 89/104/EEC, O.J. L40/1 of Feb. 11, 1989, and First Council Regulation (EC) No. 40/94, O.J. L11/1 of Jan. 14, 1994, with subsequent amended versions, the last being Directive (EU) 2015/2436, O.J. L336 and EU Regulation 2017/1001, O.J. L154/1 of June 16, 2017.

[7] Joined Cases C-56/64 & 58/64, Consten & Grundig v. Comm'n, 1966 E.C.R. 00429.

[8] *See also* Case C-24/67, Parke, Davis & Co. v. Probel, Reese, 1968 E.C.R. 00081 (concerning patents, where this distinction appeared for the first time. Initially, the interface and division of competence between the TFEU's antitrust rules and the IPRs system were interpreted with reference to art. 222 TEEC/art. 295 TEC/art. 345 TFEU, which stipulated, "The Treaties shall in no way prejudice the rules in Member States governing the system of property ownership"). For a historical analysis, see DAWID MIĄSIK, STOSUNEK PRAWA OCHRONY KONKURENCJI DO PRAWA WŁASNOŚCI INTELEKTUALNEJ 348–52 (2012).

[9] Case C-40/70, Sirena v. Eda, 1979 E.C.R. 03169, 1971 C.M.L.R. 260. The ECJ refined later the practice on agreements involving trademark assignments by requiring continuous effects aimed at partitioning of markets. *See* CATHERINE SEVILLE, EU INTELLECTUAL PROPERTY LAW AND POLICY 459–60 (2d ed. 2016) (discussing cases C-51/75, EMI v. CBS, 1976 E.C.R. 00811, and C-9/93, IHT v. Ideal Standard, 1994 E.C.R. I-02789).

[10] *Sirena v. Eda. supra* note 9.

thesis that a mere grant or existence of an IPR cannot be prohibited under Article 102 TFEU.[11]

Another important step in EU practice was the development of the doctrine of specific subject matter of an IPR. This doctrine is aimed at preserving the possibility of enforcing certain types of exclusive IPRs. It is also aimed at avoiding enforcement practices incompatible with the rules laid down in the TFEU. With respect to trademark protection, this doctrine was specifically applied to circumstances involving parallel importation and repackaging.[12] Still, the doctrine is not a stable safe-harbor for IP owners, as the ECJ has invoked abuse of a dominant position in order to impose an obligation to license the asset to competitors in certain circumstances.[13]

On the other hand, the major rulings on the so-called "refusal to deal" doctrine—a typical issue that can lead to the application of EU competition law—do not relate to trademark deals. Still, mergers or acquisitions of undertakings or of their assets with specific business turnover involving IPRs require reporting to the EU Commission, and clearance based on provisions of the EU Merger Regulation.[14] In particular, this control aims at guaranteeing that new "concentrations" of business power, including relevant IPRs, do not lead to a significant impediment of competition.[15] Could this cover trademarks and entail specific obligations with regard to trademark licensing? That is could these control measures address the concentration of IPRs in one company and raise the question of whether the company would abuse a dominant position if it refuses to license its trademarks?

As emphasized by several authors, exclusive rights granted by trademarks with strong selling power may strengthen (and initially generate) market dominance on the part of the companies controlling these marks.[16] In past years, the EU Commission

[11] MARIA TERESA MAGGIOLINO, INTELLECTUAL PROPERTY AND ANTITRUST: A COMPARATIVE ECONOMIC ANALYSIS OF US AND EU LAW 102 (2011).

[12] The specific subject matter of a trademark is the owner's exclusive right to use the mark for the purpose of putting affixed goods into circulation for the first time, as well as to prohibit further marketing of repackaged goods. The exact scope of this right must be established with regard to the essential (i.e., source-identification) function of a trademark. *See, e.g.*, Case C-102/77, Hoffman La Roche v. Centrafarm, 1978 E.C.R. 011139; Case C-16/74, Centrafarm v. Winthorp, 1974 E.C.R. 001183; Case C-192/73, Van Zuylen v. Hag, 1974 E.C.R. 00731; Case C-10/89, SA CNL-Sucal v. HAG, 1990 E.C.R. I-03711.

[13] Giandonato Caggiano, *Competition and Regulation of Intellectual Property Rights for the Achievement and Functioning of the Internal Market*, *in* COMPETITION LAW AND INTELLECTUAL PROPERTY: A EUROPEAN PERSPECTIVE 3, 12 (Giandonato Caggiano, Gabriella Muscolo, & Marina Tavassi eds., 2012); KATARZYNA CZAPRACKA, INTELLECTUAL PROPERTY AND LIMITS OF ANTITRUST: A COMPARATIVE STUDY OF US AND EU APPROACHES 98 (2009) (referencing C-241/91, RTE (Magill), 1995 E.C.R. I-00743; C-418/01, IMS Health, 2004 E.C.R. I-05039; and T-201/04, Microsoft, 2007 E.C.R. II03601).

[14] *See* Council Regulation (EC) No. 139/2004 of Jan. 20, 2004, on the Control of Concentrations Between Undertakings, arts. 2–3 2004 O.J. L24 (replacing previous Regulation (EEC) No. 4064/89); *see also* Thomas Vinje, *European Union*, *in* THE INTELLECTUAL PROPERTY AND ANTITRUST REVIEW 34, 47–50 (Thomas Vinje ed., 2016) (discussing recent EU practice).

[15] *See* Council Regulation (EC) No. 139/2004 of Jan. 20, 2004, on the Control of Concentrations Between Undertakings, arts. 2–3 (replacing previous Regulation (EEC) No. 4064/89).

[16] Gustavo Ghidini, *The Bride and the Groom: On the Intersection Between Intellectual Property and Antitrust Law*, *in* COMPETITION LAW AND IP, *supra* note 13, at 27, 4243 (discussing Italian cases *PepsiCo Foods & Beverages Int'l v. IBG S./Coca-Cola Italy* (A224 Dec. 17, 1999) and *Henkel v. Loctite* (order no. 4993 C 2641)).

has monitored the concentration of market power in the case of mergers that may result in the creation of a larger manufacturing entity, or in the combination of strong consumer brands in the hands of one business entity. The EU Commission feared that these mergers could lead to a concentration of brand power in the marketplace. For example, one such merger was between Kimberly-Clark and Scott, which created one of the largest manufacturers of tissue products.[17] The concern was that this new company would be able to obtain the leading position for tissue products and, at the same time, pursue a branding strategy that would tie together essential branded products and private-label products. Ultimately, the merger was permitted under the condition of divestment of certain brands and businesses that were part of the merger, including the grant of exclusive trademark licenses in the framework of coexistence agreements.

Apart from requiring a commitment to divest (the preferred remedy of the EU Commission), a concentration may also be allowed under an alternative approach that also seeks to remedy the concentration of IPR-related power. Such an alternative approach should involve agreements that enable effective competition similarly to a divestiture; in particular, the company at issue may be requested to grant an exclusive license to a third party without imposing on the licensee any restriction with respect to the field or geographical extent of use.[18] This was the case with respect to the use of the trademark "Nimenrix." The purchaser of the mark, GlaxoSmithKline (GSK), was granted an exclusive and perpetual license after the acquisition of the global human vaccines business (excluding the vaccines related to Influenza) from Novartis. Such license was necessary because the suffix *–rix* was used for a variety of GSK's own vaccines, and thus a divestiture for Nimenrix was impossible.[19] Hence, the terms of the license were sufficient to ease the EU Commission's concerns that the acquisition would constitute a practice contrary to EU competition law.

Along similar lines, interesting aspects on compatibility of the so-called "no-challenge" prohibition clauses in trademark licenses with EU competition law have emerged from the interpretation of application of Article 101 (81/85) of the TFEU, beyond mergers and acquisitions. An important example in this respect dealt with a set of agreements that combined licensing of know-how and trademarks, based on which an English manufacturer was able to brew and sell Canadian beer in the UK under the trademarks of the proprietor (Moosehead).[20] The exclusive trademark license at issue included, apart from selling restrictions, the licensee's obligation not to challenge the ownership of the trademark on grounds such as prior use or prior registration of an identical trademark. The EU Commission cleared this contractual provision on the consideration that the question of whether the licensor or the licensee is the person entitled to enforce the trademark right against third

[17] Commission Decision 96/435, 1996 O.J. L183, 1 (Case No. IV/M.623, Kimberly-Clark/Scott), ¶¶ 5, 87, 105, 128, 138.

[18] Commission Notice on Remedies No. 2008/C 267/01, 2008 O.J. C267/01, ¶ 38.

[19] Commission Regulation (EC) No. 139/2004, 2015 O.J. C539 (Case No. COMP/M.7276), ¶ 366.

[20] Commission Decision No. 90/186/EEC, 1990 O.J. L100/32 [hereinafter *Moosehead/Whitbread*].

parties is irrelevant from the perspective of market competition.[21] However, the EU Commission took a different position regarding the prohibition of challenging the validity of the trademark, and held that "[s]uch a clause may constitute a restriction of competition within the meaning of Article 85 (1), because it may contribute to the maintenance of a trademark that would be an unjustified barrier to entry into given market."[22] In general, the EU Commission stated that a competition restriction within the meaning of the TFEU had to be appreciable, and this would be the case for well-known trademarks capable of conferring an important advantage to new entrants in the market. The EU Commission specifically emphasized that the purpose of challenging the validity of a mark can have an important role, such as when the challenge is based on the existence of an absolute ground for refusing registration. Absolute grounds include refusal if a sign is generic or descriptive, as there is a need to enable free use of generic and descriptive terms. Still, the EU Commission ultimately found that the "no-challenge" clause at issue did not restrict competition because Moosehead trademarks were presumed to be "comparatively new" to the lager market in the territory and thus unable to constitute an appreciable barrier of entry.[23]

One commentator criticized the finding of the EU Commission, especially the second part of the decision where the contract was qualified as not falling under the block exemption set forth in Regulation 556/89,[24] because the trademark agreement was said not to have an "ancillary" character to that concerning know-how.[25] The EU Commission reasoned that the principal interest of the parties lay in exploiting the trademark, and not the know-how per se. This position was quite controversial because the company was producing a new type of beer in the UK. Usually, know-how and trademark aspects are complementary in franchise agreements. Hence, it is hardly possible to establish a dichotomy of ancillary versus substantial.[26]

It is conceivable that new versions of the Technology Transfer Block Exemption (TTBER) were adopted in the light of this criticism with the aim to consolidate previous acts containing block exemptions.[27] New versions included trademarks among the category of IPRs which may be exempted in case of ancillary licensing[28]—although (again) trademarks were not mentioned in the legal definition of a

[21] *Moosehead/Whitbread, supra* note 20 (Whitbread had a restriction to sell outside the territory and to produce or promote any other Canadian beer within the territory).

[22] *Moosehead/Whitbread, supra* note 20, ¶ 15(4)(a).

[23] Finally, the contract as a whole, although found restrictive within the meaning of art. 85(1), was cleared in the light of the exemption set in art. 85(3) of the TFEU, *supra* note 4.

[24] Commission Regulation (EEC) No. 556/89 of Nov. 30, 1988 on the application of art. 85(3) of the Treaty to certain categories of know-how licensing agreements of Mar. 4, 1989, 61 O.J. L1.

[25] VALENTINE CORAH, INTELLECTUAL PROPERTY RIGHTS AND THE EC COMPETITION RULES 126–28 (2006) (ancillary character means that it does not constitute the primary object of such agreements).

[26] *Id.* at 128.

[27] *See* TTBER, *supra* note 5 (replacing, inter alia, Commission Regulation No. 556/89 concerning know-how and trademarks).

[28] *See* WALTER FRENZ, HANDBOOK OF EU COMPETITION LAW 451 (2016) (however, in order to be exempted by TTBER, the agreement (e.g., license) must be directly linked to the use, sale, or resale of goods or services covered by the technology). Similarly, Commission Regulation No. 330/2010 of Apr. 20, 2010 on the application of Article 101(3) of TFUE, 102 O.J. L1 (replacing Regulation No. 2790/1999), which exempts vertical distribution agreements, applies the exemption only to so-called ancillary

technology transfer agreement.[29] However, new official guidelines clearly specify that a trademark license agreement improving the exploitation of the licensed technology may be covered by the TTBER exemption, even if the principal interest of the parties lies in the exploitation of the trademark rather than in the technology.[30]

Another relevant case involves a trademark coexistence agreement which also contained a no-challenge validity clause. This contract is between different holders of potentially confusingly similar marks who agree to delimitate their respective use of the marks in order to avoid further conflicts.[31] In the case at issue, a Dutch manufacturer of tobacco and the owner of the trademark "Toltecs Special" entered into an agreement with a German owner of the presumably dormant trademark "Dorcet." Under the terms of the agreement, the owner of the mark "Dorcet" was expected to not oppose the registration of the same trademark in Germany for the Dutch manufacturer, provided that the Dutch manufacturer used its trademark with respect to a narrow category of goods, and refrained from initiating cancellation proceedings for non-use of the mark against the German manufacturer.[32] The ECJ confirmed the EU Commission's decision that the agreement restricted competition within the meaning of Article 85 (currently Article 101) of the TFEU, and that the real effect was to hinder distribution of Dutch goods in Germany. However, the ECJ took the position that delimitation agreements are not unlawful per se if their main purpose is to avoid confusion and to solve an (existing) conflict between parties. Still, these agreements are not excluded from an anticompetitive inquiry if the analysis of the entire contractual relationship shows that restrictions are not well calibrated by the coexistence agreement.[33]

In light of these examples, what then is the impact of competition law provisions and case law on NTTMs? At the outset, it does not seem that these marks are more vulnerable to anticompetitive assessment than other categories of trademarks. As in other cases of IPRs, the mere procurement and possession of a trademark right is not considered to be a matter of concern from a competition law perspective. This is only different in the rare situation where monopolists acquire rights via mergers or exclusive licenses, and combination with other factors leads to the risk of impairing

provisions on the assignment or use of an IPR, here including trademarks (*cf.* art. 2(3) in relation to recital 3 of this regulation).

[29] *See* TTBER, *supra* note 5, arts. 1(1)(c), 1(1)(h), 2(3).

[30] *See* Guidelines on the application of Article 101 of TFUE to technology transfer agreements, 2014/C 89/03, ¶¶ 6 and 47.

[31] *See* case *Airam/Osram* in the Eleventh Report on Competition Policy, ¶ 97 (1981) (covering another settlement concerning the use of trademarks "Airam" versus "Osram" following a prior investigation carried by the Commission against a defensive registration by a German entity with dominant position of a trademark used earlier by a Finnish competitor in order to hamper his possibilities to penetrate the market); with reference to other EEC cases on delimitation agreements, *see* Decision *Sirdar-Phildar*, 1975 O.J. L125; Decision *Penneys*, Mar. 2, 1978 O.J. L60; cases settled informally include *Persil, in* Seventh Report on Competition Policy, ¶¶ 138–40; *Bayer-Tanabe, in* Eighth Report on Competition Policy, ¶¶ 125–27.

[32] Case C-35/83, BAT Cigaretten-Fabriken GmbH v. Comm'n of the European Cmtys., 1985 E.C.R. 00363, ¶¶ 32–37 (appealing from Commission Decision of Dec. 16, 1982, Case IV/C-30.128).

[33] This approach is considered relevant for the present practice. *See* Vinje, *supra* note 14, at 41.

competition.[34] This exercise of trademark rights could constitute a practice relevant to competition law provisions, especially in anticompetitive agreements. Hence, this incorporation of competition law generally happens due to specific factual aspects of the contractual relationship (e.g., misconduct in the policy of pricing or of tying practices) and not because of the nature of the trademark;[35] however, brands may constitute a barrier to entry. This is even more true with respect to NTTMs. Interestingly, compulsory licenses are generally prohibited under trademark law,[36] because these licenses jeopardize the interests of a trademark owner who would lose control over the source-identifier used with regard to her products.[37] Yet, compulsory licensing could function as a remedy in merger cases, especially with respect to NTTMs, which tend to cover the shape or other characteristics of products.

No-challenge clauses and coexistence agreements may also raise serious anticompetitive concerns in NTTM cases, as these marks sometimes remain "weak" due to their inherently low distinctiveness or their desirable features for the general type of products. A restriction to challenge the validity of a NTTM, especially when taking into account higher chances of applying an absolute ground of refusal (such as functionality, genericness, and descriptiveness), may almost certainly confer anticompetitive advantages on the trademark proprietor. A similar consideration could apply to restrictions on challenging the validity of NTTMs in opposition or infringement proceedings for lack of distinctiveness. A coexistence agreement between owners of similar NTTMs, or between the owner of a NTTM and a third party using a similar sign, could lead to market concentration in the hands of a few companies, and prevent other parties from using a sign not valid from the start. An action could be based on the claim that these marks are generally used in combination with the

[34] For a discussion in EU and U.S. law of the problem of acquiring IPRs by an entity not via own research, but thanks to superior technologies developed by competitors (Case T-51/89, Tetra Pak v. Commission, 1990 E.C.R. II-00309 (concerning patent license)) or to fraudulent procurement (Case C-457/10, Astra Zeneca v. Commission, 2012 EURLex 62010CJ0457 (concerning, inter alia, abuse of administrative procedures for obtaining a supplementary protection certificate for medicinal products)); *see* MAGGIOLINO, *supra* note 11, at 103–12.

[35] *See* Case C-385/07 P, Der Grüne Punkt—Duales System v. Commission, 2009 E.C.R. I-06155 (finding abuse of dominant position consisting in imposing unfair prices and trade conditions, here a trademark's licensing scheme imposing a double fee. The ECJ confirmed the Commission's restriction of the terms of the trademark license, emphasizing that it did not constitute a "compulsory license"; however, a commentator saw this as having a similar effect); *cf.* Christopher Stothers, *ECJ Upholds "Compulsory Licenses" of Green Dot Trade Mark*, 4 J. INTELL. PROP. L. & PRAC. 854 (2009), https://doi:10.1093/jiplp/jpp181.

[36] Agreement on Trade-Related Aspects of Intellectual Property Rights, Apr. 15, 1994, Marrakesh Agreement Establishing the World Trade Organization, Annex 1C, 1869 U.N.T.S. 299 33 I.L.M 1197 [hereinafter TRIPS Agreement]. Pursuant to art. 40(2) of the TRIPS Agreement, members may take measures against anti-competitive licensing practices, provided that such measures are consistent with other provisions of TRIPS, whereas art. 21 forbids compulsory licensing of trademarks. A different regulation was adopted for patents, *cf.* art. 31 of the TRIPS Agreement.

[37] Apostolos Chronopoulos, *Goodwill Appropriation as a Distinct Theory of Trademark Liability: A Study on the Misappropriation Rationale in Trademark and Unfair Competition Law*, 22 TEX. INTELL. PROP. L.J. 253, 229 (2014). There are also studies with an economic calculation showing that licenses may reduce a holder's incentives in trademarks' promotion, accompanied by a reduction of consumers' trial, which may not be counterbalanced by the advantages of a lower price under the licensing scheme. *See* W.J. Lane, *Compulsory Trademark Licensing*, 54 S. ECON. J. 643 (1988).

products' main marks, and thus are not capable of distinguishing the products independently. For instance, shapes of containers are most often put on the market with appropriate labeling. These actions could still be blocked under coexistence agreements, and for this reason, these agreements remain questionable.

B. Can a law and economics perspective reveal anticompetitive effects of non-traditional trademarks?

The query over a possible competition law intervention in trademark cases is directly linked to the economic rationale and understanding of the function of trademarks in the marketplace. In the past decades, the economic analysis of anti- or procompetitive effects of trademarks has evolved. The status quo in the debate is that trademarks are regarded as procompetitive, and the growth of brands is seen as a positive development. This current approach, in favor of trademark and brand protection, has contributed to a general tendency of extending the scope of trademark protection beyond the traditional threshold of unfair competition (based on a likelihood of consumer confusion) in favor of protecting trademarks, and thus the brand image of the firm per se (based on a likelihood of trademark dilution).

Still, trademarks are generally perceived as a positive tool to enhance market transparency and consumer information by enabling consumers to recall a mark and its associated product features. Trademarks are believed to reduce consumers' search costs with regards to both product origin and quality due to their ability to convey information about the commercial origin of the products they identify. At the same time, trademarks are seen as an incentive for right holders to invest in the quality of products, develop goodwill in the firm, engage in advertising featuring the products, and possibly expand to other markets by producing related or collateral products.[38] These activities result in product differentiation and a state of imperfect competition, which is a matter long and intensively discussed in literature concerning the effects of trademark protection on economic and social welfare.[39] Certainly, trademarks allow consumers to make better informed choices, or at least choose products that consumers believe are better tailored to their needs or preferences. Even though consumer choice allows companies to charge higher prices than for near identical and non-branded products, these higher prices are

[38] *See* ANNETTE KUR & MARTIN SENFTLEBEN, EUROPEAN TRADE MARK LAW 6–10 (2017); Andrew Griffiths, *A Law-and-Economics Perspective on Trade Marks*, *in* TRADE MARKS AND BRANDS: AN INTERDISCIPLINARY CRITIQUE 241, 246–55 (Lionel Bently, Jennifer Davis, & Jane C. Ginsburg eds., 2008) [hereinafter TRADE MARKS AND BRANDS].

[39] Even Nicholas Economides, a strong proponent of trademarks' beneficial role on competition, discusses the possible distortions that result from an over-optimal number of differentiated products (brands), underproduction of each brand, and distorted purchase decisions by persuasive advertising. *See* Nicholas S. Economides, *The Economics of Trademarks*, 78 TRADEMARK REP. 523, 532–35 (1998). The opposite view—that strong trademarks enforced by persuasive advertising leads to product differentiation, high barriers to entry, and monopoly power—goes back to EDWARD CHAMBERLIN, THE THEORY OF MONOPOLISTIC COMPETITION (1st ed., 1933); *see also* Ioannis Lianos, *Brands, Product Differentiation and EU Competition Law*, *in* BRANDS, COMPETITION LAW AND IP 146, 147–61 (Deven R. Desai, Ioannis Lianos, & Spencer Weber Waller eds., 2015).

compensated by the saving in consumers' search costs. Trademarks also function as indications of product quality. Without trademarks, it would not be possible to monitor consistent quality, which could lead to producers not having an incentive to trade in equally good or better products, and the "lowest common denominator of quality would prevail."[40]

In order to fulfill their informational function, trademarks should be non-deceiving; that is, they should be able to communicate correct information to consumers. To the same end, marks should not be generic or descriptive. Otherwise, they would not fulfill the informative function and would instead raise the costs for competitors who would be deprived of the generic and descriptive terms necessary to communicate about their own products. Similarly, protection should not be granted to signs that are functional, especially when these marks comprise of shapes or other product features. Like the issues raised by protecting generic and descriptive signs, granting exclusive rights to these signs would prevent competitors from copying a product's shape or other features, which in turn could prevent competitors from offering a close substitute product at a comparable price.[41] These considerations directly apply to the registration and enforcement of NTTMs, as NTTMs are often functional product features or comprise of functional features whose protection as trademarks could easily bar competitors from copying and making substitutable products at the same or lesser costs.

The focus on product substitutability remains crucial in the assessment of NTTM protection. In particular, IPRs are often justified on the basis that even though the existence of IP protection may prevent competition by imitation (therefore reducing the level of price competition), this protection generally enhances competition by substitution, as competitors are stimulated to create different and better products that do not infringe existing IPRs. In turn, this would simultaneously put pressure on the IPR owner to further innovate and continue competing in the marketplace. However, problems could arise and distort dynamic competition in the absence of competition by substitution. In some instances, these problems are unavoidable, as in the case of the existence and exercise of IPRs with a limited term of protection, such as patents or industrial designs, or because of specific market circumstances external to IPRs.[42]

[40] WILLIAM CORNISH, INTELLECTUAL PROPERTY: OMNIPRESENT, DISTRACTING, IRRELEVANT? 82 (2004) (referencing U.S. doctrine and George A. Akerlof, *The Market for "Lemons": Quality Uncertainty and Market Mechanism*, 84 Q. J. ECON. 488 (1970)). On the contrary, Jonathan Aldred expresses a critical view, sustaining that a proprietor may calculate the balance between cost savings from producing a lower-quality product with less market expenditure and future losses from damage reputation—therefore, his interest may lay in building "a good reputation at least cost" while compensating it with sophisticated marketing that makes consumers believe in a consistent quality of the branded goods. *See* Jonathan Aldred, *The Economic Rationale of Trade Marks: An Economist's Critique, in* TRADE MARKS AND BRANDS, *supra* note 38, at 267, 269–71.

[41] *See* Richard A. Posner, *Intellectual Property: The Law and Economics Approach*, 19 J. ECON. PERSP. 57, 62, 66–67 (2005) (illustrating that this matter is clear even for advocates of the Chicago School liberal policy toward trademarks).

[42] *See* Josef Drexl, *Is There a "More Economic Approach" to Intellectual Property and Competition Law?*, *in* RESEARCH HANDBOOK ON INTELLECTUAL PROPERTY AND COMPETITION LAW 27, 45–47 (Josef Drexl ed., 2008).

Yet, trademarks are generally not perceived as rights that confer market dominance or power, and rarely involve anticompetitive conduct. This includes instances of consumer loyalty to a trademarked product, including the case of famous marks, which does not amount to an entry barrier for competitors per se. Thus, as long as a range of available substitute products is available in the market, courts are unlikely to find that a mark can lead to market dominance and anticompetitive market effects.[43] In the famous U.S. case concerning the alleged monopoly in the processed lemon juice market resulting from extensive promotion of a renowned trademark ("ReaLemon"), the Court found that the abuse was based on selective geographic predatory pricing, and not on the use of the mark per se.[44] In particular, the violation of antitrust provisions was corroborated by the following factors: dominant share of the market; differentiated products through extensive trademark advertising; geographically manipulating prices; and discriminating customers for maximizing advantages over competitors.[45] In the end, the case was settled and the previous order was reversed, due to a change of administrations including commissioners of the Federal Trade Commission, and also because the ascendency of economic theories of the Chicago School supporting a more "pro-competitive" view of the role of trademarks.[46]

Still, it is undeniable that granting exclusive trademarks in certain situations does have anticompetitive effects. One of these cases refers to the strategies (named as "rent-seeking activities") of using trademark protection as a leverage tool for extending and continuing the market dominance acquired from patents in order to maintain supra-competitive prices in the same market, after the expiration of the patent protection. This practice is particularly visible in the pharmaceutical sector, where companies have increasingly used heavy promotion of word trademarks and trade dress to the point of absorbing funds that would otherwise presumably be allocated to R&D for new product development. Hence, this practice does not lead to enhanced innovation, but rather to "harm price competition with generic producers."[47]

[43] HERBERT HOVENKAMP, MARK D. JANIS, & MARK A. LEMLEY, IP AND ANTITRUST: AN ANALYSIS OF ANTITRUST PRINCIPLES APPLIED TO INTELLECTUAL PROPERTY LAW, VOL. I, 1–14; 4-4 and 4-5; 4-10 and 4-11; 4-56 (2009 SUPPLEMENT) (making reference to the U.S. changing practice about the status of brands as barrier to entry); *see also id.* at 203 & n.13.

[44] Borden v. F.T.C., 495 F.2d 785 (7th Cir. 1974); Borden, Inc. v. F.T.C., 674 F.2d 498 (6th Cir. 1982), *vacated*, 461 U.S. 940 (1983).

[45] *Id.*

[46] *Cf.* Daniel M. McClure, *Trademarks and Competition: The Recent History*, 59 L. & CONTEMP. PROBS. 13, 17–37 (1996) (discussing how the influence of Chicago School's thinking on trademarks was embraced by prominent scholar Thomas McCarthy and conducted to a dismissal of all other FTC complaints on trademarks cases, as well as to a liberal practice of courts in protecting functional trade dress or descriptive/generic marks).

[47] *Cf.* Josef Drexl, *Real Knowledge Is to Know the Extent of One's Own Ignorance: On the Consumer Harm Approach in Innovation-Related Competition Cases 19–20*, Max Plank Institute for Intellectual Property, Competition & Tax Law Research Paper Series 09-15, http://ssrn.com/abstract=1517757; KLAUS JENNEWEIN, INTELLECTUAL PROPERTY MANAGEMENT: THE ROLE OF TECHNOLOGY-BRANDS IN THE APPROPRIATION OF TECHNOLOGICAL INNOVATION 25 (2005) (discussing Bayer Aspirin as an example of successful branding policy aiming at long-term appropriation of revenues generated by initial technological innovations and consolidating of firm's market position. For example, in 1996, Bayer Aspirin

The same considerations and concerns apply to NTTMs consisting of product features covered by prior or present patents or utility models, and possibly industrial designs. This issue is of particular significance both under EU and U.S. law. To date, courts on both sides of the Atlantic have emphasized the importance of keeping access to certain signs free—not only because alternative IPRs may already protect the same signs, but also because these signs consist of essential product features, technically or as otherwise needed by consumers. Thus, courts have highlighted the importance of allowing these signs to be copied (also) as a means to ensure market competition.[48]

Moreover, branding strategies can be anticompetitive in that the popularity of a brand may induce "network effects," as consumers need to choose the brand in order to be accepted by a community sharing similar social benefits. The more frequently such a choice occurs, the stronger the brand, and with less of the choice, the brand becomes less susceptible to competitive pressure.[49] In other words, brands diminish the substitutability of products and hamper the entry of new competing alternatives. This, however, is a relevant factor in cases dealing with violation of competition rules.[50] In this respect, branding strategies may be built on the appeal of NTTMs, as it was pointed out in a series of cases regarding protection of the color orange brand for telecommunication services, a transparent clear bin for a vacuum (Dyson), the shape of the Lego brick, or the red sole of Louboutin shoes.[51] Unquestionably, these features help sell the products, since they are appealing for consumers and are often marketed as "the one and only."[52] Hence, protecting

was 300% more expensive than the cheapest alternative on the German market, and its high absolute margins stimulated the vendors (pharmacies) to sell it more than ASA branded substitute); *id.* at 54–55.

48 *See* Case C-30/15 P, Simba Toys GmbH & Co. KC v. EUIPO, 2016 EURLex 62015CJ0030; Case C-205/13, Hauck GmbH & Co. KC v. Stokke A/S, 2014 EURLex 62013CJ0205; Case C-48/09 P, Lego Juris A/S v. OHIM, 2010 E.C.R. I-08403; Case C-299/99, Philips v. Remington, 2002 E.C.R. I-05475. Also see, for instance, opinions of Advocate General Maciej Szpunar in Case C-163/16, Christian Louboutin SAS v. Van Haren Schoenen BV, 2017 EURLex 62016CC0163, ¶¶ 22–26, or in Case C-205/13, *Hauck*, ¶¶ 57–58, 79–80. For a concise but valuable discussion of trademarks' hampering innovation, see Jennifer Davis & Spyros Maniatis, *Trademarks, Brands and Competition*, *in* TRADEMARKS, BRANDS, AND COMPETITIVENESS 119, 127–30 (Teresa da Silva Lopes & Paul Duguid eds., 2010). For an ample U.S. study against mainstream liberal practice of trademarks' overprotection—by sustaining the view that products artificially differentiated through brands equating "more choice" does not always mean competition and that allowing copying does not necessarily conduct to "inefficient incentives"—*see* Glynn S. Lunney, Jr., *Trademark Monopolies*, 48 EMORY L.J. 368, 421–54 (1999).

49 Daniel A. Crane, *Brands and Market Power: A Bird's-Eye View*, *in* BRANDS, COMPETITION LAW AND IP, *supra* note 39, at 128, 132–33; Lunney, *supra* note 48, at 427–31.

50 This fact is mentioned by: *e.g.*, Council Regulation (EC) No. 139/2004, 2004 O.J. C 31, guidelines on the assessment of horizontal mergers, art. 2, ¶¶ 36, 71(c); EC Guidelines on Vertical Restraints, 2010 O.J.C 130/01, ¶ 104. Another important antitrust issue concerns the mix of horizontal and vertical competition between producers' brands and retailers' private brands. *See* Paul W. Dobson & Ratula Chakraborty, *Assessing Brand and Private Label Competition*, 36 EUR. COMPETITION L. REV. 76 (2015).

51 *See* Jennifer Davis, *Between a Sign and a Brand: Mapping the Boundaries of a Registered Trade Mark in European Union Trade Mark Law*, *in* TRADE MARKS AND BRANDS, *supra* note 38, at 65, 65–66, 70.

52 DARIUS C. GAMBINO & WILLIAM L. BARTOW, TRADE DRESS: EVOLUTION, STRATEGY AND PRACTICE 159 n.19 (2014) (characterizing Apple's advertisements as highlighting the uniqueness of its products, as a commercial for iPhone 4 summarized "Yep, if you don't have an iPhone, well, you don't have an iPhone.").

these features can lead to creating a case of single-product markets with unsuitable substitutes. When this may occur, we witness an unacceptable monopoly without substitutes, potentially for a perpetual length of time, as trademark rights may last as long as the mark is in use.

III. Product Substitutability as Evidence of Sufficient Competition and Application to Non-Traditional Trademarks

Substitutability of goods is a key concept for the purpose of defining the relevant product market. This in turn is an essential tool for analyzing market power (dominance), which has been adopted as a judiciary prerequisite in all competition proceedings, be these proceedings related to anticompetitive agreements, abuse of dominant position, or merger control.[53] Availability of substitutable goods has possible relevance in trademark law as well, especially for functionality cases featuring NTTMs. In particular, this triggers a *mutatis mutandis* consideration as to whether competition law perspective on products' substitutability may be of some use for trademark practice.

A. Functionality in trademark law and product definition

In the U.S., trademark decisions on utilitarian functionality apply a "competitive necessity test"—underlying a so-called "need-to-copy" approach—for delineating cases where copying functional or aesthetical features was restricted to circumstances with a need to produce competitively comparable alternatives.[54] According to an alternative school of thought, the finding of functionality simply denies trademark protection in the name of a "right-to-copy" product features unprotected by patents or copyright, without any inquiry over possible alternatives.[55] Although the latter approach was preferred by the U.S. Supreme Court for interpreting utility functionality,[56] lower courts and scholars still find advantages in a market-orientated perspective, which evaluates the effectiveness or commercial feasibility of alternatives and the implicit necessity and cost to design around given features, for all types of functionality.[57]

On the other side of the Atlantic, EU judicial decisions have resolved the problem of the interface between trademarks and (lapsed) patents similarly to the right-to-copy

[53] *See also* CHRISTIAN A. MELISCHEK, THE RELEVANT MARKET IN INTERNATIONAL ECONOMIC LAW: A COMPARATIVE ANTITRUST AND GATT ANALYSIS 29–56 (2013).

[54] *In re* Morton-Norwich Prods., Inc., 671 F.2d 1332 (C.C.P.A. 1982) (utility functionality of a container's shape); Qualitex Co. v. Jacobson Prods. Co., 514 U.S. 159, 170 (1995) (aesthetic functionality of a color standing alone).

[55] For more on the U.S. functionality doctrine, *see* GRAEME B. DINWOODIE & MARK D. JANIS, TRADE DRESS AND DESIGN LAW 107–210 (2010); *see also* Mark P. McKenna, *(Dys)Functionality*, 48 HOUS. L. REV. 823 (2011).

[56] TrafFix Devices, Inc. v. Mktg. Displays, Inc., 532 U.S. 23 (2001) (a road sign's spring mechanism).

[57] Robert G. Bone, *Trademark Functionality Reexamined*, 7 J. LEGAL ANALYSIS 183, 227–43 (2015); *see also* GAMBINO & BARTOW, *supra* note 52, at 109–32.

approach in the U.S. by relying on a presumption of functional determination, based on prior patent documentation. However, in the *Lego* case, Advocate General Mengozzi suggested verifying market alternatives in order to see whether the exclusivity conferred by registering such a trademark puts competitors at a significant non-reputation-related disadvantage.[58] Similarly in the *Hauck* case, with respect to other functional exclusions, Advocate General Szpunar recommended to focus on features that a consumer "is likely to seek … [because] there is no equally good substitute (perfect substitute feature)" on the market.[59] Ultimately in *Hauck*, the CJEU adopted a compromise solution navigating between objective criteria—meant to identify the "essential characteristics" of a product that are "inherent to its generic function(s)"—and a subjective consumer perspective focusing on product characteristics "look[ed] for in the products of the competitors" by consumers.[60] While such an approach seems to shift slowly toward a consumer demand test looking into market alternatives, it remains an issue to be clarified by future EU practice.

In general, analysis of substitutable alternatives requires product demarcation, according to the following criteria for interdependence: the narrower the product category defined by specific product features, the more difficult to find other products with different features considered acceptable substitutes by clients, and thus there is a higher need for competitors to have free access to copy those specific features. Conversely, a broader product category increases the chances of finding comparable competitive products. To date, EU case law has avoided conducting an in-depth product analysis in the decisions adopted in this area. Instead, existing decisions have mostly focused on the semantic definition of the products as listed in a trademark's application for registration.[61] This is different than the early U.S. cases, where courts made the outcome of a functionality ruling strictly dependent on the assessment of the relevant product category. This was emphasized in a case about ice cream beads, the trade dress (shape, size, and color) of which was found functional in a market narrowly defined as "flash-frozen ice cream business," as compared to a larger soft-served ice cream or general ice cream market.[62] However, a recent U.S. judgment shows that a narrowly construed product category (high-end shoes with a red sole contrasting with upper coloring) may help passing over the aesthetic functionality defense raised in infringement proceedings, and redirect the assessment to the issue of acquired distinctiveness.[63]

[58] *Lego, supra* note 48, ¶ 74 (opinion of Advocate General Paolo Mengozzi).

[59] *Hauck, supra* note 48, ¶ 57 (opinion of Szpunar); *see also Louboutin, supra* note 48, ¶ 54 (delivered on June 22, 2017) (opinion of Szpunar) (considering that "monopolisation of colour … remove[s] the freedom of competitors to offer goods incorporating the same functionality").

[60] *Hauck, supra* note 48, ¶ 27.

[61] *See Simba Toys, supra* note 48 (concerning the problem of admitting evidence about the actual use of product (features)).

[62] Dippin' Dots, Inc. v. Frosty Bites Distribution, LLC, 369 F.3d 1197 (11th Cir. 2004); *see also* DINWOODIE & M. JANIS, *supra* note 55, at 170–72 (discussing *Dippin' Dots v. Frosty Bites Distribution*).

[63] Christian Louboutin S.A. v. Yves Saint Laurent Am. Holding, Inc., 696 F.3d 206, 224–28 (2d Cir. 2012). The Court dismissed the argument implying an industry-based per se rule for aesthetic functionality, while considering the importance of colors for the fashion industry. A different result may bring CJEU proceedings on the validity of Louboutin positioning trademark.

This kind of fluctuation between tests adopted by courts confirms the scholarly view that courts generally define relevant market by intuition, while more precise methodology may be needed.[64] A solution recently advanced by scholars is thus to explore the notions and methods of describing the competition relationship between producers, by relying on market definition and evaluation of the degree of substitutability between products.[65] This is an attempt to adjust tools from competition law to the specific situation of IP cases, instead of transposing them in exactly the same way. In particular, it was proposed that IPRs deal at large with interfirm rivalry and product delineation with a frequent focus on small, single-branded markets, rather than involving the typical concepts of market definition and market power.[66] Without denying the specificity and complexity of these cases, the approach based on the assessment of the substitutability between products could become ("*toute proportion gardée*") a promising approach in IP law in general, and to the suitability of protecting NTTMs in particular, especially regarding the registrability and resolution of conflicts related to these marks.

B. Market definition and product substitutability under competition law

Competition law deals with situations of market dominance and power. This is generally interpreted as the power to charge anticompetitive prices (i.e., higher than marginal cost) by reducing market output where competitors cannot respond with a corresponding increase in offering other products that consumers would perceive as substitutes.[67] The U.S. and EU have established a three-step method to determine market power by defining the relevant market, proceeding to a computation of shares among competitors, and analyzing entry barriers.[68] In particular, the EU legislation formulates the purpose of market definition as "to identify those actual competitors of the undertakings involved that are capable of constraining those undertakings' behaviour and of preventing them from behaving independently of effective competitive pressure."[69] Such constraints are possible only if products that exist on the market, or are expected to be introduced with ease, function as close substitutes.

[64] McKenna, *supra* note 55, at 832.

[65] Graeme B. Dinwoodie, *The Death of Ontology: A Teleological Approach to Trademark Law*, 84 Iowa L. Rev. 611, 726–27 (1999); Mark A. Lemley & Mark P. McKenna, *Is Pepsi Really a Substitute for Coke? Market Definition in Antitrust and IP*, 100 Geo. L.J. 2055 (2012).

[66] Herbert Hovenkamp, Response, *Markets in IP and Antitrust*, 100 Geo. L.J. 2133 (2012) (generally assuming that an IPR gives only the power to exclude duplication and its value depends on the value of the protected asset, but this does not amount as such to market power).

[67] *See* Hovenkamp, Janis, & Lemley, *supra* note 43, § 4-2.

[68] Melischek, *supra* note 53, at 37–39 (noticing possibilities of direct measurement of market power without prior market definition, if exercise of already acquired market power has already produced anticompetitive effects); For another critical view, see Dennis W. Carlton, *Market Definition: Use and Abuse*, 3 Competition Pol'y Int'l 3 (2007), http://ssrn.com/abstract=987061.

[69] Commission Notice on the Definition of Relevant Market for the Purposes of Community Competition Law, 1997 O.J. C 372/3, ¶ 2.

Generally, substitutability is considered from two angles under competition law. First, on the demand side, substitution refers to the possibility for consumers to choose among existing alternative products in case of a price increase, which is understood according to the Small but Significant Non-Transitory Increase in Prices (SSNIP) test as set around 5–10%, depending on industry, and for a time of approximately one year.[70] This switching mechanism may be calculated either from the point of "own elasticity" of demand—volume of products likely to be lost with an increase of price, because consumers switch to alternatives or stop buying them—and from the point of "cross-elasticity of demand"—asking to what other products the lost sales are diverted.[71] The second perspective is that of supply-side substitution. Under this perspective, one should evaluate the possibility of alternative suppliers to shift production effectively and immediately start producing relevant products and increase output (i.e., to introduce substitutes) in the short term as a response to a SSNIP. On this basis, a relevant product market is meant to be one that encompasses all goods and services considered "interchangeable or substitutable" by consumers, by reason of the "products' characteristics, prices, and intended use."[72] Finally, it should be noted that product substitutability also takes a geographical dimension, as it should be verified whether producers from different areas can represent an alternative source of supply for consumers, and if they can produce effectively substitutable products.[73]

In practice, market definition remains a complicated finding that is highly fact-determined, and therefore requires corroboration of several different pieces of evidence. These may comprise the following: industry studies directly from producers showing how they place their product among competing products according to business strategies (i.e., pricing decisions, promotions, product innovation); non-econometric empirical analysis from agencies (reports discussing product attributes and substitutes) or private entities gathering data about sales, prices, competitive activities, or conducting consumers surveys in order to show preferences, substitution behavioral patterns (brand loyalty); econometric analysis meant to calculate possible demand for a product, according to a SSNIP test modeled differently depending, for instance, on how heterogenic consumer preferences are; and to estimate the impact of important market events, such as introduction or exit of products, natural disasters, or expansion in productive capacity of a competitor.[74]

70 The SSNIP test was first introduced by the U.S. 1982 Merger Guidelines, https://www.justice.gov/archives/atr/1982-merger-guidelines, and later applied for market definition in other antirust cases, also by EU agencies.

71 *See* Luc Peeperkorn & Vincent Verouden, *The Economics of Competition*, *in* THE EU LAW OF COMPETITION, §§ 1.139–1.174 (Jonathan Faull & Ali Nikpay, 3d ed. 2014). The authors note: "[T]he higher the cross-price elasticity of product B with respect to the price of A, the more product B forms a competitive constraint for product A, and the less likely is that product A is a relevant market on its own." *Id.* § 1.158.

72 Commission Notice, *supra* note 69, ¶ 7. *See* Brown Shoe Co. v. United States, 370 U.S. 294 (1962) (the US seminal case introducing criteria for a relevant product market, and discussing also the possibility of "submarkets").

73 Commission Notice, *supra* note 69, ¶¶ 28–31.

74 The following factors were mentioned as type of evidence admissible for market definition of the category of "differentiated consumer products"—i.e., products sold for direct use to individual

In the EU, courts and adjudicators generally follow the EU Commission Guidelines on market definition. In this respect, the inquiry seeks to identify the specific market as comprising the totality of the products that are particularly suitable for satisfying specific consumer needs due to specific characteristics, and are interchangeable with other products only to a limited extent, while taking into account the competitive conditions and/or the structure of supply and demand in that specific market.[75] In this respect, there have been several decisions in which the relevant market was narrowly determined. For example, the CJEU found that single-wrapped "impulse" ice creams intended for immediate consumption constituted a market that could be separated from take-home ice creams due to production technology, high-level of branding, and distribution conditions.[76] Or, moving to pharmaceuticals, the CJEU found that different groups of vitamins constituted distinct markets because of specific metabolizing functions and possible uses,[77] or that the famous "Losec" AstraZeneca's drug (a proton pump inhibitor) formed an autonomous market vis-à-vis other anti-acids medicines (blockers) used for ulcer treatment by relying on the different modes of action of the drug, and not on common therapeutic indications for the same category of medicines.[78]

In the context of narrowly defined markets, it is also worth noting that branding strategies—which generally underlie specific choices in product development, publicity, and promotions—were considered an important factor to induce low responsiveness to price changes, resulting in a smaller degree of elasticity of demand and smaller degree of product substitutability. This was the case, in the view of the EU Commission, for sparkling mineral waters forming a market distinct from

end consumers, featuring similar functionality, but highly differentiated in attributes offered to consumers and perceived as such by them—by US ABA Section of Antitrust Law, MARKET DEFINITION IN ANTITRUST: THEORY AND CASE STUDIES 99–112 (2012). Different industries involve specific means and methods of assessment. *See* certain similarities in the Commission Notice, *supra* note 69, ¶¶ 36–52.

[75] For the purpose of assessing abuse of dominant position, *see, e.g.*, Case T-321/05, AstraZeneca v. Commission, 2010 E.C.R. II-02805, ¶ 31 (delivered on July 1, 2010) (further Case C-457/10 P); Case T-219/99, British Airways v. Comm'n of the European Cmtys., 2003 E.C.R. II-05917, ¶ 91 (delivered on Dec. 17, 2003); Case T-504/93, Tiercé Ladbroke SA v. Comm'n of the European Cmtys., 1997 E.C.R. II-00923, ¶ 81 (delivered on June 12, 1997); Case T-83/91, Tetra Pak Int'l SA v. Comm'n of the European Cmtys., 1994 E.C.R. II-00755, ¶ 63 (delivered on Oct. 6, 1994); Case T-30/89, Hilti AG v. Comm'n of the European Cmtys., 1991 E.C.R. II-01439, ¶ 64 (delivered on Dec. 12, 1991); Case C-322/81, NV Nederlandsche Banden Industrie Michelin v. Comm'n of the European Cmtys., 1983 E.C.R. 03461, ¶ 37 (delivered on Nov. 9, 1983); Case C-31/80, NV L'Oréal & SA L'Oréal v. PVBA "De Nieuwe AMCK," 1980 E.C.R. 03775, ¶ 25 (delivered on Dec. 11, 1980).

[76] Case T-65/98, Van den Bergh Foods Ltd. v. Comm'n of the European Cmtys., 2003 E.C.R. II-04653, ¶¶ 133–138 (delivered on Oct. 23, 2003) (in relation to European Commission decisions IV/34.073, IV/34.395, and IV/35.436).

[77] Case C-85/76, Hoffmann-LaRoche & Co. AG v. Comm'n of the European Cmtys., 1979 E.C.R. 00461, ¶¶ 27–31.

[78] *AstraZeneca, supra* note 75, ¶¶ 61–107. The assessment of lack of substitutability between those drugs, due also to a discretionary application of Anatomical Therapeutic Chemical classification, raised many critics. *See, e.g.*, Ilaria Ottaviano, *Industrial Property and Abuse of Dominant Position in the Pharmaceutical Market: Some Thoughts on the AstraZeneca Judgment of the EU General Court, in* COMPETITION LAW AND INTELLECTUAL PROPERTY: A EUROPEAN PERSPECTIVE 191–200 (Giandonato Caggiano, Gabriella Muscolo, & Marina Tavassi eds., 2012).

soft drinks or bottled purified tap water,[79] and for whisky, which the Commission separated from other main spirit types.[80] Even in an earlier ruling concerning bananas—which constituted a distinct market from other fresh fruit markets, due to specific characteristics of appearance and taste meeting constant needs of an important section of the population—the EU Commission found that branding efforts to increase product distinctiveness had made Chiquita the "premier banana brand name" on the relevant mark. As a result, every distributor had to supply Chiquita bananas, and this element helped sustain the EU Commission's finding of a dominant position in the case.[81]

Another problem with branded products is that they may falsify the substitutability test based on SSNIP. In particular, long-term use of well-known brands can increase the prices of the generic products in that market. Thus, all companies selling that type of product may be able to charge higher prices. Therefore, the cross-elasticity measured at the level of current market prices in those markets may show that substitutes exist. However, this would not have been the finding if measured at lower, more competitive prices for the categories of products as a whole. In technical terms, this situation is called "the cellophane fallacy," which stands for a market that is wrongly defined as a wide market. This definition comes from a famous U.S. case in which cellophane was found substitutable with other wrapping materials; on this basis, the U.S. Supreme Court denied market power of the company concerned, even though the company already charged monopolistic prices.[82]

C. Non-traditional trademarks and product substitutability

The previous remarks on EU competition law decisions demonstrate that there have been cases where substitutability of products was assessed within the frame of a narrowly defined market restricted to the parameters of one product. Reading this in a trademark context means that it is not unusual for companies, and their respective trademarks, to be considered as a separate market for antitrust purposes. For example, this could be the case for a company owning a NTTM on product features that could be functionally important for competitors. This company could engage (or desire to engage) in a rent-seeking strategy of licensing this NTTM to competitors, thus reaping the economic advantages that could otherwise be granted by another set of IPRs, such as patents, designs, and copyright. In this respect, the critical inquiry is how to avoid a generalization vexing the status of NTTMs as

[79] Commission Decision 92/553/EEC, 1992 O.J. L356, ¶¶ 10–12 (discussing Case No. IV/M.190—Nestlé/Perrier).

[80] Commission Decision 98/602/EC, 1997 O.J. L288, ¶¶ 8–19 (discussing Case No. IV/M.938—Guinness/Grand Metropolitan) (stating that: "[B]rands do not appear to be easily transferable between spirit types; for example, there is no Johnnie Walker gin or Gordon's whisky. This behaviour is consistent with product markets based on each spirit type, since it implies that manufacturers have adopted a strategy of branding for, and within, each spirit type in order to satisfy specific consumer demands in terms of taste, price and image.").

[81] Case C-27/76, United Brands Co. & United Brands Continentaal BV v. Comm'n of the European Cmtys., 1978 E.C.R. 00207, ¶¶ 12–35, 90–94 (delivered on Feb. 14, 1978).

[82] United States v. E.I. du Pont de Nemours & Co., 351 U.S. 377 (1956).

always anticompetitive, while also identifying aspects of these marks that could pass the muster for protection.[83] As suggested by prominent scholars, the evaluation of the effect on competition by trademarks should focus on the "quality" of available substitutes.[84] This means that product substitutability should be determined, as explained above, by taking into account both traditional functional criteria—that is, analyzing a product's function and its methods and costs of production—and more specific aspects of consumer demand, namely by showing consumers' brand-motivated choices, insensitiveness to price, and a low degree of interchangeability.

An objection that could be voiced at this point is that such a factual finding is highly dependent on the industry sector. In turn, this may be an obstacle in the work of the judge or administrative body assessing the case. Notably, to assess the case from a particular industry sector's perspective may require time- and money-consuming evidentiary proceedings, including expert opinions from different fields (for instance, containing marketing studies or econometric analysis) and interpretations of market data and consumer surveys. The fact that evidence-gathering and assessing is a lengthy and expensive process is demonstrated also by the fact that, at the registration stage of verifying absolute grounds of refusal, most examiners and trademark offices would rather refrain from delving *ex officio* into this kind of exercise. Hence, trademark applications can be opposed, and are often opposed by competitors with a legal and economic interest and determination to fight for their market position. After an opposition, there is more willingness, and often a need, to gather such evidence. Accordingly, at the litigation stage courts may also become more willing to take on more evidence-gathering and assess the benefit of market competition. This would require that the court allows such evidence, takes time to evaluate it, and makes a sensible judgment about the availability and closeness of substitutes.

In particular, the court, as well as the trademark offices at the moment of deciding whether to grant the mark, should inquire whether there are good substitutes with regard to specific demands of targeted consumers. The additional inquiry should be whether the type of consumer preference at issue deserves special attention in the context of efficient business activities of competitors.[85]

Hence, it should again be noted that such an approach may require an elaborated set of evidence, which may presumably protract proceedings and increase litigation costs. For instance, consumer interviews and surveys conducted by private vendors are generally known to be expensive. Still, an adjudicator would need more

[83] The present chapter discusses substitutes with regard to NTTMs' grounds of invalidity. Another possible issue is to take into account substitutes while tailoring (i.e., reducing) the scope of protection of NTTMs in infringement cases, Lemley & McKenna, *supra* note 65, at 2103; Hovenkamp, *supra* note 66, at 2150. To a similar direction aims the argumentation suggesting a reduced scope of protection (i.e., against quasi identical signs) for marks "deriving protection exclusively from one weak element," *cf.* KUR & SENFTLEBEN, *supra* note 38, at 231, ¶ 4.353 (a situation that may involve a NTTM).

[84] Lemley & McKenna, *supra* note 65, at 2102.

[85] The criterion of "consumer's choice" (of products meant to satisfy his needs in terms of better performance/functional diversification/lower price) developed in recent EU competition case law remains subject for further analysis. For an invitation to discussion, *see* Paul Nihoul, *Freedom of Choice: The Emergence of a Powerful Concept in European Competition Law*, 3 CONCURRENCES REV. 55 (2012).

information about the concentration of capital and ownership of NTTMs in the industry sector and about the competitors' position and their actual status to reach a balanced solution (here a legal assessment), one that could be optimal from a competition perspective. This could become an obstacle, as only larger companies may dispose of a budget sufficiently large to collect favorable market studies that could support the registration of NTTMs based on proof of existing substitute products. The same observation applies to litigation. In other words, only deep pocket litigants may be able to secure sufficient proof to support or oppose the registration of these marks in litigation against third parties—based on the proof of existing or the absence of substitutability of similar product features. Accordingly, it is hard to say at this time whether this competition-driven approach could favor big economic players in the quest to secure or oppose the granting of trademark rights to NTTMs.

In addition to these concerns and due to the fact that NTTMs are often not inherently distinctive, a decision on trademark registration to these marks is usually granted after the applicants can prove acquired distinctiveness or secondary meaning. Generally, this requires a period of active presence on the market, combined with intensive advertising and promotion. This can again be to the advantage of large companies that can easily allocate funds to these activities. In this context, a review of all business activities showing how the applicants have been presenting their newly launched product and targeting consumer demands, and whether there is evidence of market segmentation tending to a "one-product" market, may be very informative about the degree of substitution without carrying out more advance measurements of supply and demand elasticity. To return to ice creams, a market study discussing Unilever activities since the 1970s which were undertaken in response to the challenge of private labels showed the development of branded ice cream products, which supermarkets could not easily imitate, and addressed different consumer needs under specific conditions of consumption. The products at issue in the study were the "dessert" ice cream brands Carte D'Or (initially sold only in restaurants) and Viennetta, an ice cream cake in the shape of a mille-feuille cake.[86] The producers of Viennetta had sought trademark protection for the product configuration—the wavy shape—of the ice cream cake. This request led to a well-known decision in the UK dealing with issues of distinctiveness and functionality featured by a sign, which were presumably determined by the nature of goods.[87] Ultimately, the shape was found not to be registrable based on the trademark statute. The Court also discussed the problems for competition that such trademark protection could have entailed.

In summary, in many cases, adjudicators can gather relevant information to assess whether a sign is functional, and thus should be excluded from protection, based on the assessment of other types of products available in the market and whether these

[86] Paul Miskell, *Unilever's (Other) Brand Wars*, *in* TRADEMARKS, BRANDS, AND COMPETITIVENESS 228 (Teresa da Silva Lopes & Paul Duguid eds., 2010).

[87] Société de Produits Nestlé SA v. Unilever Plc, [2002] E.W.H.C. 2709 (Ch.); W. CORNISH & D. LLEWELYN, INTELLECTUAL PROPERTY: PATENTS, COPYRIGHT, TRADE MARKS AND ALLIED RIGHTS 709 (6th ed. 2007) (discussing *Société de Produits Nestlé*).

products could indeed be substitutable products. This kind of information may not necessarily come from private sources and be financed by a NTTM owner; it can also be publicly accessed via industry reports prepared by governmental agencies or directly from the Internet, which is nowadays a popular medium for any marketing campaign and selling technique. As I mentioned before, brands may have a psychological lock-in effect on consumers that diminishes the degree of products' substitutability, and therefore affects competition on the merits. Despite this psychological effect, however, past cases indicate a series of objective measurement tools for courts and trademark offices in the assessment of the potential impact of NTTMs on competition. Thus, courts and trademark offices should exercise a higher degree of scrutiny on these marks based on the general principles of competition law.

IV. Conclusion

Granting trademark protection to a NTTM is a decision that can directly impact market competition. This is why the choice of legal criteria to interpret the requirements for the protection of these marks should include, as much as possible, an objective method to quantify the extent of this impact. An assessment based on the substitutability of products may be a promising solution, and this assessment can offer relevant information about the existence and quality of alternative products for customers in the marketplace. This type of assessment requires a clear product demarcation, that is, a market definition, which may be conducted with a type of assessment based on methods and proofs modeled on those used in competition law cases.

However, as with other types of assessments, assessing market definition remains an inquiry that is highly dependent on the parties' ability to provide relevant proof in each specific case and on the adjudicator's willingness to take this proof into consideration. Thus, despite the potentials of this type of assessment, the high cost of gathering evidence and conducting lengthy proceedings should not be underestimated. In particular, large businesses may have larger resources to turn to this type of assessment as compared to small and medium-sized enterprises.

Nevertheless, even though applying the substitutability test may require caution, an analysis based on substitutability remains an important tool that can be used to counter the expansionist trend of registration and use of NTTMs. In particular, this approach can address situations where the use of NTTMs affect customers' preferences and create price insensitiveness on the part of consumers. These are circumstances in which a "brand magnetism" may impede significant competition in the market and where courts and administrative bodies of law should react by denying protection to these marks. In such cases it is also conceivable that the above-described measures ranging from divesting to cross-licensing could be applied to keep the scope of NTTM protection within reasonable limits. This could apply especially to a NTTM consisting of product features which became a standard on the market and should remain available for competitors.

13

The Economics and Management of Non-Traditional Trademarks

Why, How Much, What, and Who

*Carolina Castaldi**

I. Introduction

Court cases about non-traditional trademarks (NTTMs) do well in the popular press, as the general public is amazed by how far companies can go in protecting elements associated to their brands. While these isolated news items may give the impression that the registration of NTTMs is a rare event, an emerging legal literature is reporting a more widespread trend. This trend is already attracting steady critique from authors claiming that NTTMs go beyond the boundaries of what the trademark system was originally designed to do.[1]

This critique complements a more general debate on the problematic side-effects of intellectual property right (IPR) regimes.[2] A major concern is the stretching of the boundaries of what can be registered in any of the IPR systems. An acute observer has talked about the "propertization of just about everything"[3] that has come together with the increasing relevance of intangibles in current economies.[4] While many are concerned about the increasing possibilities for patenting,[5]

* I thank Amanda Myers at the United States Patent and Trademark Office for offering kind and precious guidance on the use of the Trademark Case Files database. I also thank Irene Calboli for her enthusiasm and support throughout the process and for the opportunity to have an economic chapter in this book.

[1] In this respect, *see, e.g.*, Chapters 10, 11, 15, and 16 in this volume.

[2] A book that spurred this debate is DAVID LEVINE & MICHELE BOLDRIN, AGAINST INTELLECTUAL MONOPOLY (2008).

[3] The phrase comes from Robert P. Merges, *The Uninvited Guest: Patents on Wall Street, in* PROPERTY RIGHTS DYNAMICS. A LAW AND ECONOMICS PERSPECTIVE 116 (2006).

[4] Giovanni B. Ramello & Francesco Silva, *Appropriating Signs and Meaning: The Elusive Economics of Trademark*, 16 INDUS. & CORP. CHANGE 937 (2006).

[5] Robert P. Merges, *As Many as Six Impossible Patents before Breakfast: Property Rights for Business Concepts and Patent System Reform*, BERKELEY TECH. L. J. 577 (1999).

the underlying questions resonate with the ones being asked about NTTMs as well.

Economists have mostly directed their objections toward patents and copyrights[6] and have been less concerned about the consequences of trademark systems.[7] Only a few economic studies, which I will review in this chapter, have started to ponder possible unintended consequences of trademark use. When it comes to NTTMs and their effects, the extant literature is almost exclusively a legal one. Studies within the larger field of economics and management have incidentally investigated NTTMs for their ability to generate additional private returns in well-designed company strategies to leverage intangible assets. The more specialized literature on branding offers several clues on the reasons why companies would wish to file NTTMs, even though empirical economic studies including NTTMs are rare. As for the social returns of NTTMs, the economic perspective has systematically disregarded the issue. As a result, neither economic tools nor data to assess the social returns of NTTMs are currently available. Instead, a few attempts have been made to define and measure both private and social returns of trademarks in general. These studies have shaped an emerging field of empirical economic studies using trademarks.[8]

The main aim of this chapter is to offer a first systematic empirical analysis of the extent of the phenomenon of NTTM filings. Such an analysis is expected to inform the debates in the legal literature by complementing the case-based evidence with general empirical findings. The analysis is also expected to inform economists and provide them with insights on NTTMs.

To introduce the empirical analysis, the chapter first reviews the basic economic and managerial considerations around the use of trademarks in general and NTTMs in particular. This first part reviews arguments that answer the question of why firms would file NTTMs. Next, the chapter presents a first systematic assessment of the use of NTTMs by looking at all filings for non-visual marks at the United States Patent and Trademark Office (USPTO). The empirical analysis will focus on the overall volume of filings (i.e., on the "how much?" NTTMs are registered), the type of marks being filed (i.e., the "what?" type of NTTMs), and the applicants behind the filings (i.e., the "who?" are the filers). As this analysis is only a first step toward establishing empirical regularities, avenues for further empirical research will be sketched in the conclusions.

[6] For example, Giovanni Dosi, Luigi Marengo, & Corrado Pasquali, *How Much Should Society Fuel the Greed of Innovators?: On the Relations Between Appropriability, Opportunities and Rates of Innovation*, 35 Research Policy 1110 (2006).

[7] *See* David W. Barnes, *A New Economics of Trademarks*, 5 Nw. J. Tech. & Intell. Prop. 22 (2006).

[8] *See* Philipp Schautschick & Christine Greenhalgh, *Empirical Studies of Trademarks–The Existing Economic Literature*, 25 Econ. Innovation & New Tech. 358 (2016).

II. Economics of Trademarks

A. Economic function of trademarks

When it comes to the economic rationale behind using trademarks in markets, the classical reference is *The Market For "Lemons"* by George Akerlof.[9] There he describes how a market failure can emerge in case of information asymmetries: these are circumstances when the quality of the good cannot be (entirely) assessed before purchase and the seller may withhold information from the buyer. Trademarks can help overcome such possible market failures through two mechanisms.[10] First, they help reduce transaction costs by signaling the origin of the good, thereby reducing the consumers' search costs. Second, they provide incentives for producers to invest in the quality of their products in order to maintain the informational value of the brand.[11] In this interpretation, trademarks are basically signs that convey in an economical way a wider set of informational content about what the company stands for.[12] This second effect also means that consumers are given options for retaliation in case they are not satisfied with the products' quality, something that also adds to the theorized positive welfare effect of trademarks.

Economic studies of trademarks tend to emphasize the positive welfare effects of trademarks.[13] Their use decreases both consumers' search costs and transaction costs between producers and consumers. Such effects relate directly to their informational role. Other authors are more critical when it comes to the welfare effects of trademarks. In particular David Barnes suggests that the economic analysis of trademark systems is ill-conceived when it assumes that trademarks are private goods with a rivalrous nature.[14] Instead, trademarks also entail non-rivalrous use typical of public goods, to the extent that they are used by any economic actor (consumer, competing and non-competing firm, analyst) for their mere communicative and informational value. Failing to protect this non-rivalrous use makes the monopoly rights granted to trademark owners problematic from a societal perspective. From an economic perspective this non-rivalrous use enables positive social returns to trademarks, that is benefits to actors other than the trademark owner.[15]

[9] George A. Akerlof, *The Market for "Lemons": Quality Uncertainty and the Market Mechanism*, 84 Q. J. Econ. 488 (1970).

[10] Nicholas S. Economides *The Economics of Trademarks*, 78 Trademark Rep. 523 (1988) (another classical reference for the economics of trademarks).

[11] *See* Paul Milgrom & John Roberts, *Price and Advertising Signals of Product Quality*, 94 J. Pol. Econ. 796 (1986).

[12] *See* Ramello, & Silva, *supra* note 4, at 937.

[13] *See* William M. Landes & Richard A. Posner, *Trademark Law: An Economic Perspective*, 30 J. L. & Econ. 265 (1987).

[14] Barnes, *supra* note 7, at 22.

[15] *See* for a discussion of the differences between private and social returns to trademarks: Christine Greenhalgh & Mark Rogers, *Trademarks and Performance in Services and Manufacturing Firms: Evidence of Schumpeterian Competition Through Innovation*, 45 Austl. Econ. Rev. 50 (2012).

B. Private vs. social returns of trademarks: the existing empirical evidence

By now several econometric studies have investigated empirically the private returns of trademarks for companies. These analyses became possible as a result of efforts aimed at matching trademark data to firm-level databases.[16] There is strong empirical evidence that the use of trademarks, in particular when coupled with investment in brand equity, is positively correlated to several indicators of firm performance, including market value, profitability, and survival.[17] The main underlying mechanisms through which the purported economic benefits are obtained are basically three: (1) direct financial returns, stemming from the ability to charge higher prices, to obtain licensing revenues, or to monetize marks in different types of transactions;[18] (2) benefits from marketing, since trademarks support differentiation strategies;[19] and (3) benefits from reputation-building, as strong trademarks positively relate to customer satisfaction and thus to customer loyalty by creating so-called brand equity.[20] This last mechanism is particularly interesting because it concerns the underlying behavior of consumers, which is the realm of an extensive literature on branding and consumer behavior.[21]

Christine Greenhalgh and Mark Rogers have analyzed the welfare effects of the use of trademarks for a large sample of UK firms.[22] Their analysis proposes that while trademarks may indeed have negative social returns by damping static competition, they should have positive social returns via dynamic competition. The main mechanism is that by signaling innovation trademarks promote knowledge spillovers and trigger further imitation and innovation by competitors.

On the other hand, the industrial organizational literature demonstrates that brands can be effectively used as barriers to entry.[23] Thereby, branding allows

[16] Schautschick & Greenhalgh, *supra* note 8 (reviewing several of these empirical studies, using different methodologies).

[17] *See* Alexander Krasnikov, Saurabh Mishra, & David Orozco, *Evaluating the Financial Impact of Branding Using Trademarks: A Framework and Empirical Evidence*, 73 J. MARKETING 154 (2009); Philipp G. Sandner, & Joern Block, *The Market Value of R&D, Patents, and Trademarks*, 40 RES. POLICY. 969 (2011); Greenhalgh & Rogers, *supra* note 15.

[18] *See* Giovanni B. Ramello, *What's in a Sign? Trademark Law and Economic Theory*, 20 J. ECON. SURVS. 547 (2006) (discussing how trademarks themselves have become tradable assets); Stuart J. Graham, Alan C. Marco, & Amanda F. Myers, *Monetizing Marks: Insights from the USPTO Trademark Assignment Dataset* (2015) (providing empirical evidence on the extent of trademark transactions, https://ssrn.com/abstract=2430962).

[19] Meindert Flikkema, Ard-Pieter De Man, & Carolina Castaldi, *Are Trademark Counts a Valid Indicator of Innovation? Results of an In-depth Study of New Benelux Trademarks Filed by SMEs*, 21 INDUSTRY & INNOVATION 310 (2014) (providing empirical evidence that differentiation motives are crucial motives for companies to trademark).

[20] *See* DAVID A. AAKER, MANAGING BRAND EQUITY (2009) (discussing the concept of brand equity); Krasnikov, Mishra, & Orozco, *supra* note 17 (an empirical analysis of how companies build brand equity using different types of trademarks).

[21] *See* Kevin Lane Keller & Donald R. Lehmann, *Brands and Branding: Research Findings and Future Priorities*, 25 MARKETING SCI. 740 (2006) (reviewing this literature).

[22] *See* Greenhalgh & Rogers *supra* note 15, at 50.

[23] *See* JOHN S. SUTTON, SUNK COSTS AND MARKET STRUCTURE: PRICE COMPETITION, ADVERTISING, AND THE EVOLUTION OF CONCENTRATION (1991); Silvia Appelt, *Early Entry and Trademark Protection—An Empirical Examination of Barriers to Generic Entry*, paper presented at the DRUID Summer Conference 2009, on this matter (on file with author).

companies to avoid price competition, which results in excess profits for companies but also in higher prices for consumers. While small firms might be able to register trademarks, establishing brand value remains costly, especially if there are strong incumbents. In fact, some authors argue that the differentiation role of trademarks has become more dominant than the informational role, something that prompts policy and welfare questions about possible excesses of the use of branding in the current economy. As Ramello and Silva put it, " '[b]randing' has the outright aim of creating market power."[24]

In sum, the economic literature on the returns to trademarks has mostly focused on private rather than social returns. The conceptual neglect of the issue of social returns of trademarks has translated into a lack of empirical work in this direction.

III. The Economics of Non-Traditional Trademarks

NTTMs were not explicitly considered in the original design of trademark systems, but they have been allowed registration under the premise that they can fulfill the same economic functions as traditional trademarks. If colors, sounds, scents, or other signs can be proven to act as source identifiers, they are expected to help consumers recognize the market offerings of the trademark owner and distinguish those offerings from competing ones. While the basic economics overlap with the notions valid for all trademarks, it can be challenging to prove the distinctiveness of NTTMs.[25] Basically, the applicant has to demonstrate that a color, sound, motion, or other attribute, has acquired a "secondary meaning" in the designated market. This secondary meaning relates directly to what marketing researchers call brand associations, that is the range of meanings, perceptions, and feelings that consumers associate with a brand. Brand associations are an important part of building brand equity as they relate to the deeper subconscious sphere of how consumers perceive a brand and eventually decide to purchase it (or not). The overall benefits of brand associations are well understood in the literature and they revolve around benefitting from more satisfied customers that more often choose repeat purchases of the same brand and more often trust any brand extension from the same brand.[26] Moreover, several authors have stressed how trademarks have "psychological foundations" and the condition of secondary meaning required by trademark offices for NTTM filings is all about consumer sentiments and perceptions about the mark.[27]

[24] *See* Ramello & Silva *supra* note 4, at 947.

[25] *See* Melissa E. Roth, *Something Old, Something New, Something Borrowed, Something Blue: A New Tradition in Nontraditional Trademark Registrations*, 27 Cardozo L. Rev. 457 (2005).

[26] *See* Kevin Lane Keller, *Conceptualizing, Measuring, and Managing Customer-based Brand Equity*, 57 The Journal of Marketing 1 (1993); Vivek Srinivasan, Chan Su Park, & Dae Ryun Chang, *An Approach to the Measurement, Analysis, and Prediction of Brand Equity and its Sources*, 51 Mgmt. Sci. 1433 (2005).

[27] *See* Jacob Jacoby, *The Psychological Foundations of Trademark Law: Secondary Meaning, Genericism, Fame, Confusion and Dilution*, 91 Trademark Rep. 1013 (2001).

The immense literature on branding has not delved into the details of trademark ownership and has focused instead on the concept of brand as something much broader than the trademark itself. An interesting exception is the empirical study by Krasnikov et al.[28] They exploit data on trademark portfolio of a sample of manufacturing and service companies to investigate the effect of ownership of different types of trademarks on the financial value of companies. The originality lies in going beyond standard measures of trademark stocks typical of the econometric studies discussed in the previous section. The authors distinguish between brand identification trademarks and brand association trademarks, the latter also including NTTMs, such as motion, scent, and sound marks. These trademarks are thought to mostly affect the associations which an identified brand triggers in the minds of consumers. In other words, these marks revolve around the whole range of perceptions and sentiments activated by the brand. The authors find that these brand association trademarks, including NTTMs, are significantly positively related to cash flow variables and companies with larger efforts in these trademarks show less volatile financial results. Next to economic studies focusing on financial returns, marketing research has also embraced novel techniques to quantify the impact of non-traditional approaches to marketing. For instance, neuroscience is being increasingly applied to research in marketing to study the direct and indirect effects of advertising on consumers and their minds.[29] The more indirect effects, linked to brand associations, are exactly the ones that can be recovered from neuro markers that trace memory processes.

Research on so-called "sensory marketing" is that part of marketing concerned with the effect of sound on consumer perceptions and behavior.[30] All kinds of sounds have been investigated in this rather extensive literature, from the music used in advertisements, to the tone of the voice used, to the sound of the product itself. There is also research on the effect of touch-related properties on product perceptions.[31] In general, if companies are moving toward branding affecting all senses, then a proliferation of NTTM applications should come as no surprise.[32]

While this proliferation may be hailed by marketing practitioners as opening new opportunities, several authors are critical about the consequences. "[G]ranting trademark protection in nontraditional marks may incite rather than mitigate consumer confusion."[33] She stresses the challenges for consumers of not only recognizing color, sounds, and scents as trademarks, but also comparing them from the ones of competing firms. These difficulties become issues for trademark owners themselves but also for trademark examiners and court judges involved in opposition cases.

[28] Krasnikov, Mishra, & Orozco, *supra* note 17, at 154.

[29] Hilke Plassmann, Vinod Venkatraman, Scott Huettel, & Carolyn Yoon, *Consumer Neuroscience: Applications, Challenges, and Possible Solutions*, 52 J. Marketing Res. 427 (2015).

[30] *See* the review in Aradhna Krishna, *An Integrative Review of Sensory Marketing: Engaging the Senses to Affect Perception, Judgment and Behavior*, 22 J. Consumer Psychology 332 (2012).

[31] Aradhna Krishna & Maureen Morrin, *Does Touch Affect Taste? The Perceptual Transfer of Product Container Haptic Cues*, 34 J. Consumer Res. 807 (2007).

[32] Jerome Gilson & Anne Gilson LaLonde, *Cinnamon Buns, Marching Ducks and Cherry-Scented Racecar Exhaust: Protecting Nontraditional Trademarks*, 95 Trademark Rep. 773 (2005).

[33] Roth, *supra* note 25, at 460.

Not surprisingly, different countries take very different approaches toward NTTMs, with the United States (U.S.) being more flexible than the European Union (EU).[34]

Several contributions to the book advance important critical notes on the proliferation of NTTMs. Yet, the extent of this proliferation and its features remains unclear due to the lack of empirical studies. These empirical questions are timely and needed, as the debate about NTTMs is enlarging.

IV. An Empirical Exploration of Non-Visual Marks at the United States Patent and Trademark Office

A. Description of the data

To fill the gap in the field of empirical studies, I exploited a database recently made available by the USPTO, namely the Trademark Case Files database updated lastly in 2016.[35] The database allows user-friendly offline access to all trademark records at the USPTO. It is composed of a number of tables that can be linked through unique identifiers, either of the individual trademarks or the individual owners. For the purpose of this study, I needed a way to identify NTTMs. The database does not include an identifier for this very heterogeneous category of trademarks, but it turns out that non-visual NTTMs are most readily identifiable.

Specifically, one can rely on the *mark draw cd* field in the case file table. This field captures the type of drawing that is attached to the trademark application. Trademark applicants may submit a depiction of their marks and typically these are standard characters without design elements (in these cases the database field takes the value of 1: *mark draw cd*=1). In other cases, the drawing has instead specific design or style elements that are claimed as a feature of the mark (*mark draw cd*=2 or 3). These will include NTTMs like shape and product packaging marks but also many traditional marks with design elements, like logos. In yet other cases, the marks cannot be depicted with a drawing and this occurrence identifies in a straightforward manner non-visual trademarks. Thus I select all non-visual marks by selecting all trademark applications where no depiction is possible (*mark draw cd*=6). This results in 652 trademarks.

I then rely on the mark description in the statement table of the database. If drawing the mark is not possible, the applicant is in fact required to provide a detailed description of the mark, for instance: "The mark consists of the sound of a childlike human giggle which represents the Pillsbury Doughboy giggle" (U.S. Reg. No. 2692077).[36] I found the length of the description to vary per trademark and

[34] For example, smell marks are excluded from trademark protection in the EU. *See* Case C-273/00, Sieckmann v. Deutsches Patent und Markenamt, 55 E.C.R. I11737, ¶¶ 47 (2002). *See infra* Section IV.C.1.

[35] Stuart Graham, Galen Hancock, Alan C. Marco, & Amanda Fila Myers, *The USPTO Trademark Case Files Dataset: Descriptions, Lessons, and Insights*, 22 J. Econ. & Mgmt. Strategy 669 (2013) (presenting the database).

[36] *Id.*

some of the older trademarks have an empty field. Yet, in the large majority of cases, the statement description allows recovering the actual type of non-visual mark, most of them being sound trademarks.

B. How much?

As each trademark record in the database includes complete details of the history of the trademark application, from application to abandonment or rejection date, it is possible to reconstruct the evolution in time of filings and registrations of non-visual marks at the USPTO.

Of course, the numbers dwarf in comparison to the total number of trademark applications at the USPTO. One should consider that the requirements of non-functionality and distinctiveness that NTTM applications have to fulfill are rather tricky to prove. Yet, the totals indicate a somewhat more widespread use than the incidental cases appearing in the legal literature might suggest. At the same time, the rising trend is also in line with the increasing numbers of trademark applications worldwide.[37]

Figure 13.1 shows both the yearly numbers of new filings and the yearly new registrations. There is a structural lag between filing and registration, as trademark filings are subject to a systematic review process. Also, potential oppositions can be filed in a given period of time after publication (thirty days for the USPTO). All this implies a typical registration lag, which is for this set of trademarks an average of 1.83 years for sound marks and two years for scent marks.

Figure 13.2 reports the share of trademarks that are eventually registered for each year of filing. I calculated these rates starting from 1995 because only then the numbers of filings increases substantially. Of course the last couple of years are truncated as trademarks filed after 2015 have not had enough time to be registered yet. The figure does not show a very clear trend, as the rates oscillate in the range between 30% and 70%. There is no evidence of registration rates becoming either higher or lower, as they vary substantially across the years.

C. What and who?

1. *Types of non-visual marks*

Thanks to the trademark description provided by the applicants and included in the database, I was able to classify almost all non-visual marks into distinct types, except for seven trademarks for which the description was not available or did not allow establishing a type.

Table 13.1 reports the frequency distribution of the different types. The table also reports the distribution of each type in the category of trademarks or service

[37] *See* WORLD INTELLECTUAL PROPERTY ORGANIZATION (WIPO), BRANDS—REPUTATION AND IMAGE IN THE GLOBAL MARKETPLACE (2013), http://www.wipo.int/edocs/pubdocs/en/intproperty/944/wipo_pub_944_2013.pdf.

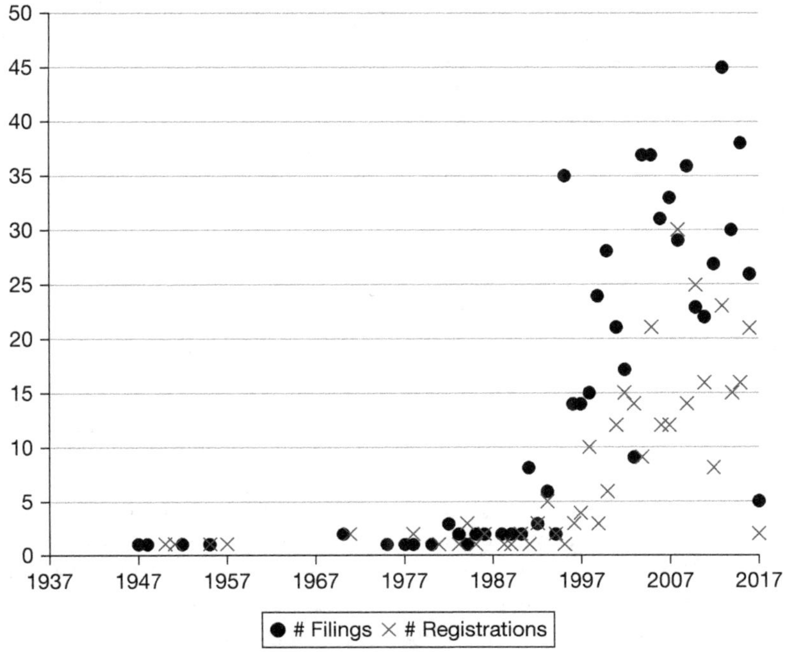

Figure 13.1 Yearly numbers of new filings and registrations of non-visual marks at the USPTO, 1947–2017

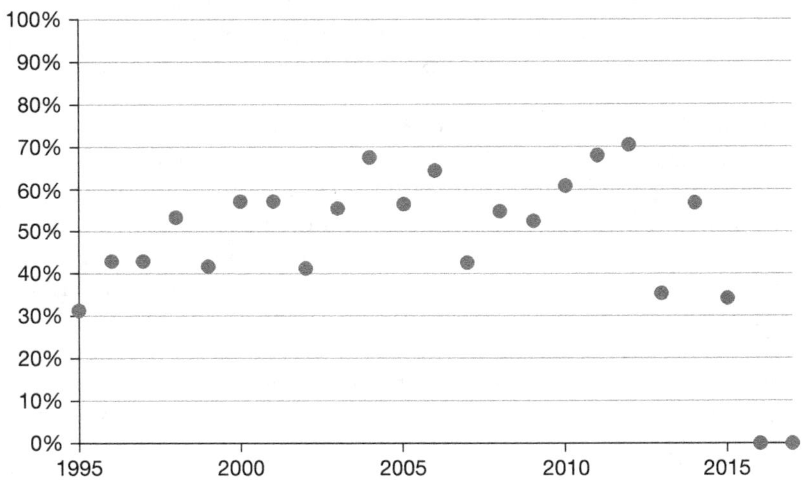

Figure 13.2 Percentage of trademark filings that are successfully registered, by year of filing, starting from 1995

Table 13.1 Types of non-visual marks and classification in trade/service marks based upon the primary class (goods vs. services).

Type	Total filings	Total registrations	Trade marks	Service marks
Sound	571	301	203	362
Scent	51	19	45	6
Trade dress	12	1	7	5
Sensory	5	2	5	0
Motion	4	0	1	3
DNA	1	0	0	1
Literary characters	1	0	0	1
Not classified	7	0	1	6
Total	652	323	262	384

marks. "Trademarks" refer here to marks with a primary class referring to goods (1–34), while "service marks" refer to marks with a primary class referring to services (classes 35–45). Creating a brand equity that transmits certain associations would seem particularly crucial in market settings where reputation impacts consumers' buying decisions. These markets are characterized by high information symmetries and, therefore, a higher risk of market failure. This could particularly be the case for services which tend to have a strong intangible component.[38] More generally, it may also be true for what economists call "experience goods" and "credence goods."[39] While "search goods" can be compared before purchase along objective dimensions, "experience goods" can only be valued after purchase and "credence goods" can only be partially valued because valuation may require expertise that consumers do not possess. In both cases, consumers tend to pick a supplier based upon its reputation.[40]

Most non-visual marks are sound marks, followed by scent marks, trade dress, and sensory marks, which are only a small fraction of the overall filings. It should be noted that the criterion of distinctiveness is easiest to prove for sound and music, which are often specifically composed for the trademark owner. Moreover, sound can be recognized objectively based on specific compositions of notes and instruments, while scents and sensory marks are more difficult to separate from each other.

Sound trademarks include jingles, whole scripts of an advertisement (dialogues, sentences), but also sounds made by the products, and have been filed by companies for many years now. Most sound marks relate to services. This is in line with

[38] Praveen R. Nayyar, *Information Asymmetries: A Source of Competitive Advantage for Diversified Service Firms*, 11 Strategic Mgmt. J. 513 (1990).

[39] Wilfred Dolfsma, *Appropriability, Services and Reputation*, 23 Tech. Analysis & Strategic Mgmt. 919 (2011).

[40] Carolina Castaldi & Marco Giarratana, *Diversification, Branding and Performance of Professional Service Firms*, 21 J. Service Research 353 (2018).

the theoretical prediction related to the intangible and experience/credence nature of services. The sound marks cover different forms of services, in particular Internet services (the distinctive sounds of YAHOO, AOL, and others), movies (including the famous case of the lion roar of Metro-Goldwyn-Mayer), financial services (Visa, Mastercard). The strong sound component of broadcasting (TV/radio) has also led to several registrations of jingles. Many sound marks also cover products: these are in most cases the very sounds made by products, such as the sounds of a Harley Davidson or a Ducati motorbike.

Scents can be registered at the USPTO since the early 1990s. The U.S. jurisdiction is more open to scents than the EU where attempts to register scent marks have failed because of the requirement of a sufficiently clear and precise graphical representation.[41] Yet, proving non-functionality and distinctiveness for scents can be very challenging for applicants.[42] This difficulty, coupled with the uncertain benefits related to the difficulty for consumers to actually recognize scents, deters most firms from even considering scent marks. If a trademark registration takes place, however, scent marks tend to cover more goods than services, as they mostly refer to a physical product.

A third category includes trade dress marks. These typically cover the overall appearance of a product, but also the appearance of stores in the case of retailers. They cover both products and services.

A fourth category is sensory marks, such as sensory marks related to the touch of materials of the product packaging. These exclusively refer to products.

Finally, I sorted the odd ones out: four marks referring to some kind of motion (serial number 86819597, 86142261, 86142303, 86213691, of which only the first one has an actual filing date), one referring to the DNA sequence of a specific person (serial number 76016924) and one referring to literary characters (serial number 86012852). All of them have been filed and then abandoned. They have never been registered. It seems that the respective applicants attempted to stretch even further the boundaries of what is eligible for trademark protection, but failed to do so successfully.

In general, sound trademarks are the most used non-visual marks at the USPTO. In this area, companies succeed in registering about half of their filings.

2. *Which firms make use of non-visual marks?*

The Trademark Case Files database includes complete information regarding ownership, including owner name. As names are not standardized, I first cleaned all the names to assign all records to the same owner. Cleaning mostly entailed matching versions of the names written with capital vs small letters or using abbreviations. After this preliminary analysis, I was able to count all trademark filings by the same owner. Table 13.2 shows the filings of the twenty owners with the highest

[41] *See Sieckmann supra* note 34, ¶¶ 47–55 (2002).

[42] Amanda E. Compton, *Acquiring a Flavor for Trademarks: There's No Common Taste in the World*, 8 Nw. J. Tech. & Intell. Prop. 340 (2009).

Table 13.2 Top 20 firms in terms of total number of filings for non-visual marks at the USPTO.

Name of owner of non-visual marks	Filings	Published	Registered	Type	Business
AT&T	24	24	5	Sound	ICT
TiVo Brands LLC	20	10	10	Sound	Home entertainment systems
Infone LLC	15	9	9	Sound	Business services
Cisco Technology, Inc.	9	9	9	Sound	ICT
MasterCard International Inc.	8	7	1	Sound	Financial services
Microsoft Corporation	8	8	8	Sound	Software
Mike Mantel, Manhattan Oil	8	7	3	Scent	Oil
Petroleo Brasileiro S.A - PETROBRAS	7	7	0	Sound	Oil
Herbal Water, Inc.	6	0	0	Scent	Beverages
Nortel Networks	6	6	0	Sound	Telecom
Powermat INC.	6	6	4	Sound	ICT
The Smead Manufacturing Company	6	6	6	Scent	Office supplies
Visa International Service Association	6	6	1	Sound	Financial services
Apple Inc.	5	5	5	Sound	ICT
Intel Corporation	5	5	2	Sound	ICT
Karen's Krystals, Inc.	5	0	0	Trade dress	Jewelry
Licon Ventures, INC.	5	0	0	Sound	ICT
Lucent Technologies INC.	5	5	0	Sound	ICT
N.V. Organon	5	3	0	Sound	Medical
Twentieth Century Fox Film Corporation	5	5	5	Sound	Movies

number of total filings of non-visual marks. These are also all owners with at least five filings in the overall period considered. The table also reports how many of the filings have been published and how many of them eventually were registered. After publication, trademarks may be abandoned as a result of opposition or because of the failure of the applicant to comply with the requirement of genuine use in the market. Publication does indicate that the NTTM met all legal requirements for registration.

Even the most active firms only end up registering few of the original applications. All non-visual marks filings of AT&T made it to publications, but only five out of twenty-four were registered. Cisco, Apple, Microsoft, and Twentieth Century Fox were instead able to successfully register all their sound trademarks and the Smead Manufacturing Company was successful in registering its six scent marks. Finding a clear pattern in these findings is challenging, as many factors might play a role and accounting for all of them is beyond the scope of this chapter. I will elaborate on the need for further research in the conclusion.

As the top-twenty firms account for a quarter of all filings, non-visual marks do not show a particularly strong concentration in the hands of only a few firms. Instead, their use seems to be widespread, as owners include firms from different sectors and firms of different sizes.

In the spectrum of other firms, one is worth mentioning: G. Pohl-Boskamp GmbH & Co (KGL). KGL is the only firm filing three different types of non-visual marks for the same product, the Nitrolingual Pumpspray: a sound (serial number 85008686, "The mark consists of a unique sound comprising a rapid and pressurized swooshing spray noise followed by a low-toned click sound"), a sensory (serial number 85007641, "The mark consists of the distinctive touch and feel of a glass pump spray bottle with a plasticized surface. The pump spray bottle has a smooth surface with a weightiness, thickness and durability imparted by the glass; simultaneously the bottle has a lightness and rubber-like quality imparted by the plasticized coating"), and a scent trademark (serial number 85007428, "The mark consists of the distinctive flavor of peppermint in connection with nitroglycerin"). Interestingly, none of these three filings made it through the application review process and all trademark filings were abandoned. The product name is simply protected with a traditional word mark (serial number 73062058, still on the register).

V. Conclusions

This chapter has reviewed the economic perspective on NTTMs and has provided empirical evidence on the amount and properties of NTTM filings, albeit for a very specific set. I have shown that trademark filings are not only steadily increasing, but also that they are common for very different types of firms. This evidence informs complementary legal literature addressed in other chapters of this book. My empirical analysis complements the one by Mitchell Adams and Amanda Scardamaglia, who were able to collect data for several trademark offices, different from the USPTO and to cover all kinds of NTTMs.[43] As their analysis shows, non-visual marks are not the most used form of NTTMs when looking at overall filings and applications. This is a reassuring result: the numbers of non-visual marks—the most controversial category from an economic perspective—are in the hundreds, rather than in the thousands.

[43] See Chapter 2 in this volume.

The empirical analysis in this chapter has three important limitations. First, I only focused on a specific set of NTTMs. Identifying other types of NTTMs in the USPTO Trademark Case Files database is possible, but requires an extensive keyword-based text analysis of all trademark descriptions. Second, I only focused on the USPTO, which remains a relevant case given the relatively high use of trademarks in the United States. Replicating the analysis for other national settings would be welcome. Mitchell Adams and Amanda Scardamaglia already report some basic descriptions on the extent of NTTM filings, but their analysis could be extended with an investigation of the firm strategies behind NTTM filings. Third, and most importantly, in this chapter I have only provided descriptive indicators of the extent and quality of non-visual mark filings and their owners. A more extensive analysis needs to match the information already included in the USPTO database with firm-level indicators capturing, for instance, size, age, market strategies, and overall IPR strategies. The latter can be accounted for by collecting all filings and registrations of patents, trademarks, design rights, and other IPRs. All these variables can then be used to understand the probability of a firm to file NTTMs or their success rate in the registration process of NTTMs.

These data efforts can also open the way for answering an even more pressing question, namely the question of the extent to which firms are active in so-called "IPR stacking." I define IPR stacking as the practice of protecting the very same object with multiple IPRs. This practice refers to the strategic cumulation of IPRs in respect of a specific product, rather than at the firm level. In the light of existing economic and management literature on IPRs, it is of course no news that large companies skillfully combine all possible IPRs to protect different elements of their business.[44] Yet a recent legal literature is highlighting the dangers of the increasing practices of stacking different IPRs on the same object.[45] Since each IPR system has been designed with a very specific goal in mind, the question is whether the extension of one into the realm of another weakens or distorts the role of both.[46] In the case of NTTMs, this issue is particularly salient for sound trademarks which may concern musical works stemming from the field of copyright,[47] and packaging and trade dress, the protection of which overlaps with the realm of design rights. The existing legal research, mostly based on selected cases, could be complemented by empirical economic research using larger samples. For this purpose, new datasets at the product, rather than the firm level will be needed.

[44] *See*, Markus Reitzig, *Strategic Management of Intellectual Property*, 45 MIT Sloan Mgmt. Rev. 35 (2004).

[45] *See* Irene Calboli, *Overlapping Rights; The Negative Effects of Trademarking Creative Works*, *in* the evolution and equilibrium of copyright in the digital age 52 (Susy Frankel & Daniel Gervais eds., 2014) (on the combination of trademark and copyrights for creative works).

[46] Laura A. Heymann, *The Trademark/Copyright Divide*, 60 SMU L. REV. 55 (2007).

[47] For a discussion of shape marks applied to famous sculptures, see Martin Senftleben, Vigeland *and the Status of Cultural Concerns in Trade Mark Law—The EFTA Court Develops More Effective Tools for the Preservation of the Public Domain*, 48 International Rev. Intellectual Property and Competition L. 683 (2017).

14

Non-Traditional Trademarks in the Pharmaceutical Sector

Non-Traditional Barriers to Access to Medicine?

*Arul George Scaria and Kavya Susan Mammen**

I. Introduction

From the scent of roses applied to tyres,[1] to floodlights moving across the sky as seen in the 20th Century Fox Film Corporation logo,[2] to the contours of the distinctive Coca-Cola bottle,[3] to the eye-catching robin's-blue jewelry boxes from Tiffany's,[4] to the hologram trademark of Upper Deck playing cards,[5] and the memorable three-note NBC chimes,[6] and so on and so forth; many such trademarks are representative of a shift that has been steadily taking place in trademark law.

* Authors would like to disclose that CIIPC has received external funding from different sources (details available at http://ciipc.org/about/funding/). However, none of the funders have played any role in the framing of research questions or in determining the outcomes in this research. The authors thankfully acknowledge the research assistance provided by Aditi Prakash, Anushka Sachdev, and Rishika Kumar. Authors would also like to thank Mathews P. George, Priyanka Choudhary, Shreyashi Ray, and Shrinkhala Jaiswal for their comments on the first draft.

1 Registration No. 2,001,416 (U.K.) (filing date Oct. 31, 1994; the registration expired in 2014). The description of the mark in the Register is as follows: "The trade mark is a floral fragrance/smell reminiscent of roses as applied to tyres."

2 20TH CENTURY FOX, Registration No. 1,928,423. The description of the mark in the Register is as follows: "The trademark is a computer generated sequence showing the central element from several angles as though a camera is moving around the structure. The drawing represents four 'stills' from the sequence."

3 COCA-COLA, Registration No. 696,147. The description of the mark in the Register is as follows: "The trademark consists of the distinctively shaped contour, or confirmation, and design of the bottle as shown."

4 The mark consists of a shade of blue often referred to as robin's-egg blue which is used on boxes, Registration No. 2,359,351.

5 UPPER DECK AUTHENTICATED MEMORABILIA, Registration No. 2,619,227. The description of the mark in the Register is as follows: "The mark consists of an oval hologram with a repeating holographic image consisting of the words upper deck authenticated memorabilia and design."

6 The mark comprises the musical notes G, E, C, played on chimes, Registration No. 0916522. The description of the mark in the Register is as follows: "The mark comprises a sequence of chime-like musical notes which are in the key of C and sound the notes G, E, C, the 'G' being the one just below middle C, the 'E' the one just above middle C, and the 'C' being middle C, thereby to identify applicant's broadcasting service."

Non-Traditional Trademarks in the Pharmaceutical Sector: Non-Traditional Barriers to Access to Medicine? Arul George Scaria and Kavya Susan Mammen. Published 2018 by Oxford University Press.

In this chapter, we seek to understand the effects of non-traditional trademarks in the area of pharmaceutical products and whether affording legal protection for non-traditional marks in this area may hamper access to medicine. In order to answer this question effectively, this chapter is divided into three parts; the first part takes a brief look at what constitutes non-traditional trademarks and how they operate in different legal landscapes; the second part explores the prevalence of non-traditional marks in the area of pharmaceuticals; and the third part analyzes whether protection for non-traditional marks could pose impediments to access to medicine.

II. What is a Non-Traditional Trademark?

The term "non-traditional trademarks" generally refers to marks other than word marks or figurative marks.[7] This includes a whole range of trademarks—from colors, shapes or packaging, smell, taste, texture,[8] to motion marks, hologram marks, etc. Although shape marks[9] have been protected for a long time, trademark protection for a single color, smell, or short animation sequence, and others are relatively new.[10] This shift arose primarily to complement the efforts of brand owners to remain memorable and distinct from their competitors by appealing to all five senses.[11]

Many jurisdictions have tried to keep up with these developments. For instance, in the EU and India, the word "mark" has been qualified by an inclusive, open-ended list of possible marks, such as words, names, letters, designs, and numerals.[12] The U.S. Supreme Court has similarly interpreted the Lanham Act to mean that a trademark can be "any word, name, symbol, or device" or "almost anything at all that is capable of carrying meaning."[13] The Court of Justice of the European Union (CJEU) echoed similar sentiments in the Shield Mark case.[14] The Agreement

[7] *See* Désirée Fields & Alasdair Muller, *Going Against Tradition: The Effect of Eliminating the Requirement of Representing a Trade Mark Graphically on Applications for Non-Traditional Trademarks*, 39 EUR. INTELL. PROP. REV. 238, 238 (2017); *see also* WIPO Secretariat, *New Types of Marks* 2 (SCT/16/2, Sept. 1, 2006), http://www.wipo.int/edocs/mdocs/sct/en/sct_16/sct_16_2.pdf.

[8] *See* WIPO Secretariat, *supra* note 7, at 11.

[9] *See* COCA-COLA, *supra* note 3; *see also* Ted Ryan, *The Story of the Coca-Cola Bottle*, COCA-COLA CO. (Feb. 26, 2015), http://www.coca-colacompany.com/stories/the-story-of-the-coca-cola-bottle.

[10] *See* Lisa P. Lukose, *Non-Traditional Trademarks: A Critique*, 57 J. INDIAN L. INST. 197, 198 (2015).

[11] *See* Lesley Matty, *Rock, Paper, Scissors, Trademark? A Comparative Analysis of Motion as a Feature of Trademarks in the United States and Europe*, 14 CARDOZO J. INT'L & COMP. L. 557, 559–60 (2006).

[12] For the Indian position, *see* Section 2(m) of the Trade Marks Act of 1999, http://www.wipo.int/wipolex/en/text.jsp?file_id=128107 [https://perma.cc/9V2G-XJ5Q]. For the European Union position, *see* art. 4 of Regulation 2017/1001 of the European Parliament and of the Council on the European Union Trade Mark, http://data.europa.eu/eli/reg/2017/1001/oj.

[13] Qualitex Co. v. Jacobson Prods. Co., 514 U.S. 159, 162 (1995). In this case, the petitioner was selling press pads in a green-gold color to dry cleaning companies and sought trademark protection over the color. The respondent was also using the same color for its products. The petitioner filed a trademark infringement suit against the respondent once it acquired trademark registration from the USPTO. The question before the Court was whether a single color could be registered as a trademark. The Court held in the affirmative.

[14] Case C-283/01, Shield Mark BV v. Joost Kist, 2003 E.C.R. I-14313, ¶¶ 35, 36, 41 (European Court of Justice on Jan. 29, 2001). This was a case in which the petitioner was the registered owner of sound marks in the Benelux area. These sound marks were used by the respondent in its business, which led to the petitioner filing a suit against them for trademark infringement and unfair competition. One

on Trade-Related Aspects of Intellectual Property Rights (the TRIPS Agreement) also takes an inclusive approach with regard to the concept of "trademark," which has provided flexibilities with regard to the registration of non-traditional marks in WTO Member States.[15] The same approach was adopted in the Singapore Treaty on the Law of Trademarks, which was significant in that it explicitly recognized non-traditional trademarks for the first time at the international level.[16] It may also be interesting to note that the U.S. has at times used preferential trade agreements to force countries to adopt smell and sound marks as registrable signs.[17]

But the extension of trademark protection to non-traditional marks has also met many challenges in many jurisdictions. For example, one of the important requirements for registration of a trademark in India is that the mark should be capable of being represented graphically.[18] Yet jurisdictions like the U.S. have been

of the main questions was whether sound could constitute a trademark. The Court held that sound could act as a mark provided that it was "capable of distinguishing the goods or services of one undertaking from those of other undertakings and are capable of being represented graphically." *Id.* ¶ 41. The Court also observed that "types of signs of which a trade mark may consist," provided under art. 2 and Recital 7 of the Directive, was neither exhaustive nor did it expressly exclude sounds from being registered as trademark. *Id.* ¶ 34.

[15] Article 15(1) of the TRIPS Agreement includes the following: "Any sign, or any combination of signs, capable of distinguishing the goods or services of one undertaking from those of other undertakings, shall be capable of constituting a trademark. Such signs, in particular words including personal names, letters, numerals, figurative elements and combinations of colours as well as any combination of such signs, shall be eligible for registration as trademarks. Where signs are not inherently capable of distinguishing the relevant goods or services, Members may make registrability depend on distinctiveness acquired through use. Members may require, as a condition of registration, that signs be visually perceptible." Agreement on Trade-Related Aspects of Intellectual Property Rights, Apr. 15, 1994, Marrakesh Agreement Establishing the World Trade Organization, Annex 1C, 1869 U.N.T.S. 299 [hereinafter TRIPS Agreement]; *see also* Qian Zhan, *The International Registration of Non-Traditional Trademarks: Compliance with the TRIPS Agreement and the Paris Convention*, 16 World Trade Rev. 111, 113 (2017).

[16] Singapore Treaty on the Law of Trademarks r. 3(5)–(7), Mar. 27, 2006, S. Treaty Doc. No. 110-2, http://www.wipo.int/wipolex/en/treaties/text.jsp?file_id=290013 [https://perma.cc/Q5FS-X5UM]; *see also* Kenneth L. Port, *On Nontraditional Trademarks*, 38 N. Ky. L. Rev. 1, 4 (2011).

[17] *See, e.g.*, Australia–United States Free Trade Agreement, U.S.–Austl., May 18, 2004, art. 17.2, cl. 2, https://ustr.gov/sites/default/files/uploads/agreements/fta/australia/asset_upload_file469_5141.pdf [https://perma.cc/P7Q9-BES7] ("Neither Party may require, as a condition of registration, that marks be visually perceptible, nor may a Party deny registration of a mark solely on the ground that the sign of which it is composed is a sound or a scent."); *id.* at n.17-6 (This related footnote adds that, "A Party may require an adequate description, which can be represented graphically."); United States–Singapore Free Trade Agreement, U.S.–Sing., May 6, 2003 art. 16.2, cl. (1), https://ustr.gov/sites/default/files/uploads/agreements/fta/singapore/asset_upload_file708_4036.pdf [https://perma.cc/VG5C-NVZB] ("Neither Party shall require, as a condition of registration, that signs be visually perceptible, but each Party shall make best efforts to register scent marks."); *see also* Zhan, *supra* note 15, at 121.

[18] For the Indian position, see Sections 2(zb) and 2(m) of the Trade Marks Act 1999. The EU also had a similar graphical representation requirement until recently. Although registration was granted early on in the EU for a scent mark ("smell of fresh cut grass" for tennis balls, CTM Registration No. 428,870, expired Dec. 2006), the stringent requirements for graphical representation laid down by the European Court of Justice in Case C-273/00, Ralf Sieckmann v. Deutsches Patent- und Markenamt, 2002 E.C.R. I-11754, subsequently have made the process for obtaining a scent mark in the EU virtually impossible. Adhering to the same strict standards for scent marks laid down in the EU, the Indian draft manual (*A Draft of Manual of Trade Marks: Practice and Procedure*, Ch. III, § 3.2.4, at 86–87 (Mar. 10, 2015)) also noted that scent marks do not meet the requirement of graphical representation under Indian trademark law. However, with the waiver of graphical representation requirement under the new trademark regulation in the EU, it would be interesting to see how courts in the EU would consider the

more lenient in this regard.[19] For example, in the U.S., an application for a sound mark can be submitted with a detailed description of the mark, accompanied by an audio file "to supplement and clarify the description of the mark."[20] In the case of visual non-traditional marks—such as color, shape, animations, and holograms—emerging international consensus suggests that they can be represented graphically in a combination of ways.[21]

Another important requirement in securing trademark protection is that the mark should be capable of distinguishing the goods or services of the trademark proprietor from those of its competitors.[22] Most non-traditional marks are not inherently distinctive and may only obtain trademark protection when they acquire a secondary meaning, commonly referred to as "acquired distinctiveness."[23] For example, in the Trademark Trial and Appeal Board (TTAB) decision *In re Clarke*, which examined the question of trademark protection for a non-functional arbitrary scent (scent of plumeria blossoms) on embroidery yarn, the applicant could get registration only when she demonstrated that her customers and distributors had come to recognize her as the sole source of those scented yarns and embroidery.[24]

III. Non-Traditional Trademarks in the Pharmaceutical Sector

To shed light on the extent of use of non-traditional marks in the pharmaceutical sector, we conducted two kinds of surveys. The first one consisted of identifying and analyzing the kinds of marks used on top ten products of the top ten pharmaceutical companies in the world.[25] The second survey consisted of analyzing case law from

question of registration of scent marks. For the new EU position, which came into effect on Oct. 1, 2017, see art. 4 of Regulation (EU) 2017/1001 of the European Parliament and of the Council on the European Union Trade Mark.

19 15 U.S.C. § 1127 defines trademark as "any word, name, symbol . . . use[d] in commerce . . . to identify and distinguish his or her goods, including a unique product, from those manufactured or sold by others and to indicate the source of the goods, even if that source is unknown."

20 In the case of a sound mark comprising music, generally, a musical score sheet should also be submitted to further describe the mark. *See* U.S. PATENT & TRADEMARK OFFICE, TRADEMARK MANUAL OF EXAMINING PROCEDURE § 807.09 (Apr. 2017).

21 *See* Dev Gangjee, *Non Conventional Trade Marks in India*, 22 NAT'L L. SCH. INDIA REV. 67, 76 (2010); WIPO Secretariat, *Representation and Description of Non-Traditional Marks: Possible Areas of Convergence* 4–9 (SCT/19/2, Apr. 28, 2008).

22 15 U.S.C. § 1127 (1946).

23 *See Qualitex*, *supra* note 13, 163.

24 *In re* Clarke, 17 U.S.P.Q.2d 1238 (T.T.A.B. 1990).

25 For identifying the top ten pharmaceutical companies at the global level, we used a list compiled by Forbes. *See World's 25 Biggest Drugs & Biotech Companies in 2016*, FORBES, https://www.forbes.com/sites/corinnejurney/2016/05/27/2016-global-2000-the-worlds-largest-drug-and-biotech-companies/#71fbdb46cf19 [https://perma.cc/T2XE-NQ7M]. For details on the methodology Forbes used in this regard, see Andrea Murphy, *2016 Forbes Global 2000: How We Crunch the Numbers*, FORBES (May 25, 2016, 6:45 AM), https://www.forbes.com/sites/andreamurphy/2016/05/25/how-we-crunch-the-numbers/#1c0ccd2a7467 [https://perma.cc/U8QA-45SJ]. For identifying the top ten products of these companies, we relied primarily on their recent annual reports. In cases where this information was not available in annual reports, we used secondary sources, such as statistica.com, to obtain the list of top ten products. This survey was conducted between Jan. 16, 2017 and Apr. 4, 2017.

different jurisdictions. This approach offered an overview of the prevalence of non-traditional marks in the pharmaceutical sector.

Our survey of current practices reveals that many pharmaceutical companies have a proclivity toward using non-traditional marks to add uniqueness to their products. Interesting examples we found in this regard include Viread[26] (Gilead Sciences), Viagra[27] (Pfizer), Aubagio[28] (Sanofi Genzyme), Xarelto [20 mg][29] (Johnson & Johnson), and Sensipar[30] (Amgen), all of which are of a unique shape and color.[31]

We were not able to determine whether all of the above-mentioned pharmaceutical products are currently receiving trademark protection for their shape, color, or a combination of both in different jurisdictions. However, it is evident that at least some shape and color marks enjoy protection.[32] The details of the trademark registration procured by Pfizer for the diamond shape of Viagra tablets are available in the European Union Intellectual Property Office (EUIPO) database,[33] and the registration details for the purple and gold colors of Nexium (commonly known as the "purple pill"), owned by AstraZeneca, can be seen in the U.S. Patent and Trademark Office (USPTO) database.[34] Our survey of case law shows that companies like AstraZeneca and Pfizer have also initiated litigation against competitors who have attempted to copy the distinct features of those tablets.

For example, in the case of Nexium, AstraZeneca's heart-burn medicine, the unique purple and gold color combination was used by Dr. Reddy's Laboratories

[26] *Medicines: HIV/AIDS*, GILEAD, http://www.gilead.com/medicines#HIVAIDS [https://perma.cc/M9GG-3UDD].

[27] *ED Medications: Cialis, Levitra, Viagra*, ADVANCED UROLOGICAL CARE P.C., https://www.urologicalcare.com/upload/ed/viagra.jpg [https://perma.cc/6ML5-QJSC].

[28] *Aubagio Images*, DRUGS.COM, https://www.drugs.com/aubagio-images.html [https://perma.cc/Q4UG-SDQR].

[29] *Xarelto Images*, DRUGS.COM, https://www.drugs.com/xarelto-images.html [https://perma.cc/DQC2-8CXW].

[30] *About Sensipar*, SENSIPAR, http://www.sensipar.com/about-sensipar/ [https://perma.cc/QHZ2-W6BX].

[31] Other interesting examples include: Truvada (Gilead Sciences, http://www.sbs.com.au/news/sites/sbs.com.au.news/files/truvada_mpx_0.jpg [https://perma.cc/EEH6-L3U2]), Ranexa (Gilead Sciences, https://www.drugs.com/ranexa.html [https://perma.cc/L4H9-PFYG]), Letairis (Gilead Sciences, https://www.drugs.com/letairis-images.html [https://perma.cc/RZ25-6WWN]), Norvasc (Pfizer, https://www.drugs.com/norvasc-images.html [https://perma.cc/MEH7-EAXH]), Isentress (Merck, https://www.drugs.com/isentress-images.html [https://perma.cc/KA5B-H3C6]), and Stribild (Gilead Sciences, https://nl.wikipedia.org/wiki/Elvitegravir/cobicistat/emtricitabine/tenofovir_disoproxil#/media/File:Stribild_bottle_Dutch_labeling.jpg [https://perma.cc/9T4W-NCRP]).

[32] *See, e.g.*, The mark consists in part of the configuration of the goods consisting of a dosage tablet in an almond shape, characterized by one end being narrower than the other, and the color blue as applied to the entirety of the goods, Registration No. 2,679,181 (owned by Gilead Sciences).

[33] The mark consists of a three-dimensional shape with the color blue, PANTONE 284U, applied to the whole of the outside surface and the word PFIZER appearing thereon, Registration No. 1,909,472 (EUIPO) (owned by Pfizer).

[34] *See, e.g.*, The marks consist of the colors purple and gold as applied to the surface of a pharmaceutical capsule, Registration Nos. 3,062,072 & 2,980,749 (both owned by AstraZeneca Pharmaceuticals). The description of the latter mark in the Register is as follows: "The mark consists of the colors purple and gold as applied to the surface of a pharmaceutical capsule. The capsule is purple with three side-by-side gold rings that encircle the top of the capsule. The drawing is lined for the colors purple and gold."

for its own generic version of Nexium, which was launched in 2015.[35] AstraZeneca promptly filed a suit against Dr. Reddy's Laboratories. By looking at the factors affecting a likelihood of confusion, the Court held that the plaintiff had proven that it was likely to succeed on the merits of the case and would suffer irreparable harm if an injunction was not granted. Thus, the Delaware District Court granted a temporary restraining order in favor of AstraZeneca and barred Dr. Reddy's from marketing its generic version of Nexium.[36] Following the order, Dr. Reddy's is reported to have changed the color of its generic tablet from purple to blue.[37]

Similarly, in the case of Viagra, the diamond-shaped, blue-colored tablets manufactured by Pfizer used to treat male erectile dysfunction, the Delhi High Court adjudicated on litigations initiated by Pfizer against many producers of generic forms in India.[38] The generic manufacturers were using brand names, such as Penegra, Kamagra, and Edagra, and had adopted a similar blue color and packaging for their products.[39] Pfizer initiated a passing off action, claiming injunction and damages. One of the main concerns expressed by Pfizer was that consumers would buy generic products like Penegra thinking it to be Viagra's equivalent that was manufactured by Pfizer in India.[40] Because Pfizer did not have a trademark registration in India for Viagra and was not marketing the product in India at the time, the Court held that there was no likelihood of confusion, as consumers would know that they were only getting an Indian equivalent of Viagra.[41] The Court also held that there was no misrepresentation by a pharmacist when he or she used the term "desi version" of Viagra, as it was a "fact that what was sold was not VIAGRA but its local equivalent."[42] The Court thereby denied Pfizer's application for a temporary injunction after determining that the balance of convenience was in favor of the defendant.[43] But it is important to note that the Court also took the position that the defendants could not use the blue color used by Pfizer.[44]

Our survey of case law also indicates that non-traditional marks have been at the center of many litigations in the pharmaceutical sector, especially in the U.S., for a long time. It is pertinent to highlight here some of the cases where protection was granted and where protection was denied.

In *Ross-Whitney Corp. v. Smith Kline & French Laboratories* (SKF), the respondent SKF was manufacturing Valentine's heart-shaped Benzedrine and Dexedrine tablets in pinkish brown and orange colors, respectively.[45] Once the patents on those

[35] Kiran George, *AstraZeneca v. Dr. Reddy's—Colour as a Pharmaceutical Trade Dress*, Spicy IP: Blog (Dec. 22, 2015), https://spicyip.com/2015/12/astrazeneca-v-dr-reddys-colour-as-a-pharmaceutical-trade-dress.html.

[36] Memorandum at 13–14, AstraZeneca AB v. Dr. Reddy's Labs., Inc., 209 F. Supp. 3d 744 (D. Del. 2016) (No. 15-988-SLR), https://www.scribd.com/document/290877170/AstraZeneca-v-Dr-Reddys#scribd.

[37] Dan Stanton, *AstraZeneca's Purple Reign? Dr Reddy's Relaunches Nexium Generic in Blue*, In-Pharma Technologist: Blog (Jan. 6, 2016), http://www.in-pharmatechnologist.com/Processing/AZ-retains-purple-reign-Dr-Reddy-s-relaunches-Nexium-generic-in-blue.

[38] Pfizer Products Inc. v. B.L. & Co., (2002) 25 PTC (Del.) 262 (Delhi High Court, India), https://indiankanoon.org/doc/145093/.

[39] *See generally id.* [40] *Id.* ¶ 10. [41] *Id.* ¶¶ 72–74.

[42] *Id.* ¶ 73 (internal quotation marks omitted). [43] *Id.* ¶¶ 83–86.

[44] *Id.* ¶¶ 87, 91, 94, 110.

[45] Ross-Whitney Corp. v. Smith Kline & French Labs., 207 F.2d 190, 192 (9th Cir. 1953).

products expired, other companies started to manufacture the tablets under different brand names. Ross-Whitney Corp. manufactured the generic version of the Dexedrine tablet with the same shape, size, and color as the respondent's Dexedrine tablet and further labeled it as "Heart Brand Dexedrine."[46] SKF filed a suit for trademark infringement and unfair competition against the respondents. The Court affirmed that Dexedrine was a valid trademark and further noted that SKF's distinctive shape and color of the Dexedrine tablet had acquired secondary meaning.[47] According to the Court, in such a situation, consumers may get easily confused between the two products, regardless of the label used by the appellant.[48] Hence, the appellants were enjoined from manufacturing their tablets in any color or shape, or combination of color and shape resembling those of the respondents.[49]

Similarly, in *SK&F, Co. v. Premo Pharmaceutical Laboratories, Inc.* (Premo), SK&F was manufacturing a patented oral diuretic under the brand name Dyazide in a maroon and white hard gelatin capsule.[50] The same drug combination was also sold in Europe in an orange-color tablet version.[51] Premo, a generic drug manufacturer, came out with a generic version of the same drug in a similar maroon and white hard gelatin capsule.[52] In response to this, SK&F filed a complaint on grounds of unfair competition and trademark infringement and sought a preliminary injunction.[53] In this case, one of the major concerns was that the availability of look-alike generic drugs would prompt "unscrupulous pharmacists" to pass off less expensive generic drugs instead of Dyazide (produced by SK&F) without passing on the benefits of the lower price to consumers.[54] In this case, the Court was of the opinion that the maroon and white colors used by SK&F were nonfunctional.[55] According to the Court, the trade dress of SK&F "was arbitrary, having nothing to do with the purpose or performance of the drug, or with its processing."[56] The Court noted that there was no industry practice for the identification of diuretic drugs through the colors or capsule form, and that even the identical diuretic drug combination was successfully marketed in an orange tablet form.[57] Further in this case, it was established that the bioavailability of the drugs differed, and so the Court was of the opinion that though the drugs were similar, they would not be functionally equivalent to each other.[58] The Court affirmed the preliminary injunction granted by the District Court, which required the trade dress to be as different as possible from that of the prescribed brand.[59]

As mentioned earlier, there are also many cases where protection for non-traditional features was denied by the courts. For example, in the case of *William R. Warner & Co. v. Eli Lilly & Co.*, Eli Lilly was manufacturing liquid quinine in

[46] *Id.* [47] *Id.* at 195–96. [48] *Id.* at 197. [49] *Id.* at 198.

[50] SK&F, Co. v. Premo Pharm. Labs., Inc., 625 F.2d 1055, 1057–58 (3d Cir. 1980).

[51] *Id.* at 1058. [52] *Id.* [53] *Id.* [54] *Id.* at 1063. [55] *Id.* at 1062–64.

[56] *Id.* at 1064. [57] *Id.*

[58] *Id.* at 1067. The term "bioavailability" generally refers to "the degree and rate at which a substance (such as a drug) is absorbed into a living system or is made available at the site of physiological activity." *See Bioavailability*, MERRIAM-WEBSTER DICTIONARY, https://www.merriam-webster.com/dictionary/bioavailability.

[59] *SK&F, Co.*, *supra* note 50, 1068.

the color and flavor of chocolate and called it Coco-Quinine.[60] Eli Lilly initiated a suit against the petitioner when they began manufacturing a less costly version of the same preparation with the color and flavor of chocolate under the name Quin-Coco.[61] Eli Lilly argued that the petitioner was infringing their exclusive right to use and sell the chocolate-flavored mixture.[62] The Court took the position that the petitioners were free to manufacture and sell the chocolate-flavored quinine mixture because the use of chocolate was functional in character.[63] The fact that the use of chocolate lent the medicine a degree of palatability, which was difficult to substitute, made it functional.[64]

Similarly, in *Norwich Pharmacal Co. v. Sterling Drug, Inc.*, the plaintiff was engaged in the production of a pink-colored liquid preparation called Pepto-Bismol for treatment of stomach disorders.[65] By 1955, it was the leading medicine in this field.[66] Around this time, the defendant started to manufacture Pepsamar, which was almost identical to Pepto-Bismol with regard to color, flavor, and chemical constitution.[67] The plaintiff filed a suit seeking injunctive relief against the defendants. In this case, the Court held that there was no proof of deception or violation of property rights of the plaintiff because the overall appearance of the defendant's product was dissimilar to that of the plaintiff's (shape of the bottle and color of the label and cap).[68] Most importantly, the Court noted that "[a]bsent confusion, imitation of certain successful features in another's product is not unlawful and to that extent a 'free ride' is permitted."[69] Interestingly enough, the Court pointed out that the color pink was also functional in its use with regard to stomach remedies, as the color lent a "pleasing appearance to the customer and to the sufferer," and thus competitors could not be restricted from using the color.[70] Considering all these aspects, the Court held that the color pink cannot be monopolized by the plaintiff alone as its exclusive property.[71]

In another instance, the respondent in *Inwood Laboratories, Inc. v. Ives Laboratories, Inc.* had a patent on the drug cyclandelate (brand name Cyclospasmol), a vasodilator used in long-term therapy for peripheral and cerebral vascular diseases.[72] It was manufactured in two dosages with 200 mgs of the drug in a blue capsule imprinted with "Ives 4124" and 400 mgs in a blue and red capsule imprinted with "Ives 4148."[73] Once the patent expired, generic manufacturers started manufacturing cyclandelate using the same dosage-color combination as practiced by Ives.[74]

[60] William R. Warner & Co. v. Eli Lilly & Co., 265 U.S. 526, 528 (1924).

[61] *Id.* at 529. [62] *Id.* [63] *Id.*

[64] *Id.* However, because there was evidence suggesting passing off by retail druggists, the Court held there was unfair competition and that the petitioners enabled such behavior. Thus, the Court decreed that the original packets sold to pharmacists should not only have labels clearly distinguishing them from the products of the petitioner, but also explicit warnings that prescriptions for Coco-Quinine should not be substituted with Quin-Coco.

[65] Norwich Pharmacal Co. v. Sterling Drug, Inc., 271 F.2d 569, 570 (2d Cir. 1959).

[66] *Id.* [67] *Id.* [68] *Id.* at 571. [69] *Id.* at 572. [70] *Id.*

[71] *Id.* at 573. [72] Inwood Labs., Inc. v. Ives Labs. Inc., 456 U.S. 844 (1982).

[73] *Id.* at 846.

[74] *Id.* at 847. There were also reports that some pharmacists were mislabeling and substituting generic drugs for Cyclospasmol.

The Court upheld the District Court's finding that the colors used by Ives were functional because it helped patients rely on colors to differentiate among medications, especially patients who had a habit of commingling medications in a container and also the elderly who associated color with therapeutic effect.[75] Additionally, Ives failed to establish secondary meaning.[76] In the light of these findings, the Court held that there was no infringement as "after patent expiration . . . a functional characteristic . . . is no more the property of the originator than the product itself."[77]

The examples of litigation mentioned above indicate that the industry has been constantly trying to protect various physical attributes of pharmaceutical products, such as color and shape, among others.

It is also important to note in this context the attempts of the industry in seeking registrations for non-visual marks, such as taste marks.[78] In the TTAB decision *In re N.V. Organon*, the company had sought trademark registration for the orange flavor of its quick-dissolving anti-depressant tablets.[79] The Appellate Board rejected this application on three grounds. Firstly, since this was a pill that dissolved on a patient's tongue, there was a "practical need for the medicine to have an appealing taste" (which was stressed by the applicant in its advertisements), and hence the orange flavor was functional.[80] Further, orange was a popular flavor, and granting a monopoly over the flavor would leave few popular alternatives for other anti-depressant medications.[81] Secondly, the Appellate Board expressed doubts as to whether orange flavor could act as a mark, since most consumers would perceive orange flavor as a common product feature used to hide any unpleasant taste of medicine.[82] Finally, the Appellate Board raised the question of how trademarks could practically function as a trademark given that consumers had no way of perceiving it prior to purchase.[83] Similarly, in the EU, Eli Lilly's application for a taste mark for the artificial flavor of strawberries for a drug was rejected on grounds similar to those seen in *N.V. Organon*.[84]

The case law discussed in this section indicates that the pharmaceutical sector has not shied away from seeking protection for non-traditional marks.

IV. Protection of Non-Traditional Trademarks and Impact on Access to Medicine

The previous section illustrates the prevalence of non-traditional marks in the pharmaceutical sector. Against this background, it is pertinent to analyze some important consequences of affording protection to non-traditional trademarks with regard to access to medicine. We would like to highlight three of these consequences.

[75] *Id.* at 853. [76] *Id.* [77] *Id.* at 863.

[78] For an interesting discussion on taste marks, *see generally* Thomas A. Gallagher, *Nontraditional Trademarks: Taste/Flavor*, 105 Trademark Rep. 806 (2015).

[79] *In re* N.V. Organon, 79 U.S.P.Q.2d 1639, at *1 (T.T.A.B. 2006). [80] *Id.* at *7.

[81] *Id.* [82] *Id.* at *11. [83] *Id.* at *12.

[84] *See generally* OHIM decision Second Board of Appeal, R120/2001-2 (Aug. 4, 2004) (Eli Lilly & Co., Appeal Relating to Community Trade Mark Application No. 1452853).

Firstly, there would be an increase in transaction costs due to protection afforded to non-traditional marks. Empirical studies have shown that patients might be reluctant to take bioequivalent drugs if the physical attributes of the branded drug and generic drug are different.[85] Studies demonstrate that some patients may even discontinue their prescribed drug regimen due to doubts over the efficacy of the drug.[86] Studies have suggested that doctors and pharmacists need to educate and reassure patients when providing a different-looking generic bioequivalent.[87] As one can imagine, this would require substantial investments, in terms of time. Some studies point out that pharmacies may need to adapt existing information technology systems in order to provide updates to the consumers when such changes occur.[88] With rising protection for non-traditional marks in the pharmaceutical sector, these transaction costs are bound to increase, thereby adversely affecting the budgets for access to medicine.

In *Hoffmann-La Roche & Co. AG v. DDSA Pharmaceuticals Ltd.*,[89] the Court made some interesting observations in this regard. The case was a passing off action relating to the black and green chlordiazepoxide capsules (brand name Librium) manufactured by Hoffmann-La Roche. One of the arguments used by DDSA was that the consumers who were accustomed to the black and green capsules would have resisted the drug if the same drug had appeared subsequently in different colors. Although the Court ultimately ruled against the defendant, it is interesting to see the observations of the Court with respect to this argument:

> Now that shows quite clearly that if the defendants were to put their C.D.P. in a blue and white container and it were prescribed, as it might be by any doctor prescribing C.D.P., there would immediately be resistance on the part of patients. Patients would come back and say "This is not what I have been taking before. I want the one I know. I want the green and black one"; and the chemist would have to spend laborious hours explaining that there was a new manufacturer on the market and that he put up his drug in a different coloured capsule although it was exactly the same drug-says the chemist. "Oh" says the patient; "I want the ones I have always had—the same again," and goes back to the doctor and makes a fuss; and there will be general sales resistance and difficulties of that sort . . .[90]

This challenge was also highlighted in a recent interview conducted by us with a pharmacist in a leading hospital in India.[91] According to the pharmacist, many

[85] *See generally* Aaron S. Kesselheim et al., *Variations in Pill Appearance of Antiepileptic Drugs and the Risk of Nonadherence*, 173 JAMA Internal Med. 202 (2013) [hereinafter Kesselheim, *Variations in Pill Appearance*]; Aaron S. Kesselheim et al., *Burden of Changes in Pill Appearance for Patients Receiving Generic Cardiovascular Medications After Myocardial Infarction*, 161 Annals Internal Med. 96 (2014) [hereinafter Kesselheim, *Burden of Changes in Pill Appearance*].

[86] *See generally* Kesselheim, *Variations in Pill Appearance, supra* note 85; Kesselheim, *Burden of Changes in Pill Appearance, supra* note 85.

[87] Kesselheim, *Variations in Pill Appearance, supra* note 85, at 206.

[88] *Id.*

[89] *Cf.* Hoffmann-La Roche & Co. A.G. v. D.D.S.A. Pharm. Ltd., [1972] R.P.C. 1, 20 (C.A.). Here, the Court held that there was a likelihood of confusion, and an interlocutory injunction was granted to the plaintiffs.

[90] *Cf. id.* at 21.

[91] Interview with a clinical pharmacist in Cochin, India (Apr. 17, 2017). Name and affiliation withheld to protect confidentiality requirements.

hours are still being spent in offering explanations to convince patients to switch from a familiar tablet identifiable in a particular color or shape to a generic equivalent in a different color or shape.[92]

Colours generally used on asthma inhalers illustrate another aspect of transaction costs. Conventionally, reliever medication inhalers were blue in color and preventer inhalers were brown in color.[93] It has been found that non-adherence to these set color codes for inhalers often resulted in confusion among the asthma patients.[94] When a particular type of inhaler is identifiable with the help of a color, transaction costs for all stakeholders, including patients, pharmacists, and doctors, for identifying the right kind of inhaler for a particular medical scenario would be much less. As rightly observed by a commentator, if a company is allowed trademark protection over the use of a particular colour in their inhalers, it would be tantamount to keeping an asthmatic patient " 'handcuffed" to that brand for life.[95] Given this, the question arises as to whether the increased transaction costs by virtue of monopoly rights over color or shape are justifiable, particularly when viewed in the context of limited social benefits that may be accrued by way of grant of monopoly rights over color or shape.

Secondly, protection of non-traditional marks may create additional barriers for entry of generic drugs. There are two important aspects to be considered in this regard. On the one hand, non-traditional marks may perpetuate the monopoly position enjoyed by the branded drugs. On the other hand, non-traditional marks may further reinforce the myth that generic drugs are low quality.

Branded drugs often enjoy a monopoly position due to patent protection, and they also undertake extensive advertising campaigns to market and promote the uniqueness of the drug during the patent term. Sometimes, such campaigns can be so successful in capturing the imagination of the customer that it becomes difficult for generic companies to break into that market with a cheaper version of the drug even after the expiry of the patent term. In such instances, the trademark is slowly metamorphosing into a "brand."[96] While there is no general definition for the term "brand," it is usually understood "to have a value which transcends the product."[97]

AstraZeneca's "Nexium" is a classic example that can illustrate how a branded drug can maintain its hold over the market via trade dress despite the presence of

[92] *Id.*

[93] B. Jayakrishnan & Omar A Al-Rawas, *Asthma Inhalers and Colour Coding: Universal Dots*, 60(578) Br J. Gen Practice 690–91 (Sept. 1, 2010), https://www.ncbi.nlm.nih.gov/pmc/articles/PMC2930224/.

[94] *Id.*

[95] Murali Neelakantan, *The Interplay Between Competition law and Intellectual Property Rights in the Indian Healthcare Sector*, 1 Nls Business.L. Rev. 32, 51 (2015).

[96] A brand is "an aggregation of assets which *includes, but is not limited to* a trade mark." Jennifer Davis, *Between a Sign and a Brand: Mapping the Boundaries of a Registered Trade Mark in European Union Trade Mark Law*, *in* trade marks and brands 65, 81 (Lionel Bently et al. eds., 2010).

[97] *Id.* at 80. Others point out that brands have a "psychological impact" in the minds of the consumers to whom it could represent a certain kind of "lifestyle," and for them, purchasing that particular branded product would "reinforce their self-image." *See* Hannah Brennan, *The Cost of Confusion: The Paradox of Trademarked Pharmaceuticals*, 22 Mich. Telecomm. & Tech. L. Rev. 1, 14 (2015).

cheaper generics in the market. AstraZeneca had a patent over a new class of acid reflux medications, which were known as proton-pump inhibitors (PPIs).[98] The particular drug omeprazole was sold under the brand name Prilosec in purple and gold trade dress and was heavily advertised with the popular sobriquet, the "Purple Pill."[99] This campaign ensured that the patients remembered the color, even if they forgot the name of the drug.[100] Prilosec was a commercial success, and when the patent on that drug was set to expire, AstraZeneca came out with a slightly modified version of omeprazole, known as esomeprazole, which was duly patented and marketed as "Nexium."[101] Though it had more or less the same effect as Prilosec, it was marketed as the "new purple pill" by giving it the same physical appearance as Prilosec.[102] The fact that Nexium was able to hold onto its customer base even after the entry of generic manufacturers into the market at much lower prices illustrates the power of branding in this sector.[103]

It is evident that if other branded pharmaceutical companies were to adopt similar practices, it could portend considerable difficulties to the generic manufacturers trying to break into the market. As pointed out by a commentator, such factors that inhibit the generic market come at a great cost to consumers and affect the efficient functioning of the healthcare market.[104] Hence, generic companies should be allowed to copy the physical appearances, such as color, shape, and size, of branded drugs.

An additional point of concern is the fact that monopoly rights over physical attributes of branded drugs may perpetuate the myth of "low-quality generics." There are regulatory mechanisms in most jurisdictions to ensure that generic drugs are manufactured under safe conditions.[105] Further, no studies have conclusively established that generics manufacture products of low quality.[106] However, there is a perception among many patients that generics are not as effective as branded drugs. In order to understand the underlying reasons behind this, a survey was undertaken by a team of researchers in the U.S. who used a random sample of commercially insured beneficiaries.[107] The survey found that over 70% broadly agreed that "generic drugs are a better value than branded drugs" and 56% agreed with the statement that "Americans should use more generic drugs."[108] However, only 37.6% agreed that they would take generics over branded drugs.[109] More interesting was that over 42% disagreed with the statement that "Generics are safer than branded drugs."[110] It was suggested that this may be due to the perceptions

[98] *See* Brennan, *supra* note 97, at 27. [99] *Id.*

[100] David M. Fritch, *Should "The Purple Pill" by Any Other Drug Company Still Be as Purple? The Changing Face of Trade Dress Protection for Pharmaceutical Manufacturers*, 47 IDEA 171, 188 (2006).

[101] Brennan, *supra* note 97, at 28.

[102] Jeremy A. Greene & Aaron S. Kesselheim, *Why Do the Same Drugs Look Different? Pills, Trade Dress, and Public Health*, 365 New Eng. J. Med. 83, 85 (2011).

[103] Nexium did not experience a considerable drop in sales, as would usually be the case when cheaper generics enter the market to compete with the branded drug. *See* Brennan, *supra* note 97, at 29.

[104] *Id.* [105] *Id.* at 22–23. [106] *Id.* at 22.

[107] William H. Shrank et al., *Patients' Perceptions of Generic Medications*, 28 Health Aff. 546, 547 (2009).

[108] *Id.* at 549. [109] *Id.* [110] *Id.*

associated with the term "generic" itself, which connoted low quality, or the belief that more expensive products are more effective.[111] A more serious aspect was that such perceptions about generics even led to non-adherence among those who could not afford branded drugs.[112] When one views non-traditional marks in the pharmaceutical sector in the light of this evidence regarding the "low quality" generic myth, it is clear why generics should be allowed to adopt the external attributes of branded drugs.

If these aspects are not given due consideration, the barriers to entry for generics may only be perpetuated with harmful repercussions for public health.

Thirdly, many of these non-traditional marks may also be serving different functions. For example, children are a significant group to which a combination of color and shape is compelling. Interviews with medical practitioners confirm that certain shapes, colors, and flavors make medicines more palatable to children.[113] In such cases, a finding of functionality would be necessary to prevent monopolization of those physical attributes by the manufacturers of branded drugs.

There also exist public health considerations that necessitate a finding of functionality. As briefly discussed above, empirical studies have indicated that changes in color, size, or shape can have negative results, such as drug regimen non-adherence, patient confusion, and prescription errors.[114]

One of those studies, which focused on adults who were on antiepileptic drugs, found that "color and shape discordance occurred infrequently but was more common preceding cases of antiepileptic drug nonpersistence."[115] This assumes significance when read in the backdrop of previous research, which has shown that non-adherence to treatment in epilepsy patients leads to "increased risk of seizure-related emergency department visits and even mortality."[116] Another study, which focused on patients who had been discharged after myocardial infarction, also came to similar conclusions with regard to non-persistence.[117] As mentioned above, apart from drug non-adherence, changes in the appearance of medications can also cause patients to doubt the efficacy of their medication or lead to confusion that could contribute to prescription errors.[118] This is a serious issue, particularly among groups such as the elderly and those with limited health literacy.[119]

In this regard, it becomes necessary to also examine the link between physical attributes of a pharmaceutical drug and placebo effects. According to Arthur Shapiro and Elaine Shapiro, placebo effects are "nonspecific, psychological, or psychophysiological therapeutic effect produced by a placebo, or the effect of spontaneous

[111] *Id.* at 554. [112] *Id.*

[113] Interview with a doctor in Cochin, India (Apr. 18, 2017); telephonic interview with a doctor (July 18, 2017). Names and affiliations withheld for protecting confidentiality requirements.

[114] *See* Kesselheim, *Variations in Pill Appearance, supra* note 85, at 204; *see also* Kesselheim, *Burden of Changes in Pill Appearance, supra* note 85, at 101.

[115] Kesselheim, *Variations in Pill Appearance, supra* note 85, at 204. [116] *Id.* at 207.

[117] "A total of 177 (3.9%) instances of nonpersistence involved color discordance, 242 (5.3%) involved shape discordance, and 110 (2.4%) involved color and shape discordance." Kesselheim, *Burden of Changes in Pill Appearance, supra* note 85, at 100.

[118] *Id.* at 101. [119] Greene & Kesselheim, *supra* note 102, at 86.

improvement attributed to the placebo."[120] Experiments conducted over time indicate that a relationship exists between the physical appearance of a branded tablet and the placebo effect to be garnered from it by patients.[121] In particular, it showcases how the placebo effect from a tablet varies with the size, shape, and color of the tablet.[122]

Patients react best when color corresponds with the intended results of the medication.[123] For example, in *Norwich Pharmacal Co. v. Sterling Drug, Inc.*,[124] the Court observed that because pink was a pleasing color to those suffering from stomach ailments, substitutes of Pepto-Bismol in different colors would not have the same effect as far as the patients were concerned.[125] Such an effect may be even more pronounced in patients suffering from psychosomatic disorders including anxiety, depression, impotence, obesity, and pain.[126]

Given the correlation between pill appearance and non-persistence in otherwise bioequivalent drugs, studies have recommended that it is advisable to have similar appearance for both the branded drugs and their generic drugs equivalents.[127] One study even proposed that the U.S. Food and Drug Administration should require generic drug manufacturers to retain the physical attributes of branded drugs.[128]

Courts have also recognized this important aspect in some cases. For example, in *Shire US Inc. v. Barr Laboratories Inc.*, Shire, a branded manufacturer of Adderall (a prescription drug for the treatment of Attention-Deficit/Hyperactivity Disorder (ADHD)) sued Barr Laboratories, a generic producer, for copying the colors and shapes used by Shire to indicate dosage.[129] In this case, the Court noted that Shire failed to show that its product configuration was nonfunctional. Interestingly enough, one of the arguments raised by the generic companies, with the help of an expert witness, was that there was "clinical functionality" when a generic drug was physically similar to the branded drugs.[130] The Court, while accepting this argument, also recognized that such similarity "materially benefitted the patient population" and denied injunction to Shire.[131]

All three aspects highlighted above demonstrate how protection afforded to non-traditional marks can pose non-traditional barriers to access to medicine.

[120] Arthur K. Shapiro & Elaine Shapiro, *The Placebo: Is It Much Ado About Nothing?*, *in* THE PLACEBO EFFECT 12, 12 (Anne Harrington ed., 1999). They defined placebo itself as "any therapy prescribed knowingly or unknowingly by a healer, or used by laymen, for its therapeutic effect on a symptom or disease, but which actually is ineffective or not specifically effective for the symptom or disorder being treated." *Id.*

[121] Greene & Kesselheim, *supra* note 102, at 87.

[122] *Id.*

[123] *See generally* Aarti T. More & R.K. Srivastava, *Aesthetic Considerations for Pharmaceutical OTC (Over the Counter) Products*, 11 INT'L J. BIOTECH. 267 (2010).

[124] *Norwich Pharmacal Co.*, *supra* note 65; *see also* Iver P. Cooper, *Trademark Aspects of Pharmaceutical Product Design*, 70 TRADEMARK REP. 1, 13 (1980).

[125] *Norwich Pharmacal Co.*, *supra* note 65, 572.

[126] Greene & Kesselheim, *supra* note 102, at 87.

[127] Kesselheim, *Variations in Pill Appearance*, *supra* note 85, at 207; *see also* Kesselheim, *Burden of Changes in Pill Appearance*, *supra* note 85, at 101.

[128] Kesselheim, *Burden of Changes in Pill Appearance*, *supra* note 85, at 101.

[129] Shire US Inc. v. Barr Labs. Inc., 329 F.3d 348 (3d Cir. 2003).

[130] *Id.* at 357.

[131] *Id.* at 359.

Policymakers would need to take into account these public health aspects while framing recommendations with regard to non-traditional marks. Unfortunately, most of the international and national health policies have not yet given due consideration to these aspects.[132]

V. Conclusion

As is evident from the discussions in this chapter, any decision on extending protection to non-traditional marks should not limit itself to the contours of trademark law, but must also explore the larger public health policy concerns. Trademark protection should not be allowed as a means to extend the monopoly of a branded drug in perpetuity. As the previous section illuminates, granting protection for non-traditional marks in the pharmaceutical sector may pose significant barriers to access to medicine. This could include an increase in transaction costs and barriers to generic entry. As discussed in this chapter, many of the physical attributes of pharmaceutical products warrant rejection of trademark protection, on grounds of functionality. Thus to prevent the rise of non-traditional barriers to accessing medicine and in view of the larger public health concerns, more rigorous use of traditional legal doctrines like functionality is desirable.

[132] For example, the Doha Declaration is silent in this regard. *See Declaration on the TRIPS Agreement and Public Health*, World Trade Org. (Nov. 20, 2001), https://www.wto.org/english/thewto_e/minist_e/min01_e/mindecl_trips_e.htm [https://perma.cc/BV64-557E].

15

Hands Off "My" Colors, Patterns, and Shapes! How Non-Traditional Trademarks Promote Standardization and May Negatively Impact Creativity and Innovation

Irene Calboli

I. Introduction

In this chapter, I continue the critique that I have started in a recent editorial vis-a-vis to non-traditional trademarks (NTTMs) and focus on three specific examples of NTTMs used and registered by fashion designers, notably: Louboutin, Gucci, and Bottega Veneta.[1] In my view, these examples best exemplify the problems deriving from the protection of NTTMs. First of all, as several of the chapters that are published in this volume have pointed out, these examples demonstrate the negative impact that the protection of NTTMs has on market competition.[2] In particular, granting exclusive rights on NTTMs frequently results in preventing competitors from copying similar styles and product features, as NTTMs generally protect product design and aesthetic product features (such as colors, patterns, and shapes). Moreover, when these marks are considered famous—and Louboutin, Gucci, and Bottega Veneta's marks certainly qualify as famous—their legal protection extends beyond confusing signs and includes anti-dilution protection.[3] Accordingly, granting exclusive rights to NTTMs equates to foreclosing competitors and third parties from using any identical and similar product design and product features when this use could "blur" or "tarnish" the protected marks.

Still, the examples I address in this chapter highlight an additional problem related to the protection of NTTMs. Notably, these examples highlight the fact that by recognizing and protecting as marks elements that are product design and aesthetic product features, the current legal provisions ultimately support a system

[1] Irene Calboli, *Chocolate, Fashion, Toys, and Cabs: the Misunderstood Distinctiveness of Non-Traditional Trademarks*, 49 Int'l Rev. Intell. Prop. & Competition L. 1 (2018).
[2] *See*, in particular, Chapters 6, 10, and 11 in this volume.
[3] *See* discussion *infra* Section II.

of intellectual property protection that not only legitimizes, but also promotes standardization, rather than creativity and innovation in product development in a variety of creative industries, including but not limited to the fashion industry. In this chapter, I refer to the potential negative effects of NTTMs on product creativity and innovation as a "monolithic effect" on product and design development. This effect has, in my view, a twofold negative impact. First, it induces businesses to standardize the aesthetic features of their products and repeatedly use them on their products to acquire the level of necessary market recognition (distinctiveness) necessary to be protected as trademarks. This trend is demonstrated by the proliferation of "trademarked" patterns, buckles, buttons, and other product accessories and designs used by famous labels and market leaders, such as Gucci, Chanel, Louis Vuitton, Hermes, and Fendi to name a few. This technique is then regularly copied by other designers, for example Michael Kors, Coach, and Guess, in order to compete with the market leaders by using similar aesthetic features to decorate their products. Second, as a result of this trend of proliferation of trademarked patterns and other NTTMs, protecting these marks may lead to less investment not only in product and design innovation for new products both by market leaders and their competitors, but also in product quality for existing products. In particular, securing trademark protection for NTTMs and enforcing this protection against potential copiers allows businesses to capitalize on and extract value from the attractive power of these aesthetic features (that are protected as trademarks). In turn, this strategy can provide better and more effective short-term means to attract consumers toward purchasing the products with these exclusive trademarked product features, and consequently can guarantee higher profitability for trademark owners, rather than investing in long-term product quality of their existing products or new products.

The chapter proceeds as follows. In Section II, I review the traditional justifications for trademark protection and discuss the difference between trademarks and other intellectual property rights within the wider context of intellectual property incentives. This review is necessary as background to the critique that I develop in Section IV. In Section III, I elaborate on the pragmatic reasons that led to the rise and growth of NTTMs, primarily the benefit of a potentially endless term of protection, coupled with the relatively low costs of registration, the advantages of the international priority system, and the possibility to also protect unregistered signs under trademark law. As mentioned above, in Section III, I refer to current examples of use of NTTMs by fashion designers—Louboutin, Gucci, and Bottega Veneta. These examples, and the legal proceedings surrounding them, demonstrate that the rise of NTTMs is driven, to a large extent, by businesses that seek to obtain perpetual protection on successful (or potentially successful) aesthetic product features. This tendency is natural, as businesses will always try to capitalize on their success and monopolize their successful product designs and features. However, this should not be the case regarding product styles and aesthetic designs. In Section IV, I conclude and repeat that protecting NTTMs may hinder creativity and innovation to the benefit of the endless extraction of value on product design and aesthetic features that, albeit being appealing, valuable, and frequently distinctive, are not meant to be protected for a virtually unlimited period of time as trademarks.

II. Allocating Incentives: The Traditional Account for Trademark Protection

As other chapters in this volume have analyzed at length, the traditional justification for trademark protection is based on economics.[4] In particular, trademarks provide consumers with information about the products to which they are affixed in terms both of commercial origin and predictable quality, and thus reduce the costs of collecting information for consumers when and if they decide to make a purchase.[5] As such, trademarks are protected to prevent unauthorized third parties from using identical or similar signs, which in turn confuses consumers.[6] However, granting trademark rights has social costs, as trademark owners can enjoy protection for a virtually unlimited period of time: trademarks are registered for an initial term of ten years in most jurisdictions, and can be renewed for additional increments of ten years, without any limit in time and number of renewals, as long as the marks are used in commerce to identify the goods and services to which they refer.[7] In addition, most countries protect non-registered trademarks based on their use as long as the signs are used in commerce. To offset these costs, trademark protection has been traditionally limited to preventing the unauthorized use of identical or similar signs affixed on identical or similar products when such use could lead to a likelihood of confusion on the part of consumers.[8] Only when a mark reaches the status of "well-known" or "famous" mark, or mark "with a reputation," then the law provides protection of the mark beyond confusion and in relation to dissimilar goods and services.[9]

Until the beginning of the twentieth century, the so-called "indicators of origin" function of trademarks was considered the only function worthy of legal protection, and "origin" was interpreted as "manufacturing origin."[10] Eventually, following the changes in the economy and the growth of the phenomenon of trademark licensing, the law was changed so as to reflect that the notion of "origin" included the

[4] *See, e.g.*, William M. Landes & Richard A. Posner, *Trademark Law: An Economic Perspective*, 30 J. L. & Econ. 265 (1987); Nicholaw Economides, *The Economics of Trademarks*, 78 Trademark Rep. 523 (1988); William P. Kratzke, *Normative Economic Analysis of Trademark Law*, 21 Mem. St. U. L. Rev. 199 (1991). *See also* my previous analysis in Irene Calboli, *Trademark Assignment "With Goodwill": A Concept Whose Time Has Gone*, 57 Fla. L. Rev. 771, 832 (2005); Irene Calboli, *The Sunset of "Quality Control" in Modern Trademark Licensing*, 57 AM. U. L. Rev. 341, 396 (2007).

[5] Landes & Posner, *supra* note 4, at 265–66.

[6] *Id.*; Lanham Act §§ 14, 16 (U.S.); TRIPS: Agreement on Trade-Related Aspects of Intellectual Property Rights, act. 16, Apr. 15, 1994, Marrakesh Agreement Establishing the World Trade Organization, Annex 1C, 1869 U.N.T.S. 299, 33 I.L.M. 1197 (1994) art. 15 [hereinafter TRIPS Agreement].

[7] TRIPS Agreement arts. 18; Lanham Act § 1058.

[8] TRIPS Agreement art. 15; Lanham Act § 114; Council Directive 2015/2436 art. 3, of the European Parliament and of the Council of 16 Dec. 2015 to approximate the laws of the Members States relating to trademarks [hereinafter TMD 2015] (current EU standard).

[9] TRIPS Agreement art. 16.3; TMD 2015 art. 16.

[10] *See generally* Elmer William Hanak, III, *The Quality Assurance Function of Trademarks*, 43 Fordham L. Rev. 363; Alex Kozinski, *Trademarks Unplugged*, 68 N.Y.U. L. Rev. 960, 961 (1993).

"sponsorship, affiliation, connection or association" with a mark.[11] Since consumers rely on trademarks as indicators of consistent quality—that is, they expect all the products identified by a certain mark to have identical characteristics and quality—a second function was also legally recognized in several jurisdictions: that marks represent a mechanism to guarantee that the product to which they are affixed meets a consistent quality. Years later, a third protected function was added to the debate: trademarks' advertising function, that is the ability of a mark to "stimulate further purchasing by the consuming public."[12] The recognition of a mark's attractive power, separate from its other functions, acknowledged that a mark can create goodwill on its own by influencing consumers through a specifically created product image.[13]

Still, central to the scope of protection is the notion of trademark distinctiveness.[14] This notion is the basis of each of the protected trademark functions. In particular, for a sign to be protected as a mark, it is crucial that the sign is able to identify and distinguish the products to which it is affixed as originating from a single business source. The fact that, to be protected as marks, signs should "be able to distinguish" or should already "be distinctive of" products, which are available in the marketplace, is directly stated in several of (if not all) the current legal definitions of what constitutes a mark, both under relevant international agreements and national laws.[15] Besides being the *sine qua non* for acquiring trademark status, the notion of distinctiveness is at the basis of trademark enforcement. Notably, a mark has to be distinctive to be protected against infringement—where confusingly similar signs are used to lure consumers toward competitors' products.[16] Additionally, trademark distinctiveness, and the protection thereof, is at the core of the justification to the enhanced protection against "trademark dilution" for marks that are well known, famous, or have a reputation in the relevant market. In order to enjoy this enhanced protection, these marks have to be highly distinctive, and it is precisely this distinctiveness that qualifies them for the additional protection.[17] In general,

[11] Kozinski, *supra* note 10, at 961.

[12] Hanak, *supra* note 10, at 363–64.

[13] Thomas D. Drescher, *The Transformation and Evolution of Trademarks—From Signals to Symbols to Myth*, 82 Trademark Rep. 301 (1992). *Cf.* Robert G. Bone, *Hunting Goodwil: A History of Goodwill in Trademark Law*, 86 B.U. L. Rev. 547 (2006).

[14] The acquisition of trademark rights is centered upon the concepts of "distinctiveness" and "priority" and is limited to marks that are in use or are intended to be used. *See* Lanham Act § 1, 15 U.S.C. § 1051 (2006); *see also* Zazú Designs v. L'Oreal, S.A., 979 F.2d 499, 503 (7th Cir. 1992) ("By insisting that firms use marks to obtain rights in them, the law prevents entrepreneurs from reserving brand names in order to make their rivals' marketing more costly."); Abercrombie & Fitch Co. v. Hunting World, Inc., 537 F.2d 4, 9 (2d Cir. 1976). "[T]he more distinctive or unique the mark, the deeper is its impress upon the public consciousness, and the greater its need for protection against vitiation or dissociation from the particular product in connection with which it has been used." Frank I. Schechter, *The Rational Basis of Trademark Protection*, 40 Harv. L. Rev. 813, 825 (1927).

[15] TRIPS Agreement art. 15.1 (offering the first definition of trademark); Lanham Act § 115(a); TMD 2015 art. 4.1.

[16] *Zazú Designs, supra* note 14, 503.

[17] Schechter, *supra* note 14, at 819. Schechter argued that a trademark has a dual function, and a mark "is not merely the symbol of good will but often the most effective agent for the creation of good will, imprinting upon the public mind an anonymous and impersonal guaranty of satisfaction, creating a desire for further satisfactions. The mark actually *sells* the goods. And, self-evidently, the more distinctive the mark, the more effective is its selling power." *Id.*

distinctiveness can be inherent or acquired through use.[18] However, the international trademark framework seems to support a low threshold for distinctiveness by requiring that trademark application be allowed without the need for a mark to be already used in the course of trade.[19] No use, or intent-to-use a mark is sufficient, under most national laws to file a trademark application.[20] Still, as the examples described in this chapter indicate, several jurisdictions require a proof of acquired distinctiveness or secondary meaning to register NTTMs. [21]

In essence, different than other types of intellectual property rights, trademark protection does not emphasize the aspect of innovation or scientific discovery of trademarks, but remains rooted in commercial concepts—the ability of traders to identify their products in the marketplace and distinguish them from similar products offered for sale by their competitors and third parties. This is a very important characteristic that qualifies trademark protection as distinct from the other forms of intellectual property rights: trademark rights are not granted to directly protect the products to which the marks are attached and that they identify. Instead, trademark law aims at protecting the signaling function of the marks—the ability to distinguish and identify goods and services—so that consumers can identify the mark and the products with a single source. Accordingly, trademark law aims at preventing as infringement any actions that may lead to consumer confusion.[22] And again, when a mark reaches the status of being famous, well known, or has an established reputation, then the law also aims at preventing that competitors take unfair advantage of, or cause detriment to, the established fame or reputation of these.[23]

On the contrary, other types of protected intellectual property, primarily patents and copyrights, directly protect products and creative works per se, or parts of these products and works.[24] In particular, both patents and copyrights grant a time-bound period of exclusivity to their owners during which third parties cannot copy the products or works per se, unless a legally provided specific limitation or exception applies.[25] In exchange for this monopoly on products and works per se, patent owners and copyright owners have to fulfill several requirements. In this respect, patent owners must disclose, in the best mode known to those skilled in the art, the characteristics of the invention and how the invention works, so that competitors can work around the terms of the patent during the time of exclusivity to develop similar products, and so that the invention can be copied when the patent expires.[26] Likewise, the incentive and reward system through which an author obtains a copyright is similarly built on the idea that the temporary monopoly granted to an author

[18] TRIPS Agreement art. 15. [19] *Id.* [20] *Id.*

[21] *See* discussion *infra* Section III.

[22] TRIPS Agreement art. 15.3. Gen. Rep. of the Assemblies of the Member States of World Intellectual Property Organization (WIPO), *Joint Resolution Concerning Provisions on the Protection of Well-Known Marks*, WIPO Doc. A/34/13 art. 2(3) (1999).

[23] Schechter, *supra* note 14, at 825.

[24] *See, e.g.*, Mark A. Lemley, The *Modern Lanham Act and the Death of Common Sense*, 108 Yale L.J. 1687 (1999).

[25] U.S. Const. art. I, § 8, cl. 8 (offering the basis for the protection of patents and copyrights in the U.S.).

[26] 35 U.S.C. § 112.

is justified by the benefit of releasing the copyrighted material during the copyright terms and ultimately the possibility for everyone to copy once this term expires.[27] Moreover, copyright protection does not extend to independent creative works.[28] Ultimately, whereas the patent system underscores the importance of innovation and the promotion of scientific progress, the copyright system is aimed at promotion of creative and artistic endeavors. Yet again, both systems of protection function differently than trademark protection, in that the time-limited nature and the societal bargain beyond these intellectual property rights lie precisely in the fact that the exclusive rights in the products or works at issue would, at the end, expire.

Besides patents and copyrights, the protection of industrial design is relevant in this context. In the European Union (EU), for example, industrial design is protected as a *sui generis* right both under a unified system under Council Regulation (EC) No. 6/2002[29] as well as under harmonized national systems.[30] In particular, industrial design is defined in the EU as "the appearance of the whole or a part of a product resulting from the features of, in particular, the lines, contours, colours, shape, texture and/or materials of the product itself or its ornamentation."[31] As with patents and copyrights, industrial design protection is time-limited, with the term of protection varying between fifteen to twenty-five years.[32] Protection is also based on the requirements of novelty or originality.[33] In the United States (U.S.), industrial design is protected under the category of design patents, again for a limited period of time and based on the requirement of novelty.[34] However, design is also protected under the notion of trade dress in the U.S., which enjoys the same protection as trademarks and only requires a proof that the design is distinctive to signal commercial origin to consumers.[35]

As I elaborate in the following section, it has been precisely the transposition of the notion of distinctiveness from traditional marks—that are usually applied onto the products to distinguish them—to the entire product design or other aesthetic product features that has led to the possibility to register as NTTMs, with all the advantages of trademark protection, elements that represent, in essence, industrial designs (or design patents) and should have been confined to this type of protection.[36] In particular, even though these designs and aesthetic product features can be found to be distinctive and characteristic of certain products, to protect them potentially in perpetuity through trademark protection does not seem to have been the intent of the legislators, who instead created specific forms of protection for these

[27] 17 U.S.C. § 106.

[28] 17 U.S.C. § 106; Feist Publications, Inc. v. Rural Telephone Serv. Co, 499 U.S. 340 (1991).

[29] Council Regulation (EC) No. 6/2002 of Dec. 12, 2001, on Community designs O.J. L3/1.

[30] Council Directive 98/71/EC of Oct. 13, 1998, on the legal protection of designs O.J. L289/28 [hereinafter Design Directive].

[31] Design Directive art. 11. [32] *Id.* art. 10. [33] *Id.* arts. 4–5.

[34] 35 U.S.C. § 171.

[35] *See* Wal-Mart Stores, Inc. v. Samara Brothers, Inc., 529 U.S. 205 (2000); Qualitex Co. v. Jacobson Prods. Co., 514 U.S. 159 (1995); Two Pesos, Inc. v. Taco Cabana, Inc., 505 U.S. 763, 765 (1992); *In re* Slokevage, 441 F.3d 957 (Fed. Cir. 2006); Rock & Roll Hall of Fame & Museum, Inc. v. Gentile Productions, 134 F.3d 749 (6th Cir. 1998).

[36] See the critique elaborated in this respect Chapters 10 and 11 in this volume.

items through *sui generis* regimes such as industrial design and design patents, both types of protection that, while granting strong rights during the life of the protection, expire within a reasonable amount of time, and later permit that any interested party may copy the design and aesthetic features at issue.

III. These are "My" Colors, Patterns, and Shapes! Non-Traditional Trademarks as Means to Protect Designs and Aesthetic Product Features

What do Louboutin red soles, Gucci monogrammed patterns and stripes, and the Bottega Veneta intrecciato pattern have in common? These signs have been, with several others, protagonists of the rising trend of applications to register shapes and other non-traditional signs as trademarks in a variety of countries.[37] In some cases, these signs were found not to be suitable to be registered as trademarks, at least at first.[38] Still, their owners managed to secure registrations after several rounds of office actions in several intellectual property offices, even though some of these registrations were later invalidated as a result of litigation.[39] In several instances, the owners of these marks ultimately relied on their acquired registrations to attack competitors who had used similar styles and aesthetic features for their own products on the basis of possible trademark infringement, dilution, and unfair competition.[40] As I will examine in the examples below, the courts involved in these cases did in fact declare several of these marks invalid or reduced their scope. Still, this was not always the case. Moreover, the lawsuits involving these marks have generally involved several degrees of litigation. This means that only plaintiffs and defendants with deep pockets are in a position to afford these lawsuits.[41] Litigants carrying on with the legal proceedings, several smaller (and less wealthy) competitors probably did cave in and settle accusations of infringement, dilution, and unfair competition with confidential out-of-court agreements.[42]

This situation begs several questions. First, is this trend of securing rights in NTTMs compatible with the traditional functions that trademarks are supposed to fulfill in the system? As I mentioned in Section II, the traditional function of a trademark is that of signaling commercial original and consistent quality to consumers in the market place. Upon these functions, trademark protection has been built with the notion of infringement and the standard to assess infringement based on consumer confusion. However, in the past decades, the domain of trademark law and the scope of trademark protection has grown exponentially. Today, any sign can be registered as a mark as the examples I address demonstrate. This includes single colors, shapes, sounds, smells, video clips, holograms, and even gestures.

[37] *See* discussion *infra* Section III. [38] *Id.* [39] *Id.* [40] *Id.*

[41] James Gibson, *Risk Aversion and Rights Accretion in Intellectual Property Law*, 116 YALE L.J. 882, 913 (2007); Stacey L. Dogan & Mark A. Lemley, *The Merchandising Right: Fragile Theory or Fait Accompli?*, 54 EMORY L.J. 461, 485–87 (2005).

[42] Gibson, *supra* note 41, at 913.

Hence, and this is the second question that we need to address in this context, how did we get here? Not surprisingly, the answer can be found in the development of the definition of "what can represent a mark" in several trademark laws worldwide. In particular, the very broad, and first international definition of trademark in the 1994 Agreement on Trade-Related Aspects to Intellectual Property Rights (TRIPS) paved the way for the possibility to protect all types of marks, including NTTMs.[43] Moreover, TRIPS simply permits, but does not mandate, that country members of TRIPS provide that signs should be "visually perceptible" to be protected.[44] This trend toward facilitating the phenomenon of "trademarking everything" was later confirmed with two additional international agreements: the Trademark Law Treaty[45] and the Singapore Treaty on the Law of Trademarks, which both facilitate the registrability of NTTMs.[46] Recent bilateral and plurilateral international trade agreements have continued on the same path and have supported the registrability of NTTMs as part of their intellectual property chapters.[47]

Still, what prompted the recent escalation of applications, registrations, and litigation in this area? As I anticipated in Section II, the reason for the proliferation of NTTMs lies at the heart of the requirement for trademark protection—the notion of trademark distinctiveness. As I elaborated above, distinctiveness has historically represented the very core of the type of protection granted through trademark law. However, in the recent decades, the original notion of distinctiveness seems to have become looser. In particular, from the recent wave of registration of NTTMs, and most marks in general, as well as many of the cases that have been litigated, it seems that the interpretation of the notion of trademark distinctiveness has gradually shifted. Notably, from a strict interpretation of distinctiveness as a requirement that is necessary for a sign to be able to identify goods or services in the marketplace, it seems that today's distinctiveness has come to mean little more than "recognizable" by the human senses—that is characteristic, typical, appealing, or just interesting to see—when it is applied to the distinctive features of a sign for which trademark protection is sought. As I just mentioned, this trend is directly reflected also in several of the legal definitions of trademarks.[48] In particular, TRIPS requires that a sign be "capable of distinguishing" a product to be registered as a mark, without even imposing a proof of acquired distinctiveness or secondary meaning of that sign before registration.[49] Also in countries, such as in the United States (U.S.), that require secondary meaning—that is, acquired distinctiveness—to register some of these signs, the bar to prove distinctiveness remains very low based on the actual cases on point.[50]

[43] TRIPS Agreement art. 15. [44] *Id.* art. 15.1.

[45] Trademark Law Treaty, Oct. 27, 1994, S. Treaty Doc. No. 105-35, 2037 U.N.T.S. 35.

[46] Singapore Treaty on the Law of Trademarks, Mar. 27, 2006, S. Treaty Doc. No. 110-2.

[47] *See, e.g.*, Burton Ong, *The Trademark Law Provisions of Bilateral Free Trade Agreements*, in RESEARCH HANDBOOK OF TRADEMARK LAW AND THEORY 229 (Graeme B. Dinwoodie & Mark D. Janis eds., 2008) (providing a detailed overview of the post-TRIPS trademark provisions in FTAs).

[48] TRIPS Agreement art. 15. [49] *Id.*

[50] *See, e.g.*, Jake Linford, *A Linguistic Justification for Protecting "Generic" Trademarks*, 17 YALE J. L. & TECH. 110 (2015); Christian Faith Fellowship Church v. Adidas AG, 841 F.3d 986 (Fed. Cir. 2016).

In other words, it seems that the current interpretation of trademark distinctiveness suffers from what I would define as "circularity." Notably, the test to protect a sign as a mark is no longer that a sign necessarily needs to be distinctive of existing products. Instead, any sign that has a potential to be distinctive—that is because it is original, interesting, and appealing to the human eye and sense—can be protected as a mark. Today, this can include, not surprisingly, product designs and a variety of aesthetic product features, which are certainly distinctive under this looser and circular definition.[51] Yet, these items are not distinctive of products, they are integral parts of the products, if not the entire products themselves.

To add to the problem, this circularity between the notion of distinctiveness and trademark protectable subject matter is coupled with a weak system both in terms of absolute grounds to refuse trademark registration as well as trademark defenses across many jurisdictions. This situation has also been addressed at length by several chapters in this volume.[52] For example, historically, shape marks could not be registered at all in several countries.[53] These prohibitions are long gone and have been replaced with a list of absolute grounds that prevent trademark registration. These include the exclusion from registration of signs are that "functional" in the U.S. Lanham Act[54] and "aesthetically functional" under U.S. case law,[55] or signs that comprise of the "shape, or another characteristics" of a product that either "results from the nature of the goods" or "is necessary to obtain a technical result" or "gives substantial value to the goods" under EU trademark law.[56] However, examiners do not seem to strictly enforce the existing absolute grounds when tasked to assess the registrability of NTTMs, at least considering the proliferation of registrations, as highlighted also in this volume.[57] Furthermore, several signs that were opposed and contested at the time of their application were ultimately registered by the trademark offices.[58]

In fairness, as the examples that I analyze below indicate, the journey of NTTMs has not been without bumps. These marks continue to be seen skeptically by many (besides academics), especially the judiciary. Notably, courts across several jurisdictions have increasingly expressed concerns toward the suitability of protecting these marks due to the relevant concerns for market competition and the overlaps with other forms of protection, primarily design protection.[59] In some instances,

[51] *See* the judgment of the House of Lords in *Coca Cola T.M.*, 1986, R.P.C., 421 (U.K.). In that decision it was stated that in the case of liquids the form of the container must necessarily be deemed to be that of the product. *Id.* at 425 and 449.

[52] In this respect, *see* the analysis elaborated, in particular, by Michael Handler, Martin Senftleben, and Lisa Ramsey in chapters 8, 16, and 17 in this volume.

[53] See the observations in this respect by Dev Gangjee in Chapter 3 in this volume.

[54] Lanham Act § 21(a).

[55] *Abercrombie & Fitch Co.. supra* note 14, 9; *Qualitex Co., supra* note 35, 165; *see also* TrafFix Devices, Inc. v. Mktg. Displays, Inc., 532 U.S. 23, 32 (2001) (quoting *Qualitex Co.* at 165).

[56] TMD 2015 art. 4.

[57] See Chapter 3 in this volume.

[58] For example, Rubik's Cube, Trademark Registration No. 5,339,260 (later cancelled by the CJEU).

[59] The London Taxi Corp. Ltd. v. Frazer-Nash Research Ltd., [2017] E.W.C.A. Civ. 1729 (Eng.); Case C-371/02, Björnekulla Fruktindustrier AB v. Procordia Food, AB, [2004] EURLex ECLI:EU:C:2004:275; Case T-629/14, Jaguar Land Rover Ltd v. OHIM, [2015] EURLex ECLI:EU:T:2015:868 (denying the shape trademark to Land Rover).

courts have canceled these marks or have reduced the scope of their protection as a result of litigation proceedings.[60] However, these cases are again a limited sample as compared to the cases that are settled or never litigated. In some instances, courts have upheld these registrations, which have then emerged even stronger.

A. Louboutin red lacquered sole shoes

The fame of Louboutin's red lacquered sole shoes is well known today. What is less well known is that their creator, Christian Louboutin, started designing shoes for the dancers of the Parisian cabaret "Les Folies Bergères," and later worked with the maison Chanel and Yves Saint Laurent.[61] In the early 1990s, Louboutin founded his own label and, inspired by his assistant's bold red nail color, designed the famous red lacquered shoes,[62] which, within a few years, were named to be the most desirable shoes in the world by independent consulting firm The Luxury Institute.[63] Renowned for their appeal, the shoes have been featured in award-winning TV series like HBO's *Sex and the City*, and celebrities like Madonna have popularized them by wearing them in multiple music videos. Jennifer Lopez even dedicated a song to "My Louboutin Shoes."[64] To date, Louboutin stores span over thirty countries. Louboutin's products are also available through numerous retailers and online marketplaces.

Not surprisingly, Louboutin has made a significant effort to protect its shoes from competitors and has filed trademark application for the red soles feature of the shoes in most countries where it has a store,[65] including: France, Mexico, Singapore, New Zealand, Australia, the U.S., Moldova, the Philippines, Cambodia, Laos, Brunei, Indonesia, Morocco, Bahrain, Chile, Israel, Switzerland, Vietnam, Malaysia, and India.[66]

The first of such applications was filed in France, in 2000, where it was initially rejected.[67] It was only after a reapplication that the mark was registered in France in 2009.[68] As I elaborate below, this registration was later canceled following litigation. Still, after obtaining the trademark in France, Louboutin filed for an EU-wide application and sought protection in a variety of countries through the international filing system administered by the World Intellectual Property Organization

[60] *See* discussion *infra* Section III.

[61] Hadley Freeman, *Christian Louboutin: How Killer Heels Conquered Fashion*, The Guardian, Mar. 19, 2010, https://www.theguardian.com/lifeandstyle/2010/mar/19/christian-louboutin-high-heels.

[62] Christian Louboutin & Phillippe Garcia, Christian Louboutin (2011).

[63] The Luxury Institute, "Most Desirable Brands", http://luxuryinstitute.com/LuxuryInstitute/.

[64] Jennifer Lopez, Louboutins (Epic Records, 2009).

[65] Rashi Gahlaut, *Louboutin's "Red Sole" Declared as a Well-Known Trademark by Delhi HC*, Khurana & Khurana, Dec. 30, 2017, http://www.khuranaandkhurana.com/2017/12/30/louboutins-red-sole-declared-as-a-well-known-trademark-by-delhi-hc/.

[66] World Intellectual Property Organization, Global Brand Database V. 2018-03-28 03:27, http://www.wipo.int/branddb/en/.

[67] LexDellmeier, *Trademark Issue: Red Sole(ly) for Louboutin?*, Lex Dellmeier: Intellectual Property Law, July 28, 2016, http://lexdellmeier.com/en/blog/trademark-issue-red-solely-louboutin.

[68] The mark consists of the red sole, Registration No. 3690945 (France).

(WIPO).[69] Like the original French application, the EU application was rejected at first, in 2010. The mark was registered following the decision of the Board of Appeals in January of 2013.[70] Here again, the validity of the EU registration was later challenged. However, after lengthy litigation, the Court of Justice of the EU (CJEU) held that van Haren, a Dutch shoe company, had infringed the brand's trademark.[71] The Court noted that Louboutin was not seeking protection on the shape of the shoe itself, but merely protection of the application of a color to a specific part of the shoe.[72] In addition, Louboutin was able to secure registrations in Germany, Belgium, and the Netherlands, even though the mark was later canceled in the Netherlands.[73] In Switzerland, the Swiss IP Office recently refused to register the mark.[74] In the U.S., Louboutin was granted federal registration in 2008.[75] The company also applied for trademark protection throughout Asia and Latin America, and obtained it in the majority of the countries in which it was applied for. For example, Louboutin filed in Japan shortly after the Trademark Act of 2014 was enacted, as the new law officially allows the registration of non-traditional marks.[76] In India, the red sole trademark has been successfully registered after surviving numerous opposition challenges. Still in India, the mark was recently defined to be a well-known mark.[77]

Empowered by the rights obtained with these registrations, Louboutin has filed numerous actions for trademark infringement in several jurisdictions. One of the most famous claims in this regard is the one that Louboutin brought in the U.S. against Yves Saint Laurent (interestingly, Louboutin's former employer). In this case, Louboutin attacked Yves Saint Laurent for producing a line of monochrome colored shoes, including a wholly red shoe.[78] YSL responded to the accusation by counterclaiming the invalidity of the mark and seeking its cancellation, based on its ornamental and functional nature of the lacquered red sole.[79] The U.S. District Court agreed with YSL.[80] However, the Second Circuit Court of Appeals did not share this view, and ruled that a single could be protected as a mark based on existing precedents.[81] Still, the Court said that Louboutin could not prevent YSL from manufacturing a whole red shoe.[82] Shortly after, Louboutin sued (ultimately unsuccessfully) Brazilian designer Carmen Steffensin in the U.S., again claiming

[69] The mark consists of the red sole, Registration No. 1031242 (WIPO International Trademarks—Madrid).

[70] The mark consists of the red sole, Registration No. 011113611 (EUIPO).

[71] Case C-163/16, Louboutin and Christian Louboutin SAS v. van Haren Schoenen BV [2018] EURLex 62016CJ0163, ECLI:EU:C:2018:423.

[72] *Id.*

[73] The mark consists of the red sole, Registration No. 0874489 (Benelux); the mark consists of the red sole, Registration No. 005282322 (Germany).

[74] LexDellmeier, *supra* note 67.

[75] The mark consists of the red sole, Registration Nos. 3376197, 3361597 (U.S.).

[76] Trademark Act (Act No. 127 of Apr. 13, 1959, as amended up to Act No. 36 of May 14, 2014) (Japan).

[77] Gahlaut, *supra* note 65.

[78] Christian Louboutin S.A. v. Yves St. Laurent Am., Inc., 778 F. Supp. 2d 445 (S.D.N.Y. 2011).

[79] *Id.* at 448.

[80] *Id.* at 458.

[81] Christian Louboutin S.A. v. Yves St. Laurent Am., Inc., 969 F.3d 206 (2d Cir. 2012).

[82] *Id.* at 229.

infringement of its mark. This case was followed by a 2013 settlement with Charles Jourdan and the retail store DSW, which agreed to discontinue their similar shoe lines.[83] As these lawsuits unfolded in the U.S., Louboutin also sued Spanish retail giant Zara in France for infringement and unfair competition.[84] Again, Zara counterclaimed that the mark was invalid.[85] Interestingly, the French courts sided with Zara. Ultimately, the French Supreme Court ruled that Louboutin's trademark was unable to be protected, because the shape was imposed by its function.[86] Still, Louboutin retains other marks in France, notably the mark on the actual color and two-dimensional shape of the sole.[87]

Elsewhere in Europe, a German shoe retailer, Roland SE, opposed the mark, but the Board of Appeal ultimately disagreed and allowed the registration.[88] The case eventually made its way to the CJEU, which affirmed the EUIPO's ruling in 2016.[89] Also in Belgium, two opponents challenged the Louboutin trademark. First, Dr. Adams Footwear obtained a favorable ruling in the Court of First Instance, but ultimately lost to Louboutin in the Court of Appeals.[90] The second opponent, Van Dalen Footwear, was also able to win in the lower Court before being defeated in the Court of Appeals.[91] The case is currently under review by the Dutch courts for further consideration of the validity of the mark.[92] Finally, Louboutin sued Van Haren (yet another shoe retailer) in the Netherlands in 2009.[93] The Hague District Court ruled that the red sole was a "hybrid mark" combination of color and shape, and held in favor of Louboutin.[94] Ultimately, the case made its way to the European Court, which initially ruled that no, Louboutin's red sole was not a valid trademark,[95] yet later reversed itself and stated that the mark was valid and infringed.[96] Also in favour of protection, in India, Louboutin was awarded over $100,000 (in U.S. dollars) in December of 2017.[97] This success has been the latest of the wins in an otherwise complex road the brand has faced in its war against infringement and invalidity. In this case, two separate retailers were held to have infringed on the red

[83] LexDellmeier, *supra* note 67.

[84] French Supreme Court, Commercial Chamber, Decision of 30 May 2012, *Christian Louboutin v. Zara France* (2012).

[85] *Id.* [86] *Id.*

[87] The mark consists of the red sole, Registration No. 3690945 (France).

[88] Case T-631/14, Roland v. OHIM, [2014] O.J. C380 (nuance of the color red for shoe soles).

[89] Case C-515/15 P, Roland SE v. EUIPO, EUR-Lex 62015CO0515 (2016).

[90] Tribunal de Première Instance [Civ.] [Tribunal of First Instance] Brussels, Louboutin tegen Dr. Adams Footwear, 2013, 482 (Belg.); Hof van Beroep [Court of Appeal] Brussels, Louboutin tegen Dr. Adams Footwear, IEFbe 1119 decision 2014/AR/734 (Nov. 2014).

[91] Christian Louboutin v. Van Dalen Footnote BV, District Court (Brussels), Mar. 20. 2014, Case AR 2013-6154.

[92] Don-Alvin Adegeest, *Louboutin Loses EU Trademark in Red Sole Court Case*, FASHION UNITED, Feb. 7, 2018, https://fashionunited.com/news/business/louboutin-loses-eu-trademark-in-red-sole-court-case/2018020719545.

[93] Aanvullende Conclusie AG HvJ EU Feb. 6, 2018, IEF 17487; IEFbe 2476; ECLI: EU: C: 2018: 64; C-163/16 (Louboutin tegen Van Haren) Merkenrecht, http://www.ie-forum.be/dossiers.

[94] *Id.*

[95] Case C-163/16, Louboutin and Christian Louboutin [2017] EURLex 62016CC0163.

[96] Case C-163/16, Louboutin and Christian Louboutin [2018] EURLex 62016CJ0163, ECLI:EU:C:2018:423.

[97] Case C-163/16, Louboutin and Christian Louboutin [2017] EURLex 62016CC0163 ¶ 73.

soled shoes in India; both received a permanent injunction against marketing or selling their infringing product.[98]

B. Gucci's monograms, patterns, and stripes

Guccio Gucci was a young hotel worker in Paris in the early 1900s, where he regularly handled the luxurious suitcases of the hotel's guest that were made with fine leatherwork.[99] Inspired, Mr. Gucci opened a small shop selling fine leather goods when he returned to his native Florence a few years later.[100] Very soon, the Gucci store became a success in Florence to the point that Mr. Gucci's son and grandsons expanded the business to Milan and Rome.[101] From these years, the Gucci stores were famous for their finely crafted leather accessories, including handbags and shoes, as well as silks and knitwear.[102] As homage to his father, Mr. Aldo Gucci created the official double-G logo in 1933.[103] Within a few decades, Gucci had become a sought-after luxury brand, and Gucci opened offices also in New York. This turned Gucci merchandise into a global status symbol, with celebrities, fashionistas, and the wealthy increasingly wearing Gucci-made goods, with the eponymous double-G logo. Still, Gucci had suffered an economic crisis in the 1980s, which was followed by a restructuring in the late 1990s. Noted designer Tom Ford was brought in to create a ready-to-wear line, and subsequently served as Gucci's creative director. Gucci headquarters were returned to Florence, and the number of Gucci products, which had swelled to 20,000, was reduced to 5,000, to return to the exclusivity and prestige for which the Gucci brand was originally known.[104]

Today, Gucci is recognized as one of the most iconic brands in high fashion. The brand is easily identifiable from their double-G logo, as well as the green-red-green racing stripes, the diamond motif repeating the inverted G pattern in each corner, the stylized G mark, and the scripted Gucci design mark. These signs are registered as trademarks and have been widely copied and infringed upon worldwide. In particular, the interlocking double-G logo has become one of the most enduring, iconic fashion symbols. The sign is a registered mark throughout the world, from Singapore to Mexico.[105] For the most part, Gucci did not have any trouble in registering its various marks. For example, in the U.S., Gucci holds forty-six active trademarks,[106] covering a wide arrangement of the iconic GG design, from the original interlocking, facing Gs to a grid of interlocking and interconnecting Gs, to

[98] *Id.* ¶ 74.

[99] Logo My Way, *The History of Gucci and Their Logo Design*, Dec. 29, 2016, http://blog.logomyway.com/history-of-gucci-and-their-logo-design/.

[100] The House of Gucci, *Gucci History—The 1920s*, http://www.gucci.com/us/worldofgucci/articles/history-1920.

[101] *Id.* [102] Logo My Way, *supra* note 99. [103] *Id.*

[104] The House of Gucci, *supra* note 100.

[105] The mark consists of the interlocking GGs, Registration No. 0119851234216 (Mexico); the mark consists of the interlocking GGs, Registration No. 4020153387S (Singapore).

[106] World Intellectual Property Organization, Global Brand Database V. 2018-03-28 03:27, http://www.wipo.int/branddb/en/.

other designs featuring the double-G emblem.[107] A comprehensive list of offices that recognize the marks includes Switzerland, Spain, Bahrain, Estonia, South Korea, Mongolia, Australia, Morocco, Germany, Chile, Laos, Israel, and Cambodia, among others, including several registration files through the Madrid international registration system.[108]

Still, while Gucci has had few issues registering their trademarks, there have been numerous infringement and invalidity contentions throughout several jurisdictions involving its marks in the past years. Recently, these cases have involved primarily the company Guess, also a manufacturer of bags, shoes, and similar apparels as those produced by Gucci (but at a considerably lower level in the luxury scale). Guess uses a design bearing a logo that is similar to the G moniker. The two brands have hashed out numerous legal battles in different countries and courts, with both sides occasionally declaring victory.

In particular, in the U.S., Gucci won $4.7 million in damages against Guess based on a ruling by the District Court for the Southern District of New York. The Court held that there was a likelihood of confusion between the two marks, and that Guess knowingly and in bad faith copied Gucci's stripe mark on shoes. The Court also stated that Guess's use of the pattern would likely cause dilution by blurring.[109] Gucci had asserted the right in its five different marks: the red-green-red stripe mark; the repeating GG pattern; the diamond motif trade dress; the stylized G design mark; and the script Gucci design mark.[110] Of those five, only the diamond motif trade dress was held not to be a famous mark.[111] However, the Court denied that Guess had counterfeited Gucci's marks, stating that "courts have uniformly restricted trademark counterfeiting claims to those situations where entire products have been copied stitch by stitch."[112] Hence, despite this success in the U.S. Court, Gucci has lost similar cases in other countries. A year after winning the case in New York, Guess filed suit in the Italian courts to cancel three of Gucci's trademarks, and in turn Gucci countered with infringement.[113] The Italian Tribunale di Milano (Court of Milan) held that Guess's products do *not* infringe on Gucci's products, and invalidated two of Gucci's trademarks.[114] The finding was based on two key differences between the Guess and Gucci products. One, the Court said, was that there are graphic differences between the marks when taking the fonts, thickness, and inclination of the letters.[115] Two, all of Guess's products have a visible presence of the well-known "Guess" trademark. This, the Court said, was enough to avoid

[107] The mark consists of two mirrored Gs, Registration Nos. 11067220, 11073110 (U.S.); the mark consists of a repeating pattern of the stylized letters "GG" surrounded by four filled squares at four corners of the letters, forming an overall diamond design pattern, Registration No. 5221475 (U.S.).

[108] For example, the mark consists of two mirrored Gs, Registration Nos. 11073110 (U.S.), M-0646473 (Mongolia), 1482967 (Australia).

[109] Gucci Amer., Inc. v. Guess?, Inc., 868 F.Supp.2d 207 (S.D.N.Y. 2012) .

[110] *Id.* at 217–20. [111] *Id.* at 229. [112] *Gucci Amer.*, *supra* note 109.

[113] Tribunale di Milano (Ordinary Court of First Instance—Milan), Gucci v. Guess? Inc., No. 6095 (2013).

[114] *Id.* ¶ 54.

[115] Kevin Bercimuelle-Chamot, *Gucci may be One Nail Away from a New Legal Battle*, IP Kat, Oct. 6, 2015, http://ipkitten.blogspot.co.uk/2015/10/gucci-may-be-one-nail-away-from-new.html.

any risk of confusion for the "particularly observant and circumspect" customer.[116] Moreover, the Court found that the mark consisting of the letter G inserted into a radial dotted pattern was invalid because it lacked distinctive character.[117]

The next showdown between the two brands occurred in the Paris High Court in France. Here again, Gucci argued infringement while Guess claimed that the trademarks were invalid.[118] The High Court dismissed Gucci's infringement claims, and revoked three of its trademarks, including the G mark.[119] In the lower Court, the Tribunal de Grande Instance (before a panel of three justices), Gucci's request for $62 million in damages was precluded.[120] Instead, the brand was ordered to pay Guess $34,000.[121] In addition, the Court found that Guess did not engage in counterfeiting or unfair competition.[122] Now with the score at Guess 2, Gucci 1, the Italian brand hoped to even things up in the Chinese and Australian courts. Interestingly, Gucci received a favorable holding in the Nanjing Intermediate People's Court of China. The Nanjing Court found the deciding factor in the infringement case was whether the marks look subjectively similar, not whether the customer will be confused.[123] This contrasts with the other case where Gucci won, when the U.S. Court hinged its decision on consumer confusion.[124] Fresh from its victory in China, Gucci opposed the registration of two registrations that Guess had filed under the Madrid Protocol on the basis of prior marks.[125] Gucci was able to adequately prove that the prior Gucci mark had established the requisite reputation, and the Officer noted that the two brand's marks share very similar design features.[126] This led to the conclusion that the degree of similarity would create customer confusion and meet the reasonable doubt standard that the trademark law required.[127] Thus, Gucci was successful in its attempt to block the registration of the Guess marks in the Australia Trademark Office.

C. Bottega Veneta intrecciato pattern

Established in 1966 in Vicenza, Italy, Bottega Veneta was initially formed by two entrepreneurs, Michele Taddei and Renzo Zengiaro. Bottega Veneta ("Venetian Shop" in Italian) was founded as an artisanal leather goods producer, and created the distinctive leather design, *intrecciato*, in the late 1960s.[128] Intrecciato is unique in that it requires super fine leather to get under the needle of the specialized sewing machines that Bottega Veneta made to produce its goods.[129] Even though the leather

[116] Tribunale di Milano, Gucci v. Guess? Inc., No. 6095. [117] *Id.* ¶ 75.

[118] Cour de Cassation [Cass.] [Court of Cassation], Mar. 19, 2015, Decision 367605.

[119] *Id.* ¶ 65. [120] Bercimuelle-Chamot, *supra* note 115. [121] *Id.*

[122] Cour de Cassation, Mar. 19, 2015, Decision 367605.

[123] TFL, *The Gucci v. Guess Case is Not Over Yet*, THE FASHION LAW, June 17, 2013, http://www.thefashionlaw.com/home/gucci-v-guess-isnt-over-yet.

[124] Gucci Amer., *supra* note 109.

[125] Guccio Gucci SpA v. Guess?, Inc., (2015) ATMO 71 (Austl.). [126] *Id.*

[127] *Id.*; Trade Marks Act 1995 (Cth) (Austl.).

[128] Megs Mahoney Dusil, *History of Intrecciato from Bottega Veneta*, PURSE BLOG, Aug. 4, 2009, https://www.purseblog.com/bottega-veneta/history-of-intrecciato-from-bottega-veneta/.

[129] *Id.*

used to create the goods is so fine, the purpose of the manufacturing method is to create a more durable material for leather accessories.[130] Widely associated with Bottega Veneta, this weave design was the starting point for the brand's evolution and is still one of the most recognizable elements of the brand.[131] Over the next decade, Bottega Veneta started to use the tagline "when your own initials are enough," a nod to the company's common abbreviation to just its initials, BV. Indeed, the Bottega Veneta initials seemed to catch on, with the brand becoming a go-to accessory for the jet set crowd by the early 1980s. This clientele included such notable figures as former first lady Jacqueline Kennedy Onassis and Empress Farah Pahlavi.[132] Even prominent artists took notice of the brand, with Andy Warhol making a short film for the brand in 1980.[133]

After this boom for the brand, the mid and late 1980s into the 1990s saw fortunes declining for Bottega Veneta. Encouraged by the now famous name, the company began to emblazon a "BV" logo on its popular bags. By 2001, the company was sold to the Gucci group for $156 million.[134] Gucci's creative director at the time, Tom Ford, made the decision to hire Tomas Maier, a German designer, as the Creative Director for Bottega Veneta within the first year of the acquisition.[135] Maier was given total creative control over all aspects of the brand—from the product and store design to overseeing advertising.[136] With this power, Maier worked to return the brand back to its original identity; he removed the garish visible logos from products, and focused on the signature weave and company's artisanal roots.[137] This move back to the brand's basics was encouraged by Vogue, calling it a form of "stealth wealth." Encouraged by the renewed positive view of the brand, Maier then presented the brand's first ever woman's ready-to-wear line in 2005, followed by a men's line in 2006.[138] The same year the brand branched into men's fashion, Bottega Veneta also released jewelry, furniture, and interior design lines.[139] To sell this new and vastly expanded product line, Bottega Veneta unveiled its first "Maison" in 2013; within a historical building, an 11,000-square foot boutique offering all of the product lines.[140] Currently, the brand has over 250 boutiques in forty-three countries, and Thomas Maier celebrated his fifteenth year as creative director in 2016, the same year as the brand's fifty-year anniversary.[141]

[130] *Id.*

[131] Deloitte, *Global Powers of Luxury Goods 2015*, 12 Deloitte Touche Tohmatsu Limited (DTTL) (2015).

[132] tomas maier, bottega veneta: art of collaboration (2012).

[133] Fashion Model Direcroty, *Bottega Veneta: History and Brand Profile*, http://www.fashionmodeldirectory.com/brands/bottega-veneta/ (2011).

[134] John Colapinto, *Just Have Less: Bottega Veneta's Tomas Maier*, The New Yorker, Jan. 3, 2011.

[135] *Id.*

[136] Nick Compton, *Bottega Veneta: The Dream Weavers' Tale*, The Telegraph, Mar. 1, 2014.

[137] Maier,, *supra* note 132.

[138] Sarah Mower, *Fall 2006 Ready-to-Wear Bottega Veneta*, Vogue, Feb. 20, 2006.

[139] Vogue, *Bottega Veneta*, Vogue, Nov. 24, 2015.

[140] Louisa Zargani, *Bottega Veneta Unveils Maison in Milan*, WWD, Sept. 23, 2013.

[141] Caroline Issa, *Bottega Veneta: 50 Years in the Making, it's all About the Clothes*, The Telegraph, Sept. 28, 2016.

Bottega Veneta currently holds 179 active trademarks from twenty-six Intellectual Property Offices.[142] Their trademarks range from the initials they found to be "enough" in their 1970s slogans, to the intrecciato pattern they claim as unique and distinctive, to the knot adornment present on many of their products, including wallets and perfumes. The weaving pattern, which does not have a logo, the "BV" initials or any other indicator that clearly states that it is a Bottega Veneta creation, has been a particularly troublesome trademark for the brand. According to Bottega Veneta, this very specific weave in itself is distinctive and serves as an indication of the source.[143] But because the weave is easily made and the Bottega Veneta logo is not present, infringers are constantly copying the intrecciato weave. Unsurprisingly, many trademark examiners are hesitant to register such a mark because of its lack of a logo or easily identifiable and unique characteristics.[144] Likewise, the knot symbol has run into some trouble as many examiners also find this hard to distinguish or generic.[145] Still, the U.S. has allowed the registration, although not without some controversy as indicated below.[146] France has also allowed the company to register this mark, as of 2009.[147] This registration was subsequent to the European Union Intellectual Property Office (EUIPO) registration in 2008.[148] The other Bottega Veneta trademark of interest is the knot symbol often adorning the company's products. Currently the following countries or regions recognize the registration: Kuwait, the U.S., EU, Chile, Indonesia, Singapore, the Philippines, and Australia.[149]

However, the perplexities over registering a weaving pattern as trademarks were palpable also in countries that allowed the registration. In the U.S., the mark was registered only after the Trademark Trials and Appeals Board (TTAB) ruled that the brand *could* register a trademark for the specific design, after the examining attorney issued a final rejection on the mark.[150] The rejection was based on the grounds that the mark was functional, and that the design does not function as a trademark because it is solely ornamental.[151] On review, the TTAB reversed both the argument that the mark was utilitarian and that the mark was merely ornamental.[152] The reversal was based on the finding that Bottega Veneta had demonstrated that the design had acquired distinctiveness as a trademark.[153] The win in the TTAB signified an upswing for Bottega Veneta, who has continued to file trademark applications on the weave with renewed vigor. However, the rights granted by the marks are limited to "identical or nearly identical" designs comprising the elements listed in the applicant's

[142] WIPO Global Brand Database, http://www.wipo.int/branddb/en/#.
[143] Lisa Wan, *Weaving a Trademark*, The IP Law Blog, Oct. 28, 2013, https://www.theiplawblog.com/2013/10/articles/copyright-law/weaving-a-trademark/.
[144] *Id.* [145] *Id.*
[146] The mark consists of the woven leather pattern, Registration No. 4527371 (U.S.).
[147] The mark consists of the woven leather pattern, Registration No. 3685850 (France).
[148] The mark consists of the woven leather pattern, Registration No. 006632905 (EUIPO).
[149] The mark consists of a knot, Registration Nos. 147923 (Kuwait), 012537081 (EUIPO), 86170650 (U.S.), D002014000894 (Indonesia), 2013063939 (Myanmar), T1407169D (Singapore), 1201398 (Philippines), 1621397 (Australia), and 1201398 (Chile).
[150] *In re* Bottega Veneta Int'l S.A.R.L., 2013 WL 5655822 (T.T.A.B. 2013).
[151] *Id.* at 1. [152] *Id.* at 2. [153] *Id.* at 13.

mark description. This excludes products that have horizontal weaves (as opposed to the diagonally situated intrecciato weave), products with a weave made out of a material that is not leather (including materials that simulate leather), or with strips that are wider or narrower than the Bottega Veneta-prescribed 8 to 12 millimeters.[154]

Other administrative bodies have also reviewed the Bottega Veneta woven leather and other applications for a three-dimensional trademark. In the EU, the General Court denied registration to the same three-dimensional trademark of the leather weaves in the shape of two bags.[155] The Court upheld two decisions of the Board of Appeals on the matter—one for either of the bag shapes. In this case, the General Court said that the bags did not pass the test for distinctive character. In order to pass, the bags must "deviates significantly ... from the standard or customs of the sector and, therefore, allows the consumer to identify the bag, corresponding to the trademark applied for, as originating from a particular undertaking, and thus to distinguish it from bags produced by other companies."[156] The overall shape of the bags in question was declared only a "simple variation" of those bags available on the market; there was nothing distinctive enough about the product to significantly prove to the Court that it could only originate from the Bottega Veneta brand.[157] While the General Court denied this three-dimensional mark, the Court did provide some guidance for future applications. Specifically, this explanation expanded on one reason that the three-dimensional mark is so hard to obtain: the average consumer is not in the habit of determining the source or origin of a good or product based only on the shape of that product.[158] This is particularly true in situations where there are no logos or brand elements on the product. Curiously the Court did not address the woven element on the surface of the bag.

IV. The Potential Negative Impact of Non-Traditional Trademarks on Creativity and Access to Styles

In this section, I conclude the chapter and attempt to draw some considerations based on the analysis of the examples above. In particular, what are the main takeaways from the analysis of the three examples described above—Louboutin, Gucci, and Bottega Veneta—and to what extent the conclusions that we could draw based on these examples could be applied, or could illustrate, some of the problems that relate, in general, to the protection of NTTMs?

First, it seems that persistence in insisting to register their colors and patterns as marks has paid off for Louboutin, Gucci, and Bottega Veneta in a variety of jurisdictions.[159] The companies were able to secure and still retain, even after some problematic outcomes of litigation proceedings in some countries, a number of trademark registrations.[160] Based on these registrations, the companies—so far

[154] TFL, *Bottega Veneta Granted Trademark for Weave Design*, The Fashion Law, Oct. 10, 2013, http://www.thefashionlaw.com/home/bottega-veneta-granted-trademark-for-weave-design.

[155] Joined Cases T-409 to 410/10, Bottega Veneta Int'l v. OHIM, 2013 EURLex 62010TJ0410.

[156] *Id.* [157] *Id.* ¶ 55. [158] *Id.* [159] *See* discussion *infra* Section III.

[160] *Id.*

primarily Louboutin and Gucci—have strictly enforced their rights and demanded that competitors refrain from using identical and similar colors style and color for shoes soles for Louboutin, similar patterns and stripes for Gucci, and similar pattern for Bottega Veneta.[161] In some instances, these demands have been met with resistance, and the companies had to face litigation. In some cases, this litigation concluded unsuccessfully. However, in other cases, the litigation proceedings concluded successfully for the companies. Moreover, as I highlighted in Section III, the litigation proceedings at issue most likely represent just a fraction of the actual claims that these companies may have made through demand and cease-and-desist letters to other competitors and third parties, which may have immediately accepted to cease to produce any products that looked similar, or may have entered into a specific transaction and settlement agreement after a short time. As the data related to the number of letters sent by these (or any other) companies are not publicly available, and the terms of any out-of-court proceedings remain confidential, it is thus not possible to assess the actual impact and effect that the NTTMs at issue may have on market competition and, in general, competitors' access to similar style and product features.

This result is certainly problematic. As several of the chapters in this volume have highlighted, protecting and granting exclusive rights on NTTMs ultimately results in preventing access to competitors and third parties to relevant and aesthetically appealing designs and product features. Even though these product features have been first created by the companies that have applied to register them as trademarks, these features are again product designs or contribute to the style and appearance of the overall products, and often they may represent the whole product at issue. In other words, these features are far more than indicators of commercial origin in the traditional trademark sense, and their signaling function far extends from the traditional trademark signaling function of commercial original and product quality. Accordingly, by granting rights that allow trademark owners to prevent access to these features to anyone else besides themselves directly translates in securing a potentially perpetual monopoly on styles and aesthetic elements that appeal to creators and consumers.

However, the potential damage to creativity and product innovation is not limited to competitors. It also affects the companies that own these trademark registrations, by paradoxically "trapping" them in having to use their NTTMs repeatedly as part of their products, lest they could be accused of using their marks inconsistently and in manners that could affect the distinctiveness of the marks. In particular, all the companies in the examples above (and many other companies in the fashion industry and other industries) have certainly built their image—past, present, and to a large extent, their future image—on the characteristic shapes, patterns, and colors that they have fought hard to register as trademarks and later enforce against as many "copiers" as possible.[162] For example, a trip to any Louboutin store worldwide, or a search online, reflects the essential value of the red soles for the designer. Every single

[161] *Id.*

[162] *See* discussion *infra* Section III.

pair of shoes in these stores, be they shoes for woman or man, now uses the famed red soles. A Louboutin shoe would not be a Louboutin without the red sole. A trip to any Gucci store, reading a Gucci catalogue, or a visit to the online retailers and outlets selling Gucci products, would prove exactly the same point for Gucci. The typical pattern and stripes is omnipresent in almost the totality of Gucci products, again projecting the message that a Gucci product would not be a Gucci product without the typical monogrammed patterns (sometimes used as a full product trade dress and other times used more discretely) and stripe. Last but not least, every single Bottega Veneta product comes as an intrecciato pattern product. Thus, while the company has a large line of product and accessories in different colors, the pattern used for these products is always the intrecciato pattern.

Is this a positive result for these companies and the creativity of these designers, and the fashion industry at large, in the long term? Clearly, these companies have no choice and have to repeat their NTTMs as part of their design if they want to continue to secure trademark protection. At this time, these companies may be eager to do so, as those designs may drive more consumers to them based on the recognition of the designs and the status that wearing these (exclusive and not possible to (legally) copy) designs may mean for the purchasers and those seeing the purchasers wearing the products after the sale. Moreover, this repetition and acquired goodwill in those NTTMs continue to drive competitors to copy the desired aesthetic elements, which in turn triggers trademark enforcement on the part of these companies, and to "sanctify" the protected elements as the desirable (but untouchable) styles of the industry. Yet, would the designers of these companies like to change because consumers have become bored with the style, or simply because they would like to follow a different type of design? At this time, the need of this constant repetition of the same colors, patterns, and style seem to severely limits designers' creativity as every shoe, bag, and any other product designed by these companies would need to carry the characteristic colored sole or patterns and stripes. Moreover, the temptation of continuing to extract value from the same shapes, colors, and patterns protected with NTTMs has the potential to also decrease investments in product quality, at least in the short term.

In other words, it seems clear that protecting NTTMs does not incentivize the creative process. In particular, any change would run against possible value extraction in the immediate term, and more relevantly would jeopardize trademark protection. As a result, protecting NTTMs seems to chill creativity and innovation for the companies that own these marks, as they find themselves almost obliged to continue repeating products with the same colors and patterns as part of their collections. Similarly, protecting NTTMs may have a very negative effect in the investment dedicated to improving product quality in product development in the long term, as extracting value through the marks becomes more profitable than investing in high product quality. These are, in my view, highly problematic results for the fashion industry, and for any industry as the trend of applying for registrations for NTTMs is common in many industries today. Even though company executives may be pleased with the extra value that NTTMs bring to their companies and profits, and (company) lawyers may be proud of having managed to secure trademark rights in NTTMs, designers may ultimately be severely frustrated in pursuing new designs and experimenting with new collections. Likewise, companies may suffer in the long term for lack of creativity and product quality investment. At the same time, as the litigations analyzed in Section IV demonstrate, competitors are once again driven toward creating copies, and often lower quality replicas, of the original designer products, which in turn flood the market with the same or similar designs over and over, to the detriment of competing creativity and creativity in general for our society. In essence, beyond representing a challenge for competition, NTTMs also do not benefit their owners and the quality of their products and design in the long term, and thus their protection should be reconsidered and severely limited.

V. Conclusion

The examples described in this chapter reinforce my previous critique regarding NTTMs, and illustrate the negative impact that the protection of these marks may have on market competition. In particular, these examples illustrate the potential chilling effect that NTTMs can have on innovation and creativity in product design and product development in the fashion industry and, in general, creative industries. As I described in this chapter, protecting NNTMs supports a system of intellectual property protection that promotes standardization and repetition, as repetition is necessary to acquire consumer recognition and, in turn, trademark distinctiveness—one of the conditions to secure protection as a mark. The use, over and over, by Louboutin, Gucci, and Bottega Veneta of their successful product designs—red lacquered soles, monogrammed patterns and stripes, and intrecciato leather patterns—for all their products demonstrates this phenomenon of repetition and product consistency to obtain trademark protection thereof. Certainly, these product features are highly valuable, and it is understandable that these businesses desire to protect them on an exclusive basis and for unlimited time. However, no matter how distinctive, original, and innovative, these product features were never meant to be protected as marks because they are integral product parts or the product per se. Instead, as other chapters in this volume have explained as length, these product features are, and should be protected, under the domain of industrial design or design patents. Ultimately, as the examples in this chapter illustrate, protecting NTTMs induces businesses to standardize instead of creating new designs. In turn, this can lead to less investment in product quality, as NTTMs allow businesses to extract value from their marks on an exclusive and potentially perpetual basis. However, neither of these effects are desirable for the fashion industry, or for any industry, and should be countered by reducing or prohibiting the protection of product designs and aesthetic features as NTTMs.

16

A Clash of Culture and Commerce

Non-Traditional Marks and the Impediment of Cyclic Cultural Innovation

Martin Senftleben

I. Introduction

In intellectual property law, overlaps of exclusive rights that stem from different protection regimes raise difficult questions. In *Dastar v. Twentieth Century Fox*, the United States (U.S.) Supreme Court held that overlaps between trademark and copyright or patent protection can have a corrosive effect on the "carefully crafted bargain" under which, once the patent or copyright monopoly has expired, the public may use the invention or work at will.[1] The Court of Justice of the European Union (CJEU) expressed similar concerns in *Hauck v. Stokke*, where it explained that the functionality doctrine in trademark law served the purpose of preventing the exclusive and permanent right that a trademark confers "from serving to extend indefinitely the life of other rights which the [European Union (EU)] legislature has sought to make subject to limited periods."[2]

Despite the awareness of the potential corrosive effect of protection overlaps on both sides of the Atlantic, the intellectual property system fails to draw a clear boundary line between the subject matter of copyright and trademark protection. Instead, character merchandising leads to cumulative copyright and trademark protection of contemporary cultural symbols (Mickey Mouse).[3] In principle, it is also possible to acquire trademark rights to cultural heritage symbols once distinctive character is acquired through use in trade (Mona Lisa).[4] The situation differs

[1] Dastar Corp. v. Twentieth Century Fox Film Corp., 539 U.S. 23, 33–34 (2003).

[2] Case C-205/13, Hauck GmbH & Co. KG v. Stokke A/S, ¶¶ 19–20 (CJEU Sept. 18, 2014).

[3] *Cf.* Irene Calboli, *Overlapping Trademark and Copyright Protection: A Call for Concern and Action*, 2014 Ill. L. Rev. Slip Opinions 25, 29–30 (2014). Examples can easily be found in trademark registers. *See, e.g., Mickey Mouse*, WIPO: ROMARIN, http://www.wipo.int/romarin/result.xhtml (International Registration No. 296478); *Superman*, DPMA REG., https://register.dpma.de/DPMAregister/marke/register/DD643100/DE (German Registration DD643100); *Miffy*, BENELUX OFF. FOR INTELL. PROP., https://register.boip.int/bmbonline/intro/show.do (Benelux Registration No. 0653451).

[4] For example, *see* CJEU, Case C-488/16 P, Bundesverband Souvenir—Geschenke—Ehrenpreise v. EUIPO (CJEU Jan. 9, 2017) (concerning "Neuschwanstein" as an indication of Neuschwanstein

markedly from the status quo reached in respect of patent–trademark overlaps. At the intersection of these two protection regimes, the doctrine of technical functionality prevents the cumulation of exclusive rights.[5] Similarly, the doctrine of aesthetic functionality can be employed to arrive at a far-reaching separation of trademark and industrial design protection.[6]

In respect to the copyright–trademark interface, by contrast, the recognition of non-traditional trademarks even broadens the area of overlap and aggravates the problems arising from cumulative protection.[7] Three-dimensional objects may

Castle), which evolved from an appeal against the confirmation of trademark rights in the General Court of the European Union, Case T-167/15, Bundesverband Souvenir—Geschenke—Ehrenpreise v. EUIPO (July 5, 2016) (Neuschwanstein); Cases 2013/7132 and 2013/7133, Anne Frank Found. v. Benelux Office for Intell. Prop. (Court of Appeals of Brussels Oct. 3, 2013) (concerning the book titles "The Diary of Anne Frank" and "The Secret Annex") and Case R 2401/2014-4, Anne Frank Fonds, ¶¶ 32–36 (OHIM App. Bd. Aug. 31, 2015) (granting trademark rights to the French indication "Le Journal d'Anne Frank"); Bundesgerichtshof [BGH] [Federal Court of Justice] Apr. 24, 2008, Case I ZB 21/06, Marlene-Dietrich-Bildnis (Ger.) (concerning a portrait photograph of the actress) [hereinafter *Marlene Dietrich*]; Bundespatentgericht [BPatG] [Federal Patent Court] Nov. 25, 1997, 1998 GEWERBLICHER RECHTSSCHUTZ UND URHEBERRECHT [GRUR] 1022, Case 24 W (pat) 188/96, Mona Lisa (Ger.) (concerning the Mona Lisa painting) [hereinafter *Mona Lisa*]. However, see also EFTA Court, Case E-5/16, Municipality of Oslo (EFTA Apr. 6, 2017) [hereinafter Case E-5/16, *Vigeland Judgment*], which seems to pave the way for a more restrictive approach based on public order and morality.

For case comments, *see*: Martin Senftleben, Vigeland *and the Status of Cultural Concerns in Trade Mark Law—The EFTA Court Develops More Effective Tools for the Preservation of the Public Domain*, 48 INT'L REV. OF INTELL. PROP. & COMPETITION L. 683 (2017); Martin Senftleben, *Der kulturelle Imperativ des Urheberrechts*, *in* KUNST IM MARKT—KUNST IM RECHT 75, 102–04 (Matthias Weller et al. eds., 2010); Katjia Assaf, *Der Markenschutz und seine kulturelle Bedeutung: Ein Vergleich des deutschen mit dem US-amerikanischen Recht*, 1 GRUR: INTERNATIONALER TEIL 5 (2009); Ansgar Ohly, *Von einem Indianerhäuptling, einer Himmelsscheibe, einer Jeans und dem Lächeln der Mona Lisa: Überlegungen zum Verhältnis zwischen Urheber- und Kennzeichenrecht*, *in* GRUNDLAGEN UND GRUNDFRAGEN DES GEISTIGEN EIGENTUMS, FESTGABE FÜR DIETHELM KLIPPEL ZUM 65. GEBURTSTAG 203 (Louis Pahlow & Jens Eisfeld eds., 2008); Friedrich Klinkert & Florian Schwab, *Markenrechtlicher Raubbau an gemeinfreien Werken—ein richtungsweisendes Machtwort durch den Mona Lisa-Beschluss des Bundespatentgerichts?*, 12 GRUR 1067 (1999); Wilhelm Nordemann, *Mona Lisa als Marke*, *in* WETTBEWERB IN RECHT UND PRAXIS 389 (1997).

[5] Case C-299/99, Koninklijke Philips Electronics NV v. Remington Consumer Prods. Ltd., ¶ 82 (CJEU June 18, 2002).

[6] *See generally Hauck, supra* note 2. This is not to say that the doctrine of aesthetic functionality has not been criticized. *See, e.g.*, Graeme B. Dinwoodie, *The Death of Ontology: A Teleological Approach to Trademark Law*, 84 IOWA L. REV. 611, 685–91 (1999); Annette Kur, *Too Pretty to Protect? Trade Mark Law and the Enigma of Aesthetic Functionality* 6–12 (Max Planck Inst. for Intellectual Prop. & Competition Law, Paper No. 11-16, 2011) [hereinafter Kur, *Enigma of Aesthetic Functionality*]. The central point here is, however, that in practice, the application of the functionality doctrine can have the effect of separating the protection regimes to a considerable extent.

[7] With regard to the trend of recognizing more and more non-traditional types of marks in the EU, see Ivo Lewalter & Paul T. Schrader, *Die Fühlmarke*, 6 GRUR 476 (2005); Felix Hauck, *Aktuelle Entwicklungen bei der Eintragung von Farbmarken*, 5 GRUR 363 (2005); Annette Kur, *Alles oder Nichts im Formmarkenschutz?*, 9 GRUR: INTERNATIONAL TEIL 755 (2004); Adrien Bouvel, *Qu'importe le flacon . . . Le droit des marques malmené par les emballages*, 13 PROPRIÉTÉS INTELLECTUELLES 863 (2004); Ruth Arnet, *Markenschutz für Formen*, 11 SIC! 829 (2004); Jochen Pagenberg, *Trade Dress and the Three-Dimensional Mark: The Neglected Children of Trademark Law?*, 35 INT'L REV. OF INTELL. PROP. & COMPETITION L. 831 (2004); Markus Bölling, *Der EuGH und die abstrakte Farbmarke: Von der bewussten Entwertung einer Markenform*, *in* MARKENRECHT 384 (2004); Senta Bingener, *Das Wesen der Positionsmarke oder Wo die Positionsmarke hingehört*, *in* MARKENRECHT 377 (2004); Alison Firth, Ellen

serve as shape marks. A short melody may constitute a sound mark.[8] A computer animation may qualify as a motion mark. Even single colors—indispensable raw material of artistic creativity—are registrable.[9] Given this broad range of signs qualifying as trademarks, new areas of double protection emerge and affect traditional work categories, in particular sculpture and plastic art, musical compositions, and audiovisual creations.

The outlined problem of copyright–trademark overlaps is not merely of a theoretical nature. The friction between copyright and trademark policies clearly comes to the fore in case law that evolved from attempts to register non-traditional marks with cultural significance. Relevant decisions shed light on the tension between the limited term of copyright protection and the trademark rule of indefinitely renewable rights: while copyright law aims at the continuous enrichment of the public domain, the grant of trademark rights entails the risk of an undesirable re-appropriation of public domain material. The famous *Shield Mark* decision of the CJEU, for example, concerned the registration of the first nine notes of Beethoven's piano piece "Für Elise" as a sound mark.[10] Discussing this registration initiative, Advocate General Ruiz-Járabo Colomer explicitly addressed the public domain dimension of the case. He stated that it was difficult to accept

> that a creation of the mind, which forms part of the universal cultural heritage, should be appropriated indefinitely by a person to be used on the market in order to distinguish the goods he produces or the services he provides with an exclusivity which not even its author's estate enjoys.[11]

In the *Vigeland* case,[12] the Court of Justice of the European Free Trade Association States (EFTA Court)[13] was called upon to assess an attempt to register several sculptures made by Gustav Vigeland—one of the most eminent Norwegian sculptors—as shape marks. The reason for the initiative to acquire trademark rights was the expiry of the term of copyright protection.[14] The municipality of Oslo sought to secure exclusive trademark rights even though Vigeland's creations had entered the public domain.[15] Among other works, the trademark application concerned Vigeland's "Monolith" (*Monolitten*) and "Angry Boy" (*Sinnataggen*)—popular works that feature prominently in the Vigeland Installation in the centre of Oslo's Frogner Park.

Gredley, & Spyros M. Maniatis, *Shapes as Trade Marks: Public Policy, Functional Considerations and Consumer Perception*, 23 European Intell. Prop. Rev. 86 (2001).

8 Case C-283/01, Shield Mark BV v. Joost Kist (CJEU Nov. 27, 2003).

9 Case C-104/01, Libertel Groep BV v. Benelux-Merkenbureau (CJEU May 6, 2003).

10 *Vigeland Judgment, supra* note 4.

11 *Shield Mark, supra* note 8, ¶ 52 (Opinion of Advocate General Ruiz-Járabo Colomer delivered on Apr. 3, 2003).

12 *Vigeland Judgment, supra* note 4.

13 The EFTA Court is the Supreme Court in matters concerning the interpretation of the Agreement on the European Economic Area with regard to the EFTA States Iceland, Liechtenstein, and Norway. *See* EFTA Court, http://www.eftacourt.int/ (last visited Nov. 18, 2017).

14 *Vigeland Judgment, supra* note 4 ¶ 20. Gustav Vigeland died on Mar. 12, 1943.

15 Case E-5/16, Municipality of Oslo, ¶¶ 36–37 (Report for the Hearing, Judge-Rapporteur Baudenbacher, delivered on October 5, 2016) [hereinafter *Vigeland Report*].

Discussing this registration attempt, the EFTA Court could not rule out that the grant of trademark rights may lead to a conflict with public policy:

> An artwork may be refused registration [because of a conflict with public policy], for example, under the circumstances that its registration is regarded as a genuine and serious threat to certain fundamental values or where the need to safeguard the public domain, itself, is considered a fundamental interest of society.[16]

Non-traditional marks with cultural significance can thus give rise to concerns about an encroachment of trademark rights upon the public domain of cultural expressions. Nonetheless, concerns about an impediment of literary and artistic creativity do not always lead to deference to cultural policies in court decisions and literature statements.

By contrast, an uncritical attitude vis-à-vis cumulative copyright and trademark protection seems to prevail, as outlined in Section II. Given the fundamental importance of a rich and robust public domain as a reservoir for cultural follow-on innovation, this uncritical approach is questionable. In particular, it is wrong to assume that copyright–trademark overlaps are less problematic than patent–trademark overlaps. Similar to technical solutions, literary and artistic works are not substitutable in the context of innovation processes leading to derivative creations. For an artist who wants to base her own work on a specific pre-existing creation, it makes a difference whether the desired source for a derivative work is in the public domain or on the trademark register. Once trademark rights are granted, the use of cultural public domain material is no longer as free as it was before. As long as public domain material remains unencumbered with intellectual property rights, the risk of a lawsuit arising from unauthorized use can be excluded from the outset. With the registration of cultural signs as trademarks, this absolute freedom is sacrificed in favor of a scenario in which trademark rights can serve as a basis for an infringement action, as addressed in Section III. The climate change with regard to the reuse and remix of cultural material is considerable. Artists are exposed to the risk of an infringement action. Moreover, the attachment of commercial marketing messages may blur a sign's genuine cultural meaning and devaluate it for purposes of cultural follow-on innovation. These concerns are the focus of Sections IV and V. A proposal for more robust grounds for refusal that allow the categorical exclusion of signs with cultural significance from trademark protection follows in Sections VI and VII.

II. Traditional Acceptance of Copyright–Trademark Overlaps

Despite the friction between divergent policies that may arise from cumulative copyright and trademark protection, a rather uncritical acceptance of overlaps seems to prevail in literature and court decisions. The possibility of combining copyright and trademark protection is often mentioned without much commentary on potential risks for cultural follow-on innovation, or accepted on the ground that trademark

[16] *Id.* ¶ 96.

rights do not offer protection for a cultural creation as such, but only for certain functions which the cultural creation fulfills as a distinctive sign in respect of goods and services to which it is attached.[17] Arguing in favor of an entitlement of rights owners to accumulate copyright and trademark protection, Tobias Cohen Jehoram, Constant van Nispen, and Tony Huydecoper posit that

> [i]n principle, there is no objection against cumulation or concurrence of trademark rights and copyrights and the benefits of the two protection regimes exist independently for the two rights. The proprietor of these rights satisfied all requirements stipulated by the different laws, so that there is no reason to limit the protection under one of the legal regimes for the sole reason that another legal protection exists.[18]

Besides this maximalist view, which readily accepts the cumulation of rights as a corollary of formal eligibility for protection under copyright and trademark law, more nuanced approaches have evolved in the debate. Annette Kur pointed out that the cumulation of different intellectual property rights was only unproblematic as long as the individual protection regimes involved were balanced in the sense that the prerequisites for obtaining protection were appropriately aligned with the contents and limits of exclusive rights.[19] Cumulation thus required a thorough scrutiny in the light of the checks and balances offered by the protection regimes involved. If these checks and balances were sufficient to prevent excessive protection that would obstruct competition, the cumulation of copyright and trademark rights could be deemed acceptable.[20] Otherwise, however, overlapping protection raised the problem of "asymmetric convergence" and required appropriate countermeasures.[21]

Turning to the spectrum of critical statements, the position taken by Feer Verkade is of particular interest. He expressed concerns about the corrosive effect of overlapping protection on the individual balance and structure of copyright and trademark law. Instead of affording rights owners the opportunity to always enjoy the "best of both worlds," they should be bound to accept the "one world" offered by each individual law.[22] Hence, potentially indefinite trademark protection should not be available as a vehicle to undermine the limited term of copyright protection, and the absence of formalities in copyright law should not allow the circumvention of the registration requirement in (Benelux) trademark law.[23] Seeking to prevent one protection regime from blurring the conceptual contours of the other, Verkade

[17] Malte Stieper, *Geistiges Eigentum an Kulturgütern: Möglichkeiten und Grenzen der Remonopolisierung gemeinfreier Werke*, 11 GRUR 1083, 1090–91 (2012); Alexander Peukert, *Die Gemeinfreiheit: Begriff, Funktion, Dogmatik*, 111–13 (2012), https://ssrn.com/abstract=2627191.

[18] TOBIAS COHEN JEHORAM, CONSTANT VAN NISPEN & TONY HUYDECOPER, EUROPEAN TRADEMARK LAW 556 (2010).

[19] Annette Kur, *Funktionswandel von Schutzrechten: Ursachen und Konsequenzen der inhaltlichen Annäherung und Überlagerung von Schutzrechtstypen*, *in* GEISTIGES EIGENTUM IM DIENST DER INNOVATION 23, 45, 50 (Gerard Schricker, Thomas Dreier, & Annette Kur eds., 2001) [hereinafter Kur, *Functional Change of IP Rights*]. *Cf.* Kur, *Enigma of Aesthetic Functionality, supra* note 6, at 9.

[20] Kur, *Functional Change of IP Rights, supra* note 19, at 44.

[21] *Id.* at 42–44.

[22] D.W. Feer Verkade, *The Cumulative Effect of Copyright Law and Trademark Law: Which Takes Precedence?*, *in* INTELLECTUAL PROPERTY AND INFORMATION LAW: ESSAYS IN HONOUR OF HERMAN COHEN JEHORAM 69, 72 (Jan J.C. Kabel & Gerard J.H.M. Mom eds., 1998).

[23] *Id.*

proposes to determine on a case-by-case basis whether the trademark or copyright aspect takes precedence.[24]

The critical comments on trademark–copyright overlaps, finally, comprise proposals seeking to eliminate cumulative copyright and trademark protection for literary and artistic works altogether. A categorical rejection of the cumulation of rights can result from a strong preference for freedom of competition based on the public interest in the optimal use of intellectual resources and the encouragement of follow-on innovation after the expiry of the limited term of copyright protection.[25] If the constant enrichment and cultivation of the public domain is qualified as an element of the *ordre public*, an amalgam of copyright and trademark rights that allows the continuation of trademark protection after copyright expiry can also be deemed impermissible because it withholds literary and artistic works from the public domain and causes a conflict with public order and morality for this reason.[26]

In practice, however, judges seem reluctant to adopt positions leading to the separation of copyright and trademark protection.[27] Even nuanced approaches, such as Verkade's proposal to determine the predominant protection aspect case-by-case, have not made their way into court decisions. Instead, judges seem to favor the rather uncritical attitude vis-à-vis cumulative copyright and trademark protection that comes to the fore in many literature statements. In *Danjaq LLC v. OHIM* ("*Mission Productions*"), the General Court of the European Union (GCEU) clearly followed this uncritical approach.[28] The case concerned an opposition brought by Danjaq against Mission Production's attempt to register the sign "Dr. No"—the title of the first James Bond film and the name of James Bond's antagonist—as a trademark. Commenting on the possibility of copyright and trademark overlaps in this context, the GCEU pointed out that

> [t]he same sign may be protected as an original creative work by copyright and as an indicator of commercial origin by trade mark law. It is therefore a matter of different exclusive rights based on distinct qualities, that is to say the original nature of a creation, on the one hand, and the ability of a sign to distinguish the commercial origin of the goods and services, on the other.[29]

Hence, the GCEU readily accepted the protection overlap on the ground that trademark rights do not offer protection for a cultural creation as such, but only for certain functions which the cultural creation fulfills as a distinctive sign in respect of

[24] *Id.* at 73.

[25] BENJAMIN RAUE, NACHAHMUNGSFREIHEIT NACH ABLAUF DES IMMATERIALGÜTERRECHTSSCHUTZES? 120–22, 199–201 (2010).

[26] Senftleben, Vigeland *and the Status of Cultural Concerns in Trade Mark Law*, *supra* note 4, at 716–17; CASPAR VAN WOENSEL, MERK, GOD EN VERBOD 412–13 (2007); Klinkert & Schwab, *supra* note 4, at 1073; Wilhelm Nordemann, *Mona Lisa als Marke*, *in* WETTBEWERB IN RECHT UND PRAXIS 389, 391 (1997); Ralph Osenberg, *Markenschutz für urheberrechtlich gemeinfreie Werkteile*, 2 GRUR 101, 102–03 (1996).

[27] *Cf.* Calboli, *supra* note 3, at 28–30.

[28] Case T-435/05, Danjaq LLC v. OHIM, ¶ 26 (GCEU June 30, 2009) [hereinafter *Mission Productions*].

[29] *Id.*

goods and services to which it is attached.[30] In this vein, the GCEU stated that "only signs which develop characteristic trade mark functions"[31] were eligible for trademark protection. It rejected trademark rights to "Dr. No" because the sign would be perceived as a mere descriptive reference to the film and not as an identifier of commercial source.[32] Nonetheless, the decision confirms the possibility of combining copyright and trademark protection in cases where a literary or artistic work also functions as a distinctive sign.

Similar considerations play a role in national court decisions. The Dutch Supreme Court, for instance, traditionally permits the cumulative assertion of copyright and trademark claims.[33] In recent decisions, the Court added that a holder of rights under trademark and copyright law could invoke both rights simultaneously only if he had a distinct interest in the protection following from each individual right.[34] However, this additional condition need not constitute a substantial hurdle. If the cumulation of rights is accepted on the ground that copyright protects a cultural creation as such, whereas trademark law protects specific trademark functions, it is easy to justify the assertion of trademark rights by pointing to the interest in preserving the trademark features of the intellectual creation concerned.[35] The Dutch Supreme Court relied on similar considerations to explain the acceptance of combined copyright and trademark claims.[36]

The result is a rather low, if not negligible, threshold for the cumulation of copyright and trademark protection. If the difference between the purpose and configuration of the two protection regimes is already sufficient to justify overlapping rights, there seems to be no substantial obstacle to the assertion of cumulative protection in case of subject matter capable of constituting both an original work and a trademark. In any case, courts do not seem hesitant to hear claims based on cumulative copyright and trademark protection. Instead, they favor elastic tests of eligibility for a combined claim, such as the test of "different exclusive rights based on distinct qualities" used by the GCEU or the "distinct interest in protection" requirement introduced by the Dutch Supreme Court.

III. Corrosive Effect on Cultural Follow-On Innovation

As pointed out above, the acceptance of copyright–trademark overlaps is highly problematic when it comes to signs with cultural significance. Pierre Bourdieu's

[30] Stieper, *supra* note 17, at 1090–91; Peukert, *supra* note 17, at 111–13.

[31] *Mission Productions, supra* note 28 ¶ 26. [32] *Id.* ¶¶ 25–28.

[33] HR Apr. 16, 1999, NJ 1999, 697 m.nt. Eerste Kamer, 9098 (R97/163HR) (Bigott-Batco/Doucal), ¶ 3.9 (Neth.). *Cf.* COHEN JEHORAM, VAN NISPEN, & HUYDECOPER, *supra* note 18, at 556.

[34] Case LJN AV3384, Benetton Grp. SpA v. G-Star Int'l BV, ¶ 3.11 (Dutch Supreme Court Sept. 8, 2006). *Cf.* R.A.M. Quanjel-Schreurs, *Enkele procesrechtelijke aspecten van cumulatie van auteurs- en merkenrecht: Naar aanleiding van het Benetton/G-Star-arrest*, AUTEURS-, MEDIA- & INFORMATIERECHT, May 1, 2007, at 76, 80–83.

[35] Stieper, *supra* note 17, at 1090–91; Peukert, *supra* note 17, at 111–13.

[36] *Benetton, supra* note 34, ¶ 3.11.

sociological analysis of the field of literary and artistic production provides a useful theoretical framework in this context. His analysis of cyclic innovation processes in the artistic domain leads to the insight that the room for possible new positions in the creation of art—the range of options available for the establishment of a new avant-garde—depends on the positions that have already been taken by previous artists.[37] For a new generation of artists to challenge the leading avant-garde, it must detect the structural gaps within the texture of already known aesthetic positions. It must formulate an alternative artistic position in the light of the weaknesses and contradictions of the present state of the art.[38] The positions that have already been taken in the literary and artistic field thus constitute potential lines of development and potential starting points for new literary and artistic productions.

This description of cyclic innovation in the artistic domain makes it possible to draw a parallel between copyright and patent law. Evidently, innovation in the field of technology is also the result of the use of pre-existing technical solutions for the purpose of developing new know-how. With regard to the regulation of overlaps with trademark protection, this functional parallel has important repercussions: the fact that both copyright and patent law regulate processes of cyclic innovation may imply that the same effort must be made to safeguard the respective cyclic innovation processes when it comes to overlaps with indefinitely renewable trademark rights. In this vein, the U.S. Supreme Court emphasized in *Dastar* that it was necessary to shield the quid pro quo underlying both—copyright and patent law—from the corrosive effect of protection regimes with potentially indefinite rights:

> The rights of a patentee or copyright holder are part of a "carefully crafted bargain," under which, once the patent or copyright monopoly has expired, the public may use the invention or work at will and without attribution. Thus, in construing the Lanham Act, we have been "careful to caution against misuse or over-extension" of trademark and related protections into areas traditionally occupied by patent or copyright.[39]

However, the argument of a need to safeguard the cultural inspiration cycle (copyright law) to the same extent as the technical innovation cycle (patent law) rests on the assumption that the respective processes of cyclic innovation are vulnerable to a comparable degree. This raises the question whether coexisting trademark protection is likely to harm the cyclic evolution of new cultural productions to the same extent as it would harm the cyclic evolution of new technical knowledge.

The answer to this question seems to be influenced by general perceptions of the domain of technology on the one hand, and the domain of culture on the other. While technical knowledge is seen as the result of exact, objective science, cultural productions are often portrayed as the result of subjective, intuitive imagination.[40] This fundamental difference—the *objective* domain of technology and the *subjective*

[37] PIERRE BOURDIEU, DIE REGELN DER KUNST: GENESE UND STRUKTUR DES LITERARISCHEN FELDES 370 (1999).

[38] *Id.* at 372.

[39] *Dastar Corp.*, *supra* note 1, 33–34 (2003) (internal citations omitted).

[40] ANTOON A. QUAEDVLIEG, AUTEURSRECHT OP TECHNIEK: DE AUTEURSRECHTELIJKE BESCHERMING VAN HET TECHNISCH ASPECT VAN INDUSTRIËLE VORMGEVING EN COMPUTERPROGRAMMATUUR 21–22 (1987).

domain of culture—may be understood to justify the further assumption that there is also a fundamental difference with regard to the substitutability of intellectual creations stemming from these distinct domains. Whereas it is often readily accepted that a technical problem can only be solved by applying one particular patent, the same assumption may appear less plausible when it comes to literary and artistic works. If a particular literary or artistic work is not available even though copyright protection has already expired, the view may be held that it can easily be replaced with a comparable work that also fits in the envisaged cultural production.

The exact, objective nature of technical know-how and the subjective, imaginative nature of artworks may thus predetermine our assessment of the need to ensure the availability of intellectual resources in the respective domains of technology and culture when it comes to overlaps with trademark law: whereas technical knowledge may be regarded as non-substitutable to an extent that justifies strong measures to keep it freely available for technical follow-on innovation, the existence of alternatives for a literary or artistic work is often readily assumed without considering a potential corrosive effect on the evolution of new cultural productions. In the context of assessing the vulnerability of processes of technical and cultural innovation, this may lead to the conclusion that technical innovation will inevitably be frustrated if a particular technical solution is not available because of coexisting trademark protection. Cultural innovation, by contrast, may be deemed unaffected even if a particular work is not available as a result of trademark protection.

This conclusion, however, is false. According to Bourdieu, it is naïve to assume substitutability of literary and artistic works in the context of the production of new works. As explained, his analysis shows that the room for the evolution of new directions in the creation of art depends on the range of options that is available in the light of the positions that have already been taken by previous artists.[41] For an artist seeking to formulate a new artistic position in the light of an aesthetic position reflected in a particular pre-existing work, the conditions of use surrounding this pre-existing work are crucial. If the work is not available as a basis for a derivative work, the envisaged cultural innovation step will simply not take place. In other words, every pre-existing aesthetic position that is not freely available for cultural follow-on innovation reduces the range of options that later generations of artists have at their disposal to find and formulate new aesthetic positions. When placed in the context of the rule of indefinitely renewable trademark rights, it can thus be said that every literary and artistic work that does not enter the public domain after the expiry of copyright protection reduces the resources that are readily available for cultural follow-on innovation.

The dilemma arising from copyright–trademark overlaps is thus not much different from the scenario in the field of technology. The objectivity of the technological domain on the one hand, and the subjectivity of the cultural domain on the other, does not imply that the cultural innovation cycle is less vulnerable than the technical innovation cycle. Nor does it imply that literary and artistic works are

[41] BOURDIEU, *supra* note 37, at 370.

substitutable to a larger extent. By contrast, it simply means that the assessment of non-substitutability is objective in the case of technical solutions, whereas it is subjective in the case of literary and artistic works. For determining whether a given technical solution is unique, pioneering, and non-substitutable, an objective assessment can be made. Persons skilled in the respective field of technology may reach agreement on non-substitutability on the basis of objective criteria. This, however, is fundamentally different in the field of culture. As the creation of new literary and artistic works is subjective, the assessment of pre-existing "masterpieces" that are indispensable (and thus non-substitutable) for follow-on creativity is subjective as well. Every artist will make her own, subjective assessment of pre-existing aesthetic positions and identify those that are relevant to her own creativity on the basis of this subjective assessment.

In contrast to specialists in a particular field of technology who can rely on objective assessment criteria, artists specializing in a particular field of art do not have shared objective criteria at their disposal because of the subjectivity of the domain of culture and creativity. Consequently, artists are unlikely to generally agree on the non-substitutability of a given literary and artistic work. A cultural expression that may be non-substitutable for one artist may appear unimportant and substitutable for another.

In terms of vulnerability of innovation processes in the domains of culture and technology, this insight does not permit the conclusion that cultural follow-on innovation need not be shielded from potential corrosive effects of trademark protection to the same extent as technical follow-on innovation. By contrast, even broader measures are necessary to safeguard cultural follow-on innovation because it is not foreseeable which aesthetic positions reflected in a literary or artistic work will be non-substitutable from the perspective of later generations of artists. As it is possible to identify unique, non-substitutable technical solutions on the basis of objective criteria, efforts to inhibit protection overlaps from interfering with technical follow-on innovation, at least theoretically, could be confined to these unique, non-substitutable solutions.[42] However, the subjectivity of the decision on relevant source materials in the field of cultural productions makes it impossible to reach general agreement on unique, non-substitutable cultural expressions. Efforts to prevent protection overlaps from interfering with cultural follow-on innovation, thus, *cannot* be confined to specific literary and artistic works. In principle, each aesthetic position may become indispensable for the creation of a new work. Therefore, it is wrong to assume that the cultural innovation cycle is less vulnerable than the technical innovation cycle when it comes to protection overlaps that may restrict the intellectual resources available for follow-on creativity. As technical solutions, literary and artistic works are non-substitutable.

[42] *But see* QUAEDVLIEG, *supra* note 40, at 40–45 (describing the profound problems arising from this approach focusing on non-substitutability in a strict sense).

IV. Reliance on Checks and Balances in Trademark Law

From the perspective of cultural innovation, cumulative copyright and trademark protection is thus undesirable and the acceptance of non-traditional marks is particularly problematic because it broadens the potential corrosive effect of trademark protection by extending the reach of trademark law to more and more categories of artistic creativity. Once this starting point is accepted, the practical impact of trademark protection on remix and reuse in the cultural domain becomes a center of gravity in the debate. Evidently, the described cultural concerns only carry weight if it is right to assume that trademark protection reduces the potential of affected literary and artistic creations to serve as a basis for new works. Surprisingly, many judges and commentators seem to be confident that they can prevent an encroachment upon cultural remix and reuse by employing balancing tools that are available in trademark law.[43] The registration requirement of distinctiveness, the impact of cultural significance on the infringement analysis, and defenses to trademark infringement claims play a central role in this context.

A. No registration because of lack of distinctiveness

To illustrate the reliance on the basic threshold requirement of distinctiveness in the context of signs with cultural significance, the *Mona Lisa* decision of the German Federal Patent Court can serve as an example. The case concerned an attempt to register the famous Leonardo da Vinci painting as a trademark.[44] Rejecting the application, the German Federal Patent Court held that the applicant had failed to establish the requisite distinctiveness. Because the painting was frequently used by third parties in advertising, the public would regard the Mona Lisa as a mere advertising instrument rather than as an indication of source.[45] The Court also held that, because of the frequent use in advertising, the painting had become customary in established trade practices.[46] However, the Court was unwilling to accept the further argument that registration of the Mona Lisa was contrary to public policy or accepted principles of morality. In the Court's view, the appropriation of the Mona Lisa on the basis of trademark law would not violate the principle that cultural expressions should remain freely available for the public after the expiry of copyright protection.[47] Instead of openly addressing the cultural

[43] See also European Copyright Society (ECS), *Trade Mark Protection of Public Domain Works: A Comment on the Request for an Advisory Opinion of the EFTA Court: Case E-05/16: Norwegian Board of Appeal for Industrial Property Rights—Appeal from the Municipality of Oslo*, 39 Eur. Intell. Prop. Rev. 457, 458–59 (2017) (summarizing this practical approach).

[44] *Vigeland Judgment, supra* note 4, ¶ 29.

[45] *See Mona Lisa, supra* note 4, at 1022.

[46] *Id.* at 1023. For case comments, see Senftleben, *Der kulturelle Imperativ des Urheberrechts, supra* note 4, at 102–04; Assaf, *supra* note 4, at 5; Ohly, *supra* note 4, at 203; Klinkert & Schwab, *supra* note 4, at 1067; Nordemann, *supra* note 4, at 389.

[47] *Mona Lisa, supra* note 4, at 1023.

dimension of the trademark application, the Court thus relied exclusively on the basic requirement of distinctiveness.

Interestingly, this focus on distinctiveness also comes to the fore in decisions on non-traditional trademarks. Regulating access to trademark protection for shape marks and color per se, the CJEU relies on distinctive character as a central gatekeeper. In *Henkel v. DPMA*, the CJEU pointed out that average consumers were not "in the habit of making assumptions about the origin of goods based on the shape of their packaging, in the absence of any graphic or word element."[48] Therefore, it could prove more difficult, according to the CJEU, to establish distinctive character in the case of product packaging for which trademark protection is sought. Only a trademark that significantly departed from the norm or customs of the sector and thereby fulfilled the function of an indication of commercial origin was not devoid of distinctive character.[49] In *Libertel v. Benelux-Merkenbureau*, the CJEU invoked the same line of argument with regard to color per se.[50] Distinctiveness without any prior use was inconceivable, save in exceptional circumstances, and particularly where the number of goods or services for which the mark was claimed was very restricted and the relevant market very specific.[51]

If an application concerns a non-traditional mark with cultural significance, such as an application for registering a famous sculpture as a shape mark, the criterion of acquired distinctive character will thus play a crucial role. Instead of openly addressing cultural concerns, such as the risk of encouraging the privatization of parts of the cultural heritage, the undesirable redefinition of important cultural expressions in commercial contexts, and unfair free-riding on the status, reputation, and favorable image of cultural creations,[52] judges are likely to hide behind considerations relating to a sign's degree of distinctiveness.[53]

B. No confusion because of cultural significance

If trademark protection is granted, a sign's cultural significance can tip the scales against a finding of a likelihood of confusion in the context of the infringement analysis. In the EU, this became apparent in *Picasso v. OHIM*, where the CJEU had to decide on an opposition against defendant Daimler's application for registration of the sign PICARO for vehicles. The opposition had been lodged by the Picasso

[48] Case C-218/01, Henkel KGaA v. DPMA, ¶ 52 (CJEU Feb. 12, 2004); Cases C-53/01 to C-55/01, Linde AG et al., ¶ 48 (CJEU Apr. 8, 2003).

[49] *Henkel, supra* note 48, ¶ 49.

[50] *Libertel Groep BV*, supra note 9, ¶ 65.

[51] *Id.* ¶ 66.

[52] Artur Wandtke & Winfried Bullinger, *Die Marke als urheberrechtlich schutzfähiges Werk*, 8/9 GRUR 578 (1997); Senftleben, *Der kulturelle Imperativ des Urheberrechts, supra* note 4, at 103–04. For a solution based on public order and morality considerations, see Klinkert & Schwab, *supra* note 4, at 1073; VAN WOENSEL, *supra* note 26, at 412–13; Osenberg, *supra* note 26, at 102–03; Nordemann, *supra* note 4, at 391. See also the critique expressed by Ohly, *supra* note 4, at 207; Fedor Seifert, *Markenschutz und urheberrechtliche Gemeinfreiheit, in* WETTBEWERB IN RECHT UND PRAXIS 1018 (2000).

[53] Admittedly, the doctrine of aesthetic functionality may be considered as well, as discussed in more detail below. For a critical assessment of aesthetic functionality as a ground for refusal, see Dinwoodie, *supra* note 6, at 685–91; Kur, *Enigma of Aesthetic Functionality, supra* note 6, at 6–12.

estate, arguing that PICARO was likely to cause confusion with the earlier word mark PICASSO, which it had registered for various goods, including vehicles.[54] Discussing the criteria for a finding of a likelihood of confusion in this context, the CJEU confirmed the first instance decision that in this particular case, conceptual differences between the PICASSO mark and the PICARO sign counteracted the low degree of visual and phonetic similarity.[55] Conceptual differences could have this mitigating effect in cases where the meaning of at least one of the two signs was "clear and specific" so that the relevant public could grasp it immediately.[56] As to the meaning of the PICASSO mark, the CJEU recalled the factual assessment of the GCEU, which had found that

> confronted with the word sign PICASSO, the relevant public inevitably sees in it a reference to the painter and that, given the painter's renown with that public, that particularly rich conceptual reference is such as greatly to reduce the resonance with which, in this case, the sign is endowed as a mark, among others, of motor vehicles.[57]

Hence, the fact that the name "Picasso" is well known as a reference to the famous painter does not imply that the trademark PICASSO is highly distinctive and enjoys broad protection against confusion.[58] The painter's fame cannot simply be transferred to the trademark as an identifier of commercial source. By contrast, the well-known cultural meaning of the sign reduces the risk of confusion because its immediate impact on the perception of the public may outweigh visual and/or aural similarities. A sign with a strong cultural connotation may thus constitute a weak trademark.[59]

C. Limitations supporting freedom of expression

Considering the statutory limitations of trademark rights, it is finally to be conceded that even if prima facie infringement is found, use of trademarked cultural material may still be found permissible in the light of available defenses, such as the defenses of "due cause"[60] and "referential use"[61] in EU trademark legislation. The case *Lila Postkarte* of the German Federal Court of Justice, for example, concerned the marketing of postcards that alluded ironically to trademarks and advertising campaigns of the chocolate producer Milka.[62] On purple background corresponding to Milka's abstract color mark, the postcard sought to ridicule the nature

54 Case C-361/04P, Picasso v. OHIM, ¶¶ 5–6 (CJEU Jan. 12, 2006). 55 *Id.* ¶ 20.
56 *Id.* 57 *Id.* ¶ 27.
58 *See id.* ¶¶ 11, 32 (discussing the rejection of this counterargument advanced by the Picasso estate).
59 With regard to examples of cases where this occurred, see Assaf, *supra* note 4, at 2–3; Senftleben, *Der kulturelle Imperativ des Urheberrechts*, *supra* note 4, at 101–02.
60 Council Directive 2008/95 art. 5(2), 2008 O.J. L299/25 (EC) [hereinafter Former Trademark Directive]; Council Directive 2015/2436 art. 10(2)(c), 2015 O.J. L336/1 (EU) [hereinafter New Trademark Directive].
61 New Trademark Directive art. 14(1)(c).
62 Bundesgerichtshof [BGH] [Federal Court of Justice] Feb. 3, 2005, Case I ZR 159/02, Lila Postkarte, 2005 GRUR 583 (Ger.) [hereinafter *Lila Postkarte*].

idyll with cows and mountains that is evoked in Milka advertising.[63] It showed the following poem attributed to "Rainer Maria Milka":

Über allen Wipfeln ist Ruh!
irgendwo blökt eine Kuh!
Muh![64]

Assessing this ironic play with Milka insignia, the German Federal Court of Justice held that for the use of Milka trademarks to constitute relevant trademark use in the sense of EU trademark law, it was sufficient that the postcard called to mind the well-known Milka signs.[65] Even though being decorative, the use in question therefore gave rise to the question of trademark infringement.[66] Accordingly, the Court embarked on a scrutiny of the trademark parody in the light of the infringement criteria of detriment to distinctive character or repute, and the taking of unfair advantage.[67] Weighing Milka's concerns about a disparagement of the trademarks against the fundamental guarantee of the freedom of art, the Court finally concluded that the freedom of art had to prevail in light of the ironic statement made with the postcard.[68] The use of Milka trademarks was found to have taken place with "due cause."[69]

Similar decisions may follow from the application of the defense of "referential use," which was broadened in the framework of the EU trademark law reform and is now laid down in Article 14(1)(c) of the EU Trade Mark Directive 2015/2436 (EUTMD) and Article 14(1)(c) of the EU Trade Mark Regulation 2017/1001 (EUTMR).[70] If a reference to a trademarked cultural symbol is qualified as actionable trademark use, this broadened defense of referential use offers the unauthorized user the opportunity to argue that the reference to the trademark is the result of an honest practice of using the sign. In the case of use in the cultural domain, this line of reasoning finds support in Recital 27 of the EUTMD and Recital 21 of the EUTMR, which explicitly state that

> [u]se of a trade mark by third parties for the purpose of artistic expression should be considered as being fair as long as it is at the same time in accordance with honest practices in industrial and commercial matters.[71]

V. Critique

At first glance, the described checks and balances may appear sufficiently robust to dispel concerns about a corrosive effect of trademark rights on remix and reuse in

[63] *Id.*

[64] "It is calm above the tree tops, somewhere a cow is bellowing. Moo!" The attribution to "Rainer Maria Milka" is an allusion to the famous German writer Rainer Maria Rilke. *See id.*

[65] *Id.* at 584. [66] *Id.* at 584–85. [67] *Id.* [68] *Id.* [69] *Id.* at 585.

[70] *See* ANNETTE KUR & MARTIN SENFTLEBEN, EUROPEAN TRADE MARK LAW: A COMMENTARY ¶¶ 6.39–.41 (2017) (discussing the considerations underlying this legislative change).

[71] For a more detailed discussion of this point, see Jens H. Schovsbo, *Mark My Words: Trademarks and Fundamental Rights in the EU*, 7 U.C. IRVINE L. REV. (forthcoming 2018).

the cultural domain. However, a closer look at the described safeguards reveals how volatile they are. It also shows the core problem underlying the debate: the traditional acceptance of trademark rights relating to cultural material is based on an understanding of trademarks as source identifiers and trademark rights as tools to ensure market transparency. After the remarkable broadening of the concept of "use as a trademark" in advanced trademark systems, such as the EU trademark system,[72] and the explicit recognition of advertising, investment, and communication functions as independent protection objectives,[73] this traditional understanding no longer corresponds with the current scope and reach of trademark rights.[74]

A. Registration requirement of distinctiveness

In the *Mona Lisa* case, the German Federal Patent Court relied on the basic requirement of distinctive character and saw no need to invoke public policy and accepted principles of morality as further grounds for refusal. This focus on distinctiveness as sole gatekeeper has far-reaching consequences. The exclusion of the Mona Lisa registration because of a lack of distinctive character following from the painting's widespread use in advertising is weak because non-distinctive, descriptive, and generic signs can acquire the requisite distinctive character as a result of use in trade.[75] The decision of the German Federal Patent Court thus offers the chance of overcoming the registration obstacle through intensive use in product marketing and advertising. Once consumers have been taught to perceive the Mona Lisa as a source identifier referring to the trademark applicant, a registration of the famous painting becomes possible.[76]

[72] For a more detailed discussion of this development, see KUR & SENFTLEBEN, *supra* note 70, ¶¶ 5.14–.15, 5.49–.56; Martin R.F. Senftleben, *Keyword Advertising in Europe—How the Internet Challenges Recent Expansions of EU Trademark Protection*, 27 CONN. J. INT'L L. 39 (2011). As to the recognition of a potential gatekeeper function of the trademark use requirement in U.S. law, *see* Stacey L. Dogan & Mark A. Lemley, *The Trademark Use Requirement in Dilution Cases*, 24 SANTA CLARA COMPUTER & HIGH TECH. L.J. 541, 542 (2008) ("By maintaining the law's focus on misleading branding, the trademark use doctrine keeps trademark law true to its ultimate goal of promoting competitive markets."). However, see also Graeme B. Dinwoodie & Mark D. Janis, *Confusion Over Use: Contextualism in Trademark Law*, 92 IOWA L. REV. 1597, 1657–58 (2007), who doubt that problems arising in the current "expansionist climate" could be solved by recalibrating the notion of trademark use: "Trademark use is simply too blunt a concept, no matter how defined, to capture the full range of values at play in these debates." For a summary of the U.S. debate, see Mark Davison & Frank Di Giantomasso, *Use as a Trademark: Avoiding Confusion When Considering Dilution*, 31 EUROPEAN INTELL. PROP. REV. 443 (2009); Mark P. McKenna, *Trademark Use and the Problem of Source*, 2009 U. ILL. L. REV. 773 (2009).

[73] Case C-487/07, L'Oréal SA v. Bellure NV, ¶ 58 (CJEU June 18, 2009). *Cf.* KUR & SENFTLEBEN, *supra* note 70, ¶¶ 1.12–.39.

[74] ESTELLE DERCLAYE & MATTHIAS LEISTNER, INTELLECTUAL PROPERTY OVERLAPS: A EUROPEAN PERSPECTIVE 328 (2011).

[75] Former Trademark Directive art. 3(3); New Trademark Directive art. (4)(4).

[76] For a detailed discussion of this conditional character of a refusal based on a lack of distinctiveness, *see* Martin Senftleben, *Public Domain Preservation in EU Trademark Law—A Model for Other Regions?*, 103 TRADEMARK REP. 775, 783–84 (2013); Lotte Anemaet, *The Public Domain is Under Pressure: Why We Should Not Rely on Empirical Data When Assessing Trademark Distinctiveness*, 47 INT'L REV. INTELL. PROP. & COMP. L. 303 (2016).

Viewed from this perspective, the *Mona Lisa* decision is unsatisfactory. While the German Federal Patent Court may have felt that the distinctiveness test is sufficient to keep signs with cultural significance free of trademark protection, the reliance on the basic protection requirement may have the opposite effect. Enterprises may regard the prospect of acquiring trademark rights as a result of use in trade as an invitation to invest in marketing and advertising activities based on cultural signs. They may strive to make a particular cultural heritage symbol part of the trademark experience they are offering to consumers. The mere possibility of acquiring trademark rights in consequence of use in trade may be sufficient to support business activities that lead to the removal of cultural material from the public domain instead of putting an end to attempts to obtain trademark rights to cultural creations.[77]

This risk must not be underestimated. Literary and artistic works in the public domain have rich and positive connotations. Investing in the acquisition of trademark rights to such a work, an enterprise can benefit from the favorable image that the cultural material already has. Given the popularity of the sign, the process of brand image creation need not be started from scratch. The establishment of a link with the cultural work offers the chance of an image transfer that may outweigh the costs of advertising necessary to acquire distinctiveness through use in trade. The enhanced value to be gained once trademark protection is acquired may allow bigger investments than in regular cases of brand development—investments capable of setting aside the cultural renown and "particularly rich conceptual reference" that the CJEU qualified as an obstacle to a strong distinctive character in *Picasso v. OHIM*.[78]

In addition, the requirement of distinctiveness as a basic threshold for the acquisition of trademark rights fails to cover the entire spectrum of cultural public domain material. The *Mona Lisa* case concerned a famous cultural symbol belonging to mankind's universal cultural heritage. In the light of the popularity of the painting and its widespread use in advertising, the court could reject the registration attempt on the grounds that the sign had become a customary marketing tool and constituted a non-distinctive, generic sign. In the case of cultural material that is not well known, this line of argument is not available.[79] For example, the registration of a culturally important but not widely known melody taken from a classical piece of music could hardly be rejected based on the argument that the sign has been used so frequently in a commercial context that consumers are unlikely to perceive it as a reference to an individual commercial source.[80] Moreover, distinctive character may be found when the goods or services, in respect of which trademark

[77] *Cf.* Anemaet, *supra* note 76, at 331–32; Senftleben, *supra* note 76, at 812–13; Lisa P. Ramsey, *Descriptive Trademarks and the First Amendment*, 70 Tenn. L. Rev. 1095, 1150 (2003); Robert C. Denicola, *Trademarks as Speech: Constitutional Implications of the Emerging Rationales for the Protection of Trade Symbols*, 182 Wis. L. Rev. 158, 170 (1981). *See also* ECS, *supra* note 43, at 460–61.

[78] *Picasso, supra* note 54, ¶ 27. *Cf.* Wandtke & Bullinger, *supra* note 52, at 578.

[79] *See* Klinkert & Schwab, *supra* note 4, at 1068 (expressing similar concerns). *Cf.* Senftleben, *supra* note 4, *Der kulturelle Imperativ des Urheberrechts*, 103–04.

[80] Examples of this kind are not of a theoretical nature. In Germany, for instance, the beer producer Licher has consistently used "Solveig's Song" from Edvard Grieg's "Peer Gynt Suite" in advertising since the nineties. *See* AlteTVSpots, *Licher Pilsner Wegung 1992*, YouTube (Dec. 14, 2012), https://www.youtube.com/watch?v=dfGGjk1QEeM.

protection is sought, are unrelated to the cultural domain and the genuine meaning of a cultural symbol.

The distinctiveness-based jurisprudence concerning non-traditional marks does not offer starting points for a satisfactory application of distinctiveness as a regulatory tool either. As explained above, the CJEU held in *Henkel* and *Libertel* that consumers were not in the habit of perceiving non-traditional marks as source identifiers and insisted on a showing of acquired distinctiveness.[81] This additional hurdle can be regarded as the result of an effort made to safeguard the public domain. The CJEU acknowledged in *Libertel* that there was a public interest in not unduly restricting the availability of colors for competitors.[82] As in the case of traditional marks with cultural significance, however, the effectiveness of this effort to keep signs available is doubtful. The mere prospect of acquiring trademark rights in consequence of use in trade may encourage marketing campaigns based on product packaging or color per se—marketing efforts that aim to change the perception of consumers. The more often the public is confronted with a shape mark or abstract color mark, the more alert it will be to the fact that, besides standard word and figurative marks, shapes and color per se may also indicate the commercial source of goods and services. The CJEU may thus have to revise its own assumptions about the distinctiveness of shapes and color per se in the near future. Arguably, the assumption of consumers not being "in the habit" of perceiving signs of this type as a badge of origin becomes more and more doubtful with every trader who succeeds in linking a specific shape or color with her enterprise as the origin of goods or services in the minds of consumers.[83]

The jurisprudence on distinctiveness in the case of non-traditional marks may even provide additional incentives for the adoption of artworks as trademarks—at least in the field of shape marks. As mentioned above, the CJEU stated in *Henkel* that only a shape that significantly departs from the norm or customs of the sector and thereby fulfills the function of an indication of commercial origin is not devoid of distinctive character.[84] Traders seeking to surmount the hurdle of distinctive character may thus look for shapes that are original enough to achieve a significant departure from shapes that are regularly used in the sector concerned. This could bring artworks into focus that are not widely known and unlikely to be qualified as descriptive or generic because of their widespread use in advertising.

The reliance on distinctive character as a gatekeeper may thus be highly problematic when it comes to non-traditional marks, particularly shape marks. However,

[81] *Henkel, supra* note 48, ¶ 52 (CJEU Feb. 12, 2004); Case C-104/01, *Libertel Groep BV, supra* note 9, ¶ 65.

[82] *Libertel, supra* note 9, ¶ 55.

[83] Given the widespread recognition of Milka lilac (CTM Registration 000031336 of Oct. 27, 1999 (Kraft Foods)) and Deutsche Telekom magenta (CTM Registration 000212787 of Aug. 3, 2000 (Deutsche Telekom)) as abstract color marks in the EU, it may already be asked whether it is still correct to deny inherent distinctiveness in the case of eccentric colors, even though there is increased consumer awareness that color may serve as an indication of commercial source. UPS brown (CTM Registration 000962076 of Sept. 17, 2001 (United Parcel Service)) constitutes an additional example indicating that an abstract color may serve as a source identifier, even if it is much less exceptional.

[84] *Henkel, supra* note 48, ¶ 49.

it must not be overlooked that in this area, distinctiveness is not the only threshold requirement. When it comes to shape marks, the functionality doctrine enters the picture as an additional ground for refusal that offers a more robust solution than a rejection based on a lack of distinctiveness: the rejection of trademark protection because of functionality cannot be overcome through use in trade.[85] A broad concept of aesthetic functionality can thus constitute an important tool to keep sculptures and other works of plastic art outside trademark law.

Against this background, it is promising that the CJEU opted for a relatively broad concept of aesthetic functionality in *Hauck v. Stokke*. The case concerned trademark protection for the so-called "Tripp Trapp" children's chair consisting of sloping uprights and an L-shaped frame of uprights and sliding plates—a minimalist design that is not only aesthetically appealing but also offers other advantages, such as flexibility, safety, and comfort. Given this mix of values inherent in the chair design, the lawsuit about the validity of a trademark registration which Stokke had obtained in the Benelux gave rise to the question whether, for invoking the exclusion of a shape giving substantial value to the goods (which represents the doctrine of aesthetic functionality in EU trademark law), it was necessary that the shape's artistic or ornamental value constituted the main or predominant value.[86]

In answering this question, the CJEU made it clear that the scope of the exclusion of substantial value shapes could not be limited "purely to the shape of products having only artistic or ornamental value."[87] Otherwise, there was a risk that products having essential functional characteristics as well as a significant aesthetic element would not be covered, which, in turn, could compromise the objective to prevent the use of trademark law as a means of artificially extending the term of intellectual property rights, which the legislator had limited in time.[88] The Court thus rejected the argument that the exclusion of substantial value shapes should only cover designs with predominant artistic or ornamental value. This decision gave rise to the further question which assessment criteria had to be taken into account when applying the shape exclusion. In this regard, the CJEU clarified that the presumed perception of the design by the average consumer was not decisive but constituted a relevant assessment criterion.[89] Other criteria to be factored into the equation included the nature of the category of goods concerned; the artistic value of the shape in question; the dissimilarity of the shape from other shapes in common use on the market concerned; a substantial price difference in relation to similar products; and the development of a promotion strategy which focuses on accentuating the aesthetic characteristics of the product in question.[90]

Hence, there can be little doubt that the CJEU aims at an open, flexible application of the doctrine of aesthetic functionality. With the development of a whole list of assessment criteria in *Hauck v. Stokke*, the CJEU clearly expressed the need for a comprehensive analysis based on various factors. A trader adopting an artwork

[85] With regard to EU legislation, this has explicitly been confirmed. *See, e.g., Koninklijke Philips Electronics NV, supra* note 5, ¶ 75.

[86] *Hauck, supra* note 2, ¶ 14. [87] *Id.* ¶ 32. [88] *Id.* ¶¶ 31–32. [89] *Id.* ¶ 34.

[90] *Id.* ¶ 35.

as a shape mark to surmount the hurdle of a significant departure from the "norm or customs of the sector" in the sense of *Henkel* may thus have difficulty to escape a finding of aesthetic functionality in the light of the flexible criteria established in *Hauck v. Stokke*, including the factor of "dissimilarity of the shape from other shapes in common use on the market concerned." As a result, the shape mark jurisprudence of the CJEU obliges traders to navigate between Scylla and Charybdis: while a significant departure from the norm may be necessary to satisfy the test of distinctiveness, it may culminate in a finding of aesthetic functionality and exclude trademark protection from the outset. Given this status quo, the risk of widespread use of sculptures and other works of plastic art as trademarks seems to have been contained in the EU.

However, the described mitigating effect of the doctrine of aesthetic functionality seems to remain confined to three-dimensional creations that are employed as shape marks, even though current EU trademark legislation has extended the scope of the doctrine to other product characteristics in Article 4(1)(e) of the EUTMD and Article 7(1)(e) of the EUTMR. The German *Marlene Dietrich* decisions shed light on the limits of the approach. Discussing a request to register a portrait photograph of Marlene Dietrich with respect to photographs, posters, postcards, and goods of a similar nature, the German Federal Patent Court argued that the photograph of the famous actress constituted a mere reproduction of these goods, and invoked the exclusion of "the shape which results from the nature of the goods themselves" to deny registration.[91] Hence, the German Federal Patent Court was of the opinion that the mark was functional because it consisted of the product itself and sought to use the shape exclusion as a vehicle to prevent the acquisition of trademark rights.

However, the decision was overruled by the German Federal Court of Justice, which tersely concluded that the sign consisted of the reproduction of the head of Marlene Dietrich and did not consist of a shape resulting from the nature of a photograph, poster, or postcard, as such.[92] Seeing no room for the application of the exclusion of shapes resulting from the nature of the goods in this case, the German Federal Court of Justice relied on the requirement of distinctiveness. It refused trademark protection with respect to goods and services concerning the work and life of the actress, such as books, magazines, photographs, posters, CDs, DVDs, musical performances, and film productions. With respect to these goods and services, the public would perceive the portrait photograph as a mere indication of product characteristics.[93] Hence, the Court argued that the genuine cultural meaning underlying the photograph—showing the head of Marlene Dietrich—rendered the sign descriptive and incapable of serving as a trademark with respect to goods and services that are closely related to the work and life of the actress.

This solution of the case has its price. In contrast to the shape exclusion that had been invoked by the German Federal Patent Court, the hurdle of a lack of

[91] Bundespatentgericht [BPatG] [Federal Patent Court] Nov. 9, 2005, Porträtfoto Marlene Dietrich, ¶ 4.2 (Ger.) [hereinafter *Portrait Photo of Marlene Dietrich*].

[92] *Marlene Dietrich, supra* note 4, ¶ 11.

[93] *Id.* ¶¶ 12–15. For relevant case precedents, see Bundesgerichtshof [BGH] [Federal Court of Justice] Dec. 5, 2002, Case I ZB 19/00, Winnetou, 6 (Ger.); Bundesgerichtshof [BGH] [Federal Court of Justice], Jan. 23, 2003, Case I ZR 171/00, Winnetous Rückkehr, 10 (Ger.).

distinctiveness because of descriptive character can be surmounted once the sign becomes distinctive as a result of the use made of it in trade.[94] Accordingly, the German Federal Court of Justice had to leave open the backdoor of acquired distinctive character: as a result of use in trade, the Marlene Dietrich photograph may become distinctive with regard to goods and services related to the life and work of the actress at a later stage.[95] The Court added that the portrait photograph was inherently distinctive with regard to merchandising articles, such as scarves, hats, shirts, and shoes. In this respect, it rejected the view expressed by the German Federal Patent Court that consumers would perceive the portrait as a mere marketing tool and fail to understand that it served as an indication of commercial source.[96] The German Federal Court of Justice emphasized instead that the photograph did not necessarily need to be placed prominently on the articles; it could also be used as a label attached to the goods. Given this option of use as a badge of origin, distinctive character could not be denied.[97] Rejecting a broader application of considerations of functionality, the decision thus leaves open several avenues for the acquisition of trademark rights to signs with cultural significance.

B. Impact of cultural significance on infringement analysis

In *Picasso v. OHIM*, the CJEU held that the renown of a cultural creation may constitute such a rich conceptual reference that it greatly reduces the recognition of the sign as a trademark.[98] Hence, it seems that in the CJEU's view, cultural significance is a factor weighing against the assumption of a highly distinctive character. This, in turn, is a factor weighing against broad protection against confusion and excluding protection against dilution.

Nonetheless, it would be wrong to jump to the conclusion that trademark rights relating to cultural signs are generally unproblematic because the scope of protection against confusion and dilution will always remain limited. By contrast, the elasticity of distinctive character as a parameter for determining the scope of protection must be factored into the equation. A relatively weak trademark may be developed into a powerful brand over time. This is inherent in the configuration of trademark law. In addition, the acquisition of a considerable degree of distinctive character and a broad scope of trademark protection does not seem particularly difficult when a trademark consists of a sign that has cultural significance but is not widely known among the consuming public. A symbol, shape, or melody

94 Former Trade Mark Directive art. 3(3) (art. 4(4) of the New Trademark Directive), which governs the application of national trade mark law in the EU (and EEA) Member States, explicitly offers the possibility of acquiring distinctive character through use with regard to non-distinctive, descriptive, and generic signs.

95 *Marlene Dietrich, supra* note 4, ¶ 17.

96 *Portrait Photo of Marlene Dietrich, supra* note 91, ¶¶ 8.1, 8.2.

97 *Marlene Dietrich, supra* note 4, ¶¶ 19–22. See also the confirmation of this point in Bundesgerichtshof [BGH] [Federal Court of Justice] Mar. 31, 2010, Case I ZB 62/09, Marlene-Dietrich-Bildnis II, ¶¶ 20–28 (Ger.) [hereinafter *Marlene Dietrich II*].

98 *Picasso, supra* note 54, ¶ 27.

stemming from a culturally important but relatively unknown work is unlikely to have a strong cultural connotation capable of weakening the recognition of the sign as an indication of commercial origin. Who thinks of Nike, the Greek goddess of victory, when seeing the trademark NIKE?[99] Who is aware of culturally important signs of indigenous communities?

Given the relatively low threshold for acquiring anti-dilution protection in many trademark systems, such as the EU system, there is also a substantial risk of unknown signs with cultural significance becoming eligible for enhanced protection against dilution. In contrast to the U.S. trademark system, requiring recognition among the general consuming public, niche reputation is sufficient under EU trademark law.[100] For a trademark to constitute a mark with a reputation in the sense of EU trademark law, it must be known by the target group of the goods or services marketed under the trademark. In the case of specific products, this target group may be a specialized public, such as traders in a specific sector. The required degree of knowledge is reached when the mark is known by a significant part of the relevant public.[101]

Once reputation is established, EU trademark law offers anti-dilution protection covering blurring, tarnishment, and unfair free-riding in competitive and non-competitive situations.[102] The evidence to be produced need not necessarily include proof of a change in the economic behavior of consumers.[103] For a claim based on the taking of unfair advantage, it suffices to argue that "a third party attempts, through the use of a sign similar to a mark with a reputation, to ride on the coat-tails

[99] With regard to these and further examples, see Assaf, *supra* note 4, at 2–3; Senftleben, *Der kulturelle Imperativ des Urheberrechts, supra* note 4, at 101–02.

[100] *Cf.* Martin Senftleben, *The Trademark Tower of Babel—Dilution Concepts in International, US and EC Trademark Law*, 40 Int'l Rev. Intell. Prop. & Competition L. 45, 50–55 (2009); J. Thomas McCarthy, *Dilution of a Trademark: European and United States Law Compared*, 94 Trademark Rep. 1163 (2004); Barton Beebe, *A Defense of the New Federal Trademark Antidilution Law*, 16 Fordham Intell. Prop. Media & Ent. L.J. 1143, 1157 (2006).

[101] Case C-375/97, General Motors Corp. v. Yplon SA, ¶¶ 24, 26 (CJEU Sept. 14, 1999). With respect to the territorial expansion required, see *id.* ¶ 28; Case C-301/07, PAGO Int'l GmbH v. Tirolmilch registrierte Genossenschaft mbH, ¶ 29 (CJEU Oct. 6, 2009).

[102] Under the former Trademark Directive 2008/95, this followed from Case C-292/00, Davidoff & Cie SA v. Gofkid Ltd. (CJEU Jan. 9, 2003). It has been made explicit in art. 10(2)(c) new Trademark Directive 2015/2436. As to the scope of protection offered in cases of marks having a reputation, see particularly *L'Oréal SA, supra* note 73. *See also* Martin Senftleben, *Trade Mark Protection—A Black Hole in the Intellectual Property Galaxy?*, 42 Int'l Rev. Intell. Prop. & Comp. L. 383 (2011); Ansgar Ohly, *Keyword-Advertising auf dem Weg von Karlsruhe nach Luxemburg*, 8 Gewerblicher Rechtsschutz und Urheberrecht 709, 711–12 (2009).

[103] This test applies in cases of blurring and tarnishment. *See* Case C-252/07, Intel Corp. v. CPM U.K. Ltd., ¶ 77 (CJEU Nov. 27, 2008); Case C-383/12P, Envtl. Mfg. LLP v. OHIM, ¶ 37 (CJEU Nov. 14, 2013). *Cf.* kur & senftleben, *supra* note 70, ¶¶ 5.223–.228; Adrien Bouvel, *Marques et renommée: À propos de l'arrêt "Intel" rendu par la Cour de justice des communautés européennes le 27 novembre 2008, in* les défis du droit des marques au xxie siècle 123 (Christophe Geiger & Joanna Schmidt-Szalewski eds., 2010); Antoon A. Quaedvlieg, *INTEL en verwatering: Economisch gedrag en juridisch bewijs*, bijblad bij de industriële eigendom 253 (2009); Antoon A. Quaedvlieg, *Herkomst- en goodwillinbreuk in het merkenrecht na INTEL en l'Oréal*, Ars Aequi 799 (2009); Susie Middlemiss & Steven Warner, Comment, *The Protection of Marks with a Reputation: Intel v. CPM*, 31 European Intell. Prop. Rev. 326, 331–32 (2009).

of that mark."[104] Moreover, the CJEU refuses to consider the need to keep protected signs freely available in the context of the infringement analysis. In *Adidas v. Marca Mode*, the Court stated that the requirement of availability was "extraneous both to the assessment of the degree of similarity between the mark with a reputation and the sign used by the third party and to the link which may be made by the relevant public between that mark and the sign."[105]

In addition to these developments in the field of specific infringement criteria, current EU trademark law is an example of an advanced trademark system in which inherent limits of exclusive rights, such as the requirements of "use in the course of trade" and "use in relation to goods or services," have lost much of their potential to contain access to trademark protection from the outset. The requirement of use in relation to goods or services is applied flexibly by the CJEU. In principle, this general prerequisite for obtaining protection could be applied to confine the scope of trademark rights to instances where the senior user's trademark is employed by a junior user as an identifier of commercial source with regard to its own goods or services. Following this approach, the requirement of trademark use could serve as a filter to exclude claims that are unrelated to the identification and distinction of goods and services from the outset. Considerable breathing space for freedom of use in a cultural context could be created in this way.[106]

However, the CJEU takes the opposite approach, weakening the trademark use requirement instead of sharpening its conceptual contours. As the above-described German decision *Lila Postkarte* shows, the requirement of "use as a trademark" is applied flexibly in the EU. It does not serve as a filter to exclude, from the outset, all instances where the trademark is not used in the traditional manner, that is to indicate the commercial source of the user's own goods or services.[107] Instead, a mere reference to the trademark[108] and a mere link with goods or services may be sufficient to satisfy the trademark use requirement and trigger an infringement action.[109]

[104] *L'Oréal*, *supra* note 73, ¶ 49. For a critical comment on intuitive protection against free-riding as a species of unjust enrichment law, see Mark A. Lemley & Mark P. McKenna, *Owning Mark(et)s*, 109 MICH. L. REV. 137 (2010).

[105] Case C-102/07, Adidas AG v. Marca Mode CV, ¶ 43 (CJEU Apr. 10, 2008).

[106] For a discussion of the concept of trademark use in EU trademark law, see: KUR & SENFTLEBEN, *supra* note 70, ¶¶ 5.14–.15, 5.49–.56; Annette Kur, *Confusion Over Use?—Die Benutzung "als Marke" im Lichte der EuGH-Rechtsprechung*, 1 GRUR: INTERNATIONALER TEIL 1, 11 (2008); Po Jen Yap, *Essential Function of a Trade Mark: From BMW to O2*, 31 EUROPEAN INTELL. PROP. REV. 81, 86–87 (2009); Ilanah Simon Fhima, *How Does "Essential Function" Doctrine Drive European Trade Mark Law?*, 36 INT'L REV. INTELL. PROP. & COMPETITION L. 401 (2005); Patricia L. Loughlan, *Protecting Culturally Significant Uses of Trade Marks (Without a First Amendment)*, 22 EUROPEAN INTELL. PROP. REV. 328 (2000). For a fundamental critique of the continuous expansion seeking to reduce the scope of trademark protection to the traditional origin function, see moreover Peukert, *supra* note 17, at 96–107.

[107] This stricter test, however, was mentioned with regard to the traditional identification function of trademarks in Case C-48/05, Adam Opel AG v. Autec AG, ¶ 24 (CJEU Jan. 25, 2007).

[108] Case C-408/01, Adidas-Salomon AG v. Fitnessworld Trading Ltd., ¶ 39 (CJEU Oct. 23, 2003); *Adidas v. Marca*, *supra* note 105, ¶ 41.

[109] Case C-17/06, Céline SARL v. Céline SA, ¶¶ 21–23 (CJEU Sept. 11, 2007); Case C-62/08, UDV N. Am. Inc. v. Brandtraders NV, ¶ 47 (CJEU Feb. 19, 2009). The emphasis on the criterion of a mere link with the goods or services offered under a conflicting sign was confirmed in cases dealing with keyword advertising. *See* Cases C-236/08 to 238/08, Google France SARL v. Louis Vuitton Malletier SA et al., ¶ 72 (CJEU Mar. 23, 2010); Case C-324/09, L'Oréal SA v. eBay Int'l AG, ¶ 92 (CJEU July

In the light of the elastic standard developed by the CJEU, even decorative use of a trademark may amount to actionable trademark use.[110] Evidently, this development is worrisome from the perspective of cultural follow-on innovation. To exclude a trademark action in cases of remix or reuse of trademarked cultural symbols in the artistic domain, it is no longer sufficient to argue that the use takes place in a cultural context and does not constitute use "as a trademark." The moment the use establishes a link with a trademarked cultural symbol, this defense strategy may already fail because of the broad concept of actionable trademark use in the EU that includes mere references to cultural signs enjoying trademark protection.[111] As a result of this inclusion of referential use in the concept of use "as a trademark," the requirement of trademark use does not prevent trademark owners from bringing lawsuits against artistic uses that are not—and are not intended to be—perceived as indications of commercial source. On the contrary, referential use is brought within the reach of the exclusive rights of trademark owners.[112] The impact of this broad concept on use for cultural purposes is considerable.

Surveying these developments, it can be said that the inherent limits of exclusive trademark rights—use in the course of trade, use as a trademark, use likely to cause confusion, and use likely to cause dilution—have become elastic and unreliable safeguards of freedom of use for cultural purposes. In many cases of use in a cultural context, it will be difficult to rule out the threat of a trademark claim on the basis of these infringement criteria.[113]

C. Limitations of trademark rights insufficient

Hence, the question arises whether the defenses in trademark law are sufficient to eliminate the risk of a corrosive effect on artistic expression. As already pointed out above, the legal uncertainty arising from a potential lawsuit distinguishes the scenario in which a sign with cultural significance is in the public domain, from the situation where the sign is re-appropriated as a result of trademark protection. Given the described elasticity of infringement criteria in advanced trademark systems, the risk of infringement can no longer be ruled out. This legal uncertainty is likely to

12, 2011). For a discussion of this development, see Martin Senftleben, *Adapting EU Trademark Law to New Technologies: Back to Basics?*, *in* CONSTRUCTING EUROPEAN INTELLECTUAL PROPERTY 137, 147–48 (Christophe Geiger ed., 2013).

110 *See Adidas v. Fitnessworld, supra* note 108, ¶¶ 39–41 (The Court established an ambiguous test by holding that "the fact that a sign is viewed as an embellishment by the relevant section of the public is not, in itself, an obstacle to the protection conferred by Article 5(2) of the Directive where the degree of similarity is none the less such that the relevant section of the public establishes a link between the sign and the mark."). For decisions illustrating the weakness of the descriptive use defence in this context, see *Adidas v. Marca, supra* note 105, ¶¶ 47–49; *Adam Opel, supra* note 107, ¶ 44; Bundesgerichtshof [BGH] [Federal Court of Justice] Nov. 24, 2011, Case I ZR 175/09, Medusa, ¶¶ 19–20 (Ger.).

111 *Adidas v. Fitnessworld, supra* note 108, ¶ 39 (CJEU Oct. 23, 2003); *Lila Postkarte, supra* note 62, at 584–85.

112 *Cf.* KUR & SENFTLEBEN, *supra* note 70, ¶¶ 5.50–.54; DERCLAYE & LEISTNER, *supra* note 74, at 328.

113 *Cf.* Irene Calboli, *Overlapping Rights: The Negative Effects of Trademarking Creative Works*, *in* THE EVOLUTION AND EQUILIBRIUM OF COPYRIGHT IN THE DIGITAL AGE 52, 52–54 (Susy Frankel & Daniel Gervais eds., 2014); DERCLAYE & LEISTNER, *supra* note 74, at 328.

have a deterrent effect on cultural follow-on innovation even if the artist can rely on a defense, such as the EU defenses of "due cause" or "referential use." These defenses merely add a further discussion point to the list of legal arguments. The claimant will assert that the use at issue is excessive and falls outside the scope of any defense. The alleged infringer will seek to convince the court that the defense is fully applicable.

In various areas of creative activity, concerns have been articulated about a growing fear of artists to be sued for intellectual property infringement because of the reuse of pre-existing cultural material that still enjoys protection.[114] These fears can have a chilling effect on creativity and cultural diversity. An artist seeking to avoid potential lawsuits will refrain from the creation of works based on pre-existing material or limit takings from pre-existing material to an absolute minimum.[115] Therefore, the legal uncertainty arising from the elastic application of trademark infringement criteria leads to a climate that is not conducive to new cultural productions. Instead, it is likely to impoverish new cultural productions in terms of creative inputs. In many cases, artists will not have sufficient confidence and financial resources to take the risk of a lengthy lawsuit. If a powerful trademark owner sends a cease-and-desist letter stating that a given form of artistic use amounts to trademark infringement, this will often suffice to put an end to the use in a cultural context.[116]

Hence, the legal uncertainty surrounding the invocation of available defenses, such as "due cause" and "referential use," must be factored into the equation. It is not sufficient that the statutory law provides for defenses and that judges are willing to hear arguments based on these defenses. It must also be considered whether artistic creators may nevertheless refrain from permissible use once the registration of an artwork leads to the acquisition of trademark rights and involves the risk of an infringement action.[117] Even if courts may finally manage to arrive at reasonable solutions

[114] WOLFGANG SAKULIN, TRADEMARK PROTECTION AND FREEDOM OF EXPRESSION: AN INQUIRY INTO THE CONFLICT BETWEEN TRADEMARK RIGHTS AND FREEDOM OF EXPRESSION UNDER EUROPEAN LAW 292–93 (2011); William McGeveran, *Four Free Speech Goals for Trademark Law*, 18 FORDHAM INTELL. PROP. MEDIA & ENT. L.J. 1205, 1206–07, 1224–25 (2008); Jesse A. Hofrichter, *Tool of the Trademark: Brand Criticism and Free Speech Problems with the Federal Dilution Revision Act of 2006*, 28 CARDOZO L. REV. 1923, 1926 (2007); James Gibson, *Risk Aversion and Rights Accretion in Intellectual Property Law*, 116 YALE L.J. 882, 913 (2007); Julie E. Cohen, *Copyright, Commodification, and Culture: Locating the Public Domain*, *in* THE FUTURE OF THE PUBLIC DOMAIN: IDENTIFYING THE COMMONS IN INFORMATION LAW 121, 156 (Lucie Guibault & P. Bernt Hugenholtz eds., 2006); Patricia Aufderheide & Peter Jaszi, *Untold Stories: Creative Consequences of the Rights Clearance Culture for Documentary Filmmakers*, CTR. FOR SOC. MEDIA 29–30 (Dec. 2004), http://archive.cmsimpact.org/sites/default/files/UNTOLDSTORIES_Report.pdf; LAWRENCE LESSIG, FREE CULTURE: HOW BIG MEDIA USES TECHNOLOGY AND THE LAW TO LOCK DOWN CULTURE AND CONTROL CREATIVITY 185–88 (2004).

[115] Arpan Banerjee, *Non-Origin Infringement: Has Trade Mark Law Gone Too Far?*, 43 INT'L REV. INTELL. PROP. & COMPETITION L. 555, 564 (2012); David M. Morrison, Bridgeport *Redux: Digital Sampling and Audience Recoding*, 19 FORDHAM INTELL. PROP. MEDIA & ENT. L.J. 75, 131–36 (2008); Hofrichter, *supra* note 114, at 1926; Cohen, *supra* note 114, at 154–56; TERESA M. AMABILE, CREATIVITY IN CONTEXT 115–20, 231–32 (1996).

[116] For a more detailed discussion of the chilling effect of cease-and-desist strategies, *see*: Calboli, *supra* note 3, at 31–32; McGeveran, *supra* note 114, at 1206–07; LESSIG, *supra* note 114, at 185–88.

[117] For an explicit recognition of the deterrent effect that can follow from the legal uncertainty surrounding a use privilege and the need to factor this legal uncertainty into the equation, see Bundesverfassungsgericht [BVerfG] [Federal Constitutional Court] May 31, 2016, Case 1 BvR 1585/13, Sampling, ¶ 100 (Ger.).

in cases involving use of trademarked cultural material, the fundamental difference remains that legal uncertainty about a potential trademark claim is surrounding the use of cultural material once it has been re-appropriated. The risk of potential trademark infringement is hanging above use made of affected cultural creations like the sword of Damocles.

VI. Need for More Robust Grounds for Refusal

Against this background, it seems advisable to strike at the root of the problem and pave the way for stricter access control that prevents the acquisition of trademark rights to signs with cultural significance from the outset.[118] To effectively ban the risk of impeding cultural follow-on innovation, it is necessary to go beyond distinctiveness-based grounds for refusal and develop more robust mechanisms to arrive at an outright exclusion of signs with cultural significance from trademark protection.

A. Functionality doctrine not sufficient

Despite the results that have been achieved with regard to the separation of trademark protection from patent protection, the functionality doctrine in trademark law does not seem an appropriate vehicle to also separate trademark protection from copyright protection. As discussed above, considerations of aesthetic functionality may lead to an effective ban on trademark protection with respect to products that incorporate an artwork, such as decorative items and furniture. However, a trademark application seems immune from a refusal based on aesthetic functionality when it is argued that the cultural signs concerned would only be attached to the goods as a label—a line of reasoning that was decisive in the German *Marlene Dietrich* decisions.[119]

If merely used as a label, a cultural sign can hardly be found to be functional. Otherwise, the brand value that the sign represents in the form of the label would be sufficient to assume aesthetic functionality. This, in turn, would lead to a circular line of reasoning and the exclusion of any sign with brand value from trademark protection. For example, the attachment of the Coca-Cola logo to soft drinks would also lead to an exclusion of trademark rights because the brand value of the logo adds

[118] For a more detailed discussion of this point, *see*: Anemaet, *supra* note 76, at 331–32; Calboli, *supra* note 3, at 34; Calboli, *supra* note 113, at 76–78; Senftleben, *supra* note 76, at 816–17, 823–25. With regard to the field of traditional knowledge and traditional cultural expressions, see: Susy Frankel, *Third-Party Trade Marks as a Violation of Indigenous Cultural Property: A New Statutory Safeguard*, 8 J. WORLD INTELL. PROP. 83 (2005) [hereinafter Frankel, *Third-Party Trade Marks*]; Susy Frankel, *Trademarks and Traditional Knowledge and Cultural Intellectual Property Rights*, *in* TRADEMARK LAW AND THEORY: A HANDBOOK OF CONTEMPORARY RESEARCH 433 (Graeme B. Dinwoodie & Mark D. Janis eds., 2008) [hereinafter Frankel, *Trademarks and Traditional Knowledge*] (discussing the concept of "cultural offence" in New Zealand and a *sui generis* protection regime that would offer grounds for opposition under trademark law).

[119] *Marlene Dietrich*, *supra* note 4, ¶¶ 19–22; *Marlene Dietrich II*, *supra* note 97, ¶¶ 20–28.

substantial value to the product. Therefore, use as a label necessarily falls outside the scope of an outright exclusion of trademark protection based on considerations of aesthetic functionality. The same may be said about the use of a melody with cultural significance as a sound mark for goods. As the sign is not incorporated in the product itself, the doctrine of aesthetic functionality is not applicable as a tool to exclude trademark rights.

B. Public order and morality

This insight brings other grounds for refusal into focus. In particular, an effective separation of copyright and trademark protection for signs with cultural significance could follow from the invocation of reasons of public order and morality. A refusal based on these grounds leads to an outright exclusion of trademark protection that cannot be overcome through use in trade and is not confined to situations where a sign with cultural significance constitutes a decisive element of the goods themselves. With regard to the further development of this ground for refusal, the aforementioned *Vigeland* decision of the EFTA Court[120] is of particular interest. Seeking to obtain trademark rights to several artworks of Gustav Vigeland, the municipality of Oslo argued in this case that

> [a]ll of the shapes have been exclusively connected to, and used by or through, the Municipality since the death of Gustav Vigeland in 1943. Many of these shapes are well known and valuable, in particular, due to the efforts and investments made by the Municipality.[121]

With this argument, the city of Oslo had little success in its own country. The Norwegian Industrial Property Office remained unimpressed and refused the trademark application on the grounds that Vigeland's works were non-distinctive, descriptive, and functional. The shape of the works added substantial value to at least some of the goods, with respect to which registration was sought.[122] Instead of dispelling these concerns, the Norwegian Board of Appeal decided to supplement the list of grounds for refusal with a further counterargument. It expressed the view that a trademark registration of works belonging to the cultural heritage may be contrary to public policy or accepted principles of morality, and wondered which factors should inform the decision on these grounds for refusal.[123]

Addressing this question, the EFTA Court contributed to the further development of public policy and principles of morality as grounds for refusal by clearly distinguishing its two branches. In the EFTA Court's view, a refusal based on grounds of public policy requires an assessment of objective criteria, whereas a refusal based on accepted principles of morality implies the examination of subjective values.[124]

[120] *See supra* note 13 and accompanying text.

[121] *Vigeland Report, supra* note 15, ¶ 32.

[122] *Id.* ¶ 27.

[123] *Id.* ¶¶ 28–30.

[124] *Vigeland Judgment, supra* note 4, ¶¶ 84–86. As to the innovative character of the decision, see Christophe Geiger & Leonardo Machado Pontes, *Trade Mark Registration, Public Policy, Morality and Fundamental Rights* 11–12 (Centre for Int'l Intell. Prop. Studies, Paper No. 2017-01), https://ssrn.com/abstract=3009170 (placing the judgment in the context of previous EU office practice).

As to the subjective criterion of a conflict with accepted principles of morality, the EFTA Court underlined the necessity to examine on a case-by-case basis how the relevant public would perceive the sign at issue. In line with previous EU case law,[125] the Court posed the question whether Vigeland's works, in and of themselves, would be considered offensive by reasonable consumers with average sensitivity and tolerance thresholds.[126] Quite clearly, this question could be answered in the negative.[127] The EFTA Court, however, went beyond this standard analysis and added an important nuance by holding that

> certain pieces of art may enjoy a particular status as prominent parts of a nation's cultural heritage, an emblem of sovereignty or of the nation's foundations and values. A trade mark registration may even be considered a misappropriation or a desecration of the artist's work, in particular if it is granted for goods or services that contradict the values of the artist or the message communicated through the artwork in question. Therefore, the possibility cannot be ruled out that trade mark registration of an artwork may be perceived by the average consumer in the EEA State in question as offensive and therefore as contrary to accepted principles of morality.[128]

This addition is remarkable. With this statement, the EFTA Court departs from the traditional focus on the scandalous nature of the sign itself. A refusal based on accepted principles of morality may also follow from a finding that the relevant public perceives the *trademark registration of an artwork* as offensive.[129] In this way, the Court substantially broadens the field of application of the ground of refusal. While in the past the offensive nature of the sign was decisive, the offensive nature of the registration attempt offers an alternative avenue for a refusal in the view of the EFTA Court. Consequently, the assessment must take into account the status or perception of the artwork in the relevant national context and the nature of the goods or services covered by the trademark application, "such that registration must be refused if the work is being misappropriated."[130]

As to the second branch of the ground for refusal—the objective criterion of a conflict with public policy—the EFTA Court noted that "public policy" referred to principles and standards regarded to be of a fundamental concern to the state and the whole of society. Therefore, a refusal based on public policy required exceptional circumstances, namely "a genuine and sufficiently serious threat to a fundamental interest of society."[131] Nonetheless, the EFTA Court saw room for applying this ground for refusal in the context of artwork registrations. As already pointed out above, it held that an artwork may be refused registration if its registration is regarded as a genuine and serious threat to fundamental values, or if the need to safeguard the public domain is considered a fundamental interest of society.[132]

[125] For an overview, *see*: Geiger & Machado Pontes, *supra* note 124, at 8–11; KUR & SENFTLEBEN, *supra* note 70, ¶¶ 4.205–.218; ECS, *supra* note 43, at 459–60.

[126] *Vigeland Judgment, supra* note 4 ¶¶ 89–90, 93. [127] *Id.* ¶ 91. [128] *Id.* ¶ 92.

[129] *Id.* For the discussion of a similar concept of "cultural offensiveness" that has evolved in New Zealand in respect of signs of indigenous peoples, see Frankel, *Third-Party Trade Marks, supra* note 118, at 87–91.

[130] *Vigeland Judgment, supra* note 4, ¶ 93. [131] *Id.* ¶¶ 94–96. [132] *Id.* ¶ 96.

As in the context of accepted principles of morality, the EFTA Court stated that a genuine and serious threat to public policy could follow from the *trademark registration of an artwork*.[133] Hence, the Court confirmed that not only the nature of the sign at issue but also the registration attempt as such could be sufficient to justify a refusal based on public policy. The scope of the ground for refusal was thus broadened substantially.

VII. Conclusion

Non-traditional types of marks offer enhanced possibilities for the cumulation of copyright and trademark rights. With the recognition of shape, sound, and motion marks, new areas of overlap emerge that affect traditional work categories, in particular sculpture and plastic art, musical compositions, and audiovisual creations. Given this growing area of overlap, the time is ripe to recalibrate the copyright–trademark interface. Instead of relying on distinctiveness as a threshold criterion and volatile checks and balances within trademark law, more robust mechanisms should be developed to exclude the acquisition of trademark rights to cultural signs from the outset—grounds for refusal that apply across all goods and services and cannot be overcome through use in trade. In the *Vigeland* decision, the EFTA Court took important steps in this direction. The decision provides exemplary lines of argument that can support an exclusion of trademark protection on the basis of public policy or accepted principles of morality. This is a welcome impulse for the future regulation of copyright–trademark overlaps.

[133] *Id.*

17

Non-Traditional Trademarks and Inherently Valuable Expression

*Lisa P. Ramsey**

I. Introduction

Trademark protection today is not just for words (e.g., NIKE for shoes), personal names (e.g., LOUIS VUITTON for handbags), logos (e.g., the Starbucks mermaid for coffee), and graphic designs applied to products, packaging, and retail store signs. Trademark laws now allow companies to obtain trademark rights in three-dimensional shapes, colors, scents, sounds, flavors, textures, and other "non-traditional" marks that identify and distinguish the source of goods or services.[1] Examples of registrations in the United States (U.S.) for non-traditional marks include the shape of the LEGO Minifigure product configuration for toy figures, the color pink for Owens-Corning's fibrous glass residential insulation, the scent of bubble gum for Grendene's shoes and sandals, the sound of a lion roaring for MGM's entertainment

* I appreciate the helpful comments on this chapter from Erin Barns, Irene Calboli, Anne Gilson LaLonde, Kayla Jimenez, Lydia Loren, Glynn Lunney, Dustin Marlan, Alexandra Roberts, Jens Schovsbo, Martin Senftleben, Edward Timberlake, and the participants at the Sixth Annual International Intellectual Property Scholars Roundtable at New York University School of Law, the 16th Annual Conference on IP Law and Policy at Golden Gate University School of Law, the Intellectual Property Scholars Roundtable at the University of New Hampshire School of Law, the Protection of Non-Traditional Marks: Critical Perspectives Roundtable at Singapore Management University, and the 36th Annual Congress of the International Association for the Advancement of Teaching and Research in Intellectual Property at Victoria University of Wellington. I also thank Kathryn Evans, Christiana Garrett, and Molly McBride for their excellent research assistance.

[1] While the United States has registered such marks for several decades, protection of non-traditional marks is a more recent development in other countries. *See* WIPO Committee on Development and Intellectual Property, *Study on Misappropriation of Signs*, CDIP/9/INF/5 (M.R.F. Senftleben ed., Mar. 14, 2012), http://www.wipo.int/edocs/mdocs/mdocs/en/cdip_9/cdip_9_inf_5.pdf [hereinafter WIPO Report]; ANNETTE KUR & MARTIN SENFTLEBEN, EUROPEAN TRADE MARK LAW: A COMMENTARY 90–104, 140–57 (2017); THOMAS P. ARDEN, PROTECTION OF NONTRADITIONAL MARKS: TRADEMARK RIGHTS IN SOUNDS, SCENTS, COLORS, MOTIONS AND PRODUCT DESIGNS IN THE U.S. (2000); Anne Gilson LaLonde & Jerome Gilson, *Getting Real with Nontraditional Trademarks: What's Next After Red Oven Knobs, the Sound of Burning Methamphetamine, and Goats on a Grass Roof?*, 101 TRADEMARK REP. 186 (2011); John A. Tessensohn, *Non-Traditional Trade Marks Thriving in Japan*, 6 J. INTELL. PROP. L. & PRAC. 413 (2016).

services, and a leather texture wrapping around bottles of wine sold by the David Family Group.[2]

Advertising experts note that "sensory branding" incorporating the five senses of sight, smell, sound, taste, and touch can be quite effective in building a strong brand message and attracting and retaining customers.[3] If the public uses these product attributes—also called the "trade dress," "get-up," or "distinguishing guise" of a product—to identify a company's products and distinguish them from other goods or services, a competitor's later unauthorized use of this distinctive subject matter as a mark may cause confusion in the marketplace and harm the distinctiveness of the mark.[4]

Yet sometimes the attributes of a product are not used by consumers to identify or distinguish that product's source. When an alleged mark is not distinctive, trademark laws promote competition by refusing to allow registration of that product feature claimed as a mark. Moreover, if the shape, color, scent, sound, flavor, or texture claimed as a mark makes the goods or services more useful or appealing, this feature may be functional under some trademark laws and ineligible for registration and protection so that others can use it to effectively compete in commerce.[5]

Even if a non-traditional mark is distinctive and non-functional under a nation's trademark laws, this chapter argues that governments should consider not granting exclusive trademark rights in certain shapes, colors, scents, sounds, flavors, and textures because this subject matter can communicate expression protected by the right to freedom of expression. These product attributes may convey information, ideas, emotions, pleasures, or other messages unrelated to source-identification, just like a sculpture, song, or other artistic work.[6] Granting trademark rights in such marks may suppress and chill protected expression without a sufficient justification, as trademark laws today are not limited to regulations of misleading commercial expression and it is difficult to predict what expressive uses of product features claimed as marks are prohibited or allowed.

For example, Globefill Inc. currently owns a U.S. trademark registration for Crystal Head Vodka's skull-shaped glass bottle for alcoholic beverages in addition

[2] U.S. Registration No. 4,903,968 (Minifigure); U.S. Registration No. 1,439,132 (pink); U.S. Registration No. 4,754,435 (bubble gum); U.S. Registration No. 1,395,550 (lion roaring); U.S. Registration No. 3,896,100 (leather). While flavors can be registered as trademarks, *In re* N.V. Organon, 79 U.S.P.Q. 2d (BNA) 1639 (T.T.A.B. 2006), the author was unable to find an example of a registered flavor mark.

[3] MARTIN LINDSTROM, BRAND SENSE: BUILD POWERFUL BRANDS THROUGH TOUCH, TASTE, SMELL, SIGHT, AND SOUND (2005).

[4] Jerome Gilson & Anne Gilson LaLonde, *Cinnamon Buns, Marching Ducks and Cherry-Scented Racecar Exhaust: Protecting Nontraditional Trademarks*, 95 TRADEMARK REP. 773 (July–August 2005). *See also* Graeme B. Dinwoodie, *The Death of Ontology: A Teleological Approach to Trademark Law*, 84 IOWA L. REV. 611 (1999).

[5] *See infra* Section III.

[6] *See infra* Section IV.A.; Ann Bartow, *The True Colors of Trademark Law: Greenlighting a Red Tide of Anti Competition Blues*, 97 KENTUCKY L.J. 263 (2009); Glynn S. Lunney Jr., *Trademark Monopolies*, 48 EMORY L.J. 367, 433–39 (1999); Kenneth L. Port, *On Nontraditional Trademarks*, 38 N. KY. L. REV. 1 (2011); *cf.* Christopher Buccafusco, *Making Sense of Intellectual Property Law*, 97 CORNELL L. REV. 501 (2012) (arguing original artistic works that communicate ideas, emotions, or pleasures to any of the five senses should be potentially copyrightable).

to a design patent and copyright for the sculpture.[7] The bottle was designed by artist John Alexander based on crystal skulls found in the Yucatan.[8] The company's majority owner, actor Dan Aykroyd, said in an interview that the biggest challenge with Crystal Head Vodka is "[g]etting people to open the bottle. Lots of times I hear that people buy Crystal Head Vodka for the bottle—that's great but please crack that skull open."[9] Not only does this bottle shape evoke the "Legend of the Crystal Skulls" featured in the movie *Indiana Jones and the Kingdom of the Crystal Skull*,[10] but a human skull design is often associated with holidays such as Halloween or the Day of the Dead. This skull shape was inherently valuable expression *before* Globefill used it as a mark for vodka and obtained trademark rights in the design. This fact, however, has not discouraged Globefill from aggressively enforcing its trademark rights in the skull shape against competitors and other companies, including a British couple selling "Bloody Hell Hot Sauce" in a similar skull-shaped bottle.[11]

Like shapes, a product's color, scent, sound, flavor, or texture can also convey inherently valuable expression. For example, the color green can communicate an environmentally friendly message and gold may convey opulence when used on products or packaging.[12] Heinz's "Power of Red" campaign created a powerful connection between the ketchup brand and "the feelings associated with the color red: energy, joy, control, and confidence."[13] The scent of coconuts wafting through a retail clothing store or a piña colada scent applied to ukuleles may evoke

[7] U.S. Copyright Registration No. VA 1-766-939; U.S. Patent No. D589,360; U.S. Registration No. 4,043,730.

[8] Geoff Kleinman, *Dan Aykroyd Talks About Crystal Head Vodka*, Drink Spirits (Sept. 23, 2010), http://www.drinkspirits.com/vodka/dan-aykroyd-talks-about-crystal-head-vodka/ (discussing how Alexander—who had "been going to the Mexican 'Day of the Dead' celebration for some time" and was "putting skulls in his artwork for years"—wanted to "put tequila in a glass skull" and then Aykroyd had the idea to "bring back the Mitchell-Hedges skull that was found in the Yucatan" and they "created Crystal Head Vodka").

[9] *Id.* The bottle shape is part of the product—and not just packaging for a product—and that is why it is included here as an example of a non-traditional mark.

[10] Jane MacLaren Walsh, *Legend of the Crystal Skulls*, 61(3) Archaeology Archive (May/June 2008), http://archive.archaeology.org/0805/etc/indy.html.

[11] Telegraph Reporters, *Dan Aykroyd Threatens to Sue Isle of Wight Hot Sauce Company After Business Pitch Goes Horribly Wrong*, Telegraph (July 21, 2017), http://www.telegraph.co.uk/news/2017/07/21/dan-ackroyd-threatens-sueisle-white-hot-sauce-company-business. *See also* Globefill Inc. v. Maud Borup, Inc., No. 0:14-cv-04776 (D. Minn. filed Nov. 17, 2014) (cocktail mixes and hot sauce sold in skull-shaped bottles); Globefill Inc. v. Elements Spirits, Inc., No. 2:10-cv-02034 (C.D. Cal. filed March 22, 2010) (skull-shaped bottle for tequila); Daniel Siegal, *Dan Aykroyd's Skull Vodka Co. Wins Booze Bottle IP Trial*, Law360 (Mar. 29, 2017), https://www.law360.com/articles/907095/dan-aykroyd-s-skull-vodka-co-wins-booze-bottle-ip-trial (discussing jury verdict for Globefill).

[12] Evert-Fresh Corporation owns registrations for the color green and the phrase GREEN BAGS for plastic storage bags that preserve fruit, vegetables, and flowers, U.S. Registration Nos. 2,280,244; 2,359,179, and has sued competitors "using similar names and the green color to mimic [the company's] shelf-life extender" sold under the brand name "Debbie Meyer Green Bags." Mary Flood, *Inventor Pockets Court Wins in Fight Over Storage Bags*, Houston Chronicle (Feb. 13, 2009), http://www.chron.com/business/article/Inventor-pockets-court-wins-in-fight-over-storage-1739011.php. After noting that "[g]old connotes opulence" and "is a natural color to use on a fancy cookbook," the Seventh Circuit held the color "is a prime example of aesthetic functionality" and is not sufficiently distinctive for protection. Publ'ns Int'l, Ltd. v. Landoll, Inc., 164 F.3d 337, 342 (7th Cir. 1998).

[13] lindstrom, *supra* note 3, at 45.

summer or a vacation to a tropical island.[14] A company may use a chocolate aroma or flavor for non-chocolate products to suggest decadence or self-indulgence. An automobile manufacturer could use the smell or texture of leather in magazine advertisements or the cars themselves to connote luxury.[15] A business could use part of a country's national anthem or traditional song in sounds emitted from its products or in advertising to convey a patriotic message. While a product feature may express different messages or nothing at all, this subject matter can communicate messages of expressive value that have nothing to do with the company which is claiming trademark rights in it.

When inherently expressive product features used as trademarks eventually identify a product's source, and are registered and protected as trademarks, this source-identifying message will often be added to the original message rather than substitute for it. For example, Globefill's skull design can identify this product as Crystal Head Vodka *and* continue to convey the expression intrinsically associated with that bottle's shape. Regardless of whether a product feature communicates source-identifying information, another message, or has more than one meaning, this chapter argues that use of non-traditional trademark subject matter in the marketplace can constitute "expression" protected by the right to freedom of expression in treaties, constitutions, and other laws.[16] Thus trademark laws regulating this expression must have a sufficient justification and should directly further the purpose of the law and not harm expressive values more than necessary to achieve that purpose.[17]

This chapter also contends that the free expression right can be harmed when governments register and protect trademark rights in expression that was inherently valuable in the marketplace *before* it was adopted or used as a trademark, which is the case for many non-traditional marks.[18] Granting trademark rights in inherently valuable expression—whether it is colors, representational shapes, or other product features that convey messages unrelated to the product's source,[19] generic or descriptive words,[20] or popular

[14] Id. at 12 (noting a Sydney retail shop pumped out a coconut scent using a concealed machine). SHS International currently owns a registration on the supplemental register for the scent of a piña colada for "musical instruments, namely, ukuleles." U.S. Registration No. 4,144,511.

[15] LINDSTROM, *supra* note 3, at 93–94 (discussing how car manufacturers create an artificial leather smell for cars).

[16] *See infra* Sections II & IV.A. *See also* Lisa P. Ramsey, *A Free Speech Right to Trademark Protection?*, 106 TRADEMARK REP. 797, 821–32 (2016).

[17] *See infra* Section IV.B. *See also* Lisa P. Ramsey, *Free Speech Challenges to Trademark Law After* Matal v. Tam, 56 HOUS. L. REV. (forthcoming 2018).

[18] *Id.* The phrase "inherently valuable" is used in this chapter to refer to an expression that had intrinsic communicative value due to its contribution to the marketplace of ideas and information before it was used as a mark, and not that this non-source-identifying message is beneficial or high-value expression (such as political messages).

[19] Lisa P. Ramsey, *Reconciling Trademark Rights and Free Expression Locally and Globally*, *in* INTERNATIONAL INTELLECTUAL PROPERTY: A HANDBOOK OF CONTEMPORARY RESEARCH 341, 361–68 (Daniel Gervais ed., 2015); Glynn S. Lunney Jr., *The Trade Dress Emperor's New Clothes: Why Trade Dress Does Not Belong on the Principal Register,* 51 HASTINGS L.J. 1131, 1176–77 (2000) (noting shapes and other product features have "inherent product value").

[20] Ralph H. Folsom & Larry L. Teply, *Trademarked Generic Words*, 89 YALE L.J. 1323, 1340–46 (1980); Lisa P. Ramsey, *Descriptive Trademarks and the First Amendment*, 70 TENN. L. REV. 1095 (2003).

slogans[21]—is more likely to harm free expression compared to registration and protection of marks whose value is primarily created by the trademark owner *after* the company began using the mark, such as the APPLE brand name and logo for electronics.

Nations can reduce the conflict between non-traditional trademark laws and expressive values by declining to register and enforce trademark rights in non-traditional marks that contain inherently valuable expression, or by providing only a narrow scope of protection for such marks. Legislatures and courts should also ensure that trademark laws regulating the requirements for registration of non-traditional marks, the scope of trademark rights, defenses, and remedies are consistent with the right to freedom of expression.[22]

II. The Right to Freedom of Expression

Many countries protect the right to freedom of expression, but there is disagreement about the purpose, content, and scope of this right.[23] Some people think a marketplace of ideas will lead to the discovery of truth, while others believe we should protect the free expression right to further democratic self-governance, promote individual autonomy, or foster tolerance.[24]

The "right to freedom of expression" is recognized by treaties protecting human rights, including Article 19(2) of the International Covenant on Civil and Political Rights,[25] Article 13 of the American Convention on Human Rights,[26] and Article 10(1) of the European Convention on Human Rights.[27] The free expression right is not absolute, however, and nations have significant discretion to determine what qualifies as "expression" and regulate the scope and boundaries of this right.[28] While these treaties do not explicitly mention "trademarks" or clarify whether trademark laws are permissible regulations of expression, the treaty provisions do allow

[21] Lisa P. Ramsey, *Intellectual Property Rights in Advertising*, 12 Mich. Telecomm. Tech. L. Rev. 189 (2006).

[22] *See* Ramsey, *supra* note 16, at 846–78; Lisa P. Ramsey, *Increasing First Amendment Scrutiny of Trademark Law*, 61 SMU L. Rev. 381 (2008). *See also* Lisa P. Ramsey & Jens Schovsbo, *Mechanisms for Limiting Trade Mark Rights to Further Competition and Free Speech*, 44 Int'l Rev. of Intell. Prop. & Competition L. 671 (2013).

[23] Larry Alexander, Is There a Right of Freedom of Expression? (2005); Eric Barendt, Freedom of Speech (2d ed. 2005); Ronald J. Krotoszynski, Jr., The First Amendment in Cross-Cultural Perspective: A Comparative Legal Analysis of the Freedom of Speech (2006).

[24] Barendt, *supra* note 23, at 1–38; Erwin Chemerinsky, Constitutional Law: Principles and Policies 969–74 (5th ed. 2015).

[25] International Covenant on Civil and Political Rights art. 19(2), Dec. 16, 1966, S. Exec. Doc. E, 95-2 (1978), 999 U.N.T.S. 171.

[26] Organization of American States, American Convention on Human Rights art. 13, Nov. 22, 1969, O.A.S.T.S. No. 36, 1144 U.N.T.S. 123.

[27] Convention for the Protection of Human Rights and Fundamental Freedoms art. 10(1), Nov. 4, 1950, 213 U.N.T.S. 222 [hereinafter European Convention on Human Rights].

[28] Ramsey, *supra* note 16, at 821–28.

restrictions of expression for a variety of reasons, including protection of the rights of others.[29]

For example, Article 10(1) of the European Convention on Human Rights states that "the right to freedom of expression" is protected and includes "freedom to hold opinions and to receive and impart information and ideas without interference by public authority and regardless of frontiers."[30] This right is limited by Article 10(2), which provides:

> The exercise of these freedoms, since it carries with it duties and responsibilities, may be subject to such formalities, conditions, restrictions or penalties as are prescribed by law and are necessary in a democratic society, in the interests of national security, territorial integrity or public safety, for the prevention of disorder or crime, for the protection of health or morals, for the protection of the reputation or rights of others, for preventing the disclosure of information received in confidence, or for maintaining the authority and impartiality of the judiciary.[31]

A trademark law interfering with "expression" is only consistent with the right to freedom of expression protected in Article 10(1) if the government can prove (1) the limitation on expression is clearly set forth in a statute, code, or line of judicial decisions, and is sufficiently accessible and predictable; (2) the law strives to achieve one of the legitimate goals contained in Article 10(2), such as protection of the "rights of others" (here trademark owners and the public); and (3) the law is "necessary in a democratic society," meaning the restriction on expression is justified by a pressing social need, the reasons for it are relevant and sufficient, and the regulation's nature and severity is proportional to the law's purpose and does not unjustifiably chill expression.[32] States in Europe have greater freedom to regulate commercial expression, and European courts are more likely to defer to national governments when the trademark law regulates infringing use of another's mark in misleading commercial expression.[33]

The right to freedom of expression is also explicitly recognized in national constitutions, including the constitutions of Canada, Japan, South Africa, and the United States.[34] In some nations where there is no constitutional right to freedom

[29] *Id.* [30] European Convention on Human Rights, *supra* note 27, art. 10(1).

[31] *Id.* art. 10(2). The Court of Justice of the European Union's analysis of free expression challenges to trademark laws would be conducted within the framework provided by the Charter of Fundamental Rights of the European Union, which protects the free expression right using identical language and contains similar limitations on this right. Charter of Fundamental Rights of the European Union arts. 11(1), 52(1), 2012 O.J. C326/391. The Charter encourages the Court of Justice to consult opinions of the European Court of Human Rights relating to similar rights in the European Convention on Human Rights. *Id.* art. 52(3). *See* Ramsey, *supra* note 16, at 826–27.

[32] Jonathan Griffiths, *Is There a Right to an Immoral Trade Mark*, *in* INTELLECTUAL PROPERTY AND HUMAN RIGHTS 309, 322–33 (Paul L.C. Torremans ed., 2008); WOLFGANG SAKULIN, TRADEMARK PROTECTION AND FREEDOM OF EXPRESSION: AN INQUIRY INTO THE CONFLICT BETWEEN TRADEMARK RIGHTS AND FREEDOM OF EXPRESSION UNDER EUROPEAN LAW 111–15, 149–80 (2011). *See* MICHEL VERPEAUX, FREEDOM OF EXPRESSION: IN CONSTITUTIONAL AND INTERNATIONAL CASE LAW 11–15, 42–46 (2010).

[33] Griffiths, *supra* note 32, at 323, 331–33; SAKULIN, *supra* note 32, at 112–13, 231–351.

[34] Canadian Charter of Rights and Freedoms, Part I of the Constitution Act, 1982, *being* Schedule B to the Canada Act, 1982, c. 11 § 2(b) (UK); Nihonkoku Kenpō [Kenpō] [Constitution] art. 21, ¶ 1 (Japan); S. Afr. Const., 1996 § 16; U.S. Const. amend. I.

of expression, such as New Zealand and the United Kingdom, the government has protected this right in legislation.[35] As with the treaties, the constitutional and statutory free expression right is not absolute and can be restricted in certain circumstances to protect other public and private interests.[36] For example, Canadian free expression law broadly defines "expression" to cover anything that conveys or attempts to convey meaning, but Canadian courts often find government limitations on expression to be reasonable and demonstrably justified in a free and democratic society.[37]

The United States uses a different approach.[38] While the Free Speech Clause of the First Amendment to the U.S. Constitution provides "Congress shall make no law . . . abridging the freedom of speech,"[39] the U.S. Supreme Court has recognized that there are certain historic and traditional categories of expression which the government can generally prohibit, punish, and otherwise regulate without violating the First Amendment. These categorical exceptions to speech-protection include obscenity, defamation, fraud, incitement to illegal activity, speech integral to criminal conduct, and misleading commercial expression.[40] If a law regulates one of these categories of "unprotected" expression and does not discriminate based on the viewpoint of the speaker, a court may hold the speech restriction is valid under the First Amendment without engaging in further constitutional analysis of whether the benefits of the law outweigh the harm to expression.[41] For example, some U.S. courts have said trademark infringement laws are constitutional under the First Amendment when they regulate misleading commercial speech.[42]

When a categorical exception to First Amendment protection does not apply, constitutional analysis of U.S. laws regulating expression often (but not always) involves application by courts of a balancing test whose level of constitutional scrutiny depends on whether the law regulates expression based on its content or viewpoint, or whether the expression is commercial or non-commercial.[43] Usually regulations of non-commercial speech, viewpoint-discriminatory laws, and other laws that target speech based on its communicative content ("content-based" laws) are presumptively unconstitutional and subject to strict scrutiny analysis, which means the restrictions are "justified only if the government proves that they are narrowly tailored to serve compelling state interests."[44] Content-neutral regulations

[35] New Zealand Bill of Rights Act 1990, § 14; Human Rights Act 1998, c. 42, § 12 (UK); *id.* sch. 1, pt. 1, art. 10.

[36] *See, e.g.*, KROTOSZYNSKI, *supra* note 23, at 183–213 (UK law); SHIGENORI MATSUI, THE CONSTITUTION OF JAPAN: A CONTEXTUAL ANALYSIS 196–211 (2011); Ramsey, *supra* note 16, at 828–32.

[37] ROBERT J. SHARPE & KENT ROACH, THE CHARTER OF RIGHTS AND FREEDOMS 166–203 (6th ed. 2017); Ramsey, *supra* note 16, at 829–30.

[38] Ramsey, *supra* note 16, at 869–70; Ramsey, *Increasing First Amendment Scrutiny of Trademark Law, supra* note 22, at 412–21.

[39] U.S. Const. amend. I.

[40] United States v. Stevens, 559 U.S. 460, 468–69 (2010); Cent. Hudson Gas & Elec. Corp. v. Pub. Serv. Comm'n of N.Y., 447 U.S. 557, 563–66 (1980).

[41] CHEMERINSKY, *supra* note 24, at 1036–37; Ramsey, *supra* note 16, at 869–70.

[42] *See, e.g.*, Facenda v. N.F.L. Films, Inc., 542 F.3d 1007, 1018 (3d Cir. 2008). *See* Ramsey, *Increasing First Amendment Scrutiny of Trademark Law, supra* note 22, at 414–15.

[43] CHEMERINSKY, *supra* note 24, at 976–87, 1144–53. *See also* Ramsey, *Increasing First Amendment Scrutiny of Trademark Law, supra* note 22, at 421–46; Ramsey, *supra* note 20, at 1147–69.

[44] Reed v. Town of Gilbert, 135 S. Ct. 2218, 2226–33 (2015). *See also* Ramsey, *supra* note 17.

of expressive conduct, laws which regulate expression based on its time, place, or manner, and other content-neutral laws are normally evaluated under a more relaxed intermediate scrutiny analysis.[45] U.S. courts have also used an intermediate scrutiny test set forth in *Central Hudson* to determine the validity of restrictions of non-misleading commercial speech, which requires the law to be "narrowly drawn" to directly advance "a substantial interest" and not regulate expression more extensively than necessary to serve that interest.[46] After the recent U.S. Supreme Court decision in *Matal v. Tam*, however, regulations of commercial speech that suppress particular viewpoints or ideas will likely be subject to heightened or strict constitutional scrutiny.[47]

In *Tam*, the U.S. Supreme Court clarified that trademark laws are content-based speech regulations subject to First Amendment scrutiny when it held that the federal trademark law denying registration to potentially disparaging marks was unconstitutional.[48] The *Tam* Court declined to decide whether the *Central Hudson* test or a different First Amendment test should be used when evaluating the constitutionality of trademark laws.[49] Still, it is clear after *Tam* that U.S. courts should evaluate the constitutionality of trademark laws to determine if they violate the free speech right.[50] In *Tam*, the Court also noted the test for determining whether a mark may be disparaging was vague and resulted in "a haphazard record of enforcement,"[51] but it did not consider whether the Court's void for vagueness doctrine applied to this law. A law may be unconstitutionally vague if a reasonable person cannot determine what expression is prohibited. Vagueness doctrine recognizes that it is unfair to punish people based on the content of their expression without giving them clear

[45] Turner Broad. Sys. v. F.C.C., 512 U.S. 622, 641–52 (1994); Ward v. Rock Against Racism, 491 U.S. 781, 791–803 (1989); United States v. O'Brien, 391 U.S. 367, 376–77 (1968).

[46] *Cent. Hudson Gas & Elec. Corp.*, *supra* note 40, 562–66. *See also* Jennifer E. Rothman, *Commercial Speech, Commercial Use, and the Intellectual Property Quagmire*, 101 VA. L. REV. 1929 (2015) (discussing how courts distinguish between commercial and non-commercial expression).

[47] Matal v. Tam, 137 S. Ct. 1744, 1751–60 (2017) (holding the ban on registration of potentially disparaging marks in 15 U.S.C. § 1052(a) was an unconstitutional regulation of expression based on its viewpoint). While four Justices said the Court need not decide whether strict or intermediate scrutiny analysis applies "because the disparagement clause cannot withstand even *Central Hudson* review," *id.* at 1764 (Alito, J., plurality opinion) (joined by Chief Justice John Roberts and Justices Clarence Thomas and Stephen Breyer), five Justices believed that heightened or strict scrutiny analysis should be used to evaluate the constitutionality of the viewpoint-discriminatory law regardless of whether it regulated commercial expression. *Id.* at 1765–69 (Kennedy, J., concurring) (joined by Justices Ruth Bader Ginsburg, Sonia Sotomayor, and Elena Kagan) (quoting Sorrell v. IMS Health Inc., 564 U.S. 552, 566 (2011)); *id.* at 1769 (Thomas, J., concurring).

[48] Lisa Ramsey, *The First Amendment Protects Offensive Trademarks*, REGULATORY REVIEW (July 25, 2017), https://www.theregreview.org/2017/07/25/ramsey-first-amendment-protects-offensive-trademarks/; Lisa Ramsey, *Symposium: Increasing First Amendment Scrutiny of Trademark Law After* Matal v. Tam, SCOTUSBLOG (June 20, 2017), http://www.scotusblog.com/2017/06/symposium-increasing-first-amendment-scrutiny-trademark-law-matal-v-tam/.

[49] *Tam*, 137 S. Ct. at 1763 n. 16, 1764 n. 17 (Alito, J., plurality opinion); *id.* at 1768 (Kennedy, J., concurring).

[50] *See, e.g.*, *In re* Brunetti, 877 F.3d 1330, 1349–50 (Fed. Cir. 2017) (holding that strict scrutiny applied to this trademark law banning registration of immoral or scandalous marks, but then concluding that this law is unconstitutional even under *Central Hudson*'s intermediate scrutiny test). *See also* Ramsey, *supra* note 17.

[51] Matal v. Tam, 137 S. Ct. 1744, 1756–57 n. 5 (2017).

notice of what language is regulated by the law. Vague laws chill expression because the threat of sanctions can deter lawful communications.[52]

If there is a free expression challenge to a trademark law in any nation, legislatures or courts will need to first decide whether that country is bound to protect the right to freedom of expression by a treaty, constitution, or statute. If so, the decision-maker must next consider whether this regulated use of a trademark constitutes "expression" protected by the free expression right. If a statute, code, judicial decision, or administrative ruling prohibits, punishes, or chills expression, or harms expression in other ways, the challenged law will likely be subject to review under the balancing tests created by courts interpreting exceptions to the free expression right in treaties, constitutions, or other laws. If laws granting exclusive trademark rights in product features and other non-traditional trademark subject matter (hereinafter called "non-traditional trademark laws") are subject to this analysis, it is likely that at least some of them will be found inconsistent with the right to freedom of expression.

III. Non-Traditional Trademark Laws

As demonstrated through a few examples below, the requirements for registration and protection of non-traditional marks can differ, but nations generally require the mark to distinguish the trademark owner's goods or services and function as an indicator of their source.[53] Generic symbols and other signs that lack distinctiveness or fail to function as a mark will usually be refused registration and protection.[54] In addition, trademarks must be capable of graphical representation or meet other criteria that provides sufficient notice of what subject matter is claimed as a mark.[55] Some—but not all—governments also refuse to protect trademark rights in matter that is functional regardless of whether the mark has become distinctive in the marketplace. Once a non-traditional mark is deemed to be a valid trademark, it will usually be protected just like "traditional" marks against infringement and other trademark violations unless a defense applies. These trademark rules can promote competition and protect the public domain,[56] but they may not be sufficient to protect expressive values for the reasons discussed later in Section IV.B.

The federal trademark statute in the United States is an example of a law which allows many types of non-verbal and non-visual marks or "trade dress" to be eligible for registration and protection. Rather than list the specific types of non-traditional subject matter that can qualify as a mark in the statute, the U.S. Congress defined the word "trademark" as "any word, name, symbol, or device, or any combination

[52] NAACP v. Button, 371 U.S. 415, 432–33 (1963) ("Because First Amendment freedoms need breathing space to survive, government may regulate in the area only with narrow specificity."); CHEMERINSKY, *supra* note 24, at 987–99.

[53] *See* WIPO Report, *supra* note 1.

[54] *Id.* For information about the difference between lack of distinctiveness and failure to function as a mark, see Alexandra J. Roberts, *Trademark Failure to Function*, 103 IOWA L. REV. (forthcoming 2018).

[55] *See* WIPO Report, *supra* note 1.

[56] *Id.*

thereof, used by a person . . . to identify or distinguish his or her goods, including a unique product, from those manufactured or sold by others and to indicate the source of the goods, even if that source is unknown."[57] The U.S. Supreme Court interpreted the words "symbol" and "device" in the statute broadly in *Qualitex*: "Since human beings might use as a 'symbol' or 'device' almost anything at all that is capable of carrying meaning, this language, read literally, is not restrictive."[58] The Court further explained that "[i]t is the source-distinguishing ability of a mark—not its ontological status as color, shape, fragrance, word, or sign—that permits it to serve" the basic purposes of trademark law.[59] Thus "almost anything" capable of carrying "source-distinguishing" meaning can qualify as a trademark in the United States, including a single color (e.g., Qualitex's green-gold for dry cleaning press pads) and other non-traditional marks such as three-dimensional shapes, scents, sounds, flavors, textures, and the exterior or interior décor of a building.[60]

Such marks can only be registered in the United States, however, if they are distinctive for the goods or services, the matter claimed as a mark is not functional, and the applicant files a "specimen" showing how the mark is used in commerce.[61] Substantial proof of acquired distinctiveness may be required for registration of certain non-traditional marks, and the mark must not consist of matter that is merely ornamental, decorative, or informational, or matter which otherwise fails to function as a mark.[62] Moreover, courts have declined to protect trademark rights in certain unregistered non-traditional marks where the alleged trademark owner failed to prove the mark acquired sufficient distinctiveness through use.[63]

U.S. courts also refuse to enforce trademark rights in functional product features regardless of whether they are distinctive. According to the U.S. Supreme Court, "a product feature is functional, and cannot serve as a trademark, if it is essential to the use or purpose of the article or if it affects the cost or quality of the article."[64] An example of a product configuration with utilitarian functionality is the shape of a dual-spring design mechanism that keeps road signs upright.[65] A feature like this currently or formerly protected by a utility patent is more likely to be found functional.[66] A product attribute desired by consumers for aesthetic rather than utilitarian reasons may also be functional under the "competitive necessity" test if granting exclusive rights to that feature "would put competitors

[57] 15 U.S.C. § 1127.

[58] Qualitex Co. v. Jacobson Products, Co., 514 U.S. 159, 162 (1995).

[59] *Id.* at 164.

[60] *Id.* at 162–64; J. THOMAS MCCARTHY, MCCARTHY ON TRADEMARKS AND UNFAIR COMPETITION §§ 7:39–52, 7:100–108, 8:1–5 (5th ed. 2017).

[61] 15 U.S.C. §§ 1051(a)(1), 1052(e)(5), 1052(f), 1053, 1127; Wal-Mart Stores, Inc. v. Samara Brothers, 529 U.S. 205, 210–16 (2000); MCCARTHY, *supra* note 60, at §§ 4:13, 7:39–108, 19:61:50.

[62] U.S. Patent & Trademark Office, Trademark Manual of Examining Procedure §§ 1202, 1202.02–05, 1202.13–15, 1212 (Oct. 2017); MCCARTHY, *supra* note 60, at §§ 3:5, 7:24–25.

[63] *See, e.g.*, Savant Homes, Inc. v. Collins, 809 F.3d 1133, 1146–50 (10th Cir. 2016) (floorplan of a home); Bern Unlimited, Inc. v. Burton Corp., 95 F.Supp.3d 184, 205–11 (D. Mass. 2015) (shape of sports helmet); Buzz Bee Toys, Inc. v. Swimways Corp., 20 F.Supp.3d 483, 497–505 (D.N.J. 2014) (shape of water gun).

[64] TrafFix Devices Inc. v. Marketing Displays Inc., 532 U.S. 23, 32–35 (2001).

[65] *Id.* at 28–32.

[66] *Id.*

at a significant nonreputation-related disadvantage."[67] Use of the color black for floral packaging in connection with bereavement is an example.[68] Such product features have aesthetic functionality and are unlikely to be protected as a mark if few or no equally effective alternatives are available to competitors.[69]

Like the United States, Member States in the European Union allow registration and protection of non-traditional marks that are distinctive and not functional.[70] The EU Trade Mark Regulation and EU Trade Mark Directive both provide that shapes, colors, sounds, and other signs are eligible for registration if they are capable of "distinguishing the goods or services of one undertaking from those of other undertakings" and the mark can be represented on the trademark register "in a manner which enables the competent authorities and the public to determine the clear and precise subject matter of the protection afforded to its proprietor."[71] Trademarks will not be registered if they are "devoid of any distinctive character," but certain marks may be registered after they have become distinctive through use of the mark with the relevant goods or services.[72] Functionality of a sign is also an absolute ground for refusal of a registration, and this rule applies to "signs which consist exclusively of: (i) the shape, or another characteristic, which results from the nature of the goods themselves; (ii) the shape, or another characteristic, of goods which is necessary to obtain a technical result; [or] (iii) the shape, or another characteristic, which gives substantial value to the goods."[73]

Some countries require non-traditional subject matter to be distinctive for trademark registration, but do not explicitly bar registration of product features which are functional. For example, in New Zealand, the Trade Marks Act provides that a "trade mark" includes "a brand, colour, device, heading, label, letter, name, numeral, shape, signature, smell, sound, taste, ticket, or word," or a combination of these signs, that is capable of "being represented graphically" and "distinguishing the goods or services of one person from those of another person."[74] The New Zealand Trade Marks Act does not contain a provision banning

[67] *Id.* at 32–35 (quoting *Qualitex Co.*, *supra* note 58, 165 (1995)).

[68] *In re* Florists' Transworld Delivery, Inc., 105 U.S.P.Q.2d (BNA) 1377 (T.T.A.B. 2013).

[69] For a discussion of functionality doctrine, see Robert G. Bone, *Trademark Functionality Reexamined*, 7 J. Legal Analysis 183 (2015); Justin Hughes, *Cognitive and Aesthetic Functionality in Trademark Law*, 36 Cardozo L. Rev. 1227 (2015); Mark McKenna, *(Dys)functionality*, 48 Hous. L. Rev. 823 (2012). *See also* McCarthy, *supra* note 60, at §§ 7:63–93.

[70] *See* Kur & Senftleben, *supra* note 1, at 90–172.

[71] Regulation (EU) 2017/1001 of the European Parliament and of the Council of 14 June 2017 on the European Union trade mark art. 4, 2017 O.J. L154/1 [hereinafter EU Regulation]; Directive (EU) 2015/2436 of the European Parliament and of the Council of 16 December 2015 to approximate the laws of the Member States relating to trade marks art. 3, 2015 O.J. L336/1 [hereinafter EU Directive].

[72] EU Regulation, *supra* note 71, arts. 7(1)(b), 7(3); EU Directive, *supra* note 71, arts. 4(1)(b), 4(4).

[73] EU Regulation, *supra* note 71, art. 7(1)(e); EU Directive, *supra* note 71, art. 4(1)(e). *See* Annette Kur, *Too Pretty to Protect? Trade Mark Law and the Enigma of Aesthetic Functionality*, *in* Technology and Competition: Contributions in Honor of Hanns Ullrich 139–59 (Josef Drexl, Reto Hilty, Laurence Boy, Christine Godt, & Bernard Remiche eds., 2009) (arguing courts should focus on competitive concerns when interpreting the law).

[74] Trade Marks Act 2002, pt. 1, § 5 (N.Z.); *id.*, pt. 2, subs 2, § 18 (N.Z.).

registration of functional product features, but the New Zealand Intellectual Property Office may deny registration of such marks on other grounds, such as lack of distinctiveness.[75] Australia also does not have a non-functionality requirement for registration of distinctive marks in its Trade Marks Act, and uses a similar approach.[76]

Even when trademark laws ban registration of functional product features and require strong proof of acquired distinctiveness through use for registration of non-traditional marks, commentators note that trademark registration, clearances, and enforcement of trademark rights in three-dimensional shapes, colors, scents, sounds, flavors, and textures can be complicated and challenging due to their non-verbal and non-visual nature.[77] Moreover, unlike patented inventions, industrial designs, and copyrighted works, which are only protected for a limited duration, the term of trademark protection can last forever if the mark continues to act as a source-identifier in the marketplace.[78] Patented features that provide a utilitarian advantage will usually be denied trademark registration and protection under the doctrine of functionality.[79] Yet governments still grant trademark rights in subject matter currently or formerly protected by copyright and design laws,[80] such as Globefill's skull-shaped bottle. This practice may make it more difficult for competitors and others to use that product feature claimed as a mark in certain ways after the copyright, industrial design, or design patent term has expired even though the subject matter has supposedly entered the public domain.[81] Not only is a robust public domain important for competition, but it also promotes expressive values, as discussed next.

[75] SUSY FRANKEL, INTELLECTUAL PROPERTY IN NEW ZEALAND 499–507, 538–44 (2d ed. 2011); Rob Batty, *Unravelling the Distinctiveness Knot in New Zealand's Trade Marks Act*, 23 N.Z. BUS. L.Q. 36 (2017); Rob Batty, *Is New Zealand's Trade Marks Law Out of Shape?*, 33(5) EUR. INTELL. PROP. REV. 281–89 (2011).

[76] ROBERT G. BURRELL & MICHAEL HANDLER, AUSTRALIAN TRADE MARK LAW 65–161 (2d ed. 2016).

[77] *See, e.g.*, Spyros Maniatis, *Scents as Trademarks: Propertisation of Scents and Olfactory Poverty*, *in* LAW AND THE SENSES 217, 224–31 (Lionel Bently & Leo Flynn eds., 1996); Amanda E. Compton, *Acquiring a Flavor for Trademarks: There's No Common Taste in the World*, 8 NW. J. TECH. & INTELL. PROP. 340 (2010); Gilson & LaLonde, *supra* note 4; LaLonde & Gilson, *supra* note 1; Kevin K. McCormick, *"Ding" You are Now Free to Register That Sound*, 96 TRADEMARK REP. 1101 (2006).

[78] KUR & SENFTLEBEN, *supra* note 1, at 168; MCCARTHY, *supra* note 60, at §§ 7:63–64.

[79] KUR & SENFTLEBEN, *supra* note 1, at 166; MCCARTHY, *supra* note 60, at § 7:89.30.

[80] MCCARTHY, *supra* note 60, at § 6:5.

[81] *See, e.g.*, Irene Calboli, *Overlapping Rights: The Negative Effects of Trademarking Creative Works*, *in* THE EVOLUTION AND EQUILIBRIUM OF COPYRIGHT IN THE DIGITAL AGE 52–78 (Susy Frankel & Daniel Gervais eds., 2014); Martin Senftleben, *Public Domain Preservation in EU Trademark Law—A Model for Other Regions?*, 103 TRADEMARK REP. 775 (2013). Some scholars are fine with overlapping copyright and trademark rights for artistic works, but note problems may arise where the trademark claimant is not originally or is no longer the copyright owner of the artistic work. *See, e.g.*, Jane C. Ginsburg, *Licensing Commercial Value: From Copyright to Trademarks and Back*, *in* THE LAW AND PRACTICE OF TRADEMARK TRANSACTIONS: PERSPECTIVES AND CHALLENGES IN A GLOBAL MARKETPLACE 53–81 (Irene Calboli & Jacques de Werra eds., 2016). For an argument that three-dimensional shapes should be eligible for protection under trademark and design patent law, see Amir H. Khoury, *Three-Dimensional Objects as Marks: Does a "Dark Shadow" Loom Over Trademark Theory?*, 26 CARDOZO ARTS & ENT. L.J. 335 (2008).

IV. Certain Non-Traditional Trademark Laws May Violate the Free Expression Right

Trademark owners may argue that registration and protection of non-traditional marks does not implicate or violate the free expression right for a number of reasons. First, they may argue the government is not regulating "expression" protected by the right to freedom of expression when it grants and enforces trademark rights in non-traditional marks because the shape, color, scent, sound, flavor, texture, or other sign is being used in a commercial context to identify a product's source. If "expression" is not being regulated by the government, then there can be no violation of the free expression right. Second, trademark advocates may contend that non-traditional trademark laws generally satisfy the relevant balancing tests created by courts interpreting the free expression provision in treaties, constitutions, and statutes because these trademark laws contain internal safeguards that sufficiently protect expression. These arguments are discussed and rejected below.

A. "Expression" capable of protection by the free expression right

When determining whether laws regulate "expression" in such a way that implicates the right to freedom of expression, courts have recognized that people communicate using symbols other than words. For example, in the United States, the First Amendment protects expressive conduct or "symbolic speech" that communicates messages, including burning a flag and wearing an armband in protest.[82] Other countries also recognize the free expression right is not limited to language, and protect expressive use of symbols and expressive conduct from unnecessary government restrictions.[83] Thus, use of a product attribute or other non-traditional subject matter as a mark should qualify as "expression" if it conveys information about a product's source or communicates other messages.[84]

Critics of using a free expression framework for evaluating the validity of trademark laws may argue that non-traditional trademark laws do not implicate the right to freedom of expression when non-traditional marks are used solely to identify and distinguish the source of commercial products for sale. This argument should fail because, by definition, a symbol such as the skull-shaped bottle for Crystal Head Vodka only qualifies as a "trademark" if it conveys a source-identifying message (even if the exact name of the trademark owner, Globefill, is unknown). In those countries that protect commercial expression within the free expression right, this

[82] Texas v. Johnson, 491 U.S. 397, 399–404 (1989); Tinker v. Des Moines Indep. Cmty. Sch. Dist., 393 U.S. 503, 505–06 (1969); CHEMERINSKY, *supra* note 24, at 1117–23.

[83] BARENDT, *supra* note 23, at 78–88; SAKULIN, *supra* note 32, at 112; SHARPE & ROACH, *supra* note 37, at 169–70.

[84] Ramsey, *supra* note 16, at 865–66; Ramsey, *Increasing First Amendment Scrutiny of Trademark Law, supra* note 22, at 409–12; Ramsey, *supra* note 20, at 1137–38.

information about a product's source is "expression" even though it is communicated in a commercial context.[85]

Moreover, it is important to recognize that trademark laws—including non-traditional trademark laws—regulate both the "expression" of trademark owners and of other people using (or interested in using) the marks without authorization. A trademark owner's "expression" is being regulated when the government denies or approves an application to register a mark based on the content of the message.[86] Yet the government is also regulating—and potentially chilling—the "expression" of many other companies and people when the trademark office grants someone exclusive rights to use a non-traditional mark with certain goods or services.[87]

In addition, courts prohibit and punish "expression" of a trademark defendant when they issue an injunction banning further use of the non-traditional mark, or award monetary damages, after finding the defendant used the mark to communicate a message that is likely to confuse consumers or harm the distinctiveness or reputation of a famous mark. Use of a competitor's mark to sell identical goods or services may be misleading commercial expression, and therefore not protected by the right to freedom of expression for that reason. However, use of an identical shape, color, or other product attribute claimed as a mark may not be misleading if the second company is using the mark to sell different goods or services and is not causing confusion about the source of its own products. Just as two companies can own trademark rights in the same word in different industries without causing confusion (think DELTA airlines and DELTA faucets), use of an identical product feature as a mark may not be misleading if the products differ and the defendant does nothing to suggest a connection between the companies.

Some expressive uses of trademarks by accused infringers are explicitly allowed under trademark laws, such as descriptive use of another's protected mark to describe a product's qualities or characteristics in a fair and honest way.[88] For example, assume a company owns a registration for the colors pink, brown, and white for ice cream shops, and this mark is distinctive and not functional for this product. If the trademark owner files an infringement lawsuit against a business that sells and advertises

[85] Griffiths, *supra* note 32, at 329; MCCARTHY, *supra* note 60, at § 31:139.25; Robert C. Denicola, *Trademarks as Speech: Constitutional Implications of the Emerging Rationales for the Protection of Trade Symbols*, 1982 WIS. L. REV. 158, 193; Mark A. Lemley & Eugene Volokh, *Freedom of Speech and Injunctions in Intellectual Property Cases*, 48 DUKE L.J. 147, 219 (1998); Ramsey, *supra* note 17; Ramsey, *supra* note 16, at 865–66; Ramsey, *Increasing First Amendment Scrutiny of Trademark Law*, *supra* note 22, at 409–12. *Cf.* Sorrell v. IMS Health Inc., 564 U.S. 552, 570 (2011) (stating that "the creation and dissemination of information are speech within the meaning of the First Amendment"); *In re* Brunetti, 877 F.3d 1330, 1338 (Fed. Cir. 2017) (trademarks "identify the source of a product or service, and therefore play a role in the 'dissemination of information as to who is producing and selling what product, for what reason, and at what price' ") (quoting Va. State Bd. of Pharmacy v. Va. Citizens Consumer Council, Inc., 425 U.S. 748, 765 (1976)).

[86] Ramsey, *supra* note 16, at 865–66; *see Tam*, 137 S. Ct. at 1758–60 (Alito, J., plurality opinion); *id.* at 1765–68 (Kennedy, J., concurring).

[87] BURRELL & HANDLER, *supra* note 76, at 160; Ramsey, *supra* note 16, at 834–46, 860.

[88] *See e.g.*, 15 U.S.C. § 1115(b)(4); 15 U.S.C. § 1125(c)(3)(A); EU Directive, *supra* note 71, art. 14(1)(b); EU Regulation, *supra* note 71, art. 14(1)(b); Trade Marks Act 1995 (Cth), § 122(1)(b) (Austl.); KUR & SENFTLEBEN, *supra* note 1, at 412–15; MCCARTHY, *supra* note 60, at §§ 11:45–49; WIPO Report, *supra* note 1.

flash-frozen ice cream with the colors pink, brown, and white, and these colors accurately describe the flavors of this dessert as strawberry, chocolate, and vanilla, respectively,[89] the accused infringer could argue that the descriptive fair use defense applies. These colors communicate information and this commercial expression implicates the free expression right.

Honest referential use or nominative fair use of another's mark is also permitted in some jurisdictions, and involves use of the protected mark to truthfully identify the trademark owner or its products.[90] For example, another business may use the mark in advertising to communicate that it is selling genuine used goods, accessories, spare parts, or repair services for the trademark owner's products. In addition, some trademark statutes specifically allow use of another's mark in parody, criticism, commentary,[91] news reporting,[92] or comparative advertising.[93] These defenses should apply to expression that incorporates another's non-traditional mark. The law should allow an artist to display an art installation at a museum that includes various scents registered as marks, or sell posters with scratch and sniff stickers of these scents in the museum gift shop, to parody, complain about, or celebrate the trademark owners' registrations or the government's decision to allow registration of scent marks. News reporters or bloggers should be allowed to display a photo of the LEGO Minifigure product configuration next to an article about LEGO Group's products. It should be legal for competitors to use a photo of the LEGO Minifigure in a legitimate comparative advertisement discussing the price of competing toys, or an advertisement for accessories compatible with the Minifigure or used toys previously sold by LEGO Group.[94]

Labeling use of a non-traditional mark as "expression" does not mean that all regulations of it violate the right to freedom of expression. It simply means courts should evaluate the free expression claims of the trademark owner, accused infringers, and the public, and the government must justify the law under the relevant free expression balancing test in that jurisdiction.

What if an accused infringer did not intend to convey a message when it used another's non-traditional mark? When a company uses a color or other product feature in the marketplace because of the product's natural attributes or for random reasons, the trademark owner may argue this is not "expression" capable of protection by the free expression right because there is no intent to communicate. A company may sell a medical device with a pink color because that is the natural color of the materials used to make the product.[95] A bank may randomly decide to use red in its logo, décor, and advertisements and later discover that a competitor

[89] *Cf.* Dippin' Dots, Inc. v. Frosty Bits Distrib., LLC, 369 F.3d 1197, 1203–06 (11th Cir. 2004) (holding colors were functional for flash-frozen ice cream and could not be protected as marks because they indicate the flavors of the product).

[90] *See e.g.*, EU Directive, *supra* note 71, art. 14(1)(c); EU Regulation, *supra* note 71, art. 14(1)(c); KUR & SENFTLEBEN, *supra* note 1, at 420–34; MCCARTHY, *supra* note 60, at §§ 23:11, 31:139, 31:156.50.

[91] *See, e.g.*, 15 U.S.C. § 1125(c)(3)(A)(ii).

[92] *See, e.g.*, 15 U.S.C. § 1125(c)(3)(B).

[93] *See, e.g.*, 15 U.S.C. § 1125(c)(3)(A)(i); Trade Marks Act 1995 (Cth), § 122(1)(d) (Austl.).

[94] Note the author made up the examples in this paragraph; they are not based on real trademark disputes.

[95] The pink color would be functional for a ceramic hip implant that contains chromium, C5 Med. Werks, LLC v. CeramTec GmbH, 249 F.Supp.3d. 1210, 1218 (D. Colo. 2017), *appeal docketed* No.

registered that color as a mark and is claiming the exclusive right to use it.[96] If there was no communicative intent when this color was used by the accused infringer, courts may question whether the defendant could later argue in a trademark dispute that it has a free expression right to use this color.[97]

Even if a particular company does not have an intent to communicate a message when it uses a color or other product feature, non-traditional marks convey expression and courts should find the free expression right is generally implicated when the government registers and protects distinctive non-traditional marks.[98] The government is regulating this trademark's message based on its content and uses trademark laws to restrict use of that specific message by others after granting trademark rights in it. "Expression" is implicated when governments regulate trademarks regardless of whether the accused infringer (e.g., the couple who makes Bloody Hell Hot Sauce) is using the non-traditional mark (e.g., a skull-shaped bottle) to identify the source of its products (e.g., Globefill, the manufacturer of Crystal Head Vodka, or the hot sauce company), describe or decorate its products, or convey other messages (e.g., this hot sauce is deadly).[99]

B. Balancing non-traditional trademark rights and free expression

To properly evaluate whether non-traditional trademark laws are consistent with the right to freedom of expression, courts will first need to identify the purpose of the specific law and determine if those trademark goals satisfy the relevant criteria for government interests in that jurisdiction (e.g., the law protects the rights of others and is necessary in a democratic society in the EU, or serves at least a substantial government interest in the U.S.).[100] For example, in the United States, the government primarily registers trademarks and protects trademark rights to facilitate the communication of truthful source-identifying product information; prevent fraudulent, deceptive, or misleading uses of marks; and promote competition.[101]

17-1173 (10th Cir. May 19, 2017), but the plaintiff may have trademark rights in the color for different goods or services where pink is not functional.

[96] Competitors of a bank challenged the distinctiveness of a registered mark for the color red in Joined Cases C-217/13 & C-218/13, Oberbank AG & Others v. Deutscher Sparkassen- und Giroverband eV, 2014 E.C.R. 2012 (June 19, 2014).

[97] In the United States, for example, expressive conduct is capable of protection by the First Amendment if "[a]n intent to convey a particularized message was present, and in the surrounding circumstances the likelihood was great that the message would be understood by those who viewed it." Spence v. Washington, 418 U.S. 405, 410–11 (1974). *See also Texas v. Johnson, supra* note 82, 403–04. Scholars criticize this test as not sufficiently protective of the public interest in free expression. *See e.g.*, Robert Post, *Recuperating First Amendment Doctrine*, 47 Stan. L. Rev. 1249, 1250–60 (1995).

[98] *See* Ramsey, *Increasing First Amendment Scrutiny of Trademark Law, supra* note 22, at 410–11.

[99] Ramsey, *supra* note 16, at 865–66; Ramsey, *Increasing First Amendment Scrutiny of Trademark Law, supra* note 22, at 409–12.

[100] *See supra* Section II.

[101] 15 U.S.C. § 1127 (setting forth the intent of the federal trademark law); Matal v. Tam, 137 S. Ct. 1744, 1751–52 (2017) (discussing the reasons for trademark protection); *id.* at 1768 (Kennedy, J., concurring) (stating that the "central purpose of trademark registration is to facilitate source identification"); *id.* at 1768 ("It is well settled, for instance, that to the extent a trademark is confusing or misleading the law can protect consumers and trademark owners."). *See also* Ramsey, *supra* note 17. For a discussion of

These trademark goals benefit consumers and trademark owners. Courts evaluating a free expression challenge to a non-traditional trademark law will likely find these primary goals of U.S. trademark law to be substantial (if not compelling) government interests.[102]

While the free expression doctrines used by courts to balance trademark goals and expressive values may differ, the analysis will likely include a determination of the importance of the government interests used to justify this specific restriction on expression, whether there is a reasonable and proportional fit between the trademark law and its purpose, and a discussion of how the law harms expression.[103] Critics of non-traditional trademark laws argue these laws generally fail to help consumers identify and distinguish among competing products, do not prevent fraud or deception in a significant way, and harm competition because product features claimed as marks are rarely distinctive and often contain useful, artistic, or otherwise desirable subject matter that should remain in the public domain for use by all traders.[104]

Non-traditional trademark laws are more likely to further the primary goals of trademark law and protect the public domain if governments require non-traditional marks to be non-functional and have strong and substantial evidence of acquired distinctiveness through use before they are registered and protected. Unfortunately not all nations have these requirements. Moreover, even if a trademark office or court determines a non-traditional mark has acquired distinctiveness, this conclusion may not require a majority of consumers to believe the product feature is a source-identifying mark rather than ornamentation, decoration, or other expression. Compared to words, logos, and other "traditional" marks, product attributes may be less likely to be perceived by consumers as marks.[105] Thus, for a significant number of consumers unaware of the source-identifying message, registering and protecting trademark rights in non-traditional marks will not directly advance the ability of those people to identify the source of products or reduce confusion in the marketplace.

In addition, requiring companies to prove acquired distinctiveness through use of non-traditional marks will favor larger companies over start-ups and individual sellers, and make it easier for famous brands to maintain their strong position in the

the primary goals of trademark law in other jurisdictions, see BURRELL & HANDLER, *supra* note 76, at 1–8 (Australia); KUR & SENFTLEBEN, *supra* note 1, at 3–25 (Europe).

102 Ramsey, *supra* note 17. Trademark laws protect limited property rights in marks and an investment in goodwill, MCCARTHY, *supra* note 60, at §§ 2:1–2; Robert G. Bone, *Hunting Goodwill: A History of the Concept of Goodwill in Trademark Law*, 86 B.U. L. REV. 547 (2006), but protection of property rights in words and expressive product attributes claimed as trademarks is not itself a substantial government interest. Ramsey, *supra* note 17. This is especially true when that expression was inherently valuable before it was adopted or used as a mark and the trademark owner is free riding off that inherent value. *Id.*; Ramsey, *supra* note 20, at 1152–56; Ramsey, *Increasing First Amendment Scrutiny of Trademark Law, supra* note 22, at 422–25.

103 *See supra* Section II. *See also* Ramsey, *supra* note 17.

104 *See, e.g.*, Bartow, *supra* note 6; Lunney, *supra* note 6; Lunney, *supra* note 19; Port, *supra* note 6.

105 *See* KUR & SENFTLEBEN, *supra* note 1, at 170–72 (discussing argument but noting this could change); Bartow, *supra* note 6, at 290; Lunney, *supra* note 19, at 1163–67; Port, *supra* note 6, at 7–11, 25–26, 47; *cf.* Wal-Mart Stores, Inc. v. Samara Brothers, 529 U.S. 205, 213 (2000) (noting a product's shape can make it more useful or appealing).

marketplace. Big firms often have more money to spend on advertising featuring the non-traditional marks, and their marketing and sales can cover more geographic areas and will likely be of higher volume. Such evidence helps prove acquired distinctiveness, and thus it is more likely that established companies will be the ones to obtain exclusive trademark rights to non-traditional subject matter. Eliminating trademark rights in non-traditional trademarks may therefore promote competition and other trademark law goals better than protecting rights in such marks, as it would allow everyone to use the desired product attribute to compete in the marketplace and distinguish their goods using words, logos, and other "traditional" marks.

Legislatures can also protect expressive values and promote trademark law's primary goals by requiring proof of fraud or misleading use of another's non-traditional mark for trademark liability. Current trademark laws regulate non-misleading expression, however, and endanger protected expression because they do not provide clear notice of what expression is prohibited or allowed.[106] The laws are vague and overbroad rather than narrowly drawn because owners of non-traditional marks can sue under trademark laws when the expression is not misleading and the parties are not competitors. Neither dilution nor infringement law requires proof of fraud or actual confusion (only a likelihood of confusion is sufficient for infringement), and both laws can apply to defendants selling dissimilar products.[107] The harm to expression is exacerbated when companies claim trademark rights in representational shapes, colors, and other product attributes that expressed inherently valuable messages before they were adopted or used as marks. Laws granting trademark rights in non-traditional subject matter that intrinsically conveys a message are akin to laws granting exclusive trademark rights in descriptive terms, which are arguably unconstitutional regulations of commercial expression in the United States.[108]

When governments are deciding whether to allow registration and protection of certain non-traditional marks, and are balancing the free expression claims of the trademark owner, other companies, and the public, they should consider the nature and severity of the limitation on expression, including whether the law bans and punishes expression or only discourages expression, and the amount of people whose expression is affected by the regulation. Trademark owners may argue that denying registration to a non-traditional mark will chill the company's use of that expression because this regulation reduces the incentive to use that subject matter as a mark, but trademark registration laws do not prohibit or penalize the company for using that product attribute. The company can still use this product feature even if it can only register words, logos, and other "traditional" marks.[109] Thus, refusing to register non-traditional trademark subject matter does not significantly harm expression.

[106] See the discussion and sources in Ramsey, *supra* note 16, at 836–43, 869–75; Ramsey, *Increasing First Amendment Scrutiny of Trademark Law, supra* note 22, at 414–57.

[107] *See, e.g.* KUR & SENFTLEBEN, *supra* note 1, at 294–310, 337–68; MCCARTHY, *supra* note 60, at §§ 23:12, 24:67–72, 24:40–48, 24:61.

[108] Ramsey, *supra* note 20, at 1146–70.

[109] Ramsey, *supra* note 16, at 832–46, 861–62.

On the other hand, granting registration of a non-traditional mark that contains inherently valuable expression causes substantial harm to freedom of expression.[110] Registration discourages use of this message by many other companies and people who may want to communicate using the same shape, color, or other expressive product feature. More importantly, infringement and dilution laws protecting non-traditional marks allow courts to ban and penalize use of the mark in expression.[111] This is a more severe restriction of expression than a law banning registration of such marks. Moreover, allowing registration of shapes, colors, and other product attributes increases the chance that a competitor's products or advertising will be removed from the websites of companies such as Amazon or Google once a trademark owner complains that its registered trade dress is being infringed by this competitor. This private censorship of commercial expression may harm competition and expressive values if this use of the registered mark is not misleading.

Non-traditional trademark laws are also more vague and unpredictable than laws granting trademark rights in words and other traditional marks, and therefore unjustifiably chill more expression, because the non-visual or non-verbal nature of certain non-traditional marks makes it more difficult to determine what is registered and protected as a mark. Many trademark registration laws do not require marks to be visually perceptible for registration, and the exact contours of a mark consisting of a scent, sound, flavor, or texture may be unclear. Moreover, shapes, colors, and other features of a product are not always used as source-identifiers, so accused infringers may not know someone else claims ownership of a trademark in a product feature until they receive a demand letter or complaint. Additional uncertainty exists under the law because the parties' non-traditional marks and goods or services need not be identical for trademark violations. Competitors, artists, news reporters, and other companies and people engaging in expression may self-censor once they are accused of infringement or dilution because they cannot determine what is protected as a mark or whether a threatened trademark lawsuit will be successful.

Trademark laws do include defenses and some contain other internal safeguards—such as a trademark use or commercial use requirement for liability—that promote competition and protect expressive uses of marks.[112] These laws should apply in disputes involving non-traditional marks, but application of these rules may be more complicated in cases involving shapes, colors, or other product attributes claimed as marks. For example, since product features are often not used as marks, reasonable people may disagree on whether a defendant is using the protected shape or color "as a mark," for decoration, or for other purposes. The rules for determining whether a

[110] *Id.*

[111] *See, e.g.*, T-Mobile US, Inc. v. Aio Wireless LLC, 991 F.Supp.2d 888 (S.D. Tex. 2014) (granting preliminary injunction after finding T-Mobile was likely to succeed on claim that competitor's use of plum color infringed T-Mobile's magenta color mark).

[112] *See e.g.*, Trade Marks Act 1995 (Cth), § 120 (Austl.) (requiring use "as a trade mark"); EU Directive, *supra* note 71, art. 10(2) (requiring use "in the course of trade"); EU Regulation, *supra* note 71, art. 9(2) (same); 15 U.S.C. § 1125(c)(3)(C) (exempting "noncommercial use of a mark" from dilution liability). *See* BURRELL & HANDLER, *supra* note 76, at 375–92; KUR & SENFTLEBEN, *supra* note 1, at 276–87; MCCARTHY, *supra* note 60, at §§ 24:128, 31:139–152. *See also supra* notes 88, 90–93 (defenses).

word mark is used otherwise than "as a mark" by the accused infringer—for example, in a sentence rather than in a brand name or slogan—do not apply when the mark is a product configuration, color, scent, sound, flavor, or texture. Another problem is that trademark defenses like descriptive fair use only apply in limited circumstances and can be fact-intensive, making it difficult for courts to dispose of frivolous trademark claims early in litigation.[113] Moreover, some national trademark laws do not contain sufficient statutory rules allowing expressive uses of another's mark. For example, the U.S. trademark statute does not explicitly require trademark use or commercial use of a mark for infringement liability, and there is no statutory defense for parody, criticism, commentary, comparative advertising, news reporting, or non-commercial use of the mark in the infringement statute.[114]

In addition, U.S. infringement and dilution laws do not contain a statutory defense allowing unauthorized use of another's mark in satire and other expression unrelated to the trademark owner.[115] Thus it is unclear whether use of another's non-traditional mark in commentary about current events would violate trademark law. For example, after a passenger was forcefully removed from an overbooked United Airlines flight, someone posted a clearly fake LEGO "Passenger Removal Playset" online that contained a photo of LEGO Minifigures.[116] If LEGO Group sued for trademark violations, a court would likely find this expression does not violate the company's trademark rights in its logo or product configuration because the message was not likely to cause confusion or is non-commercial expression. Still, the creator of this expression or a website hosting it would probably remove the photo if LEGO Group complained due to the expense of defending a lawsuit and uncertainty about whether this expression is allowed. A law that chills non-misleading or non-commercial expression like this can harm expressive values.

Aesthetic functionality doctrine in the United States may prevent registration of non-traditional marks which convey messages if there is a competitive need to use the non-reputation-related aspects of that product feature, but the functionality exclusion from registration does not adequately protect expression. This law only applies if the symbol or device claimed as a mark by the plaintiff is comprised of functional matter; functional use of the product feature by the defendant is not relevant to the functionality analysis.[117] A shape, color, or other characteristic of a product could be registered in an industry where the feature is not functional, and then the trademark owner could sue a company selling dissimilar goods or services who is using this mark in a functional way and argue this unauthorized use causes

[113] Ramsey, *supra* note 16, at 838–43; *see* MCCARTHY, *supra* note 60, at §§ 11:45–49.

[114] Ramsey, *supra* note 16, at 836, 842.

[115] *Id.* at 842; Jane C. Ginsburg, *"See Me, Feel Me, Touch Me, Hea[r] Me" (and Maybe Smell and Taste Me too): I am a Trademark—a US Perspective, in* TRADE MARKS AND BRANDS: AN INTERDISCIPLINARY CRITIQUE 92, 104 (2008). Dilution law's exemptions for parody, criticism, and commentary only apply when the mark is used to identify the trademark owner or its goods or services. 15 U.S.C. § 1125(c)(3)(A)(ii).

[116] *LEGO United Airlines Kit*, BEHEADING BOREDOM, http://www.beheadingboredom.com/lego-united-airlines-kit/ (last visited Jan. 15, 2018).

[117] 15 U.S.C. § 1052(e)(5); MCCARTHY, *supra* note 60, at §§ 7:63–84. For EU law see KUR & SENFTLEBEN, *supra* note 1, at 158–72.

confusion about affiliation or consent. If there is no functionality defense in that jurisdiction, it may be difficult for the accused infringer to get a quick resolution of the trademark dispute in its favor.

Another problem with relying on functionality doctrine to protect expressive values in non-traditional trademark laws is that the availability of alternatives can count against a finding of aesthetic functionality (but not utilitarian functionality) in some jurisdictions.[118] For example, in *Qualitex*, the U.S. Supreme Court said that color is useful for covering stains on dry cleaning press pads, but held the color green-gold is not functional for that product because other colors can serve this function equally well.[119] On the other hand, the existence of alternative language is not sufficient to justify a content-based restriction of protected expression in the United States and other countries; the right to freedom of expression includes the right to choose the vehicle of your expression.[120]

Finally the free expression interests of the public—the consuming "audience"—should be considered when governments determine whether they should register and protect trademark rights in non-traditional marks, as the right to freedom of expression includes the right to "receive" the information, ideas, and other expression.[121] Consumers may want to buy a product with a certain representational shape, color, scent, flavor, or texture because that feature expresses messages unrelated to the trademark owner. Granting exclusive trademark rights in this inherently valuable expression will likely reduce the availability of competing products with that expressive attribute and harm the right of the consuming public to receive that expression from other companies.

For all of these reasons, nations should consider not registering non-traditional trademark subject matter that was inherently valuable before it was adopted or used as a mark, or only grant such marks a narrow scope of protection. Any free expression right or trademark right of a business to register this inherently valuable expression is arguably outweighed by the rights of competitors and other companies to communicate this expression and the right of consumers to receive it.

V. Proposals for Reform of Non-Traditional Trademark Laws

Nations concerned about how non-traditional trademark laws conflict with the right to freedom of expression have various options. First, legislatures could amend their trademark laws to deny registration and protection to "matter which was inherently valuable expression before it was adopted or used as a mark."[122]

[118] *See* KUR & SENFTLEBEN, *supra* note 1, at 166–67; MCCARTHY, *supra* note 60, at §§ 7:79–81.

[119] *Qualitex Co.*, *supra* note 58, 166–69.

[120] *See, e.g.*, Cohen v. California, 403 U.S. 15, 26 (1971); CHEMERINSKY, *supra* note 24, at 976–85, 1087, 1117–18; VERPEAUX, *supra* note 32, at 40.

[121] *See supra* Part II; CHEMERINSKY, *supra* note 24, at 1145-46; SHARPE & ROACH, *supra* note 37, at 169; VERPEAUX, *supra* note 32, at 39–40; Ramsey, *Increasing First Amendment Scrutiny of Trademark Law, supra* note 22, at 410–11.

[122] This would include subject matter that consumers prefer for cognitive, psychological, or aesthetic reasons that are widespread among consumers before the trademark owner used the mark in connection

The law itself, or commentary accompanying it, could provide examples of the types of signs that contain inherently valuable expression or explain this includes matter which is intrinsically ornamental, decorative, informational, or which conveys other non-source-identifying messages. This rule should apply regardless of whether the mark has acquired distinctiveness through use, just like the United States' ban on trademark registration and protection of generic signs and functional product features.

A better option is for legislatures to use the "inherently valuable expression" concept as a guideline for determining what specific types of subject matter should not be registered or protected by trademark law. They could explicitly prohibit registration of signs consisting of three-dimensional representational shapes, single colors, scents, sounds, flavors, textures, or other subject matter they deem to be inherently valuable, or list the signs that can qualify as marks and exclude these types of subject matter from the statute.

It is admittedly difficult to precisely define what is "inherently valuable expression" before it is claimed as a mark, but just because it is difficult to draw a line does not mean that the rule is unclear at the extremes or is not effective at furthering trademark law's goals or promoting expressive values. New shapes, sounds, scents, and other non-traditional subject matter independently created by the trademark owner to identify and distinguish its goods or services would not be inherently valuable before it was adopted or used as a mark, and would therefore be capable of registration and protection if it is distinctive, not functional, and meets other requirements in the trademark law.[123] Examples include the LEGO Minifigure product configuration, a new jingle created for use in advertising and selling a product, and Play-Doh's "scent of a sweet, slightly musky, vanilla fragrance, with slight overtones of cherry, combined with the smell of salted, wheat-based dough."[124] On the other hand, all colors and pre-existing representational shapes (e.g., a human skull), sounds (e.g., a lion's roar), scents (e.g., bubble gum), flavors (e.g., chocolate), and textures (e.g., leather) all arguably have inherent value regardless of the goods or services sold in connection with the mark.[125] They should remain in the public domain for everyone to use in the marketplace unless the feature is protected by another intellectual property law. If the feature was copied from nature or another artist or inventor whose work or invention has fallen into the public domain, the party claiming trademark rights is free riding on the inherent value in that subject matter and the government should consider declining to grant exclusive trademark rights in it to protect the right of everyone to use this product feature.

with its products. Hughes, *supra* note 69 (arguing that aesthetic functionality doctrine should be limited to these circumstances).

[123] Whether this subject matter should be subject to overlapping trademark, copyright, industrial design, and/or design patent protection is beyond the scope of this chapter.

[124] U.S. Registration No. 5,467,089.

[125] While some colors may be more valuable for certain products—such as the color orange for life jackets—arguably colors and many other product attributes are valuable in any context because they can attract attention, make the product more appealing, or convey non-source identifying messages. *Cf. Qualitex Co.*, *supra* note 58, 165 (noting color can make products more desirable).

To be clear, this proposal to exclude inherently valuable expression from registration and protection under trademark law does not apply to subject matter which became valuable *after* it was adopted and used as a mark. Examples using "traditional" marks are the brand names and logos of Volkswagen and Audi for automobiles[126] and the word BARBIE for dolls.[127] Like the blocky design of the LEGO Minifigure and the invented scent of Play-Doh, these logos and word marks have value primarily due to the efforts of the trademark owner (and the public) after the mark was used in the marketplace. Even if enforcement of trademark rights in certain disputes may conflict with the free expression right,[128] the right to freedom of expression is not harmed by registration of such marks and protection of their source-identifying information and brand value against misleading use of those marks by others to sell goods or services.

If governments decide to register and protect trademark rights in non-traditional marks, the protection should be narrow in scope to protect expressive values and promote competition and trademark law's other legitimate goals.[129] Legislators should only grant exclusive trademark rights in non-traditional marks with strong and substantial evidence of acquired distinctiveness through use, and prohibit registration and protection of matter that is functional, ornamental, decorative, informational, or which otherwise fails to function as a mark. They should also require registrations (and complaints for infringement of unregistered marks filed in U.S. courts) to describe, display, or otherwise convey the content of the mark in a clear and precise way so that others have sufficient notice of what subject matter is registered or protected under the trademark laws.

Trademark laws are also less likely to conflict with the free expression right if the law only bans and punishes fraudulent or misleading use of another's non-traditional mark. Claims for dilution and other non-misleading uses of non-traditional marks should not be allowed. Infringement laws should require the trademark owner to prove the defendant is using the shape, color, or other non-traditional mark to explicitly mislead consumers in the marketplace regarding the product's source. The accused infringer must do or say something to falsely suggest that there is a connection between the parties other than simply use the product feature protected under trademark law. Moreover, requiring the parties' marks and goods or services to be

[126] Au-tomotive Gold, Inc. v. Volkswagen of America, Inc., 457 F.3d 1062 (9th Cir. 2006).

[127] ORLY LOBEL, YOU DON'T OWN ME: HOW *Mattel v. MGA Entertainment* EXPOSED BARBIE'S DARK SIDE (2017).

[128] Rochelle Cooper Dreyfuss, *Expressive Genericity: Trademarks as Language in the Pepsi Generation*, 65 NOTRE DAME L. REV. 397 (1990).

[129] *See* Dinwoodie, *supra* note 4 (recommending certain limitations on non-traditional trademark rights to further trademark law's goals). The suggestions below are similar to proposals for trademark reforms made in scholarship not focused on non-traditional marks. *See, e.g.*, Graeme B. Dinwoodie, *Developing Defenses in Trademark Law*, 13 LEWIS & CLARK L. REV. 99 (2009); William McGeveran, *The Trademark Fair Use Reform Act*, 90 B.U. L. REV. 2267 (2010); Ramsey, *supra* note 17; Ramsey, *Increasing First Amendment Scrutiny of Trademark Law, supra* note 22, at 414–46, 454–57; M.R.F. Senftleben et al., *The Recommendation on Measures to Safeguard Freedom of Expression and Undistorted Competition: Guiding Principles for the Further Development of EU Trade Mark Law*, 37(6) EUR. INTELL. PROP. REV. 337 (2015); Ramsey & Schovsbo, *supra* note 22, at 690–96.

identical or almost identical for trademark liability will increase predictability in trademark disputes and make non-traditional trademark laws less vague and overbroad. These expression-protective rules will help companies and individuals better determine the exact scope of trademark rights, and enable them to use shapes, colors, or other desirable product features in non-misleading expression.

It is also important for legislatures to enact and courts to apply statutory trademark defenses that allow legitimate use of non-traditional trademark subject matter claimed as a mark. This includes fair use of non-traditional marks to describe a product's qualities or characteristics, and honest referential or nominative fair use of another's mark. Governments should also consider specifically allowing the fair use of marks in comparative advertising, news reporting, consumer product reviews, criticism, teaching, scholarship, entertainment, parody, satire, and other editorial, educational, artistic, or literary expression. Functionality should be a defense in trademark law and not just a reason to refuse registration of a mark. Accused infringers should be able to use naturally-occurring, technical, or aesthetic features of a product that have non-source-identifying value even if that product feature is registered as a mark and is not functional for the trademark owner's products.

In addition, legislatures should protect expressive values by allowing fair use of matter which conveys "inherently valuable expression," or matter which was ornamental, decorative, informational, or which conveyed other non-source-identifying messages, before it was adopted or used as a mark. This defense would be similar to the descriptive fair use defense, which allows legitimate use of descriptive terms protected by trademark law even where some consumers might be confused about this use of the mark. Adding this defense to the trademark statute will ensure companies can continue to use inherently valuable expression conveyed by a product feature to communicate with the public. All of these defenses will protect free expression, promote competition, increase certainty, and may provide the basis for summary disposition of a frivolous lawsuit. They may also make the trademark laws less subject to a challenge on free expression grounds.

A final way legislatures can protect expression in non-traditional trademark laws is by giving courts discretion on trademark remedies. Judges should not be required to always ban unauthorized infringing use of the non-traditional mark. A more speech-protective remedy would be to allow use of the shape, color, or other product attribute if the defendant agrees to reduce consumer confusion by including its house mark (such as a brand name or logo) on the packaging or product that contains the non-traditional mark. Courts could also require use of a disclaimer.

VI. Conclusion

Nations should consider refusing to register and protect trademark rights in non-traditional marks that contained inherently valuable expression before they were adopted or used as marks. This reform of non-traditional trademark laws will better protect the right to freedom of expression and ensure a robust public domain of product features and marketing techniques remains available for use by established companies and new entrants to the market. Brands may initially and understandably resist efforts to reform non-traditional trademark laws. Yet in our global and ever-changing economy, trademark laws must help firms retain the ability to use new ways to express themselves and compete fairly when they advertise and sell goods or services desired by consumers. Companies may alter the shape of their goods or packaging, or change the colors in their store or advertising. They may choose to convey a message or appeal to our non-visual senses by incorporating a scent, sound, flavor, or texture into their products or marketing materials. Trademark laws should enable them to engage in this expression. Given the fact that companies can distinguish their products using words, logos, and other "traditional" marks, it is unlikely that brands will reduce the quality of their products, or that consumers will be unable to find the products they want, if certain non-traditional trademark subject matter cannot be registered or protected as a trademark.

18

Non-Traditional Trademark Protection as (Non-Traditional) Means of Cultural Control

Katya Assaf-Zakharov

I. Introduction

This chapter focuses on the protection of non-traditional trademarks, with a specific focus on its social implications and its interplay with different cultural traditions. The term "non-traditional trademarks" commonly refers to new trademark forms, such as product shapes, designs, or colors.[1] Such trademark protection may restrict copying of product elements that are generally not protected, no longer protected, or not protectable with patents, copyrights, or design patents. In turn, this restriction can directly affect market competition, as several contributions to the book have specifically observed.[2] In addition, since trademarked products, particularly those produced by high-end brands, are often used as status symbols in social interaction, protection of non-traditional trademarks can also have significant cultural effects. In general, the impact of trademark protection on social interactions has been intensively discussed in the literature.[3] This chapter outlines an additional perspective by focusing specifically on "non-traditionality," that is, inconsistency with traditional values, which the protection of non-traditional trademarks creates.

Western jurisdictions hold different views on imitation: while the United States (U.S.) legal system normally strives to encourage it, the legal systems of Continental Europe tend to be much more cautious.[4] This difference has to do with the more

[1] *See* Chapter 1 in this volume. [2] See Chapters 10, 11, and 12 in this volume.

[3] *See, e.g.*, Barton Beebe, *Intellectual Property Law and the Sumptuary Code*, 123 Harv. L. Rev. 809, 834 (2010); Katya Assaf, *Buying Goods and Doing Good: Trademarks and Social Competition*, 67 Ala. L. Rev. 979, 1002–03 (2016); Malla Pollack, *Your Image Is My Image*, 14 Cardozo L. Rev. 1392 (1993); Nestor M. Davidson, *Property and Relative Status*, 107 Mich. L. Rev. 757, 804 (2009); Mark P. McKenna, *Probabilistic Knowledge of Third-Party Trademark Infringement*, 2011 Stan. Tech. L. Rev. 10, 32–33 (2011); Ann Bartow, *Counterfeits, Copying and Class*, 48 Hous. L. Rev. 707, 733 (2011); Jeremy N. Sheff, *Veblen Brands*, 96 Minn. L. Rev. 769 (2012); Connie D. Powell, *We All Know It's a Knock-Off! Re-evaluating the Need for the Post-Sale Confusion Doctrine in Trademark Law*, 14 N.C. J.L. & Tech. 1 (2012); Matthew Grace, *Note: The End of Post-Sale Confusion*, 28 Harv. J.L. & Tech. 263 (2014).

[4] Ansgar Ohly, *The Freedom of Imitation and Its Limits—A European Perspective*, 41 Int'l Rev. Intell. Prop. & Competition L. 506, 507–09 (2010).

Non-Traditional Trademark Protection as (Non-Traditional) Means of Cultural Control. Katya Assaf-Zakharov. Published 2018 by Oxford University Press.

general cultural dispute between the Old and the New World on authenticity and imitation. On a subtler level, this dispute is interconnected with the tradition of preserving established social orders, typical for Continental Europe, and the ideal of social mobility, which characterizes American national ethos. The current legal tendency to protect "non-traditional" trademarks against imitation preserves status privileges, thus clashing with the ideal of social mobility. Hence, in the U.S. context, this protection is non-traditional in an additional sense: it is dissonant with a most fundamental cultural tradition of that country.

This chapter proceeds as follows: Section I explains that Intellectual Property (IP) regulations exist in different legal climates surrounding imitation. It outlines the differences between the U.S. approach, which is generally supportive of copying, and the Continental European view, which is largely adverse toward imitation. It traces this difference to the long-standing cultural dispute between the Old and the New World on the significance of authenticity and the legitimacy of imitation. Section II notes that trademarks are different in the IP landscape in that—at least originally—they were not designed to restrict imitation, but only to prevent consumer confusion. Section III reveals an interconnection between social norms regarding imitation and cultural views on tradition and social mobility. Section IV points out that copyright and industrial design protection regimes provide meaningful protection to products functioning as status symbols in Europe, whereas in the U.S., no IP right provides such a protection. This picture is in harmony with the cultural ideals of tradition and heritage in Europe, as opposed to the ideals of challenging traditional authority and fostering social mobility in the U.S. Section V breaks this harmonic picture, demonstrating that trademark law doctrines function to restrict imitation of status symbols in the U.S. The discussion in this section focuses on U.S. trademark law, since this is where the legal protection of status symbols runs counter to the general legal acceptance of imitation and the cultural ideal of social mobility. Section VI points out an overlooked aspect of non-traditionality concerning U.S. legal protection of status symbols: such protection reinforces the existing societal hierarchy and hampers social mobility, thereby clashing with a most dearly cherished traditional value of the American nation. Section VII concludes the discussion.

II. Intellectual Property, Imitation, and Cultural Traditions

IP protection is all about the idea of restricting copying. Patents restrict the copying of technology, industrial design protection limits the copying of product shapes, and copyrights restrict the copying of works of art. IP thus creates scarcity in the world of immaterial objects and ideas—a world that is naturally characterized by lack of rivalry and unlimited capability to exploit the same asset. Trademarks are somewhat different in this landscape. The objective of their protection is ensuring the accuracy of market information. Trademarks are not designed to restrict copying of products, but to prevent consumer confusion as to the source of goods.

Today's IP philosophy is predominantly utilitarian, at least on its surface. It is common to justify the restrictions on copying by a purely economic argument: promoting creativity. According to this logic, IP rights grant market exclusivity to inventors and creators, without which there would be no (sufficient) incentive to invent and create, and our society will suffer from undersupply of new technologies, works of art, etc. This is because immaterial assets, such as inventions and artistic creations, are "public goods," goods that can be used by an unlimited number of people simultaneously. As all public goods, immaterial assets may cause a "market failure": their creators cannot control their circulation and hence, cannot internalize their positive value.[5] For instance, without patent rights, a new breakthrough drug would be immediately copied by all pharmaceutical companies, leaving its inventor with no possibility to profit from her invention.

In this view, copying is the rule and IP protection is the exception. Exclusivity periods provided by IP rights are commonly regarded as the price society has to pay in the short run in order to benefit from technological progress and blossom of creativity in the long run. This price is a real one: market exclusivity granted by IP rights obstructs competition, raises consumer prices, diminishes supply, and hinders inventive and creative progress. Hence, IP legislation should strike a balance between the need to spur creativity and the need to leave enough room for free copying. Again, trademarks are different in this regard: they are not designed to promote creativity, but to preserve the accuracy of product source indicators. Traditional trademark protection usually embraces a name or a symbol, which is sheltered against confusing use by third parties. Unlike patents and copyrights, such protection involves no significant social price in terms of restricted copying and obstructed competition. Hence, the protection of trademarks is not limited in time.

The vision of spurring creativity by granting exclusivity in immaterial creations is somewhat elusive though. In fact, we cannot draw a comparison with a world without IP protection. There is no conclusive evidence that IP rights really spur technological progress.[6] However, there is some evidence that the prospect of material gain can actually hinder creativity.[7] Even if we accept the assumption that IP protection is indispensable, there is no way to determine the optimal scope of protection: one that ensures sufficient levels of inventive and creative activity with minimal restrictions on copying.[8] Traditionally, trademarks are not part of this discourse: since they neither limit imitation nor spur innovation, their protection does not require a balance between restricting competition and rewarding creativity. Yet,

[5] *See generally*, RICHARD POSNER, ECONOMIC ANALYSIS OF LAW 11–12 (2nd ed. 1977).

[6] *See, e.g.*, Petra Moser, *Patents and Innovation in Economic History*, 8 ANN. REV. ECON. 241 (2016); Kal Raustiala & Christopher Sprigman, *The Piracy Paradox: Innovation and Intellectual Property in Fashion Design*, 92 VA. L. REV. 1687 (2006); KAL RAUSTIALA & CHRISTOPHER SPRIGMAN, THE KNOCKOFF ECONOMY: HOW IMITATION SPARKS INNOVATION (2012).

[7] Diane L. Zimmerman, *Copyrights as Incentives: Did We Just Imagine That?*, 12 THEORETICAL INQUIRIES L. 29 (2011).

[8] Mark A. Lemley, *Property, Intellectual Property, and Free Riding*, 83 TEX. L. REV. 1031, 1055–56 (2005); Thomas B. Nachbar, *The Comedy of the Market*, 30 COLUM. J.L. & ARTS 453, 463–64 (2007). *See generally*, Robert P. Merges & Richard R. Nelson, *On the Complex Economics of Patent Scope*, 90 COLUM. L. REV. 839 (1990).

as will be discussed below, non-traditional trademarks, such as product shapes or colors, stroll away from the traditionally humble role of a trademark as a source identifier.[9] The protection of such trademarks does involve a restriction of copying and comes at a significant social price associated with reduced competition. In addition, as will be discussed in the following sections, over time trademark law developed several doctrines that result in a broad protection against non-confusing imitation. This protection embraces traditional and non-traditional trademarks alike. Yet, since originally trademark law is not about restricting imitation, no serious inquiry whether this price is justified by any social benefit has been made. In other words, while traditional trademarks, as well as traditional trademark doctrines, are rightly exempt from the rational cost-benefit analysis, non-traditional trademarks and extended trademark protection unjustifiably escape its scrutiny.

On a closer look, the laws of IP actually express more than purely rational concerns about a possible deficit of incentives to invent and create. They touch upon a deeper feeling of injustice arising in situations where somebody's creation is exploited by another—reaping where one has not sown.[10] This sentiment is arguably more typical for Western cultures that are much focused on individual achievements, rather than on ideals of collectivity and sharing.[11] And this is perhaps the best explanation for allowing non-traditional trademarks to creep unchecked under the roof of legal protection.

Western cultures themselves display no uniformity in their views on copying. Formally, all Western jurisdictions largely accept the general principal that copying is free unless limited by a specific IP right.[12] Yet, Continental European jurisdictions, such as France and Germany, seem to be rather adverse toward imitation as such.[13] Courts tend to bar imitation of articles not protected by IP rights, frequently finding this behavior to constitute "unfair" or "parasitic" competition, "slavish imitation," or misappropriation, unless the imitation is necessary for achieving a certain functional result.[14] For example, when examining imitation, German courts routinely inquire whether the imitator consciously sought to make an identical product, rather than creating something of her own, and whether she purposefully employed another's achievement for her own profit.[15] They ask whether the imitator could be reasonably expected to keep a greater distance from the original.[16] Exact or "slavish" copying is almost inevitably found to be wrong, unless justified by a functional

[9] *See infra* Section V.

[10] Wendy J. Gordon, *On Owning Information: Intellectual Property and the Restitutionary Impulse*, 78 Va. L. Rev. 149, 156–57 (1992).

[11] *See, e.g.*, Ron Selden, *Economic Development Attitudes Must Change*, Indian Country Today, June 13, 2001, https://indiancountrymedianetwork.com/news/economic-development-attitudes-must-change/.

[12] Gordon, *supra* note 10, at 156–57; Ohly, *supra* note 4, at 506–07.

[13] Ohly, *supra* note 4, at 507–09.

[14] *Id.*; Bundesgerichtshof [BGH] [Federal Court of Justice], Apr. 30, 2008, IZ R 73/05, 2008 GRUR 349, 353—*Klemmbausteine III.*

[15] *E.g.*, Bundesgerichtshof [BGH] [Federal Court of Justice], Jun. 19, 1956, IZ R 104/54, 1960 GRUR 244, 245-46—*Simili-Schmuck*; Bundesgerichtshof [BGH] [Federal Court of Justice], Dec. 18, 1968, IZ R 130/66, 1969 GRUR 292, 294—*Buntstreifensatin II.*

[16] *Id.*

need.[17] In restricting imitation, German courts often find it dissonant with the sense of decency.[18] In addition, German jurisprudence frequently finds that close copying inevitably causes consumer confusion, thus leaving little room for legitimate competitor adoptions.[19] Protection of non-traditional trademarks fits nicely into this legal context. If imitation without a functional reason is regarded as objectionable, there should be no special concern with protecting trademarks consisting of product design or color against copying.

Argumentation with fairness and decency can rarely be found in the context of copying in U.S. legal decisions.[20] To the contrary, a large body of American case law emphasizes that nothing is wrong with exact and wholesale copying "down to the minutest detail" of articles unprotected by IP,[21] that such copying benefits the public by driving prices down, and is thus crucial for effective competition.[22] Notably, unlike their Continental European counterparts, U.S. courts do not require that copying should be justified by a necessity to reach a certain functional result. They regard copying as a protected federal right—a necessary complement to the IP protection system.[23] Imitation has been described as "the life blood of competition,"[24] and "the essence of [the U.S.] free-market economic system."[25] In contrast to their European counterparts, American courts emphasize that they find nothing unfair, unlawful, or immoral about boldly copying a competitor's product: "[i]t is permissible in a competitive economy for the second comer to try to capture as much of the innovator's market as it can."[26] It is difficult to see how restriction of imitation associated with non-traditional trademarks can fit into this competition-welcoming legal climate. The following sections will take a closer look on this question.

The different legal attitudes toward copying most probably have to do with the more general dispute between the Old and the New World over the importance of the original and the value of its imitation. European culture puts a great emphasis

[17] *E.g.*, Bundesgerichtshof [BGH] [Federal Court of Justice], Oct. 30, 2003, I ZR 236/97, 2003 GRUR 360—*Pflegebett*; Bundesgerichtshof [BGH] [Federal Court of Justice], Apr. 2, 2009, I ZR 199/06, 2009 GRUR 1073—*Ausbeinmesser*; Bundesgerichtshof [BGH] [Federal Court of Justice], May 28, 2009, I ZR 124/06, 2010 GRUR 80—*LIKEaBIKE*.

[18] *Id.*; Bundesgerichtshof [BGH] [Federal Court of Justice], Jul. 14, 1962, I ZR 44/59, 1962 GRUR, 144, 150—*Buntstreifensatin*.

[19] *E.g.*, Bundesgerichtshof [BGH] [Federal Court of Justice], Sep. 15, 2005, I ZR 151/02, 2006 GRUR 79—*Jeans I*; Bundesgerichtshof [BGH] [Federal Court of Justice], May 24, 2007, I ZR 104/04, 2007 GRUR 984—*Gartenliege*; Oberlandesgerichte Zweibrücken [OLG] [Higher Regional Court, Zweibrücken], 2000 Az. I ZR 98/06—BeckRS; Oberlandesgerichte Hamburg [OLG] [Higher Regional Court, Hamburg], 2003 Az I ZR 75/234—BeckRS 03.

[20] *But see* Int'l News Serv. v. Associated Press, 248 U.S. 215 (1918).

[21] *See, e.g.*, Ernest Thompson Fine Furniture Maker, Inc. v. Youart, 16 U.S.P.Q.2d (BNA) 1386 (N.M. Ct. App. 1990); Gray v. Meijer, Inc., 295 F.3d 641 (6th Cir. 2002).

[22] *See, e.g.*, Roho, Inc. v. Marquis, 902 F.2d 356 (5th Cir. 1990); Dorr-Oliver, Inc. v. Fluid-Quip, Inc., 94 F.3d 376 (7th Cir. 1996).

[23] *See, e.g.*, Thomas & Betts v. Panduit Corp., 65 F.3d 654 (7th Cir. 1995); Versa Products Co. v. Bifold Co., 50 F.3d 189 (3d Cir. 1995).

[24] Am. Safety Table Co. v. Schreiber, 269 F.2d 255 (2d Cir. 1959); Smith v. Chanel, Inc., 402 F.2d 562 (9th Cir. 1968).

[25] Aromatique, Inc. v. Gold Seal, Inc., 28 F.3d 863, 875 (8th Cir. 1994).

[26] Duraco Prods., Inc. v. Joy Plastic Enters., Ltd., 40 F.3d 1431, 1448 (3d Cir. 1994); *accord*. Sassafras Enters., Inc. v. Roshco, Inc., 915 F. Supp. 1, 4 (N.D. III. 1996).

on authenticity, heritage, and tradition. As a country of immigrants that decided to break up with the traditional European culture, America is generally much more open to the idea that a good copy may be valuable, and not only "the real thing." The leaning Tower of Pisa in Illinois, Arc de Triomphe in New York, the Parthenon in Nashville, and Eiffel Tower of Las Vegas illustrate this point.

III. Imitation and Social Stratification

Social norms on imitation of objects are interconnected with deeper cultural views on society order and the place of the individual. The idea that imitation is a welcome phenomenon that brings greater efficiency and drives prices down subtly echoes the American Dream. According to this national vision, nobody is condemned to live within one's inborn social status. America is the Land of Opportunities, and each person has a possibility to reach a high social position no matter the starting point. Any legitimate way to success is accepted. A paperboy who makes all the way up to replace the newspaper's director is the hero of this tale: it's a competition, so the best legitimately and fairly wins. To become a newspaper's director, one does not have to take the regular route of studying journalism with rich parents paying for one's studies—just like one doesn't have to live in Italy to enjoy the view of Pisa tower.

Likewise, a company that efficiently copies a successful product of its rival thus improving the company's market position should be encouraged. As long as no specific IP right protects the product, it does not matter much who is its original creator—just like it does not matter whether the person was born with a certain social status or gained it later.

The idea of social mobility is connected to copying in an additional way. Throughout history, people of high classes have used various means to signal their status and to distinguish themselves from the rest. At the same time, people of lower classes have always made attempts to copy these signals, thereby improving their position.[27] During Ancient times and the Middle Ages, sumptuary laws banned such behavior, but this position was later abandoned in all Western societies.[28] The Industrial Revolution enabled mass production of fake gold, diamonds, and precious stones thus undermining the efficiency of these articles as status symbols.[29] In a market overflooded with cheap bijouterie, which looks very much like expensive jewels, precious materials obviously lose their status-signaling function.

However, the willingness of certain social groups to distinguish themselves from the others through visible status symbols remained, and to a great extent, gave rise to the phenomenon of fashion.[30] To be sure, there are many ways to communicate status: education, erudition, musical taste, place of work, a big house, to name a few. Yet, easily displayable material possessions are most practical for indicating status in

[27] Beebe, *supra* note 3, at 834; Assaf, *supra* note 3, at 1002–03.

[28] ALAN HUNT, GOVERNANCE OF THE CONSUMING PASSIONS: A HISTORY OF SUMPTUARY LAW 39 (1996). *See also* Assaf, *supra* note 3, at 985.

[29] Assaf, *supra* note 3, at 985.

[30] Georg Simmel, *Fashion,* 62 AM. J. SOC. 541 (1957).

casual social encounters. For a long time, fashion could fulfill this role: new designs circulated slowly, so that the rich enjoyed a significant period of exclusivity, until the fashion "trickled down."[31] Yet, the ever more progressive technologies of copying rendered fashion ever less reliable as a medium of status-signaling.[32] Obviously, the cheaper, the more accurately, and the quicker a new prestigious design may be copied, the less it is capable of indicating a high economic status.

The philosopher Walter Benjamin envisioned that mechanical reproduction will ultimately liquidate "the traditional value of the cultural heritage" attached to works of art, undermining the authority and the aura surrounding the original. He perceived mass copying as a process liberating art from the dictatorship of tradition and heritage, and making it available for the masses.[33] Similarly, mass copying of status goods could erase the uniqueness of these goods, making them available for large parts of the consuming public and ultimately undermining their possibility to serve as signals of material status.[34]

IV. Intellectual Property and Status-Signaling

As stated in Section II, IP laws function to preserve exclusivity in a world of easy copying. Hence, products protected by IP are natural candidates for the role of status signals. Indeed, consider the social effect of owning the latest and hottest model of an iPhone, or showing off with a designer bag.[35]

Patents fall short of preventing intentional status cheating.[36] While a patent may protect the technologies incorporated in a new iPhone, it won't help against a look-alike smartphone that uses different technologies.[37] In the U.S., copyright does not extend to utilitarian articles, such as bags.[38] By contrast, in European countries, copyright may embrace utilitarian articles if they meet the requirement of "originality," which is prerequisite for copyright protection.[39]

Design patents, as they are called in the U.S., or industrial designs, as they are called in Europe, specifically aim at protecting product shapes and seem to be a most suitable legal tool for monitoring the circulation of fashion goods. Yet in the U.S., the protection provided by design patents is inadequate for fashion because of the need to register each item.[40] The long registration process renders the protection impractical for quickly changing vogue trends. In the European Union (EU), in

[31] *Id.* [32] Assaf, *supra* note 3, at 1002–03.

[33] Walter Benjamin, *The Work of Art in the Age of Mechanical Reproduction, in* ILLUMINATIONS 221–24 (Hannah Arendt ed., 1968).

[34] Assaf, *supra* note 3, at 1004. [35] *See* Beebe, *supra* note 3.

[36] Note, *The Devil Wears Trademark: How the Fashion Industry Has Expanded Trademark Doctrine to Its Detriment*, 127 HARV. L. REV. 995, 996–98 (2014).

[37] *See, e.g.*, Lisa Eadicicco, *This Super Cheap Android Looks Exactly Like the iPhone 6*, BUSINESS INSIDER, Jan. 27, 2015, http://www.businessinsider.com/iphone-clone-android-2015-1.

[38] 17 U.S.C.A. § 101 (2010).

[39] *See* Trevor Cook, *The Cumulative Protection of Designs in the European Union and the Role in such Protection of Copyright*, 18 JIPR 83 (2013).

[40] *See* Note, *supra* note 36, at 996–98.

addition to copyright, the mechanism of "unregistered community design" provides protection to every new product shape, without registration, for a period of three years, greatly restricting the possibilities to copy new fashion items.[41] This protection is consistent with the somewhat suspicious attitude toward imitation that many Continental European legal systems share. These systems significantly restricted the imitation of articles not protected by any IP right long before unregistered community design regulation was enacted.[42]

This position is consistent with appreciation of originality and authenticity, which traditionally characterizes Continental European culture. To give another example, Article 3a(1) of the Comparative Advertising Directive forbids presenting one's goods as an imitation or a replica of goods bearing a protected trademark. Although severely criticized in the literature for curtailing legitimate competition, this clause is very much consonant with the general European cautious approach to imitation.[43]

Preventing imitation, the European regulation allows fashion items to function like status signals, at least to some extent. In addition, assuming that some people recognize fragrance smells and conclude about the status of those who wear them, the ban on describing one's product as imitation further obstructs status-cheating. Without direct information, a smell-alike is naturally very difficult to discover. The bottom line of these imitation-restricting regulations in the context of status-signaling is: if you cannot afford the original, just avoid this status symbol altogether; no cheating allowed. This legal message might be unintended. Yet it does not run counter to the European cultural climate, which gravitates more strongly toward the ideals of heritage and tradition than toward the ideal of social mobility.

As noted above, the U.S. legal system is vastly different. Notably, copyrights and design patents in the U.S. fall short of granting an adequate protection to fashion items. The U.S. Congress has repeatedly rejected bills aiming to establish a European-like protection for non-registered designs, reasoning that this would "create a 'new monopoly' having obvious and significant anticompetitive effects."[44]A large body

[41] Council Regulation 6/02/EC on Community Designs of Dec. 12, 2001, [2002] O.J. L3/1; *amended by* Council Regulation No. 1891/2006 of Dec. 18, 2006, to give effect to the accession of the European Community to the Geneva Act of the Hague Agreement concerning the international registration of industrial designs, [2006] O.J. L386/14.

[42] This was the legal situation in Germany, *e.g.*: Bundesgerichtshof [BGH] [Federal Court of Justice], Dec. 18, 1968, IZ R 130/66, 1969 GRUR 292, 294—*Buntstreifensatin II.*; Bundesgerichtshof [BGH] [Federal Court of Justice], Jun. 17, 1999, I ZR 213/96, Neue Juristische Wochenschrift [NJW] 2000, 338, [1999] GRUR 1106—*Rollstuhlnachbau*; Bundesgerichtshof [BGH] [Federal Court of Justice], Apr. 2, 2009, I ZR 199/06, [2009] GRUR 1073—*Ausbeinmesser.*

[43] *E.g.,* Frauke Henning-Bodewig, *Vergleichende Werbung—Liberalisierung des deutschen Rechts?*, 48(5) GRUR INT'L 385 (1999); Ansgar Ohly & Michael Spence, *Vergleichende Werbung: Die Auslegung der Richtlinie 97/55/EG in Deutschland und Großbritannien*, 8/9 GRUR INT. 681 (1999).

[44] H.R. Rep. No. 1476, 94th Cong., at 50 (2d Sess. 1976). *See also* H.R. 5055, 109th Cong. (2006). For discussion *see* Christine Quilichini, *Haute Couture Legislation: Tailor Made High Fashion Design Protection in the United States*, 4 U. PUERTO RICO BUS. L.J. 228 (2013). In a somewhat similar vein, Raustiala and Sprigman have argued that IP protection is unnecessary for the fashion industry, since it thrives and flourishes notwithstanding widespread copying: *see* RAUSTIALA & SPRIGMAN, *supra* note 6, Chapter 2.

of American case law finds imitation of product shapes legitimate, proclaiming the ideal of free copying.[45] In one particularly remarkable case involving imitation of an entire Christian Dior garment collection, the Court discussed whether the imitator has the right to identify the source of the copied designs:

The Lanham Act [the Trademark Act of the United States] does not prohibit a commercial rival's truthfully denominating his goods a copy of a design in the public domain, though he uses the name of the designer to do so. Indeed, it is difficult to see any other means that might be employed to inform the consuming public of the true origin of the design. . . .

Involved in the instant case is a conflict of values which necessarily arises in an economy characterized by competition and private property. The courts have come to recognize the true nature of the considerations often involved in efforts to extend protection of common law trade names so as to create a shield against competition. The interest of the consumer here in competitive prices of garments using Dior designs without deception as to origin, is at least as great as the interest of plaintiffs in monopolizing the name. [references omitted][46]

Similarly, in cases involving smell-alikes, American courts consistently uphold the right of the imitators to truthfully indicate that their perfume smells like a famous brand.[47] Thus, for instance, in one such case, the Court stated:

Since [Chanel 5] perfume was unpatented, appellants had a right to copy it . . . . There was a strong public interest in their doing so, . . . [b]ut this public benefit might be lost if appellants could not tell potential purchasers that appellants' product was the equivalent of appellees' product. . . . Appellees are not entitled to monopolize the public's desire for the unpatented product, even though they themselves created that desire at great effort and expense. . . .

Disapproval of the copyist's opportunism may be an understandable first reaction, but this initial response to the problem has been curbed in deference to the greater public good. By taking his "free ride," the copyist, albeit unintentionally, serves an important public interest by offering comparable goods at lower prices. [references omitted][48]

The rhetoric of these cases is compelling in its commitment to making equivalents of high-end products accessible for consumers who cannot afford the original. We can see that U.S. courts fully recognize the value of imitation and its ability to replace the original. Judicial acceptance of the consumer's desire to own imitations of high-end products subtly correlates with the American visions of infinite opportunities for social mobility.

So far our discussion reveals a rather coherent picture, in which Continental Europe and the U.S. largely treat imitation in accord with their perceptions of authenticity, heritage, imitation, and social mobility. Yet, as we will see in the next section, the picture is more complex, as far as the U.S. legal system is concerned.

[45] *See, e.g., supra* notes 21–26.

[46] Societe Comptoir de L'Industrie Cotonniere Etablissements Boussac v. Alexander's Dep't Stores, Inc., 299 F.2d 33, 36–37 (2d Cir. 1962).

[47] Saxony Prods., Inc. v. Guerlain, Inc., 513 F.2d 716 (9th Cir. 1975); *Smith v. Chanel, Inc., supra* note 24; Calvin Klein Cosmetics Corp. v. Lenox Labs., Inc., 815 F.2d 500 (8th Cir. 1987).

[48] *Smith v. Chanel, supra* note 24, 567–69.

V. The Special Case of Trademarks and Status-Signaling

Trademark law blurs the clarity of American pro-imitation legal policy. As mentioned above, trademarks are symbols identifying the commercial origin of goods and allowing the consumer to distinguish between merchandise of different traders. Trademarks are different from the rest of IP rights in that traditionally, they do not restrict copying, but solely prevent consumer confusion as to the source of goods. In this view, it is hard to see how trademarks, out of all IP rights, may be used to restrict the circulation of status symbols.

Yet, today it is trademarks that play an important status-signaling role in casual social encounters. This happens because at least in the U.S., trademarks are the most suitable mechanism to preserve the idea of authenticity in the reality of easy and legitimate copying. In a world where no one can be sure whether the diamonds one wears are real, and even if the latest Christian Dior dress one wears was really made by the company, trademarks—or brands—turn into relatively reliable means of signaling status. The trademark symbol is protected against copying by competitors and hence, it can be utilized as a convenient means of communicating one's status. Thus, although the initial reason to protect trademarks is providing the purchaser with valuable information about the product source, this mechanism can be employed to convey information about the purchaser herself. For example, luxury marks such as Rolex, Ferrari, or Luis Vuitton can convey the information that the users of these products are members of a selected elite, as only a small number of people can afford these products. Similarly, marks such as Apple convey the information that the users of these products are members of groups that have specific preferences toward high-end technology and design-focused products, again as part of a selected group. These examples illustrate how trademarks can take a completely new role in the economy and society: they no longer simply function as product identifiers that provide consumers with relevant information, but as personal identifiers that provide people with information about other people.

Indeed, research shows that people use brands to communicate their identity and to perceive the identity of others.[49] Of course, this does not mean that high material status is the only message a brand can communicate. Yet, connoting status, and in several instances also wealth, *is* a significant function of brands today, and this chapter critically analyzes this specific function. Research shows that individuals displaying luxury brands enjoy a higher status, which is associated with various benefits in social interactions.[50] Such individuals are perceived as competent

[49] Russell W. Belk et al., *The Sacred and the Profane in Consumer Behavior: Theodicy on the Odyssey*, 16 J. Consumer Res. 1, 15 (1989); Albert M. Muniz, Jr. & Thomas C. O'Guinn, *Brand Community*, 27 J. Consumer Res. 412, 427 (2001); Ronald W. Pimentel & Kristy E. Reynolds, *A Model for Consumer Devotion: Affective Commitment with Proactive Sustaining Behaviors*, 2004 Acad. Marketing Sci. Rev., 1, 24, http://www.expectad.com/white_paper/A_model_for_consumer_expect_advertising_inc.pdf. For discussion *see* Katya Assaf, *Brand Fetishism*, 43 Conn. L. Rev. 83, 91–96 (2010).

[50] Rob M.A. Nelissen & Marijn H.C. Meijers, *Social Benefits of Luxury Brands as Costly Signals of Wealth and Status*, 32 Evolution & Hum. Behav. 343, 348 (2011).

workers,[51] as being able to exert control,[52] and as desirable partners for cooperation and exchange.[53] When encountering conspicuous displays of wealth, people assert more social restraint and compliance and tend to be more generous and less aggressive.[54]

Because brands play such an important role in communicating status, they are ever more conspicuously displayed. It has been observed that the fashion industry is undergoing a process of "logoification," with brand logos becoming ever larger and more prominent elements of fashion designs.[55]

Not surprisingly, there are continuous attempts to copy high-end brands: where there's status-signaling, there's copying. Yet as long as the copying volume is low relatively to truthful status-signaling, the signal remains overall reliable. Consider that while some animals may deceive as to their actual size, strength, or dangerousness, the signals these deceivers employ do not lose their general reliability. Similarly, although high-end branded products are sometimes imitated, in the most cases, the volume of imitation is not so high as to impair the reliability of the brand as a status symbol: as long as replicas remain the exception rather than the rule, the brand can continue serving its status-signaling function.[56]

The reason that brands, unlike gold and diamonds, do not lose their function of communicating status in casual relations largely lies in trademark law. Although monitoring social competition for status lies far from the original purposes of trademark law, it has extended its protection to encompass the status-signaling function of brands. This expanded protection follows from an interplay of three major doctrines: trade-dress protection, post-sale confusion, and dilution. Trade dress protection encompasses the product as a whole, rather than focusing on a specific element, such as a name or a symbol, thus effectively preventing product imitation. Post-sale confusion protects trademarks against uses that do not confuse the direct purchasers, but deceive later observers into thinking that the purchaser owns an original product. This mechanism targets the market of non-deceptive brand replicas. Finally, the dilution doctrine protects famous brands against cheapening of their uniqueness and exclusivity, thus preserving their status-signaling function. In the following sections, I will elaborate on these protection mechanisms, on their impact on social interactions, and on their compatibility with U.S. traditional cultural values.

As discussed above, Continental European legal systems are cautious toward imitation, and restrict it to a large extent, which is in harmony with their traditional

[51] *Id.* at 351; Maura L. Scott et al., *Judging the Book by Its Cover? How Consumers Decode Conspicuous Consumption Cues in Buyer–Seller Relationships*, 50 J. Mktg. Res. 334, 334 (2013).

[52] Helga Dittmar et al., *Fine Feathers Make Fine Birds: A Comparative Study of the Impact of Material Wealth on Perceived Identities in England and Italy*, 4 Soc. Behav. 195, 199 (1989).

[53] Nelissen & Meijers, *supra* note 50, at 344.

[54] *Id.* at 345.

[55] C. Scott Hemphill & Jeannie Suk, *The Law, Culture, and Economics of Fashion*, 61 Stan. L. Rev. 1147, 1176–78 (2009); Lauren Howard, *An Uningenious Paradox: Intellectual Property Protections for Fashion Designs*, 32 Colum. J. L. & Arts 333, 336 (2009); Susan Scafidi, *Intellectual Property and Fashion Design*, *in* intellectual property and information wealth 121 (Peter K. Yu ed., 2007).

[56] Assaf, *supra* note 3, at 1008.

cultural values. Trademark doctrines providing further means of banning imitation continue this line. Yet, similar trademark doctrines have quite a different standing as against U.S. legal background, which—in accord with its cultural values—is generally supportive of imitation. As the following sections demonstrate, trademark doctrines restricting imitation mark a discontinuity in U.S. legal attitude and clash with its traditional values. The following discussion will thus focus on the U.S. legal system, since this is where the intriguing dissonance between cultural values and legal rules occurs.

A. Trade-dress protection

While a trademark protects an specific source identifier, such as a symbol or a name, trademark law provides additional protection through "trade dress"—the overall look of the product, including "features such as size, shape, color, color combinations, texture, or graphics."[57] Just as a trademark, a trade dress may now be registered or protected without registration in the U.S.[58] Yet, it is more difficult to obtain protection in a trade dress than in a traditional trademark, since a trade dress is regarded as inherently non-distinctive, that is, incapable of serving as a source identifier.[59] To gain trade dress protection, it is necessary to prove that the trade dress in question has acquired distinctiveness in a way that it communicates the origin of the product to the consumer.[60] In an action for infringement, it is necessary to prove that having imitated the trade dress, the defendant created a likelihood of consumer confusion, deceptively suggesting that its products originate with the plaintiff.[61]

At first glance, the protection of trade dress fits nicely into the traditional logic underlying the trademark system: preventing consumer confusion as to the source of goods is the primary goal of trademark law, and product appearance may sometimes indicate its source: Coca-Cola's classic glass bottle illustrates this point. Yet, since trade dress protection targets the overall look of the product rather than a symbol attached to it, this protection has the potential to establish a monopoly over product design where other IP rights fail to do so. Indeed, trade dress protection is now applicable in the U.S. to designs of clothing,[62] handbags,[63] and

[57] *See, e.g.*, Vision Sports, Inc. v. Melville Corp., 888 F.2d 609, 613 (9th Cir. 1989); Clicks Billiards, Inc. v. Sixshooters, Inc., 251 F.3d 1252, 1259 (9th Cir. 2001); Adidas-Salomon AG v. Target Corp., 228 F. Supp. 2d 1192, 1193 (D. Or. 2002).

[58] Glynn S. Lunney, *The Trade Dress Emperor's New Clothes: Why Trade Dress Does Not Belong on the Principal Register*, 51 Hastings L.J. 1131 (2000); Charles Cronin, *Lost and Found: Intellectual Property of the Fragrance Industry; From Trade Secrets to Trade Dress*, 5 NYU J. Intell. Prop. & Ent. L. 256, 295 (2015).

[59] *See, e.g.*, Wal-Mart Stores, Inc. v. Samara Brothers, Inc., 529 U.S. 205, 213–14 (2000); *Adidas-Salomon, supra* note 57, 1205–06.

[60] *Adidas-Salomon, supra* note 57.

[61] *Id.* at 1210–11; Abercrombie & Fitch Stores, Inc. v. Am. Eagle Outfitters, Inc., 280 F.3d 619, 635 (6th Cir. 2002); Louis Vuitton Malletier v. Dooney & Bourke, Inc., 454 F.3d 108, 116–18 (2d Cir. 2006). *See also* Kevin V. Tu, *Counterfeit Fashion: The Interplay Between Copyright and Trademark Law in Original Fashion Designs and Designer Knockoffs*, 18 Tex. Intell. Prop. L.J. 419 (2010).

[62] Wal-Mart Stores, Inc., *supra* note 59.

[63] Hermès Int'l v. Lederer de Paris Fifth Avenue, Inc., 219 F.3d 104 (2d Cir. 2000); Louis Vuitton Malletier v. Dooney & Bourke, Inc., 454 F.3d 108 (2d Cir. 2006).

shoes.[64] In a groundbreaking decision, the Court of Appeals for the Second Circuit recognized that the high-fashion French designer Christian Louboutin has an exclusive right to a red, lacquered outsole of a woman's high fashion shoe.[65]

Note that trade dress protection is available for status goods much more than for any other goods: if a small designer company comes up with a creative new dress, which is then copied by a competitor, the company will get no trade dress protection because such copying is unlikely to cause confusion. But if a large and famous corporation manages to establish a certain design as a meaningful fashion symbol, in a way that this design is exclusively associated with the corporation, then copying this design will subject the copier to liability for trade dress infringement.[66] Similarly, trade dress protection will usually apply more readily to high-end expensive goods than to more accessible items. Thus, for instance, while the famous designer corporation Hermès managed to obtain trade dress protection over its Birkin bag,[67] the much smaller Sunburst Company failed in a similar action regarding its waist pouches.[68]

B. Post-sale confusion

Post-sale confusion is another trademark doctrine that provides protection of status signals against imitation. Developed in the second half of the twentieth century by U.S. courts,[69] this doctrine protects the trademark owner against uses that do not confuse the direct consumer, but are likely to deceive third parties who later observe the product into thinking that it originates with the trademark owner.[70] This doctrine is mostly applicable to replicas of famous products that are openly sold as such. Such replicas target the market of consumers who knowingly wish to obtain a non-authentic copy of a famous product for an accessible price.

In some cases of post-sale confusion, products are copied together with their trademarked names or logos, that is, the products at issue are identical replicas or "counterfeits."[71] As it is commonly known, counterfeited products are sold at much

[64] *Adidas-Salomon, supra* note 57.

[65] Christian Louboutin S.A. v. Yves Saint Laurent Am. Holding, Inc., 696 F.3d 206 (2d Cir. 2012). In a parallel case before the Court of Justice of the European Union, it was held that the red sole mark should not be protected if its intrinsic value "affect[s] the attractiveness of the goods to such an extent that the reservation thereof to a single undertaking would distort competition on the market." Deciding on this question, national courts "must take no account of attractiveness of the goods flowing from the reputation of the mark or its proprietor": Case C-163/16, Christian Louboutin SAS v. Van Haren Schoenen BV, [2017] EUR-Lex 62016CC0163, opinion delivered June 22, 2017.

[66] Tu, *supra* note 61, at 435. [67] *Hermès Int'l, supra* note 63, 107.

[68] Sunburst Prod., Inc. v. Cyrk Int'l, 98 F.3d 1358 (Fed. Cir. 1996).

[69] The first decision to recognize post-sale confusion as actionable is Mastercrafters Clock & Radio Co. v. Vacheron & Constantin-Le Coultre Watches, Inc., 221 F.2d 464 (2d Cir. 1955). The 1962 amendment of the Lanham Act eliminated the requirement that, to establish trademark infringement, there should be confusion of "purchasers." Most courts regard this amendment as adaptation of the post-sale confusion doctrine: *see, e.g.*, Rolex Watch U.S.A., Inc. v. Canner, 645 F. Supp. 484, 492–93 (S.D. Fla. 1986); Payless Shoesource, Inc. v. Reebok Int'l. Ltd., 998 F.2d 985 (Fed. Cir. 1993).

[70] J. THOMAS MCCARTHY, MCCARTHY ON TRADEMARKS AND UNFAIR COMPETITION § 23:5 (4th ed., 2017).

[71] *E.g.*, Rolex Watch USA, Inc. v. Canner, 645 F. Supp. 484 (S.D. Fla. 1986).

cheaper prices than the original goods, and consumers seek them, of all things, because of their cheaper prices and identical, or almost identical look as compared to the original goods. Consumers are rarely confused when purchasing such products because of their low price and their selling environment (flea markets, street stands, or non-official distributors of the products).[72] In addition, these products may carry explicit notifications that they are replicas and not originals, thus excluding the possibility of confusing the immediate purchaser.[73]

In other cases of post-sale confusion, specifically in cases related to trade dress copying, defendants may copy only the distinctive features of a prestigious product without copying its name or logo.[74] In these cases, again, the immediate consumer is not confused because the name of the real producer appears either on the package or on the product itself. Yet, these identifiers can often be removed after the product is purchased;[75] sometimes they appear in an inner part of the article,[76] or cannot be properly seen when a third party observes the product from a certain distance.[77] In other words, the differences with the original products are minimal: consumers seek these goods precisely because of their striking resemblance with the originals.

Thus, for instance, the design of a prestigious "Atmos" clock,[78] Levi's jeans pocket patterns,[79] and Reebok "stripecheck" design have been protected as trade dresses on the ground that third parties, who would encounter consumers displaying products with those features, could believe that they observe original articles.[80] Furthermore, courts banned imitations of Rolex watches that were sold for as little as $25 at a flea market in one case,[81] and explicitly advertised as "replica gold watches" in another.[82] Perhaps most remarkably, in a series of automobile cases, courts enjoined the distribution of customized kits designed to make cars appear like Rolls Royce[83] and Ferrari.[84]

In addition to civil sanctions, a finding of post-sale confusion could lead a vendor of brand replicas to face criminal penalties.[85] Thus, for example, selling Rolex, Gucci, Piaget, and Movado watches for prices ranging between $13 and $17 cost the vendor five months imprisonment, five months in a community treatment

[72] *Id.*

[73] *E.g.*, Rolex Watch U.S.A., Inc. v. "Bud" Forrester, 2 U.S.P.Q.2d 1292 (SD Fla 1986); *Hermès Int'l*, *supra* note 63, 107.

[74] Lois Sportswear, U.S.A., Inc. v. Levi Strauss & Co., 799 F.2d 867 (2d Cir. 1986); Levi Strauss & Co. v. Blue Bell, Inc., 632 F.2d 822 (9th Cir. 1980); Keds Corp. v. Renee Int'l Trading Corp., 888 F.2d 215, 222 (1st Cir. 1989).

[75] *Lois Sportswear, U.S.A.*, *supra* note 74, 872–73; *Levi Strauss & Co.*, *supra* note 74, 822.

[76] Polo Fashions, Inc. v. Craftex, Inc., 816 F.2d 145 (4th Cir. 1987).

[77] *Keds Corp.*, *supra* note 74, 222 (1st Cir. 1989); Ferrari S.P.A. v. McBurnie, 11 U.S.P.Q.2d 1843, 1844–47 (S.D. Cal. 1989).

[78] *Mastercrafters Clock & Radio Co.*, *supra* note 69.

[79] *Lois Sportswear, U.S.A., Inc.*, *supra* note 74, 872–73 (2d Cir. 1986); *Levi Strauss & Co.*, *supra* note 74.

[80] Reebok Int'l Ltd. v. Sung Hwa Int'l Corp., 6 U.S.P.Q.2d 1233 (S.D.N.Y. 1987).

[81] Rolex Watch USA, Inc. v. Canner, 645 F. Supp. 484 (S.D. Fla. 1986).

[82] Rolex Watch U.S.A., Inc. v. "Bud" Forrester, 2 U.S.P.Q.2d 1292 (S.D. Fla. 1986).

[83] Rolls-Royce Motors Ltd. v. A & A Fiberglass, Inc., 428 F. Supp. 689 (N.D. Ga. 1976).

[84] Ferrari S.P.A. v. Roberts, 944 F.2d 1235 (6th Cir. 1991); *Ferrari S.P.A. v. McBurnie*, *supra* note 77.

[85] 18 U.S.C.A. § 2320 (2016).

center, and a $3,000 fine.[86] "A purchaser ... would probably not be confused as to the watch's origin. However, a casual observer viewing a counterfeit watch, on the wrist of a friend, for instance, could easily be confused," the Court observed.[87] Courts have reached similar conclusions in numerous other cases, imposing criminal punishments on various distributors of fake status symbols.[88]

Judges have given various justifications for the doctrine of post-sale confusion. Most remarkably, a consistent body of case law holds that purchasing the imitation, a consumer acquires the prestige associated with the original without paying its price. Several decisions found wrongfulness in the very fact that consumers acquire a cheap product with a "luxury design" thus deceiving people into thinking that they actually own a prestigious article.[89] As one Court stated: "[A public harm] occurs when a sophisticated buyer purchases a knockoff and passes it off to the public as the genuine article, thereby confusing the viewing public and achieving the status of owning the genuine article at a knockoff price."[90]

Furthermore, courts pointed out the need to preserve the prestige and the high value of the originals, which derives from their scarcity[91] and their high prices.[92] They reason that if imitations become commonplace, the prestige and the exclusivity of the genuine articles would be lessened, thus discouraging consumers from acquiring them[93] and harming those who already own them.[94]

The doctrine of post-sale confusion thus openly protects trademarks as status symbols. Indeed, the main reason why consumers buy status-signaling branded articles is the fact that they are relatively rare or, at the very least, not accessible for everyone. This characteristic is the very essence of a status symbol.

The fact that the legal system acts to enable and preserve social status-signaling has attracted much criticism.[95] Indeed, this goal seems to be foreign to trademark philosophy and is hardly desirable as a legal policy in general. It is hard to see what kind of a "public harm" will occur if people achieve "the status of owning the genuine article at a knockoff price."

[86] United States v. Hon, 904 F.2d 803, 804 (2d Cir. 1990). [87] *Id.* at 805.

[88] *See, e.g.*, Rolex Watch USA, Inc. v. Canner, 645 F. Supp. 484 (S.D. Fla. 1986); United States v. Gonzalez, 630 F. Supp. 894 (S.D. Fla. 1986); United States v. Gantos, 817 F.2d 41 (8th Cir. 1987); United States v. Torkington, 812 F.2d 1347 (11th Cir. 1987). For discussion *see* Zachary J. King, *Knock-Off My Mark, Get Set, Go to Jail? The Improprieties of Criminalizing Post-Sale Confusion*, 88 NYU. L. Rev. 2220 (2013).

[89] *See, e.g., Mastercrafters Clock & Radio Co., supra* note 69, 466; *Hermès Int'l, supra* note 63, 109; Louis Vuitton Malletier v. Dooney & Bourke, Inc., 340 F. Supp. 2d 415, 431 (S.D.N.Y. 2004).

[90] *Hermès Int'l, supra* note 63, 109.

[91] *Ferrari S.P.A. v. Roberts*, supra note 84, 1238; Ferrari S.P.A. v. McBurnie, *supra* note 77.

[92] *Ferrari S.P.A. v. Roberts, supra* note 84.

[93] Rolex Watch U.S.A., Inc. v. Canner, 645 F. Supp. 484, 495 (S.D. Fla. 1986); Lois Sportswear, U.S.A., Inc. v. Levi Strauss & Co., 799 F.2d 867, 875–76 (2d Cir. 1986); Gucci Am., Inc. v. Dart, Inc., 715 F. Supp. 566, 12 U.S.P.Q.2d 1912 (S.D.N.Y. 1989); *Ferrari S.P.A. v. Roberts, supra* note 84, 1244–45.

[94] *Hermès Int'l, supra* note 63, 107–08; Gen. Motors Corp. v. Keystone Auto. Indus., Inc., 453 F.3d 351, 358 (6th Cir. 2006).

[95] *See supra* note 3.

C. Dilution

Finally, the doctrine of dilution protects trademarks against uses that impair their distinctive value and lessen their uniqueness.[96] Although initially designed for other factual constellations, the doctrine of dilution may successfully prevent imitation of a high-end brand: such imitation naturally dilutes the distinctive value of the trademark. Indeed, in several cases involving copying of status-signaling goods, courts found the copier guilty of trademark dilution.[97] Yet, the finding of dilution has so far always accompanied findings of trade dress infringement or post-sale confusion, and has not yet played a decisive role for the outcome of the case.[98]

VI. What is Non-Traditional about Protecting Status Symbols?

This chapter is about non-traditional trademark protection, which usually refers to protecting non-traditional trademark forms. Indeed, product shapes, pocket design patterns, colors of shoe soles, and diagonal stripes are all relatively new, that is non-traditional, subjects of trademark protection. In addition, protection of trademarks against uses that do not confuse the direct purchaser—like the post-sale confusion and other doctrines described above do—is non-traditional in the sense that it strolls away from the traditional goals of trademark law. Yet, there is an additional reason why these legal trends are non-traditional in the U.S. context. In the remainder of this chapter, I would like to point out an alternative perspective on their non-traditionality.

As discussed at the outset of this chapter, the American legal system is generally very supportive of copying. Unlike some of their European counterparts that permit imitation only in cases of functional necessity, U.S. courts analyze imitation in light of economic efficiency. As a result, they allow imitators to capitalize on others' achievements in a broad variety of cases, because such behavior is overall socially beneficial:[99]

> Disapproval of the copyist's opportunism may be an understandable first reaction, but this initial response to the problem has been curbed in deference to the greater public good. By taking his "free ride," the copyist, albeit unintentionally, serves an important public interest by offering comparable goods at lower prices.[100]

Such statements are highly inconsistent with rhetoric of post-sale confusion cases:

[96] Trademark Dilution Revision Act of 2006, 15 U.S.C.A. § 1125(c) (2016).

[97] *See, e.g.*, Rolex Watch, U.S.A., Inc. v. Canner, 645 F. Supp. 484, 492–93 (S.D. Fla. 1986); *Ferrari S.P.A. v. Roberts, supra* note 84, 1244–45 (6th Cir. 1991); Levi Strauss & Co. v. Abercrombie & Fitch Trading Co., 633 F.3d 1158, 1159 (9th Cir. 2011). For discussion *see:* David M. Tichane, *The Maturing Trademark Doctrine of Post-Sales Confusion*, 85 Trademark Rep. 399, 422 (1995); Note, *supra* note 36, at 1007–08.

[98] See cases cited above.

[99] *See, e.g., supra* notes 21–26.

[100] *Smith v. Chanel, Inc., supra* note 24, 568–69.

[P]laintiff copied the design of the Atmos clock because plaintiff intended to, and did, attract purchasers who wanted a "luxury design" clock. This goes to show at least that some customers would buy plaintiff's cheaper clock for the purpose of acquiring the prestige gained by displaying what many visitors at the customers' homes would regard as a prestigious article.[101]

It is puzzling how American courts that are so sympathetic to the idea of imitators making expensive articles accessible to the large consuming public show concern with the practice of allowing purchasers to acquire prestige at a low price. Just consider the radical contrast between the ideal of imitation driving prices down and the concern that a brand's "reputation for rarity" and luxuriousness would be "cheapened" by widespread existence of knock-offs.[102]

Cases that allow copying differ from those restricting it in a factual finding of consumer confusion as to the source of the product (in cases of trade dress protection) and confusion of bystanders (in cases of post-sale confusion). This distinction is often razor-thin: for instance, courts were split as to the question whether a red sole unambiguously signals that the shoe originates with Christian Louboutin.[103]

Furthermore, the confusion rationale is unconvincing in these cases: as far as a purchaser's confusion is concerned, it is always possible to eliminate it using distinguishing signs and disclaimers. It is absolutely unnecessary to restrict the production of product shapes, designs, and patterns for the simple goal of preventing consumer confusion of source. As far as post-sale confusion is concerned, it is incomprehensible what kind of a "public harm" status cheating causes. Similar "harm" may be caused by luxury-looking apparel or luxury-smelling fragrances, such as replicas of Christian Dior dresses and an imitation of Chanel 5. Yet, this kind of "harm" has never been prevented by the U.S. legal system, and has nothing to do with the goals of trademark law.

So how can it happen that the U.S. legal system highly encourages imitation, including imitation that makes luxury-appearing items accessible, while at the same time restricting very similar types of copying? Perhaps, the answer is that no legal system is guided by a single ideal or principle. It always consists of a mixture of various, often conflicting, beliefs, principles, and tendencies.[104] When two conflicting legal ideals clash, the outcome is largely unpredictable, and similar factual constellations may render opposite legal outcomes.[105] In the context of imitation, the principle of free copying conflicts with another ideal of American law, which is the protection of private property. Since trademarks are categorized as "property"[106]—rather than

[101] *Mastercrafters Clock & Radio Co.*, *supra* note 69, 466. [102] *See supra* notes 91–94.

[103] The District Court found that the red sole cannot be protected as a trade dress, since fashion industry "is dependent on colors": Christian Louboutin S.A. v. Yves Saint Laurent Am., Inc., 778 F. Supp. 2d 445, 454 (S.D.N.Y. 2011), but the Second Circuit reversed: Christian Louboutin S.A. v. Yves Saint Laurent Am. Holding, Inc., 696 F.3d 206 (2d Cir. 2012). For discussion *see* Claire Guehenno, *Color War: The Louboutin Decision and Single-Color Marks in the Fashion Industry*, 4 Harv. J. Sports & Ent. L. 225 (2013).

[104] Katya Assaf, *Capitalism vs. Freedom*, 38 NYU. Rev. L. & Soc. Change 201, 211–12 (2014).

[105] Another example of such a conflict is trademark tarnishment doctrine, which lies at the crossroad between property protection and the freedom of speech. For a discussion of unpredictability of its outcomes *see* Katya Assaf, *The Dilution of Culture and the Law of Trademarks*, 49 IDEA 1, 49–74 (2008).

[106] Callmann on Unfair Competition, Trademarks & Monopolies § 17:7 (4th ed. 2017).

merely unfair competition law—the natural tendency of U.S. law is to expand their protection.[107] Simply imitating a product thus taking some of the profits from its original creator is different from imitating a product thereby diminishing the economic value of a trademark, one's private property.

In cases involving imitation, American judges consciously give preference to a rational economic analysis, suppressing their intuitive aversion against "reaping where one has not sown."[108] Yet, when a property right comes into play, this intuition gains legitimacy. Defining property right in a trademark as broad as to encompass "reputation for rarity" enables restricting intuitively bothering imitation without abandoning the strict logic of economic rationality. Property right gives a formal justification to judicial intuition, so that there is no need to suppress it with the strict logic of economic analysis.

What passes unnoticed is the dissonance between this line of jurisprudence and the American ideals of social mobility. As mentioned above, individuals displaying expensive brands are perceived as competent workers, as being able to exert control, and as desirable partners for cooperation and exchange.[109] That is, brands actually give better social and professional opportunities, whether we like it or not. Accordingly, those who do not display such brands are at a competitive disadvantage as compared to brand wearers. Acquiring counterfeits, they attempt to bridge this gap.

Social brand discrimination is undoubtedly wrong. By giving better career opportunities to the rich, it fortifies the existing stratification, hindering social mobility. Cheating in this context should be encouraged rather than forbidden, since it allows fighting a detrimental social prejudice. Rich people are not really more competent workers and better cooperation partners. No "public harm" occurs when an owner of a knock-off "confuses the viewing public and achieves the status of owning the genuine article." On the contrary, public harm occurs when the owner of a genuine article gains social advantages just because she is rich.

Choosing to protect status-signaling—whether through trade dress protection, post-sale confusion, or dilution—American trademark law actually departs from its long-standing liberal tradition. Allowing brands to function as status signals, it hinders social mobility in a most non-American way: it does not let the poor try to gain the same social opportunities as the rich enjoy. To illustrate this point, imagine Jean and Sara, who attended the same legal school, obtained similar grades, and comparable recommendation letters. Now they are looking for an internship in prestigious law firms. They both know that lawyers are impressed with high-end brands, and that a Rolex watch would be a good choice, but only Jean, whose parents are rich, can afford a genuine Rolex. In this scenario, Sara will be found at a considerable and entirely unjustified disadvantage on the labor market. She will probably

[107] Felix Cohen, *Transcendental Nonsense and the Functional Approach*, 35 COLUM. L. REV. 809, 820–21 (1935); Assaf, *Capitalism vs. Freedom*, *supra* note 104, at 224–25; Mark A. Lemley, *Property, Intellectual Property, and Free Riding*, 83 TEX. L. REV. 1031 (2005); David Fagundes, *Property Rhetoric and the Public Domain*, 94 MINN. L. REV. 652 (2010).

[108] *E.g., Smith v. Chanel, Inc.*, *supra* note 24, 568–69.

[109] *See supra* notes 51–54.

land at a less successful firm than her classmate, and the socioeconomic gap between their parents' families will reproduce itself in their generation. This will happen because U.S. trademark civil and criminal law forbids selling a Rolex replica to Sara. Hence, even if Sara *is* able to find an unlawful Rolex counterfeit on a flea market, its illegal status might prevent this morally concerned young lawyer from making such a purchase.[110] In addition, since counterfeits are illegal, their assortment is very limited and their quality unreliable, so that overall this might be a risky affair for Sara.

In other words, trademark law ultimately functions to preserve the existing social hierarchy. This form of cultural control is obviously undesirable, and it is deeply "non-traditional" in American cultural context, which traditionally proclaims the ideal of social mobility.

VII. Conclusion

This chapter outlines the interplay between cultural perceptions on heritage, authenticity, and social mobility on the one hand, and legal positions on imitation, on the other. I have asserted that there is a subtle interconnection between the U.S. legal position that encourages copying and the American Dream of social mobility. On the other hand, the cautious approach to imitation that is typical for Continental European countries echoes their cultural perceptions on tradition, heritage, and authenticity.

The U.S. legal system gradually expands the scope of its trademark law to embrace non-traditional trademarks, such as product shapes, designs, and colors. It broadens trademark protection beyond its traditional goal of preventing consumer confusion. These tendencies provide legal protection against imitation of products not protected by other IP rights. It thus contradicts the general U.S. legal policy, which is largely supportive of copying. What is more, these non-traditional forms of trademark protection actually restrict the possibilities of imitating status symbols, thereby reinforcing the existing social stratification. In U.S. context, this result is non-traditional in a deeper, yet unnoticed way: it hinders social mobility, an ideal that lies at the very heart of American national ethos.

[110] Assaf, *supra* note 3, at 981.

Index

Tables and figures are indicated by an italic *t* and *f* following the page number

abuse of a dominant position 238–39
acquired distinctiveness
bans on registration of certain types of shape marks 148, 149
in China 187, 189
color and shape marks, protecting (German/EU perspective) 92, 93, 96, 99, 101, 102
competition law 249, 255
cultural control 374
cultural innovation, cyclic 325
Golden Bunny case 96
inherently valuable expression 346, 348, 353, 354, 358, 359
innovation and creativity, possibly impeding 291, 294, 303
pharmaceutical sector 274
proof of 348, 353
registration and enforcement of non-traditional marks 40, 69, 71–72, 76, 83
shape and color marks 92
trademark use 165, 170, 171, 175, 176
see also **distinctiveness**
Adams, Mitchell 8
aesthetic functionality doctrine 8, 107–24
aesthetic preferences 107–08, 109, 120
heterogeneity of 107, 115
aesthetic value 109–13, 137
case law of importance 108–23
Brunswick Corp. and "matching" cases 115–18, 119
Deere & Co. v. Farmhand, Inc 116–18
Inwood Laboratories v. Ives Laboratories 109, 111
Keene Corp. v. Paraflex Industries 118
M- 5 Steel v. O'Hagin 117, 118
Maker's Mark Distillery, Inc. v. Diageo North America, Inc. 122–23, 138–41
Pagliero v. Wallace China Co 110, 111, 122
Qualitex v. Jacobson Products decision 111–15, 123, 129, 357
TrafFix Devices v. Marketing Displays unanimous decision 112–14
consumer tastes 120–23
deciding which marks should or should not be protected 136–37, 138
Lincoln Mark truck "hump" 121, 138–40, 142
making sense of 114–15
"matching" fact pattern 115–18
mitigating effect 327
overlaps between trademark and copyright or patent protection 310
packaging 107, 110, 119, 121
perceptual functionality of black, blue and other features 118–21
prevention of registration, in some non-traditional marks 356–57
principles, applying 121–23
Restatement of Unfair Competition 111, 112, 114
trade dress 107, 109, 110, 112, 114, 121, 122, 144
see also **functionality doctrine**
aesthetic product features 293–304
Agreement on Trade-Related Aspects to Intellectual Property Rights (TRIPS), 1994 *see* **TRIPS Agreement on Trade-Related Aspects of Intellectual Property Rights (TRIPS), 1994**
Akerlof, George 259
anti-dilution protection
China 198–200
European Union (EU) 329
see also **dilution**
Apple
applications to register interior layout/design of retail stores 70–71
applications to register retail services 72
logo 73
areas of convergence, non-traditional marks with
SCT Nineteenth Session 27–28
SCT Twentieth Session 29–31
artworks 317, 325, 334, 336
Assaf-Zakharov, Katya 10
AstraZeneca 275–76, 281–82
Australia
color marks, opponents to registration of single colors 42
distinctiveness law 41, 57, 178, 179
empirical study on non-traditional marks 8, 37, 38, 40–41, 43, 55–57
Federal Court 178–79
functional marks and trademark use 174–75
Intellectual Property Government Open Database (IPGOD) 44, 55
Madrid Protocol applications 55
national and regional applications, focus on 55–57
registration of shape marks 40–41

Australia (*cont.*)
sound marks 41–42
Trademark Office 43, 175
trademark use 170, 172, 174–75, 177–81
trend in annual trademark applications 45
see also **distinctiveness**
Austria 151–52, 154–55

Barnes, David 259
Bartow, Ann 135, 136
Belgium 152, 155
Benelux uniform laws (1971) 205–06
BMW 128
Bottega Veneta *intrecciato* leather design pattern 301–04, 307
weave design 302, 303
Bourdieu, Pierre 315–16, 317
Brancusi, Lavinia 9
brands/branding
and advertising 133
brand-specific information 227, 228, 230
competitive relationship between brands 182
complementary relationship between brands 182–83
concentration of brand power 240
concept of brand 262
and design 127, 128
drugs 281, 282
essence marks 126–29
and expansion of trademark protection 2, 8
goals 127
marketers and brand builders seeking to use and claim innate and cultural signals and meaning 141–45
sensory branding 338
social brand discrimination 380
status-signaling 372–73
strategies 237, 247–48
Britain *see* **United Kingdom**
British Commonwealth, trademark use in 169–72, 183
see also **Australia**; **New Zealand**; **United Kingdom**
Brussels Conference (1880–1900) 150, 154–56, 159

Cadbury 131
Calboli, Irene 9
Canada 135
Castaldi, Carolina 9
characterization of marks at time of registration 60, 63–80
applicant's freedom to define 68–73
channeling implications of classification 67–68
purpose of description and categorization requirements 65–67
retail store design 70–71
see also **registration and enforcement of non-traditional marks**
China
acquired distinctiveness 187, 189
Beijing First Intermediate Court 197, 198–99
Beijing High Court 198–200
Chinese Radio International (CRI) 188
Dafeng (battle with Hermès) 190–91, 193–96, 198, 199, 200
distinctiveness
acquired 187, 189
and functionality 187–90
inherent 187, 189
economy 195
Hermès litigation 9, 190
anti-confusion protection 196–97
Kelly bag 186, 188, 189
legal battle with Dafeng 190–91, 193–96, 198, 199, 200
protecting non-traditional marks in 185–200
registration and enforcement of non-traditional marks
anti-confusion protection 193, 196–98
anti-dilution protection 193, 198–200
distinctiveness and functionality 187–90
first-to-file rule 190–92
recognition of well-known marks 192–96
registrable subject matter 186–87
scope of registrable marks 186, 187
shape marks, bans on registration of certain types 148, 150–51
Supreme Court 188, 189
Judicial Interpretation Concerning the Trial of Civil Cases of Protection of Well- Known Marks (2009) 198
Well-Known Trademark Interpretation 196
Trademark Law (revised 2013) 186, 187, 188, 192, 196, 198
Trademark Office 188, 189, 190, 191
trademark squatters 190, 191–92
trademark trolls 191–92
well-known marks, recognition 192–96
word marks 186, 187, 190, 197
as world's second largest consumer market 185
WTO, joining (2001) 186
chocolate products, registration issues 83–84
Ferrero Rocher golden paper-wrapped chocolate packaging 189, 190
Kit-Kat chocolate wafer, shape 4, 41, 148
Lindt/Lindt & Sprüngli (Golden Bunny case) 83–86, 96–97, 100
Toblerone chocolate, shape 4, 189
chromo-lithography technology 62
Coca-Cola bottle 181, 182–83, 189, 231, 374
and secondary signs 215–16
Cohen Jehoram, Tobias 313
color marks
acquired distinctiveness, establishing 91
application for representation at SCT 29

combined with three-dimensional marks 22
depletion concerns 42, 57, 62
distinctiveness concerns 42–43
exhaustion 135
and functionality 57
Germany 91–94
graphical representation requirement 26, 131–32
inherently valuable expression 339
opening up to 60
opponents to registration of single colors 42
perceptual functionality of black, blue and other features 118–21
protecting from German and European perspective 89–106
representations vs. description 79*f*
scope, problem of 135
shade confusion 62
Singapore Treaty, under 19
use in a non-distinctive manner 103–04

Community Trade Mark (CTM) 96

competition law and trademarks
abuse of a dominant position 238–39
analysis 235–56
anti-competitive effect of non-traditional marks 244–48, 253–54
combined licensing of know-how and trademarks 240
competitive necessity test 346–47
competitive relationship between brands 182
EU competition law perspective 237–48
ancillary licensing 241–42
case law 238–44
and European Commission 239–41, 252
impact of competition law provisions and case law on non-traditional marks 242–43
market definition and product substitutability 236, 250–53, 256
no-challenge clauses 240, 241, 242, 243
and "non-switching effect" 237
Technology Transfer Block Exemption (TTBER) 241–42
trademark coexistence agreements 242, 243–44
see also **European Union (EU)**
law and economics perspective 244–48
non-traditional marks 248–56
potential distortion of competition resulting from registration and enforcement of non-traditional marks 236
product substitutability 248–56
"refusal to deal" doctrine 239
restrictions on challenging validity of non-traditional marks 243
three-dimensional (3D) trademarks, protecting 204–06
Treaty on the Functioning of the European Union (TFEU) 237–41
see also **unfair competition**

confusion, likelihood of *see* **likelihood of confusion**

Congress, overruling on trade-dress 219–27

copying, restricting 364, 366, 367–68

copyright
monopolies 309, 316
overlap with trademarks 309–11
traditional acceptance of 312–15
trademarks compared to 291–92

Cornish, W.R. 203

counterfeit products 375–76

Court of Justice of the European Union (CJEU) 40
aesthetic functionality doctrine 326–27
color and shape markets, protecting (German/EU perspective) 89–90, 97–102, 106
defining a non-traditional mark 272
infringement proceedings 330, 331
legal investment function "theory" 210, 212–13
Louboutin litigation 297
on packaging 132
on parallel imports, agreements seeking to prevent 238
and registration and enforcement of non-traditional marks 61, 65, 73, 76–78
three-dimensional (3D) trademarks 206
secondary signs 215
shape mark jurisprudence 327
Sieckmann criteria 131, 132, 134
and trademark functions 133
see also **European Union (EU)**

creativity *see* **innovation and creativity**

Crocs (reinvented clogs) 86, 87*f*, 88

Croze, Denis 7–8

cultural control 10, 363–81
copying, restricting 364, 366, 367–68
intellectual property
imitation and cultural traditions 364–68
status-signaling 369–71
limitation and social stratification 368–69
product imitation 363–68, 370–75, 377–81
status-signaling
and intellectual property 369–71
and trademarks 372–78

cultural cyclic innovation impediment
artistic domain, cyclic innovation in 316–17
artworks 317, 325, 334, 336
checks and balances in trademark law, reliance on 319–22
critique 322–33
critique of checks and balances analysis
impact of cultural significance on infringement analysis 328–31
legal uncertainty surrounding available defenses 332–3
limitations of trademark rights insufficient 331–33
registration requirement of distinctiveness 323–28

cultural cyclic innovation impediment (*cont.*)
cultural follow-on innovation, corrosive effect on 9, 315–18
cultural significance 312
copyright–trademark overlaps 315–16
impact on infringement analysis 328–31
no confusion due to 320–21
separation of copyright and trademark protection requirement 334
freedom of expression, limitations supporting 321–22
infringement, impact of cultural significance on analysis of 328–31
lack of distinctiveness, no registration due to 319–20
Mona Lisa decision 309, 319–20, 323, 324
objective domain of technology vs. subjective domain of culture 318
overlaps between trademark and copyright or patent protection 309–11
signs with cultural significance 315–16
technological field 317–18
traditional acceptance of 312–15
refusal, need for more robust grounds
functionality doctrine insufficient 333–34
public order and morality 334–36
technology, objective domain vs. subjective domain of culture 316–17
traditional acceptance of copyright-trademark overlap 312–15
cultural innovation, cyclic 309–36

Desai, Deven 8
description requirement
data 263–64
purpose 65–67
representations vs. description 78–80
see also **characterization of marks at time of registration**
design of product
aesthetically pleasing 127
anti-competitive effect of protecting 228–29
and branding 127, 128
and functionality 142
and marketing 128
non-traditional marks as means to protect 293–304
product categorization, affecting 143
recognizing as a trademark 226, 227
serving same function as a trademark 217
works of industrial design 207
see also **industrial designs**
design patents *see* **industrial designs**
devices 222, 224, 225, 346
dilution
anti-dilution protection 193, 198–200, 329
cultural control 378
enhanced protection against 290
and status-signaling 378
in United States 356

Dinwoodie, Graeme 114
diplomatic conferences
Brussels (1897–1900) 150, 154–56
Paris (1800–1883) 150, 151–54
Singapore Treaty on the Law of Trademarks (STLT), 2006 19, 20, 21
Washington (1911) 150, 156–58
distinctiveness
acquired
bans on registration of certain types of shape marks 148, 149
in China 187, 189
color and shape markets, protecting (German/EU perspective) 92, 93, 96, 99, 101, 102
competition law 249, 255
cultural control 374
cultural innovation, cyclic 325
Golden Bunny case 96
inherently valuable expression 346, 348, 353, 354, 358, 359
innovation and creativity, possibly impeding 291, 294, 303
pharmaceutical sector 274
proof of 348, 353
registration and enforcement of non-traditional marks 40, 69, 71–72, 76, 83
shape and color marks 92
trademark use 165, 170, 171, 175, 176
acquisition of trademark status 290–91
artworks 325
in Australia 41, 57, 178, 179
"capable of distinguishing" 4
circularity 295
color marks, concerns over 42–43
definition 3–4
elastic concept of 4
establishing through use in course of trade 90
and functionality 75, 346–47
global 13
inherent 3, 95, 179
China 187, 189
registration and enforcement of non-traditional marks 67, 70–72
lack of
fair use of non-distinctive signs and indications, exempting 8
functionality of shapes 178
indistinctive signs *see* **indistinctive signs**
registration not permitted 319–20, 323–28
shape marks, absolute bans on registration of certain types 150
trademark use in a non-distinctive manner 103–04
requirement of 294, 319, 323–28
sound marks 188
tests of distinctive character 3–4
three-dimensional (3D) trademarks 209
trademark use 176, 177

Dr. Reddy's Laboratories 275–76
Dyson 76

economic factors
economic assessment vs. legal conditions and limitations of trademark protection 212–13
economic function of trademarks 259
existing empirical evidence 260–61
non-traditional marks, economics of 261–63
private vs. social returns of trademarks 260–61
economics of trademarks 259–61
Eli Lilly 277–78, 279
emblems 151, 217, 219, 222–24, 300
empirical study on non-traditional marks 8, 37–58
application data collection 43–44
bibliographic data 44
comparative approaches to functionality and non-traditional trademarks 38–41
datasets/databases 43, 44
future research 57
leading categories of marks applied for 45–46
methodology 43–44
monopolies 39, 40, 41
national and regional applications, focus on 47–57
overview of application data 44–47
packaging 38–42, 53
policy concerns 41–43
statistical analysis 43
words/word marks 38, 39
enforcement *see* **registration and enforcement of non-traditional marks**
estoppel 8, 80–81
EUIPO (EU Intellectual Property Office)
Bottega Veneta *intrecciato* leather design pattern, registration 303
Cancellation Division 84
empirical study on non-traditional marks 44, 45, 47, 48, 52*f*
"other" category at 76
registration and enforcement of non-traditional marks 61, 67
characterization of marks at time of registration 75, 76, 78
registrability vs. infringement 81–82
trademark registration details for pharmaceutical sector 275
USPTO compared 76
see also **European Union (EU); EUTM (EU Trade Mark); Office for the Harmonization in the Internal Market (OHIM)**
European Union (EU)
aesthetic functionality test 110–11
"another characteristic" 39–40
anti-dilution protection 329
characterization of marks at time of registration requirement 66
competition law, perspective on *see* **competition law and trademarks**
connections and disconnects in trademark law 83–86, 88
current trademark law in Member States 130
deciding which marks should or should not be protected 135, 137
embracing non-traditional marks 130–31
empirical study on non-traditional marks 8, 37, 39–40, 47–48, 52*f*, 57
European Commission
on challenging validity of a trademark 241
on combined licensing of know-how and trademarks 240–41
on competition restriction within the TFEU 241
Explanatory Memorandum (1980) 205
Guidelines on market definition 252
on mergers and acquisitions 239, 240
functional marks, prohibition on 39–40
graphical/adequate or enabling representation requirement 65
harmonized trademark regime 63, 72, 97, 238, 292
indistinctive signs in EU trademark law 100–05
Intellectual Property Office (EUIPO) *see* **EUIPO (EU Intellectual Property Office)**
internal market 72
Madrid Protocol applications 47
marks with a reputation in 7
national and regional applications, focus on 47–8, 52*f*
principles of trademark law 97–100
"use as a mark" 94–95, 97–99, 105
"weak" marks, likelihood of confusion 99–100
reform of trademark law 8
shape marks, bans on registration of certain types 148
status-signaling 369–70
three-dimensional trademarks (compromise solution) 206–10
trademark law embracing non-traditional marks 133–34
Trademark Office 43
see also **Court of Justice of the European Union (CJEU); EUTM (EU Trade Mark)**
EUTM (EU Trade Mark)
distinctiveness requirement 70, 71
graphical representation requirement 76
"shape and logo" marks 88
three-dimensional (3D) trademarks 86
trademark law 83–84
exception to the rule, making
costs 217–18, 227–34
product imitation 217, 218, 220, 221, 226–27, 230

exception to the rule, making (*cont.*)
proper labeling requirement 226, 230
unfair competition 218, 220, 221, 226–28, 230, 231, 233, 234
USPTO trade dress protection as 217–34
word marks 227, 228–30
see also **trade dress**
exclusions from registration 4
abolition of categorical exclusions 63
absence of clear-cut exclusions 2–3
non-visible signs 16, 23, 59
shape marks 63
Trademark Law Treaty, under 16
see also **registration and enforcement of non-traditional marks**
exclusive rights 132–33, 239–40, 287
competitive necessity test 346–47
overlaps between trademark and copyright or patent protection 309–11
traditional acceptance of 312–15
expression, freedom of *see* **freedom of expression**

Ferrero Rocher golden paper-wrapped chocolate packaging 189, 190
figurative marks 60, 73, 74, 75*f*
combined with colors 22
"file wrapper" estoppel
patent law 80
filing of marks
first-to-file rule, China 190–92
non-visual marks, yearly numbers of new filings 264
registration by filing basis (1996–2016) 46–47*t*
"two variants" filing strategy 86
in United States 70, 264
footwear *see* **Crocs (reinvented clogs)**; **Louboutin red shoes litigation**
France
bilateral treaty with Russia 152
Bottega Veneta *intrecciato* leather design pattern 303
and copying 366
and EU competition law 238
and Gucci case 301
Louboutin litigation 68–69, 296–98
see also **Louboutin red shoes litigation**
telle quelle principle 151, 152
and Washington Conference (1911) 156, 157
see also **Paris Conference (1880–83)**; **Paris Convention for the Protection of Industrial Property (1883, revised July 14, 1967)**; **Paris Union**; ***telle quelle* principle**
freedom of expression
certain laws possibly violating
balancing non-traditional marks and free expression 352–57
expression capable of protection by free expression right 349–52
reform of non-traditional marks, proposals for 357–60
harming 340–41
and inherently valuable expression 6–7, 337–61
inherently valuable expression 340
limitations supporting 321–22
recognition in national constitutions 342–43
recognition of right in treaties 341–42
right to 341–45
certain laws possibly violating 349–57
vagueness doctrine 344–45
see also **inherently valuable expression**
functionality doctrine
aesthetic functionality doctrine 107–24
and appearance 142–43
and color marks 57
comparative approaches to functionality and non-traditional trademarks 38–41
context, looking for 75
deciding which marks should or should not be protected 136
defining a product feature as "functional" and effect of 108, 109
design choices 142
and distinctiveness 75, 346–47
effect in trademark law 309
EU prohibition on functional marks 39–40
exclusion from registration 64
"indicators of origin" function of trademarks 289–90
insufficiency of doctrine 333–34
lack of functionality doctrine in Australia 41
overlaps between trademark and copyright or patent protection 310
perceptual functionality of black, blue and other features 118–21
problems with reliance on 357
registration and enforcement of non-traditional marks 187–90
shape marks 64, 67, 178
three-dimensional (3D) trademarks 189
in trademark law 39, 43, 107–24, 248–50
trademark use and functional marks 172–78
traditional functionality 107, 108–09
in US trademark law 39, 43, 107–24, 346–47
utilitarian functionality 107, 108–09, 248
fundamental rights 6–7

Gangjee, Dev 8
Germany
acquired distinctiveness cases 92
association of savings banks (DSGV) 92
bifurcation system 92, 98
color marks 91–94
DSGV v. Santander 92–94

Federal Court of Justice (BGH) 90, 92–99, 103, 105, 321, 322, 328
Federal Patent Court (BPatG) 92, 93, 319, 320, 323, 327
infringement proceedings 85, 92
Langenscheidt v. Rosetta Stone 92–93
Patent and Trademark Office (DPMA) 92
secondary signs 215
shape marks/three dimensional marks in 63, 94–97
trademark registry 72–73
"use as a mark" 94–95, 105
gesture marks
application for representation at SCT 31
increased numbers of applications 57
opening up to 60
Seventeenth Session of SCT, under 25, 26
see also **motion/multimedia marks**
Ghidini, Gustavo 9
Glaxo 79
goods
adding substantial value to 295
aesthetic functionality dilemma 110–11
color and shape markets, protecting 90
cultural innovation, non-traditional marks possibly impeding 324, 326, 334
empirical study on non-traditional marks 39–40
EU competition law analysis 236
inherently valuable expression 347
marketing practices 137, 148
registration issues 65, 86
defining inherent form of 175–76
marketable, as not exclusively functional or aesthetic 206–07
product shape marks *see* **shape marks**
shapes of as registrable subject matter 39, 49
graphical representation requirement
as barrier to some non-traditional trademark registrations 131
characterization of non-traditional marks 65, 69–70
color marks 131–32
empirical study on non-traditional marks 41
India 134
WIPO treaties, development of non-traditional marks in 24–26
Greenhalgh, Christine 260
Gucci, Guccio 299–301

Hague Conference (1925) 158
Handler, Michael 8
harmonization of trademarks
and defining trademarks 63
in the EU 63, 72, 97, 238, 292
further harmonization requirement 34, 40
Singapore Treaty, under 19
Trademark Law Treaty, under 15, 19
TRIPs Agreement, under 130–31
Heinz
"Power of Red" campaign 339
holograms
application for representation at SCT 30
combination of individual colors and drawings 22
exclusions under Trademark Law Treaty (TLT), 1994 16
graphical representation requirement 26
increased numbers of applications 57
opening up to 60
honest commercial practices
indistinctive signs 104–05, 106
Hong Kong 148
Hughes, Justin 8, 138–40, 146
Huydecoper, Tony 313
"hybrid" trademarks 167, 298

ice cream brands 255
imitation, product
competition law analysis 245
cultural control 363–68, 370–75, 377–81
economic factors 260
exception to the rule, making 217, 218, 220, 221, 226–27, 230
pharmaceutical sector 278
and social stratification 368–69
incentives, allocating 289–93
India
bans on registration of certain types of shape marks 148
definition of "trademark" 272
marketing practices and trademark law 134
pharmaceutical sector, non-traditional marks 280–81
indistinctive signs
background 100–01
in EU trademark law 100–05
fair use, exempting 8
honest commercial practices 104–05, 106
potential scenarios 101–04
"limping" marks 101–03
use in a non-distinctive manner 103–04
industrial designs 4, 5, 6, 22, 310
anti-competitive effect 247
creativity and innovation, non-traditional marks possibly negatively impacting 292, 293, 307
cultural control 364, 369
defining 292
status-signaling 369
and three-dimensional shape marks 206–09
see also **design of product**
infringement proceedings 8
allegedly infringed mark/allegedly infringing sign 103
Coca-Cola's bottle shape 181, 182–83, 189

infringement proceedings (*cont.*)
determining what should constitute infringement 165–84
Germany 85, 92
impact of cultural significance on analysis of infringement 328–31
Louboutin litigation 297–98
of non-traditional marks, need to focus on 165–69
and registration and enforcement of non-traditional marks 80–88
color depletion 62
connections and disconnects in trademark law 83–86, 88
disclaimers, discarding 81–82
test for prima facie infringement 168
threshold requirement for infringement 171–72
trade dress 218
trademark use
in British Commonwealth 169–72, 183
and functional marks 172–78
and non-functional marks 177–83
trademark use as a condition of infringement 170–71
two-dimensional marks 73, 74, 172
see also **trademark use**
inherent distinctiveness *see* **distinctiveness**
inherently valuable expression 337–61
acquired distinctiveness 346, 348, 353, 354, 358, 359
colors 339
concept as guideline 358
freedom of expression 340
goods, adding value to 347
identifying source of product 338, 340
non-traditional marks laws 345–48
packaging 339, 361
scents 339
sounds 339
tastes 339
textures 339
see also **freedom of expression**
innovation and creativity, non-traditional marks possibly negatively impacting 9, 304–07
acquired distinctiveness 291, 294, 303
creativity and access to styles 304–07
monopolies 288, 291, 305
non-traditional marks as means to protect designs and aesthetic product features 293–304
potential negative effects as "monolithic effect" on product and design development 288
standardization, current legal provisions promoting 9, 287–88, 307
trademarks compared to patents and copyrights 291–92
unfair competition 293, 298, 301
see also **Bottega Veneta** ***intrecciato*** **leather design pattern; Louboutin red shoes litigation; monograms, patterns and stripes (Gucci)**
intellectual property (IP)/intellectual property rights (IPRs)
application information services, easy access 43
continuous expansion of IPRs 236
copying, restricting 364, 366, 367–68
distinction between existence and exercise of an IPR 238
exceptions to exclusionary effects 235
extension in scope of protection 13
imitation and cultural traditions 364–68
justification of IPRs 245
national IP offices 23, 25, 27, 33
overlaps between trademark and copyright or patent protection 309–11
traditional acceptance of 312–15
scope of rights, identifying 81
side-effects of IPR regimes 257
specific subject matter doctrine 239
status-signaling 369–71
trademarks compared to patents and copyrights 291–92
utilitarian philosophy 365
see also **copyright; non-traditional trademarks (NTTMs); trademarks; World Intellectual Property Organization (WIPO)**
IPGOD (Intellectual Property Government Open Database), Australia 44, 55
IPOS (Intellectual Property Office of Singapore) 44

Janis, Mark 114
Japan
empirical study on non-traditional marks 8, 37, 40, 43, 54–55, 57
Madrid Protocol applications 54
national and regional applications, focus on 54–55
Patent Office (JPO) 44, 45, 54
position marks, growth in 57
registration and enforcement of non-traditional marks 135
shape marks, bans on registration of certain types 148
shapes of goods and packaging as registrable subject matter 40
Trademark Office 43
trend in annual trademark applications 45
JPO (Japanese Patent Office) 44, 45, 54

Kit-Kat chocolate wafer, shape 4, 41, 148
Korea 148
Kur, Annette 8, 133, 313

LEGO product 148
Minifigure 351, 356, 358, 359
Lemley, Mark A. 81

likelihood of confusion
anti-confusion protection, China 193, 196–98
confusing effects, risk with three-dimensional shape trademarks 215–16
cultural significance, no confusion due to 320–21
inherently valuable expression 354
post-sale confusion 375–7
shape marks, assessment in case of 95–97
"weak" marks 99–100
"limping" marks 101–03
Lindt/Lindt & Sprüngli (Golden Bunny case) 83–86, 96–97, 100
Lisbon Conference (1958) 150, 154, 158–60
and WTO jurisprudence 161–62
logo marks 73
London Conference (1934) 158
Louboutin red shoes litigation 4, 307
deciding which marks should or should not be protected 141, 142
protection of designs and aesthetic product features 296–99
registration issues 60, 83
characterization of marks at time of registration 64–65, 68–70, 73
Lunney, Glynn 9, 145

McCarthy, Thomas 246
McKenna, Mark P. 81, 114
Madrid system, international registration of trademarks 16, 23, 72
Madrid Protocol applications 47, 48, 54, 55
Mannen, Kaya 9
market definition 236, 256
assessment of 256
EU Commission Guidelines 252
and product substitutability 236, 250–53
see also **competition law and trademarks**
marketing practices and trademark law 125–46
appearance and consumer preferences 142–43
branding 126–29, 133, 141–45
deciding which marks should or should not be protected 135–41
ergonomic concerns 142–43
essence marks 126–29
laws embracing non-traditional marks 129–35
marketers and brand builders seeking to use and claim innate and cultural signals and meaning 141–45
packaging 126, 127, 129, 131, 132, 134, 139, 144, 146
practical and ideal realities 145–46
sensory marketing 262
trade dress 143–45
see also **brands/branding; market definition; packaging; trade dress; trademark law**
Master Lock 127
monograms, patterns and stripes (Gucci) 299–301, 307
monopolies 9
aesthetic functionality doctrine 107
copyright, expiry of 309, 316
cultural control 370, 371, 375
economic factors 259
empirical study on non-traditional marks 39, 40, 41
EU competition law analysis 237, 242, 246, 248, 253
exception to the rule, making 218, 232
innovation and creativity, non-traditional marks possibly impeding 288, 291, 305
legal 59, 62, 63
natural 206
perpetual 173, 305
pharmaceutical sector 279, 281, 282, 283, 285
private 211
registration and enforcement of non-traditional marks 59, 62, 63
shape marks 206, 211, 212, 214
temporary 291–92
trademark use 166, 173, 174
motion/multimedia marks
application for representation at SCT 30
increased numbers of applications 57
opening up to 60
Seventeenth Session of SCT, under 25, 26
see also **gesture marks**

Nabisco and shredded wheat case 108–09
national and regional applications, focus on 47–57
applications by international class 49–51*t*
Australia 55–57
European Union 47–48, 52*f*
Singapore 53
United Kingdom 48, 52*f*, 53
see also **non-traditional trademarks (NTTMs)**
"new types of marks" *see* **non-traditional trademarks (NTTMs)**
New Zealand
marketing practices and trademark law 134
Trade Marks Act 347–48
trademark use 170, 172, 175, 177–78
Ng-Loy Wee Loon 8
Nice Agreement Concerning the International Classification of Goods and Services for the Purposes of the Registration of Marks (as amended on Sept. 28, 1979)
Classification classes 47, 53, 54, 56
non-conventional trademarks *see* **non-traditional trademarks (NTTMs)**
non-traditional trademarks (NTTMs)
anti-competitive effect 244–48, 253–54
balancing with free expression 352–57

non-traditional trademarks (NTTMs) (*cont.*)
combinations 22, 44, 57
concentration of capital and ownership of 255
creativity and innovation, possibly negatively impacting 9, 304–07
cultural significance 312
defining 272–74, 363
internationally accepted definition, lacking 13–14
economics of 261–63
empirical study *see* **empirical study on non-traditional marks**
indirect recognition in TRIPS Agreement 13
infringement of, need to focus on 165–69
international community, attitude to protection of 8
jurisdictional differences and legal controversies 37–43
as means to protect designs and aesthetic product features 293–304
Gucci monograms, patterns and stripes 299–301
Louboutin red lacquered sole shoes 296–99
multiple elements, with 137
national application process, under Singapore Treaty 18
non-functional 177–83
opening up to 60–63
Paris Convention silent on subject matter of 14–15
in pharmaceutical sector
defining 274–79
protection of marks and impact on access to medicine 279–85
product substitutability 253–56
as evidence of sufficient competition and application to non-traditional marks 248–56
publication of 31
recognition *see* **recognition of non-traditional marks**
reform proposals 8, 9, 357–60
registration *see* **registration and enforcement of non-traditional marks**
representation *see* **representations of trademarks**
standardization, current legal provisions promoting 9, 287–88, 307
and trademark law 125–46
branding 126–29, 141–45
deciding which marks should or should not be protected 135–41
essence marks 126–29
laws embracing non-traditional marks 129–35
practical and ideal realities 145–46
use of *see* **trademark use**
well-known, recognition of 7, 192–96, 246, 289
see also **signs; trademarks**

non-visual marks
data description 263–64
empirical exploration 263–69
firms making use of 267–69
sensory marks 266, 267
service marks 70, 266
sound marks 266–67
types 264, 266–67
at United States Patent and Trademark Office (USPTO) 263–69
yearly numbers of new filings/registrations 264
see also **olfactory marks; scent marks; signs; sound marks; taste marks; United States Patent and Trademark Office (USPTO)**

NTTMs *see* **non-traditional trademarks (NTTMs)**

Office for the Harmonization in the Internal Market (OHIM) 76, 89
see also **EUIPO (EU Intellectual Property Office)**

olfactory marks
application for representation at SCT 31
exclusions under Trademark Law Treaty (TLT), 1994 16
graphical representation requirement 41
opening up to 61
representation challenges 62
Sieckmann criteria, effect on 132
see also **scent marks**

packaging 22, 189, 217, 219, 220, 222, 226–32
aesthetic functionality doctrine 107, 110, 119, 121
anti-competitive effect of protecting 228–29
cultural cyclic innovation impediment 320, 325
economic factors 263, 267, 270
empirical study on non-traditional marks 38–42, 53
Ferrero Rocher golden paper-wrapped chocolate packaging 189, 190
inherently valuable expression 339, 361
marketing practices and trademark law 126, 127, 129, 131, 132, 134, 139, 144, 146
pharmaceutical sector 276
recognizing as a trademark 226, 227
as registrable subject matter 40
registration and enforcement of non-traditional marks 60, 67, 68, 74, 83, 85
repackaging 239
serving same function as a trademark 217
three-dimensional (3D) trademarks and competition law 204, 211, 216
trademark use 166, 167, 170–72, 175

packaging, product *see* **trade dress**
Pantone 131–32
Paris Conference (1880–83) 150, 151–54, 162
and Lisbon Conference (1958) 159
Paris Convention for the Protection of Industrial Property (1883, revised July 14, 1967)
Article 6 *quinquies* A(1) 15, 149–62, 164
exceptions recognized by 150
telle quelle principle 150–51, 160, 161
Final Protocol 153, 154, 156, 157
and Lisbon Conference (1958) 159–60
priority claims under 16
product shape marks outside purview of 164
relevant provisions on non-traditional marks 14–15
travaux préparatoires 8, 150, 164
and WTO jurisprudence 161, 163
see also ***telle quelle*** **principle**
Paris Union 8, 15
bans on registration of certain types of shape marks 149–50, 153, 154–55
patent law, "file wrapper" estoppel 80
"phantom marks," rejection of 76–77
pharmaceutical sector 9, 271–85
asthma inhalers 281
Attention Deficit Hyperactivity Disorder, drug for 284
brand names
Adderall 284
Benzedrine tablets 276–77
Dexedrine tablets 276–77
Dyazide 277
Nexium 275–76, 281–82
Nimenrix 240
Pepto-Bismol 278, 284
Prilosec 282
Viagra 275, 276
branded drugs 281, 282
defining a non-traditional mark 272–74
denial of protection for non-traditional features by courts 277–78
diuretics 277
examples of non-traditional marks 275
generic drugs 281, 282, 283
monopolies 279, 281, 282, 283, 285
non-traditional marks in 274–79
peripheral and cerebral vascular diseases 278–79
placebo effects and particular drugs 283–84
protection of marks and impact on access to medicine 279–85
proton-pump inhibitors (PPIs) 282
quinine 277–78
shape of tablet 148
stomach remedies 278, 284
Porter, Michael 127
position marks
application for representation at SCT 30
increased numbers of applications 57
opening up to 60
Seventeenth Session of SCT, under 26
price war 127
product substitutability
availability of substitutable products 236–37
EU competition law perspective 236–37, 245, 248–56
as evidence of sufficient competition to non-traditional marks 248–56
exception to the rule, making 227
and market definition 236, 250–53
narrowly defined markets 252–53
and non-traditional marks 253–56
Small but Significant Non-Transitory Increase in Prices (SSNIP) test 251, 253
see also **competition law and trademarks**
products
counterfeit 375–76
definition, and functionality 248–50
imitation *see* **imitation, product**
packaging *see* **packaging**
shape marks *see* **shape marks**
substitutability *see* **product substitutability**
prosecution history estoppel 8, 80–81
public order and morality 334–36

Ramsey, Lisa 9
recognition of non-traditional marks
consumer loyalty to well-known mark 246
indirect recognition in TRIPS Agreement 13
overlaps between trademark and copyright or patent protection 309–11
traditional acceptance of 312–15
Singapore Treaty, under 17
well-known marks 7, 192–96, 246, 289
Red Bull 80
reform proposals 8, 9, 357–60
refusal, grounds of
broader application of public interest-related grounds, need for 9
and functionality doctrine 333–34
public order and morality 334–36
registration and enforcement of non-traditional marks 8, 59–88
assessing impact of registration from EU competition law perspective 235–56
characterization at time of registration *see* **characterization of marks at time of registration**
China
anti-confusion protection 193, 196–98
anti-dilution protection 193, 198–200
distinctiveness and functionality 187–90
first-to-file rule 190–92
recognition of well-known marks 192–96
registrable subject matter 186–87
scope of registrable marks 186, 187
cross-over registration 221, 222

registration and enforcement of non-traditional marks (*cont.*)
disclaimers, discarding 81–82
distortion of competition, potential 236
functionality exclusions from registrability 64, 187–90
graphical representation requirement as barrier to some registrations 131
historical exclusions from registration 4
informational integrity of register 75
and infringement 80–88
connections and disconnects in trademark law 83–86, 88
disclaimers, discarding 81–82
EU trademark law 83
Japan 135
lack of distinctiveness affecting 319–20
limits to freedom
representations and restrictive framing 77–78
representations vs. description 78–80
type of mark 73–77
Madrid system *see* **Madrid system, international registration of trademarks**
by mark type and filing basis (1996–2016) 46–47*t*
monopolies 59, 62, 63
non-visual marks, USPTO 264
opening up to non-traditional marks 60–63
packaging 60, 67, 68, 74, 83, 85
predominance of technical/aesthetic features as impediment to 209
principal register, allowing trade dress on (US) 222, 223, 224
registered community design (RCD) 86, 88
registrability principle 205–06
registrable subject matter 186–87
shape marks, absolute bans on registration of certain types 147–64
absolute nature of bans 148–49
Aesthetic Shape Ban 148, 150, 163, 164
Brussels Conference (1880–1900) 150, 154–56, 159
China 148, 150–51
European Union (EU) 148
Functional Shape Ban 148, 150, 163, 164
Hong Kong 148
India 148
Japan 148
Korea 148
Lisbon Conference (1958) 150, 154, 158–62
Natural Shape Ban 148, 149–50, 163, 164
Paris Conference (1880–83) 150, 151–54, 159, 162
Paris Convention for the Protection of Industrial Property (1967) 149–62
Singapore 147–48
South Africa 148
telle quelle principle, breach of 149–51
TRIPS Agreement (Article 15) 162–64
Washington Diplomatic Conference (1911) 150, 156–58
WTO jurisprudence 161–62
Standing Committee, under 22–23, 24
on supplemental register, US 222
technologies of 61–62
three-dimensional (3D) trademarks, competition-related concerns 204–06
Trademark Law Treaty (TLT), under 16
trends in number of applications 45*f*
words/word marks 60, 61, 65, 68, 69, 71, 74, 76, 77, 83–86, 88
see also **functionality; non-traditional trademarks (NTTMs)**
representations of trademarks
applications for, at SCT
color marks 29
gesture marks 31
hologram marks 30
motion/multimedia marks 30
olfactory marks 31
position marks 30
sound marks 31
taste marks 31
texture/feel marks 31
three-dimensional (3D) trademarks 29
areas of convergence, under SCT
Nineteenth Session 27–28
Twentieth Session 28, 29–31
current challenges affecting olfactory and taste marks 62
vs. description 78–80
exceptional non-traditional marks 24
existing methods for non-traditional marks 25
graphical *see* **graphical representation of non-traditional marks**
non-visible signs *see* **signs**
and restrictive framing 77–78
Sieckmann criteria 131, 132, 134
Singapore Treaty, under 19
trademark offices, guidelines of 41–42
two-dimensional 73, 74, 172
retail store design 70–71
Rogers, Mark 260
Rubic's cube 4, 78
Russia 151, 152

Scardamaglia, Amanda 8
Scaria, Arul 9
scent marks
inherently valuable expression 339, 339–40
opening up to 61
registration of 267
representation of 41, 42, 57
see also **olfactory marks**
SCT *see* **Standing Committee on the Law of Trademarks, Industrial Designs and Geographical Indications (SCT)**

secondary meaning requirement, US 4, 42, 61, 71, 104, 167, 213
acquired secondary meaning 83, 210, 222, 261, 274, 277
aesthetic functionality 110, 117
economic factors 261
failing to establish secondary meaning 279
marketing practices and trademark law 125, 140
proving secondary meaning 217, 225, 226, 255, 291
trade dress 219, 220, 224, 231
Senftleben, Martin 9, 133
sensory marks 266, 267
service marks 70, 266
severability doctrine
trademark use 175–76
shape marks
absolute bans 150, 152, 162
acquired distinctiveness, establishing 91
bans on registration of certain types 147–64
absolute nature of bans 148–49
Aesthetic Shape Ban 148, 150, 163, 164
Brussels Conference (1880–1900) 150, 154–56, 159
China 148, 150–51
European Union (EU) 148
Functional Shape Ban 148, 150, 163, 164
Hong Kong 148
India 148
Japan 148
Korea 148
Lisbon Conference (1958) 150, 154, 158–62
Natural Shape Ban 148, 149–50, 163, 164
Paris Conference (1880–83) 150, 151–54, 159, 162
Paris Convention for the Protection of Industrial Property (1967) 149–62
Singapore 147–48
South Africa 148
telle quelle principle, breach of 149–51
TRIPS Agreement (Article 15) 162–64
Washington Diplomatic Conference (1911) 150, 156–58
WTO jurisprudence 161–62
CJEU jurisprudence 327
conflict concerning 203–04
denial of registration by Italy 205
distinctiveness requirement 74
functionality doctrine 64, 67, 178
Germany 94–97
historical exclusions from registration 4
likelihood of confusion, assessing 95–97
monopolies 206, 211, 212, 214
as most popular category of registered non-traditional marks 38, 45, 57
opening up to 60
problems inside and outside trademark law 4
protecting from German and European perspective 89–106
registration concerns 63
and trademark law 62–63
two-dimensional 73, 74, 172
"use as a mark" 94–95, 97–99, 105
see also **three-dimensional (3D) trademarks**
shoes *see* **Crocs (reinvented clogs); Louboutin red shoes litigation**
signs
allegedly infringing 103
basic 22
color marks 90
complex 22
cultural significance 315–16
descriptive 167, 168, 187, 241
eligible for trademark protection in New Zealand 134
generic 241, 358
Gucci's monograms, patterns and stripes 299–301
indistinctive *see* **indistinctive signs**
lack of actual obligation under STLT for any Member State to mandatorily accept registration of certain signs 20
legal monopolies in 59
non-visible
exclusion from registration 16, 23, 59
increasing protection of 17
lack of harmonization under STLT 19
opening up to 61
publication of 25–26
representation of 19
reproductions under STLT 23
see also **non-traditional trademarks (NTTMs); non-visual marks; olfactory marks; sound marks; taste marks; texture/feel marks**
as not exclusively functional or aesthetic 207
protection as marks, requirements for 290
restrictions for some shape signs relating to the goods 39
secondary 215
use as a badge of origin 170, 171
visible
inclusion under TLT 16
pattern marks 60–61
reproductions of 23
see also **symbols**
Singapore
bans on registration of certain types of shape marks 147–48, 163, 164
empirical study on non-traditional marks 8, 37, 43, 53, 57
functional marks, restriction on registration of 40
Intellectual Property Office (IPOS) 44
national and regional applications, focus on 53
Trademark Office 43
trend in annual trademark applications 45

Singapore Treaty on the Law of Trademarks (STLT), 2006 17–20
adoption of 17, 34
aim 17
Assembly 32–34
compared with Trademark Law Treaty 17–18, 19
Contracting Parties 18–19
Diplomatic Conference 19, 20, 21
documents on non-traditional marks 35
expansion of trademark domain 1–2
lack of actual obligation for any Member State to mandatorily accept registration of certain signs 20
list of indications and elements 18–19
national application process for non-traditional marks under 18
recognition of non-traditional marks 17
Regulations under 18, 19, 23
Resolution supplementary to 20
Rule 3(4) to (6) of Regulations under
amendments 32–33
Assembly approval of review of 32
reproductions of visible signs/representations of non-visible signs 23
Working Group on review of 14, 32–33
Small but Significant Non-Transitory Increase in Prices (SSNIP) test 251, 253
smell marks *see* **olfactory marks**
sound marks 5
application for representation at SCT 31
in Australia 41–42
distinctiveness, demonstrating 188
examples 266–67
exclusions under Trademark Law Treaty (TLT), 1994 16
graphical representation requirement 41, 57
opening up to 61
in United States 274
South Africa 148
Standing Committee on the Law of Trademarks, Industrial Designs and Geographical Indications (SCT) 8, 14, 20–31
Fifteen Session (Nov 28 to Dec 2, 2005)
issue-paper 21
Sixteenth Session (Nov 13 to 17, 2006) 20–24
additional costs of non-traditional marks 26
New Types of Marks, documentation on 20–22, 60
opening of 21–22
registration procedures 22–23
scope of work on non-traditional marks 23
SCT Report 22
Seventeenth Session (May 7 to 11, 2007) 14, 24–27
graphical representation of non-traditional marks 24–26
WIPO document "Methods of Representation and Description of New Types of Marks" 24–26, 60
WIPO document "Relation of Established Trademark Principles to New Type of Marks" 26–27
Eighteenth Session (Nov 12 to 16, 2007) 27
Nineteenth Session (July 21 to 25, 2008) 27–28
Twentieth Session (Dec 1 to 5, 2008) 28–31
application for the representation of three-dimensional marks (area of convergence No. 1) 29
application for the representation of color marks (area of convergence No. 2) 29
application for the representation of hologram marks (area of convergence No. 3) 30
application for the representation of motion or multimedia marks (area of convergence No. 4) 30
application for the representation of position marks (area of convergence No. 5) 30
application for the representation of gesture trademarks (area of convergence No. 6) 31
application for the representation of sound marks (area of convergence No. 7) 31
application for the representation of olfactory marks (area of convergence No. 8) 31
application for the representation of taste marks (area of convergence No. 9) 31
application for the representation of texture and feel marks (area of convergence No. 10) 31
publication of non-traditional marks 31
documents on non-traditional marks 35
see also **World Intellectual Property Organization (WIPO)**
Starbucks 60
status-signaling
brands 372–73
dilution 378
in European Union 369–70
and intellectual property 369–71
marks with a reputation, in EU 7
post-sale confusion 375–77
special case of trademarks and status-signaling 372–78
determining what is non-traditional about protecting status symbols 378–81
dilution 378
post-sale confusion 375–77
trade-dress protection 374–75
status symbols 299, 363, 364, 368, 377
determining what is non-traditional about protecting 378–81

trade-dress protection 374–75
in United States 369, 370–71
Steffensin, Carmen 297–98
STLT *see* **Singapore Treaty on the Law of Trademarks (STLT), 2006**
substitutability *see* **product substitutability**
Sun, Haochen 9
symbols
China, protecting non-traditional marks in 187
competition law 235
cultural 309, 331
cultural control 363, 364, 368, 372, 377, 381
cyclic cultural innovation impediment 309, 331, 345
fashion 299
generic 345
heritage 309
marketing practices and trademark law 125, 129, 130, 138
non-traditional marks possibly negatively impacting innovation 299
status 363, 364, 368, 372, 377, 381
trade dress 219, 222–24, 225
see also **emblems; signs**

tactile marks *see* **texture/feel marks**
Taddei, Michele 301
taste marks
application for representation at SCT 31
inherently valuable expression 339
opening up to 61
representation of 42, 62
Seventeenth Session of SCT, under 26
technical trademark protection
defining 221
unfair competition distinguished 219–20
see also **unfair competition**
***telle quelle* principle**
ambiguity 152
breach of 149–51
and Lisbon Conference (1958) 158
in Paris Convention, Article 6 *quinquies* A(1) 150–51, 160, 161
problem intended to resolve 151
terminology, origins 152
and Washington Conference (1911) 156
see also **registration and enforcement of non-traditional marks; shape marks**
texture/feel marks
application for representation at SCT 31
inherently valuable expression 339
opening up to 61
representation of 42
Seventeenth Session of SCT, under 26
three-dimensional (3D) trademarks 5, 203–16
application for representation at SCT 29
combined with colors/figurative elements 22
competition-related concerns 204–06
conflict concerning 203–04
confusing effects, risk of 215–16
distinctive character 209
dual proposal for a systemic reconstruction 206–10
dual protection for shapes as trademarks and as designs 207–08
European framework (compromise solution) 206–10
functionality doctrine 189
in Germany 205
graphical representation 26
implicit abrogation principle 208
increasing protection of 17
individual character concept 207
informed user concept 207
in Italy 205
market reality 206–07
as most popular category of registered non-traditional marks 38, 45
opening up to 60
possible interference of theory of trademark investment function 210–14
shape of product itself 147
Trademark Law Treaty provisions 19
in United Kingdom 205
see also **shape marks**
TLT *see* **Trademark Law Treaty (TLT), 1994**
Toblerone chocolate, shape 4, 189
trade dress
aesthetic functionality doctrine 107, 109, 110, 112, 114, 121, 122, 144
allowing on principal register 222, 223, 224
and Apple 122, 143, 144
claims 110, 219, 229, 230, 234
devices 222, 224, 225
infringement proceedings 218, 226
litigation 217, 218–19
marketing practices and trademark law 143–45
over-enforcement 219
and principles of statutory construction 222–23
proper labeling requirement 226, 230
protection 109, 112, 145
cultural control 373–75, 379, 380
misuse of 218
USPTO making an exception the rule 217–34
protection against product imitation 226, 230
registration 72, 85, 222, 223, 224
rights 219, 233, 234
symbols 219, 222–24, 225
unregistered 143, 144
USPTO and courts overruling Congress on 217, 219–27
see also **exception to the rule, making; packaging**

trademark law
absence of clear-cut exclusions from protection 2–3
British, late nineteenth-century 62
checks and balances in, reliance on 319–22
critique 322–33
concept of "trademark" 2
embracing non-traditional marks 129–35, 136
in European Union 133–34
EU law
connections and disconnects in 83–86, 88
EU vs. US practice 131, 135
exclusive rights 132–33, 239–40, 287
expansion of trademark domain 1–4, 217
functionality in 248–50
indistinctive signs in EU law 100–05
and non-traditional marks 125–46
branding 126–29, 141–45
deciding which marks should or should not be protected 135–41
defenses 355–56
embracing non-traditional marks 129–35
essence marks 126–29
freedom of expression 345–48
practical and ideal realities 145–46
vagueness of laws 355
problems inside and outside 4–7
reach of, limiting 132–33
and shape marks 62–63
tensions and inconsistencies within intellectual property protection 5–6
see also **marketing practices and trademark law; non-traditional trademarks (NTTMs); trademarks**
Trademark Law Treaty (TLT), 1994 14, 15–17
adoption of 34
Assembly, lack of 17
color trademarks under 19
compared with Singapore Treaty 17–18, 19
exclusion of non-visible signs 16
on registration and enforcement of non-traditional marks 16
Regulations under 16–17
scope 16
three-dimensional trademarks under 19
trademark use
acquired distinctiveness 165, 170, 171, 175, 176
Australia 170, 172, 174–75, 177–81
as badge of origin 170, 171
in British Commonwealth 169–72, 183
concept of trademark use 168–69
as a condition of infringement 170–71
"defensive doctrines" 168
"descriptive use" 167, 168, 187
distinctiveness 176, 177
double identity cases 98
and functional marks 172–78
Global Brand Marketing Inc. v. YD Pty, Ltd 179–80, 181
Kenman Kandy Australia Pty. Ltd. v. Registrar of Trade Marks 178–80
as a mark 94–95
monopolies 166, 173, 174, 176
in a non-distinctive manner 103–04
and non-functional non-traditional marks 177–83
orthodox test 172
packaging 166, 167, 170–72, 175
Philips v. Remington judgment 172–74, 176, 178
principles 171
recalibration of 183
severability doctrine 175–76
"use as a mark" 94–95, 97–99, 105
see also **infringement proceedings**
trademarks
Benelux uniform laws (1971) 205–06
challenging validity of 241
color marks *see* **color marks**
definition 38, 61, 63
amendment by Congress (1943) 222, 223, 345–46
applicant's freedom to define 68–73
and Lisbon Conference (1958) 162
non-traditional marks 13–14, 272–74
TRIPS Agreement, under 148, 273, 294
under US Lanham Act 130
economic function 259
erosion of traditional mark/ product dichotomy 2, 5
expansion of domain 1–4, 217
functional 172–78
harmonization *see* **harmonization of trademarks**
hologram marks *see* **holograms**
"indicators of origin" function of 289–90
legal investment function "theory" 210–14
"limping" 101–03
non-functional 177–83
overall market appearance, final products based on 216
Paris Convention silent on definition of 14
positive welfare effects 259, 260
private vs. social returns of 260–61
product shape marks *see* **shape marks**
sound marks *see* **sound marks**
and status-signaling 372–78
determining what is non-traditional about protecting status symbols 378–81
dilution 378
post-sale confusion 375–77
trade-dress protection 374–75
see also **status-signaling**
three-dimensional *see* **three-dimensional trademarks**
traditional acceptance of copyright-trademark overlap 312–15

traditional account of protection 289–93
use of *see* **trademark use**
"weak" marks, likelihood of confusion 99–100
see also **non-traditional trademarks (NTTMs); trademark law**
TRIPS Agreement on Trade-Related Aspects of Intellectual Property Rights (TRIPS), 1994 1
Article 15 (shape marks) 25, 162–64
China a member state of 186
comparative approaches to functionality and non-traditional trademarks 38
definition of "trademark" 148, 273, 294
graphical representation not provided for 25
harmonization of trademarks under 130–31
indirect recognition of non-traditional marks in 13
open-ended definition of a trademark 61, 63
tests of distinctive character 4
text 8
two-dimensional marks 73, 74, 172

unfair competition 86, 105, 244, 380
deception 220–21, 226, 230
exception to the rule, making 218, 220, 221, 226–28, 230, 231, 233, 234
innovation and creativity, non-traditional marks possibly impeding 293, 298, 301
pharmaceutical sector 272, 277, 278
proving 220
purpose of law 227
shape marks, absolute bans on registration of certain types 149, 160
technical trademark protection distinguished 219–20
three-dimensional (3D) trademarks 213, 214, 216
see also **competition law and trademarks**
United Kingdom
and Brussels Conference (1897–1900) 154–56
characterization of marks at time of registration requirement 66
definition of "trademark" 38
empirical study on non-traditional marks 8, 37, 38, 43, 48, 52*f*, 57
Intellectual Property Office (UKIPO) 44, 52*f*
late nineteenth-century trademark law 62
Madrid Protocol applications 48
national and regional applications, focus on 48, 52*f*, 53
shape marks/three dimensional marks in 63, 205
Trade Marks Act 1994 38, 39, 205
Trademark Office 43
trademark use in British Commonwealth 169–72, 183
trend in annual trademark applications 45
and Washington Conference (1911) 156–58
see also **London Conference (1934)**
United States
aesthetic functionality *see* **aesthetic functionality dilemma**
Chicago School 246
color marks, opponents to registration of single colors 42, 43
Court of Customs and Patent Appeals 224
deciding which marks should or should not be protected 135, 137, 138
Department of Justice 221, 222
dilution laws 356
disclaimers, discarding 82
drawing requirement 65
EU vs. US practice 131, 135
expansion of trademark subject matter 217
Federal Circuit 115–16
Federal Trade Commission 246
filing, experience of 70
Free Speech Clause, First Amendment 343
freedom of expression 343–45
functionality doctrine *see* **aesthetic functionality doctrine; functionality doctrine**
Lanham Act (1946) 217, 219, 221
defining a non-traditional mark 272
enactment 221–22, 229–30
prior to 129–30, 219
lower courts 112–13, 225
misappropriation doctrine and legal investment function theory 214
open-ended definition of a trademark 61
Restatement of Torts 109
secondary meaning requirement *see* **secondary meaning requirement, US**
secondary signs 215
service mark applications 70
sound mark applications 274
status-signaling 369, 370–71
Supreme Court 61, 107, 108–09, 111–12, 114, 129, 316, 346
trademark law 125
trademark registrability vs. infringement 81
Trademark Trial and Appeals Board (TTAB) 115, 116, 119, 274, 303
well-known marks 7
see also **United States Patent and Trademark Office (USPTO)**
United States Patent and Trademark Office (USPTO) 217
data from 9
EUIPO compared 76
non-visual marks at, empirical exploration 263–69
data description 263–64
firms making use of 267–69
types of non-visual marks 264, 266–67
yearly numbers of new filings/registrations 264

United States Patent and Trademark Office (USPTO) (*cont.*)
overruling Congress on trade-dress 217, 219–27
"phantom marks," rejection of 76–77
retail store design and characterization of marks 71
trade dress, efforts to constrain scope of 224
Trademark Case Files database 263, 267
see also **United States**
"unusual marks" *see* **non-traditional trademarks (NTTMs)**
use of trademark *see* **trademark use**
utilitarian functionality 107, 108–09, 248

van Nispen, Constant 313
Verkade, Feer 313–14
Vigeland, Gustav 334, 335, 336
visible signs *see* **signs**

Washington Diplomatic Conference (1911) 150, 156–58
"weak" marks, likelihood of confusion 99–100
words/word marks 2
China 186, 187, 190, 197
color and shape markets, protecting (German/EU perspective) 91, 93, 96, 97, 99, 100, 102–05
competition law and three-dimensional trademark 207, 209
competition law from EU perspective 246
culture and commerce 320, 321
economics 269
empirical study on non-traditional marks 38, 39
exception to the rule, making 227, 228–30
fanciful words 228–30
fantasy words 210
invented words 178
marketing practices 125, 126, 130–32, 134, 138–40, 144–46
pharmaceutical sector 271, 272
registration and enforcement of non-traditional marks 60, 61, 65, 68, 69, 71, 74, 76, 77, 83–86, 88
shape marks, absolute bans on 150, 152, 162
trademark uses 166–68, 174, 178, 182, 183
and TRIPS Agreement 162
in United States 217, 219, 221–25
WIPO treaties, development of non-traditional marks in 13, 17
word/picture combinations 100
World Intellectual Property Organization (WIPO)
discussions on non-traditional marks 14, 20
documents on non-traditional marks 24–27, 34–35
filing system administered by 296–97
Member States
and development of non-traditional marks under WIPO treaties 14, 18, 20, 23, 33–34
Questionnaire on Trademark Law and Practice 21
Secretariat 21, 23, 26–28, 32
Standing Committee on the Law of Trademarks, Industrial Designs and Geographical Indications *see* **Standing Committee on the Law of Trademarks, Industrial Designs and Geographical Indications (SCT)**
treaties 8, 14
development of non-traditional trademarks in 13–35
relevant provisions on non-traditional trademarks 14–20
see also **Paris Convention for the Protection of Industrial Property (1883, revised July 14, 1967); Singapore Treaty on the Law of Trademarks (2006); Trademark Law Treaty (TLT), 1994**
World Trade Organization (WTO)
Appellate Body 161, 163
China joining (2001) 186
Panel 161
shape marks, bans on registration 161–62

Yoshida Metals 77
Yves Saint Laurent (YSL) 83, 296, 297

Zengiaro, Renzo 301

The manufacturer's authorised representative in the EU for product safety is Oxford University Press España S.A. of el Parque Empresarial San Fernando de Henares, Avenida de Castilla, 2 – 28830 Madrid (www.oup.es/en or product.safety@oup.com). OUP España S.A. also acts as importer into Spain of products made by the manufacturer.

www.ingramcontent.com/pod-product-compliance
Lightning Source LLC
LaVergne TN
LVHW011904200926
848484LV00002B/523

* 9 7 8 0 1 9 8 8 2 6 5 7 6 *